Managing for Solvency and Profitability in Life and Health Insurance Companies

LOMA (Life Office Management Association, Inc.) is an international association founded in 1924. LOMA's mission is to help member companies in the insurance and financial services industry improve their management and operations through quality employee development, research, information sharing, and related products and services. Among LOMA's activities is the sponsorship of the FLMI Insurance Education Program—an educational program intended primarily for home office and branch office employees.

The **FLMI Insurance Education Program** consists of two levels—Level I, "Fundamentals of Life and Health Insurance," and Level II, "Functional Aspects of Life and Health Insurance." Level I is designed to help students achieve a working knowledge of the life and health insurance business. Level II is designed to further the student's career development by providing a more detailed understanding of life and health insurance and related business and management subjects. Upon the completion of both levels, the student is designated a Fellow of the Life Management Institute (FLMI) and is awarded a diploma.

Managing for Solvency and Profitability in Life and Health Insurance Companies

Susan Conant, FLMI, HIA, CEBS
Nicholas L. Desoutter, FLMI, ACS
Dani L. Long, FLMI, ALHC
Robert MacGrogan

FLMI Insurance Education Program
Life Management Institute LOMA
Atlanta, Georgia

LOMA®

Authors:	Susan Conant, FLMI, HIA, CEBS Nicholas L. Desoutter, FLMI, ACS Dani L. Long, FLMI, ALHC Robert MacGrogan
Project manager:	Dennis W. Goodwin, FLMI, ACS, HIA
Editors:	Sean Schaeffer Gilley, FLMI, ACS, AIAA, ALHC, HIA, CEBS David A. Lewis, FLMI, ACS
Copyeditor:	Robert D. Land, FLMI, ACS
Permissions editors:	Joyce Abrams Fleming, J.D., FLMI, ACS, AIAA, ALHC, HIA Ruth D. Handley, J.D.
Software programmer:	Geoffrey Kruse
Production coordinator:	Sally M. Farnham
Business coordinator:	Elizabeth A. Pedley
Administrative support:	Debra Bailey Helwig Linda M. Rybicki
Typography:	Puffin Typography, BJ Nemeth & Heather King
Printing:	RR Donnelley & Sons Company
Cover design:	Zoila Harmouche

ISBN 0-939921-80-4

Library of Congress Catalog Card Number 96-76706

Printed in the United States of America

This text is dedicated with gratitude to Warren A. Carter, ASA, now retired from Teachers Insurance & Annuity Association, in recognition of his magnificent contributions to insurance education in general and to the FLMI Insurance Education Program in particular over the past three decades. His long voluntary service as a LOMA Council and Committee member has been a major force in the evolution of the FLMI Program and of insurance and financial education.

Contents

ExecuView Applications

Chapter 6: Product Profitability Measures and Asset-Share Models

Chapter 7: Pricing Products to Reflect Expenses and Investment Income

Chapter 8: Pricing Products to Reflect Insurance Risk

Chapter 9: Reserves

Chapter 11: Capital Planning

Chapter 20: Keys to Profitability

Preface

The purpose of *Managing for Solvency and Profitability in Life and Health Insurance Companies* is to provide a broad overview of the concepts of solvency and profitability and to describe how life and health insurance companies in the United States and Canada pursue these key financial objectives. The text is divided into six parts. Part 1 introduces the environment of financial management for insurance companies. Part 2 introduces various aspects of product planning and product design for insurance-company products. Part 3 provides an overview of pricing for insurance-company products. Part 4 explains how insurance-company executives approach capital management. Part 5 explains how various internal and external groups monitor the financial performance of an insurance company. Part 6, the final section, describes structural and cultural changes that many insurance companies have undertaken to enable themselves to better safeguard their solvency and to more effectively pursue profitability in their stewardship of their customers' security.

This book has been designed for students who are preparing for LOMA's FLMI *Course 371* examination. Several features have been included in each chapter to help you organize your studies, reinforce your understanding of the materials, and prepare for the examination. As we describe each of these features, we give you suggestions for studying the material.

- **Learning Objectives.** The first page of each chapter contains a list of learning objectives to help you focus your studies. Before reading each chapter, review these learning objectives. Then, as you read the chapter, look for material that will help you meet the learning objectives.

- **Chapter Outline.** The first page of each chapter also provides an outline of the chapter. Review this outline to get an overview of the material that will be covered and scan through the chapter to familiarize yourself with how the information is presented. By looking at the headings and figures, you will get an idea of how various subjects relate to each other.

- **Key Terms.** This text assumes that you have a basic knowledge of the key terms and concepts associated with insurance principles and products, economics and investments, and statutory and GAAP accounting. In some cases, these basic terms and concepts are also reviewed and explained in this text. All "new" insurance and financial management terminology introduced in this text is defined or explained when it is first used. Important insurance and financial management terminology is highlighted with boldface type when the term is first used or defined and is included in a list of key terms at the end of each chapter. All key terms are also included in a comprehensive glossary at the end of the book. As you read each chapter, pay special attention to these key terms.

- **Insights.** Excerpts from industry publications and other sources appear throughout the text and are designed to amplify the text's descriptions of certain topics. These Insights should help you get a better feel for the life and health insurance industry.

- ***ExecuView* software.** This textbook includes the new enhanced 2.0 version of *ExecuView: An Asset Share Analysis/Product Profitability Model.* This disk-based software illustrates the interrelationships and complexities of pricing and valuing life insurance and annuity contracts. *ExecuView* allows the user to test the profitability of two life insurance and two annuity products under various assumptions affecting premium rates, interest rates and margins, withdrawal rates, and expenses. Moreover, *ExecuView* permits users to combine the four products into various product mix configurations in order to test the effects of different product mixes on an insurance company's overall profitability. As such, *ExecuView* approximates the kind of software actuaries use for pricing insurance and annuity products. Version 2.0 of *ExecuView* runs on any computer using Microsoft Windows Version 3.1 or higher.

- ***ExecuView* Applications.** Several chapters in the book contain *ExecuView* Applications that illustrate important concepts in insurance pricing and product portfolio management. These applications supplement and expand upon ideas presented in the chapters. Note that running *ExecuView* on a computer is not a requirement for understanding the concepts presented in the text.

- **Miscellaneous other features.** In addition, we have included thought-provoking quotes and interesting statistics or "Fast Facts" within the chapters to round out the presentation of material and enhance the learning experience.

- **Prep Pak assignment.** In addition to this book, LOMA's *Prep Pak for FLMI 371** is assigned reading for students preparing for the FLMI Program examination. Used along with this textbook, the Prep Pak will help you master the course material. Included in the Prep Pak are chapter review exercises, practice exam questions, a full-scale sample examination in both paper form and on a 3½-inch diskette, and appendices with answers to every question in the Prep Pak.

* The Prep Pak may be revised periodically. To ensure that you are studying from the correct texts, check the current LOMA Insurance Education Catalog for a description of the texts assigned for the examination for which you are preparing.

LOMA recommends that you use all of the study aids available for this course. **Studies indicate that students who use LOMA study aids consistently perform significantly better on FLMI Program examinations than other students.**

Acknowledgments

No matter how much work the authors put into developing a book, many other individuals always provide valuable expertise and assistance that make the book possible. Developing *Managing for Solvency and Profitability in Life and Health Insurance Companies* required the combined efforts of many highly qualified experts in insurance and financial services. On behalf of LOMA and its membership, we would like to express appreciation to those individuals who generously gave their time and energy and shared their considerable expertise for the development of this textbook.

Textbook Development Panel

Our foremost thanks go to the members of the textbook development panel who reviewed the outline of the entire book and each chapter as it was completed. These individuals have overseen the entire project from beginning to end and have made many valuable contributions. Their critical judgment, diligence, patience, and technical expertise were essential to the book's accuracy and completeness. The members of the textbook development panel include:

- Susan Benjamin, FSA, EA, MAAA, FLMI/M, CPA, Assistant Vice President and Associate Actuary, Ohio State Life Insurance Company
- Warren A. Carter, ASA (retired), Teachers Insurance and Annuity Association
- Julie F. Curry, FSA, FLMI, MAAA, Senior Consulting Actuary, Ernst & Young LLP
- Mark Evans, FSA, FLMI, MAAA, 2nd Vice President and Actuary, Providian Corporation
- Stephen W. Forbes, Ph.D., FLMI, Senior Vice President, Research Division, LOMA
- Stephanie L. Holowach, FLMI/M, CCIM, Regional Manager, Allstate Insurance Company
- JoAnn Rumelhart, FSA, MAAA, Vice President — Life Operations, Farm Bureau Financial Services

Additional Expert Reviewers

In addition to the members of the textbook development review panel, many other individuals contributed their considerable expertise to ensuring the accuracy and reliability of various specialized aspects of the book. Some of these were members of the textbook review panel who volunteered to provide information that far exceeded the usual demands of the role of a textbook reviewer. Others are industry experts who reviewed several chapters in the early stages of the text's development. For this effort, we owe a debt of gratitude to the following individuals:

Reinsurance

- Jack Broshar, FLMI (retired), Munich American Reinsurance Company
- Ann Godbehere, CGA, Vice President and Controller, Mercantile & General Life Reassurance Company of Canada
- William J. Hazelwood, FLMI/M, CLU, ChFC, Marketing Vice President, Mercantile & General Life Reassurance Company of Canada
- Mark Petersen, FLMI, ACF, CLU, Lincoln National Life Reinsurance Companies

Changes in Corporate Form

- Raymond E. Cummings, Second Vice President, Phoenix Home Life Mutual
- Thomas A. Player, Esq., Partner, Morris, Manning & Martin, L.L.P. (Atlanta, GA); Morris, Manning, Martin & Player, L.L.P. (Washington, DC)

Technical Product Design

- Sheryl Babcock, FSA, First Vice President and Assistant Actuary, Life and Annuity Actuarial, Mutual of Omaha
- Linh Huynh, FLMI, Individual Insurance Group Product Development, Prudential
- Tom Loftis, FSA, MAAA, Actuarial Officer, ING America Life Corporation
- Harry Ploss, FSA
- Scott Priebe, ASA, Mutual of Omaha

Other Advisors

- Robert Curry, FLMI, CPA, Controller, ING America Life Corporation
- Minda Davis, Corporate Vice President, Communications, The Canada Life Assurance Company
- Ivan J. Francis, CFA, FLMI/M, Portfolio Manager, Bonds, Standard Life Assurance Company, Ltd.
- Jerry Hogya, FLMI, Manager, Comptroller Systems Management, Mutual of Omaha
- Kenneth A. LaSorella, FLMI, FSA, Assistant Vice President, Individual Actuarial, Sun Life Assurance Company of Canada
- Barbara Lawson, FSA, FCIA, Dividends Officer, Sun Life Assurance Company of Canada
- Percy J. Marchman, Executive Director, Georgia Life and Health Insurance Guaranty Association
- Clarence J. Miller, FLMI, CPA, CIA, Manager, Financial Reporting and Performance Measurement, CUNA Mutual Group
- William A. O'Connell, CPA, Director, Examination Division, Office of Commissioner of Insurance, State of Georgia

LOMA Staff

All textbooks developed by LOMA are team projects. The following individuals deserve special mention for the work they performed on this text. Sean Schaeffer Gilley, FLMI, ACS, ALHC, HIA, CEBS, Senior Associate, Examinations Department, spearheaded the project in the sense that she undertook much research that shaped the project, assembled much of the text's review panel, and prepared early drafts of several chapters. She also reviewed the entire manuscript and made many helpful suggestions. David A. Lewis, FLMI, ACS, Senior Associate, Examinations Department, reviewed the entire manuscript and made many helpful suggestions. E. Scott Cass, formerly Assistant Vice President, Financial Management Products and Services and now Member Relations Representative, Patricia Smith, CPA, ACS, Associate, Financial Management Products and Services, and Gregory P. Storey, FLMI, ACS, CIA, Senior Associate, Financial Management Products and Services, reviewed several chapters and answered innumerable questions. Olivia Blakemore, Information Center Technical Assistant, along with other staff members of LOMA's Information Center, and Mary Kaye, ACS, Research Publications Assistant, Research Division, assisted with the extensive research required for the project. Harriett Jones, J.D., FLMI, Senior Associate, Curriculum Department, served as editor of the chapters in Part Four, as well as Chapter 19. Kenneth Huggins, FLMI/M, served as manuscript editor of Chapters 5, 15, and 18. Joyce Abrams Fleming, J.D., FLMI, ACS, AIAA, ALHC, HIA, Senior Associate, Curriculum Department, Debra Bailey Helwig, Education Communications Associate, and Ruth Handley, J.D., Assistant, Curriculum Department, obtained permissions for use of copyrighted material. Joyce also managed some aspects of production. Robert D. Land, FLMI, ACS, copyedited the entire manuscript and drafted the glossary and index. Elizabeth A. Pedley, Business Coordinator, Curriculum Department, made arrangements for printing. Zoila Harmouche, Graphics Manager, helped prepare the cover design and artwork.

We would also like to thank William H. Rabel, Ph.D., FLMI, CLU, Senior Vice President, Education Division, Ernest L. Martin, Ph.D., FLMI, Assistant Vice President, Curriculum Department, and Dennis W. Goodwin, FLMI, ACS, HIA, Assistant Vice President, Curriculum Department for their encouragement and support throughout the text's development.

And finally, special thanks to Sally M. Farnham, Editorial/Desktop Publishing Coordinator, who designed the inside of the text, coordinated the entire production process, made many helpful suggestions, and worked tirelessly to move the project through typesetting.

Susan Conant, FLMI, HIA, CEBS

Nicholas L. Desoutter, FLMI, ACS

Dani L. Long, FLMI, ALHC

Robert MacGrogan

PART 1

Overview of Solvency and Profitability

This book is about the solvency and profitability concerns of insurance companies in the annuity, life, and health insurance business. This first brief section of the text is designed to set the stage for the many topics we will be encountering as we progress through the remainder of this book. The information provided in this section should form a solid basis for your understanding of the concerns that insurance companies must balance as they allocate financial resources in support of the company's goals. Chapter 1 is designed to prepare you to understand how insurance companies manage their financial resources in order to meet their financial goals. Chapter 2 provides additional context for this textbook by describing the balance insurers must maintain between the goals of profitability and solvency.

CHAPTER

Introduction to Solvency and Profitability

1

LEARNING OBJECTIVES

After studying this chapter, you should be able to

- Interpret the concepts of profitability and solvency in an insurance company context
- Recognize some of the ways that profits affect a company's ability to grow
- Identify the primary sources of insurance industry revenues, major patterns of expenses, and major categories of insurance industry assets and liabilities
- Recall the major components of a balance sheet and an income statement and recognize how these statements are related to each other

OUTLINE

Each insurance company establishes its own major long-term corporate goals and the broad, overall courses of action that the company will follow to achieve those objectives. For most insurers, these major objectives focus on four issues: (1) meeting current and prospective customers' needs for products and services, (2) maintaining solvency, (3) enhancing profitability, and (4) being a responsible corporate citizen.

In many instances, these objectives work in concert with one another. At other times, they conflict. One crucial challenge of operating an insurance company is to meet all these goals, despite their often conflicting nature. The management team of an insurance company approaches this task by pursuing carefully chosen strategies designed to maintain an appropriate balance among the four objectives. To see how one insurer's CEO balanced his company's corporate objectives, read Insight 1-1.

Although this textbook acknowledges the challenges associated with both meeting customers' needs for products and services and being a responsible corporate citizen, the focus of this text is on the interrelationships and complexities involved in meeting the financial goals of life and health insurers. As such, our primary focus here will be on the objectives of (1) protecting solvency and (2) enhancing profitability. As we shall see, meeting these two objectives is a challenging task and involves balancing a number of often conflicting issues.

As we discuss the challenges associated with managing the financial affairs of an insurance company, this textbook usually takes the viewpoint of the company's top management. Sometimes, however, we step outside of the company and look at an insurer's financial picture from other viewpoints, such as those of a regulator, a distributor, a customer, a rating agency, an investor, or a competitor. The viewpoint used is important because, for insurance companies, different parties use different processes and standards to evaluate an insurer's financial position. Despite differences, the concern shared by all parties examining an insurer's financial affairs is to evaluate the insurer's success at enhancing profitability while protecting solvency.

To explain how insurance companies meet their financial goals effectively, this text will discuss the financial resources of life and health insurers and how those resources are managed. The process of managing a company's financial resources is called ***financial management.*** A great deal of the information in this text is information that would be covered in a financial management course. However, because meeting financial goals in an insurance company requires

Insight 1-1 Interview with Tom Welch, President and CEO, Ohio State Life

The responsibilities of the senior management of a life insurance company include communicating the goals of the organization and then managing resources to attain those goals. It sounds straightforward enough, and it would be were it not for two facts: the goals are frequently conflicting and the only certainty is that there will be inadequate resources to meet all the goals established.

At Ohio State Life, we have six long-standing operating objectives, in the areas of service to customers, policy growth, profits, expense control, public image, and developing and retaining employees and agents. The conflicts between objectives are evident: providing better services versus the cost of that service; more competitive products versus profits; the need to train staff versus the need to keep employees in production; and the list goes on.

Balancing these objectives means prioritizing the interests of the company's constituencies. These interests are not fixed in order of importance. It is fair to say that each sometimes takes its place at the head of the line. However, our experience has been that over the long term the interests of policyholders must come first, for from policyholders flow all the resources we command. Agents, shareholders, employees, regulators, and rating agencies take their turn at top billing, but in the end policyholders return to prominence.

The task then becomes one of juggling resources. We consider our resources, broadly speaking, to be products, distribution systems, administrative systems, financial resources, and people.

Meeting all the conflicting goals of a life insurance company is senior management's responsibility. It is one that requires a constant reevaluation of the interests of all constituencies and the application of resources to satisfy those interests.

Source: *Interview, January 17, 1996, Tom Welch, President and CEO, Ohio State Life.*

coordinating the efforts of a number of the company's functional and operational units, this textbook also presents information from a variety of additional subject areas, such as accounting, actuarial, investments, and marketing. As we will see, all levels and all facets of an insurer's operations affect its ability to achieve the goals of (1) pursuing profits, growth, or other returns, (2) avoiding undue risk, and (3) maintaining solvency.

No discussion of enhancing profitability or protecting solvency can begin without a clear understanding of these concepts. Consequently, we will review the meaning of these terms in an insurance company context. Next, we will provide some background for our discussion by presenting a financial profile of the insurance industry in the United States and Canada, paying particular attention to sources of revenue, major cash outflows, and the characteristics of the industry's primary assets and liabilities. Finally, we will provide an overview of how insurers track their financial performance, concentrating on the types of information found on two important types of financial statements—the balance sheet and the income statement. In this way, we will provide an overview of how insurers obtain and use their funds, and we will lay the foundation for later discussions of how insurers manage their financial performance in order to enhance profitability and promote solvency.

Enhancing Profitability and Protecting Solvency: An Overview

Because enhancing profitability and protecting solvency are crucial to the operations of financial institutions, you are probably already somewhat familiar with these concepts. As a starting point to the more detailed discussions that will follow in this text, however, let's review the meanings of the concepts and some of the applicable terminology to make sure we are all speaking the same language.

Before beginning these sections, take a look at Figure 1-1, which lists some of the terms associated with enhancing profitability and protecting solvency. Any discussion of insurance company profitability and solvency, both in this text and in other publications, is likely to use some of the terms shown there. If you do not already have a background in financial management, rest assured that you will become much more familiar with these terms as you progress through the book.

Enhancing Profitability

The concept of enhancing profitability is a particularly slippery one for insurance companies, because even within the insurance industry, not all companies employ the exact same terms when referring to *profits* and *profitability*.

One aspect of enhancing profitability is earning profits for the entire firm. In most business contexts, the word ***profit*** is used to refer to the excess of revenue over expenditures. Stock insurance companies use the word *profit* in much the same manner as do other business organizations—although stock insurers are sensitive to the need to balance

Figure 1-1. Terms commonly used when discussing profitability and solvency.

Terms often used in connection with PROFITABILITY		Terms often used in connection with SOLVENCY	
• Growth	• Interest	• Safety	• Capital structure
• Returns	• Spread	• Risk aversion	• Capital adequacy
• Income	• Expense control	• Risk management	• Write-offs
• Success	• Productivity	• Liquidity	• Declines in value
• Performance	• Revenue enhancement	• Capitalization	• Risk-based capital
• Profit margins	• Bottom line	• Quality	• Risk-adjusted capital
• Gains	• Wealth	• Consistency	• Reserve adequacy
• Yield	• Contribution to surplus	• Conservatism	• Surplus adequacy
• Earnings	• Earnings per share		

their shareholders' interests with their policyholders' interests. For a stock insurer, profit is equal to the difference between revenue and expenditures before shareholder dividends. Mutual insurance companies and fraternal benefit societies, however, generally avoid the use of the term *profit;* instead, they refer to the excess of revenue over expenditures as ***contribution to surplus.*** For these insurers, contribution to surplus is equal to revenue minus expenditures before policyholder dividends. Contribution to surplus is equivalent to *profit,* and in this text we will use the term *profit* to refer to the gains of stock, mutual, and other types of insurers.

Interpreting the term *profitability* in connection with insurance companies can be difficult. ***Profitability*** refers to a business firm's degree of success in generating returns to its owners. Thus, the term *profitability* has a broader meaning than does the term *profit;* profitability refers both to generating profits and increasing wealth. In this sense, wealth refers to the value of the company. Therefore, a related aspect of profitability is in increasing the value of the company, as reflected by events such as increases in the value of the company's stock or increases in the value of the company's capital and surplus. The distinctions between wealth and profits, and the differences among the many factors that affect wealth and profits, will be described more fully in later chapters.

In the previous paragraph, we noted that "profitability refers to a business firm's degree of success in generating returns to its *owners.*" An organization may have any number of goals related to its business interests, the public interest, or its social responsibilities. However, in the strictest sense, every organization operates for the benefit of its owners. Insurance organizations, whether they are stock, mutual, or fraternal, are no exception. The owners of a stock insurance company are its shareholders; the owners of a mutual insurance company are its policyowners; the owners of a fraternal benefit society are its members. In this text, when we use the term *owners,* we are referring to stock company shareholders, mutual company policyowners, and fraternal society members. Similarly, and unless indicated otherwise, when we use the terms *insurer* or *company,* we are including all three types of organizations.

The Importance of Profitability[1]

Every insurer must be profitable over the long run in order to succeed. Furthermore, an insurer's profits must be substantial enough to satisfy several needs. Over the long term, profits must satisfy the following needs:

- Profits must provide a suitable return to allow a company to reward its owners for the risk they have taken by investing money in the company. In stock companies, owners are rewarded through stockholder dividends and increases in the value of the company's stock. In mutual companies and fraternal organizations, owners are rewarded through policyowner dividends.

- Profits must enable a company to build up enough capital and surplus to ensure the company's ability to (1) pay current and future benefits for existing contracts, (2) safeguard the owners' investment in the company, and (3) support the costs associated with writing new business. Because of the costs associated with selling insurance and the reserve funds that must be established when a policy is sold, new insurance business—unlike new sales in most other businesses—typically results in an initial statutory loss rather than a profit. This depletion of statutory capital and surplus caused by issuing new business is called surplus strain.
- Profits must provide a company with enough resources to allow it to change and grow with the times. Companies need such resources in order to fund long-term investment projects, called ***capital investment projects.*** For an insurance company, capital investment projects include development of new products, new information systems, new distribution systems, new businesses, and other items needed for survival.
- Profits must provide a company with sufficient resources to cover any expenses that may not be explicitly included in the company's pricing assumptions.

When designing and pricing its products and taking other actions that affect profitability, a company must keep these needs in mind.

Measuring Profitability

In order to determine whether it is meeting its goals with regard to enhancing its profitability, an insurance company must be able to measure its success in increasing its profits. Measuring a company's profitability, however, involves more than simply looking at the company's monthly, quarterly, or annual "bottom line" results. To successfully measure their profitability and provide themselves with the kinds of information they need in order to make profitable decisions for the future, companies must be able to (1) determine the sources of their profits and (2) measure the magnitude of their profits.

To determine the *source* of their profits (or losses), insurers must analyze their profitability by specific segments of their operations. For example, insurers divide their measures of operating profitability into categories by product line, product type, market segment, or distribution system. Similarly, when measuring the profitability of their investment operations, insurers measure the profitability of specific categories of assets and of specific assets—for example, particular bonds or stocks. By looking at company profitability from a number of different perspectives, an insurer can determine which areas are contributing to profits and, correspondingly, to capital and surplus, as well as which areas are generating losses or are a drain on capital and surplus.

Although the relationship of operating profits to surplus will be discussed later in the chapter, this textbook assumes that you have a general understanding of the statutory accounting practices and generally accepted accounting principles (GAAP) followed by insurance companies.

Insurers also need to measure the magnitude of their profitability in order to evaluate how effectively they are employing their resources. When measuring profit, any positive result is generally better than a loss. However, simply measuring the absolute dollar amount of profits is not enough to help a company evaluate its profitability. To determine the strength of its profits, a company needs to know the *relationship* between its profit and the resources it has employed to earn the profit.

For example, suppose you learn that you have earned a return of $100 on an investment that you made three months ago. You might be extremely pleased if you had invested only $1,000 three months ago, because after only three months $100 would represent a substantial return. However, you would most likely be quite disappointed if your investment three months ago had instead been $100,000, because a return of $100 on this amount leaves much to be desired. Even if your original investment had been $100,000, though, you would most likely prefer to have even a small gain of $100 rather than a loss.

The resources an insurer has employed in order to earn a given profit are often measured in terms of some measure of capital and surplus—the amount of owners' equity in a company. Thus, one common measure of an insurer's profitability is *return on capital*. ***Return on capital*** is a ratio comparing some measure of the insurer's earnings during a period to some measure of its capital and surplus. Although this ratio can be formulated in various ways, we can express the return-on-capital ratio for insurers as

$$\text{Return on Capital} = \frac{\text{Earnings}}{\text{Capital and Surplus}}$$

The result of this return-on-capital ratio indicates an insurance company's overall success in generating profits during a given period—that is, how efficiently the company employed capital and surplus. Generally, for a given level of capital and surplus, the higher the ratio, the better or more efficiently the company's resources are being employed. (We will see in later chapters of the text that a company could have a high return-on-capital ratio because it has too little capital and surplus.) A return-on-capital ratio can be applied to an entire corporation, to a line of business, or to a specific product or product type. Thus, an insurer may have a high return-on-capital ratio for its overall operations while having a low return-on-capital ratio for a specific product line. Also, a return-on-capital ratio can be applied to a long or short time period and can be based on actual or predicted results. We will explore return on capital and related financial performance measures in later chapters.

Protecting Solvency

The other major component of an insurer's financial objectives is protecting solvency. ***Solvency*** is generally defined as a business organization's ability to meet its financial obligations on time. For insurance companies, however, regulations apply a stricter definition of solvency. For insurers, ***solvency*** refers to the legal minimum standard of capital and surplus that every insurance company must maintain.

The opposite of solvency is insolvency. ***Insolvency*** can be defined loosely as a financial failure. In a crisis situation involving an insurer, insolvency is declared by a court upon the recommendation of the appropriate insurance regulators. In the United States or Canada, a financially troubled insurer can ordinarily be declared insolvent only by a court judgment. We will discuss in greater detail the definitions of insurance company solvency and insurance company insolvency—as well as the methods used to monitor solvency—in later chapters of the text.

Financial Profile of the Insurance Industry

To provide a context for our discussion of solvency and profitability, we begin by looking at some of the key features of the financial profile of the life and health insurance industry in the United States and Canada. First, we review the industry's cash-flow patterns, including its primary revenue sources and its expense patterns. Next, we cover life and health companies' investment patterns and the asset types the industry holds. Finally, we examine the profile of the industry's obligations (liabilities). An understanding of the industry's financial profile will serve as a useful frame of reference from this point forward.

Note that our discussion here refers to actual results for the year ending 1994 and, in some cases, for the year ending 1993. However, because we discuss only the most essential characteristics of the industry's financial profile, and also because the broad-based life/

health insurance and annuity data presented here tend to change slowly, you can expect many of these financial patterns to remain relatively stable over a number of years. Also note that U.S. and Canadian data are developed using different rules for financial reporting, and that solvency regulation differs substantially between the two countries. Accordingly, you should use caution in drawing any conclusions from comparing U.S. and Canadian data.

To provide an overview of the insurance industry, Figure 1-2 shows the concentration of stock companies, mutual companies, and fraternal benefit societies in the United States and Canada.

Profile of Industry Cash Flows

An important aspect of managing a company's solvency and profitability involves analyzing and planning the cash flows necessary to satisfy the company's obligations and to acquire assets needed to achieve the company's goals. The term ***cash flows*** refers to a company's inflows and outflows of cash. The main components of a company's cash flows are (1) inflows of funds and (2) outflows of funds. Although insurers have some cash inflows from financing, for most life and health insurance companies, the main inflows (sources) of funds are typically from operations and investments. The main outflows (uses) of funds for life and health insurers are for benefit payments, new investments, and operating expenses.

Figure 1-2. Concentrations of stock companies, mutual companies, and fraternal benefit societies in the United States and Canada in 1994.

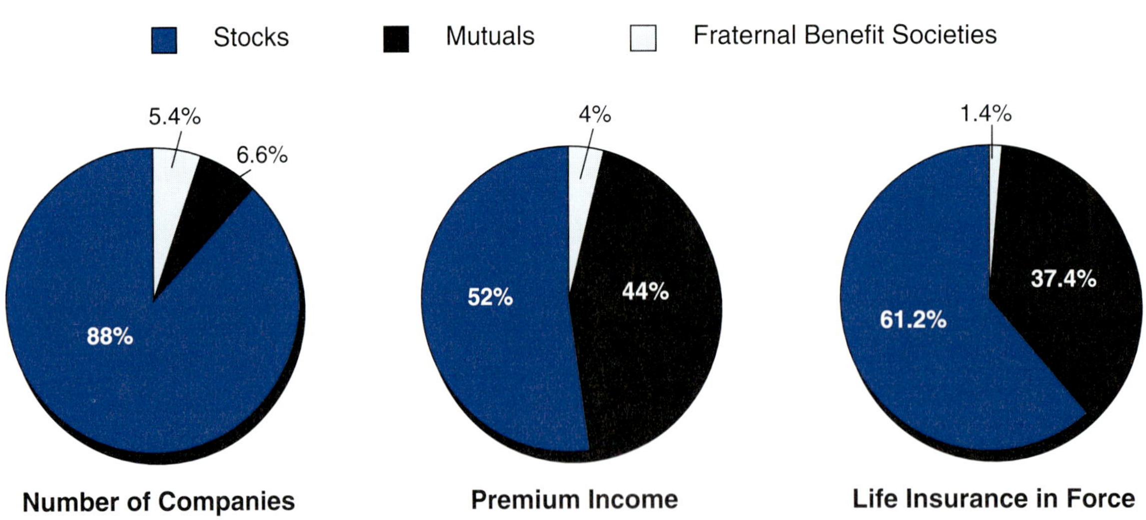

Sources: *American Council of Life Insurance; Canadian Life and Health Insurance Association, Inc.; Fraternal Congress of America.*

Figure 1-3 presents industry composite cash flow data for the life and health insurance industry in the United States and Canada. This figure also shows the important sources of industry revenue, the relative share from each revenue source, the major categories of industry expenses, and the relative importance of each expense category.

Profile of Industry Revenue Sources

The two main revenue sources of life and health insurance companies in the United States and Canada are (1) premium income and

Figure 1-3. Overview of U.S. and Canadian life and health insurance industry sources and uses of funds.

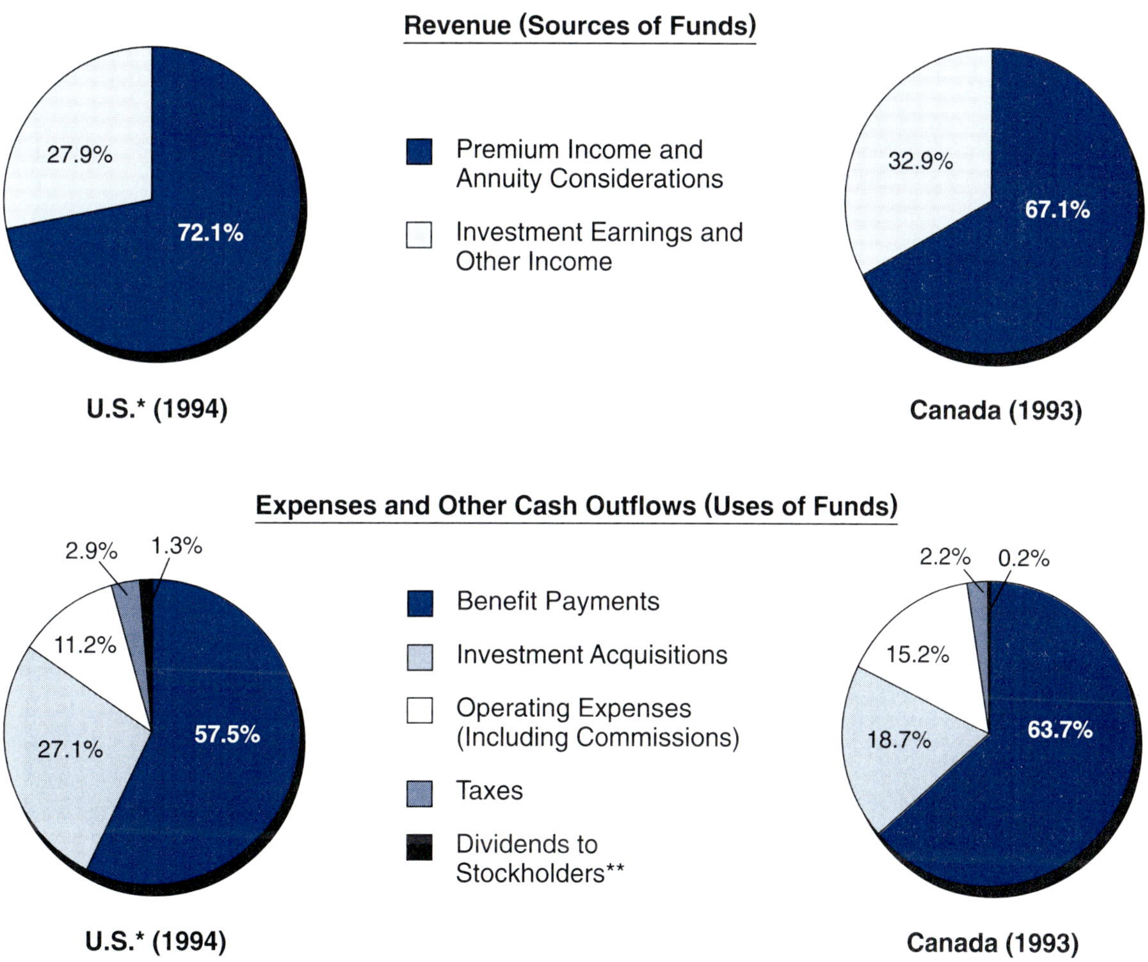

** Does not include figures from U.S. companies that sell only health insurance. Figures are for companies that sell both life and health insurance.*

*** For stock companies only, this figure would be 2.0% (U.S.) and 0.5% (Canada).*

Sources: 1995 Life Insurance Fact Book Update *(Washington, D.C.: American Council of Life Insurance, 1995), p. 37;* Canadian Life and Health Insurance Facts 1994 Edition *(Toronto: Canadian Life and Health Insurance Association, 1994), pp. 5–6.*

annuity considerations and (2) investment earnings. Roughly two-thirds to three-fourths of life and health insurers' revenue—a larger percentage in the United States than in Canada—is from premiums and annuity considerations. The remainder of their revenue is investment earnings and other income, such as income from reinsurance ceded. Thus, life and health insurers derive more than twice as much of their revenue from premiums and annuity considerations as they do from their investment earnings. A small but growing component of income for insurers is from providing services to other organizations for a fee. These service arrangements typically involve one insurer's providing specialized services, such as claims processing or data processing, to another insurer.

When broken down by product mix, an analysis of insurance industry revenue shows that annuity considerations make up the greatest share of the industry's total revenue from premiums and other considerations, followed next by life insurance premiums, with the smallest share coming from health insurance premiums. The relative shares of revenue from the three main product types are one measure of the industry's product mix. Figure 1-4 shows the relative shares of premium income from each line of business at the end of 1994. In the United States for 1994, approximately 47.1 percent of noninvestment income was from annuities and pension products, 29.5 percent was from life insurance, and 23.4 percent was from health and accident insurance. Canadian insurers earned 50 percent of noninvestment revenue from annuities and pension products, with 28 percent from life insurance, and 22 percent from health and accident insurance.

Figure 1-4. Sources of premium income for U.S. and Canadian life and health insurers.

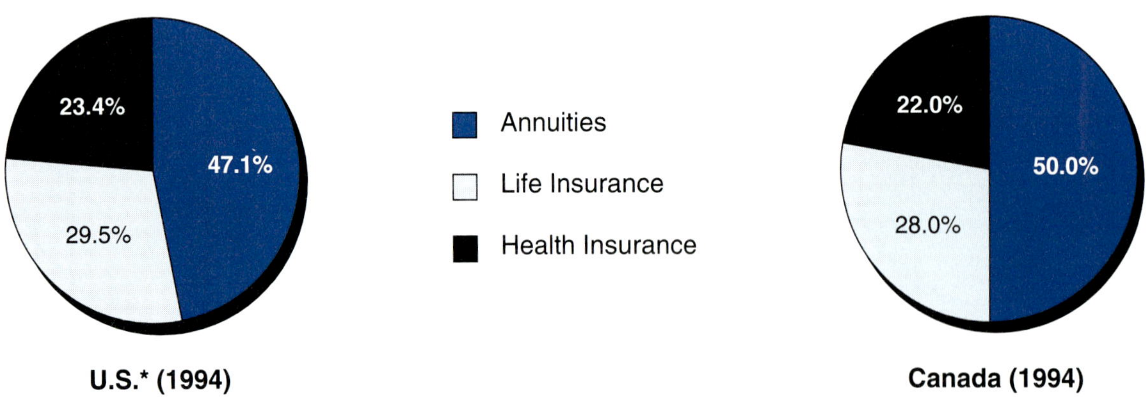

* *Does not include figures from U.S. companies that sell only health insurance. Figures are for companies that sell both life and health insurance.*

Sources: 1995 Life Insurance Fact Book Update *(Washington, D.C.: American Council of Life Insurance, 1995), p. 31;* Canadian Life and Health Insurance Facts 1995 Edition *(Toronto: Canadian Life and Health Insurance Association, 1995), pp. 19–20.*

Profile of Industry Expenses and Other Cash Outflows

In Figure 1-3, we saw a summary of the insurance industry's uses of funds, or cash outflows. The following facts about cash outflow patterns for the life and health insurance industry can give us useful insights into the operations of life and health insurers in the United States and Canada:

- The three main cash outflow categories on the income statements of life and health insurance companies are
    1. Benefit payments
    2. Investment acquisitions
    3. Operating expenses
- The largest category of cash outflows for the industry is contractual benefit payments. These benefit payments are 57.5 percent of total cash outflows in the United States and 63.7 percent of total outflows in Canada.
- Among the major outflow categories, the outflow that management has the best opportunity to control is a company's operating expenses. Operating expenses are about 11 percent of total cash outflows in the United States and about 15 percent in Canada.

Unlike businesses in most other industries, life and health insurers have very low debt service payments. The life and health insurance industry issues little or no traditional debt (corporate bonds). Thus, ***debt service***—the repaying of loans and the interest on such loans—is one expense item that usually does *not* appear on insurers' cash flow statements. Typically, in fact, insurers lend money to other businesses. However, insurers sometimes do borrow funds in order to finance mergers and acquisitions.

Profile of Industry Assets and Liabilities

The main assets of life and health insurance companies are various types of financial instruments in their investment portfolios. The main liabilities of life and health insurance companies are the policy reserve funds that companies hold to support their insurance and annuity contracts. In examining the assets and liabilities of U.S. and Canadian life and health insurers, we will thus examine their mix of investments and their mix of reserves. Not surprisingly, both the mix of insurers' policy reserves and insurers' allocation of investments reflect their product mix. For example, the composition of life company policy reserves has been changing over the years, reflecting a shift in the basic product types sold from primarily life insurance to primarily annuities and supplementary contracts. Similarly, life and health insurers' investments are allocated between both short- and long-term investments according to the nature of the insurance or annuity contracts that the investments are designed to support.

Profile of Investments

Life and health insurance companies are major institutional investors and major suppliers of funds to the capital markets. (*Capital markets* are the financial markets for long-term funds.) Institutional investors are large financial services providers that invest funds on the behalf of other investors. At the end of 1994, U.S. life insurance companies ranked third among private domestic institutional sources of funds and provided over 12 percent of the total funds flowing into U.S. financial markets.[2] Life and health insurance companies hold large investment portfolios of financial assets to back their reserves. Figure 1-5 compares the asset distributions of U.S. and Canadian life and health insurance companies. Some key facts about the investments held by life and health insurers follow.

- Far more of these assets are debt instruments (corporate bonds, government bonds, mortgages, and policy loans) rather than equities (stocks and real estate). In the United States in 1994, investment in equities represented only about 17 percent of total assets, while investment in various forms of debt represented over 77 percent of assets. In Canada in 1994, equity investments represented about 19 percent of life and health insurers' total

Figure 1-5. Comparison of asset distributions of U.S. and Canadian life and health insurers.

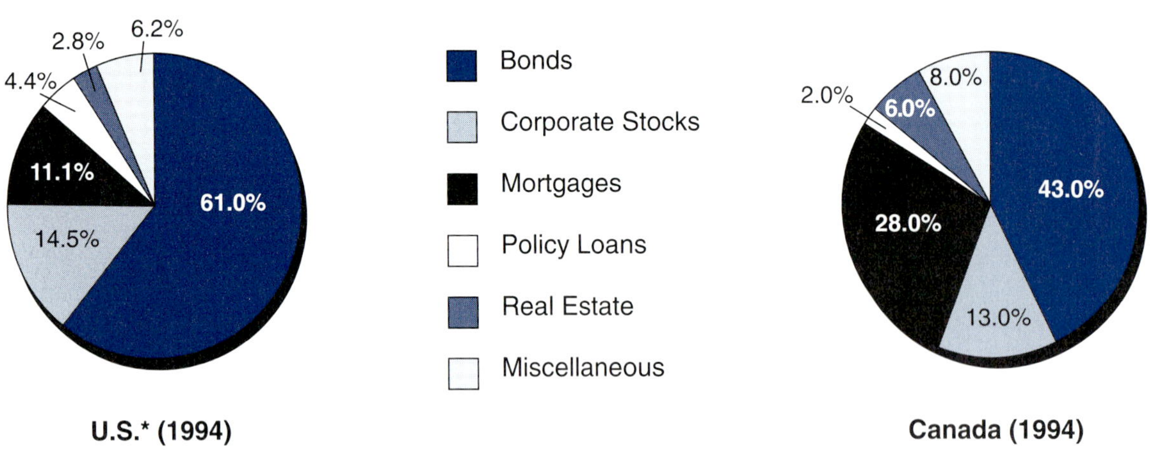

* *Does not include figures from U.S. companies that sell only health insurance. Figures are for companies that sell both life and health insurance.*

Sources: 1995 Life Insurance Fact Book Update *(Washington, D.C.: American Council of Life Insurance, 1995), p. 42;* Canadian Life and Health Insurance Facts 1995 Edition *(Toronto: Canadian Life and Health Insurance Association, 1995), pp. 21–22.*

assets, while debt instruments represented 73 percent. Because insurers' obligations are generally long-term, insurers typically hold long-term assets to back these obligations.

- In the United States, the largest category of assets is bonds, followed by stocks. The third largest category is mortgages. In Canada, the largest category of assets is also bonds. However, in Canada, mortgages represent the second largest category, with stocks being the third largest. It is interesting to note that in Canada only about 43 percent of assets are invested in bonds, while in the United States over 60 percent of assets are invested in bonds. Also, when compared with U.S. insurers, Canadian insurers have more than twice as much of their assets invested in mortgages. This difference is possibly related to widespread use in the United States of collateralized mortgage obligations (CMOs), financial instruments that bundle together many mortgages in the form of a bond issue. CMO holdings of U.S. insurers are classified as bonds.
- Insurers' policy loans are considered a type of investment. For U.S. companies, these loans make up more than 4 percent of total invested assets—a greater share than real estate. In Canada, the opposite is true. Policy loans make up only about 2 percent of total invested assets, a much lower percentage than real estate.

Profile of Obligations (Liabilities)

As we noted earlier, the obligations of life and health insurance companies consist mostly of policy reserves. Policy reserves of U.S. life insurance companies totaled $1,644 billion at the end of 1994. This total included $1,118 billion for annuities and other miscellaneous types of investment contracts, $468 billion for life insurance, and $58 billion for health insurance.[3] In Canada, life companies' policy reserves totaled $143.6 billion (in Canadian dollars) at the end of 1994.[4]

In addition to policy reserves, other liabilities of U.S. life companies at the end of 1994 included $161.5 billion consisting of items such as policy dividend accumulations, funds set aside for the following year's policy dividend payments, incurred expenses, mandatory reserves for fluctuations in the value of securities, unpaid claims, and premiums paid in advance.[5] Figure 1-6 shows the relative shares of the various types of policy reserves and other obligations for U.S. and Canadian companies. In comparing the obligations of U.S. and Canadian companies, it is interesting to note the following facts:

- For U.S. insurers, annuity reserves are 68 percent of policy reserves. For Canadian companies, annuity reserves are an even greater percentage—almost 75 percent of policy reserves.

- For U.S. insurers, life insurance reserves are slightly over 28 percent of policy reserves. For Canadian companies, life insurance reserves are less than 20 percent of policy reserves.
- In terms of total obligations, U.S. life insurance companies' policy reserves account for slightly over 91 percent of total obligations. Canadian life companies' reserves account for slightly over 77 percent of total obligations.

Figure 1-6 shows that the percentage of health insurance reserves for U.S. companies is lower than for Canadian companies.

Now that you have a financial profile of the overall U.S. and Canadian life and health insurance industries, we turn our attention to how each insurer keeps track of its own financial picture.

Figure 1-6. Shares of policy reserves (by lines of business) and total policy reserves and other obligations of U.S. and Canadian life insurers.

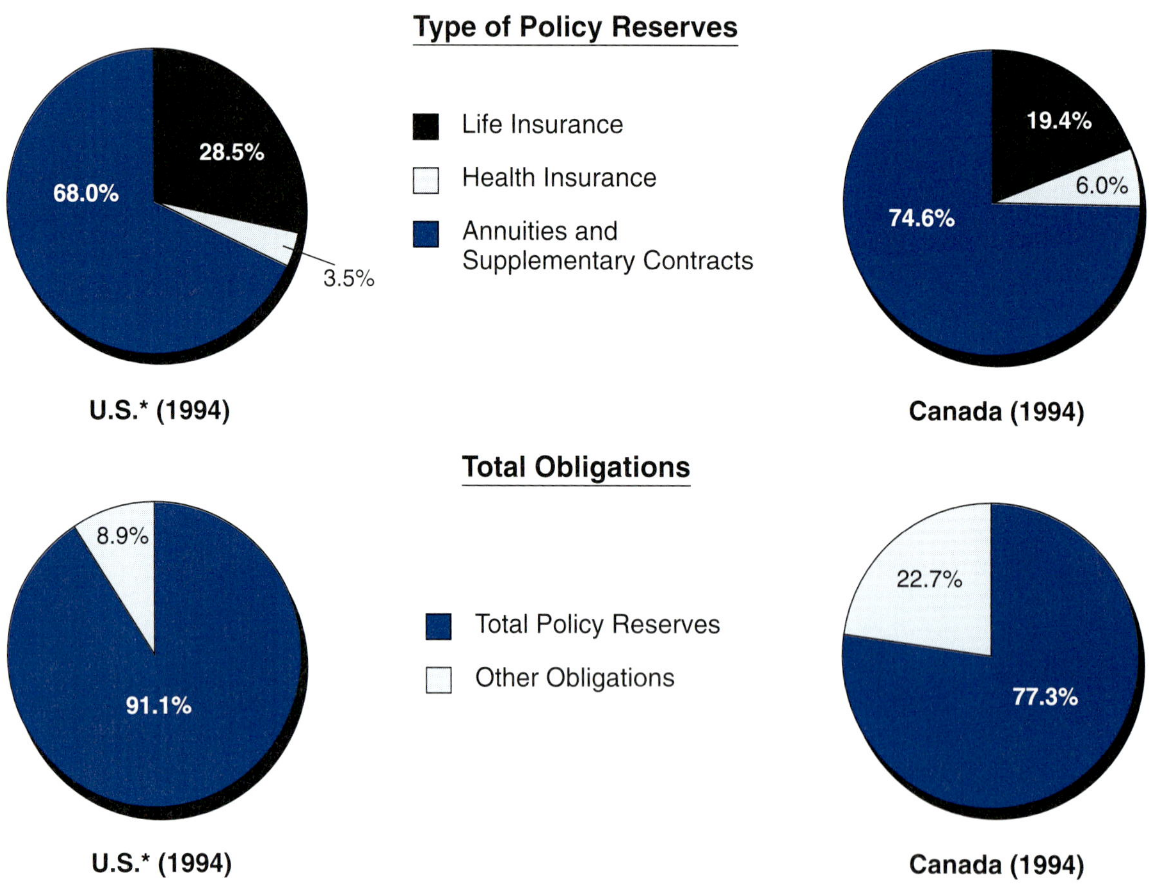

** Does not include figures from U.S. companies that sell only health insurance. Figures are for companies that sell both life and health insurance.*

Sources: 1995 Life Insurance Fact Book Update *(Washington, D.C.: American Council of Life Insurance, 1995), pp. 39–41;* Canadian Life and Health Insurance Facts 1995 Edition *(Toronto: Canadian Life and Health Insurance Association, 1995), p. 23.*

Tracking Financial Performance

To determine whether an organization is successful in meeting its objectives, particularly its financial objectives, some method must be used to track its performance. For insurance companies, the methods used to measure financial performance in terms of profitability and solvency are quite complex, and many of these methods will be discussed in more detail throughout the text.

The following sections present a foundation for these later discussions. We begin by reviewing the two main financial statements used to track a company's financial performance. These statements—the balance sheet and the income statement—will be referred to often in this text as we describe the impact of various financial transactions on an insurer's financial position. After describing the balance sheet and the income statement, we discuss the relationship between these financial statements and how profits reported on the income statement enhance an insurer's balance-sheet profile. When we present balance-sheet or income-statement examples, we generally use very simplified versions of these financial statements. Because this text focuses on financial management, the accounting viewpoint presented here is that of a company's unique internal financial reporting system. Thus, the rules of U.S. statutory and GAAP accounting are rarely issues in this text. Because our presentation takes the viewpoint of an internal financial reporting system, our approach reflects management's needs rather than the needs of regulators, potential investors, or other parties external to the firm.

Balance Sheet

The ***balance sheet,*** which is composed of assets, liabilities, and owners' equity, provides a snapshot of a company's financial position at a given point in time. The basic format and key elements of a balance sheet are illustrated as follows:

LOMA Life and Health Insurance Company Simplified Balance Sheet	
Assets	**Liabilities**
Cash	Reserves
Other assets	Other liabilities
	Owners' Equity (Capital and Surplus)
	Capital
	Surplus
Total Assets =	**Total Liabilities + Owners' Equity**

Recall from your studies of accounting that ***assets*** include the items of value owned by a company and that ***liabilities*** represent the company's obligations. ***Owners' equity,*** generally called ***capital and surplus*** by insurers, refers to the excess of assets over liabilities. Owners' equity includes two components: (1) ***capital*** investments by owners, usually through a purchase of stock, and (2) ***surplus,*** which represents the total net profits that have been earned from a company's operations and left to accumulate since the company's inception. Mutual and fraternal insurers generally have a balance only in their surplus account because these companies do not issue stock.

Before we proceed further, note that the terminology used in the insurance industry to describe capital and surplus is often inconsistent. For example, the term *capital* is often used to mean *surplus,* and vice versa. In this text, because we are employing a financial rather than an accounting focus, we will generally use *capital* or *capital and surplus* rather than *surplus* alone to refer to these items. The term *capital* also has several other meanings that we encounter later in this book. To review some of these meanings, refer to Insight 1-2.

In this text, the main purpose of the balance sheet is to measure the owners' wealth—that is, at a given time, what remains after subtracting what a company owes from what it owns. Thus, a balance sheet answers the general question: As of a certain date, what and how

Insight 1-2 Financial Management Terminology

Capital can have several meanings depending on the context of a discussion. The word *capital* sometimes appears within other financial terms, and in these contexts it often refers to all of a company's long-term financing, from both debt and equity sources. These other financial terms appear in the following glossary.

For now, our main purpose in mentioning these different meanings is to prepare you for the fact that every time you see the word *capital,* you cannot rely upon it to mean just capital and surplus. Throughout the book, as each *capital* term appears in its natural context, we alert you to the particular meaning intended at that point in the discussion.

- *Capital assets:* Long-term assets or long-term investments. For insurers, the term refers to investments in subsidiary corporations, buildings, mainframe computer equipment, and the activities involved in developing and offering a new product.
- *Capital budgeting:* Planning for long-term investments, regardless of how the investments are financed.
- *Capital markets:* The markets for long-term debt and equity funds; stock and bond markets.
- *Cost of capital:* The rate of interest that a company pays to obtain long-term financing, including both debt and equity. Whenever an insurer issues common stock, issues surplus notes, or borrows money from a bank, then the interest the insurer pays to secure these funds is the insurer's *cost of capital* for those funds.

much does a company own and what and how much does a company owe? Note that from a statutory viewpoint, a balance sheet addresses the question: As of a specific date, how *solvent* is the insurer?

As its name implies, both sides of a balance sheet must be equal. Thus, the left-hand side of a balance sheet (assets) must be equal to the right-hand side (liabilities and owners' equity). Let's look at the components of the basic accounting equation.

Basic accounting equation:

Assets = Liabilities + Owners' Equity

or as is more commonly stated by insurers:

Assets = Liabilities + Capital and Surplus

- *Assets* are all things of value owned by the company. Examples of assets include cash and investments.
- *Liabilities* are the company's debts and future obligations. A large portion of an insurance company's liabilities consists of the company's *policy reserves,* which represent the amount the insurer estimates it will need to pay policy benefits as they come due.
- *Owners' equity* is the difference between the company's assets and its liabilities and represents the owners' financial interest in the company. Owners' equity consists of the company's capital and surplus.

Further, because both sides of a balance sheet must remain equal, changes in any one balance-sheet category must reflect changes in either another balance-sheet category or else an offsetting change within the same balance-sheet category. For example, an increase in liabilities must be accompanied by either a decrease in capital and surplus or an increase in assets. Otherwise, the balance sheet would become "unbalanced."

Although insurers develop balance sheets for both GAAP and statutory financial reports, when you look at an insurer's U.S. Annual Statement, you will not see the term "balance sheet" on any of the exhibits or schedules. Instead, the Annual Statement's equivalent of a balance sheet appears on two pages: (1) an *Assets* page and (2) a *Liabilities, Surplus and Other Funds* page. The corresponding pages on the Canadian Annual Return are (1) an *Assets* page and (2) a *Liabilities, Policyholders' and Shareholders' Equity* page. The *Assets* page format and the types of assets that are admitted for statutory financial reporting purposes differ from the assets portion of a company's GAAP-based balance sheet. Except when we indicate otherwise, those differences are not a focus of this text.

The relationships between the various components of a balance sheet are primary measures of a company's solvency as well as its profitability. A company with too little capital and surplus in comparison to its liabilities, for example, may come under regulatory supervision because of solvency concerns.

Income Statement

The basic format and key elements in an income statement are illustrated in Figure 1-7. Before discussing the income statement, we need to establish some additional terminology. The income statement is called the *Summary of Operations* on both U.S. GAAP financial statements and on the statutory U.S. Annual Statement. The term *income statement* is used on the Canadian Annual Return as well as in everyday language. In this text, we will generally use the term *income statement.* The ***income statement*** is used to determine the increase or decrease in capital and surplus—that is, the profit earned or loss incurred from business operations during a given time period, such as one year.

Stated even more simply, the income statement or profit/loss equation for insurers would be

	Revenue
−	Expenses
=	**Net gain from operations (before policyowner dividends and taxes)**
−	Policyowner dividends
−	Taxes
=	**Net income**

As both Figure 1-7 and the diagram above illustrate, revenue minus expenses equals ***net gain (loss) from operations,*** also called *operating income (loss),* or *earnings before interest and taxes (EBIT).* Amounts paid out in dividends to policyowners and taxes are deducted from operating income in order to arrive at ***net income*** (also called *net earnings, net gain,* or *net profit).* A company's income statement answers the question, Did the company's revenues exceed its expenses? Net income (profit) recorded on the income statement is added to the company's capital and surplus. Likewise, losses recorded on the income statement reduce the company's capital and surplus.

By inspecting the relationships in the profit equation, we can see that an increase in profits would result from either (1) increasing revenue items or (2) reducing expense items, policyowner dividends, or taxes. Conversely, a decrease in profits would result from either (1) reducing revenue items or (2) increasing expense items, policyowner dividends, or taxes.

Figure 1-7. A simplified income statement.

LOMA Life and Health Insurance Company
Simplified Income Statement
For the period ended December 31, XXXX

Revenues
+ Premium income
+ Annuity considerations
+ Net investment income
+ Other income/adjustments

} **TOTAL REVENUES**

= **Total revenues**

minus

Expenses
+ Policy benefits
+ Annuity benefits
+ Increase in policy reserves
+ Operating expenses

} **TOTAL EXPENSES**

= **Total expenses**

= **Net gain (loss) from operations before policyowner dividends and taxes**
– Policyowner dividends
= **Net gain (loss) before taxes**
– Taxes
= **Net income (loss)**

Insurers' Revenue and Expense Accounts

Insurance companies' three main revenue sources are revenue from insurance and other contracts, income from investments, and revenue from reinsurance ceded. In the absence of other changes, increases in revenues from any or all of these sources can produce an increase in profitability. These revenue categories can be subdivided as follows:

- *Income from insurance contracts:* insurance premiums, annuity considerations, considerations for supplementary contracts with and without life contingencies, and amounts left on deposit to accumulate at interest.
- *Net investment income:* interest collected on bonds, income collected from mortgages, dividends collected from stock investments, net rent collected from property investments, and income collected from investments in subsidiaries. (Net investment income does *not* include gains or losses from the sale of invested assets.)

- *Adjustments on reinsurance ceded:* expense allowances, reinsurance commissions, and reserve adjustments on reinsurance ceded. (This category reflects revenues from sales of blocks of business by means of reinsurance transactions, a topic that will be covered in detail in Chapter 13.) On an insurer's income statement, all revenue amounts except those related to reinsurance ceded are shown net of the effects of reinsurance transactions.

A survey of the expense items offsetting these income items provides a quick key to the major sources of profitability improvement—and thus capital and surplus increases—achievable through expense control. Any reduction in an expense item, taken in isolation, would have the effect of improving or increasing net income. The major expense categories for an insurance company include

- Payments of claims for contractual benefits
- Increases in policy reserves
- Payments of sales commissions
- Expenses arising from reinsurance assumed
- Payments of general insurance (business) expenses
- Distributions of policy dividends
- Payments of taxes

In summary, net income can be calculated as shown:

LOMA Life and Health Insurance Company **Simplified Income Statement** For the period ended December 31, XXXX	
Revenues	
+ Revenue from insurance premiums and annuity considerations	**REVENUE**
+ Net investment income	
+ Income from other sources	
+ Adjustments for reinsurance	**minus**
Expenses	
– Policy benefits	
– Increases in policy reserves	**EXPENSES**
– Sales commissions	
– Adjustments for reinsurance	
– Operating and other general business expenses	**equals**
– Policyowner dividends	
– Taxes	
= **Net Income (or loss)**	**Net Income (or loss)**

Net income is not the only cause for changes in a life and health insurance company's capital and surplus. As we noted earlier, capital gains or losses from investments are not included in the amount of net gain from operations; capital gains or losses from investments do, however, affect capital and surplus. We will discuss other items that affect capital and surplus in later sections on profitability and solvency.

Before proceeding, let's review the income terminology covered thus far:

- **Revenue – Expenses = Operating Income *or* Net Gain from Operations**
- **Operating Income – Policyowner Dividends – Taxes = Net Income**
- Net income is also called *net earnings, net gain,* and *net profit.*
- If the net income figure is negative, it is called a *net loss.*

Sources of Income-Statement Figures

Note that the income statement shows the results of the organization as a whole. To obtain a finer breakdown of profits by product line or business unit, companies prepare a number of other financial documents or exhibits. One of these exhibits is the Analysis of Operations by Product Line.

Analysis of Operations by Product Line

Information concerning the revenue and expenses associated with a specific product line can be found by looking at various exhibits in a company's U.S. statutory Annual Statement or Canadian Annual Return.* From an accounting viewpoint, a ***line of business*** is a segment of products that has a cost pattern distinct from that of other segments. These cost patterns are usually determined by the product segment's distribution and servicing methods. An example of an insurer's lines of business appears in Figure 1-8. (The subdivisions provided here are loosely based upon those required in the United States by statutory regulation. For its own internal performance measurement or analysis purposes, a company can subdivide its lines in any way it deems appropriate.)

For each line of business, the insurer develops the same income and expense information as it does for the company as a whole. This

* Product-line information is found in the *Analysis of Operations by Lines of Business* part of the U.S. Annual Statement, where it appears as a worksheet in the "Gain and Loss Exhibit." In Canada, the equivalent exhibit is titled *Analysis of Income by Line of Business.* Both exhibits are designed to show an allocation of the organization's overall revenues and expenses to various distinct lines of business. The content of U.S. statutory exhibits reflects the usual lines of business identified with life insurance, health insurance, and annuities. The Canadian *Analysis* page shows the gains in each line of business separately for participating and nonparticipating insurance policies and uses broader categories for grouping lines of business.

Figure 1-8. One way an insurer might subdivide its lines of business for financial analysis.

Lines of Business

Industrial Business
- Industrial life insurance

Ordinary Business
- Individual life insurance

Ordinary Annuities
- Deferred annuities
- Immediate annuities

Supplementary Contracts
- Settlement contracts

Credit Business
- Group credit life insurance
- Individual credit life insurance

Group Business
- Group life insurance
- Group annuities

Accident and Health Business
- Group accident and health insurance
- Group credit accident and health insurance
- Individual credit accident and health insurance
- Other

Aggregate of All Other Lines of Business
- Other business

information is useful to management in determining sources of gains or losses from insurance operations. Such information is also useful for both internal and external comparisons. For example, if different companies sell similar products, serve similar markets, have similar operations, and have business of a similar age, these companies' lines of business can be compared to determine specific internal operational strengths and weaknesses at each company. A company can also use line-of-business income and expense information internally to make profitability comparisons among its own different lines of business. (Often insurers operate separate lines of business as self-contained *profit centers* or *cost centers*, and these profit centers naturally are most strongly interested in seeing the isolated results that are attributed to their own operations.)

Although this section has introduced only the product line information that insurers prepare, you should be aware that insurers prepare many types of reports and conduct various studies to track the performance of specific lines of business or other operational areas. As we progress through the text, we will investigate some of these additional means of tracking operational performance.

Connecting the Income Statement with the Balance Sheet

As we noted earlier, income statement gains (net profits) or losses are transferred to the balance sheet.

The following four rules relate items reported on an income statement to changes reported on a balance sheet:

1. Revenue items, such as premiums, produce an increase in capital and surplus.
2. Expense items, such as benefit payments, produce a decrease in assets.
3. Reserve increases produce an increase in liabilities.
4. A net profit produces an increase in capital and surplus.

As illustrated in Balance Sheet 1 that follows, a net gain on the income statement can appear on the balance sheet as (1) an increase in cash assets with (2) no change in liabilities and (3) a corresponding increase in the insurer's capital and surplus. To increase capital and surplus in this manner, an insurance company must bring in more revenue than it recognizes in expenses.

Balance Sheet 1 LOMA Life and Health	
Assets *Increase*	**Liabilities** *No change* **Capital and Surplus** *Increase*

Alternatively, as illustrated in Balance Sheet 2 below, a net gain on the income statement can appear on the balance sheet as (1) a decrease in liabilities with (2) no change in assets and (3) a corresponding increase in the insurer's capital and surplus. To increase capital and surplus in this manner, an insurance company must reduce liabilities more than it increases assets.

Balance Sheet 2 LOMA Life and Health	
Assets *No change*	**Liabilities** *Decrease* **Capital and Surplus** *Increase*

Although an income statement focuses on the financial outcome of only one period of operations, a company's capital and surplus accounts on the balance sheet record the cumulative effects of a company's operations over the years—accounting period after accounting period, the insurer's successive income statement net gains have been posted to the balance sheet, where each net gain has the effect of increasing capital and surplus. Thus, income statement gains improve both the company's profits and its wealth. Over the long term, such improvements also help safeguard the company's solvency position. In this way, a company is able to meet its financial objectives regarding both solvency and profitability.

In Conclusion

This chapter has set the stage for the rest of the text by introducing the concepts of solvency and profitability and providing an overview of the financial profile of the life and health insurance industry, including its major sources of revenue and expenses and its major categories of assets and liabilities. The approach in this chapter has been a broad-based one designed to reacquaint you with basic accounting and financial measurement concepts and how key financial statement components—revenues, expenses, net income, assets, liabilities, surplus, and capital—relate to each other. This information should prepare you to understand how insurance companies manage their financial resources in order to meet their financial goals. The next chapter provides additional context for the rest of the text by describing in more detail exactly what is meant in an insurance company by the objectives of *enhancing profitability* and *protecting solvency,* and why these two goals can conflict.

Key Terms and Concepts

financial management
profit
contribution to surplus
profitability
capital investment projects
return on capital
solvency
insolvency
cash flows
debt service
balance sheet
assets
liabilities
owners' equity
capital and surplus
capital
surplus
income statement
net gain (loss) from operations
net income
line of business

References

1. Adapted from David B. Atkinson, FSA, *Course G-340 Study Note—Pricing Individual Life Insurance* (Schaumberg, IL: Society of Actuaries, 1989), pp. 1–2.
2. ACLI *1994 Life Insurance Fact Book,* p. 83.
3. ACLI *1994 Life Insurance Fact Book,* p. 79.
4. CLHIA *1994 Canadian Life and Health Insurance Facts,* p. 31.
5. ACLI *1994 Life Insurance Fact Book,* pp. 80–81.

CHAPTER

2

Balancing Returns with Solvency

LEARNING OBJECTIVES

After studying this chapter, you should be able to

- Recognize the importance of wealth and returns for insurance companies
- Distinguish between profit maximization and wealth maximization strategies
- Interpret the importance of capitalization and liquidity to an insurer's solvency
- Demonstrate understanding of the risk-return tradeoff in general and in the context of insurance operations
- Recognize and apply the concept of the solvency-profitability tradeoff for insurers

OUTLINE

In the last chapter, we noted that a primary goal of financial management for insurance companies is to generate a return—that is, to earn a profit—while protecting solvency. In this chapter, we look at (1) approaches companies can follow in generating returns, (2) why generating returns is important to a company's survival, (3) how risk is inherent in the pursuit of profit, and (4) what is meant by solvency. The chapter concludes with a description of the delicate balance insurers must maintain between the conflicting goals of profitability and solvency.

Generating and Measuring Returns

A key financial goal of every investor—regardless of whether the investor is an individual, a business organization, or a business organization's owners—is to earn a return. In this context, a ***return*** is the reward, profit, or compensation an investor hopes to earn for taking a risk. For an investor, ***risk*** is defined as the possibility of experiencing a loss or failing to earn a return. For a company developing a new product, the return might be in the form of new product sales revenue and the increase in net income and capital and surplus resulting from those sales. The risk to the investor would be the possibility of expending many resources to develop and introduce the new product and then have it fail to generate an acceptable return. As another example, a company or an individual might invest in a particular stock, earn dividends from that stock, and then sell the stock at a capital gain. The investor's return would be the dividends earned from the stock and the capital gain realized from the increase in the stock's value. The investor's risk would be the possibility that the stock might pay lower-than-expected dividends or no dividends at all and that the stock's value might drop rather than increase.

An ***investment*** is any expenditure of money or assets in an effort to earn a return. Thus, when an insurer develops and offers a new product, the insurer is considered to be making an investment—that is, taking a risk in an effort to earn a return.

From a company's and its owners' perspectives, two of the most important measures of return focus on the company's financial performance. One popular way to measure a company's financial performance is in terms of the company's profits as represented by the company's annual net profit. As we noted in Chapter 1, profits represent an organization's net gain from one period of operations. Another popular way to measure a company's performance is in terms of *wealth.*

Wealth is the combination of *goodwill* and the monetary value that a company has built up over the years from profits and investments. ***Goodwill*** refers to the value of a company's name; its relations with its customers; the knowledge, skills, and morale of its workforce; and all the other intangible assets a company possesses. Both increasing the wealth of a company and increasing the company's profits are financial objectives that a company can set as part of its attempt to generate returns.

Distinctions between Wealth and Profits

Some people believe that, theoretically, the major focus of a business's financial operations should be to maximize profit; others believe that maximizing wealth is a superior goal. The fundamental distinction between these two approaches to managing a company resides in an important difference between profits and wealth. Because *profit* for an organization refers to the gains from one period of operations, a focus on *profit* can sometimes take a short-term view of generating returns. Because *wealth* refers to the value that a company has built up over the years, a focus on *wealth* takes a long-term view of generating returns. Though seeking profits and seeking wealth are often compatible goals, when a company focuses exclusively on profit, the company faces the danger of placing too much emphasis on maximizing returns for the current period and losing sight of the negative impact that current profit-taking activities can have on the company's future.

Conventional financial theory supports wealth maximization as the most appropriate and comprehensive financial goal for business organizations to pursue. For most stock corporations, ***wealth maximization*** is generally interpreted to mean maximizing the company's stock price, which in turn maximizes the return that the organization's owners receive for their investment in the company. Unfortunately, conventional financial theory has not been able to provide managers with clear tools or guidelines for achieving wealth maximization through everyday business decisions. One reason for the absence of practical tools and guidelines is that the effect of managerial decisions on stock price has never been established in any absolute sense. In contrast, the short-term effects of everyday business decisions on profits are much easier to measure. Therefore, although conventional financial reasoning supports focusing on wealth maximization rather than profit maximization, profit maximization sometimes becomes the goal of real-world decision making.

A firm that follows a goal of wealth maximization seeks to provide the best possible returns to the company's owners by maximizing the company's long-term value. A firm that follows a goal of profit maximization seeks to generate the highest operating profit in a period. The danger in following a goal of profit maximization is that profit maximization often ignores the effect of risk on returns and, as a result, may expose a company to too much risk. Overexposure to risk can damage a company's long-term value.

An emerging school of financial theory supports a goal of maximizing customer or client satisfaction. This goal reflects the underlying belief that customer satisfaction is the primary determinant of a company's value, its stock price, and its profits. Stated another way, this position holds that the primary financial goal of a business should be to maximize the lifetime value to the company of a customer's business, a goal that can be accomplished through maximizing customer satisfaction. The more satisfied that customers are with a company and its products, the more likely they are to continue to buy those products, the less likely they are to complain about or bring suit against the company, and the more likely they are to recommend the company and its products to others. According to this position, all of these factors serve to (1) increase the company's sales, (2) increase the company's profits, and (3) increase the value of the company's stock. When a company satisfies its customers, profits and increased wealth should follow.

The Importance of Wealth to Insurance Companies

Although profits are obviously important to insurers, most insurers pursue wealth maximization as a primary goal for several reasons—the first being that a very small life and health insurance company often cannot survive. Most jurisdictions in North America allow most types of businesses to begin operations with a minimal amount of capital invested—perhaps as little as a few hundred dollars. In contrast, before insurance regulators will permit a new insurance company to do business, they require the new company to have a relatively large capital investment—typically millions of dollars. Insurance regulators work to preserve the interests of insurance consumers, and they judge that a company starting without a sufficient capital investment would not be able to sustain operations.

The second reason most insurers pursue wealth maximization as a primary goal is that, once an insurance company begins operating on a relatively small scale, it cannot easily continue operations unless it grows. For insurers, small size can be a competitive disadvantage. Some experts refer to the idea that insurance companies must achieve critical mass, a term borrowed from physics. In this context, ***critical mass*** means that each insurance company must grow to a minimum size, depending on its particular situation, in order to survive and prosper and be able to take advantage of *economies of scale.* (You should recall that *economies of scale* refers to the savings available from large-scale operations.) The expression *critical mass* summarizes the viewpoint that, for a life and health insurance company, achieving this minimum size can be a *critical success factor*—that is, one of the few truly critical goals that the life and health insurance company must achieve in order to succeed. Experts do not agree, however, on any specific guidelines for determining a company's minimum size or critical mass. The practical minimum size for each company's survival depends on several factors, including the competitive marketplace, the company's target markets and product lines, and the nature of the company's distribution system.

Third, increasing a company's wealth also helps the company avoid solvency problems. Over the long term, as companies grow, they typically improve their levels of capital and surplus. As we shall see later in this chapter, capital and surplus play an important role in solvency formulas, and companies with inadequate capital and surplus can be subject to regulatory action. Actions life and health insurance companies can take in order to strengthen their capital and surplus are covered throughout this book.

The Importance of Profits for Insurers

As noted in Chapter 1, a life and health insurance company's ability to earn a profit has important implications for the company, whether the company is a stock company answerable to stockholders or a mutual or fraternal company answerable to policyowners.

A stock insurance company must earn a profit so that it can reward the individual and institutional investors who own the company. Owners of stock expect to be compensated through dividend payments and increased stock value. Investors choose the stocks of companies, insurance or otherwise, that they expect to provide the greatest return for the amount of investment risk inherent in the stock. In order to raise capital by selling stock, insurers must earn profits that are comparable to the profits of other companies that are subject to the same or a similar degree of risk.

Although mutual and fraternal insurers do not compete in the stock market for investors' funds, a mutual or fraternal insurance company must also earn a profit in order to be able to reward the company's owners. The policyowners of mutual and fraternal insurance organizations have supplied these organizations with capital by purchasing the organizations' products. Like stockholders of stock companies, mutual insurance company policyowners expect the company to generate enough returns to be able to pay dividends, even though (as with stockholder dividends) policyholder dividends are not guaranteed. Further, policyowners are mutual companies' primary source of funds. Just as most investors are unlikely to choose to invest in a company that is not profitable, most customers do not consciously buy insurance or other financial products from a mutual company of questionable profitability. An insurance company's profits affect its *quality ratings*—letter grades indicating financial soundness and assigned by independent agencies—which in turn significantly affect consumers' buying decisions. If a mutual or fraternal insurer is not profitable, customers may stop buying its products, and the company will not be able to generate the income it needs to maintain its necessary contributions to surplus. Without these new sales and increases in surplus, the company will find it difficult to grow.

Effects of Strong Profits

A company's profitability can help it earn even more profits. The public and the financial community take note of a firm's profits, and they see a significant change in profit levels as indicative of an overall change in an insurer's performance. In response to an improvement in profits, a company often benefits from a "halo effect" in that an insurer's financial picture can become even brighter as a result of strong profits. In addition to the obvious benefit of simply increasing capital, strong returns can benefit insurance companies in many other ways, such as

- Providing the company with investable cash from the profits themselves;
- Allowing insurers to make investments on favorable contractual or financial terms and thus realize *financial economies of scale (financial economies of scale* are cost savings that accrue from conducting financial operations on a large scale);
- Generating higher quality ratings from the firms that issue quality ratings of insurance companies;
- Providing funds needed to back new sales of current products and also to allow for expansion into new products or product lines and additional methods of distribution;
- Making for more efficient operations, resulting in lower expenses;
- Allowing a company to pay policyowner dividends and to offer products at competitive rates, resulting in higher customer loyalty and fewer withdrawals from and surrenders of insurance policies and other contracts;
- Helping a company attract and retain higher-quality agents and employees, resulting in lower turnover and lower expenses of recruiting and training because people want to be associated with a successful organization;
- For stock companies, generating high demand for the company's outstanding common stock and, thus, increasing the firm's overall value; and

- Reducing the insurer's ***cost of capital***—the overall rate of interest that a company pays for obtaining funds.

Effects of Weak or Inadequate Profits

In a similar fashion, inadequate profits—or even worse, losses—can have a "snowball effect" in that an insurer's financial problems can worsen as a result of poor profits. The public and the financial community are at least as quick to take note of inadequate profits as they are strong profits. Inadequate profits are regarded as a symptom of ineffective performance. Among the problems caused by poor profits are

- Less capital available for investment;
- Higher cost of obtaining funds (cost of capital), less favorable investment terms, and financial diseconomies of scale;
- Lower quality ratings;
- A diminished ability to sell new insurance contracts, partly as an outcome of lower quality ratings;
- Unexpected withdrawals of funds from the insurance company, possibly provoking a cash flow (liquidity) crisis;
- Higher levels of scrutiny by insurance regulators about an insurer's liquidity and solvency positions, requiring the insurer to incur additional costs related to financial examinations of the company by the NAIC (National Association of Insurance Commissioners) or OSFI (the Office of the Superintendent of Financial Institutions);
- Higher employee turnover and diminished loyalty of sales representatives and other customers;
- Sales of large blocks of stock by disenchanted stockholders; and
- A low market price for the insurer's stock and a resulting low overall value for the company.

Balancing the Profit Motive with Concern for Safety

Constraints such as regulatory limitations, particularly solvency regulations, and the nature of the insurance business itself prevent life and health insurance companies from pursuing all-out maximization of profits or wealth. For insurance companies, the goal of generating returns must always be balanced against the need to protect the company's solvency. As illustrated in Insight 2-1, insurance companies must place as much emphasis on safety and solvency as they do on profitability. A large part of the appeal of an insurance company's products and services is the consumer's perception of an insurance product's security. For insurance companies and other financial institutions, successful financial performance consists of an appropriate balance between achieving good returns and maintaining appropriate safety and solvency.

The Risk-Return Tradeoff in Finance

As we mentioned at the beginning of this chapter, a *risk* is the possibility that an investor will fail to earn a return or will lose all or part of an investment; a *return* is the reward an investor hopes to receive for taking a risk. Investors generally seek returns. However, most investors want both to avoid risk and seek returns. These two goals—avoiding risk and seeking returns—inevitably come into conflict in financial matters because it is impossible to earn an adequate return without taking on some amount of risk. The only way to avoid risk altogether is not to invest. Investors, including insurers, must decide how much risk they are willing to take and how much return they require as a reward for taking that risk.

The higher the risk associated with an investment, the greater the anticipated return must be in order to offset the risk the investor is taking. If a higher risk investment did not offer greater potential returns, no one would choose such an investment over a safer one. The lower the risk on an investment, the lower the potential return can be and yet still attract investors. The interplay between these forces is called the ***risk-return tradeoff.*** Investors must find a satisfactory compromise between their conflicting preference for risk avoidance on the one hand and their desire for returns on the other hand. Every financial or business decision a company makes is subject to the risk-return tradeoff.

In order to better understand the risk-return tradeoff, consider the following example. When reviewing a loan application, a bank consults a credit rating agency to learn about the applicant's credit history. Based on the information it receives, the bank will decide whether the borrower's probability of defaulting is high or low. If the bank decides to make the loan, it will charge a higher interest rate to a borrower having a poor credit rating than it would to a borrower with a spotless credit history. The higher interest rate compensates the bank for the additional risk it is taking by making the loan. By the same token, a

Insight 2-1 What 'Fiduciary' Should Mean to Insurers

How would you answer these questions:

What is the reason insurers are in business?

For what group do insurers have a higher obligation—stockholders or policyholders?

If you answered the first question "to make a profit," you'd be counted among many senior executives and managers in the industry. If you answered the second question, "A company's first obligation is to its stockholders before its customers," you would also have a sizable group standing with you. A senior underwriting officer for a major U.S. insurer recently told me that, in company meetings, numerous officers and managers firmly held to these beliefs about their company's purposes and obligations. When asked about their company's *fiduciary* responsibilities to policyholders, many admitted they didn't understand the word. These were people with their CLUs, FLMIs, and other designations.

Within this episode lies a partial answer to the troubles plaguing the industry today. Everyone knows that stockholders are the nominal owners of the company they've invested in. Everyone easily understands that stockholders have *risked* their money. But we seem to have stopped teaching that when policyholders *entrust* us with their premiums, we accept a fiduciary responsibility for the proper management of those funds. We have a sacred obligation to ensure that the money is there when benefits must be paid. That's our Holy Grail.

As for the role of profit, it is the indispensable means to serving the needs of our policyholders. But it is not the reason we're in business. Peter Drucker had it right 45 years ago when he wrote that the purpose of a business is to serve a customer. But the world of that time seems remote today—almost quaint and simple. Twenty-five years ago, on the day I started my first job at an insurance company, I was given a textbook written in 1958, *Selection of Risks* by Andy Webster, the esteemed actuary of Mutual of New York. It served as my introduction to the principles of insurance. Another was the *Life and Health Insurance Handbook* edited by Davis Gregg and Vane Lucas of the American College in 1959. Throughout these texts were phrases like "economic security," "human life value," "safety of principle," "guaranteed values," "company's obligation to the policyowner," and so on. Today we read of "capital accumulation," "taxpayer's adjusted basis," "indexed rates," "synthetic stable value," ad nauseam.

Of course, the senior executives of our business in the 50s had memories of the cataclysm that was the Great Depression and how insurers survived it. The lessons of the Armstrong Investigation and the appropriate role of industry regulation were more keenly understood and accepted. Today we're immersed in talk of increased privatization, shrinking government, less regulation, and totally free markets. We had better beware of unbridled capitalism that caters to the worst instincts of man in pursuit of his commercial activities.

A generation of insurance professionals has been educated to see the insurance business as analogous to any other enterprise. Increased profit margins and larger market share have been pursued as priority goals for their own sake rather than as part of a strategy focused on our customers. Recently tightened underwriting, more conservative investments, and reengineering to reduce expenses aren't really meant to ensure we meet our fiduciary obligations to policyowners. They are means to increase shareholder value, achieve competitive rates of return, and publish quarterly reports that show rising sales and falling claims.

Our market conduct problems have grown out of this single-minded focus on profit and growth. The real needs and interests of policyholders are easily subordinated in this climate. Is it any wonder that the insurance industry is held in such low public esteem? If insurers want to avoid front page scandals in the press, RICO class action suits, and stifling regulatory oversight, we must revisit the lessons our predecessors learned. Fair and honest dealing with our customers means delivering what you promised. It means we shun the "bait and switch" tactics of other marketers. It means we gain our customers' trust and never do anything to betray it.

Hyped illustrations, vanishing premium gimmicks, and so forth are only part of the problem. Creating 10 classes of preferred pricing out of what used to be one standard class is a recipe for disaster. It fuels the perception that we cherry-pick the risks we insure and are restricting availability and affordability. It means that the premium quoted at point of sale is

Insight 2-1 What 'Fiduciary' Should Mean to Insurers (continued)

more likely to be changed by the underwriters. It either violates the buyer's trust or confirms his suspicions about insurers and their agents.

Overaggressive claims management is often focused on reducing benefits rather than uncovering fraud. This encourages cynicism about insurers and perpetuates popular notions that insurers will readily take your money but fight any claims you submit. It's too easy for insurers to forget what a sensible claims executive recently posted on the Internet with regard to fair claim handling—"After all, it's their money." Yes. That's what fiduciary means. It's their money.

Source: *John J. Krinik, "What 'Fiduciary' Should Mean to Insurers,"* Probe *42, no. 8, April 24, 1995, pp. 2–3. Reprinted by permission of the publisher.*

loan applicant with an excellent credit history can usually negotiate a lower interest rate from the bank because a loan to such an applicant typically would involve a lower level of risk.

A similar principle holds true in insurance company investments. Investment-grade U.S. government bonds pay a low rate of return to the investor. Investment-grade U.S. government bonds represent little or no risk to an investor, and so they return a lower rate than do junk bonds. In contrast, junk bonds represent a high level of risk to an insurer and these bonds must pay high rates of return to compensate the insurer for the investment risk it is taking.

In general, the higher the risk connected with an investment, the greater the potential for loss, and therefore, the higher the rate of return demanded for accepting the risk. The lower the risk, the less the potential for loss, and therefore, the lower the rate of return required for accepting the risk.

Sources of Investment Risk

The specific elements associated with a particular investment transaction in combination with the economic environment can act as sources of risk for the investor. These elements, which can each serve either to decrease both risk and potential return or else to increase both risk and potential return, include the following:

- An investment's term-to-maturity
- A borrower's credit rating
- An asset's marketability
- An asset's liquidity
- Provisions of the agreement between the provider of funds and the user of funds

- The industry of a borrower
- The presence of collateral (security) for a loan
- The amount of owners' equity associated with a transaction

The following chart summarizes how these elements typically influence an investor's risk and return on any given investment decision or transaction:

Lower risks that offer lower potential return	Higher risks that offer higher potential return
• A *short-term* investment • A borrower with *good credit* • An investment with *good liquidity* or good *marketability* • An insurer that has *higher capitalization* • A loan that is *secured* by collateral • A product that has a short break-even period • The selling of a product in a familiar market	• A *long-term* investment • A borrower with *poor credit* • An investment with *poor liquidity* or *poor marketability* • An insurer that has *lower capitalization* • A loan that is *unsecured* by collateral • A product that has high up-front costs

The Solvency-Profitability Tradeoff for Life and Health Insurers

Insurance companies face a special balancing act similar to the risk-return tradeoff. In this text we call this tradeoff the solvency-profitability tradeoff. Because of its fiduciary responsibilities to its customers, an insurance company's solvency is viewed as being extraordinarily important. However, profitability is key to an insurer's financial health and success. The pursuit of the dual objectives of profitability and solvency presents a fundamental challenge to insurance company managers in that there is a natural tension between these two financial objectives. Pursuing profitability requires risk taking; protecting solvency requires avoiding or setting limits on risk taking. Pursuing profits means seeking returns; protecting solvency can reduce a company's potential returns. Yet these two goals are not polar opposites. It is possible for an insurance company to earn acceptable returns and remain solvent. The task is to find an appropriate balance.

Protecting Solvency

In this section, we introduce some of the methods used to evaluate an insurer's solvency and financial strength and we examine some very broad measures of solvency and financial stability. Although this section emphasizes the measures insurers take to protect solvency, keep in mind that, for the vast majority of insurers, insolvency is not an imminent threat.

Defining Solvency for Insurers

In Chapter 1, we defined solvency, generally, as a business organization's ability to meet its financial obligations on time. As such, solvency refers to a company's general financial strength and stability. We also noted that for insurers, solvency can be defined as the legal minimum dollar amount of capitalization or other financial standard that an insurance company must maintain. The main impetus behind the extensive regulation of the life and health insurance industry is to ensure the solvency of insurance companies. For example, statutory accounting and financial reporting systems are designed to satisfy regulators that the insurer is able to pay contractual benefits. Regulatory measures such as minimum capital and surplus requirements have the same objective. Our discussion here will serve as an introduction to solvency and insolvency standards. Both of these topics will be covered in much more detail in Chapter 18.

An Insurer's Financial Strength Is Based on Its Capitalization and Liquidity

Capitalization sometimes refers to the strength of a company's capital and surplus relative to the company's risks. When an insurer has adequate or more than adequate capital for the operating risks it faces, the company is said to be *well-capitalized.* ***Liquidity*** refers to the ease with which an asset can be converted into cash for an approximation of its true value. When a company can convert an asset into cash quickly without a significant loss in the asset's value, the asset is considered to have *liquidity.* As an example, investments in money market funds and listed stocks can be converted into cash more quickly and therefore are more liquid than are investments in real estate.

Adequate capitalization and adequate liquidity are twin supports of a life and health insurer's financial strength and solvency. ***Adequate capitalization*** refers to an insurer's having enough financial resources to conduct its business over the long run. Even if an insurer has enough capital to meet its long-term business needs, the insurer still may not be able to fulfill its current obligations or address emergency situations if it does not also have adequate liquidity. ***Adequate liquidity*** refers to an insurer's having enough cash—or assets that can easily be converted to cash—available as needed to pay bills and meet other obligations as they come due. Both adequate capitalization and adequate liquidity are needed to maintain solvency and avoid bankruptcy. The following sections explore ways in which capitalization and liquidity are measured to ensure that they are adequate. We discuss capitalization first.

Measuring Capital and Surplus for Insurers

In measuring capital and surplus for insurers, we are primarily interested in the level of an insurer's capital as an indication of the insurer's financial strength. Capital and surplus are crucial to an insurer's financial strength because insurers use capital and surplus as a safety cushion to finance growth and meet emergencies, regulatory demands, and commitments in general.

As noted in Chapter 1, *capital* can be defined as the sum of an insurer's capital stock, if any, and surplus. For accounting purposes, the amount of an insurer's capital is found by subtracting a company's liabilities from its assets. Although measuring the amount of an insurer's capital might seem to be a fairly simple process, at any one time, an insurer could measure its capital and find several different amounts, reflecting the several accounting methods used to calculate insurers' assets and liabilities. Statutory accounting and GAAP accounting prescribe different methods of valuing an insurer's assets and liabilities. In addition, an insurer's unique internal accounting system, developed for internal management purposes, may rely on still other methods of valuing assets and liabilities. Consequently, several different amounts of capital can be calculated for the same insurer, and an insurer may use some or all of these values for capital depending on the particular accounting purpose.

The amount of capital that is sufficient for one insurer may not be adequate for another insurer. Once the dollar amount to be assigned to an insurer's capital has been determined based on the accounting method being used, an additional step must be taken to determine whether that capital amount is adequate to provide a safety cushion for the insurer's liabilities for business currently on the books. The relationship between an insurer's capital and its liabilities indicates—to some extent—the insurer's financial strength. Generally, the higher the level of an insurer's capital relative to its liabilities, the better capitalized the company will be, and the greater the insurer's financial strength will be.

The level of a company's solvency or capitalization is often measured using financial ratios. Financial ratios, such as the *return-on-capital ratio* mentioned in Chapter 1, are useful for expressing a relationship between two financial statement amounts. Financial ratios are frequently used to express the relationship between an insurer's capital and its liabilities. Ratios that serve this purpose are sometimes called *capital ratios, capital and surplus ratios,* or *capitalization ratios.* For mutual insurers, they are sometimes called *surplus ratios.* The official Risk-Based Capital ratios discussed in the following section are examples of financial ratios. (We discuss financial ratios in greater detail in Part 5 of this book.)

Minimum Capitalization Requirements

Two important coexisting sets of minimum capitalization requirements apply to life and health insurers in the United States and Canada. These are (1) the minimum capital and surplus requirements, which exist in both countries, and (2) the statutory Risk-Based Capital (RBC) ratio requirements in the United States, or, in Canada, the minimum continuing capital and surplus requirements (MCCSR). Insurers in each country must meet both types of requirements. Each of these requirements helps regulators to protect consumers and the public at large from the effects of potential or actual insolvencies.

Long in effect in all U.S. and Canadian jurisdictions, ***minimum capital and surplus requirements,*** also called *minimum capitalization requirements,* set a specific minimum dollar amount of capital and surplus for a whole company and for each product line. In many jurisdictions, one minimum dollar amount is required for *initial* capital and surplus and another minimum amount is required for *continuing* capital and surplus.

Because these minimum capital and surplus requirements are expressed as a flat dollar amount, and in a given jurisdiction, the same flat dollar amount applies to all insurers regardless of their size, the task of determining whether an insurer meets one of these tests is relatively straightforward. For example, suppose the minimum requirement in one jurisdiction is $6 million. A company with actual capital and surplus of $10 million, $100 million, or any amount at least equal to $6 million would meet this requirement. A company with capital and surplus of less than $6 million would fail this requirement.

The statutory ***Risk-Based Capital (RBC) ratio requirements*** in the United States and Canada's similar ***minimum continuing capital and***

surplus requirements (MCCSR) are more complex. These ratio tests apply a minimum ratio value that each company must meet in order to be considered solvent. Under the RBC rules and the MCCSR, each insurer must meet a unique minimum dollar amount of capital and surplus. All insurers, however, are required to meet the same absolute minimum value of the RBC ratio or MCCSR.

The ratios themselves compare the insurer's actual capital and surplus to an amount that an official risk-weighting formula shows that the insurer should have. The calculations proceed as follows:

1. It is necessary to find the unique required minimum level of capital and surplus for each insurer, using a prescribed formula for weighting the values of assets and liabilities to reflect the inherent riskiness of an insurer's business. The result of the weighting process is a risk-weighted amount of capital and surplus.

2. The risk-weighted capital and surplus amount is then compared to the insurer's actual capital and surplus by means of a ratio calculation. The result of the ratio calculation expresses the insurer's actual capital surplus as a percentage of the required risk-weighted capital and surplus.

3. The outcome of this ratio calculation is then compared to the required minimum value for the RBC test.

Measuring Liquidity for Insurers

Earlier, we noted that an insurance company is considered to have adequate liquidity when it has the financial capacity to meet its short-term obligations on time. An insurance company's liquidity is quite similar to that of an individual. For example, an individual's ability to pay bills on time depends on several factors:

- The size of his or her bank account (or liquid assets)
- The amount of the individual's income
- The predictability of his or her income
- The amount of his or her expenses, bills, and various other obligations
- The predictability of these various obligations

An insurer's ability to pay its bills depends on similar factors, including

- The insurer's capital
- The amount of the insurer's income

- The certainty of the insurer's income
- The amount of the insurer's various obligations and expenses
- The certainty of the insurer's obligations and expenses

The primary short-term obligations for which life and health insurers need liquid assets include (1) paying claims and other contractual benefits, (2) covering investment losses, and (3) meeting general business expenses. The key sources of liquidity for insurers are (1) cash inflows from premiums and annuity considerations, (2) investment income, and (3) cash inflows from selling invested assets. An insurer with adequate liquidity can meet its short-term financial obligations by having cash on hand from strong and stable net cash inflows and by holding a combination of investment-grade assets that are marketable, liquid, diversified, and otherwise sound. Such an insurer rarely needs to make unplanned sales of long-term investments in order to meet current cash needs. In contrast, an insurer with poor liquidity may need to suddenly make an unplanned sale of assets and in so doing might encounter poor market values or adverse tax consequences. In a worst-case scenario, an insurer with extremely poor liquidity might be unable to raise enough cash to meet its obligations.

Measures of an insurer's liquidity often focus on solvency by measuring either the strength of the insurer's assets or the size of and the uncertainty in the insurer's obligations. In evaluating an insurer's liquidity, a financial analyst would look for strong net cash inflows, marketable assets, and sound investment practices, including diversification of invested assets with respect to such factors as maturity dates of securities, geographic representation of investments, industry representation of investments, and shares of the total portfolio invested in the various types of assets.

Risks Affecting Solvency

A thorough analysis of solvency concerns and the risks in the insurance business can easily become complicated and is beyond the scope of this chapter. We can, however, take a broad and somewhat simplified view of solvency and potential threats to it. We have already noted that the two main threats to an insurer's solvency are inadequate capital and inadequate liquidity. As an additional effort to ensure their financial strength, insurance companies must also focus their attention on a few crucial areas of risk that actuaries have identified as being vital to insurance company cash flows. Exposure to these risks, called *contingency risks,* or more often, ***C risks,*** can cause an insurer to have problems either with its level of capital or with its liquidity.

Actuaries have developed a classification system that officially recognizes four C risks—C-1, C-2, C-3, and C-4.

- ***C-1*** concerns ***asset risk*** or the risk that the insurer will lose money on its investments in stocks, bonds, mortgages, and real estate. Insurers can control C-1 risk by evaluating investment risks realistically, investing a high proportion of their assets in high-quality securities, and generally maintaining sound investment practices.
- ***C-2*** concerns ***pricing risk*** or the risk that the insurer's experience with mortality, morbidity, or expenses will differ significantly from expectations, causing the insurer to lose money on its products. Insurers can control C-2 risk by evaluating mortality and morbidity risks realistically, maintaining sound underwriting and reinsurance practices, controlling their expenses, and designing and pricing products sensibly.
- ***C-3*** concerns ***interest-rate risk*** or the risk that interest rates will shift, causing the insurer's assets to lose value. Insurers can control C-3 risk through effective asset-liability management (ALM), which we discuss in later chapters of this book.
- ***C-4*** concerns ***general management risk*** or the risk of losses resulting from ineffective general business practices. Such losses include those resulting from fraud and litigation. C-4 risk can be controlled by a high-quality and experienced management team that exercises sound managerial judgment, supports ethical behavior, prevents internal dishonesty, and controls operating costs. Nurturing an ethical culture is especially important in order to support an insurer's valuable reputation and goodwill and also to avoid costly legal settlements.

Figure 2-1 shows some examples of each of the four C risks.

Conservative and Aggressive Financial Strategies

In understanding an insurance company's quest for success, it can be helpful to view profitability as the objective of a company's offensive or growth strategy and to view solvency as the objective of a company's defensive or survival strategy. A company that de-emphasizes profitability and places unusually strong emphasis on solvency is regarded as having a ***conservative financial strategy.*** A company that de-emphasizes solvency and places unusually strong emphasis on profitability is regarded as having an ***aggressive financial strategy.*** Generally, strategies that are either too aggressive or too conservative can lead to problems for insurers.

Figure 2-1. C risks for life and health insurers, and examples of each.

C-1 Asset Risks	• Loss in assets' market value, except if caused by interest rate movements • Borrower's default in payment of interest • Borrower's default in payment of principal
C-2 Pricing Risks	• Adverse change in mortality or morbidity experience • Increase in cost of providing health care • Increase in company's operating expenses • Pricing deficiencies
C-3 Interest-rate Risks	• Assets' loss of value because of interest-rate increases; loss on forced sales of assets when interest rates rise • Withdrawals by customers when interest rates rise • Loss on bond calls and mortgage prepayments when interest rates fall • Losses due to asset/liability mismatches
C-4 General Management Risks	• Market risk from expansion into new lines of business • Market risk from geographic expansion • Changes in tax law • Fraud • Mismanagement • Lawsuits • Guaranty fund assessments • Runs on assets caused by fear of insolvency

A sudden improvement in profitability is not necessarily good for an insurance company. Although one of an insurance company's goals is to earn a high return while maintaining a high level of solvency, an insurance company's financial strength can suffer when it earns too much profit too quickly. Rapid increases in an insurer's capitalization or its profitability can indicate that the company is taking on too much risk. Insight 2-2 tells of an insurer whose aggressive strategy and tremendous short-term profitability came at the price of tremendous risks that eventually caused the insurer's downfall.

For insurance companies, we can also say that there is such a thing as too much safety. Unnecessarily high capitalization indicates a low level of risk, and extremely low risk is not necessarily good either. Too high a level of capitalization could indicate that a company is

Insight 2-2 The Collapse of Confederation Life

Canadians woke up on Friday, August 12, 1994, to the shocking news that a big Toronto life insurer had collapsed overnight.

Confederation Life Insurance, Canada's fourth-largest life insurer—one with a proud 123-year history in Canada and growing branches in the U.S. and Britain—turned into the biggest-ever liquidation in the North American insurance industry. Confed's 275,000 individual policyholders and about 2 million people covered by group insurance were left stranded. Canadian insurance consumers from coast to coast fretted over their investments.

Aggressive Growth

In the early 1980s, Confederation Life launched an aggressive growth and diversification strategy, convinced it was the way to arm itself for a looming showdown with the big banks, who were clamoring to get into the insurance business. Caution, once the watchword at Confed, was sacrificed. Largely due to booming sales of savings and investment products, as opposed to traditional life insurance, the company averaged about 23 percent annual growth between 1982 and 1992, making Confed one of the fastest growing life insurers in North America in the 1980s.

But a reckless pace of growth had led Confed into a calamitous over-exposure in the real estate market. Crushing setbacks would ensue when the market went sour.

By 1989, when real estate values peaked, 65 percent of Confed's $11 billion in assets were in mortgages—twice the industry's norm. And 70 percent of those mortgages were on commercial buildings—the sector hit hardest when real estate prices collapsed in the 1990s.

"It was unheard of that you would have a life company be so aggressive and reckless," said Brian Cass, Ontario's financial watchdog.

The Trust Company Gambit

With one eye focused on Ontario's soaring real estate market and the other fixed on new opportunities in the financial industry, Confederation Life bought Halifax Trust in 1987. Renamed Confederation Trust, the company was to be Confed's counter-attack at the banks, which would soon be exerting their financial muscle in the insurance field.

Confed's aggressive growth strategy was quickly applied at Confederation Trust. Mortgage approvals at the trust jumped from $287 million in the first year after Confed's takeover, to $454 million in the second. Deposits at the trust were turned into $1.1 billion in loans by 1989.

By 1990, as the real estate market began to collapse and defaults on these loans increased, Confed was steadily losing strength. Debt levels had risen from virtually nothing in 1984 to $1.5 billion in 1990. In the same period, surplus or emergency funds had declined from 14.1 percent of liabilities to 6.7 percent.

By 1991, nearly 30 percent of Confed's trust borrowers had stopped paying interest on their loans. In that year, Confed's profit nose-dived by 85 percent—to $19 million from $106 million. Then the cash-strapped parent was forced to inject $70 million into the trust company between December 1991 and October 1992. That drain of cash, on top of losses on the life insurer's big real estate loans, worsened its capital woes.

For years, Confed had failed to heed federal disaster warnings of reckless management. Ottawa had first warned Confed's board of trouble in 1989, but it was difficult for the board to believe that the circumstances were really catastrophic. After all, as late as January 1992—just 30 months before the insurer was liquidated—Confed still retained its coveted triple-A rating from Standard and Poor's of New York. The life insurer was profitable (if less so than before) and still exceeded minimum capital demands.

However, by 1994, it was clear that Confederation Life was in big trouble. The company attempted to save itself by selling off assets and then by seeking a bailout from the Canadian insurance industry. In August of that year, after the rescue operations failed and media reports began to surface, Confed's executives and federal regulators, fearing a "run on the bank" as policyowners rushed to yank out their investments, shut the company down.

One Year Later

The fallout from the failure of Confederation Life Insurance was still being felt and absorbed a year later. Twenty-five past executives and directors at Confed had been named in a massive lawsuit, and industry experts were still asking how such a disaster had been allowed to occur.

Fortunately, few consumers suffered large financial losses as a result of the failure. An industry compensation plan fully protected

Insight 2-2 The Collapse of Confederation Life (continued)

more than 90 percent of Confed's Canadian customers, covering up to $60,000 in savings, $200,000 of life insurance, and $2,000 per month of annuity benefits. Canadian consumers not covered fully by the plan were assured of 70 percent of their money and will likely get 90 percent or more.

Industry executives maintain that most Canadian life insurers are financially healthy and that Confed is not the tip of an iceberg. Brian Moore, president of North American Life Insurance, believes Confed's comedown was so damaging that a repetition is unthinkable.

"The industry and the regulators will never let it happen again," he said.

Source: *Reprinted with permission—*The Toronto Star Syndicate. *This is an excerpt of a series of articles that originally appeared in* The Toronto Star *on November 12, 13, and 14, and December 3, 1994.*

missing opportunities for growth. When an insurer takes inadequate risk, the insurer is unnecessarily limiting potential returns to its owners or its policyholders. It may also be preventing itself from earning the higher levels of profit needed to contribute to its growth and continued competitiveness.

There are no hard and fast rules for determining the ideal balance of the factors involved in helping an insurer remain solvent and profitable. Improvements in solvency can contribute to profitability, and increases in profitability can improve solvency. Similarly, within a certain range, both strong profitability and strong solvency are usually good for the success of an insurance company. However, an extreme emphasis on solvency or the reckless pursuit of profitability can have negative effects. The essential challenge in the financial management of life and health insurance companies is to determine the appropriate balance between aggressive and conservative strategies, between risk and return, and between solvency and profitability. We will be exploring these topics throughout the remainder of this text.

In Conclusion

In this chapter, we have provided you with an overview of the essential tensions that must be balanced in the pursuit of the financial goals of life and health insurance companies. This information should lay the foundation for your understanding of the competing concerns that insurance companies must balance as they allocate financial resources in support of the company's goals.

Key Terms and Concepts

- return
- risk
- investment
- wealth
- goodwill
- wealth maximization
- critical mass
- cost of capital
- risk-return tradeoff
- liquidity
- adequate capitalization
- adequate liquidity
- minimum capital and surplus requirements
- Risk-Based Capital (RBC) ratio requirements
- minimum continuing capital and surplus requirements (MCCSR)
- C risks
- C-1 (asset risk)
- C-2 (pricing risk)
- C-3 (interest-rate risk)
- C-4 (general management risk)
- conservative financial strategy
- aggressive financial strategy

PART 2

Product Planning and Design

This section of the text introduces you to the environment of product planning and product design for insurance companies. Chapter 3 presents an overview of forecasting for insurance companies. Chapter 4 describes the processes of designing the financial products that insurance companies offer, including generating new product ideas, preparing the product for the consumer, and pricing the product. Before you can clearly interpret the operations of life and health insurance companies, you must understand the time value of money and be comfortable with time value techniques. Therefore, Chapter 5 covers the basic concepts of the time value of money, including interest rates and present and future value. Following Chapter 5 is a user's guide to the *ExecuView* software provided with this textbook. Then, Chapter 6 goes into detail about various ways insurers measure and evaluate product profitability and examines the behavior of insurance product models under various scenarios.

CHAPTER

Creating Forecasts and Generating Assumptions

3

LEARNING OBJECTIVES

After studying this chapter, you should be able to

- Recognize the purpose and applications of capital budgeting in insurance companies
- Interpret the significance of adverse deviations from actuarial assumptions
- Identify the types of forecasts insurers typically create and distinguish one from another
- Recognize methods insurers use to analyze how changes in their forecasting assumptions affect their expected cash flows and their expected financial condition

OUTLINE

Any time an insurer commits its capital in an effort to earn a return, the insurer is making an investment. When an insurer invests in its business operations, such as by purchasing major new technology, the insurer wants to see a return—often in the form of lower expenses—from that capital investment. Likewise, when an insurer commits its capital to develop a product or product line, the insurer does so because the insurer expects a return from that investment.

Any profitable investment brings with it some form of risk, and investments in an insurer's products are no exception. In Chapter 2 we described the risk-return tradeoff, noting that as the risk associated with an investment rises, the investor's expected return from that investment typically also rises. Otherwise, investors would have no incentive to risk their money in that investment. Similarly, a company's investment in its product line is accompanied by risk; the greater the risk associated with such an investment, the greater the return the company typically requires from the investment.

The processes that insurers use to evaluate the likely profitability of any investment of long-term funds are collectively known as capital budgeting. ***Capital budgeting*** is the analysis of decisions about investing in long-term projects. In a capital budgeting context, long-term investment projects are sometimes called *capital investment projects.* Capital budgeting has many applications in life and health insurance companies. For example, new insurance products, like business development opportunities in any other business, are important capital investment projects. Insurers' other business development activities, such as acquiring another company or obtaining a new information management system, also require a long-term investment. All of these investment activities can be viewed as capital investment projects. Figure 3-1 presents some examples of applications of capital budgeting.

Financial analysts approach capital budgeting by applying a number of traditional approaches. Common capital budgeting methods include

- Payback period analysis
- Validation period analysis
- Net present value (NPV) analysis
- Internal rate of return (IRR) analysis
- Risk-adjusted discounting
- Financial management rate of return (FMRR)

Figure 3-1. Applications of capital budgeting in life and health insurance companies.

- Allocating investable general account funds to investments in specific assets or projects
- Allocating product-line capital to investments in specific blocks of business, customer groups, geographic markets, or new products
- Allocating corporate capital to investments in new product lines, existing product lines, or even in purchasing businesses
- Allocating corporate capital to investments in expense reduction strategies such as new information systems, reengineering efforts, and corporate reorganization
- Evaluating the profitability of alternative investment projects
- Evaluating the profitability of proposed new products

Most of these methods are based on an application of present values of cash flows. In essence, though, these methods approach measuring or predicting an investment project's profitability by measuring the *discounted value of its net cash flows*—that is, the difference between its discounted cash inflows and its discounted cash outflows. Additionally, capital budgeting analysis usually involves comparing the discounted cash flows for any proposed capital investment project with established criteria such as

- A corporate minimum standard or hurdle rate for project acceptability,
- Projected returns from other capital investment projects under consideration, and
- A decision rule that applies in connection with the method of analysis being applied.

Examples and explanations of these criteria are presented in some detail in Chapter 6 of this textbook.

If the measures show that an investment project's predicted profitability is below the company's requirements, the company needs to either abandon the investment idea or else restructure the investment idea in a manner that (1) increases the investment's cash inflows, and/or (2) decreases the investment's cash outflows.

With regard to cash flow analysis for capital budgeting, the only cash flows taken into consideration are those that qualify as relevant cash flows. ***Relevant cash flows*** can be defined as the cash flows that the company would not experience except for making the investment. For example, the relevant cash flows associated with an investment in a financial product generally take the form of an *initial investment,* which is a cash outflow, plus a stream of cash inflows and outflows. From a capital budgeting standpoint, the initial investment for insurance and other financial products typically consists of product development costs and product distribution costs.

For a clear introduction to capital budgeting analysis, we also should mark the distinctions between accounting profits and the cash flows measured by capital budgeting analysis. One essential difference between these two concepts is that the cash flows considered for capital budgeting purposes consist of only actual transfers of money or near-cash assets, whereas accounting profits are somewhat broader in scope. Specifically, accounting profits include revenues and expenses paid in cash, revenues earned and expenses incurred that have not yet been received or paid in cash, and noncash items such as depreciation and reserves. Another essential difference is that accounting statements generally cover periods of one year or less, whereas capital budgeting analysis generally covers the lifetime of an investment project. In the case of insurance products, the lifetime of the investment is typically a number of years.

Later, this textbook covers asset/liability management, which requires analysis of an insurer's cash flows. At this point it bears noting that the cash-flow analysis performed for the purpose of evaluating product profitability is substantially different from the cash-flow analysis performed for asset/liability management. In the upcoming section, we concentrate on sources of risk in a company's product portfolio.

Risk and the Product Portfolio

Most people can easily understand that each sale of an insurance product brings risk to an insurance company. For example, upon issuing a life insurance policy, an insurer accepts the risk that the insured person will die prematurely. In that case, the company will be obligated to pay a death benefit amount that far exceeds the premiums the company has collected for the policy and the company's investment earnings on the invested portion of those premiums. This type of risk is easily seen. Less obvious, however, is the risk insurers incur in connection with offering an entire product line. As with deciding to issue a single policy, deciding to offer any type of product requires insurers to make an investment of capital and surplus. In making such an investment, the insurer risks either losing that capital or else earning a return that is far lower than the same capital could have earned if invested in a different manner.

Much of the risk that an insurer accepts in connection with its product portfolio reflects the uncertainty inherent in its cash flows from its products and its investments. *Cash flows* refers to any payment of cash, whether coming into the company or going out of the company. Four important characteristics of cash flows are as follows:

1. The *amounts* of the cash flows
2. The *life* of the series of cash flows
3. The *timing* of the cash flows
4. The *predictability* of the cash flows

Examples of the *amounts* of cash flows are the amount of a premium payment and the amount of an annuity income payment. Examples of the *life* of a series of cash flows are how long the customer will keep an insurance contract in force, and how long an annuitant will continue to collect annuity payments. Examples of the *timing* of cash flows are the timing of premium payments (a single payment, annual payments, or monthly payments) or the amount of time that passes before a product earns a profit. Examples of the *predictability* of cash flows are related to the likelihood that a debtor might default on interest payments on a bond, or the likelihood that a renter might fail to pay lease payments.

Although insurers routinely make predictions or assumptions about cash flows, these assumptions reflect varying degrees of uncertainty. For insurance companies, the exact *amounts* of the cash inflows and cash outflows associated with many products and assets cannot be known in advance; these amounts can only be estimated, and all estimates are subject to error. Likewise, the *timing* of these cash flows is unpredictable for many products and assets; the timing of the cash flows can only be estimated, and all such estimates are also subject to error.

Unexpected outcomes in any of these dimensions of a product's cash flows can produce financial results that are far different from those projected. In general, the greater the uncertainty associated with a product's cash flows, the greater the risk associated with the product. The more predictable a product's cash flows, the lower the risk associated with the product.

Balancing Product Profitability and Risk

Taking risks is an essential part of seeking profits. Insurance companies are, by their nature, risk-taking organizations. No insurer can or should attempt to eliminate risk from its product portfolio. Instead, an insurer's goal in managing its product portfolio is to ensure that the company's product profitability goals are accompanied by an *acceptable* level of risk. For each company, the acceptable level of risk is determined by the company's policy—either conservative or aggressive—toward risk-taking.

For example, suppose the Dade Financial Corporation is considering introducing a new line of medical expense insurance products. One of Dade's primary objectives for the product line is to achieve a large sales volume. However, Dade should avoid any misguided effort to stimulate sales by setting the product's price so low that the product's total income streams will not cover the expenses associated with the product. Recall from Chapter 2 that the risk of charging inadequate premiums is C-2, or pricing risk. Dade must also provide for an adequate safety margin in case its cash flow forecasts are too optimistic. In addition, Dade should establish an asset management strategy that fits the product's likely cash flow patterns. In this case, a medical expense insurance product has a short duration, and thus any assets purchased to support the medical expense insurance product would need to be short-duration assets.

Within this context of balancing product profitability objectives and risk concerns, each insurer operates within its own comfort zone. As we noted in Chapter 2, some companies follow a conservative strategy and avoid risks that other, more aggressive companies would find acceptable. In the effort to control the level of risk they assume, insurers apply fundamental concepts of risk management. A risk management approach requires the insurer to first identify and understand the many risks it faces. In essence, risk management identifies the following alternatives for coping with risk:

1. *Avoid the risk.* First, the insurer must decide whether it can or should *avoid* a given risk. For example, an insurer avoids a risk when it denies an application for coverage or decides not to bring a particular product to market.

2. *Transfer the risk.* For example, an insurer transfers a portion of a risk when it obtains conventional indemnity reinsurance on a policy it has issued. (We discuss this mechanism in greater detail in Chapter 14.)

3. *Assume the risk without attempting to control it.* For example, an insurer assumes a risk without attempting to control it when the insurer issues a life insurance policy or a life annuity and does not obtain reinsurance on the risk.

4. *Assume the risk and attempt to control it.* For example, a health maintenance organization (HMO) assumes a risk and then attempts to control that risk when it accepts members into the HMO and then provides preventive care to HMO members.

When an insurer designs a product, the insurer makes a number of actuarial assumptions about the product's cash flows. In particular, the insurer forecasts the amount, timing, length, and predictability of a product's cash flows, and incorporates those forecasts into the product's pricing assumptions. Most of an insurer's business decisions are ultimately based on assumptions about future economic activity and the demand for a company's products and services. Staffing decisions, information systems decisions, investment decisions, capital management decisions, pricing decisions, and strategic decisions about the company's future direction are also based on assumptions about future conditions. By anticipating the future, an insurer can identify business opportunities and prepare itself to take advantage of those opportunities; it can also identify threats and take steps to avoid or overcome them. Thus, insurers must take strong measures to ensure that their assumptions are as accurate as possible.

Note the phrase "as accurate as possible." Although a goal of 100 percent accuracy would be ideal, insurers must be realistic—especially when making assumptions about money. All assumptions are based on predictions of the future, called *forecasts.* Sometimes, future conditions may differ significantly from a company's forecasts as a result of contingencies.

Contingencies are unexpected events that cause conditions to vary significantly from company forecasts. When interest rates, mortality rates, morbidity rates, or any other conditions that affect a company's cash flows vary from expectations so as to reduce revenue or increase costs, the variation is often referred to as an ***adverse deviation.*** For an insurance product, if actual cash flows differ significantly from the cash flows assumed when the product was priced, the product's actual profitability can be vastly different from the projected profitability. Large adverse deviations can be caused by such contingencies as epidemics, natural disasters, severe swings in interest rates, and unfavorable regulatory decisions or unfavorable tax legislation. Smaller adverse deviations result inevitably from the uncertainty associated with the forecasting process. Different types of forecasts tend to have different levels of reliability. In general, the broader a forecast is, the more likely it is to be reliable over time. Figure 3-2 compares the general levels of reliability of forecasts concerning several different types of trends.

Insurers can reduce the possibility that adverse deviations from their forecasts will result in financial disaster by

- Using simulation models and sensitivity testing to predict how altering various assumptions will affect results,
- Applying conservatism in selecting assumptions,
- Building margins into the prices of their financial products, and
- Holding adequate reserves and capital to cover any adverse deviations that exceed the margins built into the company's pricing assumptions.

Figure 3-2. Relative reliability of forecasts concerning various types of trends.

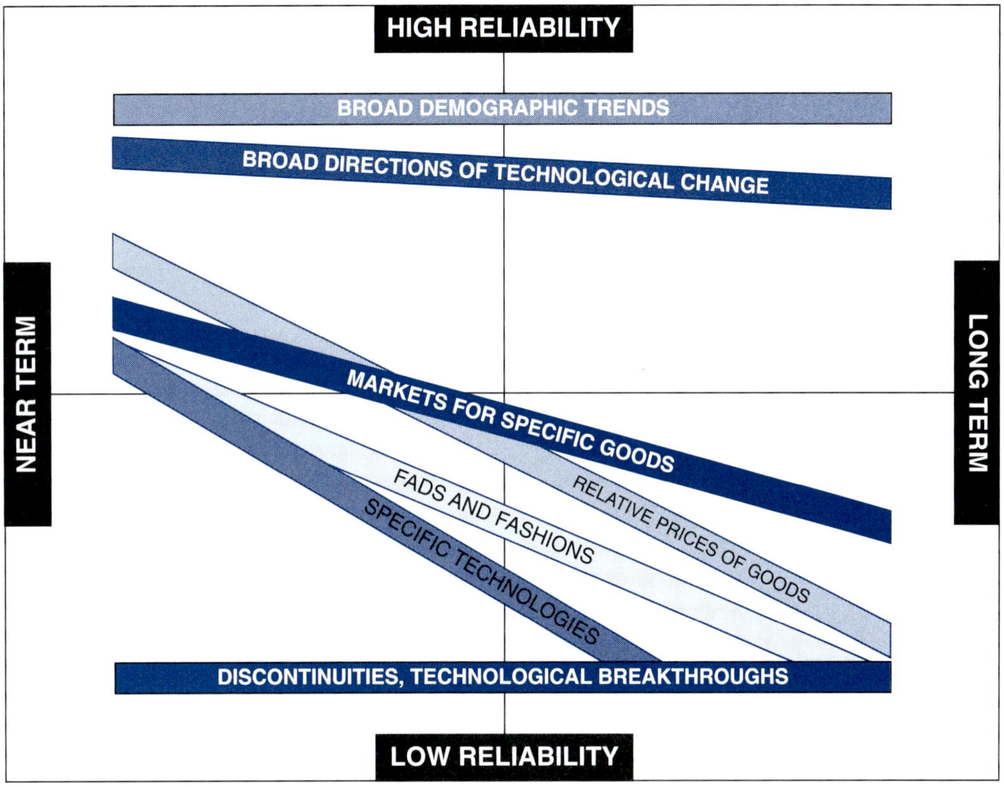

Source: *John B. Mahaffie, chart "Tomorrow and Beyond" in "Why Forecasts Fail,"* American Demographics, *March 1995, p. 36.* American Demographics *magazine, copyright © 1995. Reprinted with permission.*

Such actions work to reduce the risk inherent in a business that operates under conditions of uncertainty about the future.

Simulation modeling and sensitivity analysis make insurers aware of the potential effect that errors in their assumptions could have on the company's financial condition and permit the insurers to plan to minimize negative consequences.

In this chapter, we take a close look at the many methods insurers use to set the assumptions when making financial decisions. These assumptions are typically based on forecasts. Accordingly, we begin by describing the most common forecasts created by insurers and the importance of those forecasts. We then describe approaches to forecasting, including both qualitative and quantitative forecasting. Finally, we examine various methods insurers use to test the impact of changes in assumptions on results. Specifically, we concentrate on how insurers apply models and conduct simulations to see the impact of assumption changes on cash flows. An insurer's cash flows are an essential determinant of the insurer's profitability and solvency, and insurers make every effort to ensure that cash flows will be positive even under adverse conditions.

What Is a Forecast?

A ***forecast*** is simply a prediction of future conditions or events. On the basis of forecasts, an insurance company makes a variety of assumptions about future conditions, and uses those assumptions when making decisions. Thus, the more reliable an insurance company's forecasts, the better and more effective its decision making is likely to be. Insight 3-1 describes five essential elements of successful forecasts.

Insurers use forecasts to help them make decisions about what to do in the future. Nearly all of an insurance company's plans are based on forecasts. Forecasting provides the basis a company uses for making both short-term operational decisions and long-term strategic decisions. Real estate purchases, plans for new information systems, and other capital expenditure plans are based on forecasts. Marketing decisions concerning which products to develop, how to market those products, and which distribution systems to employ, are typically based on forecasts. So are hiring, training, and other human resource plans. Furthermore, a company's entire structure for pricing its products and managing its capital is based on forecasts. The importance of forecasting should not be underestimated.

Forecasting errors can have far-reaching consequences. Often, one forecast will be used as the basis for additional forecasts. Any errors in the initial forecast can cause additional errors in the forecasts that are

Insight 3-1 Five Essentials of Successful Forecasts

To be useful, every forecast should have most or all of the following elements. Any forecast that fails to cover them is suspicious, or at least flawed in its presentation.

A Clear Statement of Purpose
Why was the forecast made? The purpose should give the user a clearer sense of how the forecast is meant to be taken. Is it, for example, just a mind-stretching provocation, or does the author see the forecast as highly probable?

Clear Assumptions
The technological and social assumptions on which the forecast depends should make it possible for users to evaluate the forecast and decide if they agree or disagree. Without them, users can only take the analyst's word that the forecast is plausible.

A Time Horizon
Users cannot effectively interpret a forecast if they do not know when the developments it describes are supposed to happen. If the forecast has no time frame, the analysis should at least explain why.

Attention to Discontinuities
Things that could speed up the forecast or push it off track should be discussed. Nearly every forecast assumes that certain developments will not occur. If, for example, a massive asteroid strikes the Earth, or the U.S. economy collapses, all bets are off. Less catastrophic jolts and bumps can also have a big impact on a forecast.

Adequate Accounting for Social and Technological Forces
Social forces in technological forecasts and technological forces in social forecasts must be accounted for. This ensures that the forecaster has not come up short in considering the full context in which developments will happen.

Source: *John B. Mahaffie, "Why Forecasts Fail,"* American Demographics, *March 1995, pp. 38, 40.* American Demographics *magazine,*

based on the erroneous data. Flawed assumptions can lead to costly and unprofitable financial outcomes. For example, many operational decisions within insurance companies rely on forecasts of sales of the company's products. Insurers use these forecasts when deciding which products to develop and introduce, which commission schedules to use, how many employees to hire, and what and how much computer equipment to purchase. Incorrect forecasts of product sales could lead to poor decisions regarding these and other factors. If forecasting errors are large enough, they can lead to disastrous performance levels for a particular functional area or an entire company. Insight 3-2 describes eight common errors forecasters can make.

Overview of Insurance Company Forecasting

The main purpose of an insurer's forecasting activities is to provide information that the insurer can use to try to assure its future financial strength. Most of an insurer's forecasting efforts thus contribute to forecasting two factors that indicate an insurer's financial strength: the insurer's future *cash flows* and the insurer's future *financial account* values. These forecasts are, in turn, based on a number of other forecasts about various factors in an insurer's internal and external environments.

Forecasting Cash Flows

Insurers have a variety of cash flows, both in and out, associated with their products and their assets, and forecasts are used for modeling these cash flows. Insurers need to forecast the amount, life, and timing of both their asset-related and their product-related cash flows. By forecasting cash flows, an insurer can make sure that it is prepared to fulfill its cash outflow obligations when they need to be fulfilled. The insurer can also ensure that its activities will add to the company's overall value and thus contribute to the insurer's long-term financial strength. As we see in this chapter, insurers typically make many different forecasts, each one based on a specified set of assumptions about future conditions.

Forecasting Financial Account Values

Insurers also need to forecast the future values of their asset and liability accounts. Using these values, they can forecast the value of their capital and surplus account, which is equal to the difference between assets and liabilities. The strength of an insurer's capital and surplus is an important indicator of the insurer's overall financial strength. Regulators examining a company's financial condition and solvency require information about predicted financial account values. Insurers providing such forecasts must follow certain guidelines and rules when creating such forecasts for regulators. For ex-

Insight 3-2 Eight Common Errors in Forecasting

The most basic and common errors in forecasting are overestimating the speed at which developments will become important to society and underestimating wider implications and secondary effects. Some forecasts fail to connect two events and look at how they will affect one another. Others fail because they are too enthusiastic about one particular outcome, such as technology they admire or own patents on, a social outcome they would like to see, or success for a product they sell.

Almost everyone who thinks about the future tends to look enthusiastically toward desirable changes in technology, government, or other human institutions. When this "normative forecasting" is done on purpose, it can be useful. Making such forecasts sometimes motivates people into taking actions that could lead to the desired outcomes. But normative forecasting slips into many forecasts that are supposed to be detached, objective examinations of possible futures.

Here are the eight biggest reasons for forecast failure, along with the issues to consider before using any forecast.

Failure to Examine Assumptions

On what does the forecast rest? Are there specific social or technological developments that will be required for the forecast to come true? Does the forecast assume things that seem unlikely, given your view of human nature or economic realities?

Limited Expertise

Some enthusiasts overshoot their expertise when making a forecast. For example, someone might suppose that it would benefit society if goods and people were transported as they are on *Star Trek.* However, there is no reason to believe that the phrase "Beam me up, Scottie" will ever leave the realm of science fiction.

Lack of Imagination

Other forecasters may have the opposite problem. They may fail to explore the more interesting possibilities for the future out of conservatism or timidness of thought. These tendencies misguide a forecast just as easily as overenthusiasm.

Neglect of Constraints

This failure may often be summed up in the idea that "people just are not going to go for that." Or, "the economics just are not there to pay for that." Even if technology advanced to a point where a *Star Trek*–type transporter could be built, who would be the first to try it? And how much research and development would be needed before people were satisfied that this conveyance would be safe for them, their children, and their most precious belongings?

Excessive Optimism

An excessively optimistic forecaster does not weigh the "downside risk." If a forecast does not consider the offsetting of limiting factors in a given potential future, it is likely to be flawed.

Reliance on Mechanical Extrapolation

Extrapolation works well when it has identifiable limiting factors. That's why it is widely used in such areas as population growth or the market penetration of a technology. The assumption is that if we are at a certain level today and rising, we will continue to rise at a discernible rate. However, any progress or change has limits at which the curve levels off or reverses itself. Also, extrapolations will miss any acceleration in the pace.

Premature Closure

When developing forecasts, some researchers finish their work before all factors are considered. As a result, the more creative and far-reaching possibilities are never explored. Fear may be the reason for early closure and other narrowness of thinking. What organization, for example, wants to put its own death on the table when building a forecast?

Overspecification

The danger in making a concrete forecast—the level of some statistic in a given future year, or a fashion trend in the future—is that it pushes the science of forecasting beyond its capabilities. It is not possible to have control over all the variables and imponderables driving change, so no one can be utterly specific about most developments. The real value of forecasting is in showing the directions and characteristics of change.

Source: *John B. Mahaffie, "Why Forecasts Fail,"* American Demographics, *March 1995, pp. 38, 40.* American Demographics *magazine,*

ample, for some purposes insurers must base forecasted financial account values on the values of a company's current ***book of business***—the total amount of financial product business in force at a particular time. For other purposes, insurers base forecasts on current business and expected future business.

When forecasting future account values for its own internal purposes, an insurance company is free to base those values on the book of business it expects to be carrying in the future and the cash flows it expects that book of business to generate. The future value of an insurer's financial accounts depends in large part, although not completely, on the insurer's future cash flows.

External and Internal Forecasts

In order to forecast cash flows and financial account values, an insurer needs to be able to forecast a number of other factors that affect cash flows and account values. Some of these factors are *external* factors whereas others are *internal*. ***External forecasts*** concern factors beyond the insurer's control. ***Internal forecasts*** concern factors that are at least partially within the insurer's control. (Most internal forecasts are also influenced by external developments.) Figure 3-3 summarizes the important internal and external factors that insurers need to forecast.

Forecasting External Developments

Insurers can forecast external developments themselves, or they can use information available from outside sources. Insurance industry forecasters, for example, often can benefit greatly from studying industry outlook reports. An ***industry outlook report*** discusses the likely impact of external factors on firms operating in a given industry. Such industry outlook reports are periodically published by industry associations, government information services, and consulting firms. In addition, several investment research services develop industry overview reports for use by investors. The most important external factors

Figure 3-3. Summary of important external and internal factors for forecasting.

External	Internal
• Interest rates • Economic conditions • Regulatory and political forces • Social factors	• New business • Persistency • Benefits • Expenses

insurers must forecast are *economic conditions, market interest rates,* and *regulatory, social, and political factors.*

Economic Condition Forecasts. Expected economic conditions are among the most complex of an insurer's forecasts. Economic conditions include all the factors affecting production, distribution, and consumption of goods and services. Key economic conditions that must be predicted include the forces of supply and demand, the prices of goods and services, business cycles, interest rates, and the level of business activity.

Economic conditions affect virtually all areas of an insurance company, and forecasts about expected economic conditions are essential to companies as they develop insurance products, price those products, market those products, underwrite applicants, and design investment strategies to support the products and company profitability goals. Consequently, insurance company forecasting typically starts with one or more econometric forecasts. ***Econometric forecasts,*** also called *macroeconomic forecasts,* provide information about the expected general level of activity for the economy as a whole. Econometric forecasts can concern the regional, national, or world economy, and typically cover such factors as expected market interest rates and inflation rates, rates of economic growth, unemployment rates, and so on. Econometric forecasts are routinely provided by a number of public and private organizations.

Economic conditions and the overall strength of the economy also influence an insurer's investment and product cash flows. The projected strength of the economy influences the asset portfolio in many ways. For example, the strength of the economy influences the following economic outcomes:

- Inflation rates and market interest rates. Market interest rates are possibly the most important economic factor affecting an insurer's cash flows. Market interest rates, in turn, affect rates of prepayments on loans for bonds and mortgages and policy loan and surrender activity. (This factor relates to C-3 risk.)

- Rates of default on loan or bond payments. The weaker the economy, the more borrowers are likely to default. (This factor relates to C-1 risk.)

- The market values of stock and real estate investments. A weak economy depresses the value of most such investments. (This factor also relates to C-1 risk.)

General economic strength also influences an insurance company's product-related cash flows. Simply put, if the economy and employment are strong, potential customers will have more resources to commit to all types of products, including insurance and financial services products.

The factors influencing the economy's strength are numerous, and many methods are used to forecast the course of the economy. Typically, forecasters look at a number of *economic indicators* when making forecasts of future conditions. For example, real growth rates, inflation rates, and unemployment rates are important indicators of the general direction of an economy.

Forecasts of Market Interest Rates. Interest rates can be predicted by methods that range from sophisticated models to a knowledgeable person's hunch. Interest rates affect cash flows and account values related to an insurer's investment activities and its financial products. Market interest rates affect an insurer's investment cash flows and asset account values primarily through their impact on bond and mortgage returns, but also through their effect on market values of equity investments. As noted in Chapter 1, the majority of insurers' investment portfolios is composed of bonds, and a substantial portion is composed of mortgages.

An insurer's investment earnings on bonds and mortgages are extremely sensitive to fluctuations in market interest rates. Fluctuating market interest rates have the following effects on bonds and mortgages:

- As prevailing interest rates increase, the interest rates insurers can earn by lending also increase; when market interest rates decrease, the interest rates available on new loans—for bonds and mortgages, for example—also decrease.
- As market interest rates increase, the market value of outstanding bonds and mortgages decreases.
- As interest rates fall, borrowers from the insurance company, including bond issuers and mortgagees, are likely to pay off their loans early. An early repayment of a loan is known as a ***prepayment.*** When borrowers prepay their loans, the insurer loses future interest income.

Fluctuating interest rates also influence the cash flows related to an insurer's products. Changes in the interest rates that insurers can earn on their investments influence insurers' crediting rates on their products. As crediting rates fluctuate, an insurer's products become more or less attractive to customers compared to products offered by other insurers or other financial institutions. Thus, because fluctuations in market interest rates affect insurers' crediting rates, these fluctuations also influence insurers' new product sales and the persistency rates and policy loan rates of in-force business.

Interest-rate levels for the economy as a whole depend on a number of factors. Some important factors driving market interest rates include the following:

- *Inflation.* High inflation generally leads to increases in market interest rates.
- *Economic growth.* Moderate economic growth tends to promote moderate interest rates, but very rapid economic growth can lead to inflation and thus to higher interest rates.
- *Actions by a country's central bank.* The amount of credit made available by a central bank can directly effect market interest rates. A central bank's tight control of credit tends to increase interest rates, whereas less control of credit leads to lower interest rates.

Because interest rates are affected by so many economic factors, they are almost impossible to predict realistically. As a result, insurers do not generally try to forecast how interest rates will change over time. Instead, they forecast profitability under numerous interest-rate scenarios to understand where the risks are and find ways to control the risks.

Regulatory, Social, and Political Factors. Many regulatory, social, and political factors influence an insurer's financial situation. The introduction of risk-based capital (RBC) requirements by the NAIC in 1993 is an example of the kind of regulatory change that can affect the way insurers do business. RBC requirements prompted many insurers to concentrate their general account portfolios in very conservative investments. An example of a social factor that has influenced insurance company cash flows occurred in the 1980s and early 1990s, when many insurance customers became willing to take on higher investment risk in exchange for higher potential returns than had previously been available from insurance company products. In response, many insurers began to aggressively market universal and variable life insurance, variable annuities, separate account GICs, synthetic GICs, and mutual funds. These products generally pass a significant portion of the investment risk on to the consumer, but offer high potential returns. Figure 3-4 presents other prominent examples of social, regulatory, or political factors that affect insurers' financial strength or cash flows.

Many regulatory, social, and political developments are one-time changes that cannot be predicted with any degree of accuracy. Some such changes are so influential that the past is no longer a reliable predictor of the future. Such changes are referred to in current management literature as ***discontinuities.*** Examples of discontinuities that have recently or are currently influencing insurers include the

Figure 3-4. Examples of social, regulatory, and political events affecting insurers.

- **Health-care costs.** Social and political reactions to the rising costs of health care in the United States influenced the development of health insurance product innovations like managed care, including utilization review, HMOs, and PPOs.
- **Potential deregulation of roles of financial institutions.** The various financial service industries are differentiated and kept to their separate roles by a number of regulations. However, if certain regulations are relaxed, insurers may face increased competition from other providers of financial services, such as banks and mutual funds. In Canada, banks are already permitted to sell insurance, though they are somewhat restricted in the ways they can market insurance. Even these restrictions may be removed. Various judicial and legislative decisions that will be made in the coming years will strongly influence competition for insurers' products.
- **Changing demographics.** Changes in family structures and population median ages strongly affect the composition of an insurer's business. For example, the demographic characteristics of the insurer's target markets play a substantial role in determining which products will be successful. As the average age of the North American population has increased, an increasing percentage of the contracts sold by insurers have been annuities.
- **Trends in consumer behavior.** Changes in consumer opinions and preferences affect both product sales and persistency.
- **Taxation of insurers.** Insurers must pay numerous taxes, including income tax and premium tax. Changes in tax rates influence insurers' tax liabilities and hence their cash outflows.
- **Taxation of customers.** Changes in the tax rules for individuals and corporations open and close windows of opportunity for various products offered by insurers. In addition, there is a lingering threat that the U.S. federal government may declare the cash value build-up of insurance products to be taxable, or that it may repeal the taxes that currently affect other types of investment income. Either change could potentially reduce the attractiveness of cash-value insurance products to customers.

actual and potential incursion of banks and mutual funds into markets previously dominated by insurers, the rapid advances in technology, the increasing globalization of financial markets, and the shift in the North American economy from an industrial basis to a service and information basis. Each of these developments could diminish the reliability of many forecasts created by insurers, particularly forecasts based on extrapolation of trends. Insurers can prepare for discontinuities by keeping abreast of evolving trends and by maintaining the flexibility to respond to such developments.

Forecasting Internal Developments

The most important internal factors insurers must forecast are *sales of new business, surrenders and withdrawals, benefits,* and *expenses.*

Forecasting Sales of New Business. The level of product sales, or new business, is one of the main factors determining the amount of an insurer's cash inflows. In addition, insurers would find it difficult, perhaps impossible, to continue to increase the company's value and to maintain its financial health in the absence of profitable new business. Forecasting new business is an essential part of an insurer's overall forecasting efforts.

Both internal and external influences affect the level of an insurer's new business. Internal factors that influence sales include the price and design of the company's products, the company's promotion of its products, the distribution systems the company uses for its products, and the compensation the company pays producers for selling various products. External factors that influence sales include the economy and the characteristics of the marketplace in which products are to be sold. Marketplace developments have made new business more complicated to forecast than it once was, and insurers must now depend upon the knowledge and judgment of actuarial and marketing experts more so than was necessary in the past. Insight 3-3 provides an example of an economic outlook report for the life insurance industry, developed by the U.S. federal government.

FAST FACT

Two approaches to facing change. "Given that change is inevitable, the real issue for managers is whether that change will happen belatedly, in a crisis atmosphere, or with foresight, in a calm and considered manner; whether the transformation agenda will be set by the company's more prescient competitors or by its own point of view; whether the transformation will be spasmodic and brutal or continuous and peaceful."[1]

Forecasting Surrenders and Withdrawals. Policy surrenders and customer withdrawals of funds have a significant influence on an insurance product's profitability. Consequently, an insurer needs to forecast how many surrenders and withdrawals will occur, and when they will occur. Marketplace developments have made persistency, like new business, more complicated to forecast than it once was, and insurers must apply more analysis to persistency forecasts than was necessary in the past.

An insurance company's predicted level of surrenders and withdrawals depends on several external forecasts. Among the external forecasts influencing surrenders and withdrawals are forecasts of market interest rates and economic conditions. As interest rates rise or economic conditions change, insurance products may experience *disintermediation*. ***Disintermediation*** is a process in which customers remove money from a financial intermediary. Generally, customers remove money in an effort to gain a higher yield elsewhere. Another important external factor that insurers must consider is the actions of competitors. If an insurer's competitors introduce more attractive products that meet the same needs as the insurer's in-force products, the insurer is likely to see a decrease in its products' persistency. Insurers typically use a number of methods to gain information about competitors' actions in order to prepare to meet or beat the competition.

Forecasts of Benefits and Other Contractual Obligations. For most insurers, benefit payments represent the company's largest product

Insight 3-3 Economic Outlook for the Life Insurance Industry: Long-Term Prospects

The life insurance industry will go through considerable changes over the next few years. The long-term prospects for life insurance and annuity products of life insurance companies are good. Demographic variables, such as income growth, wealth accumulation, population and work-force changes, and home ownership will determine the demand for insurance products over the long term. The rate of personal savings in the United States is expected to rise with the movement of the baby-boom population into middle age. The aging of the baby-boom population will raise the demand of individuals for products that provide for retirement income and for health care financing.

Competition for these markets, however, will increase. Banks may get additional powers to sell and underwrite insurance. Banks, mutual funds, and other financial institutions will be offering investment and savings products that directly compete with insurance and annuity products. Foreign insurers will continue to expand into the largely unrestricted U.S. market.

Other means of financing and delivering health care—for example, employer self-insurance government programs, and managed care services—will diminish the growth of private health insurance, especially indemnity insurance. Moreover, new products and markets, such as long-term health care, will not replace business lost elsewhere. Instituting national health insurance could end private health insurance altogether.

On the tax front, the Federal government, in a search for revenue, may tax the investment income of annuity products, the so-called *inside build-up.* Lawmakers, however, are also looking at increasing tax benefits of Individual Retirement Accounts to spur long-term investment. This could be a boost to insurers.

Increased competition and lingering problems in real estate for some insurers should keep the rate of insolvencies at the same level as recent years. Real estate problems will persist as commercial mortgages mature over the next couple of years, but diminish as insurers restructure their portfolios and real estate markets recover. Mortgages should become a smaller part of insurers' portfolios.

The problem of insolvencies has already prompted state-level action to strengthen financial standards and tighten regulation. A larger Federal role in insurance regulation may follow, if pending congressional legislation is enacted. The Federal government may set basic financial standards for the states to follow or may regulate the industry itself. A national guaranty fund for insurance is possible, although Federal support seems unlikely.

These conflicting forces and issues will change the nature of competition in the industry. Profit margins will likely remain thin and returns on equity will remain below historical levels over the next few years. To compete, life insurance companies may have to consolidate operations, specialize in market segments, reduce operating costs, increase efficiency and service quality, and better manage their assets and liabilities. Larger, better capitalized companies will get a bigger share of the market, but smaller niche players will be strong competitors in selected markets.

To reduce costs there will be much pressure on the distribution system. Agents will have to accept less compensation or increase production. Insurers will look for cost-efficient marketing alternatives, such as direct mail, alliances with other financial institutions, financial advisors, and consultants. Insurers will be seeking new information and communications technology to increase efficiency in underwriting, distributing, investment, claims, and administrative activities.

Diminished returns on life insurance in the United States also will prompt the stronger insurance companies to look for other investment opportunities. Many life insurance companies, mainly through holding companies, have moved, or will move, into related financial services including securities, banking activities, and real estate. More U.S. life insurance companies will take advantage of expanding foreign markets, especially Europe, Asia, and—with the North American Free Trade Agreement—Mexico.

Source: *U.S. Department of Commerce,* Industrial Outlook 1993, Insurance—Life Insurance.

cash outflow. The accuracy of an insurer's forecasts of the amount of benefits it will have to pay can have a substantial effect on the insurer's ability to maintain its financial strength.

Insurers forecast the amount and timing of benefits they will have to pay using the historical data contained in mortality and morbidity tables and in other data sources. In Chapter 8, we examine in depth how insurers use morbidity and mortality information to forecast the amount and timing of cash outflows that result from benefit payments. Insurers must also take into account emerging factors that historically based mortality and morbidity data do not reflect. For example, most insurers in the 1990s must factor into their life and health benefit forecasts the increasing incidence of AIDS. In addition, actuaries must constantly monitor trends in the costs of U.S. health care as well as regulatory trends in areas such as mandated benefits.

Forecasts of Expenses for Distribution and Administration. The other primary product cash outflow for an insurer is the expense of selling and administering products. The American Council of Life Insurance (ACLI) estimated that, in 1994, sales commissions accounted for approximately 41 percent of the industry's selling and administrative expenses. A large portion of the remainder was spent on information systems (IS) and human resources (HR). Increasingly, as technological capabilities increase, insurers must invest in information systems in order to be able to offer the kind of customer service that will allow them to remain competitive. Likewise, insurance companies have found that a more productive, well-trained and highly skilled staff is as essential as a powerful information system. HR and IS are likely to continue to be key expense factors for insurers.

An insurer's expense forecasts depend to a great extent on the insurer's predicted sales volume. A large number of customers and a substantial amount of assets under management require higher total administrative costs—though potentially lower costs per unit of coverage—than a small number of customers and a smaller amount of assets under management. Also, sales volume affects commission expenses because first-year commissions are generally calculated as a percentage of new premium and renewal commissions as a percentage of renewal premium.

In most insurance companies, the accounting department performs detailed analyses of the insurers' costs of supporting specified activities or functions. So long as the business environments do not change dramatically, these analyses are also used to forecast future expenses. However, if the environment changes substantially, new cost analyses will have to be performed. Major product changes that can affect such costs include changes in the complexity of products, the frequency of customer transactions, and the size and type of potential loss a product represents. Further, if an insurer reorganizes the company or reengineers the way work is done, then its expenses could also change. As new technologies are introduced and their costs evolve, an insurer's IS expenses are likely to change. Such changes require forecasters to apply their knowledge and judgment in order to make accurate expense forecasts.

To ensure that all its forecasts are as reliable as possible, insurers use a number of different forecasting methods. Each method has its advantages and disadvantages, and companies attempt to select the method or methods most suited to the particular situation. In the following section, we describe a number of these methods and the types of forecasting situations most suited to each.

Forecasting Methods

In the past, business decisions were often based simply on educated guesses about the future based on the knowledge, experience, and intuition of the person making the forecast. In today's environment, however, the factors affecting the accuracy of a forecast are so complex that a *formal forecasting method* is usually preferred. A ***formal forecasting method*** is a standardized procedure for making predictions based on objective data or the opinions of more than one expert.

Formal forecasting methods range from simple, inexpensive analyses of data to sophisticated processes that require much time, effort, and money to complete. Some forecasts use only past data to predict the future; others use complex models that incorporate much additional data and many interdependent relationships. The most appropriate forecasting method for an insurance company to use in a given situation depends on many factors, including the

- Cost to develop or use the forecast and the benefits expected from its use,
- Time period (short-term or long-term) that the forecast covers,
- Time and other resources available for preparing the forecast before a decision must be made,
- Quality and availability of the data required for developing the forecast,
- Level of detail and degree of accuracy needed, and
- Number and complexity of the relationships to be predicted.

Generally, the greater the complexity and level of accuracy required, the more time-consuming and expensive the forecast will be. By assessing the strengths and weaknesses of each forecasting method, an insurance company can choose the methods or combination of methods most appropriate for a given situation.

Forecasting methods are commonly subdivided into quantitative and qualitative methods. We begin our discussion of forecasting methods by discussing the (1) general characteristics of each type and (2) specific methods within each type that insurers use most frequently.

Quantitative Forecasting Methods

Quantitative forecasting methods use mathematical models to predict future events. These models, consisting of equations and symbols representing the relationships between the components of the events being modeled, incorporate numerical data about past events and values in order to project future events. These components are called ***variables.*** The values that are predicted by a forecasting model are called ***dependent variables;*** the values used as inputs to a forecasting model are called ***independent variables.***

Forecasters create quantitative models by examining historical or other numerical data and identifying relationships between dependent and independent variables—that is, forecasters identify how changes in one or more independent variables cause changes in a dependent variable. Then, assuming that the relationships they have identified will continue in the future, they use those relationships to forecast the future values of the dependent variables.

Because quantitative forecasting methods require forecasters to recognize relationships in historical data, insurers can use quantitative methods only when they possess a sufficient quantity of accurate and reliable data. When such data is limited or unavailable, forecasters must use qualitative forecasting methods.

The two main categories of quantitative forecasting methods are (1) *time series models,* which use historical data about the variable being forecast as the sole basis for estimating future conditions, and (2) *causal models,* which estimate future conditions using historical data about the variable being forecast as well as data about other, related variables.

Time-Series Models

A ***time-series model*** forecasts the future value of a variable by performing some mathematical operation on the value of the same variable in one or more past periods. In a time-series model, past values of a variable are extrapolated into the future. One simple time-series model is the *moving average model.* A simple moving average might base a forecast of next year's sales volume on the average sales volume of the last three years. This simple moving average model can be expressed mathematically as follows:

$$S\,[\text{Year } t] = \frac{S\,[\text{Year } t-1] + S\,[\text{Year } t-2] + S\,[\text{Year } t-3]}{3}$$

where S [Year t] is the level of sales in the year to be predicted, and S [Year $t-1$], S [Year $t-2$], and S [Year $t-3$] are the sales volumes from each of the previous three years.

Most time-series models involve much more complex mathematical manipulation than this simple example. Other well-known time-series methods include *exponential smoothing, extrapolation, decomposition,* and the *Box-Jenkins methodology.*

Causal Models

A ***causal model*** expresses the value of one variable—the dependent variable—as a function of the value of one or more *different* variables—the independent variables. For example, most insurers assume that the amount of investment income they earn depends heavily on prevailing interest rates. A causal model reflecting this assumption would forecast the value of one variable, investment income, based on the value of another variable, the prevailing rate of interest.

Generally, the calculations in causal models involve more than one independent variable. For example, a more sophisticated causal model might forecast investment income based not only on interest rates, but also on gross domestic product (GDP) and the value of the dollar.

Some causal models incorporate large numbers of independent variables. One type of causal model that generally uses large numbers of variables is the type of model used to make econometric forecasts, which we described earlier. Econometric models often predict economic conditions based on the values of *hundreds* of independent variables.

Qualitative Forecasting Methods

Qualitative forecasting methods, also known as *judgment forecasting methods,* rely primarily on expert opinion and other subjective factors to predict future events. Qualitative methods are typically used when (1) accurate numerical or historical data is limited or not available or (2) there is reason to believe that the past is not a reliable indicator of future behavior. For example, qualitative forecasting is generally used whenever external factors, such as technological and political developments, may have a significant impact on future operations. Qualitative methods are sometimes used to supplement quantitative forecasts, especially forecasts of consumer behavior or future economic development. By themselves, qualitative forecasting methods are usually not used if the information needed can be provided by a quantitative forecasting method.

Frequently used formal qualitative forecasting methods include market survey methods and expert opinion polls.

Market Survey Methods

Market survey methods are research activities, such as telephone surveys, mail questionnaires, and interviews with consumer panels, that are used to gain information about businesses' and consumers' future purchase and other plans. Using such surveys, researchers gather information that allows them to forecast businesses' intentions to make capital expenditures and consumers' intentions to purchase major consumption items or take other actions likely to affect the demand for many types of goods and services. Insurers use the results of such surveys to help them forecast future demand for insurance products.

Most market surveys are large-scale surveys and are conducted by educational or government agencies, such as the University of Michigan's Survey Research Center, the U.S. Department of Commerce, the Bureau of the Census, and the Securities and Exchange Commission. Large private organizations, such as McGraw-Hill, Inc., Dun and Bradstreet, and the National Industrial Conference Board, also conduct market surveys.

Expert Opinion Polls

The second major category of formal qualitative forecasting methods involves the use of expert opinion polls. When expert opinion polls are used for forecasting, various groups of knowledgeable experts are asked for their opinions about the topic being studied; the goal is to develop a forecast based on a consensus of the opinions from the various experts consulted.

Expert opinion polls may be used for individual company forecasts as well as industry or national forecasts. For example, on a company level, an insurer might poll its sales force regarding their views on the sales outlook for a new product the company plans to introduce. On an industry level, experts from many insurance firms might be polled regarding their views on the potential effects of deregulation, where the industry is headed in terms of key players and product offerings, and how the industry might look five to ten years into the future. On a national or international level, experts from many areas might be polled regarding their views on future economic trends, regulatory and political changes, technological advancements, and other areas that affect business decisions.

Two formats commonly used for expert opinion polls are the Delphi method and the panel consensus method. With the ***Delphi method,*** a questionnaire is sent to a number of experts who are knowledgeable about the activity to be forecast. Each expert then provides his or her individual forecast, and also explains any supporting arguments or assumptions that he or she might have made. After the experts return their forecasts, the forecasting staff studies the information received, summarizes the responses of the experts, and then formulates a second questionnaire. The second questionnaire provides the experts with feedback on their original forecasts and also asks additional questions. These additional questions attempt to clarify and refine the responses to the first questionnaire. This cycle of questions and responses may continue for several rounds until the experts reach a consensus.

In the ***panel consensus method*** of forecasting, a group of experts is brought together face-to-face to discuss a question. Like the Delphi method, the aim of the panel consensus method is to reach a group consensus as to what the forecast should be. A potential disadvantage of the panel consensus method, however, is that during face-to-face meetings, those experts with more forceful personalities, or who have stronger opinions, may influence the opinions of some of the other panel members. A forecast that is obtained by panel consensus may be less balanced or objective than one reached by the Delphi method. Insight 3-4 contains an example of the results of a forecast obtained by means of panel consensus.

Insight 3-4 Forecast Based on Executive Opinion

Strategic-level issues were the focus of the 1995 survey of insurance industry CEOs summarized here. In this survey, conducted for the January 1996 issue of LOMA's *Resource* magazine, 12 LOMA board members responded to questions about the future of the insurance industry. (This forecast produced comments on industry sales, premiums, and profits; key issues; and financial, technological, and human resources trends.)

Industry Forecast: Continuation of Recent Trends

Relatively flat sales, mergers/acquisitions/company failures, public image and increased competition from banks will have an impact on the life/health insurance industry over the next few years, according to a number of industry chief executives. Almost every one of the 12 industry chief executives responding to this 1995 survey predict that sales of traditional industry products will be flat but sales of investment and savings-types of products will rise. This product shift trend has been established over the last few years, reflecting changes in demographics and other factors. Says one executive, "The industry's growth for the next decade or so will come from our ability to understand and respond to our customers' concerns for well-crafted solutions to address their needs."

Here are some of the executives' other key forecasts for the industry:

- Mergers and acquisitions will continue unabated. Large capital resources will be needed to compete in the changing environment.
- Profitability, distribution, understanding customer needs (and the changing nature of competition), selling practices, and disclosure are just some of the key issues/trends these executives foresee for the industry.
- Service quality will continue to be important as service continues to improve throughout the industry, due, in large part, to increasing pressures from non-traditional competitors.
- The use of new technology continues to play a larger and larger role in the daily operation of today's life/health companies.
- Banks will impact the industry on three fronts by causing changes in (1) corporate structures, (2) product development and design, and (3) distribution and marketing methods.

Comparison of Forecasting Methods

Forecasting is as much an art as it is a science, requiring a great deal of judgment from the forecaster. As we have discussed, qualitative forecasting is based almost entirely on judgment. But even quantitative forecasting, which makes use of complex mathematical formulas and sophisticated computer equipment, requires considerable judgment. When creating a model for quantitative forecasting, forecasters must use judgment in analyzing the historical basis for the model and in deciding how to express the relationships among the variables in the model. Once a model has been created, forecasters must then use their judgment to analyze the applicability of the model to various forecasting situations. At any step in the process, the judgment may be wrong and the resulting forecast may be inaccurate.

Another reason forecasts are often wrong is that forecasting methods typically do not allow for the consideration of discontinuities. Most forms of forecasting assume that the future will not differ significantly from the past. As we noted earlier, certain events can cause future patterns to depart markedly from the patterns of the past, and forecasting methods that ignore the impact of such events will not be reliable. Figure 3-5 summarizes the characteristics of qualitative and quantitative forecasting methods.

Creating Multiple Forecasts

Insurance companies are not limited to creating one forecast and using that forecast as its assumption about future conditions. After all, if an insurer bases its business plans and decisions on a single forecast, and the forecast turns out to be wrong, then the insurer could encounter serious trouble. Instead, insurers typically create a number of different forecasts or they create an entire set of predicted values; they then evaluate the likelihood that each different forecast or predicted value will accurately predict future conditions.

Figure 3-5. Characteristics of qualitative and quantitative forecasting methods.

Qualitative	Quantitative
• Based on human knowledge, experience or judgment • Best method when no reliable numerical data is available	• Based on mathematical models • Uses relationships in historical or numerical data • Models express relationships among dependent and independent variables

When forecasters assign a single value to a variable, the forecasters are creating a ***point estimate.*** For example, a predicted first-year lapse rate of 15 percent is a point estimate. If an insurer bases its business decisions on one point estimate, then the insurer is effectively putting all its eggs in one basket. Many analysts believe that this situation encourages forecasters to be highly cautious and conservative, because they are afraid to be wrong.

Alternatively, forecasters can create a ***range estimate*** of possible values for a variable by specifying a range of values for the expected outcome. For example, a predicted first-year lapse rate of 10–20 percent is a range estimate. If an insurer forecasts a range of values, then the insurer can take steps to protect itself against potential unfavorable situations and to position itself to take advantage of potential favorable situations.

When forecasters create range estimates, they can also assign probabilities to various individual outcomes within each range; each probability would represent the likelihood that a particular outcome will come to pass. For example, suppose Rachel Robins works for an insurance company and is asked to forecast what the prime interest rate will be at the end of the next quarter. She might forecast that the prime rate will fall somewhere between 7.25 percent and 7.75 percent. In addition, she might attach the following probabilities to various interest rate outcomes within that range:

Prime interest rate	Probability
7.25%	15%
7.50%	60%
7.75%	25%

A second approach forecasters often use when creating range estimates employs a statistical tool called *confidence limits.* A ***confidence limit*** is an expression of the probability that a specific outcome will fall within a certain range. For example, suppose that Richard Radcliff, like Rachel Robins in the example above, also needs to forecast what the prime rate will be at the end of the next quarter. Mr. Radcliff decides to apply confidence limits to this forecasting problem. Thus, his forecast might look like the following:

Prime interest rate	Confidence level
Between 7.25% and 7.75%	68.0%
Between 7.00% and 8.00%	95.0%
Between 6.75% and 8.25%	99.7%

Notice that, the wider the range of outcomes, the more confident the forecaster can be that the actual outcome will fall within that range.

Even when the insurer has predicted a range of possible outcomes, the insurer may want to analyze what conditions will be under each predicted situation. Or, the insurer may want to analyze what will happen if conditions fall outside the range predicted. In this way, insurers can test how variations in assumptions affect the company's economic condition.

Testing Assumptions

Insurers use a number of methods to test the effect of varying assumptions on their financial results. In some situations, insurers enter both a range of predicted values and the confidence limits associated with those values into a computer model, and the model then runs a number of simulations based on those different inputs. The insurer can analyze the results to determine whether any of the simulated conditions will cause financial distress. Insurers use simulations in a number of ways. ***Simulation*** is the use of models to represent a complex system in order to study how the system behaves under various circumstances. The objective of simulation is not to produce a single forecast based on a known or expected set of conditions, but to explore a number of "what if" situations. For example, insurers typically like to explore "best case," "worst case," and "most likely case" situations. A simulation model can thus be thought of as a testing ground for trying out different possibilities.

Using a process called *sensitivity analysis,* insurers can gain an understanding of the impact that changes in each of a model's *independent* variables has on the model's *dependent* variables. ***Sensitivity analysis*** involves measuring the impact that changing any one independent variable has on the results of the model. For example, to test the sensitivity of *dependent variable Y* to changes in *independent variable A,* an analyst would ascertain how a change of a given magnitude in *A* would affect the value of *Y.* One type of sensitivity analysis, called *duration analysis,* measures the sensitivity of the value of an insurer's assets or liabilities in response to interest-rate changes. We discuss duration analysis in more detail later in this text, when we discuss asset/liability management.

At other times, an insurer may alter assumptions in a model in order to determine how such changes will affect results. Called ***scenario analysis,*** such exercises are an important part of an insurance company's financial and strategic planning process. If an insurance company expects a specified set of circumstances to have a disastrous impact on the company's financial condition, the company can then take steps to avoid the danger.

Interest-Sensitive Cash-Flow Analysis

For the remainder of this chapter, we concentrate on how insurers use *interest-sensitive cash-flow analysis* to analyze how changes in various assumptions will alter their cash-flow forecasts. ***Interest-sensitive cash-flow analysis*** is an approach that insurers use to analyze the sensitivity of cash flows to the changed assumptions of various scenarios. Interest-sensitive cash-flow analysis incorporates many of the types of internal and external forecasts we discussed earlier in this chapter. Interest-sensitive cash-flow tests are used quite frequently in the insurance industry to help ensure solvency and to evaluate profitability.

Interest-sensitive cash-flow analysis can be performed on a number of levels. For example, an insurer might perform interest-sensitive cash-flow analysis at any of the following levels:

- On a single product
- On a line or block of business
- On a business unit
- On an insurer's entire product portfolio

Interest-sensitive cash-flow analysis can also be performed for a number of reasons. For example, insurers use interest-sensitive cash-flow analysis for the following purposes:

- To meet regulatory requirements
- To evaluate product pricing strategies
- To evaluate product design strategies
- To evaluate investment strategies
- To evaluate a potential acquisition
- To evaluate the insurer's overall prospects for financial strength

Product pricing and design strategies as well as investment strategies strongly influence an insurer's cash flows. If interest-sensitive cash-flow analysis suggests that a selected scenario produces unsatisfactory results, then the insurer probably would endeavor to avoid the parameters reflected in that scenario.

Two significant types of interest-sensitive cash-flow analysis are *cash-flow testing* and *dynamic solvency testing*. ***Cash-flow testing (CFT)*** can be defined as a process of projecting and comparing, as of a

Figure 3-6. Applications of interest-sensitive cash-flow analysis for insurance companies.

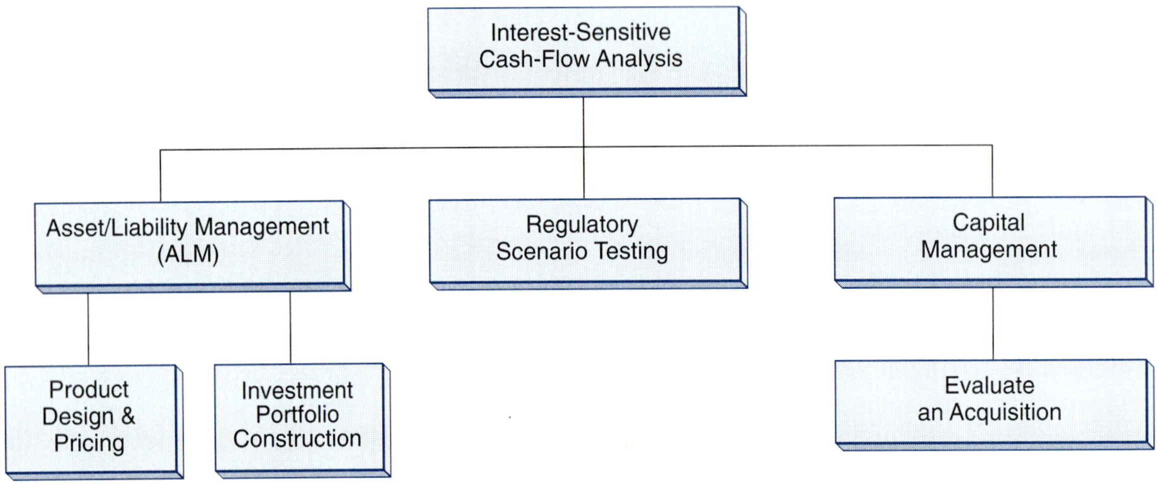

given valuation date, the timing and amount of asset and liability cash flows after the valuation date. ***Dynamic solvency testing (DST)*** is the use of simulation modeling to project into a future period an insurance company's existing and future business in terms of assets, liabilities, and owners' equity. We discuss both CFT and DST in the next several sections.

Figure 3-6 illustrates some of the many ways in which interest-sensitive cash flow analysis is applied in insurance companies.

The Cash-Flow Testing Process

As summarized in Figure 3-7, the process of cash-flow testing can be divided into four steps:

1. *Match the products or product segment liabilities to be tested with the assets (investments) corresponding to those products.* If the cash-flow testing is being performed for an entire company, then this step is not necessary, because all the insurer's assets and products are tested. However, if an entire company is not being tested, then the insurer must identify which assets are backing the products being tested.

2. *Select the scenarios to be tested.* Most often, cash flows are tested under a variety of scenarios.

3. *Project the cash flows.* The insurer would accomplish this by testing the different scenarios in its cash-flow testing model. The model would account for the ways that changes in one variable cause changes in other variables.

Figure 3-7. The cash-flow testing process.

1. Match assets with products to be tested
2. Select scenarios
3. Project cash flows
4. Analyze results

4. *Analyze the results.* The insurer would compare the cash-flow testing results to the insurer's desired results. For example, the insurer's desired results might be that total cash inflows exceed total cash outflows under all plausible scenarios, or under a certain percentage of plausible scenarios.

Insight 3-5 illustrates the use of cash-flow testing in evaluating the profitability of a universal life product.

Required Cash-Flow Testing

U.S. insurers are required to use cash-flow testing to test the adequacy of the assets backing their reserves. The NAIC's Revised Standard Valuation Law, adopted by most states, requires insurers to test cash flows under seven interest-rate scenarios. The scenarios are sometimes called the "New York Seven" because they were first enumerated in New York's Regulation 126. Whereas Regulation 126 required insurers only to test cash flows related to some types of annuities, the Standard Valuation Law requires insurers to test the cash flows related to all their products. The required scenarios include level interest-rate scenarios, scenarios in which interest rates rise or fall gradually, scenarios in which interest rates *spike* (rise or fall rapidly), and scenarios in which interest rates rise, then fall, or fall, then rise. Figure 3-8 shows the seven required scenarios. The required cash-flow testing is intended to ensure that a company's policy reserves are adequate, given the assets backing the reserves.

Once this mandatory cash-flow testing is completed, the insurer's ***valuation actuary***—an actuary who specializes in rendering opinions as to the proper values for an insurance company's assets, reserves, and capital and surplus—is required to sign an actuarial opinion and memorandum (AOM). The ***actuarial opinion and memorandum (AOM)*** is a declaration that the valuation actuary has tested the insurer's cash flows under the required scenarios and that, in the valuation actuary's opinion, the insurer's reserves make adequate provision for the insurer to meet future obligations to customers, given the assets backing the reserves. The AOM that insurers use in Canada makes broader statements than the U.S. AOM.

Insight 3-5 Illustration of Cash-Flow Testing for a UL Product

Cash-flow testing of an insurance product typically involves the testing of more than 40 scenarios. The simple CFT example reproduced in this insight shows the results of just one scenario test. This test includes assumptions as to

1. Market interest rates expected for the life of the product
2. Percentage of the investment portfolio devoted to policy loans
3. Withdrawal (lapse) rates
4. Investment matching strategy
5. Crediting strategy for investment earnings

In the following table, a set of product design assumptions is contrasted with a scenario test reflecting a revised set of assumptions. For instance, the original product design assumptions state that market interest rates will remain level at 9 percent for the life of the product. The scenario test instead makes the assumption that market interest rates will rise gradually from 9 percent to 12 percent over the life of the product. The pricing assumptions as to the crediting rate strategy and the investment matching strategy are retained unmodified in the cash-flow testing scenario. However, the withdrawal rate (lapse rate) assumption and the policy loan assumption are modified for purposes of testing the product design under stress.

In the product design, the withdrawal rate is assumed to be 14 percent each year for the life of the product, whereas for the cash-flow testing scenario the withdrawal rate is assumed to increase from 14 percent annually to 25 percent annually. Similarly, the product design assumption for policy loans is that 10 percent of policy funds would be on policy loan at any given time, whereas the cash-flow testing scenario uses an assumption that the percentage of policy funds on policy loan would begin at 10 percent but would rise to 15 percent as the product ages. The combined effect of these changes in assumptions is that the cash-flow testing scenario produces a forecast for an unprofitable outcome, whereas the pricing assumptions produce a forecast for a profitable outcome. By evaluating the results of many similar scenarios, an actuary might learn of a need to change the product design, product pricing, investment strategies, or reserve levels.

One Scenario Test of Pricing Assumptions for a Universal Life (UL) Insurance Product

Product characteristics	Pricing assumptions	Scenario assumptions
Market interest rates	Level at 9%	Beginning at 9%, increasing to 14%
Crediting rate formula	Investment portfolio rate of return minus 0.5%	Investment portfolio rate of return minus 0.5%
Investment matching strategy	High-grade bonds with 7–10 year maturities	High-grade bonds with 7–10 year maturities
Lapse (withdrawal) rates	13% each year	Beginning at 13% per year, increasing to 25%
Percent of cash value on policy loan	10%	Beginning at 10% per year, increasing to 18%
Product's Ending Surplus	POSITIVE	NEGATIVE

Source: *Excerpted and adapted with permission of the publisher from Mark A. Milton, FSA, "Cash-Flow Testing Importance Grows,"* Resource, *December 1991, p. 37.*

For internal management purposes, insurers also perform company-level cash-flow testing based on numerous scenarios other than the New York Seven. Insurers use this internal cash-flow testing to test not only their solvency prospects, but also their likely future profitability. To analyze future profitability, insurers examine how their

Figure 3-8. The seven interest-rate scenarios.

1. Interest rates remain level.
2. Interest rates increase 0.5% per year for 10 years and then remain level.
3. Interest rates increase 1% per year for 5 years; decrease 1% per year for 5 years; then remain level.
4. Interest rates increase 3% immediately and then remain level.
5. Interest rates decrease 0.5% per year for 10 years and then remain level.
6. Interest rates decrease 1% per year for 5 years; increase 1% per year for 5 years; then remain level.
7. Interest rates decrease 3% immediately and then remain level.

business is likely to contribute to surplus and add to the company's value.

Dynamic Solvency Testing

The use of dynamic solvency testing is voluntary for U.S. insurers, but mandatory for Canadian insurers.* As the term is applied in the United States and Canada, DST involves modeling the company's future financial condition under a number of business-growth scenarios and a number of interest-rate scenarios. One function of DST is to identify scenarios that would threaten a company's solvency. Standards of professional practice established by the Canadian Institute of Actuaries (CIA) require that, in Canada, each insurer's valuation actuary perform DST annually. In addition, Canada's 1992 Insurance Companies Act requires each insurer to file a statement about the insurer's financial prospects based on the results of dynamic solvency testing. The dynamic solvency testing required in Canada is more far-reaching than the cash-flow testing required in the United States. In practice, many U.S. insurers perform dynamic solvency testing voluntarily for their own management purposes. In addition, the NAIC is considering requiring that insurers perform dynamic solvency testing. However, in the United States, dynamic solvency testing is not required.

The Canadian Institute of Actuaries' DST standards require an insurer's valuation actuary to first test the insurer's financial condition based on a best estimate of actual future conditions, and then to test ten additional required scenarios. Each of the ten prescribed scenarios requires the actuary to change a single element of the best-guess

* Some practitioners prefer to call this activity ***dynamic analysis of financial condition*** or, in Canada, ***dynamic capital adequacy testing.***

scenario, such as mortality or morbidity, withdrawal rate, interest rate, expenses, or new business. The actuary should additionally use the results of the ten mandated scenarios to select a wide variety of other scenarios to test. These additional scenarios may involve altering one of the assumptions of the base scenario, or two or more assumptions in combination. The actuary is also expected to test the effects of changes in the insurer's operating strategies. For example, the actuary might project the effects of new product introductions, policyholder or stockholder dividends, or changes in investment or marketing strategy or in underwriting standards. Generally, the actuary's objective is to determine whether the insurer would be able to maintain sufficient surplus in each scenario. The appropriate amount of surplus is calculated using the Minimum Continuing Capital and Surplus Requirements (MCCSR), the Canadian equivalent of the U.S. risk-based capital (RBC) requirements.[2] MCCSR and RBC requirements are discussed in detail in Chapter 18. Insight 3-6 discusses the benefits and features of the Canadian DST law.

Comparison of CFT and DST

Dynamic solvency testing is similar in many ways to the cash-flow testing required in the United States. Like this cash-flow testing, dynamic solvency testing involves projecting an insurer's cash inflows and outflows and their effect on the insurer's financial situation under a variety of scenarios. However, as summarized in Figure 3-9, several points of contrast between DST and CFT include the following:

- Whereas U.S. mandatory CFT primarily tests the adequacy of an insurer's reserves, Canadian mandatory DST also tests the adequacy of the insurer's capital and surplus.
- Whereas U.S. mandatory CFT involves testing the insurer's in-force business only, Canadian mandatory DST requires the insurer to project its new business and the effects of future developments on that new business.

Figure 3-9. Contrasts between cash-flow testing (CFT) and dynamic solvency testing (DST).

	CFT	DST
Tests adequacy of . . .	Reserves	Reserves and surplus
Business considered . . .	In-force business only	In-force and new business
Scenarios tested . . .	Interest-rate based only	Various types
Testing criteria . . .	Pass/fail basis	Diagnostic purposes

Insight 3-6 Canadian Dynamic Solvency Testing Requirements and Benefits

Dynamic solvency testing has been a requirement in Canada since 1991. Its primary purpose is to force managements of insurance companies doing business in Canada into an ongoing awareness of their companies' surplus position and of the potential future impact of business plans and external events on this surplus position. By gaining a greater understanding of the sensitivity of the company's surplus to various contingencies—such as changes in pricing factors or management policies—the company may realize the necessity to adjust its business plans in order to avoid undue strain and/or adopt strategies to reduce the likelihood of occurrence of the contingencies that would cause a threat to surplus.

The examination is to be conducted by the company's appointed actuary, and the results are to be communicated to the company's board of directors (or, in the case of a foreign company doing business in Canada, to the chief agent of that company's Canadian branch); beginning with year end 1993, the report must also be filed with OSFI (Office of the Superintendent of Financial Institutions).

The DST requirement is stated in the Insurance Companies Act in only one sentence, but a detailed explanation is contained in the appropriate Standard of Practice of the Canadian Institute of Actuaries. Briefly, the appointed actuary

- Must define the surplus requirement that is appropriate for the company's situation. More than one definition may be used; an appropriate MCCSR (Minimum Continuing Capital and Surplus Ratio) should be one requirement, but a company's internal definition of target surplus, if higher, may also be appropriate.
- Must analyze the company's current surplus position based on the most recent financial statement, and compare it to the defined surplus requirements.
- Must determine an appropriate projection mechanism—such as cash flow testing or examination of past results—and then develop or acquire such a projection system for the company. The projection mechanism should provide information at the appropriate level of detail to permit analysis; for example, desired breakdowns might include line-of-business and in-force and new business.
- Must examine the trend of surplus adequacy for the previous three years to use as a base line and to validate the projections.
- Must, using the company's business plan and assumptions deemed appropriate as best estimates, project the level of surplus and the required surplus for five years or some longer period if appropriate.
- Must test sensitivity of surplus to changes in assumptions. There are ten prescribed scenarios—for example, changes in interest rate, changes in mortality, morbidity, lapse rates, asset default rates, and increased new business—to be tested and compared with the base scenario. Each scenario tests the effect of the change in that one assumption. By the end of the projection, valuation assumptions used in each scenario must reflect the assumptions used in the projection for that scenario.
- May develop additional scenarios to test the impact of changes of multiple assumptions, based on his or her assessment of likely situations.
- Must (as already noted) document in a report to the board of directors or the chief agent, as well as the OSFI, the results of this testing, including significant findings and conclusions

The DST law does not require additional capital, but it causes company management to be aware that additional capital probably will be required in the future. Actuaries have discussed the regulation's impact on their work and on their companies, and most comments have been very positive. Benefits they point out include

- Business plans now are less subjective and instead are based more frequently on rigorous calculations and modeling of results.
- The actuary is brought into the corporate planning loop much earlier and much more completely, and as a result there is better communication between actuarial and other areas of management.
- There is greater appreciation and understanding on the part of actuaries and management about how the company operates, its exposure to risks, and the impact on surplus of various deviations from the business plan.
- It affords early identification of potential problems—new business strain, insufficient return on equity, etc.
- Early warning allows more time to arrange alternatives—e.g.,

Insight 3-6 Canadian DST Requirements and Benefits *(continued)*

reinsurance, selling off a block of business, etc.

- It provides the company with confirming evidence in cases when current plans have appeared to be unacceptable or when it appears time to exit a line of business.

Dynamic solvency testing has made the managements of Canadian companies receive more information about and be more aware of their companies' surplus and the impact of business plans and external events on it.

Source: *Reprinted with permission of the publisher from Regina V. Rohner, FLMI, FSA, MAAA, "Solvency Regulation in the Canadian Insurance Industry,"* Resource, *February 1996, pp. 20–21.*

- Whereas U.S. mandatory CFT requires insurers to test scenarios only based on different interest rates, Canadian mandatory DST requires insurers to test scenarios based on changes in other variables in addition to interest rates.
- Whereas U.S. mandatory CFT is akin to a pass/fail test, Canadian mandatory DST does not require insurers to pass any test but instead to use the DST to identify potential threats to its solvency; the insurer can then make changes designed to lessen its exposure to any threats identified.

In Conclusion

In this chapter, we discussed the importance of forecasting to an insurer's financial management. We began with an overview of the external and internal factors that insurers need to forecast in order to analyze their future financial prospects. We then discussed forecasting methods, including qualitative and quantitative methods. Following that, we discussed interest-sensitive cash-flow testing, which includes cash-flow testing and dynamic solvency testing. In the next chapter we look at the product design process and the basics of product pricing.

Key Terms and Concepts

capital budgeting
relevant cash flows
contingencies
adverse deviation
forecast
book of business
external forecasts
internal forecasts
industry outlook report
econometric forecasts
prepayment
discontinuities
disintermediation
formal forecasting method
quantitative forecasting methods
variables
dependent variables
independent variables
time-series model
causal model
qualitative forecasting methods
market survey methods
Delphi method
panel consensus method
point estimate
range estimate
confidence limit
simulation
sensitivity analysis
scenario analysis
interest-sensitive cash-flow analysis
cash-flow testing (CFT)
dynamic solvency testing (DST)
valuation actuary
actuarial opinion and memorandum (AOM)
dynamic analysis of financial condition
dynamic capital adequacy testing

References

1. Gary Hamel and C. K. Prahalad, "Competing for the Future," *Harvard Business Review*, July-August 1994, p. 128.

2. Allan Brender, "The Evolution of Solvency Standards for Life Insurance Companies in Canada," Research Report 91-10, Institute of Insurance and Pension Research, University of Waterloo, Ontario.

CHAPTER

Designing Financial Products

4

LEARNING OBJECTIVES

After studying this chapter, you should be able to

- Recognize the activities that constitute the product development and design process
- Recognize the factors that influence a product's price and sales volume
- Identify specific acquisition and distribution expenses
- Identify features of insurance products that affect product-related expenses
- Interpret the various elements of an insurance product's gross premium
- Interpret the relationship between a reserve and the net amount at risk

OUTLINE

In Chapter 1 we profiled the primary revenues and expenses of the insurance industry. Here in Chapter 4 we see how insurance companies approach product development, and how they take revenues and costs into consideration when designing products and setting premium rates for their products. We begin Chapter 4 by introducing the product development and design process, including technical product design. The chapter then describes the basic elements of insurance pricing. Finally, the chapter looks at the revenues and costs generated by insurance products and explores some of the product design features that can affect the size and timing of these revenues and costs.

Product Development and Design Processes[1]

The many activities that go into taking a new product idea from the initial phase of idea generation to the final phase of its introduction in the marketplace represent an important expense for an insurance company. This expense, known as ***product development expense,*** is an important part of a company's investment in the growth and future of its business. Chief among these new product activities are product development and technical product design. ***Product development*** refers to the entire process of taking an idea for a new product all the way to consumers and the marketplace. For insurance contracts and other financial products offered by insurance companies, ***technical product design*** refers to just one important phase of the product development process, the phase of creating the product language, product provisions, pricing and dividend structures, and underwriting and issue specifications. Figure 4-1 illustrates the product development process.

The work of designing insurance and annuity products is typically performed by the members of a product development team. The team members represent every different area of technical expertise that is important to insurance companies, including marketing, investments, legal, and actuarial staff. Figure 4-2 presents the roles that the many different functional areas of an insurance company fulfill in the technical design phase of product development.

Developing New Product Proposals

An insurance company's product development team examines any product ideas that survive an initial screening process. The team then evaluates the feasibility of implementing a new product idea. If

Figure 4-1. Product development and design process.

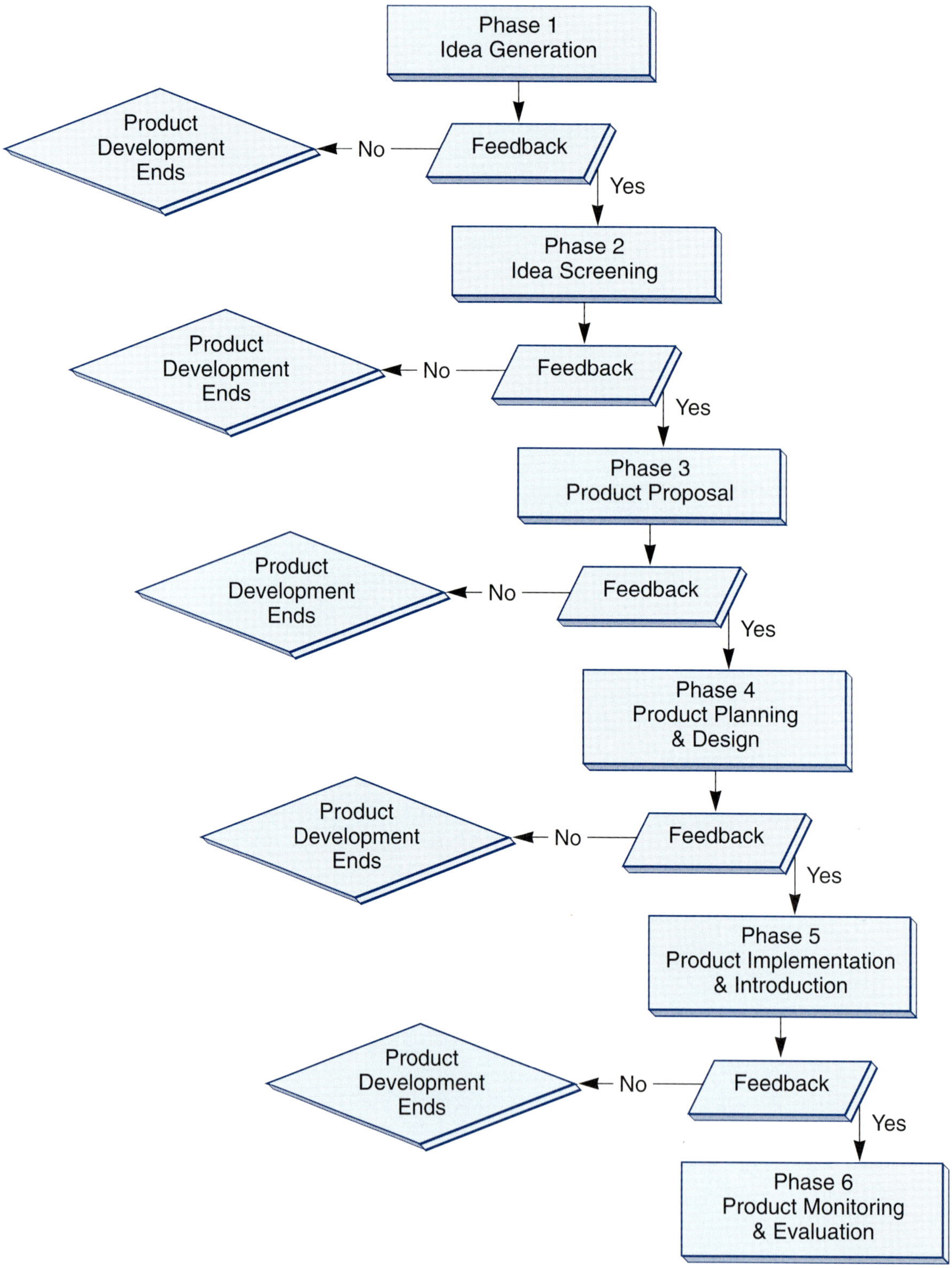

Figure 4-2. Role of each functional area during technical design of insurance products.

- **Actuarial.** Actuarial staff assess the product's rate structure (premiums, cash values, and dividends), risk factors, asset-share calculations, projected reserves, strains on surplus, profit estimates, payback and start-up costs, tax implications, and policy wording.

- **Marketing.** Marketing staff are concerned with the product's price, its consumer appeal, the competitiveness and complexity of the product, the difficulty of promoting the product and introducing it to the field, and how consistent the product's marketing and financial projections are with overall corporate objectives for growth and profit.

- **Sales Force** (If separate from marketing and if applicable). Field or agency representatives are concerned with how difficult the product will be to sell, how well it meets clients' needs, the competitiveness of the product's pricing, and the adequacy of the product's compensation schedule.

- **Information Systems.** Administering most insurance products requires extensive systems support. Information systems staff are concerned with (1) the hardware and software requirements of the new product, (2) modifying current systems to process transactions for the new product, (3) developing any new systems, (4) evaluating whether new systems should be developed in-house or purchased outside, and (5) whether any new systems should stand alone or be integrated with the company's present systems.

- **Legal.** Legal staff are usually responsible for policy drafting and ensuring policy compliance with all applicable regulations.

- **Investment.** Investment staff advise the product developers on types of investments required to make the product successful and to earn a suitable rate of return. The investment staff considers (1) the rate of return needed to make a product successful, (2) the patterns of liabilities for the product, and (3) the product's projected cash flows.

- **Accounting and Finance.** If development and introduction are particularly costly, the comptroller may establish a separate budget for the product. Special reporting of the financial results of the new product may also be required. If so, new accounting procedures would be developed. An entire set of new accounts may have to be established.

- **Administration.** Underwriting, customer service, policy issue, and claim administration staff design procedures to accommodate the new product, estimate the cost of providing administrative support, assess their staffing requirements for the new product, and evaluate the quantity and types of staff training required to service the new product.

Source: *Portions of this material are adapted from Francois Genest, "Product Myopia,"* Journal of the American Society of CLU, *July 1986, p. 67.*

the team finds that a new product idea is feasible, then the team develops a *product proposal* and presents the proposal to top management for approval.

The amount of research conducted in order to develop a product proposal varies from one product to another. If the proposed product represents a revision of a product the company currently offers, very little analysis may be required. A great deal of research may be required if the product type has never before been offered by the company. Developing a product proposal for a new type of product can require the product development team to develop additional analysis and documentation such as

- Conducting a market analysis
- Establishing product design objectives
- Conducting a feasibility study
- Developing a marketing plan
- Preparing preliminary sales or financial forecasts

Market Analysis

A ***market analysis*** is a study of all factors that might affect sales. In many cases, a company can prepare a market analysis using information already gathered during its ongoing marketing research activities or while preparing market analyses for other new product ideas. Figure 4-3 presents some of the many topics that typically would be included in a market analysis.

Product Design Objectives

Although many aspects of a new product will have been conceptualized before a market analysis is done, the market analysis provides a foundation for a concrete set of product design objectives. ***Product design objectives*** for a proposed insurance product specify the product's basic characteristics, features, benefits, issue limits, age limits, underwriting classes, and the manner in which the benefits will be provided. (*Underwriting philosophy,* discussed later in this chapter, is an example of product design objectives.) These specifications then serve as guidelines during the technical design of the product.

Feasibility Study

Once product design objectives are established, the company conducts further investigation into the operational and technical feasibility of producing and offering the product. A feasibility study can include a review of the results of another company's introduction of

Figure 4-3. Topics typically investigated in a market analysis.

- Consumer or organizational **needs** to be met by the product.
- **Nature and size of the target market(s).** If the target market is not compatible with overall corporate objectives, an analysis must be made of whether current distribution systems can reach the target market, and the reasons for deviating from corporate objectives must be presented in the product proposal.
- **Projected sales and expected persistency.**
- **Nature of price competition.** This competition could take the form of other products, other private insurers, other industries, or government-sponsored insurance programs.
- **Consumer appeal.** How is this product unique? What attributes differentiate this product from those offered by competitors? These attributes must be recognizable, credible, important enough, and relatively easy for agents or direct mail copywriters to communicate to prospects.
- **Agent/distributor appeal.** Why will the existing sales force, if there is one, want to sell this product? Will this product be easier or harder to sell than comparable products? Will this product increase agent hiring or retention, increase closing rates or value per sale, or merely increase the time required to make a sale? Will new distribution channels need to be created and, if so, at what cost?
- **Product's relationship to other products currently offered.** Will this product complement, supplement, or replace other products the company currently offers?
- **Potential legal or regulatory problems.** Can the product legally be produced and sold? Does the product have any features that regulators or consumer groups might view as negative, that might hurt the company's image, or that might not comply with regulations?
- **Special tax considerations.** Are any special tax advantages or problems associated with the product? How long are these advantages or problems likely to remain in effect?
- **Economic considerations.** What is the current economic forecast regarding inflation? Interest rates? Employment? All of these factors can affect the success of a new product.
- **Product/company fit.** Does the product fit the company's mission and objectives? How well does the product fit the company's corporate culture? Can existing systems support the product?

Source: *Portions of this material are adapted from Francois Genest, "Product Myopia,"* Journal of the American Society of CLU, *July 1986, p. 67.*

a similar product, or a discussion with key agents and other market experts to determine if the product will sell well.

Marketing Plan

The product proposal will also include a marketing plan for the new product. A ***marketing plan*** is a tactical plan that deals primarily with the product, price, distribution, and promotion strategies that a company will follow in order to reach potential customers and meet their needs. Marketing plans establish the steps required to implement and control the day-to-day marketing activities of a company.

The development of a marketing plan draws heavily on the information collected during the market analysis discussed earlier.

Sales and Other Financial Forecasts

After developing a marketing plan, the team can make rough preliminary sales and financial forecasts. These forecasts provide estimates regarding unit sales, revenues, costs, and profit, and will be useful input for setting actuarial assumptions and pricing the product during the technical design phase. These forecasts contain a great deal of uncertainty at this early stage in the product development process, and thus they are refined as better information becomes available.

Much of the remainder of Chapter 4 is about technical design and product pricing. If a product is approved, the product proposal can serve as an overall guide for the design, testing, and introduction of the product; the marketing plan will guide the marketing of the product. Here, we present an overview of technical design and how it fits into the overall process of developing and introducing a product.

Technical Product Design

The technical design stage for an insurance product consists of writing the policy contract; choosing a reserve valuation method; setting the product's actuarial assumptions as to investment earnings, persistency, expenses, mortality or morbidity, and, for interest-sensitive business, policy charges and crediting strategy; and establishing the product's rate structure, benefit levels, commission schedule, and underwriting standards. The technical design and pricing of a product should reflect the product's design objectives and should be acceptable to each member of the product development team. The design of a product, its sales estimates, and its actuarial assumptions usually undergo several adjustments before the various functional areas affected by the product can reach an acceptable compromise.

Once a reasonable consensus has been achieved, the product development team presents the product design to the marketing committee. The marketing committee is a senior management group generally consisting of key company executives—for instance, the president, the chief financial and marketing officers, the director of product development, and others—whose primary function is to (1) provide overall guidance and control of the product development process and (2) review and approve or reject product proposals prior to their implementation and introduction. The actions the marketing committee may take with respect to a proposed product are to

- Approve the product
- Call for design revisions
- Reject the product

The product development team also usually obtains feedback from the head of agency operations and selected agents to make sure that the product meets their needs and those of the marketplace.

Scheduling and Budgeting for a New Product

The scheduling and budgeting process consists of (1) allocating human, financial, and computer resources to each activity necessary to implement the product design and (2) developing a project schedule that shows the time frames required for the completion of each activity and the interrelationships among each of the activities.

The product development team must then develop a budget showing the costs associated with each product development activity and the anticipated revenue for the new product. In some cases, assigning additional resources to product development activities can speed up the expected completion date. Therefore, a product development team can also establish several schedules and alternative completion dates based on assigning different levels of resources and corresponding budgets to the product. Using these budget and scheduling projections, the marketing committee can choose the most appropriate schedule and budget for the product.

Implementing and Introducing a New Product

Once a product proposal has been approved and planning has been completed, the staff can move ahead with *implementing* the new product. By ***implementing*** the product, we mean establishing all of the administrative structures and processes necessary to take the product to market. In order to implement the product, the staff first must

- Obtain legal approval for the product from all appropriate jurisdictions—a process called ***policy filing;***
- Design promotion and training materials; and
- Develop and put in place all information systems necessary to market and administer the product.

After implementing the new product, the staff is then ready to introduce it. By ***introducing*** the product, we mean offering the product for sale to consumers.

Policy Filing

During the policy filing stage, the finished policy form and any other legally required forms and documents are filed with the state and provincial insurance departments in those jurisdictions in which the product will be issued and sold. Most companies establish a minimum number of jurisdictions in which a new product must be approved before the company will introduce the product in any jurisdiction. In some jurisdictions, approval of the policy form is not required, and the policy form is filed for the insurance department's information only. For example, in Canada, only the policy forms for variable contracts usually require approval by provincial insurance departments. In most U.S. states, however, the insurance department must approve a policy form before the policy can be introduced there. The specific filing requirements that a company must meet to obtain insurance department approval of a policy vary among states. For example, most states require that an actuary sign a form certifying that the policy complies with all applicable nonforfeiture laws. Other states require that the policy form be approved by the insurance company's home state before they will grant approval. In many states, a readability certification, which certifies that the policy is written in direct, comprehensible language—must accompany the policy when it is submitted for approval. Often, before granting approval of a policy form, a state insurance department will require a company to change contractual language. For administrative ease, insurers try to keep variations in policy wording to a minimum. However, because of variations among state regulations, companies often end up with five, six, or even more versions of the same policy for use in different jurisdictions.

State regulators can be quite helpful to insurers filing for approval of new products—especially when the benefits of the new products to consumers are readily obvious—and often assist companies through the legal complexities of filing. On the average, securing policy approval takes about two to three months. However, the process can take a year or longer.

Financial products with variable contract values may require approvals from additional regulatory authorities. In Canada, the information folders that accompany variable contracts must also be approved by the provincial insurance departments before the contracts can be introduced. Many variable contracts in Canada also require approval from the provincial securities commissions. In the United States, these variable contracts, as well as the sales material to be used with them, must be approved by the Securities and Exchange Commission (SEC). The ***Securities and Exchange Commission (SEC)*** is a federal authority charged with regulating transactions in financial securities in the United States.

Design of Promotion and Training Materials

While policy filing continues, the marketing department's promotion and training units begin their share of product implementation activities. The promotion unit's product implementation activities include the following:

- Designing sales materials and information kits for sales agents, customer service staff, and customers
- Selecting a name for the product
- Creating product-specific advertisements, often with the assistance of an outside advertising agency
- Placing advertising and publicity materials about the product in insurance, general business, and consumer publications

For insurers employing a direct response distribution system, the promotion stage consists primarily of developing and testing advertising materials, because no agent is involved in the selling process. In such cases, the promotion unit is often assisted by outside advertising agencies. Companies that use a personal selling distribution system may develop special sales programs to encourage agents to sell a new product. If agents are not properly educated about the new product, they may not be enthusiastic or effective in selling it. Thus, an insurer generally offers training about new products to its sales forces. The sales training unit's product implementation activities may include the following:

- Creating computer sales illustrations, sales/training materials, and incentive awards for product sales
- Developing a presentation to be used by the local agency head at meetings, showing where the new product fits into the overall portfolio
- Designing sample sales presentations for the new product
- Developing visual aids for agents to use with their clients

An important part of technical product design is product pricing. To form a foundation for our later discussions of pricing financial products in Part 3 of this book, the next section of this chapter reviews some of the fundamental concepts and vocabulary related to pricing insurance products.

Basics of Insurance Pricing[2]

Insurance companies employ *actuaries* to calculate the premium rates the company will charge for its products. An ***actuary*** is an expert in the mathematics of insurance, annuities, and financial instruments. In addition to calculating premium rates, actuaries perform many other mathematical calculations needed in the insurance business.

Figure 4-4. Types of actuaries.

- **Appointed actuary.** An actuary who (1) has been duly appointed by a corporation's board of directors to render an official Actuarial Opinion and Memorandum as to the insurance company's financial condition and also (2) possesses the professional qualifications necessary for the appointment.
- **Enrolled actuary.** An actuary in the United States who possesses the requisite professional qualifications and has been duly registered to sign a pension plan's required regulatory filings.
- **Illustration actuary.** An actuary specializing in certifying whether an insurer's product illustrations conform with regulations.
- **Investment actuary.** An actuary specializing in performing calculations and making decisions relating to an insurance company's investment portfolios.
- **Marketing actuary.** An actuary specializing in performing calculations and making decisions relating to the marketing of an insurance company's product portfolio.
- **Product actuary.** An actuary specializing in performing calculations and making decisions relating to designing and pricing an insurance company's insurance products and other financial products. Also known as a *product design* actuary or a *pricing* actuary.
- **Valuation actuary.** An actuary specializing in rendering opinions as to proper values for an insurance company's reserves.

For example, actuaries calculate the amounts of policy dividends for participating contracts, calculate investment crediting rates for universal life policies, establish values for reserves, and create mathematical models of the company's expected future net cash flows. Figure 4-4 presents a glossary of types of actuaries.

In this textbook we encounter the work of actuaries in all of these fields of specialization. However, in this chapter our interest is mainly in product actuaries' role in setting prices for insurance and other financial products. The prices insurance companies charge for insurance products are known as ***premiums.*** The prices insurance companies charge for annuity products are sometimes known as *annuity considerations,* but in this textbook we use the term *premium* in reference to prices for annuity and insurance products. This section discusses some of the basic elements of insurance product pricing. The insurance product pricing process is explained in detail in Chapters 7, 8, and 9.

The premium rates that actuaries establish for life insurance coverage are often expressed in terms of the charge per $1,000 of life insurance coverage. In reference to life insurance, $1,000 of coverage is known as a ***unit of coverage.*** The premium rate that an actuary establishes per unit of coverage in the process of rate making is usually

Source: By M. Swain. Reprinted with permission of copyright © 1996 the Actuarial Digest.

a gross premium. A product's ***gross premium*** is the amount the insurer charges a policyowner for that product. The gross premium is composed of two elements: the net premium and the loading. The gross premium is also influenced by another important element: the product's reserves.

The Net Premium

When actuaries price insurance products, one of their first steps is to estimate the ***cost of benefits.*** An insurance product's cost of benefits is the total amount of contractually required benefits the product is expected to pay. The cost of benefits calculated for the purpose of pricing must take into account any provisions allowing policyowners to withdraw all or part of their accumulated account values, as well as the potential mortality or morbidity losses that the insurer assumes relative to a given contract or, in the case of an annuity, the potential losses from annuitants' continued survival.

A ***net premium*** is the amount calculated to cover a product's expected cost of benefits. The cost of benefits is generally not equal to the net premium, because expected investment earnings are used to partially offset the cost of benefits. The net premium is the amount per unit of coverage that will precisely pay for the product's cost of benefits, net of expected investment earnings. Net premium calculations are based on assumptions as to mortality or morbidity rates, investment earnings rates, and lapse rates. In many cases, customers are unaware of the net premium rate for a contract. The customer is generally only aware of the gross premium, which is the premium amount the customer pays, because insurers do not list the components of the gross premium—the net premium and loading—separately.

The net premium differs from the gross premium in that a *net* premium rate does *not* cover the company's business expenses for issuing contracts and operating the company. In other words, the net premium calculation does not make a provision for loading.

Loading

In addition to the cost of benefits, the gross premium an insurance company charges for an insurance product must cover the expenses the insurer incurs in issuing the product and the cost of the company's operations. To pay for the expenses of doing business, insurers add to the net premium an amount called the ***loading.*** The amount of loading that an actuary adds to the net premium is based on an estimate of the company's operating expenses and product distribution expenses, with an additional amount added as the company's profit. The gross premium of a product is equal to the net premium plus the loading.

Net Premium + Loading = Gross Premium

Policy Reserves

An additional factor that actuaries consider when establishing the gross premium for an insurance product is the rate at which the product accumulates policy reserves. A ***policy reserve*** is a liability that identifies the amount that, together with future premiums and investment income, is expected to be needed to pay the future benefits of an insurance policy or annuity contract. Because they take into account future income from premiums and investments, policy reserves are generally less than the total amount of coverage promised by a policy. For life insurance policies, the difference between the amount of coverage promised by the policy and the policy reserve is known as the ***net amount at risk.*** In essence, the net amount at risk represents the insurance company's unfunded exposure to contractual liabilities. For whole life policies, the net amount at risk is generally highest in a policy's earliest years, decreasing over time as the policy reserve grows. For term life policies, the net amount at risk is generally high both at the beginning and at the end of the term. The basic relationship between net amount at risk and policy reserve can be illustrated as follows:

Net Amount at Risk = Coverage Amount – Policy Reserve

Figure 4-5 shows the relationship, over time, of the net amount at risk and the policy reserve of a whole life policy.

When setting gross premiums, actuaries are aware of the rate at which reserves will grow and the effect of this growth on the timing of a product's earnings. The entirety of Chapter 9 of this textbook is about various types of reserves and other aspects of reserves.

An Earnings View of Products

From an earnings viewpoint, we can look at the operation of a life insurance product as consisting of revenues, costs, and earnings, as follows:

Revenues	–	Costs	=	Earnings
• Premiums and other payments from customers • Investment earnings		• Operating expenses, including (a) Distribution & acquisition expenses (b) Administrative expenses • Claims and other benefits • Reserve increases • Reductions in reserves (considered a "negative cost")		• Profit margin

Figure 4-6 compares relative shares of insurance industry revenue from premiums versus investment earnings in the United States and Canada. Figure 4-7 compares the relative shares of expenses for op-

Figure 4-5. The net amount at risk and policy reserve of a whole life policy.

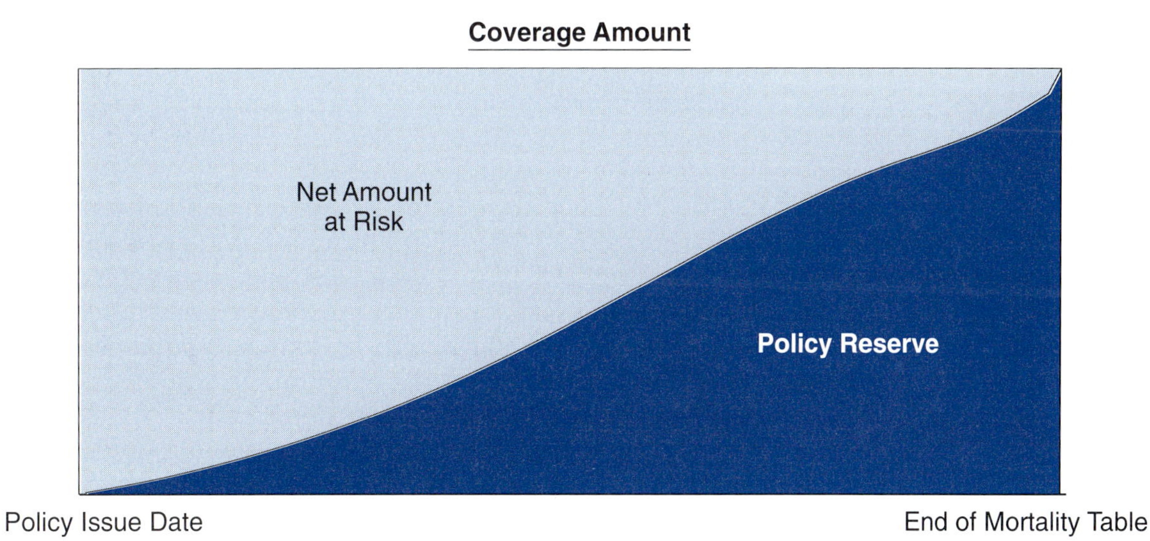

Figure 4-6. Relative shares of income from premiums versus investment earnings, U.S. and Canadian life and health insurers.

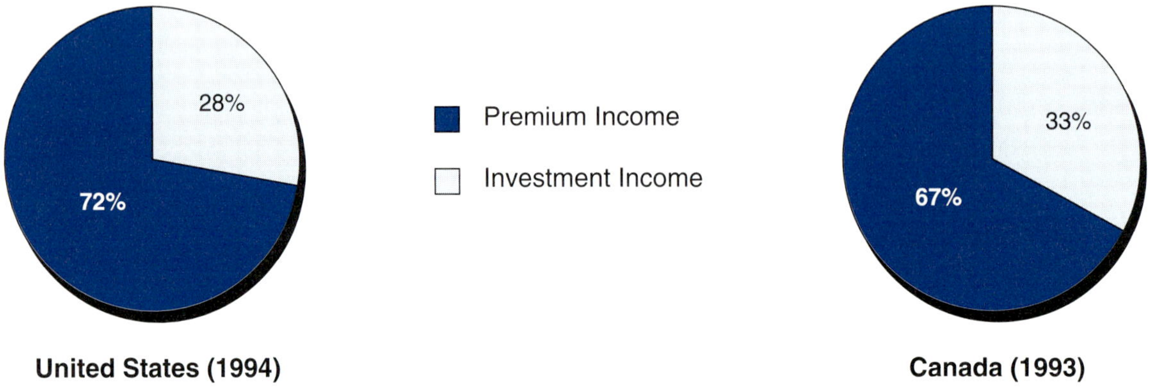

Sources: *ACLI* 1995 Life Insurance Fact Book Update, *p. 37; CLHIA* 1994 Canadian Life and Health Insurance Facts, *p. 5.*

erations versus expenses for benefits and reserve accumulations, also for the United States and Canada.

In the remainder of Chapter 4 we review the components of revenues and costs that affect the earnings and, therefore, the pricing of insurance and other financial products. We look at revenues from investments, revenues from premiums, costs of providing benefits, and operating expenses.

Product-Related Revenues

When designing products, actuaries consider product revenues from two main sources: (1) premiums and other payments from customers, and (2) investment earnings from assets backing policy reserves. Figure 4-8 shows some of the kinds of individual products offered by life and health insurance companies.

Life and health insurance companies receive payments from their customers in the form of insurance premiums, annuity premiums, contributions to retirement plans, contributions to other savings plans, service fees for contract administration, and service fees for investment management. Life and health insurance companies earn investment revenues from their investment of premium revenues in a variety of real and financial assets. These investments produce payments of interest, repayments of principal, rental income, and capital gains for insurers. Before we discuss premiums and other payments from customers, we briefly discuss investment earnings.

Figure 4-7. Relative shares of expenses and reserve accumulations for operations versus expenses for benefits, U.S. and Canadian life and health insurers.

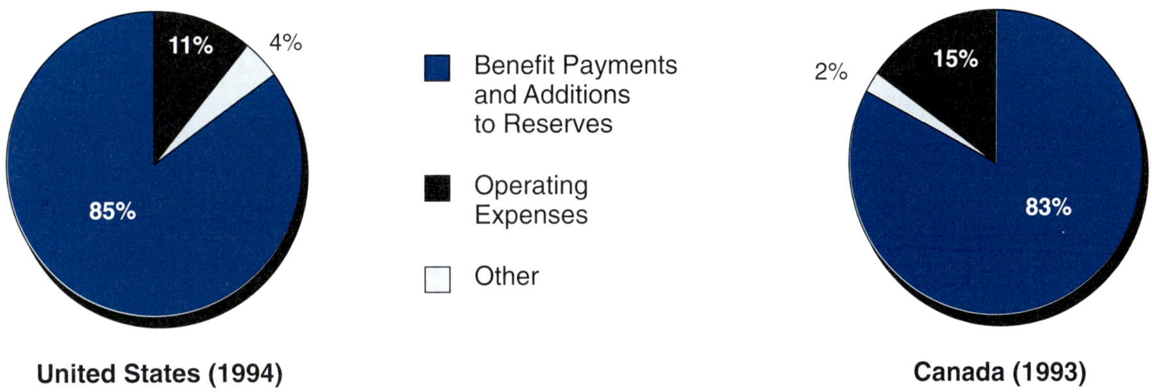

Sources: *ACLI* 1995 Life Insurance Fact Book Update, *p. 37; CLHIA* 1994 Canadian Life and Health Insurance Facts, *p. 5.*

Investment Earnings

Net investment income—from the asset portfolio—is one of two major revenue sources that insurers take into account when designing products. Product design actuaries generally take this factor into consideration by making an *actuarial assumption* about the rate of return the insurer will earn on its investments. Product design actuaries do not generally make an in-depth analysis or projection of investment earnings. Instead, product design actuaries establish multiple assumptions relating to these factors and use

Figure 4-8. Individual products offered by life and health insurance companies.

Annuity contracts	Life insurance	Health insurance
• Guaranteed (traditional) • Interest-sensitive annuities • Variable annuities • Immediate/matured annuities and supplementary contracts • Structured settlements (jury settlements, lottery winnings)	• Ordinary life • Universal life • Variable life • Variable universal life • Term life	• Disability income • Hospital/surgical/medical expense • Long-term care • Medicare supplement

models to test the profitability of products under each of these assumptions.

Investment returns have far more impact on the earnings of a long-term product than a short-term product for the simple reason that, in a long-term product, the investment earnings have a much longer period in which to accumulate. Examples of long-term products are whole life insurance, investment plans, or retirement products. Examples of short-term insurance products are annually renewable group medical expense insurance and yearly renewable term insurance.

Payments from Customers

With reference to a single life insurance product, total revenues from customers are determined by (1) premium rates and (2) the amount of business in force. In turn, the amount of business in force is related to (1) the product's sales volume and (2) how long the business remains in force.

Along with the premium rate, a product's sales volume determines the *amount* of the product's revenues, whereas how long the product remains in force (the product's *persistency)* determines *how long* those revenues will continue. Thus, to improve a product's revenues from customers, a company would typically focus on ways to enhance sales volume, persistency, or both.

Some factors influencing an insurer's sales reserves are classified as *external factors* to reflect the fact that an insurer has little or no control over them, and can only attempt to accurately forecast their effects. In contrast, influencing factors that the insurer can control are classified as *internal factors.* Some of the internal and external factors influencing an insurer's sales revenues are illustrated in Figure 4-9.

Figure 4-9. Factors affecting a product's sales volume and sales revenues.

Internal	External
• Price (premium rate per $1,000)	• Customer needs
• Product features	• Economic conditions
• Distribution system	• Social conditions
• Advertising and publicity	• Demographic conditions
• Compensation of sales force	• Political conditions
• Credited interest rates relative to competition	• Regulatory conditions
• Reputation and financial strength of company	• Competitive conditions

The sales revenue insurers collect from customers can be related to *unit price* and *quantity of units sold,* as expressed in the following equation:

Sales Revenue = Unit Price × Units Sold

For an insurance product, the *unit price* would be the premium per unit of coverage, and a *unit sold* would be represented by a premium payment for a unit of coverage either for a new policy or an in-force policy paying a renewal premium. As a rule, whenever more units of a product are sold at a given premium rate, the insurer's sales revenue increases. Likewise, whenever the product's price is increased and the same quantity is sold, sales revenue increases. However, in a competitive market, raising a product's unit price would generally cause sales volume to decrease. The reason that consumers may be able to find a competitor's product at a lower price.

Influences on Price

Like the demand for most types of products, the quantity demanded for most insurance products responds to price. Typically, the quantity sold of the product *decreases* as the price of the product *increases,* and vice versa. Economists also recognize a concept known as ***price elasticity,*** which is calculated as the percentage change in quantity demanded resulting from a change in price divided by the percentage change in price. For example, if the quantity demanded for a product decreased by 10 percent as a result of a 20 percent increase in price, the price elasticity of this change in price would be calculated as follows:

$$\textbf{Price Elasticity} = \frac{\textbf{\% Change in}}{\textbf{Quantity Demanded}} \div \frac{\textbf{\% Change in}}{\textbf{Price}}$$

$$= 10\% \div 20\%$$

$$= 0.5$$

Price elasticity is a measure of how sensitive demand is to a change in price. Demand for a product is said to be ***price elastic*** if the percentage change in quantity demanded is greater than the percentage change in price—in other words, if the price elasticity ratio is greater than 1.0. If demand is price elastic, then an increase in price will cause total sales revenue to decrease. Demand for a product is said to be ***price inelastic*** if the percentage change in quantity demanded is less than the percentage change in price (or the price elasticity ratio is less than 1.0). If demand is price inelastic, then an increase in price will cause total sales revenue to increase. The following tables show examples of price elastic demand and price inelastic demand:

Price Elastic Demand **Revenue decreases as price increases.**		
Price	$ 100	$ 120
Quantity	× 100	× 70
Revenue	$10,000	$8,400

Price Inelastic Demand **Revenue increases as price increases.**		
Price	$ 100	$ 120
Quantity	× 100	× 90
Revenue	$10,000	$10,800

Most products tend to be *price elastic* over certain price ranges, and *price inelastic* over other price ranges.

Theoretically, every product has an optimum price. A product's ***optimum price*** is the price at which the seller will maximize revenue from the product. In practice, product pricing for insurance companies is generally not so clear-cut as simply finding this optimum price. Instead, an insurance company often sets a price that it expects to provide a satisfactory sales volume and sales revenues. Nevertheless, when pricing its products, an insurer must keep in mind the relationships among price, quantity sold, and sales revenue.

Influences on Sales Volume

In general, a company's sales revenue increases whenever the company increases its sales volume, given that prices don't decrease. Because revenues are influenced by sales volume, insurers need to know how they can influence sales volume. Some of the keys to selling products are to offer products that meet customers' needs; to keep customers aware of the products that are available; to have an effective distribution system; to offer competitive commissions; to remain conscious of competing products offered by other companies; and to have a good image, good name recognition, and a good quality rating.

In addition, several aspects of a product's design, administration, and distribution affect sales volume. For insurance products, the *extent of coverage* provided by the policy is one important selling point. Products that offer more extensive coverage without charging higher premiums tend to create better sales volume than products with less extensive coverage.

A second important selling point for many financial products is the crediting rate on a product's investment or savings element. Purchasers use many financial products primarily as vehicles for saving or investment. For this reason, the expected or actual crediting rate on these products is a major consideration for consumers deciding whether to purchase or keep such products. Similarly, whether an insurer offers any guarantee at all in connection with crediting rates can affect product sales and persistency. Typically, these crediting rates and the associated guarantees, if any, can be structured as follows:

- *A fixed and fully guaranteed crediting rate,* so that the customer bears no investment risk, whereas the insurer bears the full investment risk
- *A fully variable and non-guaranteed crediting rate,* so that the customer bears all of the investment risk, whereas the insurer bears none
- *A flexible annual crediting rate with a guaranteed minimum,* so that the customer and the insurer share the investment risk

A flexible annual crediting rate with a guaranteed minimum appeals to customers who are not comfortable bearing the full investment risk. Additionally, companies can often charge a higher price for products that contain such guarantees; the higher price works both to increase product revenues and to compensate for the additional risk the companies incur in offering a crediting rate guarantee. Accordingly, in order to attract new purchasers or larger purchases, an insurer might distinguish itself from competitors by either paying a higher non-guaranteed crediting rate or offering stronger guarantees as to a minimum crediting rate.

Influences on Persistency

One important characteristic of an insurance company's product revenues is that each policy typically generates a stream of revenues—in the form of premium payments and interest income—that continues for a period of time, rather than a single payment at the point of sale. Once a company sells a policy, the company generally would like for the policy to continue in force so that the revenue stream associated with the product will continue, at least until the company recovers its investment in the policy. For business on the books, the ***persistency rate*** is the share of the business that remains in force for a specified period. The flip side of persistency is the lapse rate. A ***lapse rate*** (or *withdrawal rate)* for business on the books can be defined as the share of the business that is voluntarily terminated over a specified period. The relationship between the lapse rate and the persistency rate for the same product can be expressed as follows:

FAST FACT

In 1994, persistency in the U.S. life insurance industry reached a 20-year high. In 1994, lapse rates reached a low of 8.3% for ordinary life policies, down from an all-time high in 1984 of 14.1%. Persistency rates at mutual companies are traditionally better than those at stock companies.[3]

Lapse Rate + Persistency Rate = 100%

An insurance or annuity product with a high persistency rate generates revenues for longer than does a product with a lower persistency rate. As a rule, for a given sales level, the higher a product's persistency rate, the larger the total revenues from that product. From another viewpoint, the lower the product's lapse rate, the larger the total revenues from that product. Unexpectedly poor persistency—which is the same as an unexpectedly high lapse rate—might cause a product to produce losses rather than profits.

Insurers know that 100 percent product persistency is unrealistic. When actuaries price products, they establish an actuarial assumption for the product's persistency rate—that is, they assume that a given percentage of a block of business will remain in force for a given period. This persistency rate assumption implies that a complementary percentage of the business will lapse. The persistency rate will ordinarily cause a product's expected profitability to suffer only if persistency is worse than assumed.

In general, the keys to attaining good persistency rates are effective product design, effective marketing, and effective administration. Products with the following features tend to have good persistency rates:

- The product meets customers' needs for insurance protection and investment risk and return
- Customers can afford the product
- The product's price makes it a good value, compared to competing products
- The insurer's customer service is convenient, courteous, prompt, professional, and meets the customer's needs
- Making premium payments is convenient and administratively simple

In addition to the factors influencing revenues from investment earnings and from customers' payments, insurers must also carefully consider product-related costs when designing new products. For more information about factors that affect persistency, see Figure 4-10.

Product-Related Costs

The product-related costs that actuaries consider when constructing premium rates take two general forms: (1) payments to customers and (2) product-related business expenses. Payments to customers

Figure 4-10. Factors that affect persistency.

The following factors (when adjusted for their relationship with mode of premium payment and income level) have been shown to affect persistency.

Buyer	Higher-than-average persistency is found among buyers who are • Between the ages of 40 and 65 • Professionals, executives, and proprietors • Current owners of other policies from the same company • Insuring the lives of juveniles or students • Initiating the sale themselves • Nonsmokers • Female • Previous non-lapsers
Product	Higher-than-average persistency is found among policies that are • Permanent rather than term • Level premium • Higher in premium • Without policy loans • Underwritten on a medical basis • Sold with an insurability option rider • Purchased for business reasons • Issued as applied for
Agent	• Persistency increases as the agent's length of service increases. • Poor persistency is often associated with the business produced by new agents who leave the industry. • Persistency is positively related to the level of an agent's product knowledge.
Sales Process	Higher lapse rates occur if • No initial premium payment accompanies the application • The selling agent emphasizes savings and thrift • Policies are not delivered personally to the insured • Post-sale service is not employed
Other Factors Affecting Persistency	• Persistency tends to be poorer during periods of unemployment and high interest rates. • Persistency tends to improve when personal savings and effective buying incomes are high. • Growing competition offered by competitive investment media increases replacements.

Source: *Adapted from "Factors Affecting Persistency of Ordinary Business,"* 1978 Proceedings of the National Association of Insurance Commissioners, *Volume II, pp. 384–385.*

primarily include contractual obligations related to benefits and withdrawals, as well as dividends on participating policies. Product-related business expenses primarily involve product development expenses, distribution expenses, administrative expenses, taxes, and the expense of setting up new reserves. This section presents the product design elements that insurers can use to manage these expenses.

Expenses for Payments to Customers

The benefit payments that insurers make to customers are triggered by three types of events:

1. An insured event (the death of the insured under a life insurance policy or a covered medical expense under a health insurance policy, for example) occurs, a contractual benefit arises, or a product matures.
2. The customer prematurely withdraws all or part of the cash value in a product.
3. A dividend is payable on a participating policy.

Each of these events triggers a product-related expenditure. We first examine the expenses that result from benefit payments made in support of insurance policies and the methods companies use to manage those expenses. We then address account value withdrawals and the methods insurers can use to limit such withdrawals. Finally, we review policy dividend payments, a non-guaranteed type of product-related expenditure.

Payments of Contractual Benefits

In Chapter 1 we saw that aggregate payments for contractual benefits represent the largest component of the insurance industry's expenses. Likewise, in most cases, payments for contractual benefits represent the largest component of an insurer's expenses for each single product.

In a general sense, two variables determine the amount of contractual benefits for each product:

1. The number of occurrences of insured events
2. The extent of a product's coverage

Occurrences of Insured Events. The number of occurrences of insured events is among the most important of an insurer's pricing assumptions. When pricing products, an insurer makes assumptions about the number of insured events that will occur. The reliability of these pricing assumptions, however, depends on an insurer's underwriting and claim practices.

An insurer's ***underwriting philosophy,*** also called *underwriting objectives,* is a body of standards and goals for guiding the risk assessment process. An insurer's underwriting philosophy serves to guide all of the insurer's risk selection and risk classification procedures. The underwriting philosophy generally reflects the insurer's strategic business goals and the company's conservative or aggressive attitudes toward risk taking. Underwriting philosophy generally guides product pricing decisions. An insurer's underwriting philosophy strongly shapes the *underwriting guidelines* established for each product.

Underwriting guidelines are general rules that the underwriting staff uses in assigning applicants to the different premium classifications. The product design team, pricing actuary, and underwriting staff work together during the product design phase to set underwriting guidelines for each product. Such underwriting guidelines are intended to ensure that the underwriting staff's decisions are consistent with the risks anticipated during a product's pricing process. An insurer's underwriting guidelines for each product address

- The level of risk to accept as standard, preferred, or rated
- Retention limits, indicating the level of risk to reinsure
- The level of risk to decline

Underwriting guidelines for individual coverages generally establish broad risk classifications. Underwriting guidelines for group insurance do not define risk classes. Instead, underwriting guidelines for group coverages typically address such factors as the group's industry affiliation, employee classes, and the age demographics of the group.

Underwriting guidelines influence a product's benefit cash flows in several ways. Generally, lenient underwriting guidelines reflect an aggressive stance toward risk-taking, and strict underwriting guidelines reflect a conservative stance toward risk-taking. Either type of guideline can be effective, as long as the company's pricing structure is developed accordingly. Product revenues and costs can be adversely affected if underwriting guidelines are described or applied in a manner inconsistent with pricing assumptions. For example, *overly lenient* underwriting guidelines can result in expenses for benefit payments that far exceed the expenses expected when the product was priced. Conversely, *overly strict* underwriting guidelines would result in lost sales volume, lost profits because of lost sales, and, potentially, excessive reinsurance.

Additionally, underwriting guidelines setting the level of risk the company will reinsure are very important in managing and predicting the company's product benefit cash flows. Chapter 14 describes reinsurance and provides more details on the use of reinsurance in managing risk in the product portfolio.

An insurance company's claim procedures are also important in managing the company's benefit costs. Paying legitimate claims is an insurance company's most important responsibility to its customers. On the other hand, without adequate safeguards in a company's claim procedures, the company might incur the unwarranted expense of paying a large number of invalid or fraudulent claims. Paying illegitimate claims would increase the company's expenses and, moreover, would represent a breach of the insurer's duty to its customers and shareholders.

Extent of Coverage. Earlier, when discussing sales revenues and sales volume, we mentioned that the extent of coverage provided under a contract influences a product's sales. The extent of coverage also influences the product's benefit costs. An insurer can employ special contractual provisions either to increase or decrease the extent of coverage under an insurance product. Such contractual provisions can increase the profitability of the product for the insurer while also increasing the value of the product to the customer. Two examples of policy provisions that can affect the extent of coverage under a policy are exclusions and policy riders.

Life and health insurance policies often contain various types of exclusion provisions. ***Exclusion provisions*** limit the insurer's liability if the insured loss results from specified causes. For example, the suicide exclusion in a life insurance policy typically states that if the insured dies as a result of suicide during a specified period, then the insurer's liability will be limited to the total amount of premiums paid for the policy, or to the policy's cash surrender value at the time of death. In medical expense policies, exclusion provisions typically specify that benefits are not provided for certain types of procedures, such as cosmetic surgery or experimental treatments. Medical expense policies may also exclude coverage of expenses that arise from specified pre-existing conditions.

A ***policy rider*** is an amendment to an insurance policy that either expands or limits the benefits payable under the policy. Policy riders benefit both the customer and the insurer because riders offer flexibility for both parties. An insurer can add riders to a basic contract in order to customize the basic plan of insurance to suit different clients. Riders can be instituted at a contract's inception, or they can be added or dropped after the contract has remained in force for some time.

By including policy riders that *increase* the extent of a product's coverage, the insurer can add value by providing additional coverage that customers desire; the insurer can then charge higher premiums for the additional coverage. Examples of coverages that insurers often add to life policies are accidental death benefits and waiver of premium for disability benefits. When life insurance policies include these coverages, the insurer charges an additional premium amount for the added coverage. In this way, the companies earn additional premium income and customers gain additional coverages.

By including policy riders that *limit* a product's coverage, the insurer can often decrease its costs and thus can decrease the price of the product. The insurer may be able to decrease the product's coverage by (1) limiting the length of time that coverage continues or (2) excluding risks with a very high likelihood of occurrence or whose occurrence is likely to lead to very high benefit costs. For example, in connection with health insurance coverages, insurers can offer a variety of waiting and elimination periods, as well as different deductible and coinsurance amounts. Insurers also often exclude coverage for known health problems in order to issue policies to people who would otherwise not be eligible for coverage. Figure 4-11 shows some of the contractual provisions that can influence the number of events covered by a policy and others that can influence the amount of coverage per event.

Insight 4-1 illustrates how product features related to the extent of disability income (DI) coverage increased some companies' revenues from DI business in the early 1980s, but then later caused their expenses for benefits to increase excessively.

Figure 4-11. Contractual provisions that can affect a product's extent of coverage.

	Provisions extending coverage		Provisions limiting coverage	
	Life	**Health**	**Life**	**Health**
Covered events	• Accidental death and dismemberment • Guaranteed insurability • Waiver of premium for disability	• Prescription drug benefits • Preventive care benefits • Vision care benefits	• Suicide exclusions (limited to two years in most states) • War exclusions • Aviation exclusions • Exclusions of deaths that occur while insured is committing a crime	• Pre-existing condition exclusions • Other exclusions • Waiting periods • Provider networks
Coverage period	• Renewability of term policy • Convertibility of term policy • Portability of group benefits	• Renewability • Portability of group benefits	• Nonrenewability of term contract • Nonconvertibility of term contract	• Cancellable coverage
Coverage per event	• Accidental death and dismemberment • Paid-up additions	• High maximum benefit amounts	• Limits on the face amount customers can purchase	• Low maximum benefit amounts • Co-payments

Insight 4-1 Making DI More Appealing

Over much of the last 10 years, the noncancellable disability income market experienced an upheaval caused by significant losses among virtually all companies selling the coverage. The nine leading writers experienced increases in total claims costs from 50 percent of premium in 1984 to almost 65 percent in 1990. Overall before-tax gain fell nearly 10 percent and was negative for 1986 through 1990 despite record investment income.

Problems began when companies, in the push to garner mar-ket share, increased income replacement ratios and added built-in features. Increased replacement ratios meant that the policy would indemnify a greater portion of the insured's income. When the coverage was introduced, the replaced maximums were between 60 percent and 70 percent, but over time rose even higher. This encouraged adverse selection and extended disability durations. Many companies lessened requirements that overall coverage be integrated with Social Security benefits. The policy benefits also were increased if they were taxable. Typical waiting periods of 30 to 90 days meant insureds did not have to wait long to receive benefits. This expanded the number of claims as minor disabilities were covered.

Added features included an "own occupation" definition of disability. This powerful marketing tool provided that if insureds could not work in their own occupation, they could work in another. For example, if a doctor could no longer practice medicine because of a hand injury, he or she could teach instead and still receive the monthly disability benefit—even if he or she were earning more teaching. Extra-cost riders contributed to the problems as well. Many policies offered cost of living adjustment riders that indexed benefits to a flat rate or to inflation, further encouraging claimants to remain on disability.

Source: *Roger L. Blease, "Making DI More Appealing," Best's* Review *(February 1994), p. 41. Reprinted by permission of the publisher.*

Withdrawals of Account Values

Customer withdrawals occur when the customer prematurely removes money from an insurance product, such as by surrendering the product for its entire cash value, by removing some funds from the product, or by taking a loan against account values. Withdrawals of account values are classified as ***premature withdrawals*** if they occur prior to an insured event or a scheduled payout date. Partial withdrawals of account values differ from policy loans in that the insurer earns no interest on the withdrawn money. When a customer takes out a policy loan against the account values, the insurance company continues to earn interest on the money, but perhaps at a lower rate than would have been available to the insurer's investments staff. Surrender of a product for its account value results in an immediate cash outflow, the elimination of expected future premium payments, and the elimination of expected future investment earnings.

As we discussed in Chapter 3, when market interest rates rise, withdrawals of account values usually increase through disintermediation. When market interest rates rise, unless the insurer's crediting rates rise to match market rates, customers often withdraw their money from the insurance company and invest their funds in higher-yielding opportunities elsewhere. Figure 4-12 identifies types of insurance

Figure 4-12. Products subject to withdrawal when market interest rates rise.

Product Type	Description
Individual life insurance	Cash value life insurance is subject to full or partial withdrawal or to policy loan at the option of the policyowner.
Single-premium deferred annuities (SPDAs)	Annuities are subject to full or partial withdrawal and sometimes to policy loan at the option of the contract holder.
Guaranteed investment contracts (GICs)	Some GICs permit withdrawals by plan participants at book value. GICs themselves typically are not surrenderable by plan sponsors.
Market-value adjusted annuities	Market-value adjusted annuities are surrenderable at the option of the contract holder, but subject to a market-value adjustment that protects against C-3 risk.

company products that are particularly susceptible to withdrawal risk when interest rates rise.

Fortunately, when designing products, insurers can include several contract features to discourage withdrawals. For example, insurers can offer variable crediting rates that change along with changes in market interest rates, so that customers have little incentive to seek higher crediting rates elsewhere. Moreover, insurers can employ various lapse or withdrawal fees and surrender fees. Finally, some contracts pay customers a ***persistency bonus*** upon completion of a tenth or twentieth contract year. Insurers can apply a similar persistency bonus to agents' commissions, as discussed in Chapter 20. Figure 4-13 identifies several types of contract provisions that can restrict or discourage withdrawals, and thus limit the insurance company's exposure to disintermediation risk.

Charging Fees for Withdrawals and Surrenders. Several types of contract provisions impose various fees on consumers in connection with withdrawals. Withdrawal fees and surrender charges encourage customers to leave funds with the insurance company for at least a minimum time. ***Withdrawal fees*** are amounts that customers must pay if they withdraw part of their money from a financial product within a given period after the purchase. These fees are intended to help the company recover policy acquisition expenses. For example, a universal life policyowner may have to pay a withdrawal fee upon withdrawing any of the policy's cash value before the tenth policy year. ***Surrender charges*** are amounts that customers must pay if they withdraw all of their money from a financial product and termi-

Figure 4-13. Contract provisions that can restrict withdrawals.

- **Withdrawal fees** (surrender charges). A charge applied upon the premature distribution of funds.
- **Tiered interest crediting rates.** Provisions for retroactively decreasing interest crediting rates at the time of a premature withdrawal of funds. These provisions appear in some pension products.
- **Payout schedule provisions.** Provisions setting a fixed schedule of annual payouts of the full account balance over a period of years. These provisions appear in some pension products.
- **Withdrawal prohibitions.** Provisions prohibiting premature withdrawals for any reason. These provisions appear in some immediate annuities, terminal funding contracts, and GICs.
- **Market-value adjustment of account values.** Provisions for adjusting account values in the event of premature withdrawals to reflect investment results and adverse or favorable deviations. These provisions appear in group and individual pension products.
- **Fee-for-service contracts** (investment only contracts) (administrative service contracts). Contracts under which the insurer offers no insurance or investment guarantees and, thus, passes along all insurance or investment risk to the customer.

nate the contract within a given period after the purchase. Annuity contracts often impose a surrender charge if the contract owner surrenders the annuity for cash, usually within a specified period after the inception of the contract.

Policy Loan Activity

On an insurance company's balance sheet, policy loans are classified as an investment. For many purposes related to profit testing, policy loan activity is folded into the total investment return assumption. From a cash flow viewpoint, though, policy loans are a cash outflow. Insurers are required to make policy loans upon a policyowner's request, in accordance with the policy's policy loan provision. From the insurance company's perspective, however, making investments in policy loans is often an unprofitable investment of the insurer's funds. Policy loan activity often rises when market interest rates rise, particularly if policyholders can borrow against their insurance at a low rate of interest and then can invest that loan money elsewhere at the current higher market interest rate. If an insurer is forced to make increased policy loans during a time of rising market interest rates, the insurer will have less money to invest in other, more lucrative assets. Further, unexpected increases in policy loans can force an insurer to sell assets on unfavorable terms in order to meet the cash demands of its policyowners.

Policy Loan Charges. To discourage fluctuations in policy-loan activity, insurers have the option of setting a relatively high policy-loan interest rate. In general, the higher the policy-loan interest rate, the less likely that policyowners will borrow money from their insurance policies during times of rising interest rates in order to earn a better return elsewhere. When an insurer knows that a product's consumers look for a rapid build-up of cash value and the ability to take policy loans, the insurer may design a product so that it meets these preferences. However, in such situations, the insurer often charges a relatively high policy-loan interest rate, at least during the policy's early years. Various insurance regulations, however, limit the maximum policy-loan interest rate an insurer is permitted to charge.

An insurance product can also impose a ***variable policy-loan interest rate,*** in which case the interest rate that the policyowner must pay on policy loans fluctuates according to prevailing interest rates in the economy. Thus, when the interest rates available from other investments rise, the variable interest rate that a policyowner must pay on policy loans also rises correspondingly. This helps prevent sudden, unpredictable increases in policy loan activity. An additional benefit that the variable interest rate offers to insurers is that when policyowners borrow in times of rising interest rates, their correspondingly higher policy-loan interest rate also increases the insurer's interest earnings from policy loans.

Policy Dividends

Policy dividends can be viewed as a product-related cost for participating insurance policies. A ***policy dividend*** is an amount that the insurer credits to policyowners at the end of a policy year, and which represents a return of premiums. A policy dividend is a mechanism that insurers use for, in effect, adjusting the price of a contract after the contract has been sold and issued. By paying a policy dividend, the insurer is returning a portion of the price paid for the contract.

Policies on which policy dividends are payable are called ***participating (par) policies.*** The owner of a participating policy has a right to a share in the insurer's divisible surplus. ***Divisible surplus*** is a portion of the insurer's capital and surplus, set aside annually from current earnings and earmarked for distribution to owners of participating policies. Generally, a dividend represents a portion of realized earnings that have resulted from better than expected claim experience, expense experience, and interest earning experience.

Because an insurer does not guarantee to pay policy dividends, the insurer has a degree of control over this cash outflow. Although a policy dividend is technically an optional payment for the insurer, insurers generally pay a policy dividend on participating policies if financial performance meets or exceeds the insurer's pricing assumptions. In designing and pricing participating insurance products, insurers include an actuarial assumption for a product's *policy dividend rate.* In general, the higher the assumed policy dividend rate, the higher the product's price. Insurers and their sales representatives are prohibited from guaranteeing future policy dividends. However, agents and other producers are permitted to show customers illustrations of a company's past and present policy dividend payments. If a company has a consistent track record of paying generous policy dividends, this record may go a long way towards counteracting the potentially negative effect on sales of the product's higher initial premium.

Because dividends are not guaranteed, the policy dividend rate assumption gives the insurer an added safety cushion in case actual performance does not meet the actuarial assumptions. For example, if benefit payments under the product exceed the insurer's assumptions, the insurer could pay a smaller policy dividend than the product's actuarial assumption for policy dividends. For instance, for a policy having a policy dividend assumption of 8 percent, the insurer could pay a policy dividend of only 6 percent to reflect the poorer-than-expected claim experience. The insurer would use the other 2 percent to cover the unexpected benefits.

Insurers who have traditionally paid generous policy dividends, however, must be careful not to reduce them drastically. An insurer's reducing its policy dividend rate below customer expectations could damage customer goodwill toward and confidence in the insurer. Insurers must weigh the negative public perception and possible damage to sales and persistency associated with reducing their usual policy dividend rate.

Insurers must moreover be careful about advertising product features, such as offsetting premiums, which in the event of adverse deviations may not operate as planned. A ***premium offset policy*** is a type of policy with a rapid build-up of cash values that is structured so that, after the policy has remained in force for a stated period, no further premiums are necessary. Premium offset policies make premium payments unnecessary after a certain point by (1) borrowing premium payments from the policy's cash value, (2) using dividends to pay premiums, (3) purchasing enough paid-up additions to equal the policy's face value, or (4) in some universal life policies, accumulating an account value large enough to fund the product to maturity. Premium offset policies are often participating policies, and the policy dividend build-up is often an important factor in the availability of an *inside build-up* for making the later premium payments, purchasing the paid-up additions, or accumulating the necessary account value. Premium offset policies have sometimes been called *vanishing premium policies.* However, because insurers generally cannot guarantee that dividend payments and account value accumulations will always be high enough so that future premiums will actually *vanish,* the NAIC's Model Illustration Regulation now forbids use of the word *vanishing premium* in sales illustrations.

Once a policy begins operating with an offset premium, and customers have come to rely on the dividend to make the premium payments, the loss of this feature due to inadequate dividends can seriously damage customer goodwill and public confidence in the insurer. Addressing such issues in a direct manner generally makes sense both financially and ethically. Efforts to correct such a situation can be costly, but choosing to demonstrate loyalty to customers in a difficult situation can in turn be rewarded by customers' loyalty to the company. Insight 4-2 concerns how one insurer addressed such a problem in a head-on effort to control public relations damage and to address customer concerns related to premium offset policies with non-vanishing premiums.

Operating Expenses

Life, health, and annuity companies must also spend money to support the company's operations. To ensure profitability, insurers seek to control their operating expenses. Earlier in the chapter we saw that the two main parts of an insurer's operating expenses are various administrative expenses and product development expenses.

Administrative Expenses

The administrative expenses of issuing and supporting a product ordinarily are conceptualized as a share of business overhead that is allocated to the product. In Chapter 7, we review the types of expenses

Insight 4-2 Manulife Addresses Issue of Non-Vanishing Premiums

Manulife Financial, Toronto, among the first to start reducing its [policy] dividend scale in 1988, is again taking the lead in addressing its U.S. policyholders directly with the problem of non-vanishing premiums.

As of July 1, the insurer began a one-year program of face-to-face policy reviews with 34,884 participating policyholders.

The purpose of the review meetings, according to a release, "is to help policyholders understand and deal with the effects of falling [policy] dividend crediting rates on existing coverage."

Salaried representatives have been hired to conduct the reviews. Agents participating in the program will be paid $200 per client for what could be a two-visit process.

During the meetings, representatives will offer an "extensive" consumer education program as well as six options for responding to the impact of dividend decreases: additional in-force deposit capability, face amount reductions, enhanced term insurance, recommencing premium payments where the premium vanish has already taken place, term-to-permanent conversion and variable life conversion.

Over the next two years, the "hard" costs for the program—field support and implementing the options—are expected to run to about $10 million to be paid from surplus, according to Simon Curtis, financial vice president for U.S. operations. Other less straightforward costs, he said, might include additional mortality costs for coverage options provided without underwriting review.

"Obviously there are some risks with the program," he said. "It's hard to gauge whether sales will be depressed," but the greater risk, he said, is that the program could increase the anger of in-force policyholders.

Source: *Carole King, "Manulife Addresses Issue of Non-Vanishing Premiums." Reprinted with permission from* National Underwriter, *copyright © 1996, The National Underwriter Company* Life & Health/Financial Services Edition, *July 18, 1994, p. 3.*

considered in the pricing of products, and we discuss how these expenses are allocated to products. Here we can also note that an insurer's administrative expenses are an important product cash outflow. In Chapter 20 we describe in detail some of the steps that insurers take to control their administrative expenses. Now we can turn to a discussion of distribution expenses and their impact on a product's profitability.

Distribution Expenses

Life, health, and annuity companies must spend considerable money to support the company's new products. The beginning of this chapter covered the many activities that insurers must undertake in developing a new product. A company must spend money to develop a product, have a new product approved, advertise it, and take it to the marketplace. Likewise, insurers must spend considerable money for sales distribution of the company's products. The expenses an insurer incurs in distributing and selling its products are often referred to as ***distribution expense.*** The specific types of distribution expenses a company incurs, and the amount of those expenses, depend on the exact type of distribution system used.

Insurers use a number of different forms of distribution systems, including the agency system, the brokerage system, salaried sales systems, and direct response systems. Insurers may use only one, several, or all of these systems in combination. For insurers, the predominant form of distribution involves personal selling through an agency or a brokerage. Agency or brokerage systems are relatively expensive, particularly when contrasted with the distribution systems of competing financial institutions. The commissions paid to insurance agents and brokers can account for most or all of an individual life insurance product's first-year premium. In some cases, the first-year commissions of individual life products actually exceed first-year premiums. Although the services provided by agents and brokers are expensive, they are valued by customers. Insurance is a complex product, and personal sales efforts are a key element of life and health insurance marketing.

In Conclusion

Chapter 4 provides a foundation for this textbook's coming discussions of many technical aspects of insurance companies' product portfolios. Chapter 4 introduced the environment within which insurers make decisions concerning their product portfolios, and also introduced the basic vocabulary of pricing for insurance products. In

Chapter 4, we first presented an overview of product development and technical product design. We then reviewed the most basic elements of the gross premiums of insurance products. (Later chapters of this textbook go into far greater detail about product design and pricing.) Finally, we covered the revenues and costs generated by financial products and presented some of the product features that insurers can employ to influence these revenues and costs. Chapter 5 reviews time value of money concepts—concepts that play an important role in Chapter 6, which is about the capital budgeting approaches that insurers employ for forecasting and evaluating the expected profitability of new products.

Key Terms and Concepts

product development expense
product development
technical product design
market analysis
product design objectives
marketing plan
implementing
policy filing
introducing
Securities and Exchange Commission (SEC)
actuary
premiums
unit of coverage
gross premium
cost of benefits
net premium
loading
policy reserve
net amount at risk
price elasticity
price elastic
price inelastic
optimum price
persistency rate
lapse rate
underwriting philosophy
underwriting guidelines
exclusion provisions
policy rider
premature withdrawals
persistency bonus
withdrawal fees
surrender charges
variable policy-loan interest rate
policy dividend
participating (par) policies
divisible surplus
premium offset policy
distribution expense

References

1. Adapted and reprinted with permission of the publisher from Dennis Goodwin, *Life and Health Insurance Marketing* (Atlanta, GA: LOMA, 1989), pp. 194–199.

2. Harriett E. Jones and Dani L. Long, *Principles of Insurance: Life, Health, and Annuities* (Atlanta, GA: LOMA, 1996), pp. 88–101.

3. Michael A. Farinella, "Lapse Ratios Improved to 20-Year Low in 1994," *Best-Week Life/Health Supplement*, December 4, 1995, p. L/H 5.

CHAPTER 5

The Time Value of Money

LEARNING OBJECTIVES

After studying this chapter, you should be able to

- Distinguish between simple interest and compound interest
- Find the future value of a single amount using the *FVIF* table
- Compare an ordinary annuity to an annuity due
- Find the future value of an ordinary annuity and an annuity due using the *FVIFA* table
- Find the present value of a single amount using the *PVIF* table
- Find the present value of an ordinary annuity and an annuity due using the *PVIFA* table

OUTLINE

Suppose you could choose to have either \$1,000 today, or \$1,000 one year from now. Most people would take the money sooner rather than later. But what if, instead, you could choose to have either \$1,000 today or \$1,100 one year from now? The choice would not be quite so simple.

An important concept affecting all financial decisions is that the timing of cash flows affects their value. This chapter describes the concept of the time value of money. The ***time value of money*** is the concept that the value of a sum of money at one point in time will be different from its value at another point in time as a result of the effect of interest. Put another way, money in your hand today may have a different value than money promised to you in the future. Insurance companies constantly make decisions based on time value of money concepts.

Underlying the concept of the time value of money is the fact that an amount of money can be invested so that it will earn interest and, over time, grow to a larger amount. Thus, any amount of money can be said to have a *future value* equal to the amount that it would be worth at a given point in the future if it were to accumulate interest. Similarly, any amount of money promised to be paid in the future can be said to have a *present value,* which is the amount of money that would have to be invested on a specified date (usually today) to accumulate to that future amount. Present value and future value are mathematically linked so that present value can be used to calculate future value, and future value can be used to calculate present value. Suppose you have \$1,000 and can invest it so that you will have \$1,200 in a year's time. The \$1,000 you have today is the present value of the \$1,200 you will have in a year. Also, the \$1,200 you will have next year is the future value of the \$1,000 you have today. In this example, you will earn \$200 in interest in one year's time. Figure 5-1 shows how time, interest, present value, and future value are all related.

It is important to note that a given present value can have any number of future values, and a given future value can have any number of present values. The present or future value of an amount of money is determined by two factors: (1) the assumed interest rate and (2) the length of time between the present and future dates.

In practice, insurance companies' present and future value calculations are generally performed quickly and easily by computers. Our discussion of the time value of money will rely on financial tables, but will also present the mathematics behind present and future value calculations so that you can understand these concepts. Several

Figure 5-1. Present and future value timeline.

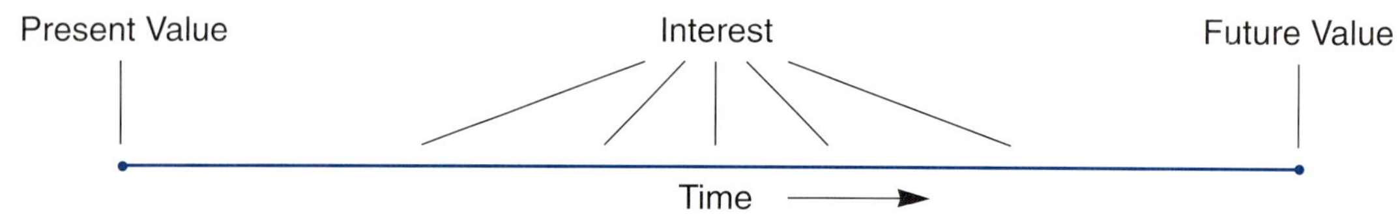

mathematical equations appear in our discussion. The notation we use in these equations is summarized in Figure 5-2.

We begin our discussion of the time value of money with an explanation of interest rates. Then we cover present and future value, explaining how to calculate the present and future value of a single payment and of a series of payments, and the way financial tables can be used to simplify such calculations. The main purpose of this chapter is to provide a review of time value of money concepts. Because this chapter functions as a review, it contains a minimal number of example problems. Students who want more practice with the math presented in this chapter should refer to the *Prep Pak* associated with this course.

The Effect of Interest

The primary reason that time affects the value of money is that, over time, money can earn interest. ***Interest*** is compensation paid for the use of money. For example, when we deposit money in a savings account in a bank, we are loaning our money to the bank. The bank

Figure 5-2. Time value of money notation used in this book.

i = interest rate

n = number of compounding or discounting periods

FV = future value of a single amount

FVA = future value of an annuity

FVAd = future value of an annuity due

FVIF = future value interest factor

FVIFA = future value interest factor of an annuity

PV = present value of a single amount

PVA = present value of an annuity

PVAd = present value of an annuity due

PP = periodic payment of an annuity

PVIF = present value interest factor

PVIFA = present value interest factor of an annuity

pays us a certain amount of interest for the use of our money. As time passes, interest causes the amount of money in the account to grow. In turn, the bank takes our money and invests it, often by loaning it to other individuals or to corporations. In return for the use of its money, the bank charges interest. The interest earned by the bank is used to compensate the bank for its loans and to pay interest to the savings account holders, who supplied the money.

Interest Rates

An ***interest rate*** is the percentage factor that is applied to a sum of money to derive the amount of compensation paid for the use of that money. An interest rate can be expressed either in percentage or decimal form. Thus, a 5 percent interest rate is equivalent to 0.05 in decimal form; similarly, a 2½ percent interest rate is equivalent to 0.025.

The amount an investor pays for an investment is called the ***principal.*** The amount of interest that will be earned on an investment in one period is equal to the principal multiplied by the interest rate for that period, as expressed in the following equation:

Interest Earned = Principal × Interest Rate

Suppose an investor deposits $100 in a bank for one year at 5 percent annual interest. The amount of interest the bank will pay on this $100 investment can be calculated as follows:

$$\textbf{Interest Earned} = \$100 \times 0.05$$
$$\textbf{Interest Earned} = \$5$$

The Effect of Compounding

When a sum is left to accumulate interest for more than one period, that sum can earn either simple or compound interest. ***Simple interest*** is interest payable only on the original principal. In contrast, ***compound interest*** is interest payable both on the principal and on all accumulated interest. Figure 5-3 compares $1,000 invested at 10 percent simple annual interest with $1,000 invested at 10 percent compound annual interest. The figure demonstrates that, for periods of greater than one year, compound interest results in a higher return than simple interest, given the same principal amount and interest rate. Notice that, as the years progress, the amount of interest earned each year under compound interest grows while the amount earned under simple interest remains the same from year to year.

Figure 5-3. $1,000 accumulated at 10 percent simple interest and 10 percent compound interest.

Simple Interest				Compound Interest			
{1} Year	{2} Amount subject to interest	{3} Interest earned ({2} × 0.10)	{4} Principal + Interest ({previous 4} + {3})	{1} Year	{2} Amount subject to interest	{3} Interest earned ({2} × 0.10)	{4} Principal + Interest ({2} + {3})
1	$1,000	$100	$1,100	1	$1,000	$100	$1,100
2	$1,000	$100	$1,200	2	$1,100	$110	$1,210
3	$1,000	$100	$1,300	3	$1,210	$121	$1,331
4	$1,000	$100	$1,400	4	$1,331	$133	$1,464
5	$1,000	$100	$1,500	5	$1,464	$146	$1,610

In reality, investments rarely earn simple interest. Rather, compound interest is the standard used in most business transactions. Unless otherwise stated, this text uses the term *interest* to mean compound interest.

Calculating Future Value

As we have discussed, the ***future value (FV)*** of a sum of money is the amount that the sum is expected to be worth at a certain point in the future, given a certain rate of interest. The term *accumulated value* is also used to refer to future value.

Future Value of a Single Amount

When calculating future values, we can substitute the term *present value* for *principal* because, like principal, present value refers to an amount of money before it is affected by interest. If present value is represented by PV and interest rate is represented by i, then the formula for interest earned on a one-year investment can be expressed as follows:

$$\text{Interest Earned} = PV \times i$$

Thus, we can calculate the future value of a one-year investment using the following equation:

$$\textbf{Future Value} = \textbf{Present Value} + \textbf{Interest Earned}$$

or

$$FV = PV + (PV \times i)$$

or more commonly

$$FV = PV(1 + i)$$

We can then calculate the future value of a one-year investment of \$100 earning 5 percent interest as follows:

$$FV = \$100(1 + 0.05)$$
$$FV = \$100(1.05)$$
$$FV = \$105$$

To calculate the future value of an investment earning interest for more than one year, the present value is multiplied by one plus the interest rate $(1 + i)$ once for each period that the investment accumulates interest. In the example discussed above, if the \$100 were invested for five years, the formula could be expressed as

$$FV = \$100(1.05)(1.05)(1.05)(1.05)(1.05)$$

or

$$FV = \$100(1.05)^5$$

Recall that $(1.05)^5$ is read "1.05 to the *fifth power.*" *Fifth power* simply means that 1.05 is being multiplied by itself five times. No matter how it is written, the result of the calculation is the same.

$$FV = \$100(1.27628)$$
$$FV = \$127.63 \text{ (rounded)}$$

We can use this example to derive a general formula for finding the future value of an investment earning compound interest for more than one year. If the future value after 5 years is found by multiplying the present value by $(1 + i)$ five times, then the future value after n years is found by multiplying the present value by $(1 + i)$ n times. Thus, the general equation for finding the future value of a single amount can be expressed as follows:

$$FV = PV(1 + i)^n$$

So far we have assumed that all interest is *compounded*—that is, calculated and applied to the principal and accumulated interest—on an annual basis. However, it is common for interest to be compounded quarterly, monthly, weekly, daily, or even continuously. In such situations, n refers to the number of compounding periods, and i is the interest rate per compounding period. To find the interest rate per compounding period when the compounding period is less than a year, you need to divide the annual interest rate by the number of compounding periods per year. For example, if the annual interest rate is 4 percent compounded semiannually, then the interest rate for half a year is 2 percent (4 percent ÷ 2 compounding periods = 2 percent). Also, the value of n is calculated by multiplying the number of years over which money accumulates by the number of compounding periods per year. For example, for a 20-year investment with quarterly compounding, n would equal 80 (20 years × 4 compounding periods per year = 80). The future value of $100 invested for one year at 4 percent interest, compounded semiannually, will accumulate as follows:

$$\begin{aligned} FV &= PV(1 + i)^n \\ FV &= \$100(1.02)^2 \\ FV &= \$100(1.0404) \\ FV &= \$104.04 \end{aligned}$$

Future Value Interest Factors

Calculating the value of $(1 + i)^n$ can be very tedious, especially when the number of compounding periods is as high as 5, 10, or 100. Computers and financial calculators can make such calculations quickly and easily. Tables are also available showing the future value of $1.00 for numerous interest rates and numbers of compounding periods. The future value of $1.00 is generally referred to as the ***future value interest factor (FVIF)*** and a table that lists such values is called a *future value interest factor (FVIF) table.* The future value interest factor (FVIF), also sometimes called the *compound value interest factor,* can be used to replace $(1 + i)^n$ in the future value equation, so that

$$FV = PV \times FVIF\ (n, i)$$

Note that *FVIF* is *not* being multiplied by n and i. The n and i show the interest rate and number of compounding periods and indicate where the *FVIF* can be found in the *FVIF* table. Figure 5-4 presents a portion of the future value interest factor table that appears in the appendix of this book. To use the *FVIF* table, find the column with the appropriate interest rate *(i)*, then find the row for the appropriate number of compounding periods *(n)*. The cell that represents the intersection of column i and row n is the correct *FVIF* to use. Thus, you can think of the *(n, i)* notation as the column/row coordinates for the proper cell in an *FVIF* table.

Figure 5-4. *FVIF* table: Future value of \$1.00 at the end of n periods, earning interest rate i, $\$1.00(1 + i)^n$.

Period (*n*)	Interest Rate (*i*) 1%	2%	5%	10%
1	1.010	1.020	1.050	1.100
2	1.020	1.040	1.103	1.210
3	1.030	1.061	1.158	1.331
4	1.041	1.082	1.216	1.464
5	1.051	1.104	1.276	1.611

All interest factor tables have the same format: (1) the interest rates shown in the tables represent the interest rates per period, and (2) the periods shown represent the number of compounding periods. In Figure 5-4, the number highlighted, 1.464, is at the row and column intersection of 4 periods and 10 percent interest per period. This could be written *FVIF* (4, 10%) and the number 1.464 is equivalent to 1.10^4. If you have a calculator, you can try raising 1.10 to the fourth power. The result of this calculation is actually 1.4641, but because our table shows only three decimal places, we rounded to 1.464. Note that, because n is the number of compounding periods and i is the interest rate per period, *FVIF* (4, 10%) could be the *FVIF* for a number of different investments, such as a four-year investment that pays 10 percent interest compounded annually, or a two-year investment that pays 20 percent interest compounded semiannually.

The future value of \$5,000 invested for five years at 5 percent interest compounded annually can easily be calculated using the *FVIF* table. First, substitute the information from this problem into the future value equation.

$$\boldsymbol{FV} = \$5{,}000 \times \boldsymbol{FVIF}\,(5,\ 5\%)$$

Next, find the appropriate *FVIF* from the *FVIF* table and substitute this in the equation.

$$\boldsymbol{FV} = \$5{,}000 \times 1.276$$

Then multiply to obtain the result.

$$\boldsymbol{FV} = \$6{,}380$$

Thus, the future value of \$5,000 invested at 5 percent interest compounded annually for five years is \$6,380.

Suppose you invested \$10,000 and expected it to earn interest at an 8 percent annual rate, compounded quarterly for two years. How could you use the *FVIF* table to calculate the future value of this investment? First, determine the interest rate per compounding period: 8 percent ÷ 4 = 2 percent. Then determine the number of compounding periods: 4 periods per year × 2 years = 8. The future value of your \$10,000 can then be calculated as follows:

$$\boldsymbol{FV} = \$10{,}000 \times \boldsymbol{FVIF}\,(8,\, 2\%)$$
$$\boldsymbol{FV} = \$10{,}000 \times 1.172$$
$$\boldsymbol{FV} = \$11{,}720$$

Standard tables of interest factors depict interest rates from 1 percent to 20 percent or higher, compounding periods from 1 to 50 or more, and interest factors that have been rounded to three or four digits or more beyond the decimal point. If you look at an *FVIF* table, you'll notice three things about *FVIF*s: (1) they are always greater than 1.0 (they would equal 1.0 only if i or n were zero); (2) at a given interest rate (i), the *FVIF*s increase as the number of compounding periods (n) increases; and (3) at a given number of periods (n), the *FVIF*s increase as the interest rate (i) increases.

Most financial services companies use computers and calculators, rather than tables, to calculate interest factors. Time value of money calculations are vital to the operations of such companies, so they use as many compounding periods as a calculation calls for, and, if necessary, base calculations on fractional rates such as 7½ or 7¼ percent. Simplified interest factor tables, however, are acceptable for the purposes of our discussion. You may encounter situations in which you will need to use interest factors for i and n that are fractional or are greater than those available in the tables. However, the sample problems associated with this text can be solved using the set of interest factor tables contained in the appendix of this book.

Future Value of an Annuity

Insurance companies often encounter situations in which they must calculate the future value of a series of payments, rather than the future value of a single amount. In actuarial terminology, an ***annuity*** is any series of equal payments made over equally spaced time periods. Insurers often use the term *annuity* to refer to a specific type of insurance product that makes payments to all surviving members of a group of original contract owners. In fact, these two definitions are not as different as they might seem to be. An annuity *product* is called an annuity because it involves regular, periodic payments to the contract owners. In this section, when we refer to an annuity, we are using the term to mean any series of equal payments. Note that in our discussion of the future value of an annuity, when we refer to interest earned on an annuity, we refer to the interest that could be earned if each annuity payment received were invested at a given interest rate.

The ***future value of an annuity (FVA)*** at a given point in time is the amount that a series of payments plus the interest earned on these payments will grow to by that point in time. Before we begin to explain how the future value of an annuity is calculated, we first review two different types of annuities that you may encounter.

An ***ordinary annuity,*** sometimes called an *annuity immediate* or an *annuity in arrears,* is one for which the payment occurs at the end of each payment period. The semiannual interest paid on most bonds is an example of an ordinary annuity because the first interest payment is made after the bond is issued. Another example of an ordinary annuity is the paycheck a worker receives after the work period has been completed.

An ***annuity due,*** also called an *annuity in advance,* is an annuity for which the payment occurs at the beginning of each payment period. Examples of annuities due include rent, lease payments, and life and health insurance premiums, all of which involve payments made at the beginning of the period concerned. The difference between an ordinary annuity and an annuity due centers on the timing of the payment—whether it occurs at the end of the payment period (ordinary annuity), or at the beginning of the period (annuity due).

In order to visualize a series of periodic payments, it may be helpful for you to draw a simple line diagram. Many actuaries and investment analysts begin their analysis with a line diagram of each investment's expected cash flows. A ***line diagram,*** or *time line,* is a visual device that allows you to see the essential elements of a particular financial transaction. It marks the end of each compounding period, the frequency and amount of each cash flow, and the timing of the valuation date. The ***valuation date*** is the date as of which the value of the financial transaction is determined.

Sometimes it is difficult to determine whether a series of periodic payments is an ordinary annuity or an annuity due. Drawing a line diagram and marking the valuation date makes this determination easier. The future value of an ordinary annuity is evaluated as of the date of the last periodic payment. The future value of an annuity due is evaluated as of the date one period after the last periodic payment.

The future value of an ordinary annuity of $100 per year for three years can be represented by the following line diagram:

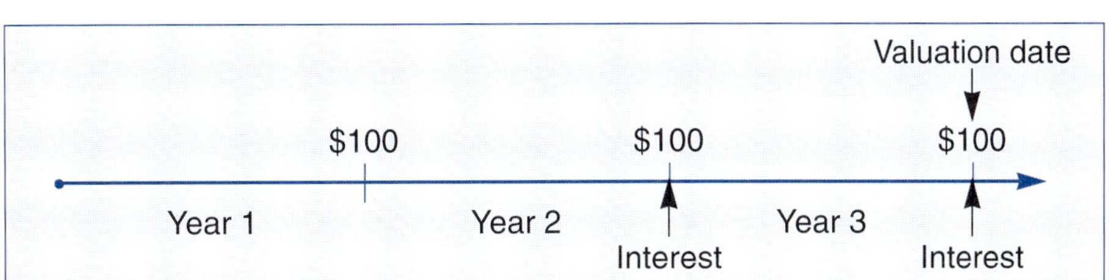

Note that the interest accrues twice for the ordinary annuity. No interest accumulates in Year 1 of the ordinary annuity, because the first payment does not occur until the end of Year 1. Compare the diagram of the ordinary annuity just presented with that of an annuity due, which follows:

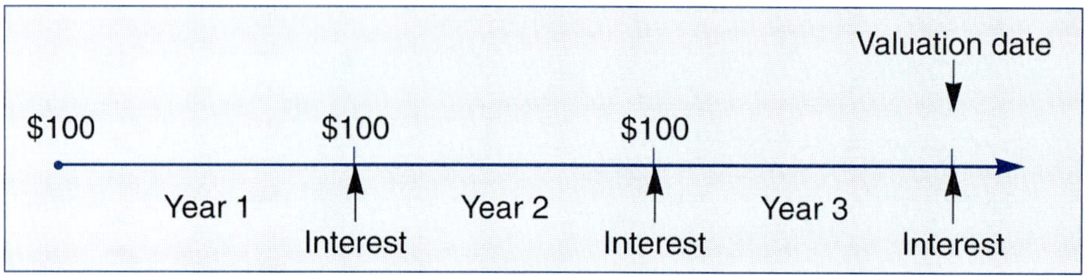

For the annuity due, the first payment occurs at the beginning of Year 1 and interest accrues in each of the three periods.

Future Value of an Annuity Interest Factors

The future value of an annuity (FVA) can be calculated by adding together the future values of each periodic payment. For a three-year ordinary annuity of \$100 earning 5 percent interest compounded annually, the future value can be calculated as shown here. (Refer to Figure 5-4 to see the values of the *FVIF* table.)

$$\begin{aligned} \textbf{\textit{FVA}} &= [\$100 \times \textbf{\textit{FVIF}}\,(2,\,5\%)] + [\$100 \times \textbf{\textit{FVIF}}\,(1,\,5\%)] + \$100 \\ \textbf{\textit{FVA}} &= (\$100 \times 1.103) + (\$100 \times 1.050) + \$100 \\ \textbf{\textit{FVA}} &= \$110.30 + \$105.00 + \$100.00 \\ \textbf{\textit{FVA}} &= \$315.30 \end{aligned}$$

For this ordinary annuity, the first \$100 payment would earn two years of interest and thus is multiplied by *FVIF* (2, 5%). The second \$100 payment would earn one year's interest, and so it is multiplied by *FVIF* (1, 5%). The final payment is made on the valuation date, and so it earns no interest.

If the annuity in this example were an annuity due instead of an ordinary annuity, the first payment would earn interest for three full years, the second payment would earn interest for two years, and the final payment would earn interest for one year. As a result, the future value of the annuity due would be greater than the future value of the corresponding ordinary annuity, as demonstrated in the calculation below. To distinguish it from a calculation involving the future value of an ordinary annuity, we are using *FVAd* to indicate the future value of an annuity due.

$$\boldsymbol{FVAd} = [\$100 \times \boldsymbol{FVIF}(3, 5\%)] + [\$100 \times \boldsymbol{FVIF}(2, 5\%)] + [\$100 \times \boldsymbol{FVIF}(1, 5\%)]$$
$$\boldsymbol{FVAd} = [\$100 \times 1.158] + [\$100 \times 1.103] + [\$100 \times 1.050]$$
$$\boldsymbol{FVAd} = \$115.80 + \$110.30 + \$105.00$$
$$\boldsymbol{FVAd} = \$331.10$$

When an annuity involves a large number of compounding periods, calculating the future value of the annuity by adding together the future value of each payment can be laborious and time-consuming. Consequently, ***future value interest factor of an annuity (FVIFA)*** tables have been created to make the calculation of the future value of an annuity simpler. Such tables are similar to the *FVIF* tables. A sample of an *FVIFA* table appears in Figure 5-5, and a more complete table appears in the appendix of this book.

The general formula for using the *FVIFA* table to solve for the future value of an annuity is as follows:

$$\text{Future Value of an Annuity} = \text{Periodic Payment} \times \text{FVIFA}(n, i)$$

or

$$\boldsymbol{FVA = PP \times FVIFA(n, i)}$$

The future value of the three-year ordinary annuity earning 5 percent interest described in the previous example can be calculated using the FVIFA table as follows:

$$\boldsymbol{FVA} = \$100 \times \boldsymbol{FVIFA}(3, 5\%)$$

Substituting the single value from the *FVIFA* table shown in Figure 5-5, we get almost the same result as we did using multiple values from the *FVIF* table. The $0.10 difference is due to rounding.

Figure 5-5. *FVIFA* table: Future value of a $1.00 annuity per period for *n* periods at *i* interest.

Period	Interest Rate (*i*)			
(*n*)	1%	2%	5%	10%
1	1.000	1.000	1.000	1.000
2	2.010	2.020	2.050	2.100
3	3.030	3.060	3.152	3.310
4	4.060	4.122	4.310	4.641
5	5.101	5.204	5.526	6.105

$$\textbf{\textit{FVA}} = \$100 \times 3.152$$
$$\textbf{\textit{FVA}} = \$315.20$$

The factors in *FVIFA* tables are calculated for ordinary annuities. To use the *FVIFA* table to find the future value of an annuity due, we need to use a slightly different method than the one described above. The future value of an annuity due is equal to the future value of a corresponding ordinary annuity of one additional period, minus the amount of one payment. To find the future value of an annuity due of n periods, we first need to find the *FVIFA* for the current interest rate and $n + 1$ periods. Then we subtract 1—remember that the interest factor tables are based on a \$1.00 payment—from this factor and multiply the periodic payment by the result. The method of calculating the future value of an annuity due using the *FVIFA* table can be summarized in the following equation (recall that we are using *FVAd* to indicate the future value of an annuity due):

$$\textbf{\textit{FVAd}} = \textbf{\textit{PP}} \times [\textbf{\textit{FVIFA}}\,(n + 1, i) - 1]$$

As an example, how would we calculate the future value of a four-payment \$1,000 annuity due earning 10 percent interest? In this example, n is 4, i is 10%, and *PP* is \$1,000. Substituting these numbers into the *FVAd* equation yields the following results:

$$\textbf{\textit{FVAd}} = \$1{,}000 \times [\textbf{\textit{FVIFA}}\,(4 + 1, 10\%) - 1]$$
$$\textbf{\textit{FVAd}} = \$1{,}000 \times [\textbf{\textit{FVIFA}}\,(5, 10\%) - 1]$$
$$\textbf{\textit{FVAd}} = \$1{,}000 \times (6.105 - 1)$$
$$\textbf{\textit{FVAd}} = \$1{,}000 \times (5.105)$$
$$\textbf{\textit{FVAd}} = \$5{,}105$$

Note that the techniques we have described for calculating the future value of an annuity using the *FVIFA* table apply only to annuities for which the length of the annuity payment period and the length of the compounding period are the same. It is possible to calculate the future value of annuities involving payment periods and compounding periods of different lengths, but such calculations are extremely complicated and are not covered in this chapter.

Future Value of an Uneven Stream of Payments

What is the future value of an investment project earning 5 percent interest if the expected cash flows are uneven—say \$12,000 at the end of Year 1, \$13,000 at the end of Year 2, \$11,000 at the end of Year 3, and \$10,000 at the end of Year 4? Remember that future value of an annuity formulas apply only to periodic payments of equal amounts and an evenly spaced number of periods. Normally, the way to calculate the future value of an uneven stream of cash flows using interest factor tables is to calculate the future value of each payment separately using the *FVIF* table and then add these future values together. In this example, assuming that each payment is made at the end of the compounding period, interest would accumulate on the first payment for three years, on the second payment for two years, on the third payment for one year, and the final payment would accumulate no interest because it is made on the valuation date. Thus, we would calculate the future value of this stream of cash flows as follows:

$$\begin{aligned} \$12{,}000 \times \textbf{\textit{FVIF}}\,(3,\ 5\%) &= \$13{,}896 \\ \$13{,}000 \times \textbf{\textit{FVIF}}\,(2,\ 5\%) &= \$14{,}339 \\ \$11{,}000 \times \textbf{\textit{FVIF}}\,(1,\ 5\%) &= \$11{,}550 \\ \$10{,}000 &= \underline{\$10{,}000} \\ & \$49{,}785 \end{aligned}$$

Calculating Present Value

In many situations, an insurance company knows or can predict the amount of a future cash flow. For example, insurers often estimate the amount and timing of future profits, expenses, benefit payments, and premium income. But because a sum of money payable in the future is not equivalent to that same sum today, insurers typically need to calculate the present value of such future cash flows. By definition, the ***present value (PV)*** of a future sum is the amount of money that, if invested at a specified interest rate on a certain date, called the *valuation date,* would grow to equal that future sum. Because the present value of a sum is generally less than its future value, the present value is often called the *discounted value.* Theoretically, all other factors being equal, it would make no difference to a company whether it received the present value of a sum on the valuation date, or the future value at the specified point in the future.

Present Value of a Single Amount

Finding present value is similar to finding future value, and the formula used to determine present value can be derived from the formula used to calculate future value. Recall the basic formula for calculating the future value of a one-period investment.

$$FV = PV(1 + i)$$

Using a little algebra, we can solve for *PV* to come up with the following formula for calculating present value when the future value is known:

$$FV = PV\,(1 + i)$$
$$FV \div (1 + i) = PV$$

which is most commonly expressed as

$$PV = FV\left(\frac{1}{1+i}\right)$$

Suppose you knew you were going to have to pay \$1,050 one year from now and that you could earn 5 percent interest, compounded annually, on an investment. How much would you need to invest today to have \$1,050 one year from now? We know the future value (\$1,050) and the interest rate (5 percent), so we can use our present value formula to find the answer.

$$PV = \$1{,}050\left(\frac{1}{1.05}\right)$$
$$PV = \$1{,}050\,(0.9524)$$
$$PV = \$1{,}000.02$$

In this equation we have *discounted* \$1,050 to its present value of \$1,000.02 (note that if we had not rounded 1 ÷ 1.05 to 0.9524, the present value would be exactly \$1,000). ***Discounting,*** which can be considered the opposite of compounding, is the process of converting a future value to its present value.

Suppose the \$1,050 payment wasn't due until two years in the future. We can use the same formula as before, except that, because two discounting periods are involved, we must perform the calculation as demonstrated below:

$$PV = \$1{,}050\,[(1 \div 1.05)(1 \div 1.05)]$$

which is mathematically equivalent to

$$PV = \$1{,}050\,[1 \div (1.05)(1.05)] \text{ or}$$
$$PV = \$1{,}050\,[1 \div (1.05)^2]$$
$$PV = \$952.38$$

The general formula for determining the present value of a future sum when more than one discounting period is involved is

$$PV = FV\left[\frac{1}{(1+i)^n}\right]$$

Present Value Interest Factors

As with future value, tables can make the calculation of present value much simpler. Called *present value interest factor tables,* such tables show the value of the present value interest factor for many possible interest rates and numbers of periods. The ***present value interest factor (PVIF)*** is the present value of $1.00 discounted at an interest rate of i for n periods. The *PVIF* can be substituted for $[1 \div (1 + i)^n]$ in the present value equation. Thus the present value of an amount to be paid at a specified later time can be calculated by multiplying that amount by the appropriate *PVIF* from the *PVIF* table as shown in the following equation:

$$PV = FV \times PVIF\ (n, i)$$

A sample *PVIF* table appears in Figure 5-6, and a more complete *PVIF* table appears in the appendix of this book. Notice that all of the numbers in the *PVIF* table are less than 1. The reason is that the present value of any amount is generally less than its future value. Thus the present value of a future value of $1.00 is generally less than $1.00. The only time this would not be the case would be if the investment in question were expected to earn no interest or to lose money. An investment that earns no interest would have a future value *equal to* its present value. An investment that loses money would have a negative interest rate and future value that is *less than* the present value. In looking at a *PVIF* table, you'll also notice that, at a given interest rate, the *PVIF*s decrease as the number of discounting periods increases, and that, at a given number of compounding periods, the *PVIF*s decrease as the interest rate increases.

We can use the present value interest factor to determine the present value of the $1,050 future amount from our earlier example.

Figure 5-6. *PVIF* table: Present value of $1.00[1 ÷ (1 + i)^n].

Period	Interest Rate *(i)*			
(n)	1%	2%	5%	10%
1	0.990	0.980	0.952	0.909
2	0.980	0.961	0.907	0.826
3	0.971	0.942	0.864	0.751
4	0.961	0.924	0.823	0.683
5	0.951	0.906	0.784	0.621

Assuming a 5 percent interest rate and two compounding periods, the present value can be found as follows:

$$\begin{aligned} \boldsymbol{PV} &= \$1{,}050 \times \boldsymbol{PVIF}\,(2, 5\%) \\ \boldsymbol{PV} &= \$1{,}050 \times 0.907 \\ \boldsymbol{PV} &= \$952.35 \end{aligned}$$

The present value we calculated using the *PVIF* table ($952.35) is very close to the amount we calculated using exponents ($952.38). The difference of $0.03 results from the rounding of the factors in the *PVIF* table.

Present Value of an Annuity

Insurance companies and other businesses often need to calculate the present value of a series of payments, evenly spaced over a specified time period. In such cases, the value being calculated is the present value of an annuity. The ***present value of an annuity*** is the amount that must be invested now in order to provide for a specified series of equal future payments, given a specified interest rate and a specified number of periods. The present value of an annuity also represents the amount that, if invested at a given interest rate, would, as of the end of the last annuity period, produce a future value equal to the sum of the future values of each periodic payment. As we have discussed, the sum of the future values of each periodic payment of an annuity is equal to the future value of that annuity. Thus, the mathematical relationship between the present value and future value of an annuity can be expressed as follows:

$$\boldsymbol{PVA \times FVIF(n, i) = FVA}$$

Our discussion of the present value of an annuity applies both to a series of payments *received* and to a series of payments *paid out.*

The valuation date for the present value of an ordinary annuity occurs at the beginning of the first period, which is one period before the first payment is made. For an annuity due, the valuation date is the beginning of the first period, which corresponds to the timing of the first payment.

Present Value of an Ordinary Annuity

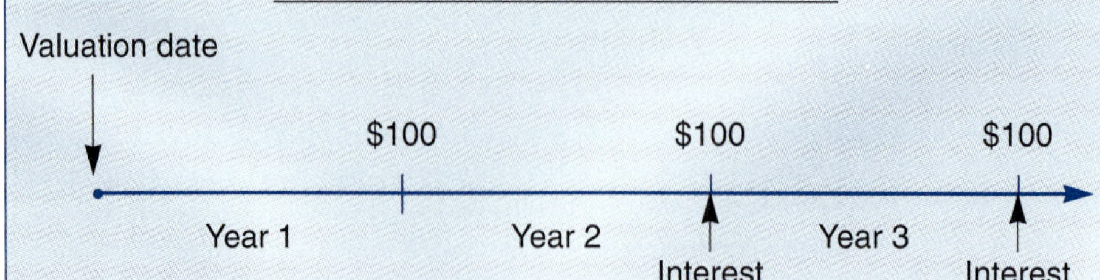

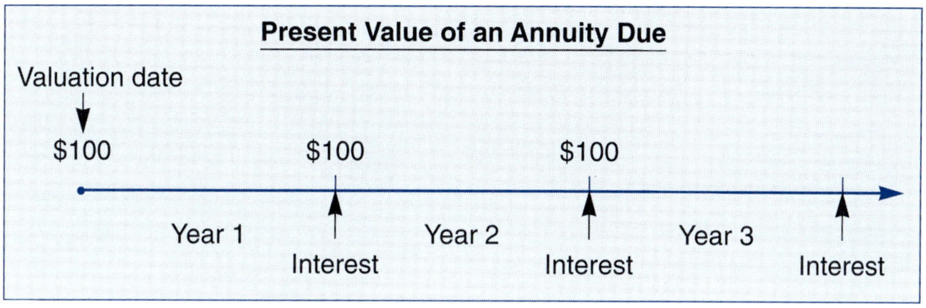

Present Value of an Annuity Interest Factors

The present value of an annuity can be found by adding together the present values of each individual payment. This process is similar to finding the future value of an annuity by summing the future values of each payment. Calculating the present value of an annuity by separately calculating the present value of each payment is a time-consuming process. Therefore, tables are available that provide the ***present value interest factor of an annuity (PVIFA).*** A sample *PVIFA* table is shown in Figure 5-7, and a more complete *PVIFA* table appears in the appendix of this book. As with the *FVIFA* table discussed earlier, the numbers in the *PVIFA* table apply only to ordinary annuities. Using the *PVIFA,* the formula for calculating the present value of an ordinary annuity is

$$PVA = PP \times PVIFA\,(n, i)$$

Applying this formula, we can determine the present value of an ordinary annuity of $1,000 for three periods at 5 percent interest.

$$\begin{aligned} \mathbf{PVA} &= \$1{,}000 \times \mathbf{PVIFA}\ (3, 5\%) \\ \mathbf{PVA} &= \$1{,}000 \times 2.723 \\ \mathbf{PVA} &= \$2{,}723 \end{aligned}$$

Figure 5-7. *PVIFA* table: Present value of a $1.00 annuity per period for *n* periods at interest rate *i*.

Period (*n*)	Interest Rate (*i*) 1%	2%	5%	10%
1	0.990	0.980	0.952	0.909
2	1.970	1.942	1.859	1.736
3	2.941	2.884	2.723	2.487
4	3.902	3.808	3.546	3.170
5	4.853	4.713	4.329	3.791

The present value of an *annuity due*—for which we substitute *PVAd*—is equal to the present value of a corresponding ordinary annuity of one less period plus the amount of one periodic payment. Using the *PVIFA* table to find the present value of an annuity due, we first find the *PVIFA* factor for the interest rate and $(n - 1)$ compounding periods. Then we add 1 to the appropriate interest factor and multiply by the amount of the periodic payment. The following equation illustrates this process:

$$PVAd = PP \times [PVIFA\,(n-1, i) + 1]$$

Suppose you wanted to know the amount you would have to invest today in a 5 percent single-premium annuity due in order to receive \$15,000 per year for the next five years. You could use the *PVIFA* table to calculate the amount of the lump sum payment needed now in order to achieve your goal:

$$\begin{aligned} PVAd &= \$15{,}000 \times [PVIFA\,(5-1, 5\%) + 1] \\ PVAd &= \$15{,}000 \times [3.546 + 1] \\ PVAd &= \$15{,}000 \times 4.546 \\ PVAd &= \$68{,}190 \end{aligned}$$

As with the techniques we described for calculating the future value of an annuity, the techniques we have described for calculating the present value of an annuity apply only to annuities for which the length of the annuity payment period and the length of the compounding period are the same.

Present Value of an Uneven Stream of Payments

If you needed to calculate the present value of a stream of uneven cash flows, you could not use the *PVIFA* table. Normally, this calculation would be made by calculating the present value of each payment separately. For example, if an investment project were expected to yield \$500 at the end of its first year, \$600 at the end of its second year, and \$200 at the end of its third year, and the going interest rate were 10 percent, the present value of this investment's cash flows could be calculated as follows:

$$\begin{aligned} \$500 \times PVIF\,(1, 10\%) &= \$\ \ 454.50 \\ \$600 \times PVIF\,(2, 10\%) &= \$\ \ 495.60 \\ \$200 \times PVIF\,(3, 10\%) &= \underline{\$\ \ 150.20} \\ &\ \ \ \ \$1{,}100.30 \end{aligned}$$

A Note about Interest Factors

The style of notation we have used to represent the various interest factors we have discussed is designed to help you remember and understand the mathematical concepts underlying these interest factors. Actuaries use a different style of notation. The following table compares the notation used in this chapter with the equivalent actuarial notation:

Textbook notation	Actuarial notation
FVIF (n, i)	$(1 + i)^n$
FVIFA (n, i)	$s_{\overline{n}\rceil i}$
PVIF (n, i)	v^n
PVIFA (n, i)	$a_{\overline{n}\rceil i}$

Figure 5-7 presents some general tips on using numbers effectively. You may find these tips useful as you study this textbook and as you perform any work that requires the use of numbers.

In Conclusion

Time affects the value of money. This concept has an impact on many of the functions of a life and health insurance company, including the accounting, actuarial, investment, claim processing, and customer service functions. In addition, determining the present value or future value of cash flows is associated with many management decisions, such as whether to develop a new insurance product or service, to lease or purchase equipment or real estate, or to purchase or sell financial investments.

In this chapter, we discussed how interest rates affect the time value of money. We then explained techniques for calculating the present and future value of a single amount and of a series of payments. Understanding these concepts will help you to understand many of the discussions that follow in this book.

Figure 5-7. Tips for using numbers effectively.

- Approach your search for data in a planned manner. Decide what data will help you understand the business situation you are studying. Then determine if the data is available and where you can find it. Find out if you have colleagues who can help you locate the proper data and analyze it.
- Choose which statistical measures will most help you analyze the data and the situation.
- Identify the types of calculations you will need to do and the units of measure—time, dollars, policies, claims, etc.—in which the calculations must be made.
- Proceed with your calculations slowly, not rushing. Whether you are doing calculations manually, on a calculator, or on a computer, don't rush.
- Don't take shortcuts. Do all calculations step by step, and write down your calculations as you go along. Spreadsheet software for PCs offers the convenience of keeping a record of your data. These spreadsheet files can be used both as rough worksheets and as final reports of calculations.
- Label your data and your calculations. Even with spreadsheets, you must be careful to identify all your data. Otherwise, you risk the danger of returning to a spreadsheet file only to find that the columns of numbers that you created in the file have become just that—merely columns of numbers for which you have forgotten the meaning and significance.
- Once you complete a calculation, write down in narrative form what the results of that calculation mean to you. Otherwise, you run the risk of forgetting some of the insights that your analysis has provided you.
- When you can, draw a picture. When dealing with present value factors especially, drawing a time line and indicating on the time line when payments are received can help you determine what formula you need to use.
- Experience is a great help in understanding the results of statistical calculations. As you become more experienced in your work or as you study more business literature, you develop a sense of what is normal in different situations. Sometimes these *norms* or *standards* are recorded and are well-known throughout an industry. Sometimes norms are less formal, more like rules of thumb. Nonetheless, norms help you judge the results of your statistical analysis. Numbers have meaning only when you compare them with other numbers, particularly standard numbers. Are your results above the norm or below the norm? Does the mean, median, or mode seem reasonable or typical?

Key Terms and Concepts

time value of money
interest
interest rate
principal
simple interest
compound interest
future value *(FV)*
future value interest factor *(FVIF)*
annuity
future value of an annuity *(FVA)*
ordinary annuity
annuity due
line diagram
valuation date
future value interest factor of an annuity *(FVIFA)*
present value *(PV)*
discounting
present value interest factor *(PVIF)*
present value of an annuity
present value interest factor of an annuity *(PVIFA)*

User's Guide to *ExecuView*

LEARNING OBJECTIVES

After studying this chapter, you should be able to

- Successfully install *ExecuView* onto your computer's hard disk drive
- Maneuver through the five *ExecuView* models
- Use *ExecuView*'s input/output, chart, and results table windows
- Save and load *ExecuView* data files
- Print an *ExecuView* model

OUTLINE

On the inside back cover of this textbook is a 3½-inch floppy disk containing a computer program called *ExecuView v. 2.0: An Asset-Share Analysis/Product Profitability Model. ExecuView* is a type of simulation software. It consists of five interactive models that allow you to test the profitability of four insurance products. Using *ExecuView* you can simulate the role of an insurance company executive and a product actuary. You can adjust the assumptions on which an insurance company's products are based. You can adjust commission rates and project new lapse rates. You can estimate the rate of return on the investments of your virtual "company." You can establish the product mix that you think will produce the most favorable results. And through *ExecuView,* you can see the effects that these and other adjustments have on profitability.

In various parts of the textbook, we refer to *ExecuView* examples to illustrate important concepts and to reinforce key lessons. All of the *ExecuView*-based examples in this book are explained so that you can understand them whether or not you run them through the computer model. The examples provide valuable insights into the topics discussed throughout the text.

This user's guide explains how to operate the *ExecuView* models on a computer. If you do not have access to a computer that can run *ExecuView,* you do not need to read this user's guide. Chapter 6 describes all aspects of *ExecuView* that you need to know to understand the *ExecuView* applications in this book, whether or not you plan to run *ExecuView* on a computer. The only purpose of this user's guide is to explain how to operate *ExecuView* on a computer. Full explanations of the product models and assumptions that make up *ExecuView* appear in Chapter 6 of this book.

Figure UG-1 shows the system requirements for running *ExecuView.* Figure UG-2 tells how to install *ExecuView* to your computer's hard disk drive under Windows 3.1 and Windows 95.

ExecuView's Features and Functions

ExecuView has several important functions that you will need to access as you work with this program. This section of the user's guide shows how to

- Select one of the five *ExecuView* models
- Save and retrieve data files recording your own demonstrations on *ExecuView*

- Reset the assumptions in *ExecuView*'s models to their default values
- Print the output
- Use *ExecuView*'s on-line help feature

Selecting a Model

When you begin using *ExecuView,* you will notice along the bottom of the screen a series of icons that resemble the tabs on file folders. On each of these tabs is the name of one of the five *ExecuView* models. The tab representing the model you are currently viewing appears in the foreground and is highlighted in light gray. The other tabs appear in darker gray in the background. You may select any one of the five models at any time by clicking on its tab with your mouse; you can also select a model from the keyboard by holding down the Alt key and pressing the key corresponding to the underlined letter in each tab—for example, Alt+W selects the Whole Life Model.

Save File Icon

Saving Files

As you experiment with various sets of product assumptions, you may want to save your assumptions for future reference. To save the assumptions you have created, select *Save* from the File menu or click on the floppy disk icon at the top of the screen and follow standard Windows procedures for naming and saving files. You should note that the current assumptions of all five models will be saved as one *ExecuView* data file.

Open File Icon

Opening Files

You may retrieve a file you have previously saved by selecting *Open* from the File menu or by clicking on the open file folder icon at the

Figure UG-1. System requirements for running *ExecuView.*

- A 3½-inch floppy disk drive
- An IBM/PC 100% compatible computer
- An 80/386 or faster processor
- Windows 3.1 or higher
- At least 4 MB of RAM
- At least 5 MB of free hard disk space

Figure UG-2. Installing *ExecuView.*

Windows 95	Windows 3.1
1. Start *Windows 95.* 2. Click on the **Start** button in the task bar. 3. From the menu that appears, click on **Settings,** then **Control Panel,** then **Add/Remove Programs.** 4. When the *Add/Remove Programs* window appears, click on the **Install** button. 5. Insert the *ExecuView* diskette into your computer's floppy disk drive. 6. Click on the **Next** button. The command line for the installation should automatically appear. 7. Click on **Finish** at the bottom of the window. 8. Follow the on-screen instructions until the installation is complete.	1. Start *Windows 3.1* or *3.11.* 2. Insert the *ExecuView* diskette into your computer's floppy disk drive. 3. Select the **Windows Program Manager.** 4. Select **Run** from the File menu. 5. In the command line, type the *letter designating your floppy disk drive* followed by a backslash (\) and the word *setup.* For most PCs, the floppy disk drive is the A drive, and the command should be A:\SETUP. 6. Follow the on-screen instructions until the installation is complete.
The *ExecuView* setup routine will now install *ExecuView* onto your PC's hard drive and will automatically place the *ExecuView* icon in the LOMA program group. To start *ExecuView,* double-click on the *ExecuView* icon.	

top of the screen. The data from the file you open will replace the current assumptions in all five models.

Resetting to Default Assumptions

You can reset *ExecuView* at any time to its default assumptions—that is, to the initial set of assumptions that are loaded into *ExecuView* whenever you first start the program. This feature will be especially handy when you begin working with the *ExecuView* applications in later chapters. To reset *ExecuView* to its default assumptions, click on the Action menu at the top of the screen and select *Reset.* You will then have the option of either resetting all of the models or only the currently selected model.

Printing

Print Icon

ExecuView's print feature allows you to print the information that appears in the input/output window. It also allows you to print the results tables of each of the five product models. To print, click on the print icon at the top of the screen or select *Print* from the File menu. A window will appear that asks you what you would like to print. You may select the input/output window, the results tables, or both, and you may select as many of the five models as you would like to print. Click on *Print,* and *ExecuView* will print your selections. You may change the setup of your printer by selecting *Printer Setup* from the File menu. *ExecuView v. 2.0* cannot print graphs or charts.

On-Line Help

ExecuView's on-line help feature works just like the on-line help feature of any other Windows-based application. It can provide instant information about *ExecuView* as you use the program. To access *ExecuView's* help function, click on the Help menu at the top of the screen.

The Five Models

ExecuView consists of four product models and an aggregate model. Full descriptions of all five models appear in Chapter 6. Briefly, the five models are

- A whole life insurance product model
- A 10-year term life insurance product model
- A single-premium deferred annuity (SPDA) product model
- An immediate annuity product model
- An aggregate model that combines the results of all four product models

In several places, *ExecuView* refers to certain values "per $1,000," as in "Gross Annual Premium per $1,000." For the Term Life and Whole Life Models, whenever *ExecuView* refers to an amount "per $1,000," the figure represents an amount per $1,000 of face value. Thus, a policy with a face value of $100,000 and a gross annual premium of $6.00 per $1,000 would have a total gross annual premium of $600. For the Single-Premium Deferred Annuity and Immediate Annuity Models, the "per $1,000" refers to $1,000 of premium paid. Thus, a policy with a $100,000 premium and an annual benefit of $180 per $1,000 would pay $18,000 a year in benefits.

The Product Models

ExecuView's product models demonstrate the growth and profitability of four fairly common insurance products. Within the product models it is possible to adjust the gross premium (for the life insurance models), interest margin (for the annuity models), mortality rate, expense rate, commission rate, and lapse rate that apply to that product. Interest rates can be adjusted only through the Aggregate Model.

The Aggregate Model

The Aggregate Model combines the results of the four product models to create a "company-level" model that allows you to control the overall product mix and the interest rates that apply to all of the *ExecuView* models. All of the product models except for the Term Life Model have profit test periods of 30 years; that is, the models are designed to show the projected profitability of each product over a period of 30 years. The Aggregate Model assumes that all funds earned by the term life product will continue to collect interest for an additional 20 years after the 10-year term expires. This assumption makes it possible to compare the results of the Term Life Model with the results of the other three models in Years 11 through 30.

How to Adjust Interest Rates in *ExecuView*

The interest rates in *ExecuView* are meant to represent a *composite* of the rates of return an insurance company would earn on the investments in its asset portfolio. The interest rates for all four product models can be controlled only through the Aggregate Model.

The interest rate input cells in the Aggregate Model are set up so that you can set a beginning interest rate and control the rate of increase or decrease in this rate. The *Initial* cell sets the interest rate for the first year. The cells labeled *Change, 2nd Year,* etc., control the number of percentage points by which the interest rate will fluctuate in each of the years listed. For example, if the initial interest rate is set at 7 percent and the *Change, 2nd Year* cell is set at 0.1 percent, then the interest rate for the second year will be 7.1 percent. Similarly, if the *Change Years 3–5* cell is set at –0.1 percent when the interest rate in the second year is 7.1 percent, then the interest rate for the third year will be 7 percent, for the fourth year will be 6.9 percent, and for the fifth year will be 6.8 percent.

The interest rates earned from Year 1 through Year 15 are displayed on the input/output window of the Aggregate Model, along with a line graph that shows the fluctuation in interest rates through this same period. Interest rates can also be viewed in the column labeled *Current Interest* in the *Cash Flow* section of the calculation tables for each of the product models.

How to Adjust the Product Mix

The Aggregate Model assumes that a combined total of 400,000 policies are sold at the beginning of the first policy year. The percentage entered next to each product in the *Percentage of Policies Sold* section controls the percentage of the 400,000 policies sold that will be attributed to each product. For example, if 50 percent is entered under *Percentage of Policies Sold, Whole Life,* in the Aggregate Model, all aggregate calculations will assume that 200,000 whole life policies were sold in the first policy year. Setting the percentage of policies sold for each type of product allows you to experiment with various types of product mixes. Note that the numbers entered under *Percent of Policies Sold* must add up to 100 percent. If these numbers do not add up to 100 percent, *ExecuView* will give you the option of changing the input yourself or allowing *ExecuView* to change the input for you. The product mix you create in the Aggregate Model will affect only the results of the Aggregate Model. Each of the four separate product models always assumes that 100,000 policies are sold at the beginning of the first policy year.

Three Ways of Viewing *ExecuView*

ExecuView gives you three different ways to view each model. Each of these views provides a different perspective on the growth and profitability shown in the model. The three views are the

1. Input/Output (I/O) window
2. Results table window
3. Charts window

I/O Window Icon

Input/Output Window

The window you will probably use most often is the input/output (I/O) window for each model. Through each model's I/O window, you can adjust assumptions such as gross premium, mortality rate, expense rate, and lapse rate. The I/O window is the only part of *ExecuView* that allows you to input adjustments to the models' assumptions. From the I/O window, you can also observe the effect of each adjustment on profit margin, internal rate of return (IRR), surplus strain, and so forth. These are the models' output. You can switch to the I/O window of the model you are currently viewing by clicking on the I/O icon or by selecting *I/O Window* from the View menu. Figure UG-3 shows the layout of the I/O window for *ExecuView*'s Term Life Model.

Input

As you look at the I/O window, you will notice a number of white cells on the left half of the screen (or the top half of the screen in the case of the Aggregate Model). In these white cells, you can enter new assumptions for each product. To maneuver through these white cells, press the <tab> key or click on the desired cell with your mouse.

Figure UG-3. Input/Output window for *ExecuView's* Term Life Model.

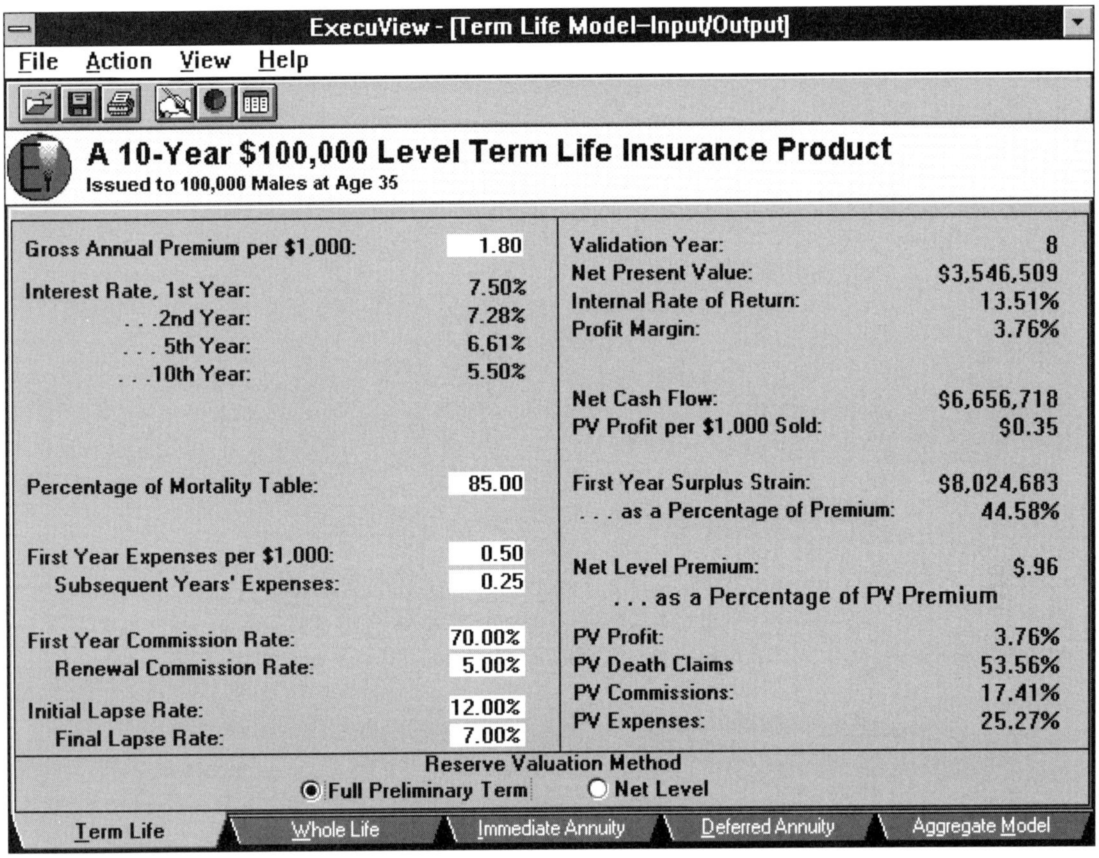

You can change the data in any of the white cells by selecting the cell and typing in a new assumption. For the Whole Life and Term Life Models, you can also select one of two reserve valuation methods by clicking on the check box next to the reserve valuation method you want to use.

When you are ready for *ExecuView* to calculate the results of your new assumptions, press the <enter> key. *ExecuView will not recalculate the model's output based on your new assumptions until you press the <enter> key.* Once the <enter> key has been pressed, *ExecuView* may take several seconds to re-compute the results. A progress bar appears at the top of the screen to graphically depict *ExecuView's* progress in re-computing the model's output.

Output

The output on the I/O window presents summary measures showing how your adjustments affect profitability. Many of these profit measures—such as *validation year, net present value (NPV), internal rate of return (IRR),* and *profit margin*—are explained in Chapter 6.

Results Table Icon

Results Table Window

While the I/O window provides you with summary information, the results table window provides you with the details behind the summary. It allows you to view the results of all a model's calculations for every policy year in the profit test period. The output displayed in the I/O window is determined by applying a complex series of calculations to the assumptions you have entered. Each of *ExecuView*'s four product models operates in essentially the same way. At the beginning of policy Year 1, a stated number of customers are assumed to have purchased the product. As each year passes, premiums are collected and added to the model's *total fund.* The ***total fund*** is a common aspect of asset-share models, and it represents the total assets that a product has accumulated. This use of the word *fund* should not be confused with the fund or account value that a policyowner accumulates under an SPDA or universal life policy. Expenses, commissions, benefits, and surrenders are all paid and their amounts subtracted from the total fund. After that, investment income is added. Finally, year-end reserve, surplus, asset share, and profit amounts are calculated. This process continues for each policy year until the end of the profit-test period, at which point totals are calculated. From these totals, *ExecuView* calculates the profitability output displayed in the I/O window. The Aggregate Model uses the results of the four product models to calculate its results.

To use the results-table window, click on the table icon or select *Results Table* from the View menu. When you enter the results-table window, you will see an array of numbers in columns and rows. Each *row* represents a policy year. Each *column* represents a different annual calculation. Each number in the table shows the result of a single calculation. Labels at the top of each column describe what the numbers in those columns represent.

The results-table window is divided into five "pages" in each of the four product models. In the Aggregate Model, it has four. Each page shows a set of related calculation results. You can select any of these pages by clicking on the appropriate tab at the top of the screen. Each product model consists of the following five pages:

1. *Policies in Force.* This page shows the results of calculations related to the number of policies in force, such as the number of policies lapsing, and the number of death claims that occur.

2. *Totals per $1,000.* On this page, all of the most important annual calculations are shown at the $1,000 unit level. The asset share is included on this page.

3. *Cash Flow 1.* The net annual cash flow (premium income, surrender payments, benefit payments, expenses, growth of total assets, etc.) is shown here.

4. *Cash Flow 2.* Simply a continuation of *Cash Flow 1.*

5. *PV Calculations.* This page shows the present values of annual cash flows.

Figure UG-4 shows the layout of the Totals per $1,000 page of *ExecuView*'s Whole Life Model.

Chart Window

Chart Window Icon

Each of the five models also contains two graphical charts—a pie chart and a line graph—that summarize some of the important output of that model. You can view the charts of the current model at any time by clicking on the chart icon at the top of the screen or by selecting *Charts* from the View menu. Within the four product models,

Figure UG-4. Totals per $1,000 results table page of the Whole Life Model.

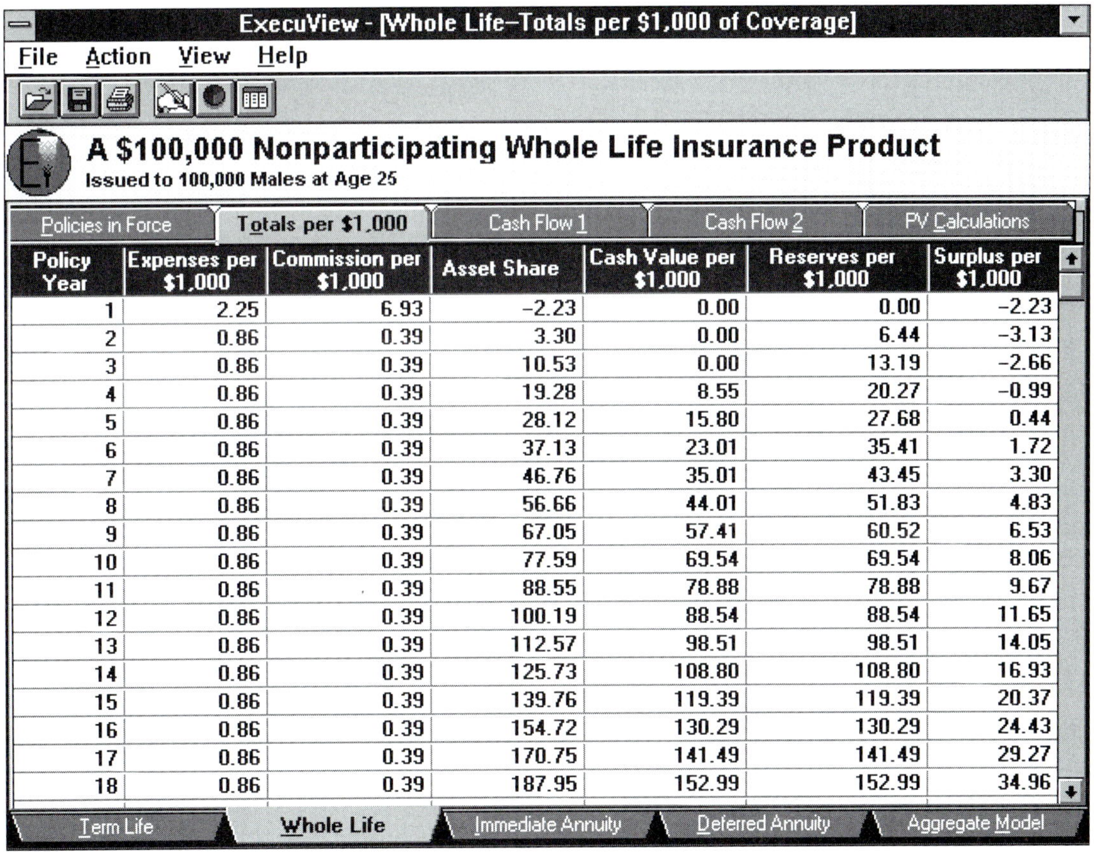

Policy Year	Expenses per $1,000	Commission per $1,000	Asset Share	Cash Value per $1,000	Reserves per $1,000	Surplus per $1,000
1	2.25	6.93	-2.23	0.00	0.00	-2.23
2	0.86	0.39	3.30	0.00	6.44	-3.13
3	0.86	0.39	10.53	0.00	13.19	-2.66
4	0.86	0.39	19.28	8.55	20.27	-0.99
5	0.86	0.39	28.12	15.80	27.68	0.44
6	0.86	0.39	37.13	23.01	35.41	1.72
7	0.86	0.39	46.76	35.01	43.45	3.30
8	0.86	0.39	56.66	44.01	51.83	4.83
9	0.86	0.39	67.05	57.41	60.52	6.53
10	0.86	0.39	77.59	69.54	69.54	8.06
11	0.86	0.39	88.55	78.88	78.88	9.67
12	0.86	0.39	100.19	88.54	88.54	11.65
13	0.86	0.39	112.57	98.51	98.51	14.05
14	0.86	0.39	125.73	108.80	108.80	16.93
15	0.86	0.39	139.76	119.39	119.39	20.37
16	0.86	0.39	154.72	130.29	130.29	24.43
17	0.86	0.39	170.75	141.49	141.49	29.27
18	0.86	0.39	187.95	152.99	152.99	34.96

the pie chart, which is labeled *Use of Funds,* shows how each dollar of premium collected has been used by the end of the profit test period. The chart shows the percentage of each dollar of premium that was used to pay (1) policy benefits, (2) expenses, (3) commissions, and (4) surrender benefits (if applicable), as well as (5) the amount of each dollar that contributed to profit. The pie charts in the annuity models show a sixth use of funds—reserves—because these products are still holding reserves for their surviving annuitants at the end of the 30-year profit test period. In each model, the line graph labeled *Cash Flow* shows the growth of the total fund, the reserve fund, and the surplus fund from the first policy year until the end of the profit test period.

The charts in the Aggregate Model are different from those in the product models. The pie chart in the Aggregate Model shows the percentage of assets attributable to each of the four products. The line graph shows the growth of total surplus for each of the four products. Figure UG-5 shows the charts contained in *ExecuView*'s Deferred Annuity Model.

Troubleshooting

Although *ExecuView* has been tested extensively, you may encounter some difficulties with the way it runs on your computer. Not all computers are the same. Some run more slowly than others. Some experience problems with certain software that others do not. Figure UG-6 presents some common problems that you may experience and the most likely solutions to these problems.

After you have successfully installed *ExecuView,* you may encounter some of *ExecuView*'s own error messages. We describe these next.

Infeasible IRR Result

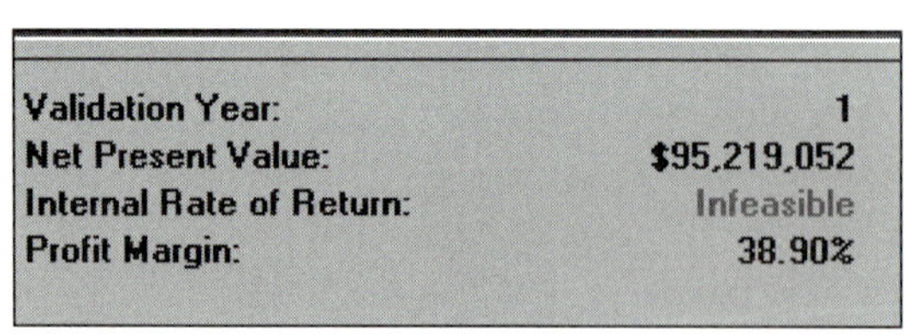

One of *ExecuView*'s error messages involves the *internal rate of return (IRR)* calculation. IRR calculations are extremely long and complicated, and sometimes it is not possible to come up with a reasonable IRR. For example, if a product never makes a profit, there will be no feasible IRR. The same holds true if a product does not experience a loss in at least one year. Whenever the assumptions you have entered cannot produce an IRR, *ExecuView* will print the message "Infeasible" in the IRR cell of the I/O window.

Figure UG-5. Chart window of the Deferred Annuity Model.

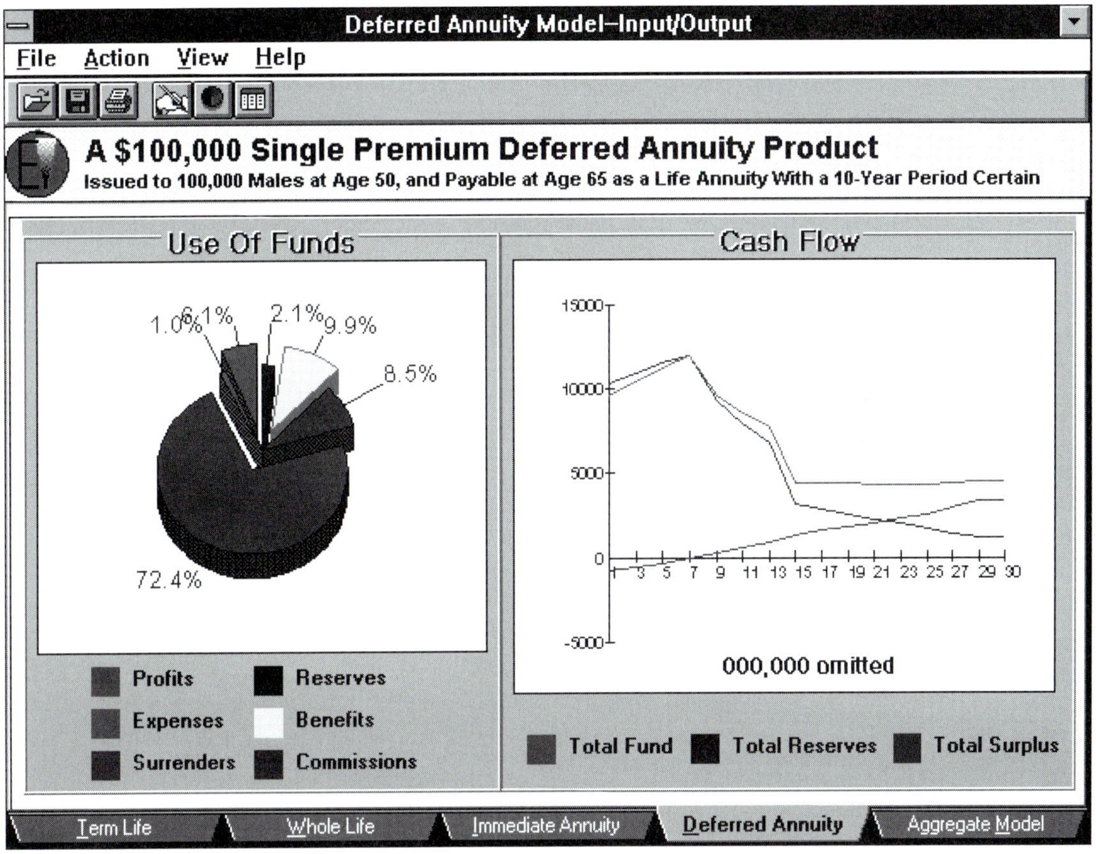

Percent of Policies Sold Result Not 100 Percent

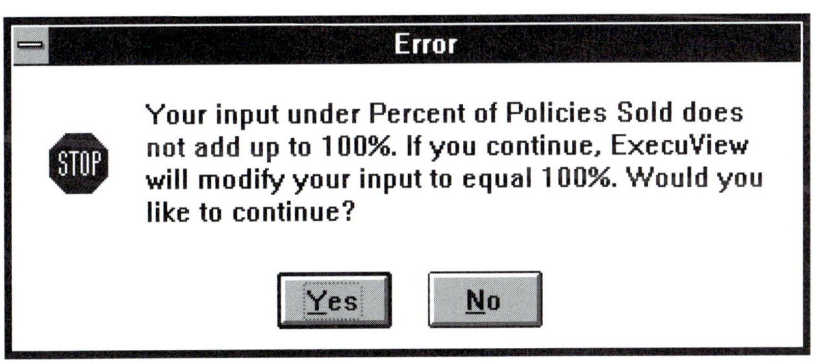

Another error message occurs only in the Aggregate Model. The series of input cells labeled *Percent of Policies Sold* requires that you enter four percentages that add up to 100 percent. If you enter four numbers that do not add up to 100 percent, a dialogue box will appear notifying you of this error. *ExecuView* will give you the choice of

Figure UG-6. Troubleshooting guide.

If you have trouble running or installing *ExecuView,* try the following suggestions:

- *ExecuView* and the *ExecuView* installation program both contain elements that sometimes conflict with certain other Windows-compatible software. If you are having trouble installing *ExecuView* or running *ExecuView* after it has been installed, the first step you should take is to shut down all other applications that are open. This includes screen savers and utilities.
- If, after shutting down all other Windows applications, you still cannot install *ExecuView,* you should exit and re-start Windows in "safe" mode. Starting Windows 3.1 or Windows 95 in safe mode prevents any applications that normally run automatically during your Windows session from starting. To run Windows 3.1 or Windows 95 in safe mode, hold down the <shift> key as soon as the Windows logo, hourglass icon, or the words "Starting Windows 95 . . ." appear on your screen, and continue holding it down until Windows has finished loading. Once you have installed *ExecuView,* you should exit Windows again and re-start normally.
- If you try both of the previous two suggestions and you continue to have trouble with *ExecuView,* you should consult the README file on the *ExecuView* diskette. The README file contains additional troubleshooting information and information about any last-minute changes to *ExecuView.* Once you have successfully installed *ExecuView,* the READ ME icon will appear along with the *ExecuView* icon in the LOMA program group. To view this file, double-click on the README icon.

If you have trouble installing *ExecuView,* you can run the README file directly from the *ExecuView* diskette in one of two ways.

1. Insert the *ExecuView* diskette into your computer's floppy disk drive. Start the Windows Notebook program. Select File, Open. Select the letter of your floppy disk drive. Select README.TXT. Click on OK.
2. Insert the *ExecuView* diskette into your computer's floppy disk drive. Start File Manager (Windows 3.1) or Windows Explorer (Windows 95). Select the letter of your floppy disk drive. Double-click on README.TXT.

(1) fixing the error yourself or (2) having the error fixed automatically using a proportional method.

Non Numeric Data Error

If you accidentally enter more than one decimal point or minus sign in one of the input cells, *ExecuView* will not be able to understand your input. In this case, *ExecuView* will print an error message notifying you that you have entered non-numerical data. You may then correct your error and try again.

In Conclusion

The next several chapters of this book contain *ExecuView* scenarios that help demonstrate some of the important concepts of this book. Working these scenarios on your computer will help illustrate certain key points about profitability and product pricing. However, you are not limited to using *ExecuView* with only these scenarios. Feel free to create scenarios of your own, experiment with different pricing strategies, and test your products with adverse or favorable conditions. Within the limits of its four product models, *ExecuView* is flexible enough to illustrate an infinite number of situations.

CHAPTER

6

Product Profitability Measures and Asset-Share Models

LEARNING OBJECTIVES

After studying this chapter, you should be able to

- Recognize the uses and limitations of asset-share analysis
- Interpret the meaning of a validation point and a validation period
- Calculate the net present value of an insurance or annuity product
- Interpret the results of an internal rate of return calculation
- Interpret the meaning of profit margin as it applies to insurance products
- Assess the likely effect on product profitability, as reflected in a forecasting model, of a given change in a product assumption

OUTLINE

When insurers price insurance and annuity products, they forecast the long-term impact of their pricing decisions before the products are actually sold. In Chapter 3 we discussed some of the different types of forecasts insurers make when they price their products. This chapter introduces you to the various ways that a specific type of model, called an *asset-share model,* can be used for profit testing the design of life insurance and annuity products. The chapter also shows you how to interpret the profitability measures that are the output of an asset-share model.

The discussion of product models in this chapter makes reference to the computer-based asset-share model—*ExecuView: An Asset-Share/Product Profitability Model, version 2.0*—that is included with this textbook. Reading this chapter **does not** require you to use *ExecuView* on a computer. Tables and screen images within the text clearly demonstrate how the *ExecuView* models behave under the various scenarios discussed in this chapter. It is not necessary for you to test these scenarios on your own computer to understand the objectives of this chapter. However, *ExecuView*-based examples appear frequently as illustrations in this chapter and in the next several chapters. Thus, a good understanding of the way the *ExecuView* models function can help you learn many concepts discussed throughout this book. This chapter provides all of the information about *ExecuView* you need to make sure you completely understand the relevant illustrations.

If you have access to a computer that can run the *ExecuView* program, we encourage you to use the program to demonstrate the *ExecuView* examples discussed in this book. Experiencing the interactive approach that *ExecuView* offers can considerably enhance the effectiveness of your study time. *ExecuView* approximates the type of software that product designers use on the job and provides an opportunity for you to learn by doing. If you intend to use *ExecuView* as you study this course you are advised to read the *User's Guide to ExecuView* supplemental section that precedes this chapter.

This chapter begins with an overview of asset-share modeling. Next, the chapter discusses some of the most important profit measures insurers use when testing the profitability of products. Then the chapter explains some of the assumptions insurers make when they create asset-share models, specifically describing the assumptions that are used in the *ExecuView* models. Finally, the chapter demonstrates how changes in some asset-share model product assumptions result in changes in profitability.

Asset-Share Models

Insurers typically evaluate a proposed product's profitability by testing the product under a number of different sets of actuarial assumptions. To test several sets of assumptions, insurers often use asset-share models. An ***asset-share model*** is a mathematical simulation model used by insurance companies to indicate how a product's assets should grow and when the product should become profitable. Asset-share models use asset shares to calculate the cash inflows and outflows created by an insurance product. An ***asset share*** is the net amount of cash per unit of coverage—often per $1,000 of face value in force—that a product has accumulated at a given time.

Asset-share models test the growth of a product's assets based on assumptions about the product and the economic environment. The assumptions insurers make when developing asset-share models for life insurance products include

- The type of product and product features included
- The gross premium
- A reserve valuation method
- The investment income rate
- The mortality table to use in calculating projected benefits
- An expense assumption
- A commission schedule
- A lapse rate assumption
- A method of calculating dividends and cash values (if any)
- A set of profit objectives
- A rate of taxation

Companies employ similar assumptions when creating asset-share models for other insurance products, such as annuities, health policies, and disability policies. The *ExecuView* models employ all of the above assumptions *except* the assumption of a tax rate.

An asset-share model allows the insurer to change the underlying actuarial assumptions and see the effect of those changes on the product's profitability. An insurer can use an asset-share model to learn whether a proposed pricing structure should generate enough revenue to cover the product's costs. Asset-share models take into account all three elements that affect an insurance product's costs: expenses, investment income, and the cost of benefits.

The Limitations of Asset-Share Models

Sometimes asset-share models are criticized because they do not automatically account for the demand for a product in their analysis of a pricing structure. Generally, asset-share models allow insurers to set the assumptions concerning number of policies sold and the number of policyowners surrendering their policies—the *lapse rate*—independent of the other assumptions. However, asset-share models do not usually calculate the effect that changes in other assumptions would have on the lapse rate and sales volume of a product.

An asset-share model might allow an insurer to set the gross annual premium per $1,000 of coverage for a life insurance product as high as it would like—to $10, $100, or even $100,000. A high premium-rate assumption can show astronomical profits because the model can continue to assume that a large number of policies are sold. Yet it is unlikely that products priced very much higher than current market rates would attract any customers at all. Therefore, insurers do not rely solely on the results of an asset-share model to choose the optimum price for a product. They use the asset-share model to evaluate the effects of various proposed premium structures on the product's ability to cover its costs and they use other forecasting methods to evaluate the effects of the various pricing structures on the product's likely sales performance and persistency. Insurers then use all data sources available to them as a basis for deciding upon the appropriate pricing strategy for the product.

Approaches to Measuring Product Profitability

Methods of measuring product profitability are based on either the *net cash flows* or the *earnings* that a product generates or is expected to generate. An insurance product's ***net cash flows*** are the cash inflows (from premiums, investments, and other sources) generated by that product minus the cash outflows (benefit payments, commissions, expenses, etc.) generated by the product. An insurance product's ***earnings*** are the amount that the product adds to the company's capital and surplus in a given period. The definitions of these two terms may sound similar, but there is an important difference. Unlike *net cash flows, earnings* takes into account non-cash items, such as a product's contributions to reserves.

Insurers typically incur considerable costs in a product's first year. Among these first-year costs are the cost of underwriting the policy, issuing the policy, establishing records, setting aside reserves for the policy, and compensating the producer who sold the policy. Because first-year costs are high, product sales usually cause an initial net cash outflow, rather than a net cash inflow. In effect, product sales require an insurer to invest its capital in its product line. An ***initial investment*** is the amount of its capital that an insurer must invest to establish a new product.

Determining the exact amount of an insurer's *initial investment* in a product is often not a straightforward process. For many products the initial investment is equal to the loss, or negative earnings, the product incurs in the first year that it is offered. In other words, a product's initial investment is sometimes equal to its surplus strain. However, some products may experience negative net cash flows for longer than one year, while others may never experience a negative annual cash flow. The exact amount of a product's cash flows that is considered to be the insurer's initial investment depends on the accounting system in use and the practices of the insurance company. Note that an insurance product need not have repaid its initial investment in order to produce earnings in a given period. If a product has not yet repaid its initial investment, then its earnings for a given period can be viewed as the amount of the initial investment that was repaid during that period.

An asset-share model generates a number of different profitability measures based on a given set of assumptions affecting the product's cash flows, earnings, and initial investment. In this section, we describe five measures commonly analyzed by insurance companies. These five measures are

1. Payback period
2. Validation period
3. Net present value (NPV)
4. Internal rate of return (IRR)
5. Profit margin (ratio of the present value of profits to the present value of premiums)

These five profit measures are basic capital budgeting tools that apply to any investment of long-term funds. These tools can be used for measuring performance in a model or for a real-world investment. In fact, insurers use most of these basic approaches when measuring the profitability of their investments in the financial markets and in various administrative systems, such as computer systems, as well as their investments in their insurance products.

Profit measures are often used by insurers when they are deciding whether to accept or reject a proposed investment. Whether a proposed investment is accepted or rejected based on a profit measure depends on the decision criteria the insurer employs. A ***decision criterion*** is a rule that helps determine which of two or more possible decision alternatives to select. For an insurance company deciding whether to accept or reject a proposed product, two decision criteria might be to accept the product if (1) the validation period is not longer than eight years and (2) the profit margin is not less than 10 percent.

Insurers can evaluate the results of the various profit measures by examining how well a measure reflects some of the important characteristics of the cash flows that generate earnings. Some of these characteristics are the

- *Amounts* of the cash flows
- *Expected life* of the series of cash flows
- *Timing* of the cash flows
- *Predictability* of the cash flows

The more precisely and completely a method of evaluating profitability takes into account these characteristics, the more useful the information the method provides.

The following sections look at the profit measures commonly used by insurance companies and discuss which elements of a product's cash flow each measure automatically considers. For your reference throughout the remainder of this chapter, Figure 6-1 shows these profitability measures and the specific cash flow elements each automatically takes into account, and briefly explains each method.

Payback Period

Regardless of how the initial investment is calculated, insurers often want to determine the period of time required to recover their capital investment. For a given insurance product, the ***payback period*** is defined as the number of years that pass before the *earnings* that the

Figure 6-1. Summary of capital budgeting techniques for insurance products.

	Cash flow features accounted for . . .				
Method	**Amount**	**Timing**	**Expected life**	**Predictability (risk)**	**Evaluation factors**
Payback period	Yes	No	No	No	Time to break even
Validation period	Yes	Yes	No	No	Time to break even
Net present value (NPV)	Yes	Yes	Yes	Yes	PV of profits
Internal rate of return	Yes	Yes	Yes	Yes	Return on initial investment
Profit margin	Yes	Yes	Yes	No	PV profits/PV premiums

product produces for the insurer equal the insurer's *initial investment* in the product. The payback period is the time it takes for an investment to produce a net contribution to the insurer's capital and surplus. The point at which an insurance product's earnings equal its initial investment is known as the ***break-even point.***

Insurers often calculate a payback period when deciding whether to purchase new equipment, such as new computer equipment. In such a situation, the payback period would be the length of time before the savings that result from a purchase will equal the equipment's purchase price.

To illustrate the use of payback period for evaluating insurance products, we consider two products offered by the Manhasset Insurance Company. The data concerning Manhasset's two products is presented in Figure 6-2.

When a product's earnings are uniform from year to year, the payback period can be calculated by dividing the initial investment by the yearly earnings. As an example, look at Manhasset's mutual fund product described in Figure 6-2. The insurer's initial investment in the product is $22,000. The insurer's yearly earnings from the product are $5,000. Therefore, the product's payback period is found by dividing $22,000 by $5,000, for a result of 4.4 years, which means that the company will earn back its initial investment by the end of 4.4 years.

More often, the earnings generated by a product are not uniform from year to year. In such situations, the insurer must break down the yearly earnings accordingly. For example, suppose the Manhasset Company introduces the variable product described in Figure 6-2, which has an initial investment of $22,000 and which generates earnings in its first three years of $6,000, $8,000, and $12,000. After two years, the product has generated earnings equal to $14,000, which is less than the initial investment. After three years the product has generated earnings equal to $26,000 (or $6,000 + $8,000 + $12,000), which is more than the initial investment. The payback period is therefore between two and three years.

To calculate the precise payback period, find the proportion of the third year's earnings that is necessary to complete the payback of the initial investment. The amount needed in the third year to complete the payback of the initial investment is $8,000, which is found by subtracting the $14,000 already earned on the investment from the $22,000 initial investment (or $22,000 – $14,000 = $8,000). By dividing the $8,000 yet to be paid off by the $12,000 earned in Year 3, we find that the remainder of the investment is paid off in 0.6 of a year. Thus, the payback period is 2.6 years.

Benefits and Limitations of Payback Period

The main advantage of the payback period is that it provides a quick and easy way to estimate how long a product will tie up the insurer's capital before the product begins to make a net contribution to capi-

Figure 6-2. Data for Manhasset's payback period calculations.

	Mutual fund (Level payments)		Variable product (Mixed stream)	
	Annual flows	**Cumulative totals**	**Annual flows**	**Cumulative totals**
Initial investment	–22,000	NA	–22,000	NA
Year 1	5,000	5,000	6,000	6,000
Year 2	5,000	10,000	8,000	14,000
Year 3	5,000	15,000	12,000	26,000
Year 4	5,000	20,000	NA	NA
Year 5	5,000	25,000	NA	NA

tal and surplus. The drawback of the payback period as a measure of profitability is that it automatically takes into account only the *amounts* of cash flows. It does not usually take into account any of the other elements of the nature of a product's cash flows. For example, the payback period does not automatically take into account the likelihood that projected earnings will actually materialize. The payback period also ignores the timing of cash flows because it does not automatically distinguish between cash flows earned in different years. By ignoring timing differences, the payback period also ignores the time value of money. To illustrate, consider the following two sets of earnings, each from an initial investment of $10,000:

	Alpha Product	Beta Product
Initial investment	$10,000	$10,000
Year 1	$ 7,000	$ 1,000
Year 2	$ 2,000	$ 2,000
Year 3	$ 1,000	$ 7,000

Both streams of earnings pay back the initial investment in three years. However, the Alpha Product's cash flow stream is more desirable than the Beta Product's, because the Alpha Product earns more money earlier, and thus its cash inflows have a higher present value.

The payback period, unless modified, also ignores the length of time cash flows are expected to continue. Consider the following streams of earnings, each generated by an initial investment of $15,000:

	Gamma Product	Delta Product
Initial investment	$15,000	$15,000
Year 1	$ 5,000	$ 5,000
Year 2	$ 5,000	$ 5,000
Year 3	$ 5,000	$ 5,000
Year 4	0	$ 5,000
Year 5	0	$ 5,000

Both cash flow streams have the same payback period ($15,000 ÷ $5,000 = 3 years), but the Delta Product's stream is clearly more valuable because it contributes a more attractive total return. Payback does not automatically provide a mechanism for showing that the Delta Product's income stream is more valuable.

The payback period is not generally used in conjunction with asset-share models. Instead, asset-share models employ an insurance-specific version of the payback period, called the *validation period.*

Validation Period and Asset-Share Models

The key comparison in an asset-share model is the comparison of reserves to asset shares. Initially, a product's policy reserve exceeds its asset share. In this situation, the product is a drain on the insurer's capital and surplus because liabilities (reserves) exceed assets. The first year that the asset share is greater than the reserve is known as the ***validation point.*** The time before a product reaches its validation point is known as the *validation period.* During the validation period, the insurance company must cover the gap between assets and reserves by allocating existing surplus to the new product's policy reserve account. Once a product's asset share exceeds its policy reserve, the validation period has ended and the product has paid off its initial investment.

To illustrate, suppose the Long Life Insurance Company is planning to offer a new whole life insurance product. Figure 6-3 represents an abbreviated asset-share model for this product.

For the sake of this example, premium and interest income have been combined into Column 3, labeled *Total Cash Inflows,* and expenses, benefit payments, and commissions have been combined into Column 4, labeled *Total Cash Outflows.* The difference between the inflows and the outflows determines the size of the fund. The fund for each year is shown in Column 5 of the figure.

At the end of the product's first year, the fund is equal to the cash inflows generated by the product during the year minus the cash outflows for the year. For each succeeding year, the fund is equal to the fund at the end of the previous year plus the cash inflows for the year

Figure 6-3. Simplified asset-share model of a whole life product.

{1} Policy year	{2} Policies in force at end of year	{3} Total cash inflows	{4} Total cash outflows	{5} Total fund (Previous {5} + {3} – {4})	{6} Asset share ({5} ÷ {2})	{7} Reserve per $1,000	{8} Surplus per $1,000 ({6} – {7})
1	100	800	1,024	–224	–2.24	0.00	–2.24
2	80	660	157	279	3.49	6.44	–2.95
3	66	582	128	733	11.11	13.19	–2.08
4	57	530	185	1,078	18.91	20.27	–1.36
5	52	500	183	1,395	26.83	27.68	–0.85
6	48	488	167	1,716	35.75	35.41	0.34
7	45	473	197	1,992	44.27	43.45	0.82
8	41	458	211	2,239	54.61	51.83	2.78
9	38	442	224	2,457	64.66	60.52	4.14
10	36	425	234	2,648	73.56	69.54	4.02

minus the cash outflows for the year. The method of calculating the fund can be summarized as follows:

1. Fund at End of First Year	=	**First-Year Cash Inflows**	–	**First-Year Cash Outflows**		
2. Fund at End of Subsequent Years	=	**Fund at End of Previous Year**	+	**Cash Inflows for the Year**	–	**Cash Outflows for the Year**

In its third year, Long Life's new product has cash inflows of $582 and cash outflows of $128. The product's fund at the end of its second year was $279. Therefore, the fund for the third year is calculated as follows:

Fund at End of Year = **Fund at End of Previous Year** + **Cash Inflows** – **Cash Outflows**
= $279 + $582 – $128
= $733

The fund is used to calculate each policy's asset share, as follows:

Asset Share	=	**Fund at End of Year**	÷	**Number of Units of Coverage in Force at End of Year**

In this example we are calculating the asset share per policy, so each policy in force functions as a unit of coverage in force. Column 2 shows that 66 policies are in force at the end of the product's third year. The asset share for the third policy year, shown in Column 6, is calculated as follows:

$$\text{Asset Share} = \text{Fund at End of Year} \div \begin{matrix}\text{Number of Units of Coverage} \\ \text{in Force at End of Year}\end{matrix}$$
$$= \$733 \div 66$$
$$= \$11.11$$

The product's asset share at the end of each policy year is compared to the policy reserve, shown in Column 7. The policy reserve represents the amount of liability per policy that the insurer must keep on its books. The asset share represents the amount of assets that each policy remaining in force has generated for the insurer. Asset share and reserve can be compared along the lines of the basic accounting equation. Recall that the basic accounting equation is

Assets = Liabilities + Owners' Equity

For an insurance product, we can substitute *asset share* for *assets* in the accounting equation, and *reserve* for *liabilities.* The insurance company's owner's equity in a single insurance policy is that policy's total surplus, or the amount of the insurer's capital and surplus that is attributable to that policy (Column 8). Thus, for an insurance policy we can express the following relationship:

Asset Share = Policy Reserve + Policy Surplus

or

Asset Share – Policy Reserve = Policy Surplus

The validation point for Long Life's whole life product can be identified from Figure 6-3 as the first year that the asset share exceeds the policy reserve. To find this point, compare Column 6 to Column 7. The validation point can also be identified as the first year that the product maintains a positive surplus (see Column 8). Figure 6-3 shows that the validation point for Long Life's whole life product is Year 6, and the product's validation period is six years. This information indicates that this product takes six years to return Long Life's initial investment in it.

Benefits and Limitations of Validation Period

The validation period, in contrast to the payback period, explicitly takes into account the time value of money by (1) including investment income among the cash inflows which are entered into the model, and (2) comparing the asset share and the policy reserve *for the same year.* However, like the payback period, the validation period does not automatically take into account the expected life of cash flows and does not explicitly account for the risk—the likelihood that the projected earnings will not actually materialize—associated with the cash flows.

Net Present Value

The ***net present value (NPV)*** of an investment project is generally calculated by subtracting the project's initial investment from the present value of the project's earnings, as follows:

Net Present Value = Present Value of Earnings – Initial Investment

An NPV calculation yields a dollar figure representing the present value of the profit that a project is expected to earn. Figure 6-4 illustrates the calculation of the net present value of an insurance product.

As shown in Figure 6-4, the initial investment in this product is $150. The earnings for this product have the following characteristics:

- *Amounts.* $50 per year.
- *Expected life.* Five years.
- *Timing.* The earnings occur at the end of each product year.

Figure 6-4. Net present value (NPV) of an insurance product—10% discount rate.

Initial Investment = $150

Year	Annual earnings	Present value interest factor (at 10%)	Present value of annual earnings
1	$50	× *PVIF* (1,10%) =	$ 45.45
2	$50	× *PVIF* (2,10%) =	$ 41.30
3	$50	× *PVIF* (3,10%) =	$ 37.55
4	$50	× *PVIF* (4,10%) =	$ 34.15
5	$50	× *PVIF* (5,10%) =	+ $ 31.05
		Total PV Earnings =	$189.50

Net Present Value = Present Value of Earnings – Initial Investment

= $189.50 – $150

= $39.50

When we add together the present value of earnings for each year and subtract the initial investment, we find that the NPV for this product is $39.50.

Note that the discount rate used to calculate the present value in this example was 10 percent. When using the NPV approach, the insurer selects the discount rate by considering the risk associated with the product. The higher the risk associated with the product, the higher the discount rate the insurer will use to calculate the present values. In Figure 6-4, for example, the 10 percent discount rate shown indicates that the insurer, in compensation for the amount of risk the cash flows represent, is willing to accept the risk as long as the return is at least 10 percent. A higher discount rate—say 15 percent—would indicate that the insurer felt that the product was riskier than a product whose cash flows were discounted at only 10 percent. Generally, the higher the interest rate used for discounting, the lower will be the resulting NPV. As Figure 6-5 shows, a 15 percent discount rate produces a lower NPV than the 10 percent rate used in Figure 6-4 ($17.60, as opposed to $39.50).

Benefits and Limitations of NPV

The NPV approach explicitly provides for all four elements of a product's cash flows. NPV takes into account the *timing* of cash flows by discounting all cash flows to the same date. In addition, because calculating NPV consists of discounting all of a product's cash flows, NPV explicitly takes into account both the *amount* of these cash

Figure 6-5. Net present value (NPV) of an insurance product—15% discount rate.

Initial Investment = $150

Year	Annual earnings	Present value interest factor (at 15%)	Present value of annual earnings
1	$50	× *PVIF* (1,15%) =	$ 43.50
2	$50	× *PVIF* (2,15%) =	$ 37.80
3	$50	× *PVIF* (3,15%) =	$ 32.85
4	$50	× *PVIF* (4,15%) =	$ 28.60
5	$50	× *PVIF* (5,15%) =	+ $ 24.85
		Total PV Earnings =	$167.60

Net Present Value = $167.60 – $150

= $17.60

flows and the full *length* of time that the product's cash flows continue. The NPV calculation also addresses the *predictability* or *risk* associated with the cash flows by means of the interest rate used to calculate the present values of the cash flows.

A product's projected NPV must always be considered in comparison to the initial investment required to produce the NPV. For example, consider the two products illustrated in the following table:

	Product A	Product B
NPV	$10,000	$ 10,000
Initial investment	$20,000	$100,000

Both products have an NPV of $10,000, but Product A has an initial investment of only $20,000, compared to Product B's initial investment of $100,000. The NPV measure, considered alone, would rank these products as equally desirable. However, the difference between the initial investments of products A and B amounts to $80,000. Insurers generally would prefer to invest in Product A, and to use the $80,000 difference between the initial investments in the two products to earn a return from another source.

Internal Rate of Return

For an insurance product, the ***internal rate of return (IRR)*** is defined as the percentage rate at which the product's earnings must be discounted in order to exactly repay the insurer's initial investment in the product. This percentage represents the rate of return that the insurer will earn on its investment in the product.

IRR is commonly used as a measure of product profitability among insurers. Figure 6-6 illustrates the use of IRR by stock and mutual companies for various types of products. Product actuaries often refer to IRR as *return on equity (ROE)* or *return on investment (ROI)*. You may remember the term ROE as used in the context of the profitability of an entire organization. Note that the term ROE is used somewhat differently in the context of product profitability than it is in the context of the profitability of an entire organization.

Figure 6-7 presents a set of cash flows for a hypothetical product to illustrate the concept of IRR. The figure shows that the insurer's initial investment in this product is $150. The figure also illustrates the following characteristics of the set of earnings associated with this product:

Figure 6-6. IRR as a primary company objective by product and company type.

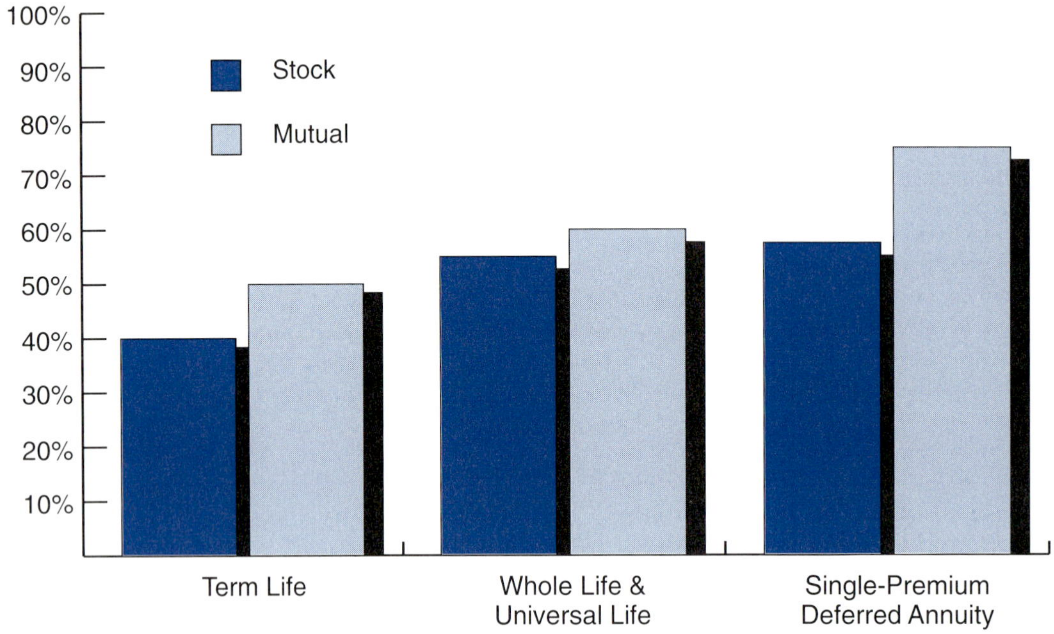

Source: *Douglas C. Doll, Tillinghast, 1994; from a presentation at LOMA's Financial Inforum, May 16, 1994. Reprinted with permission.*

- *Amounts.* $50 per year.
- *Expected life.* Five years.
- *Timing.* Earnings occur at the end of each product year.

The IRR for this hypothetical product is the specific discount rate that causes the present value of earnings to equal the initial investment of $150. Figure 6-7 shows the present values of the earnings for this product with discount rates of 15 percent, 20 percent, and 25 percent. Multiple discount rates are shown because, when calculated by hand, using present value tables, the exact IRR can only be arrived at through a process of trial and error. When the discount rate for this hypothetical product is 20 percent, the present value of earnings is $149.53, only $0.47 less than the initial investment. Therefore, the product's IRR is slightly less than 20 percent. Further trial and error would show that the IRR is approximately 19.86 percent.

Benefits and Limitations of IRR

Like NPV, internal rate of return automatically takes into account all four of the crucial elements of a product's cash flows. The IRR

Figure 6-7. Earnings and IRR of a hypothetical product.

Initial Investment = $150

Year	Annual earnings	Present value at 15%	Present value at 20%	Present value at 25%
1	$50	$ 43.48	$ 41.67	$ 40.00
2	$50	$ 37.81	$ 34.72	$ 32.00
3	$50	$ 32.88	$ 28.94	$ 25.60
4	$50	$ 28.59	$ 24.11	$ 20.48
5	$50	+ $ 24.86	+ $ 20.09	+ $ 16.38
Total PV Earnings =		**$167.62**	**$149.53**	**$134.46**

method takes the *timing* of cash flows into account by using present value calculations to view on an equal footing cash flows that occur at different points in time. IRR also takes into account the *amount* and *length* of a product's cash flows by calculating the present values of all the product's cash flows. An insurer can take cash-flow *predictability* or *risk* into account by comparing a product's estimated IRR to the product's required return, or hurdle rate.

In order for a product's IRR to be acceptable for the level of risk the product represents, the IRR must exceed the insurer's required return for the product. To illustrate, consider a hypothetical product (Product A) whose predicted IRR is 12 percent. Suppose the insurer considers the amount of risk associated with the product's expected cash flows to be relatively low. Given this risk, the insurer will proceed with developing the product if its expected IRR exceeds 10 percent. In other words, the product's required return is 10 percent. Because the product's predicted IRR of 12 percent exceeds the required return of 10 percent, the insurer will proceed with developing the product.

		Product A		
Predicted IRR	**12%**	>	**10%**	**Required Return**
		ACCEPT		

On the other hand, suppose another, riskier product (Product B) has a required return of 14 percent. If its predicted IRR were also 12 percent, the insurer would not proceed with developing the product.

		Product B		
Predicted IRR	**12%**	<	**14%**	**Required Return**
		REJECT		

Profit Margin for Insurance Products

In a general business sense, ***profit margin*** is the ratio of profit to sales revenue. Many types of businesses calculate profit margins for a wide variety of products. Profit margin can also be used to compare profit to sales revenue at the company-wide level. Regardless of the situation to which it is applied, the general formula for profit margin is

Profit Margin = Profit ÷ Sales Revenue

The method used to calculate *profit* for this formula will vary depending on the situation, the accounting methods used, and the practices of the company.

For insurance products, profit margin must take into account the time value of money. Insurance products usually generate streams of premium income and profits over many years. In order to compare these streams, insurers must use present value calculations.

The profit margin of an insurance product is calculated by taking the *ratio of the present value of profits to the present value of premiums.* In other words, the present value of the profits earned on a product is divided by the present value of the premiums collected for the product, as follows:

Profit Margin = PV Profits ÷ PV Premiums

In the calculation of this ratio, *profit* is equal to a product's net cash flows, adjusted for interest income and contributions to reserves. The discount rate used in the calculation is usually equal to the investment return the insurer earns or expects to earn on the portfolio of assets that supports the product. Profit margin helps the insurer understand what portion of the premiums paid is contributing to the insurer's profitability. Figure 6-8 shows that, like IRR, the profit margin ratio measure is widely used by insurers.

Suppose Forsythia Insurance is developing a new term insurance product. Figure 6-9 shows the expected cash inflows and outflows for the product.

Figure 6-8. Profit margin as a primary company objective by product and company type.

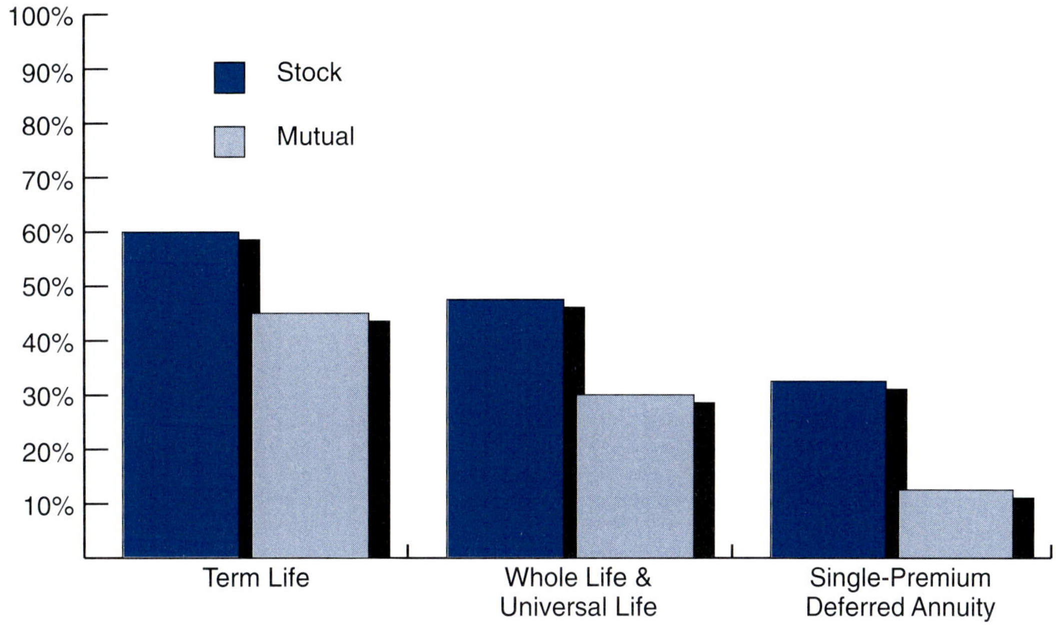

Source: *Douglas C. Doll, Tillinghast, 1994; from a presentation at LOMA's Financial Inforum, May 16, 1994. Reprinted with permission.*

Because we need to find the present value of premiums, in this figure we have separated total product cash inflows into two categories: (1) inflows from premiums and (2) inflows from investments. Figures 6-10 and 6-11 show the calculations of the present value of premiums and the present value of profits for the product.

Note that premiums are paid at the beginning of the policy year while profits are earned at the end of the year. This difference is reflected in the different *PVIF*s that are applied when calculating the present value of profits and the present value of premiums. The profit margin for this product is equal to the ratio of the present value of profits to the present value of premiums, as follows:

Figure 6-9. Cash flows for the Forsythia term life product.

Policy year	Premium income	Cash outflows	Interest income	Profit
1	$1,000	$1,400	–$40	–$440
2	$ 800	$ 600	–$24	$176
3	$ 750	$ 550	–$ 6	$194
4	$ 700	$ 500	$13	$213
5	$ 650	$ 450	$34	$234

Figure 6-10. Present value of premiums for Forsythia's term life product.

Policy Year (*n*)	Premium Income	×	*PVIF* (*n*–1, 10%)	=	Present Value of Premiums
1	$1,000	×	1.000	=	$1,000.00
2	$ 800	×	0.909	=	$ 727.20
3	$ 750	×	0.826	=	$ 619.50
4	$ 700	×	0.751	=	$ 525.70
5	$ 650	×	0.683	=	$ 443.95
			Total PV Premiums	=	**$3,316.35**

Profit Margin = PV Profit ÷ PV Premiums
= $181.90 ÷ $3,316.35
= 5.48%

Benefits and Limitations of Profit Margin

The profit margin method of measuring the profitability of an insurance product takes into account most, but not all, of the important elements of a product's cash flows. The use of present values ensures that this method considers the *timing* of cash flows. Further, because the calculation includes all the cash flows related to the product, it also takes into account the *amount* and the *length* of time the cash flows continue. However, this measure does not take into account the *likelihood* that the cash flows will occur, and thus it fails to explicitly address the *risk* associated with the cash flows.

Figure 6-11. Present value of profits for Forsythia's term life product.

Policy Year (*n*)	Profits	×	*PVIF* (*n*, 10%)	=	Present Value of Profits
1	–$440	×	0.909	=	–$399.96
2	$176	×	0.826	=	$145.38
3	$194	×	0.751	=	$145.69
4	$213	×	0.683	=	$145.48
5	$234	×	0.621	=	$145.31
			Total PV Profits	=	**$181.90**

Other Profit Measures

Different insurance companies place different emphasis on the various profit measures available to check the profitability of their products. Some insurers use additional measures we have not covered. However, validation period, net present value, internal rate of return, and profit margin are the measures most commonly used.

It would be impossible for us to cover every profit measure in use today. Figure 6-12 defines several additional measures, which are used by *ExecuView,* the computer-based asset-share analysis included with this textbook.

Assumptions Used in Asset-Share Models

Asset-share models and other computer-based product models generally use two different types of assumptions: user-defined assumptions and fixed assumptions. ***User-defined assumptions*** are the assumptions that the end-user of an asset-share model can control. Such assumptions can usually be changed quickly to test a wide variety of scenarios. ***Fixed assumptions*** are the assumptions that are built into the model when it is designed. The calculations that a model uses to produce its output are part of the model's fixed assumptions. It is possible to

Figure 6-12. Additional profit measures used by *ExecuView.*

- **Total profit on product.** The total profit that a product has generated by the end of the profit test period, ignoring the time value of money.
- **Present value of profits per $1,000 of coverage sold.** The present value of profits divided by the number of $1,000 units sold at the beginning of the profit test period. This measure shows the amount that each unit sold contributed to profitability by the end of the profit test period.
- **Surplus strain.** The net loss in the first year that a product is offered.
- **Surplus strain as a percentage of first-year premium.** Surplus strain divided by the premium income for the first policy year, in percentage form.
- **Net annual premium.** Net annual premium shows the exact amount of premium that is necessary from each policy to pay for the mortality and surrender expenses of the entire product.
- **As a percentage of present value of premiums.** Insurers can calculate the ratio of the present value of each cash outflow to present value of premiums. Profit margin (PV profits divided by PV premiums) is the most common of these measures. In addition, insurers can calculate the ratio of PV expenses, PV commissions, PV policy benefits, and PV surrender benefits to PV premiums. The results of these various ratios, expressed in percentage form, show the portion of premium income devoted to each outflow. Thus, if the ratio of PV policy benefits to PV premiums is 30 percent, then 30 percent of premiums collected over the life of the product are used to pay policy benefits.

adjust the fixed assumptions in an asset-share model, but this is a longer, more complicated process than changing the user-defined assumptions, and may involve some computer programming.

User-Defined Assumptions

An asset-share model usually allows users to change a number of assumptions very easily, so that a product can be tested under a number of possible scenarios. The assumptions that insurers plug into an asset-share model are designed to test a product's profitability under both favorable and unfavorable conditions.

A model's user-defined assumptions typically include the following:

- *Gross premium.* An insurer must determine what it intends to charge for an insurance product, or what pricing structure it wishes to test in the model. The gross premium is the amount an insurer charges each policyowner for a unit of insurance coverage. Some products involve a gross annual premium while others may involve a single premium, or a limited number of premium payments. By testing a number of premium rates, an insurer can estimate the optimal pricing strategy for a product.

- *Interest margin.* Insurance products with a significant investment component, such as annuities and universal life insurance policies, generally establish an interest margin. When insurers calculate the account value of an annuity or other investment-based insurance product, they generally pay their contract holders a rate of interest that is slightly less than the amount of interest the company is actually earning or expects to earn on its asset portfolio. A ***crediting rate*** is the rate of interest insurers pay their contract holders. A crediting rate can be determined by subtracting a given number of ***basis points,*** or one one-hundredths of a percent (0.01 percent), from the interest rate the insurer is earning on its asset portfolio. The actual method an insurer uses to calculate a crediting rate can be quite complicated, but the result of such calculations is called an interest margin. An ***interest margin,*** also called an *interest spread,* is the difference between the interest rate the insurer is earning and the rate it is crediting to its customers. For example, if an insurer is earning 8 percent interest on its asset portfolio and maintains an interest margin of 150 basis points on an annuity product, then the crediting rate the insurer is offering its customers is 6.5 percent:

Interest Rate	8.0%
– Interest Margin	–1.5%
Crediting Rate	6.5%

The higher the interest margin of a product, the lower the crediting rate of that product, assuming the interest rate remains the same. For insurance products with a large investment component, the interest margin can be the insurer's primary source of profits. As with gross premium, testing a number of interest margins can help an insurer to determine the optimal pricing strategy for a product.

- *Interest rates.* The insurer may anticipate a level interest rate, a rising interest rate, a falling interest rate, or a rate that rises and falls over time. By testing a number of interest scenarios, an insurer can test the soundness of its pricing strategy.
- *Expenses.* Introducing a product to a market generates expenses. Also, each policy that an insurer sells results in expenses. Insurers must determine how expenses will be allocated to each policy. Generally, for each policy sold and each policy renewed, an insurer determines a fixed expense per policy and a percentage of premium expense.
- *Commission rates.* Insurance products marketed through traditional insurance agents and brokers involve commission expenses. When modeling a product, insurers must determine what commission rate, if any, will be paid. For life insurance products, first-year commissions are generally very high (50 percent of premiums or more), and renewal commissions are much lower. Because most annuity products have very high initial premiums, commission rates on annuity products tend to be lower than those on life products. A $100,000 premium annuity (such as those described in the *ExecuView* models) with a 50 percent commission rate would pay a commission of $50,000! Such exorbitant rates would destroy any hope of earning a profit or allowing a contract owner to recover his investment. Annuity commissions are usually less than 10 percent.
- *Lapse rates.* Lapse rates describe the percentage of policies in force that are voluntarily terminated each year. The lapse rate experienced by a product can have a tremendous effect on profitability. Therefore, insurers must be especially careful when forecasting the lapse rates to be used in their product models. Testing a number of lapse rate scenarios can help insurers predict the effects different rates will have on profitability.

Fixed Assumptions

The way in which the model applies the user-defined assumptions to calculate the output is determined by the model's fixed assumptions. The fixed assumptions an insurer uses when developing a product model come from a variety of sources. Some are the result of forecasting techniques. Some are based on an insurer's previous experience with similar products in similar markets. Others are simply the reflection of an expert's hunch. A model's fixed assumptions reflect how the model's designer expects an insurance product to behave in the real world.

The model's fixed assumptions are mainly reflected in the mathematical formulas that calculate the model's output. Some specific types of fixed assumptions insurers make when constructing a model include the following:

- *Product description.* One of the first decisions an insurer needs to make is the type of product it will model. Will it be a life, health, or annuity product? Will it be participating or nonparticipating? To what age group will the product be sold?

- *Reserve valuation method.* The amount of reserves a product accumulates has a great effect on that product's profitability. An insurer must decide what method of reserve valuation it will use when modeling a product. Different reserve valuation methods will result in different reserve amounts for each policy year. Additionally, an insurer must decide what mortality table it will use when valuing reserves.

- *Cash value/dividend valuation method.* If the product is a participating insurance policy or a product that accumulates a cash value, the insurer must decide on a method of computing dividend payments or cash value accumulations.

The lists of fixed and user-defined assumptions provided here are by no means complete. All asset-share models are different. Depending on the kind of product an insurer is modeling and the kinds of scenarios it wants to test, a model can include different sets of assumptions. What serves as a fixed assumption in one model may be a user-defined assumption in another.

A model's purpose is to test the user-defined and fixed assumptions that have been programmed into the model in order to determine the profitability of a product. The accuracy of the model's outcome necessarily depends on the accuracy of the assumptions used in the model. Most of the assumptions are based on forecasts of one type or another. An entire set of actuarial pricing assumptions can virtually never be correct because at least some of these forecasts are certain to be incorrect. Because the outcome a model predicts is only as accurate as the assumptions that go into it, a model will never be 100 percent accurate in its projections. However, if properly constructed and programmed with reasonable assumptions, a model can approximate what is likely to happen to an insurance product under various scenarios. Thus, the information that models provide can be a great help to insurers when they are making pricing decisions.

Assumptions Used in the *ExecuView* Models

To illustrate the kinds of assumptions insurers make when creating asset-share models, this section presents the fixed and user-defined assumptions used in *ExecuView.* In addition to providing examples of the assumptions insurers use in asset-share models, this section can serve as a reference for information about *ExecuView* as you work with the *ExecuView* examples and illustrations in this and future chapters.

At the heart of *ExecuView* are five models—four product models and an aggregate model combining the results of the product models. Each of the four product models depicts a fairly common insurance product. Descriptions of the products depicted in *ExecuView* are summarized in Figure 6-13. Figure 6-14 summarizes the assumptions of the Aggregate Model. Italics indicate user-defined assumptions.

Some assumptions are the same for all four product models. Each product model assumes the following:

- One hundred thousand policies are issued at the beginning of the first policy year.
- The average policy has a face value of $100,000 for the life insurance models, and an initial premium of $100,000 for the annuity models.
- All deaths occur in the middle of the policy year.
- All premiums, expenses, and commissions are paid at the beginning of the policy year.
- Interest is compounded annually.

Term Life Insurance Model

A term life insurance product provides insurance coverage for a specified, limited period of time called a *term.* The length of the term may vary from a few hours to 20 years, 30 years, or longer. In a level term life insurance product, the premium and death benefit do not change for the length of the term.

ExecuView's Term Life Model depicts a block of 10-year term life policies issued to male insureds at age 35. The profit test period for this product is the length of the 10-year term.

Figure 6-13. Descriptions of *ExecuView's* four product models.

10-Year Term Life Product Model

- **Product summary.** 10-year term life with level premiums and level death benefits issued to a male age 35
- **Number of policies.** 100,000
- **Average face amount.** $100,000
- **Profit test period.** 10 years
- **Mortality basis.** The 1975–80 Basic Select and Ultimate table
- **Lapse rates.** *Initial* rate at beginning of Year 2; adjusts to *Final* rate by beginning of Year 6
- **Commission rates.** *First Year* for the first policy year; *Subsequent Years* every year thereafter
- **Expenses.** 15% of gross annual premiums plus the amount entered in *First Year* for the first year; 7.25% of gross annual premium plus the amount entered in *Subsequent Years* for all subsequent years
- **Reserve basis.** Either *net level* or *full preliminary term* method, both calculated assuming 4.5% interest on reserves and 1980 Commissioners Standard Ordinary (CSO) table mortality rates
- **Cash value.** N/A
- **Miscellaneous assumptions.**
  - Death claims occur in the middle of the year
  - Lapses occur at the beginning of each policy year, before premiums are collected

Whole Life Product Model

- **Product summary.** A nonparticipating whole life policy with level premiums and level death benefits issued to a male age 25
- **Number of policies.** 100,000
- **Average face amount.** $100,000
- **Profit test period.** 30 years, at the end of which all policies in force are assumed to lapse
- **Mortality basis.** The 1975-80 Basic Select and Ultimate table
- **Lapse rates.** *Initial* rate at beginning of Year 2; adjusts to *Final* rate by beginning of Year 6
- **Commission rates.** *First Year* for the first policy year, *Subsequent Years* every year thereafter
- **Expenses.** 15% of gross annual premiums plus the amount entered in *First Year* for the first year; 7.25% of gross annual premiums plus the amount entered in *Subsequent Years* for all subsequent years
- **Reserve basis.** Either *net level* or *full preliminary term method,* both calculated assuming 4.5% interest on reserves and 1980 Commissioners Standard Ordinary (CSO) table mortality rates
- **Cash value.** Based on amounts calculated using adjusted premiums, assuming 5.5% interest and CSO table mortality
- **Miscellaneous assumptions.**
  - Deaths occur in the middle of the year
  - Lapses occur at the beginning of each policy year, before premiums are collected

Figure 6-13. Descriptions of *ExecuView's* four product models *(continued)*.

Single-Premium Deferred Annuity Product Model

- **Product summary.** A single-premium deferred annuity paid in by a male at age 50 with an accumulation period of 15 years, after which the annuity is payable for life with a 10-year period certain
- **Number of policies.** 100,000
- **Average premium.** $100,000
- **Crediting rate.** The interest applied to cash value is the current interest rate minus the *Interest Margin*
- **Minimum crediting rate.** 4%
- **Surrender charges.** A 7% surrender charge is levied in the first year. This rate drops one percentage point a year for 7 years. From Year 8 no surrender charges apply
- **Profit test period.** 30 years
- **Mortality basis.** The 1983 Basic Table for annuities
- **Lapse rates.** The *Initial* rate applies for the first seven years. The *Middle* rate applies in the eighth year, the first year with no surrender charges. Half of the *Middle* rate applies in Years 9 through 14. In Year 15, the last year lapses are allowed, the *Final* rate applies
- **Commission rates.** The percentage in *Commission Rate* is applied to the initial premium only
- **Expenses.** *First Year* for the first policy year, *Subsequent Years* for every year thereafter
- **Cash value.**
  - Accumulation period: ° Initial premium accumulated at the crediting rate
  - Payout period: ° N/A

Reserve basis.
- Accumulation period: ° Equal to cash surrender value
- Payout period: ° Calculated using mortality rates from the 1983 Table *a* and 7.25% interest

Miscellaneous assumptions.
- Death claims result in surrenders without penalties
- Lapses and deaths occur in the middle of the year

Immediate Annuity Model

- **Product summary.** An immediate straight life annuity issued at age 65
- **Number of policies.** 100,000
- **Average premium.** $100,000
- **Crediting rate.** The interest applied when calculating the benefit is the current interest rate minus the *Interest Margin*
- **Minimum credited interest rate.** None
- **Profit test period.** 30 years
- **Mortality basis.** The 1983 Basic Table for annuities
- **Commission rates.** The percentage in *Commission Rate* is applied to the initial premium only
- **Expenses.** *First Year* for the first policy year, *Subsequent Years* for every year thereafter
- **Reserve basis.** Calculated using mortality rates from the 1983 Table *a* and 7.75% interest
- **Miscellaneous assumptions.** Deaths occur in the middle of the year

Figure 6-14. Assumptions of *ExecuView's* Aggregate Model.

- **Description.** An aggregate model, combining the output of four product models based on the product mix set by a user
- **Number of policies sold.** 400,000
- **Percent of policies attributable to each product.** Controlled by users; the percentage of all policies sold attributableto any one product equals the percentage a user inputs
- **Basis of calculations.** The total assets, reserves, and surplus generated by each of the four product models are multiplied by the percentages users set under *Percentage of Policies Sold* and then multiplied by 4 and added together to produce the aggregate assets, reserves, and surplus
- **Interest rates.** Equal to the *First Year Interest Rate* for the first year. In subsequent years the interest rate for a given year equals the interest rate for the previous year plus the *% Change* applicable to that year

Mortality Rates

The mortality rates used for the Term Life Model are taken from the 1975–80 Basic Select and Ultimate table. Figure 6-15 shows the 1975–80 Basic Select and Ultimate mortality rates used in *ExecuView*'s Term Life Model.

Expenses

The Term Life Model calculates expenses attributable to each policy using percent of premium expenses, and a set expense per policy. The user can set the *first year* expense per policy and the *subsequent years* expense per policy. Expenses for the Term Life Model are calculated as follows:

Figure 6-15. Mortality table for *ExecuView's* Term Life Model.

From the 1975–80 Basic, Select, and Ultimate Table 3 for Males			
Age	**Mortality per 1,000**	**Age**	**Mortality per 1,000**
35	0.63	40	1.40
36	0.76	41	1.58
37	0.99	42	1.78
38	1.14	43	2.01
39	1.28	44	2.24

Source: *Reprinted, with permission, from Paquin, C.Y., "An Extension of the 1975–80 Basic Select and Ultimate Mortality Tables, Male and Female. Actuarial Note,* Transactions of the Society of Actuaries XXXVIII *(1986): 210–211. Copyright © 1987 by the Society of Actuaries.*

- *First year.* (1) Acquisition expenses calculated as 7.75 percent of the gross annual premium, plus (2) maintenance expenses of 4.75 percent of the gross annual premium, plus (3) premium taxes, licenses, and fees, calculated as 2.5 percent of the gross annual premium, plus (4) the *first year's* expense per policy set by the user.
- *Subsequent years.* (1) Maintenance expenses of 4.75 percent of gross annual premium, plus (2) premium taxes, licenses, and fees, calculated as 2.5 percent of the gross annual premium, plus (3) the *subsequent year's* expenses per policy defined by the user.

Commissions

ExecuView's Term Life Model allows users to enter a *first year* and a *renewal* commission rate. The *first year* commission rate is applied to the first year only. The *renewal* commission rate is applied to every year thereafter.

Lapse Rates

Life insurance products tend to experience their highest lapse rates in the first few policy years. After this initial period, lapse rates usually fluctuate at a much lower level. *ExecuView* demonstrates this typical trend in life insurance lapse rates by allowing users to enter an *initial* and a *final* lapse rate. The *initial* rate applies to the first policy year. This rate decreases steadily until policy Year 6 when it is equal to the *final* lapse rate. The lapse rate remains constant at this *final* rate for the remainder of the profit test period.

Policy Reserves

Users can select which of two possible methods—the net level method or the full preliminary term method—the Term Life Model will use to calculate policy reserves. Both methods calculate reserves assuming 4.5 percent interest and 1980 Commissioners Standard Ordinary (CSO) table mortality rates. A more thorough explanation of the methods insurance companies use to calculate reserves appears in Chapter 9 of this book. See Figure 6-16 for a list of the mortality figures used to calculate reserves for *ExecuView*'s Term and Whole Life Models. Figure 6-17 shows the net level and full preliminary term reserve amounts used by *ExecuView*'s Term Life Model.

Whole Life Insurance Model

A whole life insurance policy provides insurance coverage for a lifetime at a premium rate that is guaranteed not to increase once the policy has been purchased. As a result of the level premium approach, whole life insurance builds a savings element as time passes and

Figure 6-16. Reserve mortality rates for *ExecuView*'s Term and Whole Life Models.

From the 1980 Commissioners Standard Ordinary (CSO) Mortality Table					
Age	**Mortality per 1,000**	**Age**	**Mortality per 1,000**	**Age**	**Mortality per 1,000**
25	1.77	35	2.11	45	4.55
26	1.73	36	2.24	46	4.92
27	1.71	37	2.40	47	5.32
28	1.70	38	2.58	48	5.74
29	1.71	39	2.79	49	6.21
30	1.73	40	3.02	50	6.71
31	1.78	41	3.29	51	7.30
32	1.83	42	3.56	52	7.96
33	1.91	43	3.87	53	8.71
34	2.00	44	4.19	54	9.56

Source: *"Report of the Special Committee to Recommend New Mortality Tables for Valuation,"* Transactions of the Society of Actuaries XXXIII *(1981): 617–654.*

more premiums are paid. This savings element is called a policy's *cash value* and represents the policyowner's stake in the funds accumulated as policy reserves. When policyowners surrender whole life policies, they receive the cash value as a refund.

The product depicted in *ExecuView*'s whole life insurance model is a nonparticipating whole life product issued to male insureds at age 25. The cash value of each whole life policy is based on values calculated using the adjusted premium method, assuming 5.5 percent interest and 1980 CSO mortality. The profit test period for this product is 30 years, at the end of which time all surviving policies are assumed to lapse. It is common for asset-share models of whole life insurance products to assume that all policies lapse after 20 or 30 years.

All other assumptions in the Whole Life Model mirror those in the Term Life Model. Mortality rates for the Whole Life Model are shown in Figure 6-18, and end of year cash value amounts and net level and full preliminary term reserve amounts are shown in Figure 6-19.

Single-Premium Deferred Annuity Model

A single-premium deferred annuity (SPDA) is an annuity purchased with a single amount paid at least one period before the first annuity benefit payment becomes due. Because the amount paid to purchase the annuity accumulates interest for a certain period of time before the first benefit payment is made, a larger annual benefit is purchased

Figure 6-17. Reserve amounts for *ExecuView's* Term Life Model.

Policy year	Net level reserves	Full preliminary term reserves
1	0.81	0.00
2	1.52	0.79
3	2.11	1.46
4	2.55	1.98
5	2.80	2.31
6	2.83	2.43
7	2.59	2.29
8	2.07	1.86
9	1.22	1.11
10	0.00	0.00

than would be possible if the same amount of premium were used to purchase an immediate annuity. Deferred annuities allow policyowners to withdraw their account values during the accumulation period only, and generally a surrender charge applies to all withdrawals that occur during the early years of the policy.

Figure 6-18. Mortality rates used in *ExecuView's* Whole Life Model.

From the 1975–80 Basic Select and Ultimate Table					
Age	Mortality per 1,000	Age	Mortality per 1,000	Age	Mortality per 1,000
25	0.71	35	1.01	45	2.74
26	0.71	36	1.09	46	3.07
27	0.72	37	1.18	47	3.43
28	0.74	38	1.33	48	3.82
29	0.75	39	1.47	49	4.24
30	0.77	40	1.63	50	4.69
31	0.80	41	1.79	51	5.18
32	0.82	42	1.97	52	5.72
33	0.87	43	2.19	53	6.31
34	0.95	44	2.45	54	6.94

Source: *Reprinted with permission, from Paquin, C.Y., "An Extension of the 1975–80 Basic Select and Ultimate Mortality Tables, Male and Female. Actuarial Note,* Transactions of the Society of Actuaries XXXVIII *(1986): 210–211. Copyright © 1987 by the Society of Actuaries.*

Figure 6-19. End of year reserve and cash value amounts for *ExecuView's* Whole Life Model.

Policy year	Cash value	Net level reserve	Full preliminary term reserve	Policy year	Cash value	Net level reserve	Full preliminary term reserve
1	0.00	6.07	0.00	16	130.29	135.58	130.29
2	0.00	12.47	6.44	17	141.49	146.70	141.49
3	0.00	19.18	13.19	18	152.99	158.14	152.99
4	8.55	26.22	20.27	19	164.80	169.87	164.80
5	15.80	33.58	27.68	20	176.92	181.92	176.92
6	23.01	41.27	35.41	21	189.35	194.27	189.35
7	35.01	49.26	43.45	22	202.10	206.94	202.10
8	44.01	57.59	51.83	23	215.17	219.94	215.17
9	57.41	66.22	60.52	24	228.58	233.26	228.58
10	69.54	75.19	69.54	25	242.31	246.92	242.31
11	78.88	84.47	78.88	26	256.38	260.90	256.38
12	88.54	94.07	88.54	27	270.75	275.18	270.75
13	98.51	103.99	98.51	28	285.40	289.74	285.40
14	108.80	114.21	108.80	29	300.30	304.55	300.30
15	119.39	124.74	119.39	30	315.43	319.58	315.43

ExecuView's Single-Premium Deferred Annuity Model depicts an annuity product with a single $100,000 premium paid by a group of males at age 50. The annuity accumulates for a period of 15 years and then becomes payable as a life annuity with a 10-year period certain. A life annuity continues to provide periodic benefits for at least the life of the annuitant. A *period certain* is a period over which the insurer guarantees to make benefit payments whether or not the annuitant is still alive. Many insurers would only model the accumulation period of a deferred annuity product such as this one because nearly all contract owners generally withdraw from such products before the payout period begins.

Mortality Rates

Mortality rates for the SPDA and Immediate Annuity Models are taken from the 1983 Basic Table for annuities. During the accumulation period, deaths result in policy surrenders. Figure 6-20 shows the mortality rates used in the SPDA and Immediate Annuity Models.

Cash Values, Annual Benefits, and Reserves

During the accumulation period, the product depicted in the SPDA Model accumulates cash value at a crediting rate equal to the current

Figure 6-20. Mortality rates used in *ExecuView's* SPDA and Immediate Annuity Models.

From the 1983 Basic Table for annuities					
Age	**Mortality per 1,000**	**Age**	**Mortality per 1,000**	**Age**	**Mortality per 1,000**
50	4.52	65	14.25	80	63.12
51	4.94	66	15.76	81	69.52
52	5.37	67	17.47	82	76.55
53	5.81	68	19.37	83	84.23
54	6.26	69	21.49	84	92.50
55	6.72	70	23.81	85	101.26
56	7.18	71	26.35	86	110.42
57	7.66	72	29.12	87	119.89
58	8.15	73	32.12	88	129.61
59	8.67	74	35.40	89	139.64
60	9.27	75	38.99	90	150.10
61	9.96	76	42.93	91	161.08
62	10.79	77	47.27	92	172.70
63	11.77	78	52.05	93	185.05
64	12.92	79	57.33	94	198.22

Source: *Reprinted, with permission, from "Report of the Committee to Recommend a New Mortality Basis for Individual Annuity Valuation (Derivation of the 1983 Table a),"* Transactions of the Society of Actuaries *XXXIII (1981): 695. Copyright © 1982 by the Society of Actuaries.*

interest rate minus the number entered in the *Interest Margin* cell, but with a minimum guaranteed crediting rate of 4 percent. Thus, if the interest rate is 6 percent and the interest margin is 150 basis points, the crediting rate will be 4.5 percent. However, if the current interest rate is 5 percent while the interest margin is 150 basis points, the crediting rate will be the minimum guaranteed rate of 4 percent.

A surrender penalty of 7 percent applies to withdrawals in the first accumulation year. This penalty decreases 1 percentage point each year for 7 years. Starting in Year 8, surrender charges no longer apply. No penalties apply to a surrender resulting from the death of an annuitant. During the accumulation period, reserves equal cash values. During the payout period, reserves are calculated using Table *a* mortality rates and a 5.75 percent interest rate.

At the beginning of the first year of the payout period (the *16th* policy year), *ExecuView* calculates the cost of a $1 life annuity with a 10-year period certain, based on the mortality rates in the model and the crediting interest rate from the 15th policy year. *ExecuView* then calculates the amount of annual benefits that each surviving contract owner's account value can purchase. In this way the model calculates the annual benefits that are payable through the life of the payout period.

Lapse Rates

Annuity products with surrender charges, such as the one illustrated in *ExecuView*'s Single-Premium Deferred Annuity Model, tend to experience very low withdrawal rates as long as surrender charges apply. Once surrender charges no longer apply, lapse rates increase markedly.[1] At the end of the accumulation period, during the last year lapses are allowed, many deferred annuities experience even greater withdrawal activity.

ExecuView adheres to real-world trends in deferred annuity lapse rates in the way it allows users to set three lapse rates—an *initial,* a *middle,* and a *final* lapse rate. The *initial* rate is applied during the first seven years of the accumulation period. In the eighth year, the first year no surrender charges apply, the *middle* rate is used to calculate the number of policyowners withdrawing. From accumulation Year 9 until accumulation Year 14, one-half of the *middle* rate is applied to calculate the number of lapses. The *final* rate applies only in the 15th accumulation year, the last year lapses are allowed by the product.

Expenses

The Single-Premium Deferred Annuity Model applies user-defined *first year* expenses to the first year and user-defined *subsequent years* expenses to every year thereafter. No percent of premium expense is assumed.

Commissions

The commission rate the user sets applies to the initial $100,000 premium only. No renewal commissions are applied.

Immediate Annuity Model

In contrast to a deferred annuity, an immediate annuity begins paying benefits exactly one period after the initial premium is paid. *ExecuView*'s Immediate Annuity Model depicts a straight life annuity (one with no period certain) purchased at age 65. The first benefit payment is paid at the end of the first year, and all subsequent benefits are also paid at the end of the year. The assumptions in this model are the same as those in the Single-Premium Deferred Annuity Model except for the following differences:

- The cost of benefits is calculated at the beginning of the first policy year.
- There is no period certain.

- The initial $100,000 premium is used to purchase the annuity before the premium accumulates any interest.
- The product prohibits withdrawals.
- The crediting rate is implicit in the calculation of the annual payment and thus remains constant for the life of the contract.
- Benefits are paid at the end of the year.

Aggregate Model

ExecuView's Aggregate Model functions differently from the four product models. The purpose of this model is to provide a "company-wide" picture of profitability based on the profitability of the four products in the product models. The Aggregate Model assumes that a total of 400,000 policies are sold at the beginning of the profit test period. The user can control the portion of these 400,000 policies that are attributable to each product by entering a *% of policies sold* for each product. For example, if a user wants the model to assume that 50,000 whole life policies are sold, the user would enter 12.5 percent for *% of policies sold, whole life.* Based on the percentages that users enter, *ExecuView*'s Aggregate Model calculates the total net cash flows, IRR, and NPV of all four products. The Aggregate Model also displays the percentage of aggregate assets attributable to each of the four products.

The Effects of Changes in Product Assumptions

As mathematical approximations of real-world processes, models inevitably simplify the processes they attempt to recreate. The processes that determine the profitability of a real-world insurance product are extremely complex and almost impossible to predict accurately. Often, a change in one factor causes changes in many others. For example, an increase in the premium of an insurance product would most likely result in reduced sales and higher lapse rates. Asset-share models do not generally account for such interrelationships automatically. Generally an asset-share model would only show an increase in income as a result of the increase in premium and not the loss of potential income that might be experienced in the real world. The projections made by asset-share models will almost never exactly reflect the behavior of a product being marketed. However, asset-share models, when coupled with other forecasting techniques that make up for the limitations of asset-share models, can be used to predict what is likely to happen if a given set of circumstances occurs.

In this section we explain the effect on profitability of changes in certain user-defined assumptions in asset-share models. Our discussion refers to *ExecuView* for examples. The exact effects of the changes in assumptions that are discussed in this section only apply to the *ExecuView* models in which these effects are demonstrated. This section discusses each assumption in isolation, though in the real world all assumptions affect one another. Each of the general *trends* we discuss—for example, a trend showing that a decrease in gross premium results in a lower profit margin—shows part of the complex real-world picture. By understanding the effect that changes in each assumption have in isolation, insurers can better predict the outcome when many interrelated changes are combined.

If you would like to use *ExecuView* to test the scenarios in this section on your own computer, be sure to reset the models before each scenario by selecting "Reset, All Models" from the Action menu.

Changes in Premium

As you might expect, higher premiums in life insurance product models result in higher profit margins, higher internal rates of return, and earlier validation points, whereas lower premiums generally result in lower profit margins, lower IRRs, and later validation points. However, keep in mind that asset-share models do not automatically demonstrate the effect that higher premiums have on product sales. A premium rate that shows increased or excessive profits might be priced too high to result in many sales.

Asset-share models show the sensitivity of insurance products' profits to even moderate changes in premium. Figure 6-21 shows the effect that various premium rates have on *ExecuView*'s Term Life Model. Scenario 1 in the figure shows that when the term model is set to its default premium assumption of $1.80 per $1,000 of face value, the model shows modest but acceptable profitability, with a profit margin of 3.76 percent and a validation period of eight years. A slight decrease in the premium to $1.69 in Scenario 2 causes the product to become unprofitable. Increases in premium show a similar sensitivity in Scenarios 3 and 4.

Changes in Interest Margin

As with changes in premium, increases in the interest margin in an asset-share model cause increases in profitability as reflected by the model's profit measures, and decreases in the interest margin cause decreases in profitability. Insurers must be careful that, in an effort to increase profitability, they do not set interest margins too high, because a product with too high an interest margin will have trouble attracting new customers. The effect that a change in interest margin

Figure 6-21. Effects on profit measures resulting from various changes in gross premium for *ExecuView*'s Term Life Model.

Scenario 1	
Gross premium	**$1.80**
Validation year	8
Net present value	$3,546,509
Internal rate of return	13.51%
Profit margin	3.76%

Scenario 2	
Gross premium	**$1.69**
Validation year	N/A
Net present value	–$709,837
Internal rate of return	5.23%
Profit margin	–0.80%

Scenario 3	
Gross premium	**$1.95**
Validation year	6
Net present value	$9,350,629
Internal rate of return	25.51%
Profit margin	9.15%

Scenario 4	
Gross premium	**$2.05**
Validation year	5
Net present value	$13,220,034
Internal rate of return	34.16%
Profit margin	12.31%

has on an asset-share model is greatly affected by any guarantees in the crediting rate that are built into the model. For example, *ExecuView*'s Single-Premium Deferred Annuity Model contains a guaranteed minimum crediting rate of 4 percent. No matter how high the interest margin assumption is set, the crediting rate will never be lower than 4 percent.

Figure 6-22 shows the effect that various interest margins have on the profitability of *ExecuView*'s SPDA product when the interest rate starts at 7.5 percent and declines each year. Notice that the results when the interest margin is 350 basis points (bp) (Scenario 3) are the same as when the interest margin is 400 bp (Scenario 4). The reason is that an interest margin of 350 bp creates a crediting rate of 4 percent (or 7.5% – 350 bp = 4 percent), the minimum crediting rate guaranteed by the product. Any interest margin greater than 350 bp would still produce a crediting rate of 4 percent, and thus would show the same results as the 350 bp interest margin. The high IRR and profit margin that an interest margin of 350 bp yields show that this margin is probably too high to attract many customers.

Changes in Interest Rates

The effect that changes in interest rates have on profitability varies greatly depending on the type of product being modeled. As a general rule, products that maintain more assets for longer periods of time

Figure 6-22. Changes in interest margin in *ExecuView's* SPDA Model.

Scenario 1	
Interest margin	150 bp
Validation year	7
Net present value	$648,300,061
Internal rate of return	19.15%
Profit margin	6.48%

Scenario 2	
Interest margin	80 bp
Validation year	N/A
Net present value	–$22,064,454
Internal rate of return	5.94%
Profit margin	–0.22%

Scenario 3	
Interest margin	350 bp
Validation year	3
Net present value	$1,360,468,031
Internal rate of return	52.81%
Profit margin	13.60%

Scenario 4	
Interest margin	400 bp
Validation year	3
Net present value	$1,360,468,031
Internal rate of return	52.81%
Profit margin	13.60%

will be more greatly affected by fluctuations in interest rates. Another general rule is that higher interest rates will show increased profitability in asset-share models, and lower interest rates show decreased profitability. In the real world, however, higher interest rates can actually decrease profitability because of *disintermediation.* As we discussed in Chapter 3, disintermediation is a process in which customers remove money from a financial intermediary. Disintermediation can occur because, when interest rates are high, traditional insurance products often do not offer yields as high as other financial products. Asset-share models generally do not automatically account for the effects of disintermediation, nor do asset-share models account for the effect that changes in market interest rates might have on the value of an insurer's existing assets.

Figure 6-23 shows the effect of various interest scenarios on the profitability of *ExecuView's* four product models. The Term Life Model, which involves relatively small amounts of invested assets, shows moderate sensitivity to changes in interest rates, with a profit margin of 3.76 percent under falling rates, 4.18 percent under level rates, and 4.57 percent under rising rates. The Whole Life Model, with much larger and longer-term assets, shows a strong sensitivity to interest rates, with a 7.64 percent profit margin under falling interest rates, 15.67 percent under level rates, and 21.57 percent under rising interest rates. The Immediate Annuity Model, with even larger assets, shows a similar sensitivity to changes in interest rates, with a 2.35 percent profit margin under falling rates, 9.39 percent under level rates, and 15.10 percent under rising rates.

Because the Single-Premium Deferred Annuity Model has the greatest amount of assets of all four models, you might expect it to increase in profitability the most as interest rates increase. However, as Figure 6-23 shows, such is not the case. The deferred annuity's profit margin actually *decreases* when interest rates rise. The reason for this opposite effect has to do with the way the product applies the interest margin to produce a crediting rate. During the accumulation period, the amount of interest credited to contract owners varies with the interest rate. Thus, when interest rates are higher, contract owners earn more interest and accumulate larger account values. The larger account values can then purchase a greater amount of annual benefits. As a result, the insurer pays out more in benefits when interest rates are higher. In fact, the insurer pays out a greater percentage of its assets in benefits and surrenders when interest rates are higher. Although the *amount* of profit the insurer earns on the SPDA product increases as interest rates rise, the *profit margin* (or the present value of profits as a percentage of present value of premium) decreases. Not all deferred annuities will necessarily show a decreased profit margin in the wake of rising interest rates.

Figure 6-23. The effects of interest rates on profitability in *ExecuView's* four product models.

Interest Rates Starting at 7.5%, Falling 0.222% per Year			
Product model	Validation year	Profit margin	Annual benefit
Term Life	8	3.76%	
Whole Life	5	7.64%	
Immediate Annuity	12	2.35%	$ 94.53
Deferred Annuity	7	6.48%	$150.49
Interest Rates Level at 7.5%			
Term Life	8	4.18%	
Whole Life	5	15.67%	
Immediate Annuity	6	9.39%	$ 94.53
Deferred Annuity	7	6.39%	$211.91
Interest Rates Starting at 7.5%, Rising 0.222% per Year			
Term Life	8	4.57%	
Whole Life	5	21.57%	
Immediate Annuity	5	15.10%	$ 94.53
Deferred Annuity	7	6.24%	$292.35

Figure 6-24. Changing mortality rates in *ExecuView*'s Whole Life and Immediate Annuity Models.

Whole Life Model			
% of mortality table	**85.00%**	**% of mortality table**	**95.00%**
Validation year	5	Validation year	6
Net present value	$34,535,285	Net present value	$29,187,407
Internal rate of return	24.44%	Internal rate of return	21.46%
Profit margin	7.64%	Profit margin	6.46%
Immediate Annuity Model			
% of mortality table	**100.00%**	**% of mortality table**	**110.00%**
Validation year	12	Validation year	8
Net present value	$234,537,600	Net present value	$481,218,000
Internal rate of return	11.81%	Internal rate of return	16.81%
Profit margin	2.35%	Profit margin	4.81%

Changes in Mortality Rates

A change in the mortality assumption of an insurance product will have a different effect on profitability depending on the type of product in question. For life products, as mortality rates increase, more policyowners will die each year and thus the insurer will have to pay a greater number of benefits. As a result, increasing mortality for a life product causes a decrease in profitability.

Changes in mortality assumptions have the opposite effect on annuity products. As mortality rates increase and more annuitants die, the number of benefit payments an insurer makes each year decreases. The result of this is an increase in profitability. Figure 6-24 compares the effect of a 10 percent increase in mortality rates in *ExecuView*'s Whole Life and Immediate Annuity Models.

Changes in Expense Rates

Insurers often try to improve the profitability of insurance products by reducing their expenses. Asset-share models can demonstrate how even a slight adjustment in an expense rate can have a powerful effect on profitability. As expenses come down, profitability can improve dramatically, and as expenses increase, profitability can suffer. Figure 6-25 shows the profitability of *ExecuView*'s Term Life Model under various expense scenarios.

Figure 6-25. The effect of changes in expense rates on *ExecuView's* Term Life Model.

Scenario 1	
First-year expenses	**$0.50**
Subsequent years	**$0.25**
Validation year	8
Net present value	$3,546,509
Internal rate of return	13.51%
Profit margin	3.76%

Scenario 2	
First-year expenses	**$0.60**
Subsequent years	**$0.35**
Validation year	N/A
Net present value	–$1,692,134
Internal rate of return	3.54%
Profit margin	–1.79%

Scenario 3	
First-year expenses	**$0.48**
Subsequent years	**$0.20**
Validation year	7
Net present value	$5,865,831
Internal rate of return	18.28%
Profit margin	6.22%

Scenario 4	
First-year expenses	**$0.42**
Subsequent years	**$0.18**
Validation year	7
Net present value	$7,313,560
Internal rate of return	22.01%
Profit margin	7.76%

Changes in Commission Rates

Not all insurance products involve commission payments. Among those products that pay commissions, commission rates are generally set by the insurance company or in some instances may be negotiated with an agency or broker. Sudden, drastic changes in commission rates would likely cause friction between the insurance company and its sales force, so insurers are always cautious when adjusting commission rates.

As would be expected, asset-share models show improved profitability as commission rates are lowered and show poorer profitability as commission rates increase. In the real world, the relationship between commission rates and profitability is more complex. A well-compensated sales force is likely to sell more products than a sales force that is less well compensated. However, there is a limit to how much increasing commissions can improve sales. After a certain point, increased commissions will have no positive effect on product sales. An insurer must strike the right balance between the maximum level of sales that can be generated and the level of commissions that must be paid to generate maximum sales.

Figure 6-26 shows the effect of several different commission schedules on *ExecuView's* Whole Life Model.

Figure 6-26. The effect of changes in commission rates on *ExecuView*'s Whole Life Model.

Scenario 1	
First-year commission	**90.00%**
Renewal commission	**5.00%**
Validation year	5
Net present value	$34,535,285
Internal rate of return	24.44%
Profit margin	7.64%

Scenario 2	
First-year commission	**75.00%**
Renewal commission	**5.00%**
Validation year	4
Net present value	$46,085,286
Internal rate of return	53.65%
Profit margin	10.20%

Scenario 3	
First-year commission	**100.00%**
Renewal commission	**4.00%**
Validation year	7
Net present value	$30,585,158
Internal rate of return	18.44%
Profit margin	6.77%

Scenario 4	
First-year commission	**55.00%**
Renewal commission	**6.00%**
Validation year	1
Net present value	$57,735,414
Internal rate of return	Infeasible
Profit margin	12.77%

Changes in Lapse Rates

The relationship between lapse rates and profitability is extremely complex. In general, higher lapse rates reduce profitability, though this is not always the case. The effect that a given change in lapse rate assumptions in an asset-share model has on profitability is in large part determined by whether this change is in an early policy year or a later policy year. As we have discussed, most insurance products maintain a net loss for the first several years after issue, until the validation or break-even point. Policies that lapse before the validation point will never pay off the insurer's initial investment in them. Policies that lapse after the validation point have made a net contribution to the insurer's capital and surplus. For this reason, high lapse rates during the validation period have more of a negative effect on profitability than the same lapse rates in later policy years. Figure 6-27 shows the effects of high lapse rates in the early and in the later product years on *ExecuView*'s SPDA Model. In Scenarios 1 and 3, the highest lapse rates occur late in the profit test period, and the product's profit measures demonstrate high profitability. The highest lapse rates in Scenarios 2 and 4 are early in the profit test period and the product shows poor profitability.

Figure 6-27. The effect of changes in lapse rates in *ExecuView*'s SPDA Model.

Scenario 1	
Initial lapse rate	**2.00%**
Middle lapse rate	**20.00%**
Final lapse rate	**50.00%**
Validation year	7
Net present value	$648,300,061
Internal rate of return	19.15%
Profit margin	6.48%

Scenario 2	
Initial lapse rate	**50.00%**
Middle lapse rate	**20.00%**
Final lapse rate	**2.00%**
Validation year	N/A
Net present value	–$5,334,763
Internal rate of return	6.21%
Profit margin	–0.05%

Scenario 3	
Initial lapse rate	**20.00%**
Middle lapse rate	**90.00%**
Final lapse rate	**45.00%**
Validation year	7
Net present value	$50,758,243
Internal rate of return	10.23%
Profit margin	0.51%

Scenario 4	
Initial lapse rate	**45.00%**
Middle lapse rate	**40.00%**
Final lapse rate	**20.00%**
Validation year	N/A
Net present value	–$532,627
Internal rate of return	6.96%
Profit margin	–0.01%

Changes in Reserve Valuation Methods

Insurers have many ways to calculate policy reserves for insurance products. Some methods result in higher reserve amounts, some result in lower reserve amounts. A product's net cash flows will be the same in the end regardless of the reserve valuation method chosen. However, the reserve valuation method has a pronounced effect on the timing of a product's *earnings.*

ExecuView's Whole Life and Term Life Models allow for two possible reserve valuation methods—the *net level reserve valuation method,* and the *full preliminary term reserve valuation method.* For any given policy year, the net level method produces a higher reserve amount than does the full preliminary term method. Figure 6-28 compares the profitability of *ExecuView*'s Whole Life Model under these two valuation methods. The net level method results in a product that (1) validates later and (2) produces a lower IRR than does the full preliminary term method. Notice, however, that under both methods the net cash flow, net present value, and profit margin are exactly the same. Reserve valuation methods and the many factors

Figure 6-28. Comparing reserve valuation methods in *ExecuView's* Whole Life Model.

Full Preliminary Term Method	
Validation year	5
Net present value	$34,535,285
Internal rate of return	24.44%
Profit margin	7.64%
Net cash flow	$189,206,454

Net Level Method	
Validation year	9
Net present value	$34,535,285
Internal rate of return	13.05%
Profit margin	7.64%
Net cash flow	$189,206,454

that influence insurers' decisions regarding which reserve valuation method to use are explained in detail in Chapter 9.

Changes in Multiple Assumptions

While asset-share models can be used to test the effects of changes in a single assumption, insurers more often use asset-share models to test whole sets of assumptions, or scenarios. By testing changes in multiple assumptions and incorporating forecasts about the way assumptions are likely to affect one another, insurers can more accurately picture the way an insurance product is likely to behave once it is marketed.

When insurers develop new products, they must establish minimum profit objectives that they require their products to achieve under a variety of circumstances. Using typical insurance industry standards, we have created profit objectives for each of the four *ExecuView* product models. As you try the *ExecuView* scenarios in this book, keep these objectives in mind. A product that fails to achieve its profit objectives could adversely affect an insurance company's solvency. The profit objectives for the four *ExecuView* products are listed in Figure 6-29.

Figure 6-29. Profit objectives for *ExecuView's* product models.

	Ranges of acceptable values:		
Profit test	**10-Year Term Life**	**Whole Life**	**SPDA & SPIA**
Validation year	4th to 8th	4th to 10th	2nd to 15th
IRR	12% to 20%	12% to 25%	10% to 25%
Profit margin	3% to 12%	2% to 15%	1½% to 10%

The following scenario shows how multiple assumptions can be tested together to price a new insurance product. Although we have simplified the process of asset-share analysis somewhat, the *ExecuView* models and the following example provide a basic overview of how companies use asset-share models when pricing products. If you have access to a computer that can run *ExecuView*, we suggest that you follow this example on your computer. If you do not have access to *ExecuView*, you may follow the example by reading along and examining the *ExecuView* screens that show the results of the changes in assumptions. Special instructions for *ExecuView* users will be preceded by the ➢ symbol.

Scenario: Pricing an Insurance Product Using an Asset-Share Model

Suppose the EV Life Insurance Company is in the process of developing a new insurance product. Certain basic assumptions have already been established for this product. It is to be a 10-year level-premium term life product that the company hopes to market to higher-than-average-risk individuals. Also, some profit objectives have been established for this product. It should validate in four to eight years, show an internal rate of return of 12 to 20 percent, and earn a profit margin of 3 to 12 percent. If the product does not meet these objectives, it will not be considered successful.

➢ If you wish to demonstrate this example on your computer, start *ExecuView* and select the Term Life Model. Be sure to select *Reset, All Models* from the Action menu to return *ExecuView* to its default settings.

To aid in the development of this product, EV Life has created an asset-share model. A set of assumptions has been entered into the asset-share model as a suggested starting point for pricing this product. Figure 6-30, an *ExecuView* screen shot, shows these basic assumptions and the profitability results projected by EV Life's asset-share model.

The gross annual premium for the term life product suggested in the model is $1.80 per $1,000 of face value; the model assumes a mortality rate of 85 percent of the rates contained in the 1975-80 Basic Select and Ultimate table. Because EV Life intends to market this product to higher-than-average risk individuals, it is necessary to increase the mortality rates in the model. A rate of 150 percent of the Basic Select and Ultimate table has been suggested. With such a high mortality assumption, it will no longer be necessary to have insurance applicants take a medical examination. By not requiring a medical examination, EV Life can reduce the first-year expenses for this product. According to the accounting department, this change should

Figure 6-30. Default assumptions for *ExecuView's* Term Life Model.

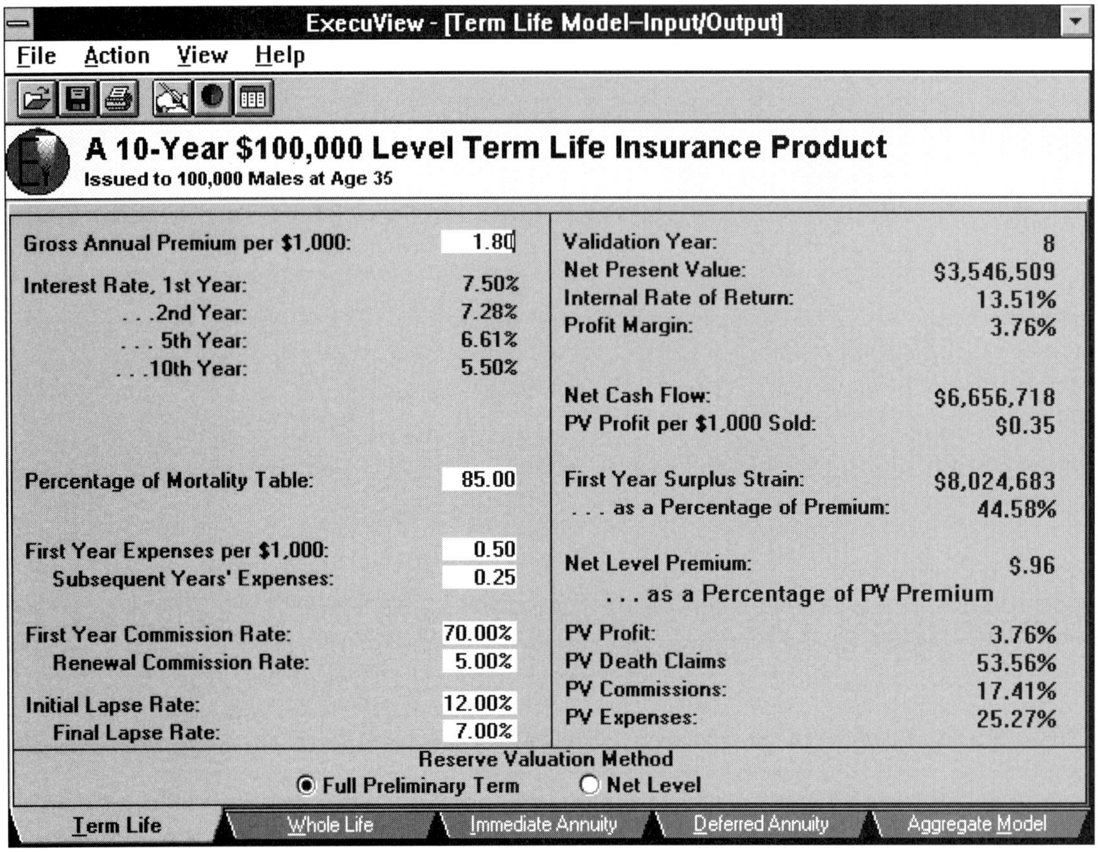

permit EV Life to reduce the model's assumption for first-year expenses to $0.35 per $1,000 of face value.

> Use the <tab> key or your mouse to highlight the *Percentage of Mortality Table* cell. Set this assumption to 150%. Now select the *First Year Expenses* cell and change this value to 0.35. Hit the <enter> key to view the results of these changes.

The asset-share model shows that these changes in assumptions result in a product that loses money for 10 years. Figure 6-31 shows the annual cash flows the product experiences using these assumptions. Notice in the graph that surplus is always negative and that by the end of the 10-year term the product has lost more than $60 million.

> Click on the Chart icon at the top of the screen to view the outcome of this scenario in a graphical form. To return to the input/output screen, click on the I/O icon.

It is apparent that the gross annual premium for this product should be higher than $1.80 per $1,000 of face value. To compensate for the higher mortality assumption, EV Life tries raising the gross annual premium per $1,000 in the asset-share model to $2.50. The marketing department expects the initial lapse rate to be 2 percentage points higher because of this change in premium.

> Change the *Gross Annual Premium* to $2.50. Change the *Initial Lapse Rate* to 14%. Hit the <enter> key to view the results of these changes.

Despite the higher premium, the product is still losing money, experiencing a profit margin of –4.99 percent, so EV Life raises the gross annual premium in the model again, this time to $3.00.

> Change the *Gross Annual Premium* to $3.00. Hit the <enter> key to view the results of this change.

Figure 6-31. Chart from *ExecuView's* Term Life Model.

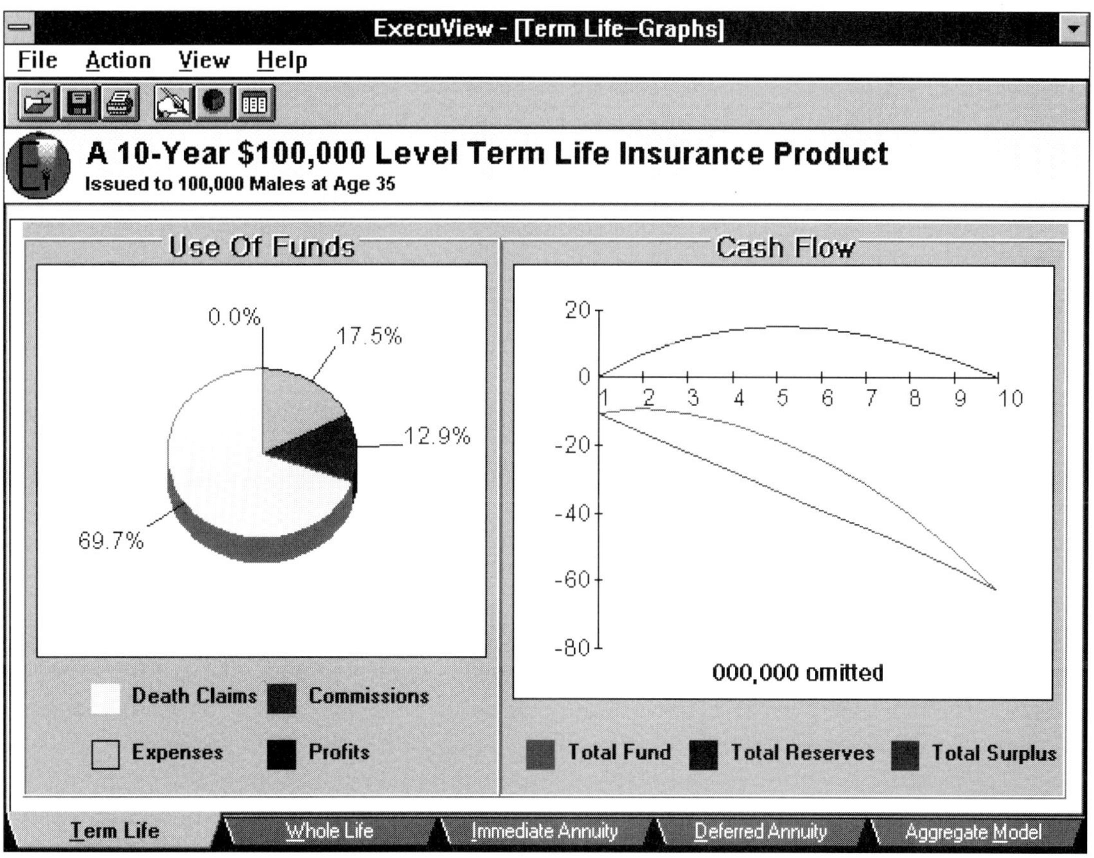

With this premium, the product shows a substantial profit, with an IRR of nearly 45 percent and a profit margin greater than 8 percent. However, the marketing department indicates that $3.00 per $1,000 of coverage is too high a premium for the product to sell well. Eventually, it is decided that the product will have a gross premium of $2.78. The marketing department expects that, with this premium, the initial and final lapse rates for this product will be 15 percent and 8 percent, respectively.

➢ Change the *Gross Annual Premium* to $2.78, the *Initial Lapse Rate* to 15%, and the *Final Lapse Rate* to 8%. Hit the <enter> key to view the results of these changes.

These latest changes cause the product to meet its profit objectives. The assumptions and outcome for this new term life product are summarized in Figure 6-32.

Figure 6-32. Results of *ExecuView* term life scenario.

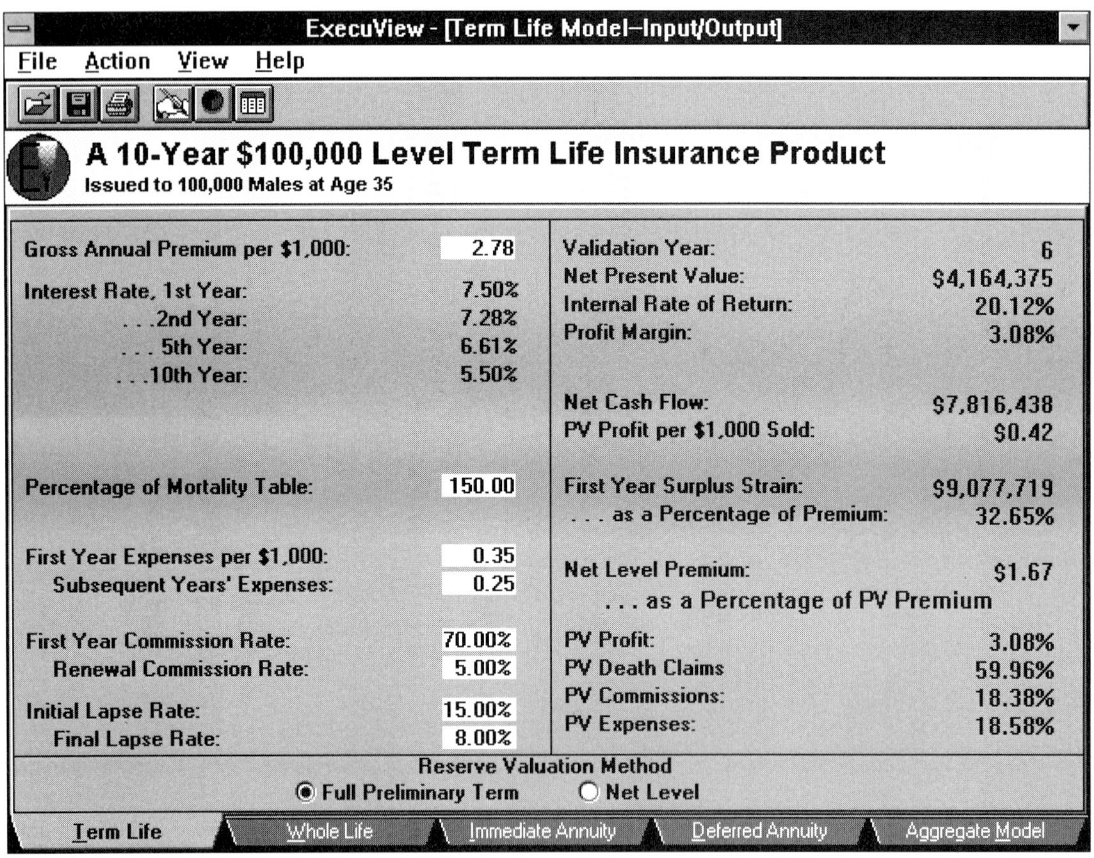

In Conclusion

In this chapter we showed some of the ways that profit measures can be used to measure the effects of changes in the assumptions in asset-share models. In addition, we described the assumptions that underlie the five *ExecuView* models. Later chapters of this book contain a number of *ExecuView* scenarios much like those illustrated in this chapter. These scenarios illustrate key points about profitability and product pricing. To learn more about how *ExecuView* can illustrate the profitability of insurance products under changing conditions, read *ExecuView* Application 6-1 (which begins on the next page) and, if you have *ExecuView* loaded into a computer, apply the example to the appropriate model.

Key Terms and Concepts

asset-share model
asset share
net cash flows
earnings
initial investment
decision criterion
payback period
break-even point
validation point
net present value (NPV)
internal rate of return (IRR)
profit margin
user-defined assumptions
fixed assumptions
crediting rate
basis points
interest margin

Reference

1. Samuel H. Cox, Paul D. Laporte, Steven R. Linney, and Lucian Lombardi, "Single-Premium Deferred Annuity Persistency Study," *Transactions of the Society of Actuaries*, 1991–92 Reports, p. 290.

Application 6-1 Pricing a Deferred Annuity

If you wish to demonstrate this example on your computer, start *ExecuView* and select the Single-Premium Deferred Annuity Model. Be sure to select *Reset, All Models* from the Action menu to return *ExecuView* to its default settings. The default assumptions and profitability outcome for this model are shown on the following *ExecuView* screen.

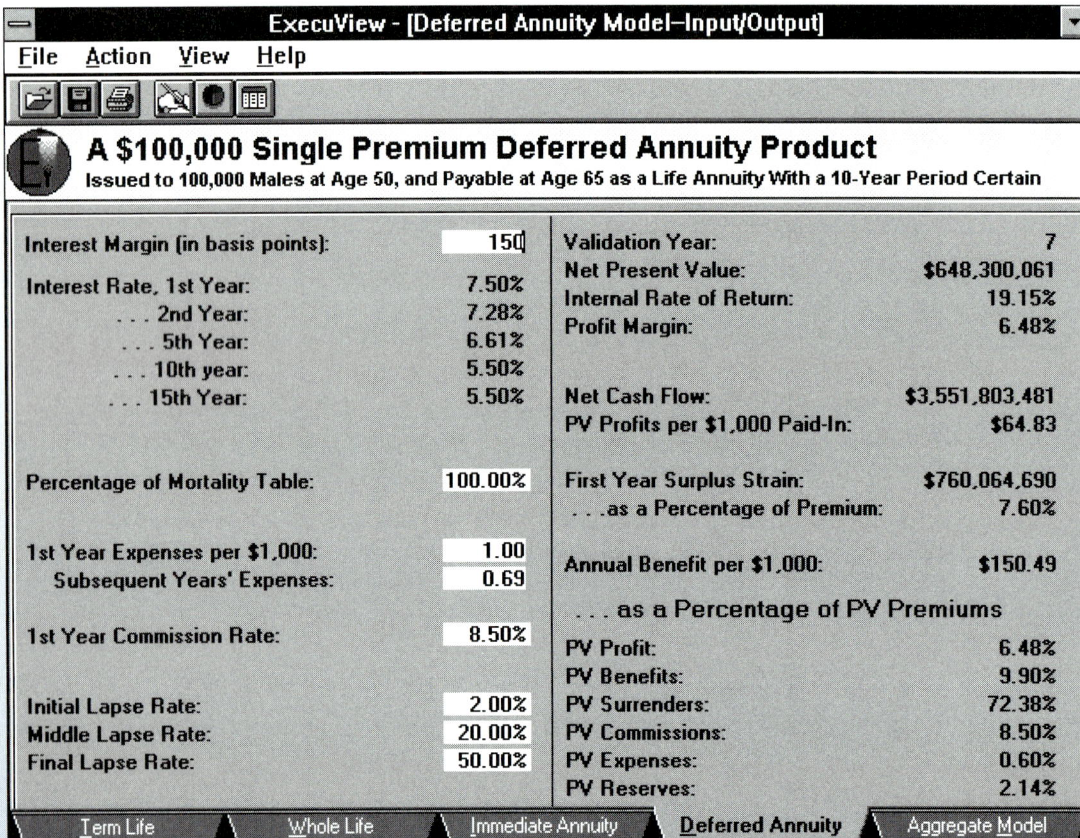

The EV Life Insurance Company is developing a new single-premium deferred annuity product that it plans to market to males in their early fifties. This product will have a 15-year accumulation period, and become payable as a life annuity with a 10-year period certain. The minimum crediting rate EV Life plans to offer on this product is 4 percent. The profit objectives for this product are a validation period of between 2 and 15 years, an internal rate of return between 10 and 25 percent, and a profit margin between 1½ and 10 percent.

EV Life is trying to establish the crediting rate it will offer on this product. Originally, the product was expected to offer a crediting rate 150 basis points below the rate EV Life actually earns on its investments. However, it is now the desire of the marketing department to make this product more competitive by decreasing the interest margin, thereby increasing the interest rate credited to EV Life's customers. As an experiment, EV Life decreases the interest margin in its asset-share model by 55 basis points to 95 (thus increasing the crediting rate by 0.55 percentage points).

(continued on next page)

Application 6-1 Pricing a Deferred Annuity *(continued)*

➤ Set the *Interest Margin* to 95 basis points. Hit the <enter> key to view the results of this change.

When the interest margin is thus reduced, EV Life's asset-share model shows a validation period of 14 years, an IRR of 8.87 percent, and a profit margin of 1.26 percent. The product no longer meets its profit objectives. If EV Life introduced the deferred annuity product to the market using this pricing strategy it would be in danger of suffering a loss if conditions were even slightly different from EV Life's forecasts. Making a few adjustments, EV Life's actuaries suggest an interest margin of 115 bp, which allows the product to meet its profit objectives. The profitability results of this interest margin, as demonstrated by EV Life's asset-share model, are shown in the following *ExecuView* screen.

➤ Set the *Interest Margin* to 115. Press the <enter> key to see the results of this change.

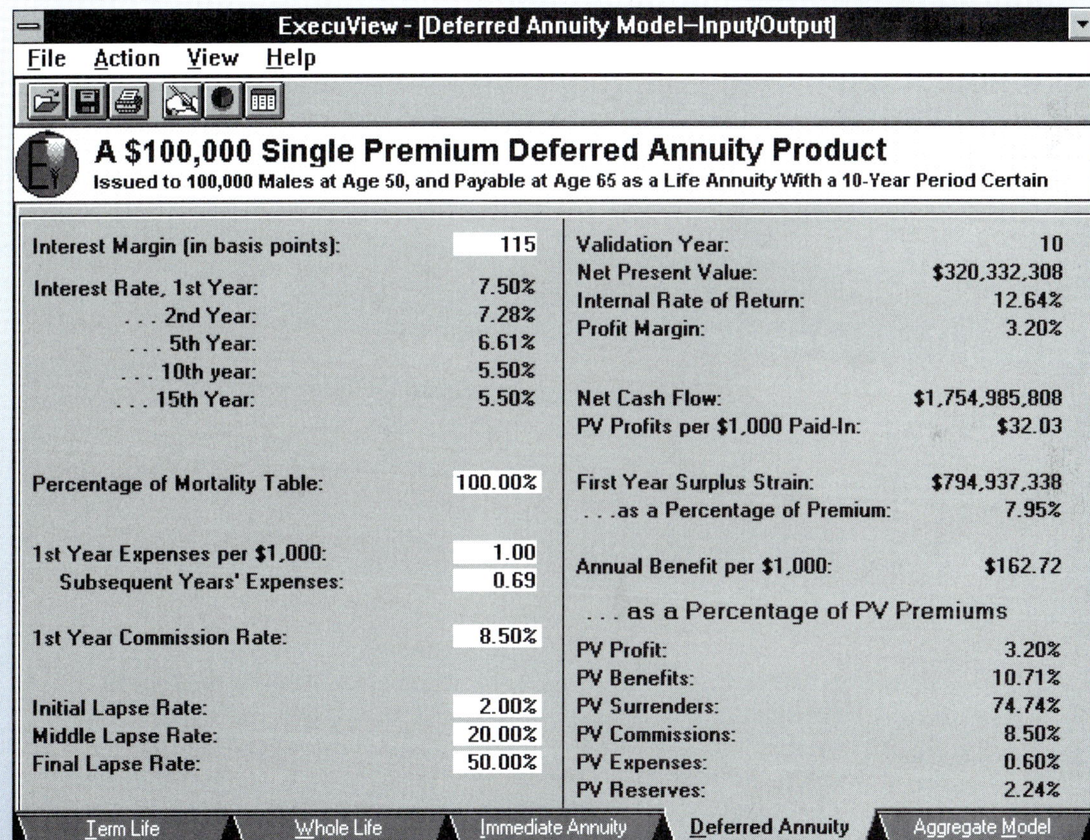

(*continued on next page*)

Application 6-1 Pricing a Deferred Annuity *(continued)*

After an interest margin is settled upon, new information becomes available about the mortality experience of EV Life's annuity products. It seems that annuitants are living longer than expected, so to compensate, EV Life needs to decrease the mortality rate in its asset-share model by at least 15 percent. Also, the latest persistency studies that EV Life's research staff can find suggest that the middle lapse rate assumption (which shows the percentage of contract owners withdrawing as soon as surrender penalties expire) is too low by at least 20 percentage points. The same studies indicate that final lapse rates (which reflect the percentage of contract owners withdrawing just before the payout period begins) are currently close to 55 percent, and initial lapse rates (which reflect the percentage of contract owners withdrawing each year that surrender charges apply) are around 4 percent.

> Set the *Percentage of Mortality Table* to 85%. Change the *Initial Lapse Rate* assumption to 4%, the *Middle Lapse Rate* to 35%, and the *Final Lapse Rate* to 55%. Hit the <enter> key to view the results of these changes.

As a result of these changed assumptions, the annuity product no longer meets its profit objectives. The validation point, at Year 10, is acceptable. IRR and profit margin, however, have fallen below profit objectives, to 9.89 percent and 1.25 percent, respectively. EV Life again increases the interest margin until the profit factors fall within an acceptable range. This time EV Life decides on a margin of 130 bp.

> Set the *Interest Margin* to 130. Press the <enter> key to view the results of this change.

The profitability outcome projected by EV Life's asset-share model is shown in the following *ExecuView* screen.

(continued on next page)

Application 6-1 Pricing a Deferred Annuity *(continued)*

ExecuView - [Deferred Annuity Model–Input/Output]

File Action View Help

A $100,000 Single Premium Deferred Annuity Product

Issued to 100,000 Males at Age 50, and Payable at Age 65 as a Life Annuity With a 10-Year Period Certain

Input		Output	
Interest Margin (in basis points):	130	Validation Year:	8
Interest Rate, 1st Year:	7.50%	Net Present Value:	$240,005,310
. . . 2nd Year:	7.28%	Internal Rate of Return:	12.91%
. . . 5th Year:	6.61%	Profit Margin:	2.40%
. . . 10th year:	5.50%		
. . . 15th Year:	5.50%	Net Cash Flow:	$1,314,902,992
		PV Profits per $1,000 Paid-In:	$24.00
Percentage of Mortality Table:	85.00%	First Year Surplus Strain:	$765,127,039
		. . .as a Percentage of Premium:	7.65%
1st Year Expenses per $1,000:	1.00	Annual Benefit per $1,000:	$157.37
Subsequent Years' Expenses:	0.69		
		. . . as a Percentage of PV Premiums	
1st Year Commission Rate:	8.50%	PV Profit:	2.40%
		PV Benefits:	4.00%
Initial Lapse Rate:	4.00%	PV Surrenders:	83.69%
Middle Lapse Rate:	35.00%	PV Commissions:	8.50%
Final Lapse Rate:	55.00%	PV Expenses:	0.50%
		PV Reserves:	0.90%

Term Life | Whole Life | Immediate Annuity | Deferred Annuity | Aggregate Model

PART 3

Elements of Product Pricing

This section of the text is about approaches to product pricing and about the factors that insurers take into account when pricing various products. Chapter 7 covers the pricing process and begins to explain the ways that insurers plan for earning a return from the risks they take in connection with their products. Chapter 7 then discusses specifically how insurers go about planning for earning returns related to the investment risks and the administrative and start-up expenses associated with various types of new life, health, and annuity products. Next, Chapter 8 covers the ways that insurers plan for earning returns from the insurance risks that they assume in connection with their life, health, and annuity products. Finally, in Chapter 9, we discuss the various types of reserves for life, health, and annuity products.

CHAPTER

Pricing Products to Reflect Expenses and Investment Income

7

LEARNING OBJECTIVES

After studying this chapter, you should be able to

- Describe how demand and costs combine to establish the upper and lower limit on product prices
- Explain how insurers price products to cover expenses and to include an expense margin
- Describe how an insurer includes an investment margin in a product's price
- Discuss how present values are used to incorporate investment income into a bundled product's price

OUTLINE

Limitations on Insurance Product Pricing
- Market Forces Set the Upper Limit on Price
- Costs Set the Lower Limit on Price
- Additional Limits on Insurance Product Prices: Regulatory Requirements

Profit Margins in Financial Products
- Margins

Pricing for Expenses
- Establishing Expense Charges
- Direct and Indirect Expenses in Pricing
- Expressing Expenses on a Unit Basis

Pricing for Investment Return
- Interest Margin
- How Investment Return is Incorporated into a Product's Price

In this chapter and the next, we discuss product pricing in life and health insurance companies. Chapter 7 introduces one common approach to the pricing of insurance, annuities, and other financial products. This approach requires insurers to estimate the future expenses, benefits, and investment performance associated with each product. Chapter 7 also discusses how insurers estimate future expenses and investment returns, and how they incorporate these estimates into product prices. In Chapter 8, we discuss how insurers price products that involve insurance risk, concentrating on how insurers estimate the cost of providing specific benefits.

In insurance, the price an insurer charges for a particular product is usually referred to as the product's *premium* for insurance products and the *premium* or ***consideration*** for annuity products. For certain other products provided by insurers, such as guaranteed investment contracts (GICs), mutual funds, and separate account funds, the product's pricing structure consists of two elements: an investment spread and an expense charge. Where possible, we will use the specific term that applies to the type of product we are discussing. At some points, however, when we are discussing products in general, we will use the generic word *price.*

Insurers use at least two different methodologies to price insurance products. Most of our discussion in Chapters 7 and 8 relates to the traditional pricing methods that insurers have used for many years. These traditional approaches to pricing are sometimes referred to as *micro pricing* or *cost-plus pricing.* We also refer to a relatively recent approach called *macro pricing.* Although we do not fully describe macro pricing, we review two features that distinguish macro pricing from traditional pricing. One feature of macro pricing is the belief that pricing should take into account both the product's expenses and the market forces that determine the demand for the product. Another feature of macro pricing is the belief that a product's indirect expenses—expenses not directly attributable to that product—should not be considered in pricing the product.

Limitations on Insurance Product Pricing

A number of factors limit the range within which a specific product's price must fall. A product's highest viable price is determined by market forces. If an insurance product's price greatly exceeds a competitor's price for the same product, then given a choice between the two products, most consumers will buy the lower-priced product. A product's minimum viable price, on the other hand, is determined by the costs the insurer incurs in developing and providing the product. With a few exceptions, prices must be high enough to cover the product's costs—both the costs of paying the benefits and the costs of selling and administering the product. For an insurance product, regulations are an additional factor that may influence a product's minimum or maximum price. In the following sections, we look more closely at how these factors influence the range of prices that can be charged for a product.

Market Forces Set the Upper Limit on Price

Although price is not the only point of competition among products, price is certainly a primary concern. Both consumers and distributors look at a product's price when deciding which product to buy or sell. In general, as the price of a particular product increases compared to the prices of competing products, the quantity sold of that product decreases.

As we mentioned in Chapter 4, the quantity sold of a product determines the revenue generated by the product:

Sales Revenue = Unit Price × Quantity Sold

If a product's price is too high relative to the prices of competing products, then the quantity sold of that product will be so low that revenues from the product will be insufficient to meet costs and contribute to profits. Thus, competition imposes an upper limit on a product's price, though the exact level of this upper limit on a product's price can change over time.

Price is not the only factor on which products compete. When making decisions among competing products, consumers consider, along with price, other characteristics of the product, the insurer, and even the specific distributor. Further, competitive forces are dynamic—not static—and the quantity demanded for a specific product or category of products can change. In this context, ***quantity demanded*** refers to the quantity of a product that consumers will buy at different price levels. Generally, the greater the demand for a product, the more of the product consumers will purchase at a given price. Therefore, the greater the demand for a product, the higher the product's maximum price.

Demand for a product type and demand for a specific product vary as different environmental factors vary. Some of the most important factors that influence the demand for insurance and financial products are

1. *Consumer resources.* If a product's potential customers are doing well financially, they have more resources available to purchase all types of products and services, including financial products. Consequently, demand increases and decreases along with corresponding changes in consumer resources.

2. *Consumer needs and desires.* Depending on their financial, demographic, and other characteristics, consumers have greater or lesser needs and desires for specific types of financial products. As these needs and desires change, the prices consumers are willing or able to pay for insurance products also change.

3. *Awareness.* The more consumers and producers know about a product and how it can fulfill their needs, the stronger the demand for the product is likely to be. Advertising and other promotional efforts are designed to increase awareness, thus increasing demand.

4. *Distribution system.* The way an insurer chooses to deliver a product to the consumer influences the product's sales. A distribution channel that makes a product easily accessible to the consumer, provides appropriate information about the product to the consumer, or meets the consumer's needs in other ways can increase demand for the product.

5. *Competing products.* Consumers are less likely to purchase a product if they are aware of a similar product that is available at a lower price or if they believe a different product will do a better job fulfilling their needs. Thus, the demand for a specific product can be reduced by (*a*) a large number of competing products, (*b*) lower-priced competing products, or (*c*) competing products with similar or more attractive features.

6. *Consumer perceptions.* The reputation of the insurance industry or of a specific insurer can have an effect on demand for a specific product or on overall demand for the products offered by insurers. Bad publicity, such as that generated in 1994 and 1995 by several high-profile cases in the United States in which agents were accused of using deceptive sales tactics, can damage the reputation of a specific insurer or of the entire insurance industry, thus lowering demand. On the other hand, bad publicity for competitors, such as that faced by the savings and loan industry in the 1980s, can serve to increase demand for the products offered by other financial services companies, such as insurance companies or savings banks.

7. *Quality ratings.* An insurer's reputation and the demand for its products can be strongly influenced by insurance rating agencies

and consumer advocacy groups. An insurer with a rating in the B range may have to sell its products at a lower price in order to compete with insurers with ratings in the A range.

Costs Set the Lower Limit on Price

Just as the demand for a product creates an upper limit for a product's price, the producer's costs associated with the product usually set a lower limit. If a product's benefits and expenses are greater than its revenues, then the insurer cannot make a profit on that product.

Figure 7-1 illustrates how market forces and product costs provide the limits of the range within which a product can profitably be priced. If a product is priced above the level dictated by the demand for the product, the product will not achieve adequate sales and thus will not provide enough revenue to fulfill the insurer's profitability goals. If a product is priced below cost, revenues will be lower than costs and the product will incur a loss.

In some situations, the price dictated by the market could be lower than the price necessary for a given insurer to cover costs. In this situation, no market price available will allow the product to be profitable. If a business finds one of its products in such a situation, the business can take one of the following courses of action:

1. Reduce the costs associated with providing the product
2. Stimulate an increase in demand for the product—for example, redesigning the product to make it more attractive to consumers but without significantly increasing the product's costs
3. Withdraw the product from the market because the product is not attractive enough to consumers to be sold at a profit

Figure 7-1. How costs and market forces set limits on a product's price.

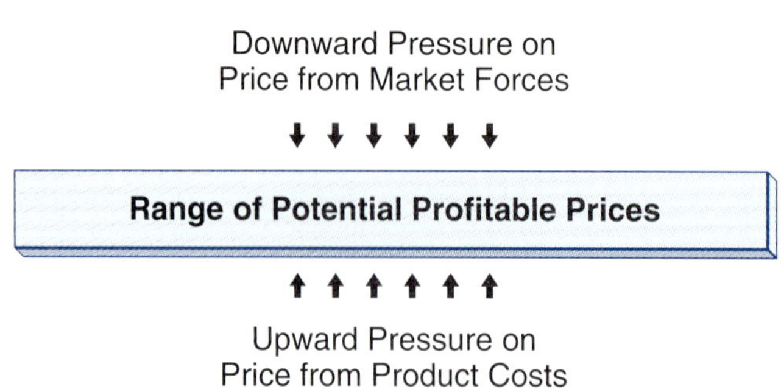

4. Sell the product at or slightly below cost in an effort to generate sales for one or more complementary, but profitable, products; the goal of this course of action is to cover any loss on the unprofitable product with the profit made on the profitable product

In this chapter, we focus on situations in which the market allows a price that is greater than product costs so that the product can be sold at a profit. Despite the possibility that, in a particular situation, an insurer might offer one or more products at a price below cost, the costs of an insurer's entire portfolio of products cannot exceed the revenue the insurer earns from all of its products. Otherwise, the insurer will be unable to operate profitably and eventually will face insolvency. Later in this chapter and in the next chapter, we discuss costs that insurers must consider when pricing their products.

Additional Limits on Insurance Product Prices: Regulatory Requirements

Costs and competitive forces impose limits on the prices of all products. However, further limits are sometimes placed by regulators on the products marketed by insurers. Regulatory requirements affect the prices of insurers' products that involve insurance risk. Additional regulations affect the pricing of insurers' investment-based products. However, our focus here is mainly on insurers' products that involve insurance risk. U.S. and Canadian regulators enforce various types of regulations that are designed to ensure, directly or indirectly, that insurance premium rates are reasonable, adequate, and equitable.

According to regulatory standards, ***reasonable rates*** are premium rates that do not exceed those rates needed to cover an insurer's expenses and provide the insurer with a fair profit. For life insurance and annuities, most jurisdictions do not directly regulate premium rates because they assume that competitive factors will ensure that rates are reasonable. However, most states require insurers to obtain approval of premium rates for individual health insurance.

Adequate rates are premium rates that are high enough to ensure that the insurer has enough money on hand to pay operating expenses and policy benefits when they come due. Although a few jurisdictions in the United States and Canada have regulations that directly address adequacy of premium rates for certain types of insurance, most such regulation is indirect. For example, regulators in Canada and the United States indirectly ensure that rates will be adequate by defining or monitoring the reserves that insurers must establish for insurance policies. To remain solvent, insurers must maintain assets that are at least equal to the amount of their policy reserves, and to obtain these assets, they must charge adequate premiums. Therefore, policy reserve requirements indirectly help ensure that insurers charge adequate rates.

Equitable rates are premium rates that vary based only on factors affecting the product's costs. For example, rates generally are legally permitted to differ among insureds on the basis of such factors as the age, sex,* occupation, health, or smoking habits of the insured because such factors affect the amount of risk the insurer is undertaking by issuing a policy to a specific insured. Similarly, premium rates are legally permitted to vary on the basis of policy size or type of insurance because such factors affect the insurer's costs. However, most jurisdictions prohibit insurers from charging different rates to different buyers of the same type of policy, unless the pricing is determined on the basis of factors affecting the insurer's costs to provide the coverage.

The following table summarizes the limits on the prices of financial products that we have discussed:

<table>
<tr><td rowspan="5">Prices must . . .</td><td colspan="2">• Be low enough to generate sufficient sales revenue</td></tr>
<tr><td colspan="2">• Be high enough to cover product costs</td></tr>
<tr><td rowspan="3">• Meet regulatory requirements as far as being . . .</td><td>▪ Reasonable</td></tr>
<tr><td>▪ Adequate</td></tr>
<tr><td>▪ Equitable</td></tr>
</table>

Profit Margins in Financial Products

As we have discussed, the limits of the range within which a product can be priced for profitability are created primarily by competitive forces and the product's costs, though regulations can also influence a product's price. Analyzing the market environment and demand for a product is generally the responsibility of an insurer's marketing staff. To forecast the probable effects of various pricing decisions on a product's sales, given anticipated conditions within the competitive marketplace, the marketing staff uses historical results on related products and demographic, psychographic, and other marketing information.

Analyzing a product's costs for the purpose of pricing is the responsibility of an insurer's pricing actuaries. A major concern of pricing actuaries is solvency. As noted in Chapter 2, C-2 risk—the risk that the insurer's experience with its products will differ significantly

* In the U.S. state of Montana, rates cannot be based on the insured's sex. Also, a recent Supreme Court decision states that employer-sponsored benefit plans cannot use sex as a basis for charging employees differing rates for the same benefits.

from expectations—is one of the contingency risks insurers must manage in order to protect their solvency. One important way that actuaries manage C-2 risk is by analyzing product costs realistically and by pricing products sensibly with respect to their cost expectations.

Actuaries and marketers often have competing objectives in the pricing process. Marketers tend to prefer lowering product prices to beat the competition and maximize sales, whereas pricing actuaries often want to raise product prices to make sure the company has covered its costs and protected its solvency. However, more and more insurance analysts are emphasizing the importance of actuaries and marketers working together to price products so that they do the best possible job of meeting all of an insurer's strategic objectives, including meeting customer needs, achieving growth in sales, and protecting solvency while maintaining profitability.

Margins

In addition to maintaining solvency, another primary concern associated with the pricing process is that the insurer make a profit. Therefore, once actuaries have forecasted a product's costs, they generally assign the product a price that exceeds the product's projected costs so as to provide the insurer with an appropriate profit or contribution to surplus. The amount by which a product's price exceeds its costs is called the product's ***margin***—also called the *spread* or *profit margin.*

To analyze product costs and margins, insurers generally divide a product's costs into two categories: (1) the costs of the benefit payments associated with the product and (2) all the other expenses associated with the product. Insurers also generally consider that a product's costs are offset, or reduced, by a third factor: the investment income the insurer earns on funds related to the product.

Accordingly, a product's overall margin can be thought of as having three components: an underwriting margin, an expense margin, and an investment margin. The ***underwriting margin,*** which applies only to products with an insurance component, is the difference between the product's benefit costs—such as the cost of death benefits or health benefits—and the benefit costs the insurer assumes in its pricing. The ***expense margin*** is the difference between the amount needed to cover expenses and the expense level the insurer uses to price the product. The ***investment margin*** is the difference between the amount of investment income the insurer earns and the investment income the insurer credits to the product or assumes when pricing the product.

At the pricing stage all product values are either assumed values or expected values. An ***expected value*** is a value that the insurer's actuaries believe is most likely to occur. Accordingly, an ***expected***

margin is the margin the insurer intends to produce and believes is most likely to occur. In contrast, ***assumed values*** are the values the actuaries use in calculating the product's price. When actuaries calculate a product's price, they frequently *assume* different values from those they *expect* to occur. Thus, a product can also be said to have an ***assumed margin*** built into its pricing structure.

Actual values are the values that actually occur after the product has been in force. Accordingly, the ***actual margin*** is the margin that emerges after the product has been in force and is the difference between the assumed values for benefit costs, expenses, or investment income, and the actual values for these components. Figure 7-2 illustrates the relationship of assumed margins to actual margins.

The actual margin may be higher or lower than the assumed margin. In addition, as illustrated in Figure 7-3, one of the components of total margin—the underwriting margin, the expense margin, or the investment margin—may be higher than expected and another component may be lower than expected. For example, the insurer may find that actual mortality experience is better than assumed but that expenses are higher than assumed. In this case, the insurer's actual underwriting margin would be larger than the expected underwriting margin, but the actual expense margin would be smaller than the expected expense margin or might even be negative; that is, the actual expenses could exceed the expense charge built into the product's price.

A product's total margin—actual as well as expected—can be composed of any combination of the three margin components. For example, a product priced with a very small expense margin might be

Figure 7-2. Assumed and actual margins.

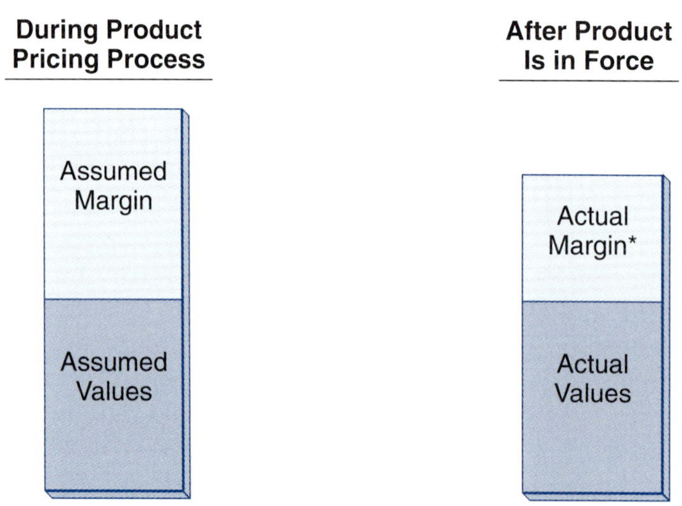

* The actual margin may be larger or smaller than the assumed margin.

Figure 7-3. Examples of products with the same overall profit margin, but different margin components.

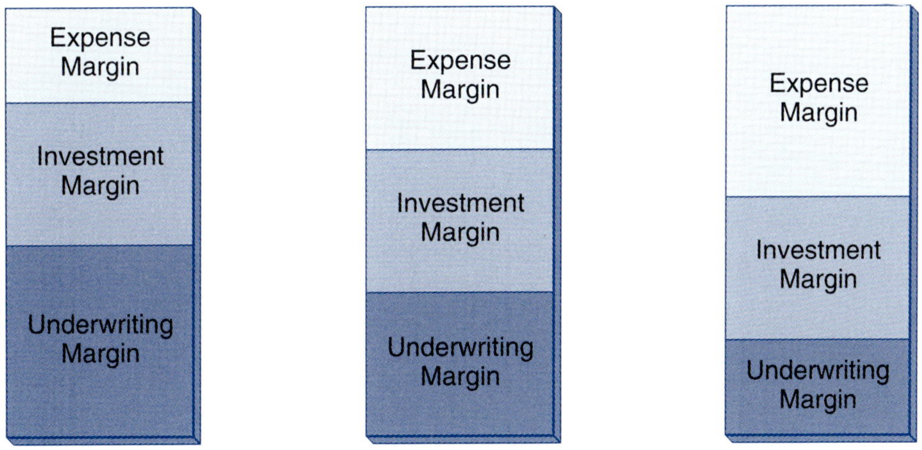

priced with a relatively large investment margin and underwriting margin. Another product might be priced with a large expense margin, a small investment margin, and a moderate underwriting margin.

Whereas it is useful conceptually to view a product as having three margin components, insurers do not always analyze all three components separately when they price a product. This is especially true for many nonparticipating bundled products. As we noted earlier in this chapter, *bundled products* are those for which the insurer charges a single premium amount that incorporates benefit costs, expenses, and investment return. When an insurer does not analyze separately its underwriting, expense, and investment margins, it relies on the tools we described in Chapters 3 and 6, such as asset-share models, to analyze the potential profitability of its products. In fact, most insurers use these tools for evaluating whether or not they analyze the separate margin components.

As we discussed in Chapter 1, insurers can analyze profitability at several different levels, including the individual product level, the product line level, and the company level. As Figure 7-4 shows, the investment, underwriting, and expense margins within a product's pricing structure combine to determine the product's overall margin. Then, the profit margins the insurer earns on each of its products combine to determine the insurer's overall net gain. The net gain then forms the basis of the insurer's profit picture.

Factors that Determine the Size of Margins

Products are often described as having either a thin margin or a wide margin. As these terms imply, a ***thin margin*** is a small margin, and a ***wide margin*** is a relatively large margin. Certain product types tend

Figure 7-4. The relationship between product margins and a company's overall profitability.

Expected Profit Margin

Profit factors within a product's pricing structure			Profit expected at the product level
Product's *expected* investment income	Product's *expected* expense charges	Product's *expected* benefit costs	Total of *expected* investment income, expense charges and benefit costs
− Investment income credited or *assumed*	− Product's *assumed* expenses	− Product's *assumed* benefit costs	− Total of *assumed* income, expenses, and benefit costs
Interest margin	**Expense margin**	**Underwriting margin**	**Product's *expected* profit margin**

Actual Profit Margin

Profit realized at the product level	Profit at the income statement level
Total product revenue received received	Total company revenue from all sources
− Total product costs incurred	− Total company costs
Product's *actual* profit margin	**Net gain from operations**
	− Policyowner dividends and income taxes
	Net income

to have relatively thin margins, whereas others tend to have wider margins.

A number of factors determine the size of a product's margin, including the following factors:

- *Competition.* As we have discussed, a competitive market often acts to force prices down. Thus, if a product is competing for consumer dollars with a number of other products, then the product's expected margin is likely to be thin. Accumulation products, such as annuities and GICs, have thin margins partly because they must compete with numerous products offered by other types of financial institutions, notably banks and mutual fund companies. Similarly, many term insurance products are fiercely competitive and, consequently, have very thin expected margins.

- *The amount of risk assumed by the insurer.* The risk-return tradeoff, which we described in Chapter 2, underlies this factor. The greater the risk an insurer assumes with a product, the greater must be the potential reward of assuming that risk. Thus, the greater the amount of risk a product represents for an insurer, the wider the product's expected margin is likely to be. The wider margin also provides a safety net, in case the insurer's experience is worse than expected. For example, the insurer assumes the entire investment risk for an ordinary life policy. Therefore, ordinary life products usually have a wider investment margin than do variable life products, for which the customer assumes most of the investment risk. Similarly, relatively little claim experience is available for an insurer to use in estimating benefit costs for long-term care (LTC) insurance. As a result, the insurer's risk in issuing such coverage is high. Thus, LTC insurance generally has a relatively wide underwriting margin.

- *The length of premium or interest guarantees.* A product's premium or interest guarantees, if any, affect the insurer's risk in issuing the product. The insurer's ability to revise a product's premium rate or crediting rate after the product has been issued reduces the risk associated with the product. The more frequently an insurer can revise a product's premium or crediting rate while the product is in force, the thinner the product's expected margin generally will be.

  For example, for a level-premium product, the insurer guarantees that the premium will remain level for the entire life of the product. If the insurer's underwriting, expense, or investment experience turns out to be worse than expected, the insurer may not be able to meet its profit objectives for the product. Neither will the insurer be able to alter the premium it charges its existing customers. An insurer must build a wide expected margin into a level-premium product's price to protect itself against the possibility of adverse experience. ExecuView Application 7-1 describes what can happen under adverse conditions if an insurer builds too narrow a margin into an ordinary life product.

For a contrasting example, with a universal life policy, the insurer can adjust the insurance charge and the crediting rate on a frequent basis. The insurer does not need to build in a wide margin to protect itself against adverse experience on this type of product. If experience is unfavorable, the insurer can adjust the product's charges or its crediting rate.

- *Customer emphasis on return.* When customers purchase investment products, they are generally drawn to products that offer the highest return available within their personal risk tolerance. Customers with a high tolerance for risk—who expect high returns—seek products, such as variable rate policies, that offer greater potential returns by shifting more of the investment risk to the customer. Shifting risk to the customer allows insurers to offer thin expected margins. Customers with a low tolerance for risk seek products that offer more investment guarantees but lower potential returns. Products with investment guarantees require insurers to build wide expected margins into their pricing.
- *Whether the policy is participating or nonparticipating.* Owners of participating policies expect to receive policy dividends. In fact, they tend to expect policy dividends to increase over time. Insurers can experience considerable negative publicity if their dividend payments do not meet customer expectations. Insurers generally incorporate wider expected margins into the prices of participating products than they do into the prices of nonparticipating policies to ensure that they will be able to pay the policy dividends that participating customers expect.
- *Demand for the product.* Products that are in great demand by consumers typically have a higher price and a higher expected margin. Economists would expect, however, that over time this higher margin would diminish as the high demand for the product attracts more suppliers, thus increasing competition. As we noted, competition acts to force market prices down and reduce margins.

As we discussed in Chapter 6 in the section on asset-share analysis, an insurer goes through many iterations until it arrives at the price and the margins that it will use for a product. In addition, after a product is introduced into the marketplace, the insurer monitors the product's profit performance and, where possible, adjusts the product's margins as needed in order to improve the product's performance.

Application 7-1 Margins Built into Pricing Guarantees

If you wish to demonstrate this example on your computer, start *ExecuView* and select the Whole Life Model. Be sure to select *Reset, All Models* from the Action menu to return *ExecuView* to its default settings. The default assumptions and profitability outcome for this model are shown on the following *ExecuView* screen.

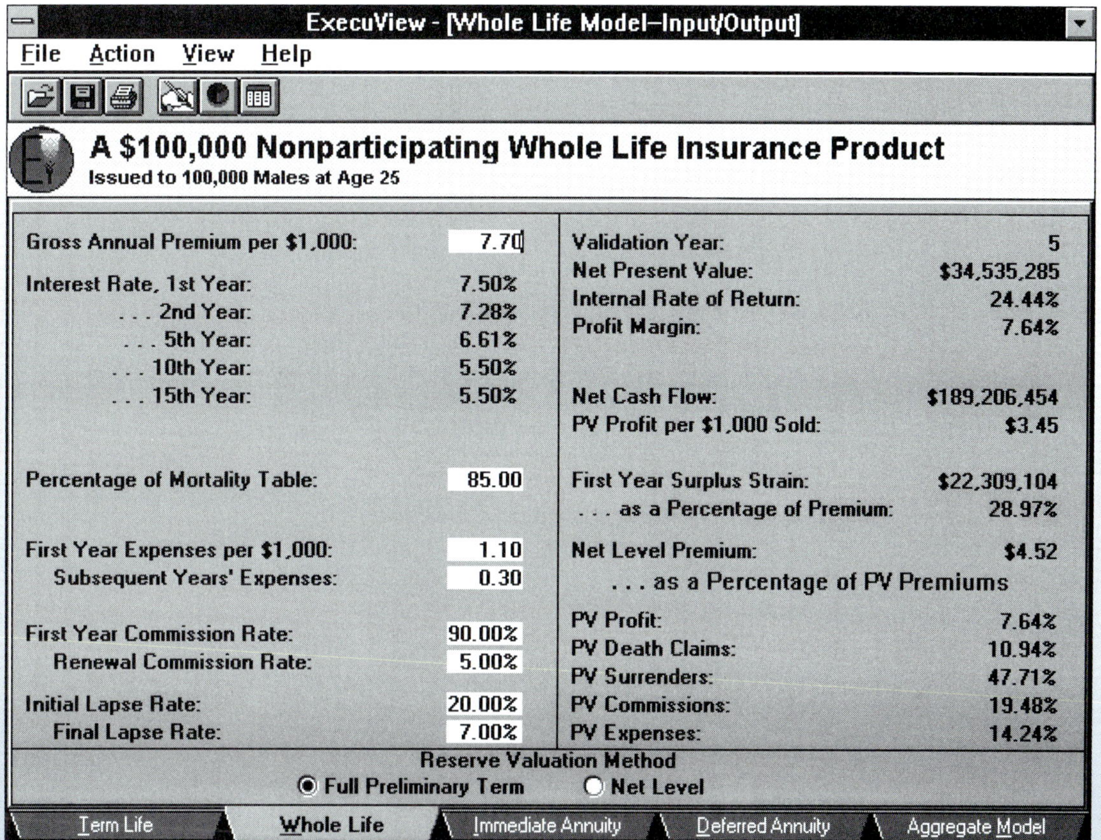

Insurers guarantee that the premium of a whole life policy will not change as long as the policy remains in force. This guarantee creates a risk for which the insurer must compensate by building relatively wide margins into the premiums of such a product.

The EV Life Insurance Company is in the process of reviewing the whole life product it markets to males in their 20s. The premium for the product is currently $7.70 per $1,000 of face value, which EV Life estimates will provide a profit margin of 7.64 percent. However, the market for whole life products for this age group is growing much more competitive, with a lot of new companies offering lower premiums. In order for EV Life to stay competitive in this area, its premium rates must be lowered. The company's actuaries have warned that it is dangerous to allow the estimated profit margin to fall below 6.75 percent, but despite their protests, it is decided that the premium for new sales of this product will be $7.55 per $1,000 of face value, which yields an estimated profit margin of 6.36 percent. Will this margin be wide enough to compensate for the risk presented by this product?

(continued on next page)

Application 7-1 Margins Built into Pricing Guarantees (continued)

> *Gross Annual Premium* is currently set at $7.70. Change this setting to $7.55 and press <enter> to view the results of this change.

The product experiences brisk sales as a result of the new low premium, but, mainly because of higher administrative costs, first-year expenses turn out to be $1.60 per $1,000, instead of the $1.10 originally projected. Subsequent years' expenses turn out higher too, at $0.55 per $1,000. When this product was priced, EV Life assumed that investment income would be 7.5 percent in the first year and that this rate would drop 0.222 percentage points each year for 9 years. By the end of the second policy year, it becomes evident that the performance of EV Life's short-term investments has declined, causing a drop of 0.75 percent in the interest EV Life earns on its investments for that year. Projections of interest fluctuations for subsequent years, however, turn out to be accurate.

> Select the Aggregate Model. Adjust *Change, 2nd Year* to -0.75 and press <enter>. Return to the Whole Life Model and change *First Year Expenses per $1,000* to 1.60 and *Subsequent Years Expenses* to 0.55. Press <enter> to view the results of these changes.

The result of these adverse experiences, shown on the *ExecuView* screen that follows, is a product that drains surplus for 30 years and never breaks even.

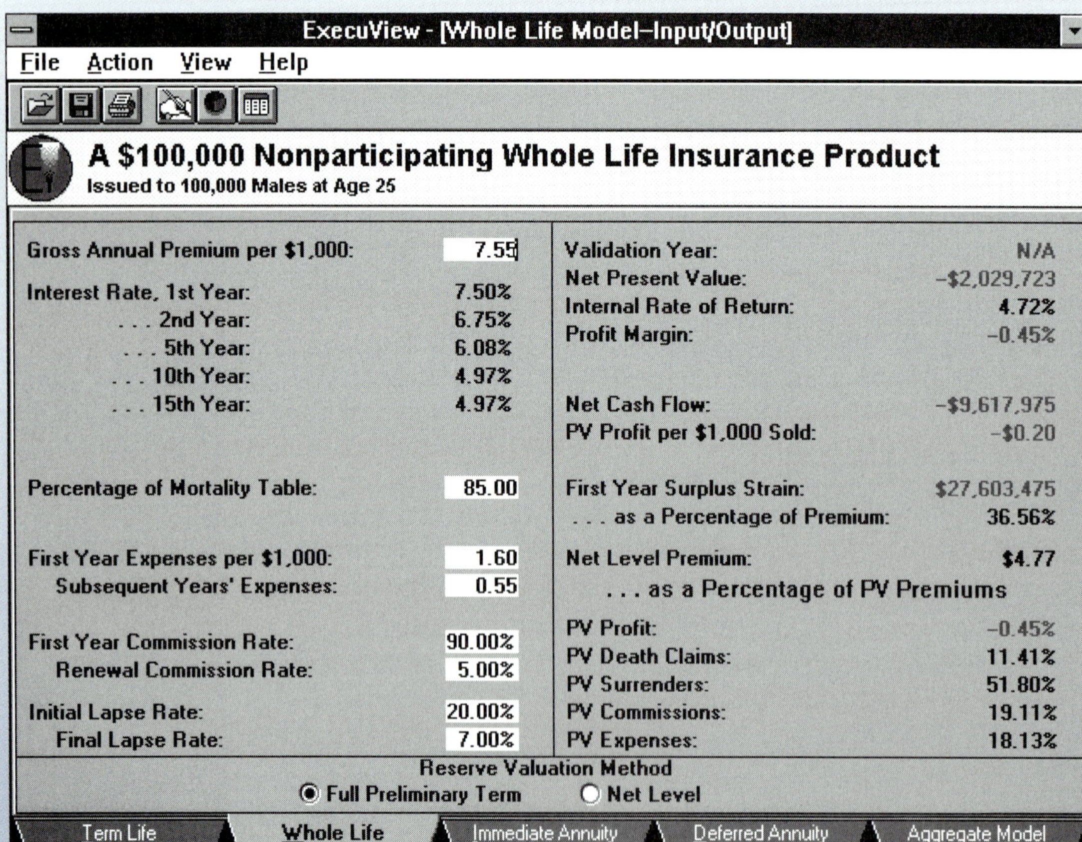

In the remainder of this chapter and in the next chapter, we discuss pricing concepts and methods that incorporate product costs and margins. We begin by discussing expenses and the expense margin. Later in this chapter, we discuss investment return and the investment margin. At the end of this chapter, we illustrate how present value calculations are used to account for investment return. In the next chapter, we examine in depth how insurers calculate the cost of benefits for products with an insurance element, and we discuss the underwriting margin. Keep in mind, though, that our descriptions of margins concern the margins built in during the pricing process, not the actual margins the company earns on a product. Actual margins are not known during the pricing process.

Even after a product is in force, determining the actual margin for the product is exceedingly difficult. Although allocating benefit costs to a particular product type or product line is fairly simple, allocating expenses and investment income to a product or product line is quite complex. Consequently, even after a product has been offered long enough for the expected and assumed values to be replaced by actual values, the determination of the product's actual margin is as much a result of the allocation method used as it is of the product's true profitability.

Margins and Loading

As we explained in Chapter 4, a gross premium is the sum of two elements: (1) the net premium and (2) the loading. According to a traditional view of insurance pricing taught by many textbooks, a product's entire profit margin is part of the product's loading. In contrast, the approach to insurance pricing we use in this book views a product's margin as consisting of three parts: (1) an underwriting margin, (2) an investment margin, and (3) an expense margin. According to our approach, only the *expense margin* is part of a product's loading. The underwriting and investment margins are both included in the net premium. Expense margins and investment margins are further explained in the next two sections of this chapter. We explain underwriting margins in detail in Chapter 8.

Figure 7-5 compares the traditional view of insurance pricing with the approach used in this book.

Pricing for Expenses

We begin our discussion of how insurers consider product costs in product pricing by discussing pricing to reflect expenses. By *expenses*, in this context, we mean the costs of doing business, but we do not include the amounts of the contractual benefits that an insurer pays

Figure 7-5. Different concepts of loading and gross premium.

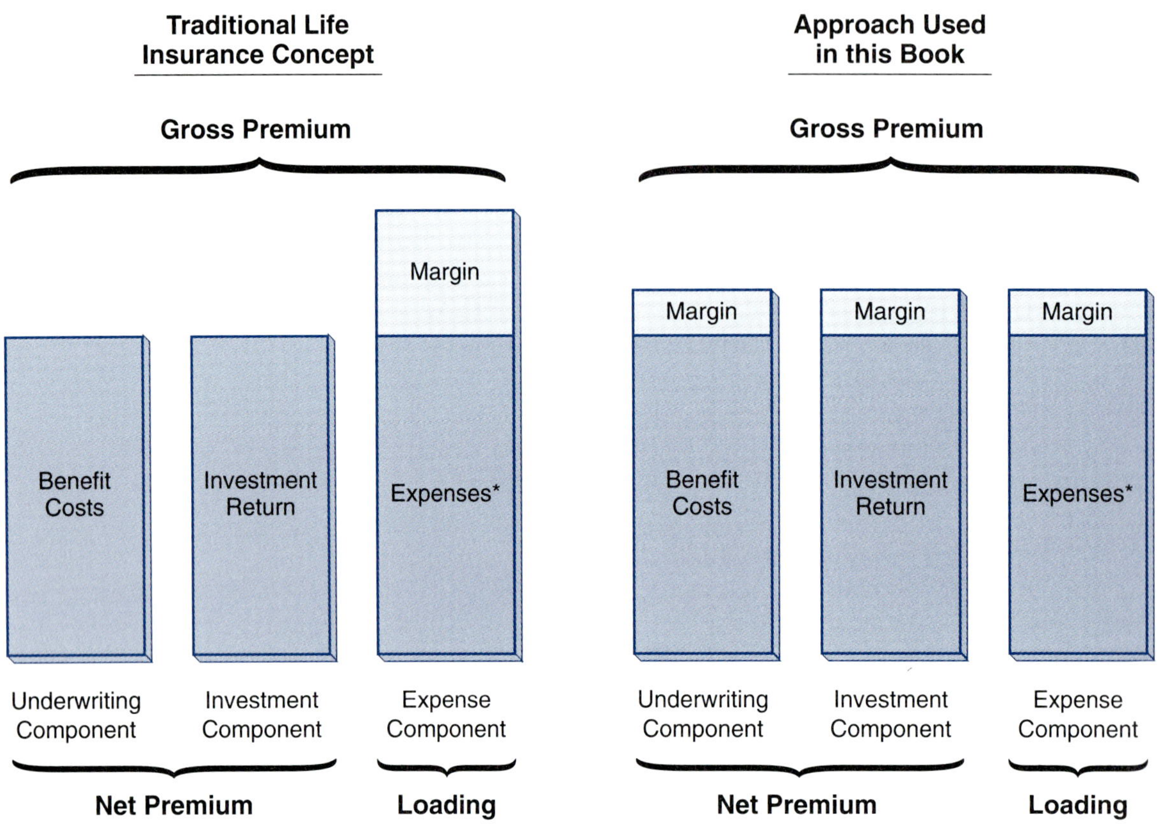

* Plus contingencies

out. Figure 7-6 includes a list of expenses insurers incur to conduct business. Our discussion of expenses initially describes the differences among various types of expenses and the difference between pricing systems that consider only direct expenses and those that consider both direct and indirect expenses. Finally, we discuss the ways that expense charges are incorporated into a product's pricing structure.

Establishing Expense Charges

The ***expense charge*** is the portion of a product's price designed to reimburse the insurer for its operating expenses, specifically, commissions, premium taxes, and general operating expenses. Note that these operating expenses do not include benefit costs or investment expenses. In traditional individual insurance products, the expense charge is frequently called ***loading.*** In group insurance, the charge for

Figure 7-6. Expenses typically associated with an insurer's business.

- Salaries, employee benefits, and bonuses of line and staff employees
- Agent and broker commissions
- Information systems development and maintenance
- Agency and other field expenses
- Underwriting expenses
- Policy issue expenses
- Customer service expenses
- Premium taxes
- Deferred acquisition cost (DAC) taxes
- Claim administration expenses
- Product development expenses
- Accounting expenses
- Actuarial expenses
- Human resources expenses, such as training, recruiting, and hiring
- Legal costs
- Marketing, advertising, and public relations expenses
- Guaranty fund assessments

expenses is generally called the ***retention charge.*** For most insurance products, the loading or retention charge also contains provisions for *contingencies.* Any amount built into a product's expense charge in excess of the amount necessary to cover operating expenses and contingencies constitutes the product's expense margin. This margin is intended to contribute to the insurer's surplus and, in the case of participating policies, to the surplus account from which policy dividends are paid.

Acquisition and Maintenance Expenses

Each insurer uses its own system for classifying expenses, but many insurers divide product expenses into two categories: acquisition expenses and maintenance expenses. ***Acquisition expenses*** are those expenses related to procuring, underwriting, and issuing new business. Some prominent examples of acquisition expenses are first-year commissions, the costs of medical examinations, and some field management expenses. ***Maintenance expenses*** are those product expenses that arise once the product is in force. Prominent examples of maintenance expenses include renewal commissions, premium taxes, claim and customer service expenses, and, again, certain field management expenses.

Although the expense figures used for pricing should approximate an insurer's actual costs, insurers often find it impractical to do a thorough cost analysis for every one of their products. Particularly if a new product is similar to one or more of an insurer's existing products, an insurer will often price a product using standard costs. ***Standard costs*** are estimates of the average expenses an insurer incurs to complete certain functions or processes. For example, most insurers know their standard costs to underwrite an ordinary individual life insurance contract or pay a life insurance claim, and companies use these standards to price their products. Although standard costs provide insurers a quick, efficient method of estimating expenses for pricing and product design, standard costs must be tested and updated periodically to ensure that they still represent with sufficient accuracy the insurer's actual costs.

Contingencies

In addition to operating expenses, an insurance product's loading is generally formulated to make allowances for contingencies. As we mentioned in Chapter 3, *contingencies* are unexpected events that cause expenses, investment earnings, mortality rates, morbidity rates, or persistency rates to vary significantly from company forecasts. When any of these factors varies from the insurer's expectations so as to reduce revenue or increase expenses or benefit payments, the variation is often referred to as an *adverse deviation.* Large adverse deviations can be caused by such contingencies as epidemics, natural disasters, severe swings in interest rates, and unfavorable regulatory decisions or tax legislation. However, smaller adverse deviations can result from the inevitable uncertainty associated with the forecasting process. Even small adverse deviations can affect a product's performance. Note that a ***favorable deviation***—a variation in key factors that result in increased revenue or reduced costs for the insurer—can also occur when actual experience varies from the company's forecasts.

Insurers usually add an amount to a product's loading to protect themselves and their customers from the potentially damaging financial results of adverse deviations. In group insurance, this amount is called the ***risk charge.*** This additional loading helps ensure that an insurer will be able to fulfill its contractual obligations even under difficult circumstances.

Expense Margin

Once the insurer determines the amount needed to cover expenses and contingencies, the insurer generally includes an additional amount—an expense margin—in the product's expense charge. This margin is intended to contribute to the insurer's profit and to provide a further cushion in case of adverse deviations. When pricing participating policies, insurers generally use a larger expense margin than they do for nonparticipating products; the additional margin is used to pay dividends. Earlier in this chapter, we discussed the factors that determine the size of the expected margin, and we noted that the actual margin is not known until after the insurer has accumulated experience.

The following graph summarizes the components of a product's expense charge:

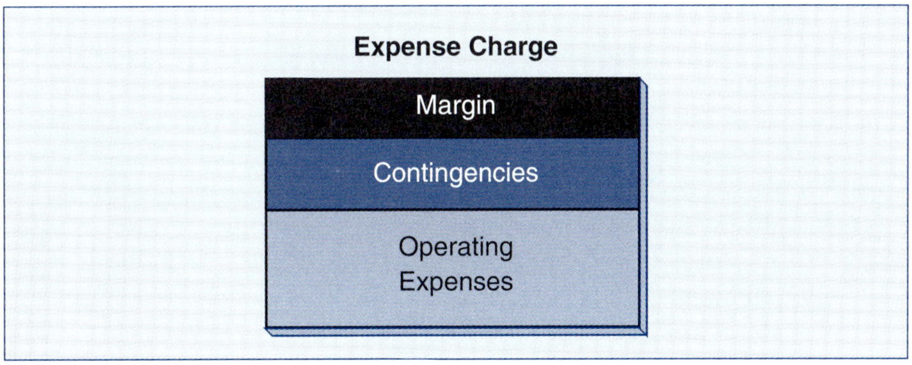

Direct and Indirect Expenses in Pricing

Expenses are often classified as either direct or indirect expenses. For our purposes, ***direct expenses*** are expenses that can be directly attributed to a specific product. A good example of a direct expense is an agent's commission. If an agent sells an ordinary life policy, the agent's commission is directly attributable to that product and is therefore a direct expense of that ordinary life product. Identifying direct expenses and allocating these expenses to a particular product line or product type is fairly straightforward; all product pricing systems include direct expenses in a product's pricing structure.

On the other hand, ***indirect expenses,*** also called *common costs,* are expenses that are not directly attributable to any specific product. Indirect expenses result from activities that relate to several or all of an insurer's products. An insurer incurs the same level of indirect expenses whether or not it offers a specific product. For example, imagine that an insurer uses the same information system to provide customer service for its individual term insurance product line and also for five other product lines. The costs of this information system are not directly attributable to the term insurance product line. Further, if the insurer canceled its term insurance product line, the costs associated with the information system would remain largely the same. The costs of this system are an indirect expense from the point of view of the term product line. Among the significant indirect expenses are information systems expenses, accounting expenses, and the salaries of some executives who have broad responsibilities that go beyond one type of product.

Identifying indirect expenses and determining how to properly allocate—that is, attribute—those expenses to a product during the pricing process is complex, difficult, and often arbitrary. Further, the narrower the focus of such allocation, the less precise the result. For example, attempts to fairly allocate indirect costs to a line of business are more likely to be successful than are attempts to allocate indirect costs to one block of policies within that line. In fact, the arbitrary nature of the allocation process is one reason some pricing systems do not attempt to allocate indirect expenses to a product when determining the product's price.

The process used to estimate a product's costs for pricing purposes is called ***costing.*** Increasingly in the insurance industry, two costing methods are used. The two methods are called marginal costing and full costing, and they differ in the way they treat indirect costs. Under ***marginal costing,*** also known as *variable costing* or *direct costing,* the only expenses that are treated as product expenses are direct expenses. Under ***full costing,*** also known as *absorption costing,* both direct and indirect expenses are treated as product expenses. Because indirect expenses are not directly attributable to any product, full costing requires the insurer to allocate indirect expenses to each product line.

For example, suppose the Geode Insurance Company sells a product line with the expense profile shown in Figure 7-7. The expense charge is the portion of the product line's price that is intended to account for the product's expenses. You should recognize that this example is a simplification, both in the numbers it uses and in the assumptions it makes about the timing of expenses and premium payments. The example assumes that all of the product's expenses are incurred and all premiums are paid at the same moment—something that rarely, if ever, occurs with financial products.

First, we assume that the insurer calculates the product's expense margin using full costing. The expense margin under full costing can be calculated by adding a product's direct and indirect expenses and subtracting this amount from the expense charge, as shown in the following equation:

Expense Margin = Expense Charge – (Direct Expense + Indirect Expense)
(Under Full Costing)

We assume here that the insurer uses a simple method to allocate indirect expenses. Because it sells three lines of products, the insurer divides its total indirect expenses by three and allocates one-third to each product line. The result of this simple calculation is that the product line we are examining is allocated $40 of indirect expenses.

Figure 7-7. Examples of how full costing and marginal costing are applied.

Expense profile of one Geode insurance product	
Expense charge	$100
Direct expenses	$ 40
Allocated indirect expenses	$ 40

Product expense allocation under . . .	Full costing	Marginal costing
Expense charge	$100	$100
– Direct expenses	– $ 40	– $ 40
– Allocated indirect expenses	– $ 40	n/a
= Product's expense margin	$ 20	$ 60

Under full costing, the expense margin for this product can be calculated as follows:

Expense Margin = \$100 – (\$40 Direct Expense + \$40 Indirect Expense)
= \$100 – \$80
= \$20

Under marginal costing, the only expenses that are treated as product expenses are direct expenses; indirect expenses are not considered. The following formula can be used to calculate expense margin under marginal costing:

Expense Margin = Expense Charge – Direct Expenses
(Under Marginal Costing)

If Geode uses marginal costing to calculate the expense margin of the same product line described in the previous example, the expense margin would be calculated as follows:

Expense Margin = \$100 – (\$40 Direct Expense)
= \$60

Note that the size and function of a product's expense margin differ depending on whether the company uses full or marginal costing. This difference is illustrated in Figure 7-8.

Figure 7-8. Different definitions of margin under full and marginal costing.

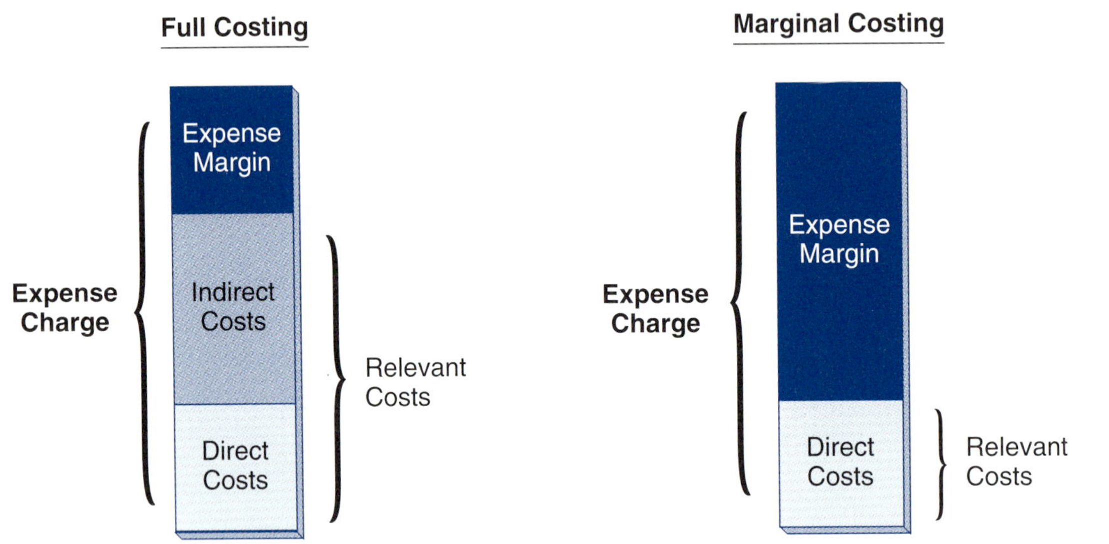

As we have already discussed, full costing assumes that both direct and indirect costs are relevant product costs, whereas marginal costing assumes that only direct costs are relevant. Under full costing, a product's expense margin is the portion of its price that contributes to profit. Under marginal costing, however, the expense margin is the portion of the product's price that contributes to indirect costs *and* profit. If you want to understand fully how much expense margin is built into a product's price, you need to know both the size of the expense margin and the costing method used. For example, if you know that one product has a \$40 expense margin and another otherwise identical product has a \$25 expense margin, you cannot determine which product will contribute more to profits, unless you also know which costing method is being used for establishing each product's expense margin.

Traditionally, the insurance industry has used full costing. However, supporters of macro pricing advocate the use of marginal costing. Figure 7-9 illustrates the proportion of insurers that use full costing, that use marginal costing, and that use a method somewhere between pure full costing and pure marginal costing, according to a 1994 survey.

Expressing Expenses on a Unit Basis

Identifying direct product costs and allocating indirect costs to products generally involves expressing expenses on the basis of a unit of product. However, in insurance and financial services, there are

Figure 7-9. Percentage of insurers using full and marginal costing (1994).

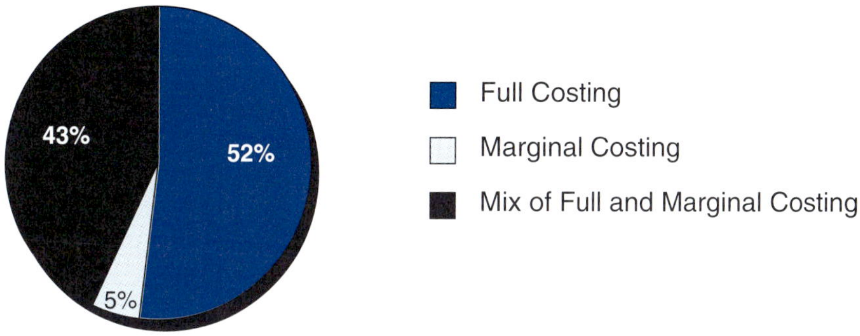

Source: *Douglas C. Doll, "Full versus Marginal Expenses," Tillinghast, 1994. Presented at LOMA's Financial Inforum, May 16, 1994. Reprinted by permission of the publisher.*

several ways to define a product "unit." When determining a specific product's expense charge, insurers generally add together three sets of expenses, allocated according to three definitions of the number of units of product sold. The three sets of expenses are

1. *Expenses that vary based on the* **dollar amount** *of the product the customer purchases.* In the case of life insurance, certain expenses are expressed per $1,000 of face amount. One example of this type of expense is underwriting expense, a portion of which often varies in proportion to the amount of insurance purchased.

2. **Per policy, per insured,** *or* **per account** *expenses.* Some expenses are assumed to be the same for all contracts of a specific type, no matter how large the contract. For example, an insurer's cost for billing a certain type of individual insurance policy once annually are the same, whether the policy is for $10,000 or for $1 million.

3. *Expenses that vary in proportion to the* **premium** *the customer pays.* The most common examples of this type of expense are sales commissions and premium taxes.

To illustrate these components of a product's total expenses, Figure 7-10 shows a simplified expense analysis for a life insurance product. As the figure illustrates, a number of expenses are frequently allocated partially on a per $1,000 face amount basis and partially on a per policy basis.

Incorporating Expense Charges into Product Prices

Insurers use different methods to incorporate the expense charge into a product's overall price depending on whether the product has a bundled or an unbundled pricing structure. A ***bundled product*** is one

Figure 7-10. Simplified expense analysis illustrating the three types of unit costs typically used for a life product.

	First year expenses		
	Per $1,000 face amount	**Per policy**	**Per $100 premium**
Acquisition expenses			
Commissions			$55.00
Underwriting	$1.00	$20.50	
Other acquisition (s)	$0.25	$21.25	
Maintenance expenses			
Premium taxes			$ 2.00
Other maintenance	$0.08	$ 9.50	

	After first year expenses		
	Per $1,000 face amount	**Per policy**	**Per $100 premium**
Maintenance expenses			
Commissions			$10.00
Premium taxes			$ 2.00
Other maintenance	$0.08	$ 9.50	

for which the customer is charged a single gross premium amount reflecting all three pricing elements—benefit costs, expenses, and investment return. The insurer does not specify what portion of the gross premium goes toward expenses, what portion goes to cover the cost of benefits, or how much interest the insurer is crediting to the customer. An ***unbundled product*** is one for which the insurer expresses pricing elements separately. The insurer specifies to the customer that part of the product's total price which reflects the insurer's expenses and that part which is intended to cover the cost of benefits. It also specifies how much interest is being credited to the customer. In the following sections, we discuss how insurers incorporate the expense charge into the price of bundled and unbundled products.

Expense Charges in Bundled Products. The most prominent examples of bundled products are traditional individual insurance products: ordinary whole life, term life, individual disability, and individual medical expense insurance. For these products, the customer is generally charged a single gross premium amount and the insurer does not specify to the customer what portion of the premium is intended to cover expenses, what portion covers benefits, or how much interest the insurer is crediting on the product.

As we have discussed, a policy's expenses are usually defined in three ways: per $1,000 face amount, per $100 premium, and per policy. However, when an insurer calculates the gross premiums it charges to customers, the insurer often converts the per policy expenses to a per $1,000 face amount basis.

When insurers convert per policy expenses to a per $1,000 basis, they usually do so based on the average policy size. For example, suppose Alspaugh Life's ordinary life product needs to be loaded for expenses of $50 per policy, and the company's average policy size for this product is $100,000. To convert this per policy expense to a per $1,000 basis, the company would divide $50 by 100, resulting in a loading of $0.50 per $1,000 face amount.

The problem with this method is that owners of larger policies end up paying more than their fair share of expenses. For example, suppose one customer buys a $50,000 policy and another buys a $150,000 policy. The owner of the smaller policy would pay $25, derived by multiplying $0.50 by 50, for this expense element. The owner of the larger policy would pay $75, derived by multiplying $0.50 by 150. Remember the assumed amount of this loading element is $50 per policy, regardless of the size of the policy. Therefore, the owner of the larger policy would be paying more than the insurer's assumed expenses for the policy. To avoid overcharging owners of larger policies for their policy expenses, insurers can use a banding system or a policy fee system. In fact, insurers often use both systems in conjunction with one another.

Banding is a pricing system under which an insurer establishes four or five ranges (bands) according to the face amount of a policy and charges different premium rates within each band. The premium rate decreases as the face amount increases. For example, a particular product might be subject to the following pricing schedule for a certain age at issue:

Face amount band	Premium per $1,000 of coverage
$0–$99,999	$5.00
$100,000–$249,999	$4.50
$250,000–$499,999	$4.25
$500,000–$999,999	$4.00
over $1 million	$3.75

The ***policy fee system*** is a pricing system whereby the policyholder pays a flat amount—called the policy fee—plus a specific rate per

$1,000 face amount. For example, a company might charge a premium based on a policy fee of $10 for every policy plus a rate of $5 per $1,000 face amount. Thus, the premium for a $100,000 face amount policy would be

$$\$10 + (\$5 \times 100) = \$10 + \$500 = \$510$$

The following table summarizes the three methods of incorporating expenses into the prices of bundled products:

1. Convert per policy expenses to per $1,000 face amount basis based on average policy size
2. Banding—charge increasingly smaller premium per $1,000 of coverage for larger policies
3. Policy fee—charge flat policy fee plus set amount per $1,000 of coverage

Expense Charges in Unbundled Products. When using an *unbundled* pricing system, the insurer specifies what part of the product's total price reflects the insurer's expenses. In addition, the insurer often charges more than one type of expense fee, and each expense fee is intended to cover a certain type of expense. Unbundled pricing is used most often in connection with investment-sensitive products, such as mutual funds and separate account funds, variable and universal life insurance, and fixed and variable annuities.

Four methods are commonly used to incorporate loading into the price of unbundled products: the front-end load, the back-end load, the periodic fee, and the one-time fee for a specific service. Each insurer, or each product, might feature one of these methods, a combination of two or three of these methods, or all of these methods.

A ***front-end load*** is an amount charged to the customer at the time the customer pays for the product. Typically, this amount is deducted from the amount of the customer's premium or investment. Note that, although many front-end load products involve annual premium payments, the front-end load is assessed only in the first year. The front-end load is intended to compensate the insurer for sales commissions and other expenses associated with acquiring the business. Front-end loads are usually calculated as a percentage of the customer's payment to the company. To illustrate, assume the Tipton Insurance Company operates a variable annuity with a 2.5 percent front-end load. If Grover Smith purchases a variable annuity from Tipton for $50,000, the company will deduct 2.5 percent of this amount and invest the remainder on behalf of Mr. Smith's variable annuity account. In this situation, the front-end load would be

$$0.025 \times \$50{,}000 = \$1{,}250$$

and Mr. Smith's annuity account value in the beginning of year 1 would be worth

$$\$50{,}000 - \$1{,}250 = \$48{,}750$$

Front-end loads were fairly common among universal life products in the early 1980s.

A ***back-end load,*** also known as a *surrender charge* or *withdrawal charge,* is an amount charged to the customer when the customer withdraws money from the product. As we discussed in Chapter 3, back-end loads discourage customers from withdrawing their money. Thus, back-end loads can decrease disintermediation and improve persistency. Back-end loads often decrease over time. For example, a product might include a back-end load of 10 percent for 5 years after the initial investment, with the load decreasing by 2 percent each of the 5 years after that. After 10 years, the customer could withdraw funds at no charge. Like front-end loads, back-end loads are intended to compensate the insurer for the costs it incurs in issuing a new policy. The rationale behind the decreasing back-end load is that if the insurer keeps the customer's business for a longer period of time, then the insurer is more likely to recoup its acquisition expenses from other sources, such as the investment spread.

Suppose the Tipton Insurance Company operates a single premium deferred annuity with the back-end load described in the previous paragraph—10 percent for the first five years, decreasing 2 percent each year after that. Assume that, seven years after Jenny Huang purchases an annuity, her account balance is \$9,000. At this point, the back-end load on the account is 6 percent.

$$10\% \text{ (First Five Years)} - 2\% \text{ (Sixth Year)} - 2\% \text{ (Seventh Year)} = 6\%$$

If Ms. Huang withdrew her entire account balance at this point, she would pay a \$540 back-end load and would receive \$8,460 of her \$9,000 account value, as demonstrated in the following calculation:

$$\begin{aligned} \textbf{Account Value} &= \$9{,}000 - (\$9{,}000 \times 0.06) \\ &= \$9{,}000 - \$540 \\ &= \$8{,}460 \end{aligned}$$

Another type of expense charge is the periodic fee. A ***periodic fee*** is an amount that must be paid at predetermined intervals, for example, every year or every month. A periodic fee is generally intended to compensate the insurer for its investment management expenses, its administrative expenses, or both. A periodic fee is generally either a flat amount or a percentage of the customer's account value.

Figure 7-11. Summary of expense charges.

	Calculated as . . .	How paid	Purpose
Front-end load	Percentage of deposit	Deducted from deposit	To cover sales commissions
Back-end load	Percentage of withdrawal	Deducted from withdrawal	To cover sales commissions/discourage withdrawals
Periodic fee	Flat amount or percentage of account value	Deducted from account value once every period	To cover investment/ administrative expenses
Fee for service	Flat amount	Deducted from account balance	To cover specific administrative expenses such as transfer expenses

Finally, some insurers might charge customers one-time fees for specific services. A common example of this type of fee is the transfer fee. A ***transfer fee*** is sometimes charged when a customer transfers money from one fund to another. For example, if a variable annuity customer wanted to transfer part of his annuity balance from one separate fund to another, the insurer might charge a fee, such as $10, to make the transfer. Fees for specific services, such as transfer fees, are generally taken out of the customer's account balance.

Figure 7-11 summarizes the expense charges that are commonly used for unbundled products.

Importance of Persistency to Expense Charges

To complete our discussion of pricing for expenses, we discuss the important impact that a product's forecasted persistency has on the size of the product's loading. As you know, an insurer's product expenses can be high during a product's early years, as the insurer pays commissions and other acquisition expenses such as underwriting and issue expenses. The insurer generally recovers the first-year expenses of a block of business over several years. If the company expects a large number of customers to allow the product to lapse, then the company must establish a higher loading charge in order to recover its expenses.

For example, suppose the Telfair Life Insurance company introduces a new product. The company plans to sell 15,000 new policies in the product's first year and to recover $1 million of its first-year expenses in the product's second year. The table below shows how much the company will have to charge each customer in order to recover these expenses under an 80 percent persistency rate scenario and under a 70 percent persistency rate scenario.

	80% Persistency	70% Persistency
Number of first-year customers	15,000	15,000
Number of customers lapsing after first year	3,000	4,500
Number of customers paying premiums in second year	12,000	10,500
Expense per customer ($1 Million ÷ Number of customers)	$83.33	$95.24

As the table shows, if the first-year persistency rate forecasted for this product is 80 percent, the amount the Telfair Company must charge each customer in the second year to cover first-year expenses is $83.33. If the forecasted persistency rate drops to 70 percent, then the charge needed to cover first-year expenses increases to $95.24 per customer.

Insurers know that some product features generally affect persistency rates. In addition, different markets exhibit different persistency rates. Any factor that influences persistency should influence loading. As we illustrated in the previous example, higher persistency generally calls for lower loading, and lower persistency generally calls for higher loading.

Pricing for Investment Return

Earlier in this chapter, we noted that insurance products can contain three different margins: an expense margin, an underwriting margin, and an investment margin. In this section, we look at the investment margin and the various factors that determine the size of a product's investment margin. We also look at how investment returns are considered when an insurer prices bundled and unbundled products.

Interest Margin

The *interest margin* of an insurance product is the difference between the product's assumed interest rate or crediting rate and the actual interest rate earned by the company on the assets supporting that product. Thus:

Interest Margin = Actual Interest Rate – Assumed (or Crediting) Rate

For bundled products, the ***assumed rate*** is the interest rate that the company assumes when pricing the product. As we discussed in

Chapter 6, a *crediting rate* is the interest rate that a company uses to credit investment return to products and customer accounts. For unbundled products, companies earn an interest margin by crediting a lower interest rate than they actually earn on their investments. For bundled products, companies build an assumed interest margin into product prices by using an assumed rate that is lower than the interest rate they actually expect to earn on their investments. As with the expense margin, the actual interest margin is determined by the actual interest rate later earned on the insurer's investments.

Interest margin is often measured in basis points (bp). As we mentioned in Chapter 6, a *basis point* is one one-hundredth (0.01) of a percent. Therefore, half a percent is equal to 50 bp, and one and a half percent is equal to 150 bp.

The size of the interest margin varies considerably among different types of products. For example, for a group health insurance policy, investment return is a minor factor in the pricing and marketing of the product; for a mutual fund, investment return *is* the product. Most other products offered by insurers fall between these extremes.

The nature of a product influences the size of that product's interest margin. Earlier in this chapter, we discussed several factors that influence the size of margins in general; here we will elaborate on those factors that influence the interest margin specifically. Among the most important of these considerations are (1) the nature and duration of the product's investment guarantees, (2) the prominence of investment return, and (3) whether the product is participating or nonparticipating.

Investment Guarantees

Investment guarantees vary from one product to another. Generally, the more generous a product's investment guarantees, the higher the assumed interest margin on the product. An ***assumed interest margin*** is the interest margin an insurer builds into the pricing structure of a product. The actual interest margin a product experiences generally differs somewhat from the assumed interest margin. The wider assumed interest margin of a product with a more generous guarantee helps offset the risk that the insurer will earn a relatively low return on its asset portfolio but still have to pay a relatively high crediting rate.

As an example, suppose that Target Life Insurance Company offers two investment-based products. Product A offers a guaranteed minimum crediting rate of 4 percent and carries an assumed interest margin of 150 bp. Product B offers a guaranteed minimum crediting rate of 5 percent and has an assumed interest margin of 175 bp. The following table shows the interest margins Target Life would *actually* earn on both products under various interest rates earned on its asset portfolio:

Interest rate earned on asset portfolio	Crediting rate		Actual interest margin	
	A	B	A	B
3.00%	4.00%	5.00%	−1.00%	−2.00%
4.00%	4.00%	5.00%	0.00%	−1.00%
5.00%	4.00%	5.00%	1.00%	0.00%
6.00%	4.50%	5.00%	1.50%	1.00%
7.00%	5.50%	5.25%	1.50%	1.75%

The table demonstrates that the assumed interest margin the company sets may not be achieved if minimum guaranteed crediting rates kick in. Product B, because it offers a higher guarantee, has a greater risk of experiencing a reduced interest margin. Insurers often compensate for this risk by setting a higher assumed interest margin.

Two aspects of a product's investment guarantee help determine the size of that product's interest margin: the nature of the guarantee and the duration of the guarantee.

Nature of the Guarantee. Products offered by insurers can generally be placed into four categories, based on the nature of the investment guarantee they offer. Most products offer either an absolute investment guarantee, a minimum investment guarantee, a guarantee of principal, or no investment guarantee.

1. *Absolute investment guarantee.* The insurer credits a specific interest rate, no more and no less. Among products with absolute investment guarantees are fixed annuities and defined-benefit pension plans. Some GICs also include this type of guarantee. Some products, including ordinary life insurance, term insurance, medical expense insurance, and disability income insurance, contain an implicit absolute investment guarantee, though the owners of these products may not be aware that their policies involve such guarantees.

2. *Minimum investment guarantee.* The insurer guarantees to credit at least a specific interest rate, and, if its investment results allow, the insurer credits a higher rate than the minimum. Universal life insurance, most general-account deferred annuities, many variable products, and many GICs feature this type of guarantee.

3. *Guarantee of principal.* The customer is guaranteed not to lose any part of an investment. The actual credited rate depends on actual investment results but can never be negative. Note that a guarantee of principal is equivalent to a minimum investment guarantee of 0 percent. Variable annuities often feature this type of guarantee.

4. *No investment guarantee.* Crediting rates reflect investment results and can be negative as well as positive. On a product with no investment guarantee, a customer can lose principal as well as interest. Most mutual funds, many separate account funds, and some variable products have no investment guarantee.

For the products for which the insurer retains the highest amount of risk and maintains the widest interest margins, the insurer faces a further risk: the risk that, in a favorable interest rate environment, the customer will withdraw funds in order to earn a higher return from a different financial institution. For example, suppose a customer purchases an annuity with a fixed rate of 6 percent. Now suppose that, one year later, the fixed rate available on many annuities has risen to 8 percent. Many customers would be interested in surrendering the 6 percent annuity in order to purchase the annuity paying 8 percent. As we discussed in Chapter 4, insurers can reduce their exposure to this type of risk through such policy provisions as surrender charges, market value adjustments, low early-year surrender values, and variable policy loan interest rates.

Duration of the Guarantee. The longer a product's investment guarantee, the greater the amount of risk the insurer assumes. Consequently, the longer the period of time for which a specific crediting rate is guaranteed, the larger the expected interest margin is likely to be on that product. For example, a product that guarantees a specified interest rate for three years typically has a higher expected interest margin than does a product that guarantees an interest rate for only one year. Therefore, an insurer might offer an annuity with a 6.5 percent rate guaranteed for one year. However, the insurer would require a larger margin in order to guarantee a rate for three years, so the equivalent three-year guaranteed rate may be only 6.25 percent.

ExecuView Application 7-2 shows how annuity products with different investment guarantees require different investment margins.

Emphasis on Crediting Rate

Consumers select many unbundled products, such as defined-contribution pension plans, mutual fund shares, GICs, fixed and variable annuities, and variable and universal life insurance, largely on the basis of the crediting rate applied to the product. Generally, the greater a customer's emphasis on a product's crediting rate, the lower the insurer's interest margin on that product will be. The insurer must keep crediting rates for such products competitive with rates offered by other financial institutions. Consequently, the insurer may have to sacrifice some interest margin in order to keep such a product's crediting rate competitive.

Application 7-2 Investment Guarantees and Investment Margins

If you wish to demonstrate this example on your computer, start *ExecuView* and select the Immediate Annuity Model. Be sure to select *Reset, All Models* from the Action menu to return *ExecuView* to its default settings. The default assumptions and profitability outcome for this model and for the SPDA Model are shown on the following *ExecuView* screens.

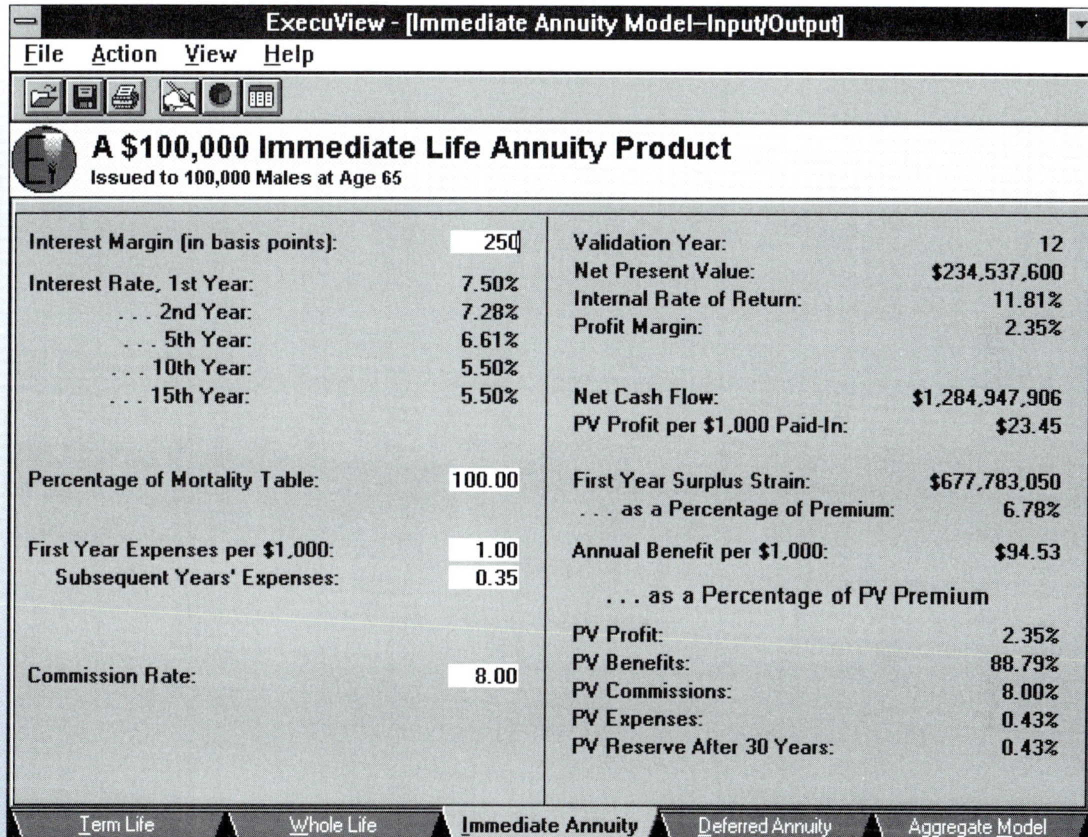

(*continued on next page*)

Further, the more easily a customer can isolate and identify a product's crediting or assumed rate, the lower the insurer's expected interest margin is likely to be. Thus, pricing structures for unbundled products typically feature lower investment margins than do premiums on bundled products. In order for insurers to earn an acceptable profit margin on unbundled products, insurers sometimes use a pricing structure that allows for a smaller interest margin but larger margins for expenses, or underwriting, or both.

Application 7-2 Investment Guarantees and Investment Margins (continued)

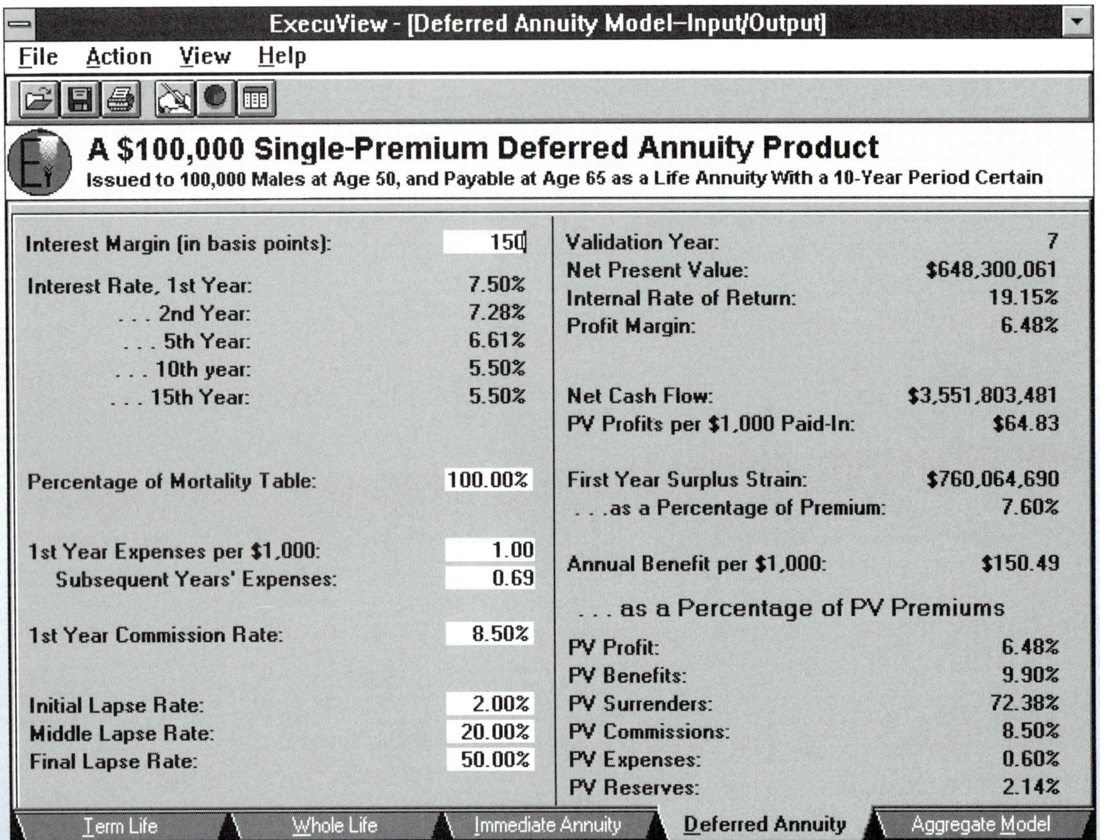

The chief actuary at the EV Life Insurance Company has become concerned about the investment margins built into the SPDA and immediate annuity products EV Life is preparing to introduce to the market. The SPDA currently offers a crediting rate 150 basis points below the rates EV Life earns on its investments, while the immediate annuity offers a crediting rate 250 basis points below the interest EV Life earns. Under current assumptions, both products meet the company's profit objectives.

The actuary's concern is with the immediate annuity product. While the SPDA product offers a floating crediting rate with a guaranteed minimum of 4 percent for all 15 years of the accumulation period, the crediting rate offered by the immediate annuity is guaranteed not to change from the time the annuity is purchased. The chief actuary believes that the immediate annuity's guarantee creates a huge risk for EV Life, since, under current assumptions, it will offer a guaranteed interest rate of 5 percent. She strongly believes that a wider investment margin needs to be built into the immediate annuity product in case of falling interest rates. Her argument is persuasive. Before the products are introduced, the investment margin of the immediate annuity product is changed to 275 basis points.

(continued on next page)

Application 7-2 Investment Guarantees and Investment Margins (continued)

➤ The *Interest Margin* of the Immediate Annuity Model is currently 250. Change this setting to 275. Press <enter> to view the results of this change.

Soon after the two annuity products are introduced, EV Life's investments begin to perform slightly less well than expected. The company earns the expected 7.5 percent interest rate on its investments for the first policy year. However, for years 2 through 10, the interest rate EV Life earns on its investments falls 0.3 percent annually, instead of falling 0.222 percentage points annually, as was assumed.

➤ Select the Aggregate Model. Adjust *Change, 2nd Year; Change, Years 3–5;* and *Change, Years 6–10* to -0.3. Press enter and return to the Immediate Annuity Model to view the results of these changes.

Under these conditions, the SPDA product breaks even in 7 years with a profit margin of 4.15 percent. The immediate annuity product breaks even in 16 years, but with a profit margin of only 1.39 percent. The return on the immediate annuity is not outstanding and is below EV Life's profit objectives, but it is within the bounds of solvency. The complete effect of these changes on the immediate and deferred annuities are shown on the following *ExecuView* screens.

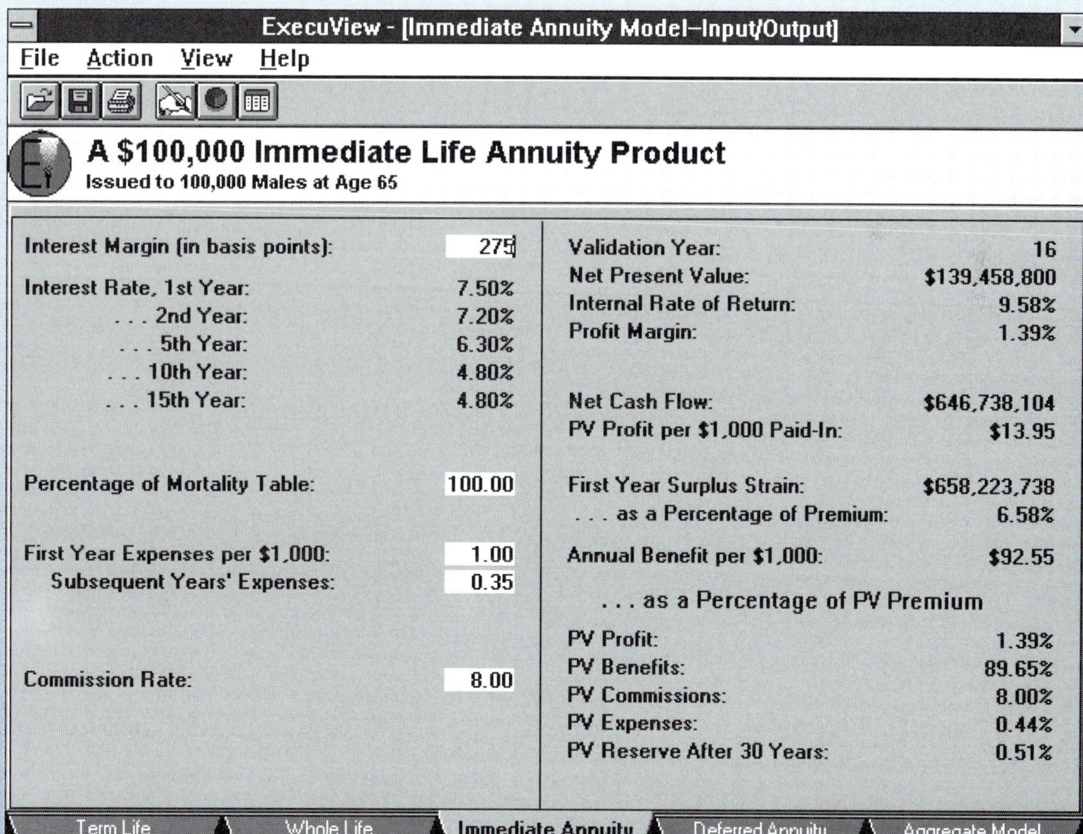

(*continued on next page*)

Application 7-2 Investment Guarantees and Investment Margins (continued)

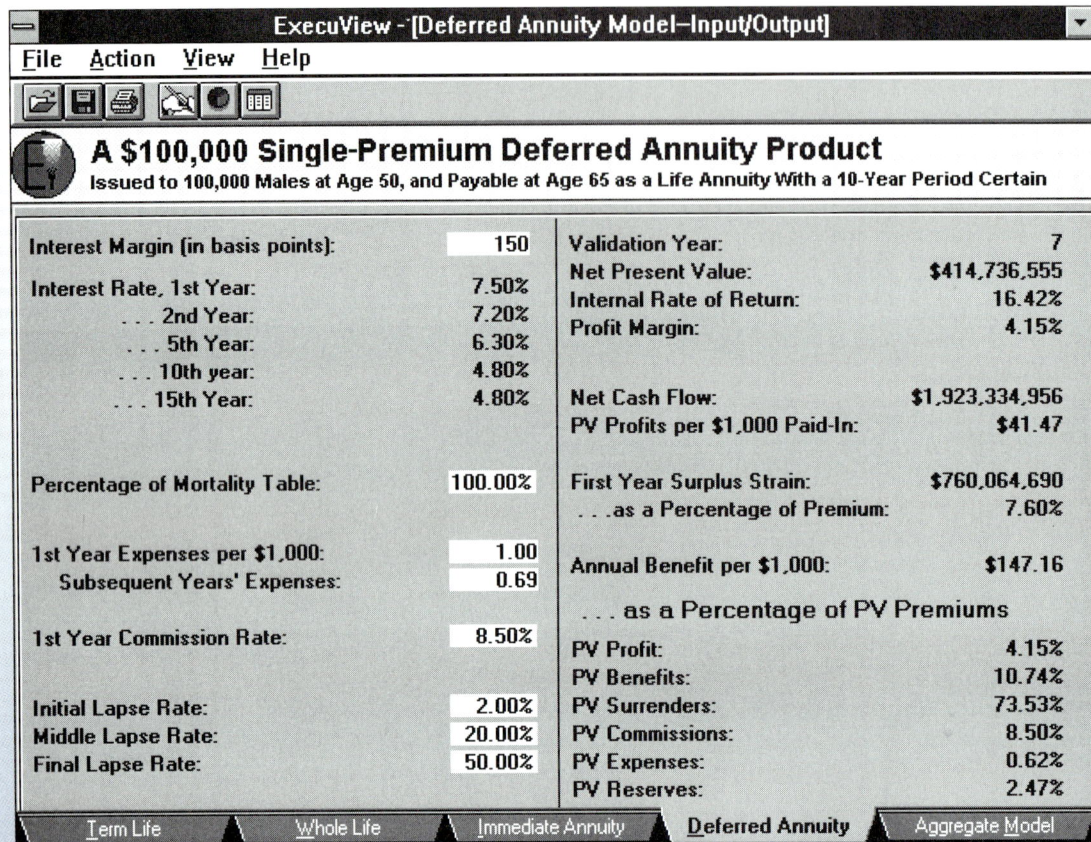

Participating Policies

Participating policies present a special case to insurers setting target interest margins. Participating policies allow insurers, in effect, to retroactively reduce a policy's price through dividend payments after the insurer's actual investment results are known. Typically, the interest margin included in the initial price of a participating policy is larger than the interest margin included in the price of an equivalent nonparticipating policy. However, the *actual* interest margin earned by the insurer after policy dividends have been paid may be smaller than the actual interest margin earned on nonparticipating products.

The following table summarizes the factors that determine the size of a product's interest margin:

Interest margin depends on . . .	• Type of product: insurance or investment
	• Whether the product is participating or nonparticipating
	• The nature of the product's investment guarantee
	• The length of the product's investment guarantee

How Investment Return Is Incorporated into a Product's Price

In general, insurers try to earn an interest margin by earning a return on their investments that is higher than the rates they credit for their products. The amount kept by the insurer—the margin—is, in effect, part of the price the customer pays for the product.

The manner in which the interest margin is incorporated into a product's price depends on the type of product. When we described how products are priced for expenses, we distinguished between how expense charges and margins are incorporated into the prices of bundled and unbundled products. Like expense charges, assumed rates and crediting rates can be bundled with the other pricing factors when the insurer is determining the gross premium amount, or they can be expressed separately. We look at both of these methods in the following sections.

Crediting Rates for Unbundled Products

For unbundled products, the insurer periodically selects a crediting rate and increases the appropriate policy values by the specified rate. For example, the cash value of a universal life policy may be credited with interest once monthly. Similarly, annuities are credited with interest at regular intervals.

An insurer must consider two important factors when it sets the crediting rate for a given period. One such factor is the effect of the crediting rate decision on the persistency of in-force products and on new product sales. If customers can earn a better crediting rate from a product offered by one of the insurer's competitors, the customers may decide to invest their funds with the competition.

The other factor the insurer must consider when setting crediting rates is its need to earn an acceptable profit margin. Sometimes, particularly when interest rates rise, this need can be in conflict with the insurer's desire to remain competitive. For example, suppose interest rates rise by 1 percent. To remain competitive with other financial institutions, an insurer would be tempted to raise its crediting rates by 1 percent. However, the insurer's investment portfolio may contain a large proportion of fixed-rate bonds that were purchased at the lower interest rate. Because of the fixed-rate bonds, the insurer's portfolio rate will not rise by 1 percent immediately. In such a situation, insurers may not be able to raise their crediting rates to keep pace with the general rise in interest rates without severely reducing margins. When setting crediting rates, insurers must balance competitive concerns with concerns for maintaining appropriate margins.

Assumed Rates in Bundled Product Premiums

Customers who purchase bundled products are generally unaware of the interest rates the insurer assumes when pricing these products. With bundled products, the insurer must establish a premium rate, based on a specific assumed interest rate, that will generate enough revenue to pay the benefit amount promised by the product when the benefit is due.

The money the insurer uses to pay a product's benefit amount comes from two sources: (1) the premiums the customer pays for the product and (2) the return the insurer earns by investing the customer's premiums. If an insurer did not earn investment income and had to pay the benefit solely from the product premium, the premium would need to be much higher. Thus, investment income reduces the price of bundled products.

Consider, for example, a GIC that promises to pay the customer $1,000 in 10 years. If the insurer had to generate funds to pay this product's benefit from customer contributions alone, then the purchaser would have to pay $1,000 for the product. On the other hand, suppose the insurer is able to earn a 12 percent investment return and, after subtracting an interest margin of 200 basis points (2 percent), credits 10 percent annual interest to the customer. The investment income allows the insurer to charge the customer far less for the product. If the customer wishes to make a single payment at the beginning of the 10 years, then, disregarding expenses, the purchaser need make only a single payment of $386—the *present value* of $1,000, assuming a discount rate of 10 percent. This is far less than the $1,000 the customer would have to pay in the absence of investment income. Alternatively, the customer could make 10 payments of $57.11 at the beginning of each year. Clearly, investment return reduces the price of this product considerably.

Figure 7-12 illustrates how investment income helps the insurer accumulate $1,000 to pay this product's benefit.

In Conclusion

In this chapter, we began our discussion of product pricing. We discussed the role that competitive forces, costs, and regulation play in

Figure 7-12. Investment income reduces the premium amount that must be charged for bundled products.

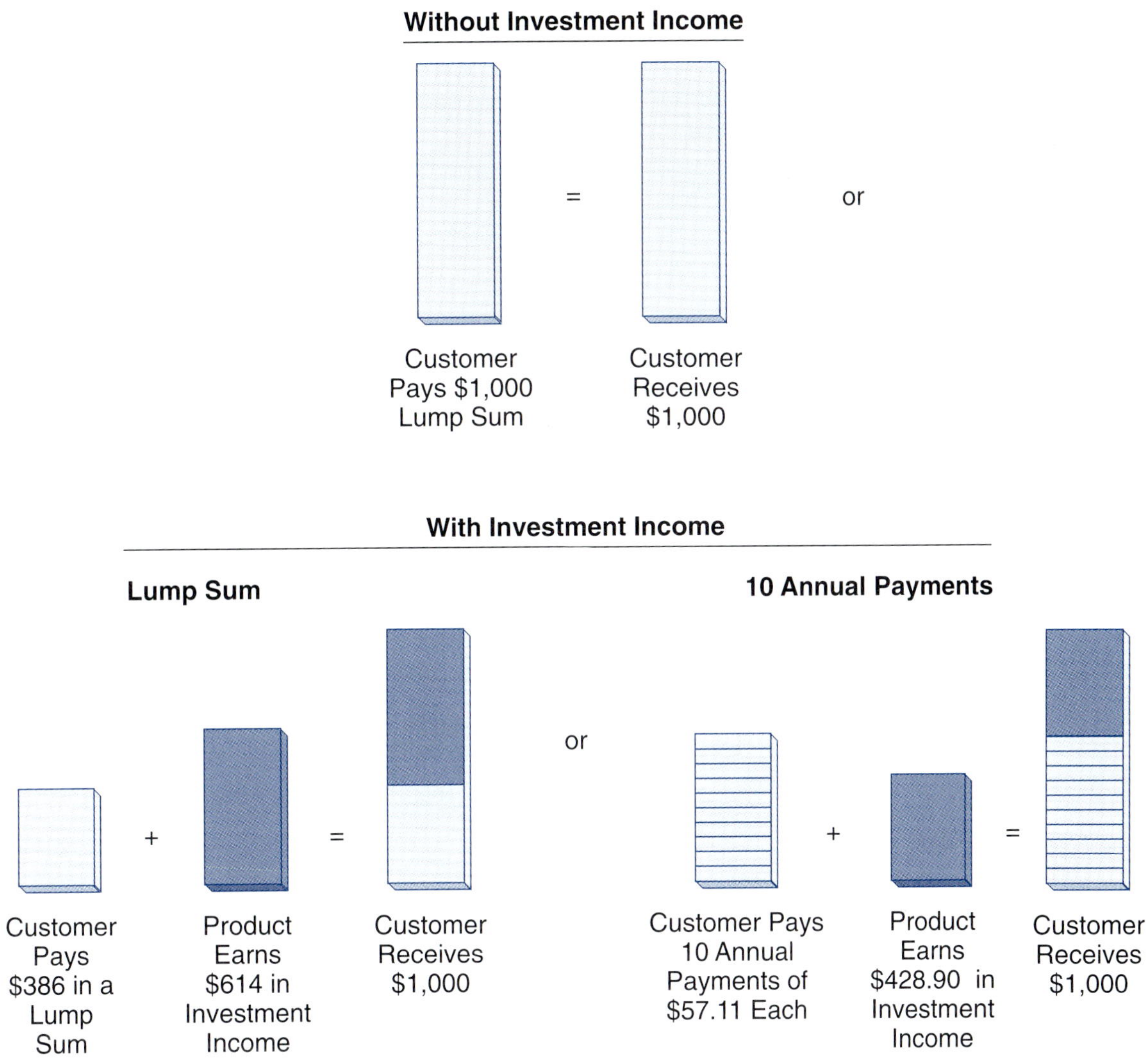

setting the upper and lower limits of a product's price. We then went on to examine the pricing elements associated with insurance and financial products. Next, we discussed expenses and expense margins, and how they are incorporated into the prices of various financial products under direct and full costing. We concluded with a discussion of investment return and interest margin, and how investments affect the prices of bundled and unbundled products.

In the next chapter, we describe how mortality and morbidity rates are used along with present value mathematics to calculate the cost of benefit payments for insurance products. In so doing, we examine the third factor in the pricing of an insurance product—the cost of benefit payments.

Key Terms and Concepts

consideration
quantity demanded
reasonable rates
adequate rates
equitable rates
margin
underwriting margin
expense margin
investment margin
expected values
expected margin
assumed values
assumed margin
actual values
actual margin
thin margin
wide margin
expense charge
loading
retention charge
acquisition expenses
maintenance expenses
standard costs
favorable deviation
risk charge
direct expenses
indirect expenses
costing
marginal costing
full costing
bundled product
unbundled product
banding
policy fee system
front-end load
back-end load
periodic fee
transfer fee
assumed rate
assumed interest margin

CHAPTER

Pricing Products to Reflect Insurance Risk

8

LEARNING OBJECTIVES

After studying this chapter, you should be able to

- Identify the purposes of different types of mortality and morbidity statistics
- Recognize how to use mortality or morbidity statistics to calculate the cost of benefit payments for various types of insurance and annuity products
- Recognize the importance of the costs of benefits to product pricing

OUTLINE

In the last chapter, we discussed how market forces, a product's costs, and regulations work together to impose an upper and lower limit on a product's price range. We also noted that an insurance product's profit margin can be viewed as consisting of three margins—an expense margin, an investment margin, and an underwriting margin. We then examined how insurers incorporate the expense and investment margins into a product's price.

In this chapter, we focus on the underwriting margin and the cost of providing benefits. As we noted in Chapter 7, the underwriting margin is the difference between the cost of providing benefits and the amount the insurer charges the customer for those benefits. Chapter 8 describes how insurers estimate a product's benefit costs and apply those costs in the pricing process to calculate net premiums.

Specifically, we discuss the techniques insurers use—with data from mortality and morbidity tables—to forecast the amount and timing of cash outflows related to benefit payments. We begin by explaining the basic methods insurers use to calculate net premiums once benefit costs are known. We then introduce mortality and morbidity tables, describe the different types of tables, and explain how they are used. After that, we describe some specific uses of mortality and morbidity data that apply to group insurance. Later in the chapter, we examine how insurers use mortality and morbidity data to forecast benefit cash flows and how insurers incorporate underwriting margins into the prices of various types of insurance and annuity products. Chapter 8 completes our discussion of the factors an insurer considers in establishing gross premiums for insurance and annuity products.

Calculating Net Premiums

As we discussed in Chapter 4, a *net premium* is the amount per unit of coverage that an insurance company must collect from customers to precisely cover a product's cost of benefits. However, the premium payments that insurers receive from customers and the benefit payments that insurers make to customers occur at different times. To acknowledge for this difference in timing, insurers use *present value* techniques.

Insurers use net premiums for at least two distinct purposes: (1) in pricing and (2) in the valuation of reserves. However, insurers do not use the same net premium amounts for these two situations. In this text, we refer to net premiums used in pricing as *pricing net premiums* and to net premiums used in reserve valuations as *valuation net premiums.* The assumptions insurers use for pricing generally differ from the assumptions insurers use to calculate reserves. Calculating reserves generally requires more conservative assumptions than does pricing, so valuation net premiums are usually larger than pricing net premiums. This chapter focuses on pricing, so for the remainder of this chapter the term *net premiums* refers to pricing net premiums.

Pricing a product to account for the timing and amount of benefit and premium payments consists of two steps:

1. The insurer uses present value techniques to calculate the amount it would need to invest at the moment the product is issued to precisely cover the estimated *cost* to the insurer of the product's *benefit payments.* This amount is known as the product's net single premium. The ***net single premium*** is commonly defined as the present value of a product's benefit costs at the moment the product is issued.

Net Single Premium = Present Value of Benefit Costs at Time of Policy Issue

2. The insurer uses present value techniques to find a set of one or more *premium payments* whose value to the insurer, at the moment the product is issued, is equal to the net single premium.

A customer could pay exactly for the cost of the product's benefits by making a single payment equal to the net single premium. Although some customers pay for an insurance product with a single payment, most prefer to make payments annually for a certain number of years, such as 5, 10, or 20 years, or for as long as the product continues in force. Calculating the net premium payments a customer would have to pay involves finding a series of premium payments whose present value, given the amount and timing of each payment, is equal to the net single premium at the moment of policy issue. There are several sets of premium payments whose present values are equal to the net single premium. An annual premium established to cover the costs of benefit payments is called a ***net annual premium.*** A net annual premium payable for 5 years is a *5-year net annual premium,* payable for 10 years is a *10-year net annual premium,* and payable for as long as the product continues in force is a *lifetime net annual premium.* However long the annual premiums continue, the present value of all the net annual premiums must equal the net single premium.

The following table summarizes the steps followed in calculating pricing net premiums:

To calculate pricing net premiums . . .	1. Find the net single premium (present value of benefit payments) 2. Find a set of premium payments whose present value equals the net single premium

In order to illustrate this process, let's assume that an insurance product will pay a benefit of $1,000 ten years after it is issued. The insurer expects to earn enough investment return to credit interest to the product at the rate of 10 percent. For simplicity, we assume that the interest is credited once a year.

STEP 1: Find the net single premium.

To pay the product's benefits, the insurer needs to have $1,000 in 10 years. The insurer therefore needs to calculate the present value of $1,000. Assume that the appropriate discount rate is 10 percent—the investment return the insurer plans to credit to the product. The discount period is 10 years—the amount of time between when the product is issued and when the $1,000 will be paid to the customer.

The net single premium needed to fund a $1,000 benefit in 10 years, discounted at 10 percent annually, is $386. This calculation is made as follows:

Net Single Premium = Present Value [10 years, 10%] of $1,000
= $1,000 x ***PVIF*** (10, 10%)
= $1,000 x 0.386
= $386

STEP 2: Find a set of premium payments whose present value equals the net single premium.

Suppose the customer wishes to pay for this product with a series of 10 annual premium payments. The insurer, then, needs to calculate the 10-year net annual premium. In order to calculate this net annual premium, the insurer needs to find the periodic payment of a 10-payment annuity at 10 percent interest that would be equivalent to a single payment of $386. In other words, the insurer needs to find the *periodic payment of an annuity whose present value is equal to the product's net single premium.* The method that an insurer would use to calculate this payment is beyond the scope of this discussion. Using present value techniques, we have calculated that the net annual premium for this product would be $57.11.

Insurers can also calculate semiannual, monthly, or weekly net premiums—or, for that matter, net premiums for periods of any length.

Note that all present value calculations require that the insurer select a discount rate. The insurer generally uses the assumed discount rate for this purpose. All other factors being equal, the higher the discount rate, the lower the present value. Thus, when using present values to calculate net premiums, the higher the assumed rate, the lower the net premium. Further, all other factors being equal, the longer the discount period, the lower the present value. Thus, when calculating net premiums, the longer the time until policy benefits are paid, the lower the net premium.

Introduction to Mortality Tables

The first step in forecasting the cost of benefits on a life insurance or an annuity product is selecting an appropriate mortality table. ***Mortality tables*** show the mortality rates, by age, among given groups of people. A ***mortality rate*** is the rate at which death occurs among a defined group of people. The mortality rates shown in mortality tables are called ***tabular rates.*** Insurers can use several types of mortality tables. The mortality table that an insurer uses in a given situation depends on a number of factors, including the following:

- *The type of product.* The mortality rates associated with one type of product generally differ from those associated with other types of products. Where possible, insurers use mortality tables that are appropriate for the type of product being priced. For example, lower mortality rates are used for annuities than are used for life insurance policies. In addition, lower mortality rates are used for products that require the consumer to provide substantial underwriting information than are used for products that require minimal underwriting information. Also, lower mortality rates are used for nonparticipating policies than are used for participating policies. These concepts are explained in later sections of this chapter.

- *The purpose for using the table.* Mortality tables are used for pricing and also for other purposes, notably for calculating policy reserves. In the United States, insurers use different mortality rates for pricing than they use for calculating statutory policy reserves. Canadian insurers usually use the same mortality tables for calculating policy reserves and for pricing but with an additional safety margin built in for the calculation of reserves. ***Statutory policy reserves*** are policy reserves established to satisfy the requirements of state insurance regulators.

- *The characteristics of the population to be insured.* Mortality rates vary among different groups of people. For example, people who have recently been through the underwriting process exhibit lower mortality than do people who have not. In addition, members of certain demographic groups, residents of certain geographic areas, and people with certain health histories exhibit historically higher or lower mortality rates than other populations. Where possible, insurers use mortality tables and rates that are appropriate for a product's target market.

Product-Differentiated Mortality Tables

Because purchasers of life insurance and annuity products exhibit different mortality patterns, insurers must use separate mortality tables for different product types. Annuity mortality tables show lower mortality rates than life insurance mortality tables because annuitants tend to live longer than life insureds.

In addition, people who purchase the various types of life insurance exhibit different levels of mortality. Thus, insurers often use separate mortality tables and rates for different types of products, such as ordinary life, group yearly renewable term (YRT), individual YRT, level-premium term, and industrial insurance. Likewise, people covered by individual annuities exhibit different mortality patterns than people covered by group annuities. Accordingly, insurers often use different tables and rates for individual annuities than they use for group annuities.

Basic and Valuation Mortality Tables

Two of the most important uses insurers have for mortality tables are

- Calculating the amount of the policy reserves insurers need to maintain
- Forecasting the cost of a product's benefit payments in order to price the product

In the United States, insurers use different mortality tables for calculating statutory policy reserves than they use for pricing. The mortality tables used to calculate statutory policy reserves are called ***valuation mortality tables.*** The valuation mortality tables used for calculating statutory reserves are conservative because they have a safety margin built into their rates. State regulators require that a safety margin be built into insurance companies' statutory reserves to ensure that, even under adverse conditions, insurers maintain enough assets to pay policy benefits as they become due. Among *life insurance* mortality tables, the more conservative the mortality table, the *higher* the mortality rate for each age. In contrast, for *annuity* mortality tables, the more conservative the mortality table, the *lower* the mortality rate for each age.

The mortality tables with no safety margin built into the rates are called ***basic mortality tables.*** Basic mortality tables are less conservative than statutory valuation tables and are used for pricing products. Basic tables are designed to provide realistic mortality estimates. By using realistic mortality estimates, an insurer can price products to reflect the actual costs of providing insurance.

Sex-Distinct and Unisex Mortality Tables

Mortality tables may be constructed on a sex-distinct or a unisex basis. ***Sex-distinct mortality tables*** show different mortality rates for males and females, reflecting the fact that women, as a group, experience lower mortality at all ages than men.* ***Unisex mortality tables*** show a single set of mortality rates to be used for both males and females.

Use of sex-distinct mortality tables to price life insurance products results in lower premium rates for female insureds than for male insureds of the same age. Use of sex-distinct mortality tables to price annuity products results in higher premiums for females than for males of the same age. However, whenever insurers use sex-distinct tables for pricing, the rates for males and females are said to be actuarially equivalent. When an insurer uses unisex tables, men and women of the same age are charged the same premiums for the same types of coverage.

Unisex tables were developed because advocacy groups, court decisions, and some legislation have argued that, in the name of equality, men and women of the same age should be charged the same premium rates for insurance and annuity products despite clear statistics showing mortality differences. In the United States, the Norris decision by the Supreme Court requires that employer-sponsored benefit plans use unisex mortality tables, and the state of Montana has legally mandated the use of unisex mortality tables for all life insurance products. However, in most circumstances, insurers use sex-distinct mortality tables to develop actuarially equivalent pricing for male and female customers.

Select, Ultimate, and Aggregate Mortality Tables

A group of insureds that has been recently underwritten generally exhibits lower mortality than does a similar group of insureds that has not been underwritten recently. Thus, a group of 50-year-olds shown to be in good health last year typically would have better mortality experience than would a group of 50-year-olds whose health had not been underwritten since they were age 30.

* Most sex-distinct mortality tables are unisex from ages 0 to 15.

Figure 8-1. Example of a select mortality table.

Age at Issue	Year of Insurance				
	1	2	3	4	5
50	4.12	4.69	5.39	6.13	6.82
51	4.45	5.09	5.90	6.72	7.50
52	4.79	5.53	6.44	7.38	8.25
53	5.21	5.99	6.96	7.97	8.93
54	5.66	6.50	7.54	8.60	9.67
55	6.15	7.06	8.16	9.30	10.49

A mortality table showing the expected mortality rates of people whose policies have been underwritten recently is called a ***select mortality table.*** Figure 8-1 illustrates a select mortality table. The select table shows mortality rates based not only on the insured's age but also based on the number of years since the policy was underwritten and issued. On a select mortality table, insureds aged 50 who were underwritten 1 year ago tend to exhibit lower mortality rates than insureds aged 50 who were underwritten 4 years ago. Figure 8-1 shows mortality rates for 5 years after policy issue. Many select mortality tables show rates for more than 5 years after issue. The correlation between recent underwriting and a lower mortality rate is generally thought to wear off between 5 and 15 years after policy issue. The length of time during which the effects of selection (underwriting) are assumed to be observable and significant is known as the ***select period.***

An ***ultimate mortality table*** shows mortality rates for people who have *not* recently been underwritten. Such people are likely to experience higher mortality than those who recently proved their good health. In an ultimate table, all insureds of the same age and sex are shown as having the same mortality.

As shown in Figure 8-2, a ***select and ultimate mortality table*** shows both select mortality rates and ultimate mortality rates. Notice that mortality rates in the first through fifth years of insurance in this table are identical to those in a select mortality table. In the portion of the select and ultimate table representing policy years after the expiration of the select period (Years 6 and later in this table), the mortality rates are identical to those in an ultimate mortality table. The *Age at Issue* on the left of the select and ultimate table applies to the select portion of the table. The *Attained Age* on the right-hand side of the table applies to the ultimate portion of the table; it is the age at which the select period ends for each *Age at Issue.*

In Figure 8-2, we can see that the mortality rate for a person aged 55 who has just been underwritten is 6.15 (*Age at Issue,* 55; *Year of*

Figure 8-2. Example of a select and ultimate mortality table.

Age at Issue	Year of Insurance						Attained Age
	1	2	3	4	5	6 and over	
50	4.12	4.69	5.39	6.13	6.82	7.64	55
51	4.45	5.09	5.90	6.72	7.50	8.42	56
52	4.79	5.53	6.44	7.38	8.25	9.28	57
53	5.21	5.99	6.96	7.97	8.93	10.24	58
54	5.66	6.50	7.54	8.60	9.67	11.32	59
55	6.15	7.06	8.16	9.30	10.49	12.53	60

Insurance, 1). The same person at the age of 58 would have a mortality rate of 9.30 (*Age at Issue,* 55; *Year of Insurance,* 4). In contrast, a person aged 58 who was underwritten at age 50 would have a mortality rate of 10.24 (*Attained Age,* 58; *Year of Insurance,* 6 and over).

Finally, an ***aggregate mortality table*** combines select mortality data and ultimate mortality data to arrive at a single mortality rate for each age. The mortality figure for each age is an average of select mortality data and ultimate mortality data and, thus, reflects the expected mortality of all insureds, those who have been underwritten recently and those who have not. This is in contrast to the ultimate mortality table, which *ignores* whether people have been recently underwritten.

Insurers use select tables, ultimate tables, and aggregate tables for different purposes. Ultimate tables show higher mortality rates than select tables and aggregate tables. Insurers use ultimate tables in situations in which conservative mortality rates are most appropriate. For example, statutory valuation mortality tables are often ultimate tables. In addition, insurers use ultimate tables (though not statutory valuation tables) to price participating policies, for which insurers can refund a portion of any excess mortality charge in the form of dividends. On the other hand, select and ultimate or aggregate tables are generally used in situations where less conservative tables are appropriate, such as in the pricing of nonparticipating policies.

Published and Proprietary Mortality Tables

Insurers use both published and proprietary mortality tables. ***Published mortality tables*** are available to the general public and are based on the experience of the public at large or of insured and annuitant populations. The mortality tables an insurer develops itself, based largely on its own experience with its insureds, are known as ***proprietary mortality tables.***

In general, larger insurers are more likely to develop proprietary tables than smaller insurers. For pricing purposes, larger insurers generally use proprietary basic mortality tables. However, some smaller insurers may not have sufficient experience with their own insureds to produce reliable mortality data. Additionally, a smaller insurer may not possess adequate resources to perform the necessary mortality studies on the experience of its own insureds. Therefore, to price their products, some smaller insurers use published basic mortality tables, such as the Society of Actuaries basic tables (discussed later in this section). Often, insurers use mortality rates based on, but not exactly equal to, those shown in the published table. For example, a company might use 85 percent of the industry average rates shown in the published table.

Among the best known and most commonly used published mortality tables are the statutory valuation tables compiled and published by the Society of Actuaries (SOA) at the request of the NAIC. The following statutory life insurance valuation mortality tables are currently in use:

- 1980 Commissioner's Standard Ordinary (1980 CSO)
- 1960 Commissioner's Standard Group (1960 CSG)
- 1980 Commissioner's Extended Term (1980 CET)
- 1961 Commissioner's Standard Industrial (1961 CSI)
- 1961 Commissioner's Industrial Extended Term (1961 CIET)

The SOA's annuity valuation mortality tables currently in use are the following:

- 1983 Table *a*
- 1983 Group Annuity Mortality (GAM)

The SOA also publishes valuation tables for disability income insurance.

Not all published mortality tables are valuation tables. For example, the SOA periodically creates and publishes a basic select and ultimate mortality table based on the mortality data of a group of established insurers. The life insurance examples we review in this chapter are based on the *1975–80 Basic Select and Ultimate* mortality table for males. The annuity examplcs in this chapter are based on an SOA basic annuity table, the *1983 Basic Table.* Figure 8-3 and Figure 8-4 show excerpts from these two tables.

Figure 8-3. Excerpt from 1975–80 Basic Select and Ultimate mortality table, male, age-nearest-birthday (mortality rates per thousand).

	Policy Year															Ultimate	
Age	1	2	3	4	5	6	7	8	9	10	11	12	13	14	15	Rate	Age
20	0.93	0.97	0.97	0.97	0.97	0.95	0.93	0.90	0.90	0.91	0.93	0.94	0.96	1.01	1.08	1.17	35
21	0.84	0.87	0.87	0.87	0.87	0.86	0.85	0.83	0.85	0.86	0.90	0.92	0.96	1.02	1.11	1.22	36
22	0.73	0.76	0.76	0.76	0.77	0.77	0.77	0.77	0.80	0.83	0.88	0.91	0.96	1.04	1.15	1.28	37
23	0.73	0.76	0.75	0.75	0.75	0.76	0.77	0.77	0.80	0.84	0.90	0.94	1.00	1.10	1.21	1.36	38
24	0.73	0.74	0.73	0.73	0.74	0.76	0.77	0.78	0.82	0.87	0.93	0.97	1.05	1.17	1.29	1.45	39
25	0.72	0.72	0.72	0.72	0.74	0.76	0.77	0.79	0.84	0.90	0.96	1.03	1.12	1.25	1.38	1.56	40
26	0.70	0.70	0.71	0.72	0.73	0.76	0.78	0.82	0.88	0.95	1.02	1.09	1.20	1.35	1.49	1.70	41
27	0.68	0.68	0.70	0.71	0.73	0.77	0.81	0.86	0.92	1.01	1.08	1.17	1.30	1.47	1.63	1.87	42
28	0.66	0.68	0.71	0.73	0.76	0.81	0.86	0.92	1.00	1.08	1.17	1.28	1.42	1.61	1.81	2.07	43
29	0.65	0.68	0.73	0.76	0.81	0.86	0.92	1.00	1.08	1.17	1.28	1.42	1.58	1.81	2.03	2.31	44
30	0.64	0.68	0.76	0.81	0.86	0.92	1.00	1.08	1.17	1.28	1.42	1.58	1.81	2.03	2.26	2.58	45
31	0.63	0.69	0.79	0.86	0.92	1.00	1.08	1.17	1.28	1.42	1.58	1.81	2.03	2.26	2.53	2.89	46
32	0.63	0.71	0.84	0.92	1.00	1.08	1.17	1.28	1.40	1.58	1.81	2.03	2.26	2.53	2.83	3.24	47
33	0.63	0.72	0.88	0.98	1.08	1.17	1.28	1.40	1.58	1.78	2.01	2.25	2.53	2.83	3.17	3.61	48
34	0.63	0.73	0.93	1.05	1.17	1.28	1.40	1.58	1.78	2.01	2.24	2.53	2.81	3.16	3.54	4.02	49
35	0.63	0.76	0.99	1.14	1.28	1.40	1.58	1.78	2.01	2.24	2.53	2.80	3.13	3.52	3.94	4.45	50
36	0.65	0.79	1.06	1.25	1.40	1.58	1.78	2.01	2.24	2.53	2.80	3.10	3.48	3.91	4.36	4.92	51
37	0.67	0.84	1.15	1.37	1.58	1.78	2.01	2.24	2.53	2.80	3.08	3.43	3.86	4.32	4.82	5.44	52
38	0.70	0.89	1.23	1.47	1.70	1.91	2.16	2.41	2.72	3.04	3.35	3.76	4.25	4.78	5.33	6.00	53
39	0.74	0.95	1.33	1.59	1.83	2.07	2.33	2.60	2.93	3.27	3.64	4.10	4.67	5.28	5.88	6.61	54

Source: *Reprinted, with permission, from Paquin, C.Y., "An Extension of the 1975–80 Basic Select and Ultimate Mortality Tables, Male and Female—Actuarial Note,* Transactions of the Society of Actuaries *XXXVIII (1986): 210–211. Copyright © 1987 by the Society of Actuaries.*

Figure 8-4. Excerpt from 1983 Basic Table (mortality rates per thousand).

Age	Males	Females	Age	Males	Females
65	14.248	8.241	90	150.099	125.936
66	15.761	9.114	91	161.082	138.997
67	17.467	10.012	92	172.699	152.469
68	19.373	10.931	93	185.049	166.187
69	21.486	11.916	94	198.219	180.008
70	23.810	13.027	95	212.291	193.795
71	26.353	14.326	96	227.346	207.411
72	29.120	15.872	97	243.467	220.718
73	32.123	17.717	98	260.903	234.236
74	35.398	19.883	99	279.903	248.485
75	38.986	22.383	100	300.716	263.985
76	42.930	25.228	101	323.592	281.255
77	47.272	28.433	102	348.780	300.815
78	52.054	32.017	103	376.529	323.185
79	57.325	36.029	104	407.088	348.885
80	63.132	40.525	105	440.707	378.434
81	69.523	45.561	106	477.634	412.352
82	76.547	51.194	107	518.120	451.160
83	84.229	57.483	108	562.412	495.376
84	92.498	64.512	109	610.761	545.521
85	101.261	72.368	110	663.417	602.115
86	110.424	81.137	111	720.626	665.676
87	119.894	90.907	112	782.640	736.725
88	129.609	101.721	113	849.708	815.782
89	139.643	113.454	114	922.077	903.367
			115	1,000.000	1,000.000

Source: *Reprinted, with permission, from "Report of the Committee to Recommend a New Mortality Basis for Individual Annuity Valuation (Derivation of the 1983 Table a),"* Transactions of the Society of Actuaries *XXXIII (1981): 695. Copyright © 1982 by the Society of Actuaries.*

The following list summarizes the characteristics of some of the types of mortality tables we have discussed.

- Valuation tables are conservative and used to calculate reserves.
- Basic tables show realistic mortality rates and can be used for pricing.
- Life insurance tables show higher mortality rates than annuity tables.
- Select tables show mortality for people recently underwritten.
- Ultimate tables show mortality for people not recently underwritten.
- Select and ultimate tables show select and ultimate mortality separately.
- Aggregate tables combine select and ultimate mortality data.
- Published tables are available to the public and are based on the mortality of the public at large or the general insured population.
- Proprietary tables are an insurer's private tables, based on the mortality of the insurer's own insureds.

Methods of Modifying Tabular Mortality Rates

Most mortality tables are based on data concerning people who were insured in the past. However, for many years mortality rates have steadily improved. Therefore, the mortality tables based on past experience alone generally provide inaccurate predictions of future mortality. For this reason, insurers often modify tabular rates using one of two methods: the projection method or the setback method.

With the ***projection method,*** the insurer multiplies the mortality rate found in a mortality table by a certain percentage. For example, if the insurer forecasts that actual mortality will be 95 percent of the tabular rate, the insurer will multiply the rate found in the table by 0.95.

With the ***setback method,*** the insurer forecasts the mortality rate for insureds or annuitants of a certain age by using the mortality rate shown in the table for people of a younger age. For example, to use a two-year setback to forecast mortality for 35-year-olds, the insurer would use the tabular mortality rate for 33-year-olds.

Actuarial Assumptions and the Underwriting Margin

As noted in Chapter 7, a product's actual underwriting margin is the difference between the insurer's actual cost of providing benefits and the assumed cost of benefits the insurer includes in the product's price to cover benefits. Insurers can build a safety margin into a product's underwriting components by setting a charge for benefits that is greater than the expected cost of benefits. Setting an assumed underwriting margin that incorporates a safety factor may provide for a profit margin and, at the very least, creates a safety margin that may help the insurer meet its benefit obligations if underwriting results are worse than expected.

Although an insurer can incorporate a safety margin into a product's assumed underwriting margin, the *actual* underwriting margin depends on the actual cost of benefits. The actual underwriting margin and actual cost of benefits may not be known for many years. Although insurers can manage their underwriting risk to a certain extent through the underwriting and pricing processes, they cannot control such factors as epidemics, environmental catastrophes, wars, terrorist acts, and health trends, all of which can greatly influence actual results. In other words, an insurer can build an underwriting margin into a product's price, but the actual underwriting margin may be considerably smaller than the assumed margin, or the actual margin may even be negative. On the other hand, the actual underwriting margin might also be larger than the assumed margin.

Insurers build a safety margin into a product's assumed underwriting margin in a number of ways. Three possible approaches include

1. *Using a conservative mortality or morbidity table.* For example, even though an insurer believes that the mortality associated with a life insurance product will be consistent with select mortality rates, the insurer could use ultimate mortality rates—which are more conservative than select mortality rates—rather than select mortality to price the product.

2. *Using a multiple of expected mortality or morbidity.* For example, the insurer might use 110 percent of expected mortality in pricing a life insurance policy or 90 percent of expected mortality in pricing an annuity contract.

3. *Adding a flat amount per $1,000 of coverage to a bundled product's net premium or an unbundled product's mortality charge.* For example, if a product's net premium based on expected mortality is $2.50 per $1,000 of insurance, then the insurer might price the product using a net premium of $3.00 per $1,000 of insurance.

Size of the Underwriting Margin

In pricing, insurers determine the size of the assumed underwriting margin on the basis of two primary factors: (1) *competition* and (2) the level of *underwriting risk* undertaken by the insurer in offering the product.

The more competition a product faces in the marketplace, the smaller the underwriting margin is likely to be. A smaller underwriting margin reduces the price of the product, helping it to be more competitive. Thus, because of the intense competition among term products, term life insurance generally includes a smaller underwriting margin than ordinary life.

An insurer's underwriting risk in connection with a given product can arise from a number of sources, including (1) lack of experience on which to forecast underwriting results, (2) the length of price guarantees, and (3) antiselection. As we discuss later in the text, insurers can reduce their exposure to these sources of underwriting risk by using reinsurance.

An insurer takes on a higher underwriting risk when it has no direct experience on which to base its mortality forecasts. For example, an insurer may have no credible mortality experience when it introduces a product in a new market or offers a product it has not previously offered. Because of the added underwriting risk, a new product or a product offered in a new market may feature a relatively high underwriting margin.

Another element of risk is the extent of the product's price guarantees. Term life products, for example, have differing premium guarantee periods. Some term products feature only a one-year premium guarantee, whereas others feature longer premium guarantee periods, such as 5, 10, or 20 years. If a product's price guarantees are limited, then the insurer can modify the product's price to account for emerging experience. However, if a product has extensive price guarantees, then the insurer's only protection against adverse mortality experience may be the product's underwriting margin. For example, a renewable term product with a five-year premium guarantee would likely have a higher underwriting margin than a term product with only a one-year guarantee and a smaller underwriting margin than a term product with a 10-year guarantee.

A third element of underwriting risk is the risk of antiselection. The higher the risk of antiselection, the larger the underwriting margin is likely to be. Thus, guaranteed-issue products generally have relatively large underwriting margins. As another example, convertible or renewable term products generally have a higher underwriting margin after the initial period of insurance because insureds in poorer health are more likely to continue their insurance than insureds in good health, who are able to shop for other insurance products.

As we have discussed, insurers use mortality rates to forecast the amount and timing of cash outflows for life insurance and annuity product benefits. To forecast health insurance benefit costs, insurers use morbidity statistics discussed in the following sections.

Introduction to Morbidity Tables

We begin this section by discussing the sources of medical expense morbidity data and then the sources of disability morbidity data. Later in the section, we discuss the nature of morbidity tables.

Sources of Medical Expense Morbidity Data

The term ***morbidity*** means sickness, injury, or failure of health. Insurers have access to both published and proprietary sources of morbidity data. For pricing medical expense insurance, by far the preferred source of morbidity data is the insurer's proprietary experience with its own insureds. Although morbidity data is available from published sources, the usefulness of published morbidity data is limited for several reasons. Among these reasons are the following:

- Numerous variables affect health care costs. For example, health care costs are much higher in some geographical areas than in others and for some socioeconomic groups than for others. Also, the specific language an insurer typically uses in its contracts may influence claim costs. Published morbidity data is generally based on a cross-section of the population and cannot account for the specific factors that influence a specific insurer's morbidity experience.
- For a number of years, health care costs in the United States have increased steadily and rapidly, leveling out only recently. Data on health care costs generally goes out of date quickly. An insurer can update its proprietary morbidity data more frequently than published data is updated.

Whenever possible, insurers forecast morbidity rates based on their own past experience—particularly their recent experience—and on their knowledge of developments in the health care environment. A ***morbidity rate*** is the rate at which sickness and injury occur among a defined group of people. Sometimes, an insurer may not have sufficient experience to effectively forecast morbidity. In these situations, various sources of published morbidity data can help the insurer with its morbidity forecasts.

Insurers can use published morbidity data to fill in the gaps if their own morbidity data is incomplete. For example, suppose an insurer has estimated a morbidity rate for 55-year-old males but does not possess adequate data for estimating morbidity rates for 55-year-old females or 45-year-old males. Using a published morbidity table, the insurer could calculate (1) the ratio between the morbidity exhibited by 55-year-old males and that exhibited by 55-year-old females and (2) the ratio between the morbidity exhibited by 55-year-old males and that exhibited by 45-year-old males. The insurer could then apply these ratios to its estimated morbidity for 55-year-old males in order to estimate morbidity for 55-year-old females and 45-year-old males. For example, if the published table shows females aged 55 experiencing 125 percent of the morbidity of males the same age, then the insurer could calculate the morbidity rate for females by multiplying its morbidity forecast for 55-year-old males by 125 percent.

Published morbidity statistics are available from various sources. The SOA regularly published, until the early 1980s, studies analyzing claim costs for various types of benefits. Published morbidity data are also available from various actuarial consulting firms.

Sources of Disability Morbidity Data

A relatively small group of insurers writes a substantial amount of disability insurance. These insurers price their products primarily using the proprietary morbidity data they have compiled based on the experience of their own insureds.

For insurers needing published disability morbidity data, the NAIC publishes public disability morbidity tables. The current individual disability morbidity tables are the *1985 Commissioners Individual Disability (1985 CID)* tables. The current group disability morbidity table is the *1987 Commissioners Group Disability (1987 CGD)* table. Although both the individual and group tables were developed primarily for valuation purposes, both show the basic morbidity rates underlying the valuation rates. In addition, the SOA periodically publishes reports of recent disability morbidity experience.

Nature of Morbidity Tables

When a customer purchases a life insurance policy, the customer generally purchases a certain dollar amount of insurance. On the other hand, when a customer purchases a disability income policy, the customer purchases a stated benefit amount per month. The length of a potential disability, and hence the total dollar value of any future benefits, is not known at the time of purchase. Likewise, under a medical expense policy, the dollar value of benefits is not known at the time of purchase. Therefore, morbidity tables are used to forecast not only the frequency of benefit claims but also the severity, size, and duration of each claim.

Figure 8-5 shows part of a medical expense table. As you can see, the table forecasts both the likelihood that a claim will occur—the claim frequency—and the average amount per claim. The table also shows the product of these two figures—the insurer's annual claim cost.

Figures 8-6 and 8-7 show two types of disability morbidity tables. Figure 8-6 shows forecasts of the likelihood that a disability will occur. This morbidity table shows disability probabilities at various ages for males and females, for various elimination periods—periods following policy issue during which the insured's medical expenses are not covered by the policy—and for various occupation classes. The table also separates disabilities caused by accident from disabil-

Figure 8-5. Medical expense morbidity table showing the claim frequency, average amount per claim, and annual claim cost.

Attained Age	Frequency	Average Claim	Claim Cost
Male			
15–19	.0215	$ 5.55	$ .119
20–24	.0325	6.31	.158
25–29	.0379	6.59	.250
30–34	.0444	7.01	.311
35–39	.0628	7.55	.474
40–44	.0705	8.10	.571
45–49	.0819	8.45	.692
50–54	.1020	8.82	.900
55–59	.1220	9.31	1.136
60–64	.1431	9.82	1.405
65–69	.2206	11.90	2.625
70–74	.3889	12.14	4.721
75–79	.4235	12.66	5.362
Female			
15–19	.0329	$ 5.41	$ .178
20–24	.0440	5.82	.256
25–29	.0700	6.21	.435
30–34	.0829	6.79	.561
35–39	.1198	7.28	.872
40–44	.1291	7.70	.994
45–49	.1325	8.19	1.085
50–54	.1364	8.75	1.194
55–59	.1402	9.12	1.279
60–64	.1480	9.72	1.371
65–69	.2035	11.88	2.418
70–74	.3622	12.08	4.375
75–79	.3785	12.63	4.780
Child			
All ages	.0469	$ 5.37	$ .252

Source: *Reprinted, with permission, from Committee on Individual Health Insurance, "Experience under Individual Medical Expense Policies, 1981–82,* Transactions, Society of Actuaries, 1983 Reports *(1987): 69. Copyright © 1987 by the Society of Actuaries.*

ities caused by sickness. Like this table, many disability morbidity tables show the likelihood of disability for many different categories of insureds, depending on the needs of the table's users. The table in Figure 8-6 demonstrates some important characteristics of morbidity data. Notice that as the length of the elimination period increases, the morbidity rate decreases. Also, the morbidity rate is substantially higher in the riskier occupation classes—Classes 2, 3, and 4—than it is in Class 1.

Figure 8-6. Disability morbidity table showing the incidence of disability per 1,000 lives exposed.

	Male-Accident						Male-Sickness					
		Elimination Period						Elimination Period				
Occupation	Age	0-day	7-day	14-day	30-day	90-day	Age	0-day	7-day	14-day	30-day	90-day
Class 1	25	33.97	25.84	13.13	4.90	.86	25	—	32.26	18.22	5.51	1.01
	35	32.88	24.42	11.99	4.23	.51	35	—	36.11	21.55	6.48	1.13
	45	30.40	20.40	9.86	4.50	.65	45	—	47.12	31.19	12.63	2.70
	55	30.19	18.32	9.63	4.71	.80	55	—	69.48	52.75	25.11	7.78
	62	33.45	16.11	10.39	5.47	1.18	62	—	91.52	74.06	41.24	15.20
Class 2	25	59.96	47.98	30.01	10.48	2.07	25	—	46.61	27.01	12.17	2.23
	35	59.96	44.62	28.83	10.14	2.09	35	—	52.79	33.37	14.47	2.56
	45	56.74	38.49	25.67	9.86	2.14	45	—	65.97	46.91	25.40	6.21
	55	51.66	31.31	20.50	10.03	2.20	55	—	92.99	71.27	41.37	15.74
	62	52.84	29.85	19.86	10.92	2.57	62	—	116.81	93.05	58.54	25.94
Class 3	25	75.80	62.68	42.87	23.69	7.04	25	—	46.83	32.22	14.75	2.99
	35	74.78	58.37	39.59	22.57	6.48	35	—	52.72	38.32	18.70	3.52
	45	69.76	50.41	34.61	20.49	5.97	45	—	67.05	51.53	29.45	7.83
	55	66.37	44.27	30.51	18.49	5.46	55	—	92.60	76.39	52.66	20.07
	62	65.04	39.98	27.96	18.56	5.30	62	—	116.23	98.78	78.56	36.04
Class 4	25	89.42	77.60	52.59	27.03	8.73	25	—	48.20	33.28	15.07	3.04
	35	91.59	73.24	50.53	26.93	8.17	35	—	53.75	39.27	19.33	3.59
	45	84.64	62.13	42.61	24.78	7.68	45	—	70.03	52.71	30.13	7.97
	55	79.77	52.03	37.34	22.78	7.27	55	—	95.01	77.91	55.87	20.45
	62	79.95	49.76	36.11	22.96	7.20	62	—	119.16	101.41	81.62	36.63

	Female-Accident						Female-Sickness					
		Elimination Period						Elimination Period				
Occupation	Age	0-day	7-day	14-day	30-day	90-day	Age	0-day	7-day	14-day	30-day	90-day
Class 1	25	23.06	19.92	12.96	6.00	1.14	25	—	61.10	39.29	14.03	2.55
	35	26.28	20.87	13.39	6.21	.91	35	—	84.38	56.89	24.75	4.37
	45	32.36	22.77	13.78	6.83	1.11	45	—	94.57	68.33	34.14	7.64
	55	45.05	26.77	14.82	8.06	1.46	55	—	90.28	61.49	34.23	10.31
	62	69.00	31.56	17.54	9.91	2.25	62	—	93.06	69.44	45.30	13.85
Class 2	25	35.05	31.48	23.39	13.40	3.22	25	—	80.97	53.57	20.03	3.75
	35	39.36	32.01	23.36	14.02	3.20	35	—	116.02	80.05	35.34	6.60
	45	47.46	33.55	24.40	15.02	3.40	45	—	134.18	92.93	47.62	10.81
	55	62.53	37.10	26.13	16.11	3.75	55	—	117.29	84.93	49.00	14.95
	62	88.91	44.31	29.27	17.88	4.46	62	—	120.40	87.53	63.15	18.86
Class 3	25	41.93	38.01	27.94	17.63	6.19	25	—	86.64	57.85	24.83	5.03
	35	46.30	38.45	28.54	18.20	6.54	35	—	124.79	96.77	44.67	8.43
	45	53.01	39.08	29.09	19.24	6.75	45	—	145.58	116.19	58.44	14.43
	55	66.71	41.96	30.86	20.99	7.08	55	—	122.98	99.89	59.99	17.86
	62	90.05	48.12	33.60	23.74	7.26	62	—	125.95	101.06	69.18	22.76
Class 4	25	52.41	47.52	34.93	22.04	7.74	25	—	90.24	60.26	25.86	5.23
	35	57.87	48.07	35.67	22.75	8.17	35	—	130.00	100.81	46.53	8.79
	45	66.26	48.86	36.36	24.05	8.45	45	—	151.65	121.04	60.87	15.03
	55	83.39	52.45	38.58	26.25	8.85	55	—	128.10	104.05	62.49	18.61
	62	112.57	60.16	42.00	29.67	9.08	62	—	131.20	105.27	72.07	23.71

Source: *Reprinted, with permission, from "Report of the Committee to Recommend New Disability Tables for Valuation,* Transactions of the Society of Actuaries *XXXVII (1985): 574. Copyright © 1986 by the Society of Actuaries.*

Figure 8-7. Continuance table showing number of disabilities (accident and sickness combined) continuing to each duration, based on 100,000 initial disabilities (male, class 3, 7-day elimination period, age 35)

Duration	Number of disabilities (accident and sickness combined) continuing	Duration	Number of disabilities (accident and sickness combined) continuing	Duration	Number of disabilities (accident and sickness combined) continuing
1 week	11,109.00	4 months	1,494.64	3 years	240.59
2 weeks	9,729.94	5 months	1,126.07	4 years	215.42
3 weeks	8,414.61	6 months	893.37	5 years	199.41
4 weeks	7,232.08	7 months	745.66	6 years	188.53
5 weeks	6,188.70	8 months	643.29	7 years	180.39
6 weeks	5,285.02	9 months	574.52	8 years	174.01
7 weeks	4,517.23	10 months	525.27	9 years	168.46
8 weeks	3,880.17	11 months	485.01	10 years	163.40
9 weeks	3,356.12	12 months	450.02		
10 weeks	2,928.27	13 months	419.97		
11 weeks	2,586.72	14 months	394.58		
12 weeks	2,316.99	15 months	373.07		
13 weeks	2,110.46	16 months	355.01		
		17 months	340.44		
		18 months	328.22		
		19 months	318.10		
		20 months	309.51		
		21 months	302.06		
		22 months	295.66		
		23 months	289.85		
		24 months	284.60		

Source: *Report of the Committee to Recommend New Disability Tables for Valuation,* Transactions of the Society of Actuaries *XXXVII (1985): 589.*

Figure 8-7 is a special type of morbidity table, called a continuance table. A ***continuance table*** shows the proportion of disabilities that are expected to last various lengths of time and is used to help forecast the length of a disability. The continuance table in Figure 8-7 shows the number of disabilities, out of an initial 100,000, that are expected to last one week, two weeks, and so on.

Adjusting Morbidity Data

Like mortality rates, morbidity rates often show benefits of selection. Many insurers use lower morbidity rates for insureds who have recently been underwritten than for those who have not been recently underwritten.

Like mortality rates, morbidity rates can be expressed on a unisex or a sex-distinct basis. Whereas women generally display lower mortality rates than men, women generally display higher morbidity rates than men.

Insurers may also adjust morbidity data to build an underwriting margin into pricing. The methods used to incorporate an underwriting margin into health insurance premiums are similar to those used for life products. The insurer can either

- Calculate net premiums using a higher morbidity rate than the insurer actually expects to materialize or
- Calculate net premiums using expected morbidity and then increase the net premiums by a specified dollar amount.

Manual and Experience Rating in Group Insurance

Life and health insurers offer life, medical expense, and disability income insurance on both a group and an individual basis. The mortality and morbidity rates used in group insurance originate from different tables than those used in individual insurance; most group insurance is not underwritten as strictly as most individual insurance, and group insureds exhibit different mortality and morbidity than individual insureds. In addition, the mortality or morbidity rates an insurer uses to price a group product depend on whether the insurer uses manual rating, experience rating, or blended rating. The word *rating,* in this instance, refers to the process of determining insurance premium *rates.*

When an insurer uses ***manual rating,*** the insurer calculates the expected cost of benefits for the group using mortality or morbidity data based on the claims experience of an "average" group. The premium rates so derived are called ***manual rates.*** An insurer's manual rates are often recorded in a book of rates, called a ***manual.*** An insurer's manual is based on either published mortality or morbidity data or on proprietary data from the insurer's experience with other groups. When manually rating a specific group, an insurer may modify its manual rates somewhat to take into account pertinent characteristics of the group, such as its industry or its geographic location.

When an insurer uses ***experience rating,*** the insurer uses morbidity or mortality rates based on the group's actual claims experience. Experience rating can be applied prospectively or retrospectively. With ***prospective experience rating,*** the insurer uses the group's previous experience to set the premium for the coming year (or other rating period). With ***retrospective experience rating,*** the insurer refunds part of a group's premium after the rating period is over if the group's experience has been better than expected during the period. The refund is called a ***dividend*** or an ***experience rating refund.***

A third approach, called ***blended rating,*** is a combination of manual and experience rating. Under blended rating, the insurer forecasts a group's cost of benefits in part based on the insurer's manual rates and in part based on the group's own experience. The relative weight assigned to the two sources in the calculation depends on the group's credibility. ***Credibility*** is a measure of how relevant the insurer believes the group's past experience to be. A group's credibility is usually expressed as a percentage between 0 and 100 or as a decimal between 0 and 1.

For example, suppose a group is covered by a medical expense product. The manual rate for the group is \$130 per member per month and the experience rate is \$115. If the group's credibility is 70 percent, then the blended rate would be the sum of 70 percent of the experience rate and 30 percent of the manual rate. The blended rate would be calculated as follows:

$$(\$115 \times 0.7) + (\$130 \times 0.3) = \$119.50$$

Whether a group is manually rated or experience rated depends on several factors. Foremost among these factors is the size of the group. Large groups are generally experience rated, unless they have little claims history. Small groups considered alone are almost always rated manually, though the experience of a number of small groups is often pooled and experience rated.

The greater the number of claims in a group's history, the more credible that experience is considered to be. Because large groups tend to make a greater number of claims than small groups, insurers tend to assign higher credibility to the claims histories of large groups. In addition, medical expense and short-term disability claims experience are generally given a higher credibility than life and long-term disability (LTD) claims experience because medical expense and short-term disability contracts generally give rise to a higher number of claims—and thus to a higher level of experience—than do life and LTD contracts.

The table below summarizes some of the differences between rating practices for small groups and those used for large groups.

The smaller the group, the more likely	The larger the group, the more likely
• The group will be rated manually • The group's experience will be given low credibility	• The group will be experience rated • The group's experience will be given high credibility

Pricing for Insurance and Annuity Products

In this section, we describe how insurers use mortality or morbidity rates to estimate the cost of benefits and then use the estimated cost of benefits to derive premium rates. We discuss a number of types of products. For each type of product, insurers follow the same basic process, although some details of the process differ for each type of product. First, we describe the basic process that is common to all insurance and annuity products. Then, we explain the modifications necessary for applying the process to different types of products. Before we begin our discussion of the pricing process, however, we first need to discuss the concept of a block of policies and why it is important to insurance and annuity product pricing.

For products involving insurance risk, the insurer pays the benefit amount only if and when a specified event happens. Sometimes the insurer does not know *if* the insured event will occur; sometimes the insurer does not know *when* the insured event will occur. Because the insurer cannot know the exact timing of a particular product's benefit payments and may not know if the benefit will have to be paid at all, insurers use the probable benefit costs of a block of policies or a block of insureds in deriving the premium to charge for each policy.

A ***block of insureds*** can be defined as a group of insureds or annuitants of the same age, sex, and risk classification. For example, all age 35 males who meet certain underwriting criteria would constitute a block of insureds. A ***block of policies*** can be defined as a group of policies issued to insureds or annuitants of the same age, sex, and risk classification. For example, a group of 10-year term policies issued to a group of age 35 males in similar health would be a block of policies. Note that a block of *policies* is NOT the same as a block of *business.* The term ***block of business*** generally refers to a distinctive group of contracts issued on the same basis, but issued on a variety of insureds. For example, a group of 10-year term policies issued to insureds of both sexes, and all ages and risk classifications would be a block of business. A block of business could also consist of all of a company's term business, or all of a company's term and whole life business.

Our discussion of the costs of benefit payments in this chapter concentrates on the approaches used to determine expected benefit costs for a block of policies. Once we have calculated the expected benefit costs for a block of policies, we use the results to calculate the appropriate values for a single insurance policy or annuity contract.

Figure 8-8 illustrates the basic pricing process that insurers use to derive gross premium rates for bundled insurance and annuity products. We discuss unbundled insurance products later in the chapter. Figure 8-8 outlines the process of deriving the investment crediting rate and the expense charge, both of which we discussed in Chapter 7. Chapter 8 concentrates on that part of the pricing process that concerns the cost of benefits, rather than those on investment return and expenses.

As Figure 8-8 shows, this part of the process can be divided into six steps as follows:

1. *Estimate the cost of benefits.* This step consists of two substeps, estimating the number of claims and estimating the average cost of a claim. Insurers use mortality and morbidity data to estimate the *number* of claims for each year of a product's term. Insurers estimate average claim *cost* differently depending on whether the product is a life or an annuity product, or a health insurance product. For life insurance and annuity products, insurers estimate the cost of benefits based on a certain benefit

Figure 8-8. The pricing process for bundled insurance and annuity products.

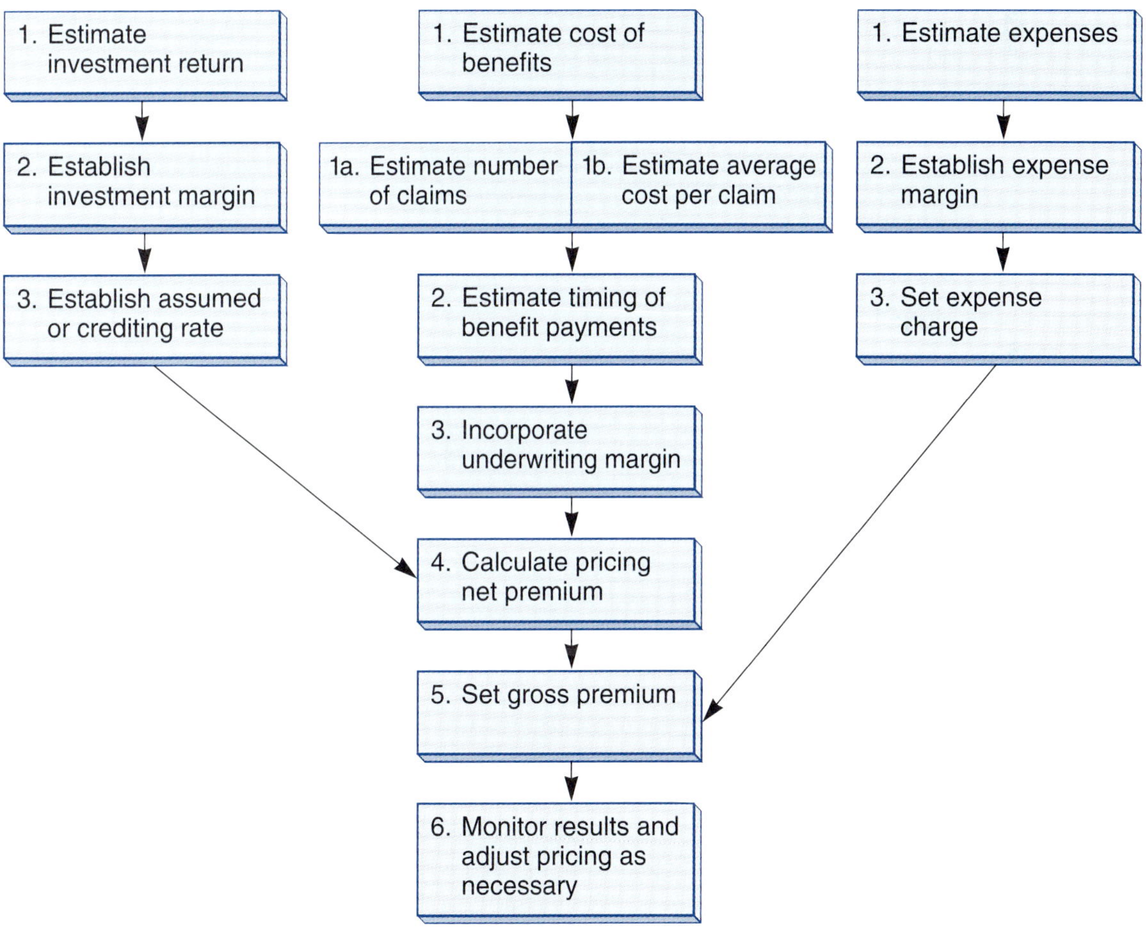

amount and then use this information to price different-sized policies. For health insurance, insurers rely on morbidity data to estimate the cost of the average claim, in addition to the number of claims.

2. *Estimate the timing of benefit payments.* The insurer next estimates or develops assumptions concerning when during the year benefit payments will occur. The timing of benefit payments affects the results of the present value calculations that insurers make in order to calculate net premiums.

3. *Incorporate the underwriting margin.* As we have seen, an insurer can incorporate an underwriting margin into a product's price by (1) calculating the net premium using a mortality or morbidity rate that is greater than the rate the insurer actually expects to realize for life and health insurance or lower for annuities or (2) increasing by a specified amount the net premium calculated using expected mortality or morbidity.

4. *Calculate the pricing net premium.* Insurers calculate the net single premium by finding the present value of the product's total benefit payments. To make this calculation, insurers use the cost of benefits and the timing of benefits estimated in Steps 1 and 2. For the discount rate in the net single premium calculation, insurers use the assumed or crediting rate selected. As we discussed, net premiums take into account the cost of benefits and investment return, but not expenses or expense margins. Having calculated the net single premium, the insurer can, if necessary, use the net single premium to calculate a net annual premium.

5. *Set the gross premium.* As we saw in Chapter 7, the gross premium reflects all three pricing elements: the cost of benefits, investment return, and expenses. After calculating the pricing net premium based on the cost of benefits and investment return, the gross premium can be calculated by adding to the net premium an appropriate loading (for individual insurance) or retention charge (for group insurance) to account for expenses and an expense margin.

6. *Monitor results and adjust premiums as necessary.* Insurers must monitor a product's results after it is on the market and adjust the product's premiums as necessary. If the insurer's actual costs to offer the product are greater than its expected costs, then the insurer may need to raise the premium on all future sales in order for the product to earn a satisfactory profit. If the product's actual costs are less than its expected costs, then the insurer might consider lowering the premium on new business.

The remainder of this chapter illustrates pricing in more detail and describes some features of pricing that are distinctive to specific types of products. We refer to Figure 8-8 throughout the rest of the chapter in order to clarify, at each point, to which part of the process we are referring.

Setting Premiums for One-Year Term Life Insurance

In this section, we illustrate the pricing process using a simple example: one-year term life insurance. We begin by estimating the cost of benefits and then discuss how this information is used to arrive at the net and gross premiums.

Estimating the Cost of Benefits

The first step in the pricing process for a one-year term product is to calculate the cost of benefits for a block of policies by first estimating the number of claims and then estimating the average cost of a claim. The amount of the benefit payments an insurer will have to make on a block of business can be calculated as follows:

$$\text{Total Benefit Payments} = \text{Number of Claims Payable} \times \text{Average Amount of Each Claim}$$

Estimating the Number of Claims

For a life insurance product, the number of claims payable is determined by the number of insureds dying during the term of the product. As we have discussed, an insurer would use a mortality table to forecast the number of insureds who will die. For this illustration, we use the *1975–80 Basic Select and Ultimate* table for males, age-nearest-birthday. We illustrate this process by finding the cost of benefits for a one-year term policy issued to a block of 100,000 35-year-old males. In the *1975–80 Basic Select and Ultimate* table (see Figure 8-3), the select mortality rate for 35-year-old males is 0.63 per 1,000 lives. To forecast how many insureds out of 100,000 will die during the year, we multiply the mortality rate for 1,000 insured by 100. The result is 63. This result means that, according to the *1975–80 Basic Select and Ultimate* table, the insurer should expect to make 63 benefit payments per 100,000 insureds during the product's one-year term.

Estimating the Average Amount of a Claim

Having determined how many claims the insurer will have to pay, we must now consider the cost of each claim. When calculating a life product's net premium, insurers generally calculate the net premium per $1,000 face amount. Once they have calculated the net premium per $1,000 face amount, it is then easy to calculate the net premium for different-sized policies. For example, if the insurer needed to calculate the net premium for $100,000 of insurance, it would simply multiply the net premium per $1,000 by 100.

In our illustration, the total benefit costs for 100,000 insureds, assuming each policy has a face amount of $1,000, can be found by multiplying the number of claims (63) by the amount of each claim ($1,000), as follows:

$$\$1{,}000 \times 63 = \$63{,}000$$

Estimating the Timing of Benefit Payments

Next we must consider the timing of benefit payments. The mortality table gives us an estimate of how many insureds will die during the year, but it gives no indication of when during the year those insureds will die. We can assume fairly safely that some will die near the beginning of the year, some in the middle of the year, and others near the end of the year. To simplify computations, insurers sometimes assume that all benefit payments are made at a certain point during the year. In the remainder of this chapter, we assume in our examples concerning life insurance that all benefit payments are made at the exact mid-point of the year. Most insurers base their calculations on either this assumption or the assumption that the benefit payments are made evenly over the entire year.

Calculating the Net Premium

Having estimated the benefit costs and having decided upon assumptions about the timing of these benefit costs, the insurer would go on to establish a net premium for the product, using the procedure we described at the beginning of this chapter. As a review, Figure 8-9 shows how to find the net single premium for this product. Recall that the net single premium is the present value of the product's benefit payments at the time of the product's issue date. Because we assume that all benefit payments are made at the mid-point of the year, we find the present value of benefits by discounting one half year. Once we find the cost of benefits for 100,000 policies, we have to divide by 100,000 to find the net premium for one policy.

Figure 8-9. Establishing the net single premium for a one-year term product.

STEP 1: Find the net single premium

Assumptions:

1. Policy size = $1,000
2. Assumed interest rate = 7%
3. All benefit payments made in the middle of the year
4. Estimated cost of benefits (100,000 policies) = $63,000

Net single premium calculation—100,000 policies:

Net Single Premium (100,000 Policies)	=	**Present Value of $63,000** (½ year, 7%)
	=	$63,000 x *PVIF*(½, 7%)
	=	$63,000 x 0.967
	=	$60,921

Net single premium calculation—1 policy:

Net Single Premium (1 Policy)	=	**Net Single Premium (100,000 Policies) ÷ 100,000**
	=	$60,921 ÷ 100,000
	=	$0.61 (or $0.60921)

The net single premium calculated in Figure 8-9, $0.61, is for $1,000 of insurance. For other coverage amounts, the net premium for $1,000 would be multiplied by the appropriate amount. The insurer would generally use the nonrounded net single premium of $0.60921 for such calculations to be more accurate. For example, the net premium for $50,000 of insurance would be equal to 50 times the net premium for $1,000 of insurance, as follows:

Net Single Premium ($50,000 Face Amount) = $0.60921 × 50 = $30.46

Setting the Gross Premium

The net premium calculated in Figure 8-9 incorporates both the cost of benefits and investment return. For a bundled insurance product, such as one-year term, the insurer could establish the product's gross premium by adding to the net premium a loading amount to account for expenses and an expense margin. The gross premium incorporates all three pricing elements—benefits, expenses, and investment return. Thus, if the insurer had calculated a loading of $0.30 per $1,000 of insurance, the gross premium per $1,000 would be calculated as follows:

$$\$0.30 + \$0.61 = \$0.91$$

Recall that, as we discussed in Chapter 7, the insurer could use the policy fee system or the banding system to set the gross premium.

Monitoring Results and Adjusting Premiums

Once a product is on the market, the insurer monitors the product's results and compares them to the assumptions used to price the product. If the product's actual results are significantly different from the insurer's expected results for the product, the insurer may choose to modify the product's premium. For example, suppose the predicted mortality rate of 0.63, taken from the *1975–80 Basic Select and Ultimate* table, turns out to be inaccurate, and the actual mortality is closer to 0.55 per year. The insurer may decide that the *1975–80 Basic Select and Ultimate* table does not accurately reflect mortality among the members of the insurer's target market. Consequently, the insurer may use a lower mortality rate, and, hence, a lower premium, for future sales of this product.

The insurer would also compare its actual expenses and actual investment performance to its pricing assumptions. Discrepancies between actual and expected expense and investment results may also cause the insurer to adjust the product's price for future issues. For products with terms longer than one year, the insurer would also monitor persistency.

Setting Premiums for Term Life Insurance with Terms Greater Than One Year

Calculating the cost of benefits of a one-year term insurance product is relatively simple compared to the task of calculating benefit costs for products with longer terms. For a longer-term product, the number of insureds in a block of policies decreases during each year of the product's existence. Specifically, the total number of insureds decreases by (1) the number of insureds who *die* and (2) the number of insureds who allow their policies to *lapse.*

The decrease in the number of insureds from year to year affects in two important ways how the insurer prices products for the cost of benefits:

1. *The decrease in the number of insureds from year to year means that the number of claims the insurer must pay each year is less than if the number of insureds remained the same.* Our calculations are based on the assumption that, initially, this block of business has 100,000 insureds. Thus, we find the number of claims the insurer must pay in Year 1 by multiplying 100,000 by the mortality rate for the group. However, in the product's second year, we have to account for the fact that the number of insureds has decreased because some insureds have died and some have allowed their policies to lapse. To calculate the cost of benefits for Year 2, we multiply the mortality rate by the number of insureds remaining—a number smaller than the number of insureds in the first year. For each year after that, we multiply the mortality rate by a still smaller number of insureds remaining.

2. *The decrease in the number of insureds from year to year means that the number of people paying premiums decreases each year.* Except for single-premium products, the insurer must take into account the decreasing number of people making premium payments as time goes on. This factor influences the calculation of annual premiums.

Next, we illustrate these two issues in an example that shows how to calculate net premiums for a 10-year term life insurance product. The assumptions we use in this example are the default assumptions from *ExecuView*'s 10-Year Term Life Model, except that, to simplify the calculation, here we are using a level interest rate of 7 percent and an average face amount of $1,000.

Estimating the Cost of Benefits

As we have discussed, the total number of insureds will decrease each year. Figure 8-10 illustrates the decrease in the number of insureds during each year of the 10-year term product's existence. The product starts out with 100,000 insureds aged 35. As in *ExecuView*'s 10-Year Term Life Model, we assume that the product's lapse rate will be 12 percent at the beginning of Year 2 (before premiums are paid), gradually decreasing to 7 by the beginning of Year 6. We assume that the mortality rate will be 85 percent of that shown in the *1975–80 Basic Select and Ultimate* mortality table for male lives. As Column 3 of Figure 8-10 shows, by the beginning of the product's tenth year, only 48,306 of the original 100,000 policies remain in force.

Estimating the Number of Claims

The expected number of claims for each year of the 10-year term product's term is calculated by applying the appropriate mortality

Figure 8-10. Benefit costs for a 10-year term product.

{1} Age	{2} Policy Year	{3} Number of Insureds (Previous {5} – Previous {7})	{4} Number Withdrawing ({3} × 12% . . . 7%)	{5} Number of Insureds Paying Premiums ({3} – {4})	{6} Mortality Rate	{7} Number Dying ({5} × {6})	{8} Death Benefits ({7} × $1,000)
35	1	100,000	N/A	100,000	0.000536	54	$54,000
36	2	99,946	11,994	87,952	0.000646	57	$57,000
37	3	87,895	9,449	78,446	0.000842	66	$66,000
38	4	78,380	7,446	70,934	0.000969	69	$69,000
39	5	70,865	5,846	65,019	0.001088	71	$71,000
40	6	64,948	4,546	60,402	0.001190	72	$72,000
41	7	60,330	4,223	56,107	0.001343	75	$75,000
42	8	56,032	3,922	52,110	0.001513	79	$79,000
43	9	52,031	3,642	48,389	0.001709	83	$83,000
44	10	48,306	3,381	44,925	0.001904	86	$86,000

rate to the number of insureds remaining at the beginning of each year. Columns 6 and 7 of Figure 8-10 show the appropriate mortality rates and the number dying each year.

Estimating the Average Cost per Claim

Once we estimate the number of claims for each year of the product's term, we can estimate the total amount of benefits the insurer should expect to pay by multiplying the number of claims by the amount per claim. Once again, we assume that the amount of each policy is $1,000. The death benefits the insurer expects to pay for each year are shown in Figure 8-10, Column 8.

The insurer then adds an underwriting margin in one of two ways: (1) by using a higher mortality rate than the insurer actually expects to achieve or (2) by adding a specified amount to the net premium calculated using expected mortality.

Estimating the Timing of Benefit Payments

Figure 8-11 illustrates the timing of benefit payments for a 10-year term insurance product. Once again, we assume that all benefit payments are made at the exact mid-point of the year in which they occur. The figure shows the insurer making a set of benefit payments in the middle of each year of the 10-year term.

Figure 8-11. Timing of benefit payments for 10-year term product.

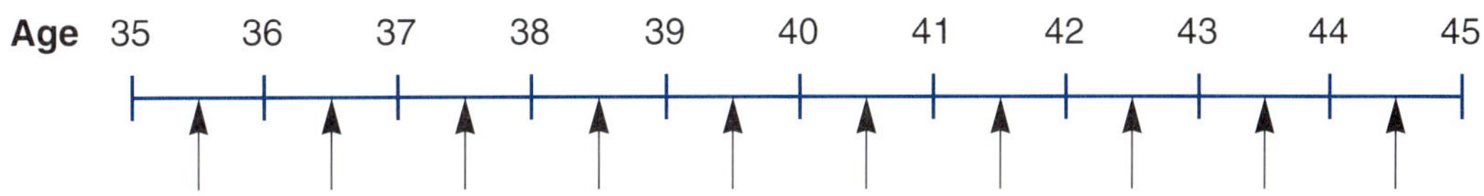

Calculating the Net Premium

The insurer can use the estimated amount and timing of the product's benefit payments to calculate the product's net single premium. As a review, Figure 8-12 illustrates the net single premium calculation. This example requires the insurer to make 10 separate present value calculations, one for each year of the product's 10-year term. Notice that the discount factors in Figure 8-12 are for each *half* year. The reason is that, in this example, we are assuming that all death benefits are paid at the mid-point of each year.

For a 10-year term product, most policyowners generally pay premiums annually or more often, rather than paying a single premium. Therefore, the insurer needs to calculate the product's net annual premium. When calculating a net annual premium for the 10-year term product, the insurer would need to take into account the fact that the number of policyowners paying premiums each year would

Figure 8-12. Net single premium calculation: 10-year term insurance issued at age 35.

{1} Age	{2} Policy Year	{3} Number Dying	{4} Death Benefits ({3} × $1,000)	{5} Discount Factor (*PVIF* [{2} – ½, 7%])	{6} Present Value of Death Benefits ({4} × {5})
35	1	54	$54,000	0.967	$ 52,218
36	2	57	$57,000	0.903	$ 51,471
37	3	66	$66,000	0.844	$ 55,704
38	4	69	$69,000	0.789	$ 54,441
39	5	71	$71,000	0.738	$ 52,398
40	6	72	$72,000	0.689	$ 49,608
41	7	75	$75,000	0.644	$ 48,300
42	8	79	$79,000	0.602	$ 47,558
43	9	83	$83,000	0.563	$ 46,729
44	10	86	$86,000	0.526	$ 45,236
				PV Total Death Benefits =	$503,663
Net Single Premium per $1,000 = $503,663 ÷ 100,000 = $5.04 [or $5.03663]					

diminish because of lapses and deaths. Figure 8-13 illustrates how the net annual premium for this product can be calculated. Note that different discount factors are used in this table than were used in Figure 8-12. The discount factors in this table apply to the premium payments that are assumed to occur at the beginning of each year.

To learn more about what net level premium figures represent, read *ExecuView* Application 8-1 and, if you have loaded *ExecuView* into a computer, apply the example to the 10-Year Term Life Model.

Completing the Pricing Process

Having arrived at the net premium, the insurer derives a gross premium by adding an appropriate loading to the net premium. Once the product is in force, the insurer monitors the product's actual performance, compares the actual performance to the expected performance, and adjusts the premium on future sales as appropriate.

Figure 8-13. Calculation of the net level annual premium for the 10-year term product.

{1} Age	{2} Policy Year	{3} Number Insureds Paying Premiums	{4} Net Level Annual Premium Amount per Insured	{5} Total Premiums {3} × {4}	{6} Discount Factor [PVIF ({2}, 7%)	{7} Present Value of Premiums ({5} × {6})
35	1	100,000	$x	100,000 ($x)	1.000	100,000 ($x)
36	2	87,952	$x	87,952 ($x)	0.935	82,235 ($x)
37	3	78,446	$x	78,446 ($x)	0.873	68,483 ($x)
38	4	70,934	$x	70,934 ($x)	0.816	57,882 ($x)
39	5	65,019	$x	65,019 ($x)	0.763	49,609 ($x)
40	6	60,402	$x	60,402 ($x)	0.713	43,067 ($x)
41	7	56,107	$x	56,107 ($x)	0.666	37,367 ($x)
42	8	52,110	$x	52,110 ($x)	0.623	32,465 ($x)
43	9	48,389	$x	48,389 ($x)	0.582	28,162 ($x)
44	10	44,925	$x	44,925 ($x)	0.544	24,439 ($x)
Net amount due to establish $1 10-year annuity for 100,000 males age 35 =						523,710 ($x)

The present value of the sum of the net annual premiums must equal the net single premium of $503,663, which we calculated in Figure 8-12. To find the net annual premium—which is represented by $x—we solve the following equation:

$$523{,}710(\$x) = \$503{,}663$$

$$\$x = \$503{,}663 \div 523{,}710$$

$$\$x = \$0.96 \text{ (rounded)}$$

Application 8-1 Understanding Net Level Premiums

If you wish to demonstrate this example on your computer, start *ExecuView* and select the Term Life model. Be sure to select *Reset, All Models* from the Action menu to return *ExecuView* to its default settings. The default assumptions and profitability outcome for this model are shown on the following *ExecuView* screen.

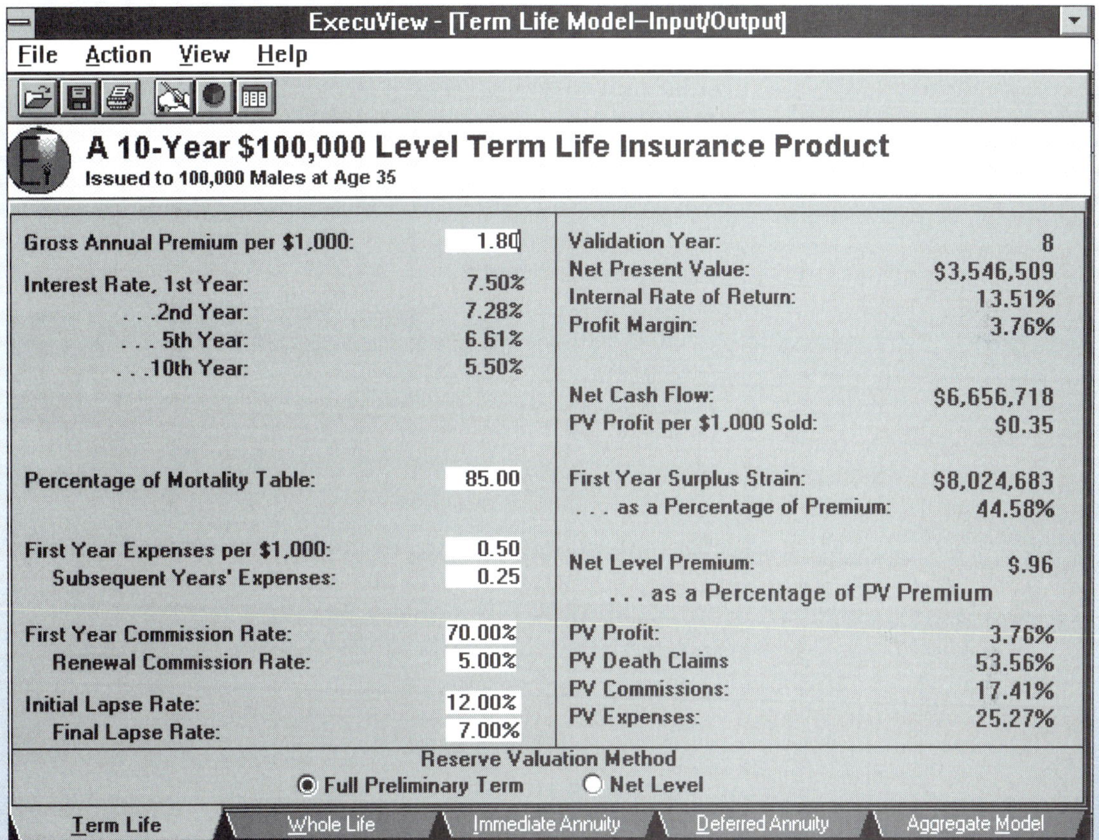

A product's net level premium is the minimum amount each policyowner must pay each year to cover all of the death claims and surrender benefits incurred by a block of policies. In Figure 8-13, we determined that the net level premium for the product described in *ExecuView's* 10-Year Term Model, assuming a level 7 percent interest rate, is $0.96 per $1,000 of face value. This means that from every gross annual premium payment, $0.96 is needed to cover the death claims that occur within the 10-year term. Recall that term insurance products do not involve surrender benefits.

To test the accuracy of this net level premium, we first need to set the interest rate in *ExecuView* to a level 7 percent. Then we can set the model's gross annual premium per $1,000 to $0.96. If $0.96 is the exact net level premium, the product should exactly pay its benefit costs and earn no profit.

(continued on next page)

Application 8-1 Understanding Net Level Premiums (continued)

➤ Select *ExecuView's* Aggregate Model. Set the *Initial Interest Rate* to 7% and set *Change, 2nd Year; Change, Years 3–5;* and *Change, Years 6–10* to 0. Press <enter> to view the results of these changes. These changes should produce a level interest rate of 7%.

➤ Next, select the Term Life Model and enter 0.96 under *Gross Annual Premium per $1,000.* Press <enter> to see the results of this change.

When we make these changes, the product shows huge losses. Remember, though, that, for a term life product, the net level premium doesn't cover any expenses aside from death claims. To see if $0.96 covers all the benefit costs for this product, we need to set all commission and expense rates to 0.

➤ Set *First Year Expenses per $1,000, Subsequent Years' Expenses, First Year Commission Rate,* and *Renewal Commission Rate* to 0. Press <enter> to view the results of these changes.

The result of these changes (summarized in the following *ExecuView* screen) is a product that makes a very small profit over the course of the 10-year term. This is close to what we would expect. When expenses and commissions are excluded, the net level premium should exactly cover all policy benefit costs.

(*continued on next page*)

To gain a better understanding of how monitoring a product's performance can affect the premium rates insurers charge, read *ExecuView* Application 8-2 and, if you have loaded *ExecuView* into a computer, apply the example to the 10-Year Term Life Model.

In the remainder of this chapter, we discuss setting premiums for a number of other insurance and annuity products. However, we do not discuss the entire pricing process for each product. Rather, we discuss how the pricing procedures for each product differ from those we have already described.

Setting Premiums for Whole Life Insurance

Setting premiums for traditional whole life insurance is similar in many ways to setting premiums for term life except for two significant differences:

1. Whole life insurance is designed to provide coverage for as long as the insured lives, rather than for a specific number of years.
2. A whole life policy builds a cash value.

Application 8-1 Understanding Net Level Premiums (continued)

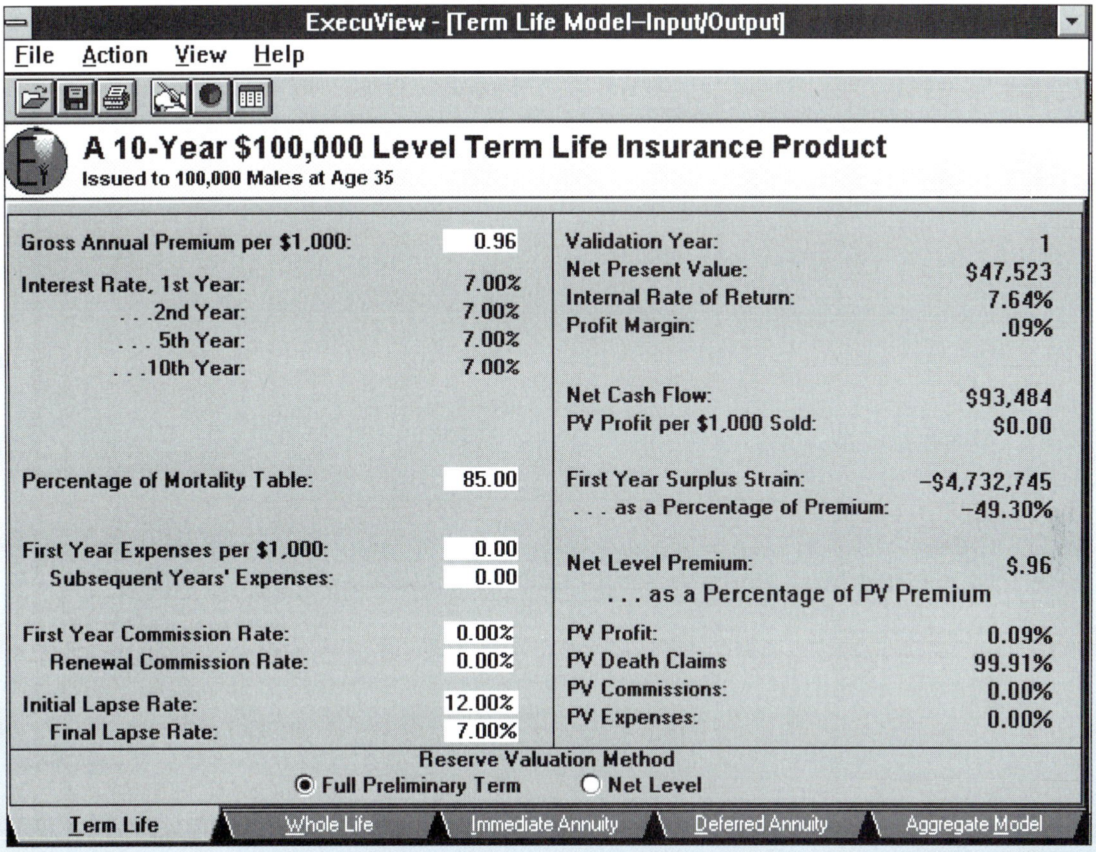

Notice, however, that the model actually shows a profit margin of –0.09 percent and a net cash flow of –$93,484 when the gross annual premium is exactly $0.96. Considering the amount of insurance issued in the first year ($10,000,000), these profits are insignificant and are simply the result of rounding the net level premium to the nearest cent. To bring all of the profit measures closer to zero, we need to enter a more precise net level premium of $0.9591, which yields a profit margin of 0.00 percent and a net cash flow of $765, as shown on the following *ExecuView* screen.

➢ Set the *Gross Annual Premium per $1,000* to 0.9501. Press <enter> to view the results of this change.

Notice that *ExecuView* has rounded the gross annual premium to $0.96. Regardless of what appears in the Gross Annual Premium cell, the output you see reflects the exact premium amount you entered.

(*continued on next page*)

Application 8-1 Understanding Net Level Premiums (continued)

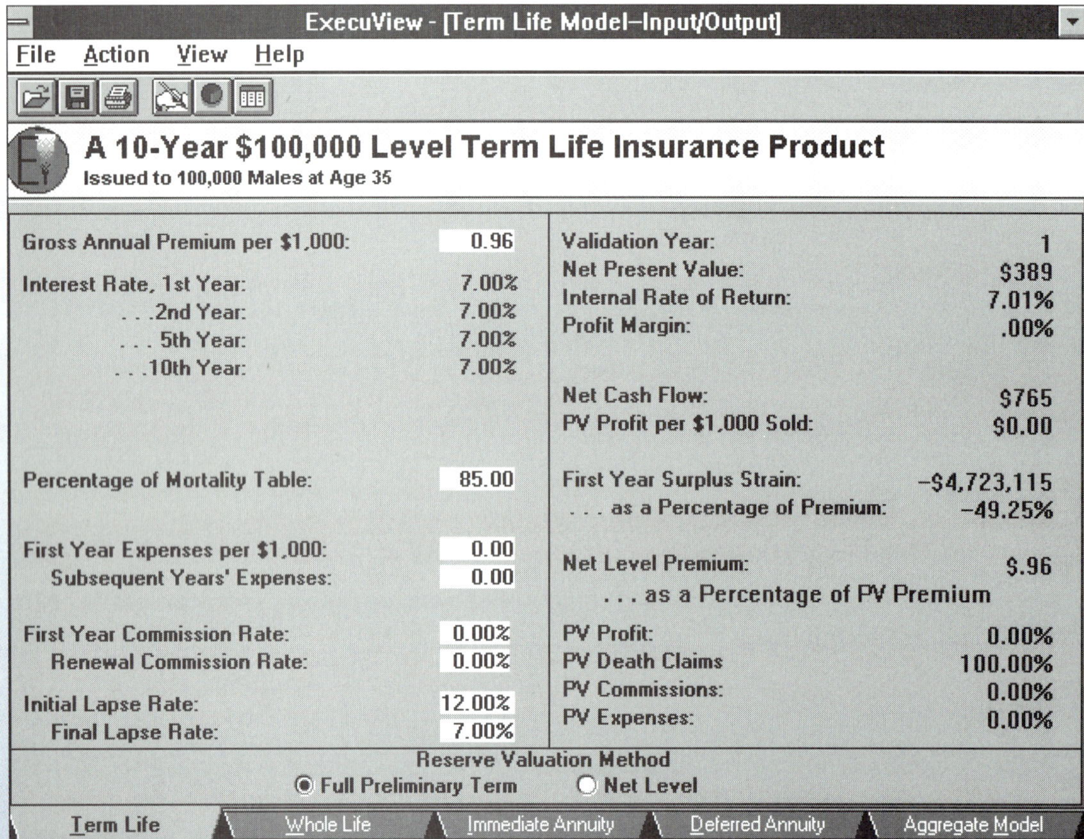

If we adjust either the interest rate or the withdrawal rate for this product, the product will begin to show either losses or profits. The net level premium for any product is based on three factors—mortality rates, interest rates, and withdrawal rates. A change in any one of these factors will change the net level premium. For example, if the interest rate goes up, the insurer will be earning more investment income on reserves and will not need as much premium income to cover the cost of death benefits. Similarly, if the withdrawal rate were to increase, fewer policyowners would be paying premiums and, because of the shrinking pool of insureds, fewer death claims would occur. Thus, the amount of premium needed from each policyowner to cover death benefits would change.

Whole life coverage, then, is priced similarly to term coverage for which the term lasts until the end of the mortality table, except that, unlike term life, whole life coverage pays surrender benefits in addition to death benefits.

Almost all whole life policies are designed so that, if the insured is still living at age 100, the insurer automatically pays the death ben-

Figure 8-14. Benefit payments for a whole life product.

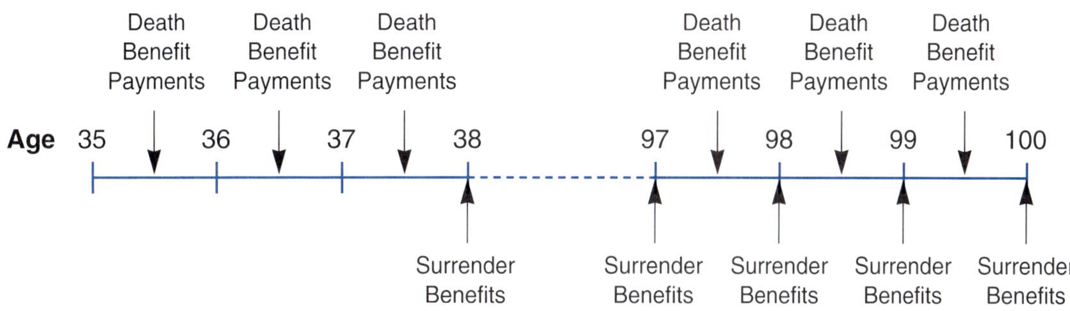

efit. The reason whole life policies automatically pay death benefits to insureds at age 100 is that most whole life policies are priced using mortality tables that end at age 100. Whole life products, then, are priced under the assumption that all insureds will die *before* they reach age 100.

When determining the cost of benefits for a block of whole life policies, the insurer must plan to pay two types of benefits: 1) death benefits and 2) surrender benefits. Figure 8-14 illustrates the stream of benefit payments an insurer would have to make for a block of whole life policies issued to 100,000 35-year-old males. For this product, the insurer assumes that it will make a set of death benefit payments at the mid-point of each year, and a set of surrender benefits at the beginning of each year, starting in the fourth policy year. In our example, annual premiums are assumed to be received at the beginning of the year. The benefit payments do not include surrender benefits in the product's early years, because most products do not build a cash value until the policy has been in force for several years. The final benefit payments would be made when the insured reaches age 100.

As with all life insurance products, the insurer would estimate the death benefits for each year using an appropriate mortality table. The product's cash value for each year is part of the product's design.* The insurer's actuaries would forecast lapse rates based on various factors, such as predicted interest rate developments and the presence or absence of various product features, such as surrender charges. The insurer would calculate the surrender benefit payments for each year based on the forecasted lapse rates for the product and based on the cash value available to the policyholder, as follows:

$$\text{Annual Surrender Benefits} = \text{Number of Insureds} \times \text{Lapse Rate} \times \text{Surrender Value}$$

* Minimum cash values are set by law.

Application 8-2 Adjusting Premium to Reflect Improved Mortality Rates

If you wish to demonstrate this example on your computer, start *ExecuView* and select the Term Life Model. Be sure to select *Reset, All Models* from the Action menu to return *ExecuView* to its default settings. The default assumptions and profitability outcome for this model are shown on the following *ExecuView* screen.

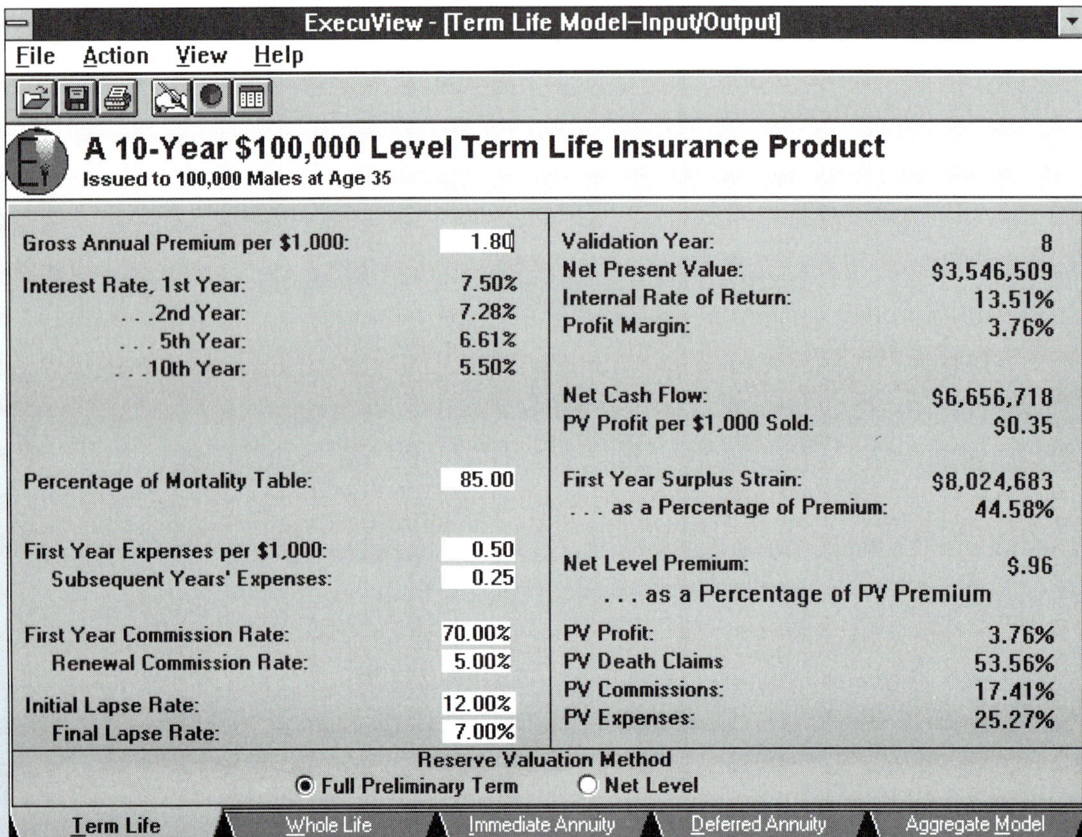

As part of their ongoing monitoring of the profit performance on existing products, the actuaries at the EV Life Insurance Company have discovered that the mortality assumptions used in pricing EV Life's 10-year term life insurance product may be too high. Thanks to very high underwriting standards, the product's mortality experience is at least 8 percent below current assumptions. The company would like to take advantage of the more favorable mortality by lowering the product's premium, thereby making the product more competitive. The first step in lowering the product's premium is to lower the product's mortality assumptions. To be on the safe side, the chief actuary has recommended that, for pricing purposes, the mortality assumption be lowered no more than 4 percentage points.

The *Percent of Mortality Table* factor is currently set to 85%. Lower this factor by 4 percentage points by setting it to 81%. Press <enter> to view the results of this change.

(continued on next page)

Application 8-2 Adjusting Premium to Reflect Improved Mortality Rates (cont'd)

This change in mortality assumptions increases the product's expected profit margin from 3.76 percent to 6.28 percent and increases the expected net profit per $1,000 of coverage sold from $0.35 to $0.59—enough of a difference that EV Life decides to lower premiums to make the product more competitive. The actuarial department cautions that it is important to keep the expected profit margin higher than 3 percent in case of unforeseen contingencies. Eventually it is decided that premiums will be lowered to $1.75 per $1,000 of face value. The marketing manager predicts that as a result of this new premium, EV Life can expect 1 percentage point decrease in the product's initial lapse rate and a 0.5 percentage point decrease in the product's final lapse rate.

➤ *Gross Annual Premium per $1,000* is currently set at 1.80. Change this setting to 1.75. Lower the *Initial Lapse Rate* by 1 percentage point by setting it to 11%. Decrease the *Final Lapse Rate* by 0.5 percentage points by setting it to 6.5%. Press <enter> to see the results of these changes.

The result of these changes in assumptions (as shown on the following *ExecuView* screen) is a product with a lower premium that validates in eight years and continues to meet EV Life's profit objectives.

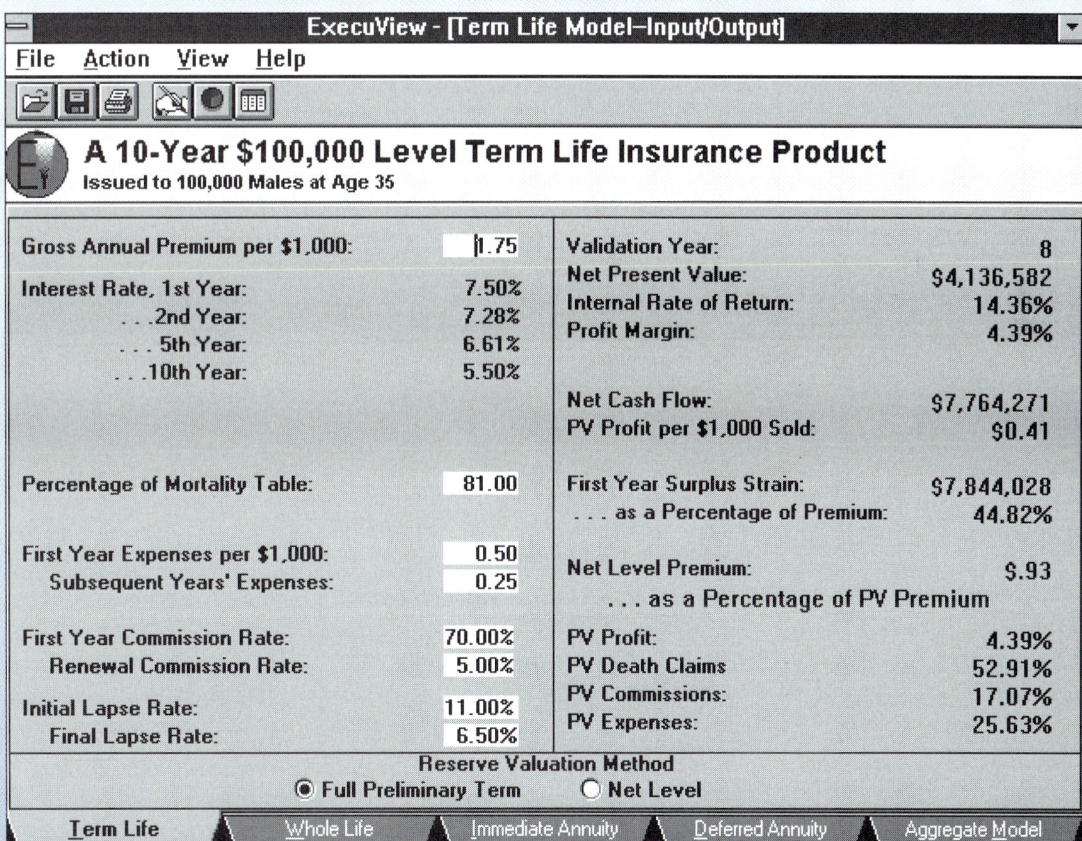

ExecuView Application 8-3 discusses some of the effects that lapse rates can have on a product's profitability.

In the next section, we discuss universal and variable universal life insurance, which are unbundled products. The process of pricing these unbundled products differs somewhat from the process used for bundled products.

Pricing Universal and Variable Universal Life Insurance

The life insurance products we have discussed so far are bundled products. For these products, the gross premium takes into account expenses, investment return, and benefit costs for the product's entire term. Universal life (UL) and variable universal life (VUL), on the other hand, are unbundled life insurance products for which the insurer expresses the product's mortality charge separately from the product's expense charge and credited investment return. Figure 8-15 shows the pricing process for unbundled life products.

Estimating the Number of Claims

A UL or VUL policy's mortality charge reflects the cost of benefits for only one period, usually a month. Thus, the mortality rate used

Figure 8-15. The pricing process for unbundled insurance products.

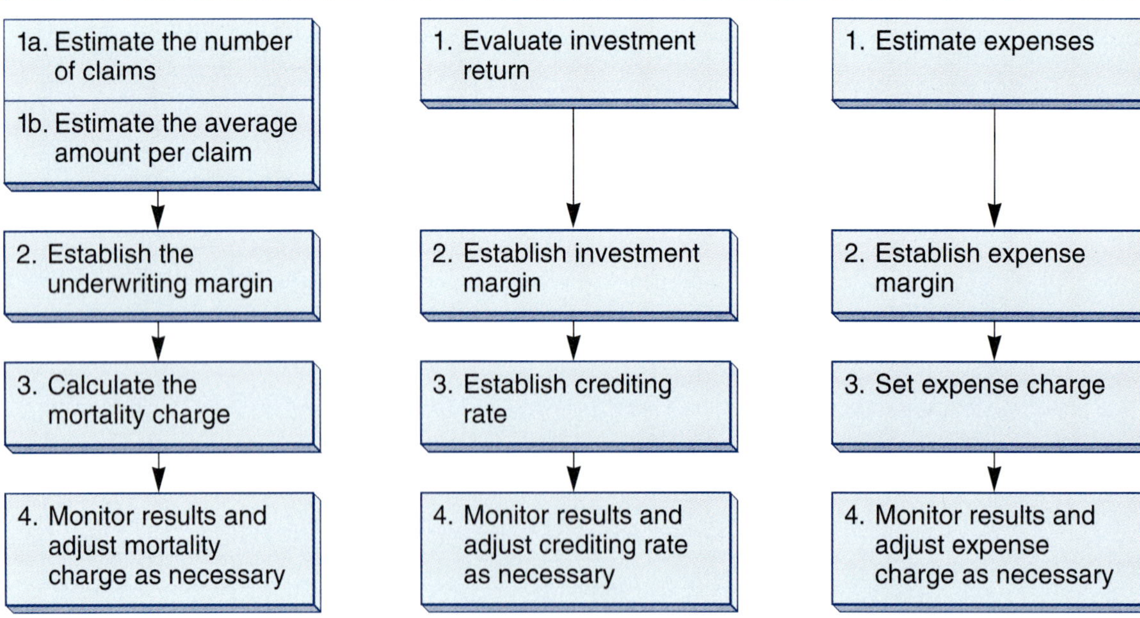

Application 8-3 Lapse-Based Products

If you wish to demonstrate this example on your computer, start *ExecuView* and select the Term Life Model. Be sure to select *Reset, All Models* from the Action menu to return *ExecuView* to its default settings. The default assumptions and profitability outcome for this model are shown on the following *ExecuView* screen.

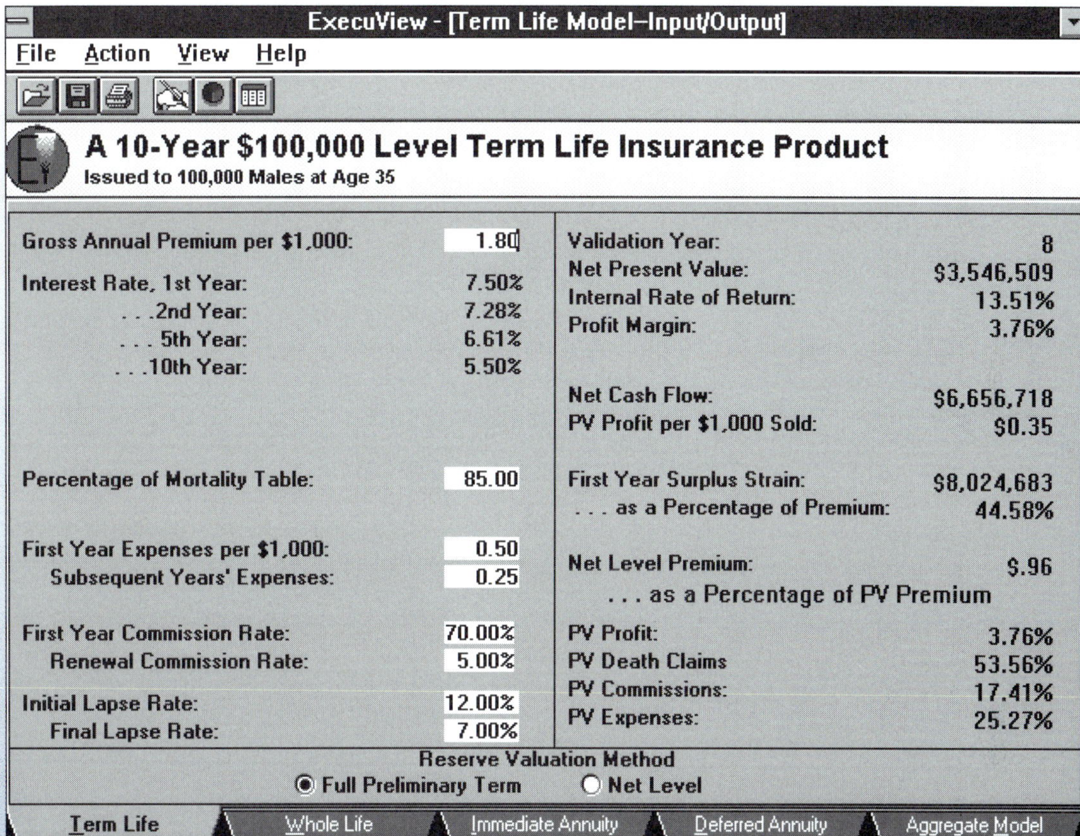

The effect that changes in withdrawal rates have on the profitability of an insurance product can be quite complex. As more policyowners withdraw, fewer policyowners remain to pay premiums and thus the income the insurer receives from premiums is reduced. However, as the pool of insureds covered by the product shrinks, fewer death claims will occur, and thus death claim expenses will be reduced. The result of these conflicting effects is that high withdrawal rates can have a very negative effect, a neutral effect, and sometimes even a positive effect on profitability. Insurers refer to products to which high withdrawal rates cause a substantial increase in profitability as ***lapse-based products.*** For most life insurance products, high lapse rates will generally have a more negative effect on profitability in the early years of a policy because in the first few years such products generally have a negative surplus and thus need future premium income to make a profit. High lapse rates in the years after a life insurance product has broken even generally have a less negative effect, and may even have a positive effect on profitability.

(*continued on next page*)

Application 8-3 Lapse-Based Products (continued)

The product depicted in *ExecuView*'s Term Life Model shows its highest present value of profits when the *Final Lapse Rate* is set to 24 percent. The effect of this lapse rate is shown in the following *ExecuView* screen.

➤ The *Final Lapse Rate* for the Term Life Model is currently 7%. Change this setting to 24%. Press <enter> to view the results of this change.

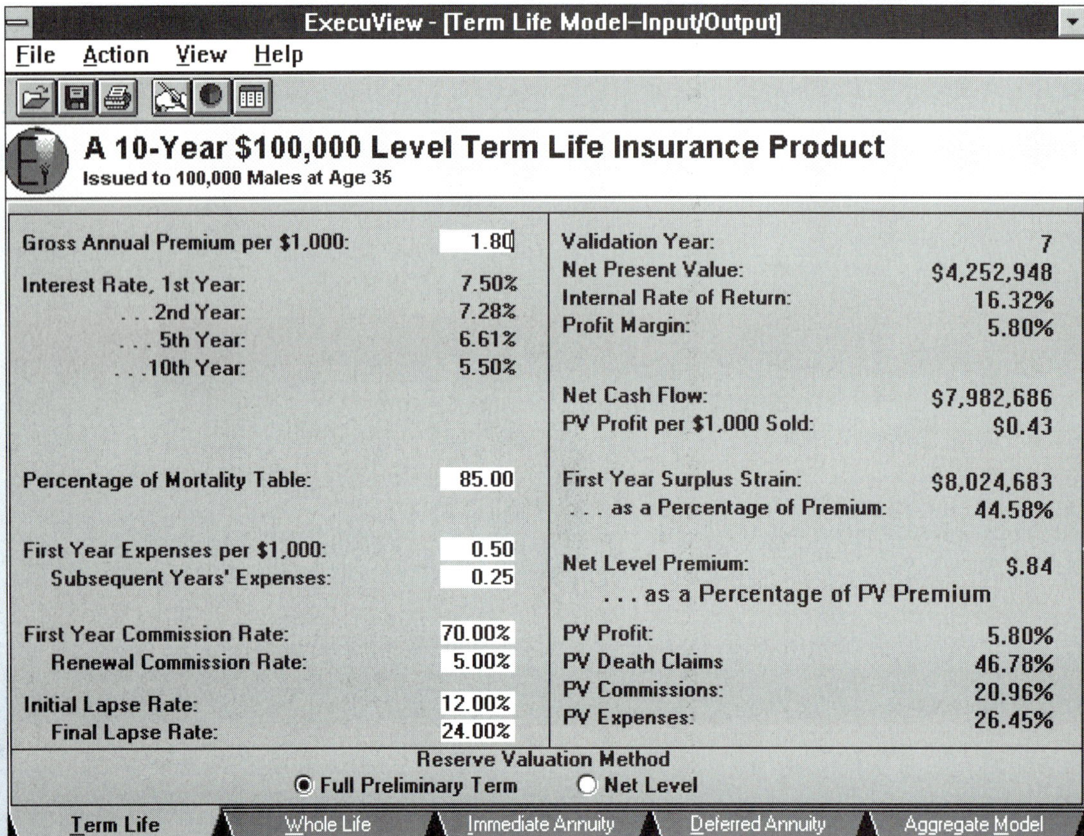

The model demonstrates that this product is, to some extent, lapse-based. With a 24 percent final lapse rate instead of the default assumption of 7 percent, the product shows a profit margin that increases by half (from 3.76 percent to 5.80 percent), and a net present value that increases by more than $700,000. When increased lapse rates cause improved profitability, it might seem that it would be in an insurer's interest to encourage policyowners to allow their policies to lapse after four or five years. However, in practice this would be very risky. If policyowners are encouraged to lapse, they might become dissatisfied with their insurance company. As a result, the company's reputation might suffer and it might have trouble attracting new customers in the future. Also, it would be difficult to control exactly when, or at what rate policyowners would lapse. Encouraging policyowners to lapse in the later years might backfire and cause them to begin lapsing in the

(*continued on next page*)

Application 8-3 Lapse-Based Products (continued)

early years as well, and at a higher rate than the insurance company intended. This could have a devastating effect. For example, if *ExecuView*'s Term Life product experiences a 35 percent lapse rate throughout its 10-year term, the result would be *negative* profitability. The full results of this scenario are shown on the following *ExecuView* screen.

➢ Set the *Initial Lapse Rate* and the *Final Lapse Rate* to 35%. Press <enter> to view the results of this change.

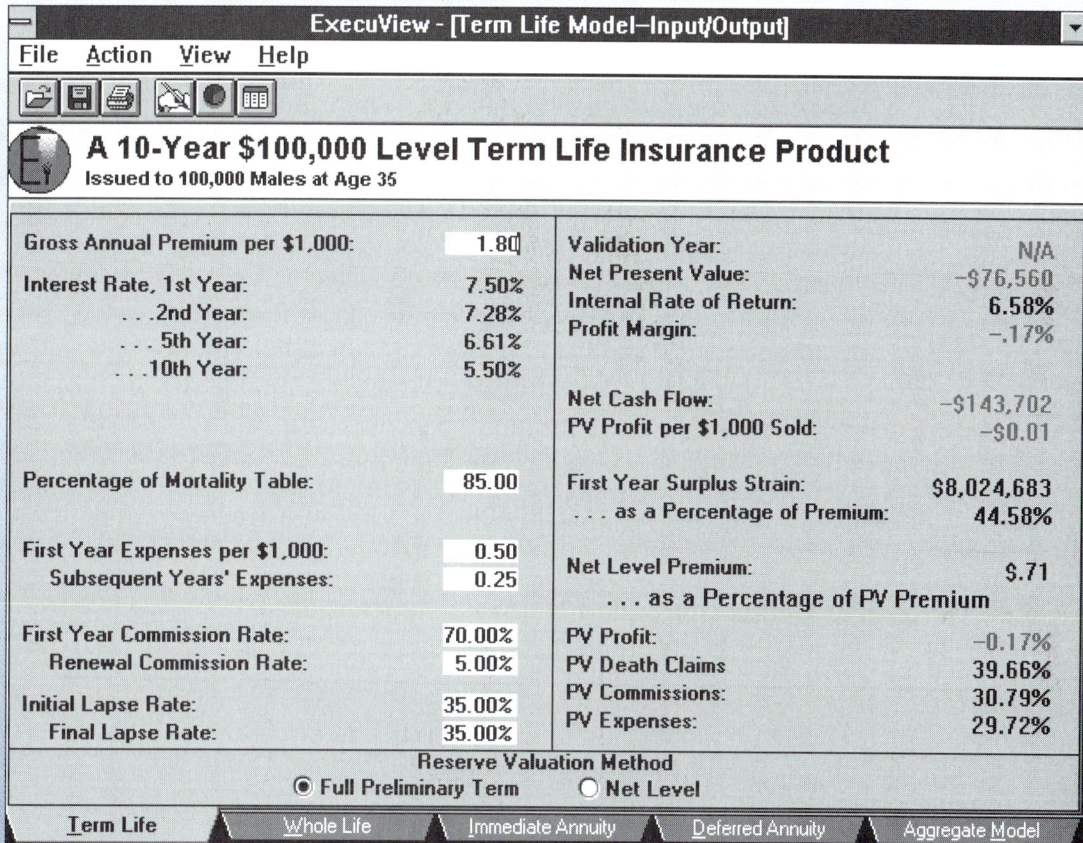

for these products is a monthly mortality rate. The mortality rate is based on the insured's age in years at the time the cost of insurance is applied. Thus, the mortality rate is not level; it increases as the insured grows older.

UL and VUL policies have two pertinent mortality rates: the guaranteed maximum mortality rate and the mortality rate used to calculate the mortality charge. The insurer guarantees not to charge a higher rate than the guaranteed maximum rate. The guaranteed maximum rate is frequently based on the 1980 CSO table, a conservative mortality table, in order to ensure that actual mortality experience will not exceed the maximum mortality rate guaranteed by the policy.

Insurers rarely calculate mortality charges using the maximum rate. The mortality rate the insurer uses to calculate the mortality charge is generally lower than the guaranteed maximum rate and represents the insurer's mortality expectations plus an underwriting margin.

Estimating the Amount per Claim

The claim amount for a UL or VUL policy is considered to be the insurer's *net amount at risk* on the policy. For some policies, called *Option A policies* or *level death benefit option policies,* the death benefit is equal to the policy's face amount. Consequently, the net amount at risk is equal to the difference between the face amount and the account value. For other policies, called *Option B policies* or *increasing death benefit option policies,* the death benefit is equal to the face amount plus the account value, and the net amount at risk is equal to the face amount of the policy. Regardless of whether the policies are Option A or Option B, the customer chooses the death benefit and may change the death benefit at any time, after showing proof of insurability in the case of large increases. The following table summarizes the differences, from the point of view of the death benefit and the net amount at risk, between Option A and Option B policies:

Option A plan:

Death Benefit = Face Amount

Net Amount at Risk = Face Amount – Account Value

Option B plan:

Death Benefit = Face Amount + Account Value

Net Amount at Risk = Face Amount

The selected mortality rate is applied to the net amount at risk to determine the monthly mortality charge. For example, suppose Ronald Feldman is insured under a level death benefit option type of UL policy. The face amount of his policy is presently $200,000. The cash value of his policy is $50,000. The net amount at risk on his policy is calculated as $200,000 – $50,000, and is equal to $150,000. If the insurer's monthly mortality charge for a male of Mr. Feldman's age and underwriting status is $0.57 per $1,000 of insurance, then Mr. Feldman's mortality charge for January would be $0.57 times 150, which equals $85.50.

If Mr. Feldman's policy were an increasing death benefit option policy, then the net amount at risk would be equal to the face amount, and the mortality charge would be based on the full face amount of $200,000. The mortality charge can be calculated by multiplying the mortality charge per $1,000 ($0.57) by 200. The result is $114.

Underwriting Margin in UL and VUL Policies

An insurer can incorporate an underwriting margin into a UL and VUL policy's mortality charge either by calculating the mortality charge using a higher mortality rate than the insurer actually expects, or by adding a specified amount to the mortality charge calculated using the expected mortality rate. UL and VUL mortality charges can vary considerably from one insurer to another, reflecting the different underwriting margins incorporated into mortality charges by different insurers. However, the insurers with the lowest mortality charges most often compensate for their low underwriting margins through higher expense or investment margins. For example, a UL product with a low mortality charge may include a front-end load and a surrender charge, whereas a policy with a higher mortality charge might not include either type of expense load.

The following table summarizes some of the important pricing elements we have discussed relating to the cost of benefits in life insurance products:

Bundled	Unbundled
• **One-year term.** Benefit costs need to be calculated for only one year. • **Multi-year term.** The present value of benefit costs needs to be calculated for all years in the product's term. • **Ordinary whole life.** The present value of benefit costs needs to be calculated for all years until the end of the mortality table. Surrender benefits as well as death benefits need to be considered.	• **UL and VUL.** The mortality charge is equal to the mortality rate multiplied by the net amount at risk.

Pricing Annuities to Account for Benefit Costs

During a deferred annuity's accumulation period, mortality (underwriting risk) is often not a pricing factor. The main pricing elements that affect the accumulation period of a deferred annuity are investment income and expenses, which are taken into account using methods described in Chapter 7. Many annuities include a death benefit during the accumulation period, and this death benefit must be taken into account in pricing. However, the cost of the death benefit is generally relatively small, so we do not discuss annuity death benefits.

When an annuity reaches its payout period, mortality is a significant factor in determining the annuity's periodic benefit.* When calculating an annuity's periodic benefit, the insurer must consider the expected cost of benefits in a manner similar to that used for life insurance. The method used is similar to that shown in Figure 8-8, which reappears here as Figure 8-16.

The pricing process for an annuity in its payout period exhibits four important differences from the pricing process for a life insurance product:

1. In general, annuities are intended to provide benefits if the annuitant lives, rather than if the annuitant dies. In order to calculate the annual cost of benefits, the amount per benefit payment is multiplied by the number of annuitants who survive, rather than the number who die.

2. Annuity benefit payments are generally divided into a number of monthly or annual payments, unlike life insurance, which is generally paid out as a lump sum. Accordingly, the insurer calculates the present value of benefit payments based on the assumption that the benefits are paid over a period of time.

3. The amount of annuity benefits depends on the accumulated value of the annuity at the beginning of the payout period. Accordingly, the insurer finds the present value of benefit payments as of the beginning of the payout period. In contrast, for life insurance, the present value of benefits is calculated as of the time the contract takes effect. Note that, for immediate annuities, the beginning of the payout period coincides with the time the contract takes effect.

4. For annuities, the insurer can create an underwriting margin by using a lower mortality rate than the insurer expects to experience; in contrast, for life insurance, the underwriting margin is created by using a higher mortality rate than expected.

We illustrate the process of pricing annuity income benefits using the example of a 10-year temporary life annuity.

* Note that our discussion of annuity pricing applies to most types of annuities, but does not apply to deferred payout annuities. A deferred payout annuity is an annuity that offers, for a single premium, a benefit that is fixed at the time of policy issue, though benefits begin sometime in the future.

Figure 8-16. The pricing process for bundled insurance and annuity products.

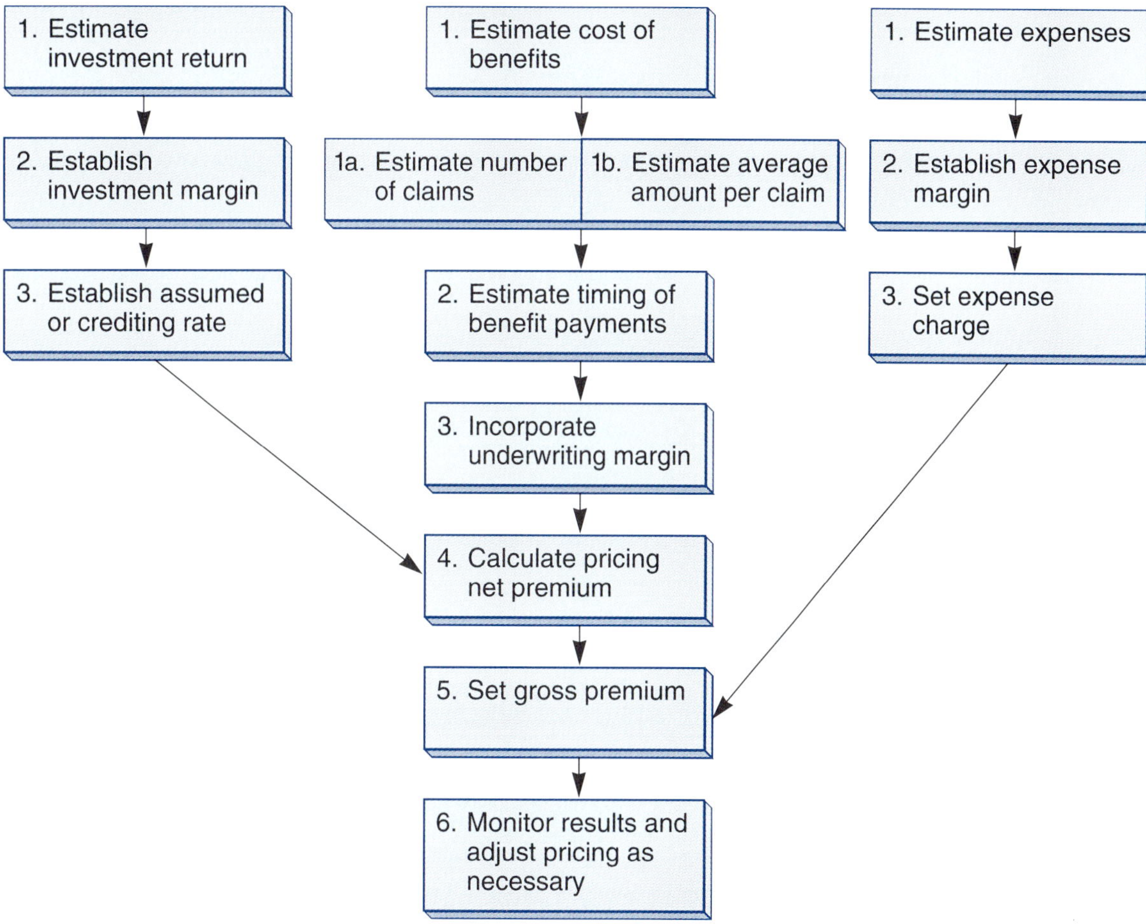

Example: Pricing a 10-Year Temporary Life Annuity

A ***temporary life annuity*** pays a benefit for a specified number of periods, as long as the annuitant is still alive. If the annuitant dies before the end of this time period, the annuity ceases paying benefits. Our example concerns a block of 10-year temporary life annuities issued to 100,000 65-year-old males. The discount rate is 7 percent. To keep our calculations simple, we assume that this annuity product makes one benefit payment of $1,000 to each annuitant who is alive at the end of each policy year.

Estimating the Number of Benefits

To estimate the number of benefit payments the insurer will make under annuity contracts other than annuities certain, the insurer must use annuity mortality tables. Figure 8-17 is based on mortality rates

Figure 8-17. Benefit amounts for a 10-year temporary life annuity.

{1} Age	{2} Payout Year	{3} Number Surviving to End of Age	{4} Annuity Benefits ($1,000 × {3})
65	1	98,575	$98,575,000
66	2	97,022	$97,022,000
67	3	95,327	$95,327,000
68	4	93,480	$93,480,000
69	5	91,472	$91,472,000
70	6	89,294	$89,294,000
71	7	86,941	$86,941,000
72	8	84,409	$84,409,000
73	9	81,697	$81,697,000
74	10	78,805	$78,805,000

from such a table, and illustrates the process of finding the cost of benefits for a 10-year temporary life annuity. The table in this figure is similar to the table in Figure 8-10, which illustrated the calculation of the cost of benefits for 10-year term life insurance. Whereas Figure 8-10 shows the number of life insureds who die during the year, Figure 8-17 instead shows the number of annuitants who *survive* the year. To calculate the annual benefits an insurer must pay for a block of annuities, the annuity amount is multiplied by the number of annuitants remaining alive at the end of the policy year. Further, note that we have used different mortality tables for life insurance and annuity calculations. As we have discussed, the tables used to forecast benefit costs for annuities generally show lower mortality rates than those used for life insurance because healthier people tend to want annuities more than life insurance.

Estimating the Amount per Claim

As with life insurance, insurers price annuities assuming a specified annuity benefit. They then use the information so obtained to price annuities of different benefit amounts. We have assumed an annuity benefit of $1,000 per year.

Estimating the Timing of Benefit Payments

As we discussed in an earlier section, annuities generally pay monthly or yearly benefits. Present value calculations involving benefit payments take into account the timing and frequency of the benefit payments.

Incorporating the Underwriting Margin

As with life insurance, an insurer can incorporate an underwriting margin into an annuity's price in one of two ways. One way is to add a specified amount to augment the net premium calculated using expected mortality. Another way is to use a mortality rate that results in a higher calculated cost of benefits than the mortality rate the insurer expects to experience. Because annuities pay benefits when people survive rather than when they die, if annuitants live longer than expected, the insurance company suffers unfavorable results. To compensate for this risk, insurers use lower than expected mortality rates in the pricing process for annuities.

Calculating the Net Premium

For life insurance, the insurer finds the net single premium by finding the present value of benefit payments at the time of policy issue. For annuities, the insurer calculates the present value of annuity benefits at the beginning of the payout period. Thus, the insurer determines the account value that the contract holder needs to have accumulated by the beginning of the payout period to fund the annuity's benefit costs. Recall that, for immediate annuities, annuity payments begin one period after the annuity is purchased; in contrast, for deferred annuities, annuity payments begin more than one period—typically a specified number of years—after the annuity is purchased, at the end of the accumulation period.

Figure 8-18, an extension of Figure 8-17, shows the present value of the benefit payments for the block of 10-year temporary life annuities of $1,000 per year in our example. Recall that our example assumes that annuity benefits are paid at the end of each contract year.

Column 4 shows the amount of benefits the insurer will have to pay each year, and Column 6 shows the present value of this amount at the beginning of the contract. The bottom of Column 6 shows the present value of all the product's benefits. Because this figure is the present value of benefits based on an initial total of 100,000 annuitants, we can find the present value of benefits per annuitant by dividing this number by 100,000, as follows:

PV Benefit Costs (1 contract) = **PV Benefit Costs** (100,000 contracts) ÷ 100,000
= $638,435,632 ÷ 100,000
= $6,384.36

Thus, disregarding expenses, an account value or single premium of $6,384.36 is sufficient to fund the benefit costs of this 10-year life annuity of $1,000 a year.

As we have discussed, whereas the payout period for immediate annuities begins one period after the annuity is purchased, the payout

Figure 8-18. The present value of total benefits for a 10-year temporary life annuity.

{1} Age	{2} Payout Year	{3} Number Surviving to End of Age (from Basic Annuity table)	{4} Annuity Benefits ($1,000 × {3})	{5} Discount Factor— *PVIF* ({2}, 7%)	{6} Present Value of Annuity Benefits ({4} × {5})
65	1	98,575	$98,575,000	0.935	$ 92,167,625
66	2	97,022	$97,022,000	0.873	$ 84,700,206
67	3	95,327	$95,327,000	0.816	$ 77,786,832
68	4	93,480	$93,480,000	0.763	$ 71,325,240
69	5	91,472	$91,472,000	0.713	$ 65,219,536
70	6	89,294	$89,294,000	0.666	$ 59,469,804
71	7	86,941	$86,941,000	0.623	$ 54,164,243
72	8	84,409	$84,409,000	0.582	$ 49,126,038
73	9	81,697	$81,697,000	0.544	$ 44,443,168
74	10	78,805	$78,805,000	0.508	$ 40,032,940
				PV Total Annuity Benefits =	$638,435,632

period for deferred annuities begins more than one period after the annuity is purchased. *ExecuView* Application 8-4 illustrates the difference between the annuity income benefits available from an immediate annuity and those available from a deferred annuity with the same premium payment.

Setting the Gross Premium and Monitoring Results

To complete the pricing process, the insurer would derive a gross premium by adding to the net premium an appropriate loading to account for expenses. After the product is on the market, the insurer would monitor the product's mortality, investment, and expense performance in order to compare them to the insurer's pricing assumptions. If necessary, the insurer would then adjust the prices of future annuities sold to account for the product's actual performance.

We have illustrated the process of calculating annuity income benefits using a temporary life annuity. For annuities with other payout options, the insurer would follow the same basic process. Next, we discuss briefly the process of estimating the cost of benefits for the following types of annuities: annuities certain; straight life annuities; life annuities with period certain; and life income with refund annuities; and we touch on variable annuity benefits.

Application 8-4 Deferred and Immediate Annuities

If you wish to demonstrate this example on your computer, start *ExecuView* and select the Deferred Annuity Model. Be sure to select *Reset, All Models* from the Action menu to return *ExecuView* to its default settings. The default assumptions and profitability outcome for this model and for the Immediate Annuity Model are shown on the following *ExecuView* screens.

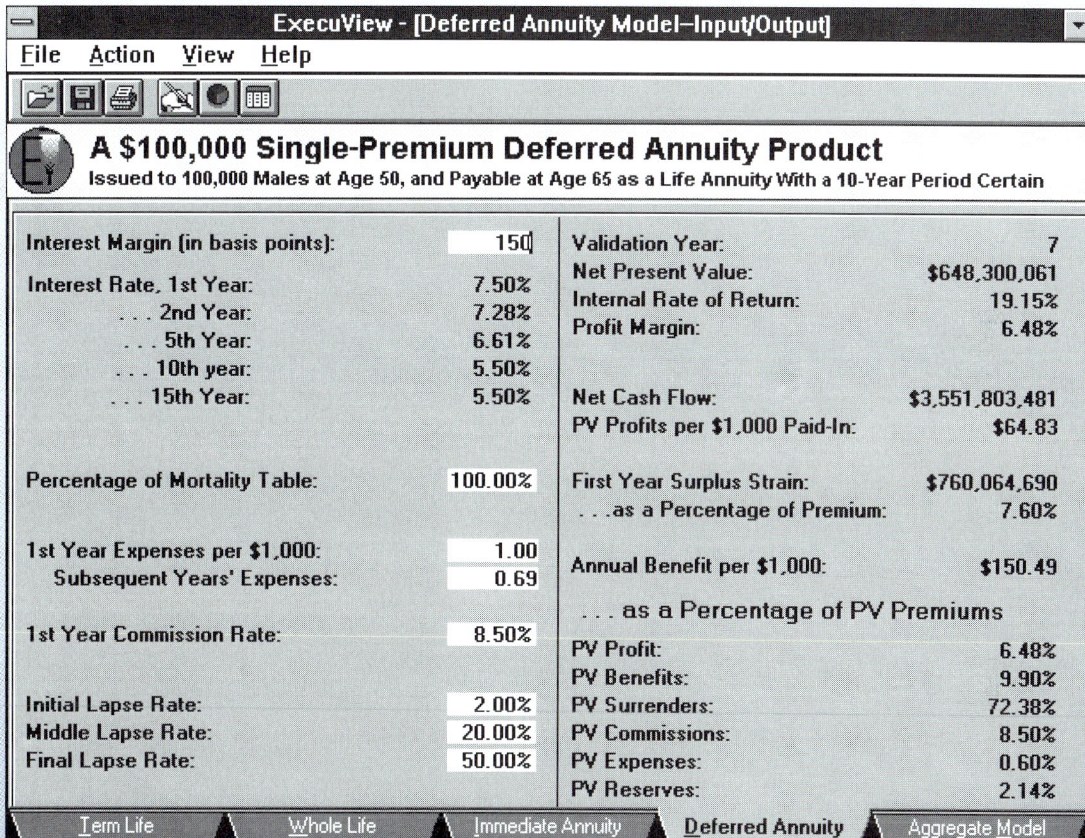

(continued on next page)

Estimating Benefit Costs for an Annuity Certain

An ***annuity certain*** is a contract requiring the insurer to pay benefits for a specified number of years, whether the annuitant lives or dies. Because the number of benefit payments is known in advance with

Application 8-4 Deferred and Immediate Annuities (continued)

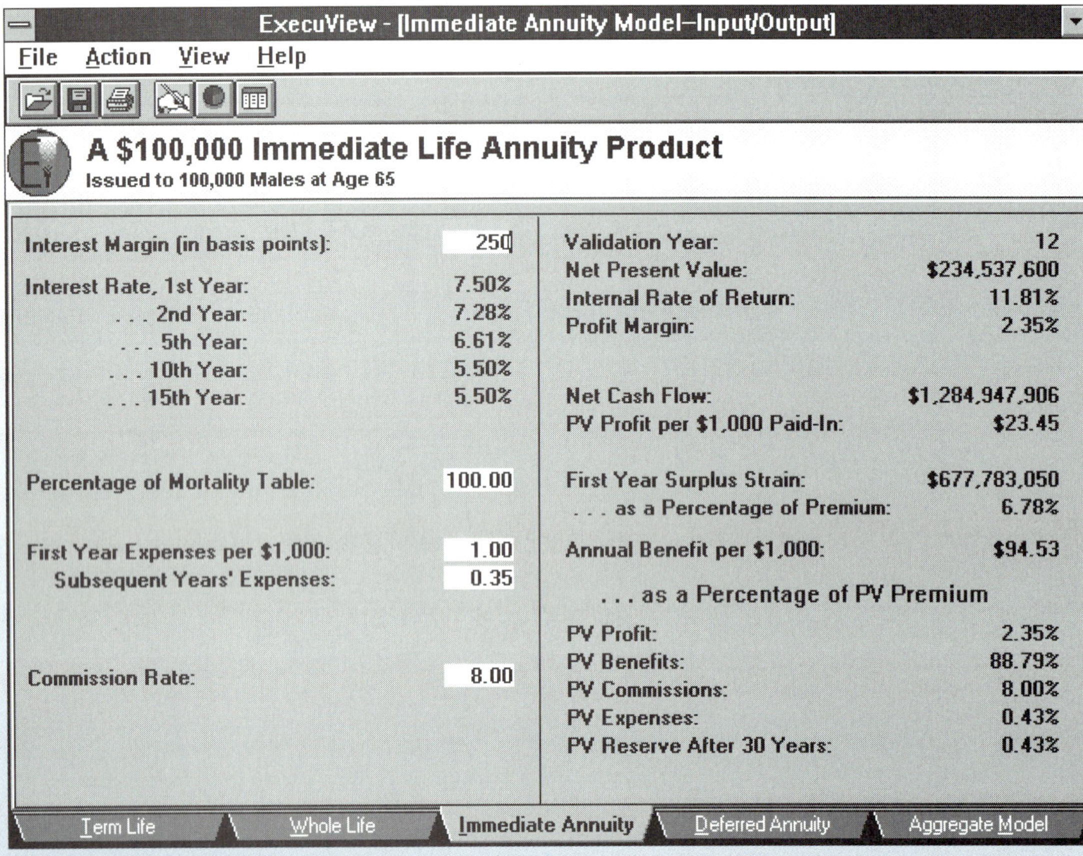

An immediate annuity begins paying benefits one period after the annuity is purchased. A deferred annuity doesn't begin paying benefits until more than one period has passed. During the accumulation period, the premium used to purchase the deferred annuity collects interest at a specified crediting rate (except in the case of a deferred payout annuity, which does not involve the accumulation of interest). The accumulation of interest makes it possible for most deferred annuities to offer much larger benefits than immediate annuities can, given the same amount of premium paid.

To illustrate this fact using *ExecuView,* we first need to make as similar as possible the assumptions for the immediate and deferred annuities. Because the Deferred Annuity Product Model doesn't calculate the annual benefit it pays until the fifteenth policy year and the immediate annuity model makes this calculation at the end of the first year, we need to make the interest rates level so that both products can offer the same crediting rate at the time benefits become payable. This gives us the consistent assumptions we need to make our comparison. We set the interest rate to a level of 7.5 percent.

➢ Select the Aggregate Model. Set *Change, 2nd Year; Change, Years 3–5;* and *Change, Years 6–10* to 0. Press <enter> to view the results of these changes. This model should show a level interest rate of 7.5%.

(*continued on next page*)

Application 8-4 Deferred and Immediate Annuities (continued)

Now we simply adjust the assumptions of the immediate annuity so that they are the same as those for the deferred annuity. The final step is to set the Deferred Annuity Model so that no withdrawals occur, since no withdrawals are possible for the immediate annuity. These steps should give us the clearest possible picture of what effect an accumulation period has on the amount of benefit that a given amount of premium can purchase.

➤ Select the Immediate Annuity Model. Set *Interest Margin* to 150 bp. Set *First Year Expenses* to $1.00 and *Subsequent Years' Expenses* to $0.69. Set *Commission Rate* to 8.5%. Press <enter> to view the results of these changes.

➤ Select the Deferred Annuity Model. Set *Initial, Middle,* and *Final Lapse Rates* to 0. Press <enter> to view the results of these changes.

The following *ExecuView* screens show the results of these two products when they both use the same assumptions. Notice that, as a result of the 15-year accumulation period, the deferred annuity offers an annual benefit per $1,000 ($211.91) more than twice as high as the annual benefit per $1,000 offered by the immediate annuity ($102.60).

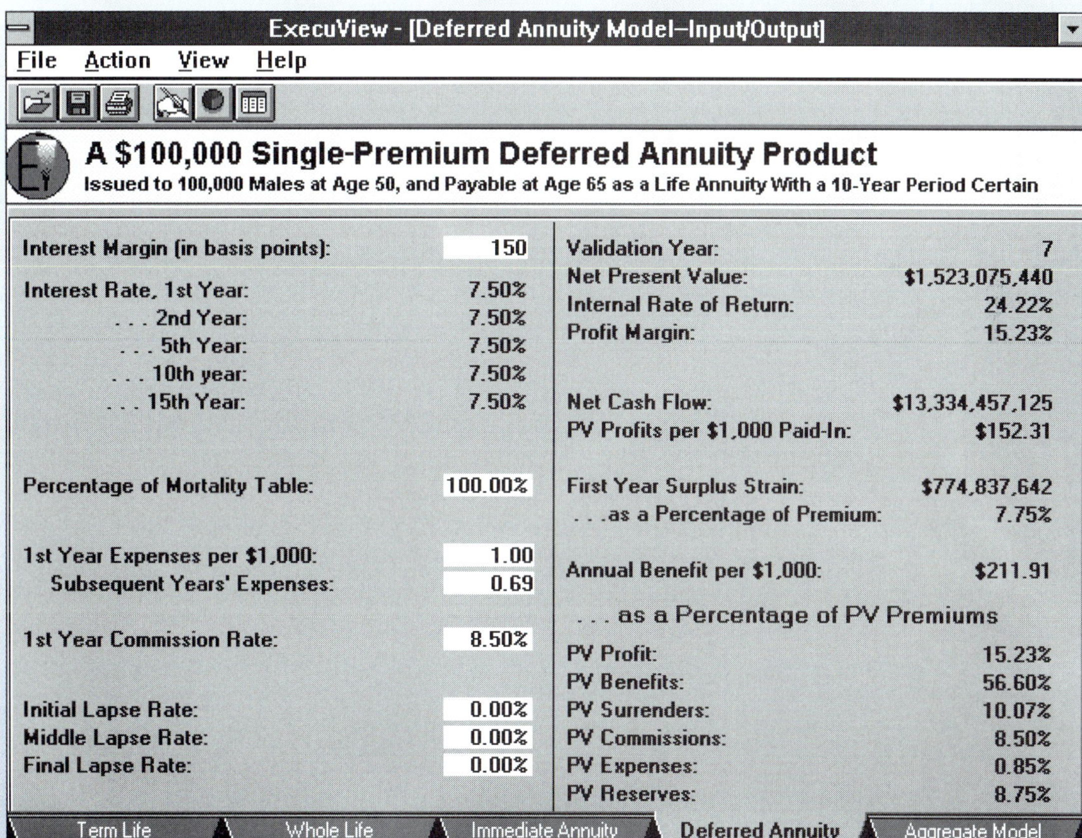

(continued on next page)

Application 8-4 Deferred and Immediate Annuities (continued)

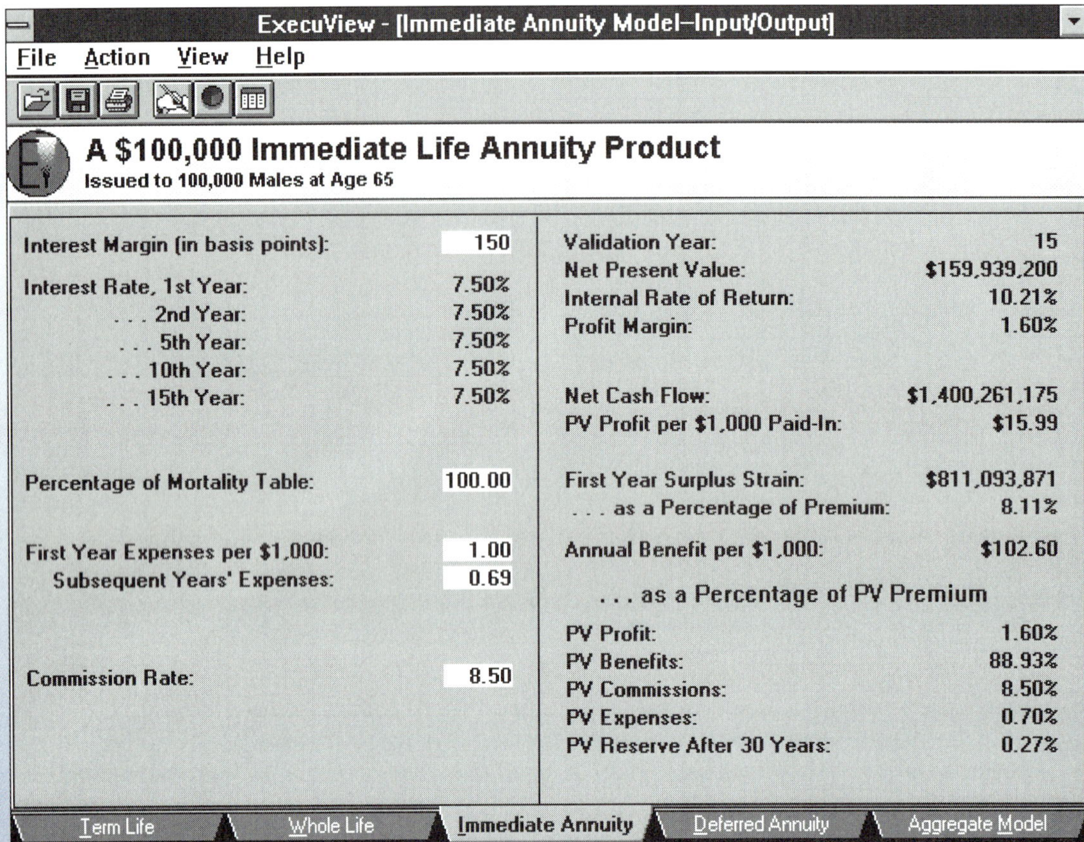

certainty, no mortality risk is involved, and the insurer does not need mortality tables. To find the benefit costs and the net single premium for an annuity certain, insurers simply add together the present values of each year's annuity benefit payments. Figure 8-19 illustrates this process for a five-year annuity certain of $10,000 that pays benefits at the end of each year.

Estimating Benefit Costs for a Straight Life Annuity

A ***straight life annuity*** contract requires the insurer to pay a benefit every year, so long as the annuitant is alive, but the annuity is not restricted to a specified number of years, like a temporary life annuity. Under a straight life annuity, annuity income payments cease when

Figure 8-19. The present value of total benefits for a five-year annuity certain.

{1} Payout Year	{2} Annuity Benefits	{3} Discount Factor at 7%	{4} Present Value of Annuity Benefits
1	$10,000	0.935	$ 9,350
2	$10,000	0.873	$ 8,730
3	$10,000	0.816	$ 8,160
4	$10,000	0.763	$ 7,630
5	$10,000	0.713	$ 7,130
	PV Total Annuity Benefits =		$41,000

the annuitant dies. Figure 8-20 illustrates the stream of annuity income payments an insurer would pay for a block of straight life annuities. As the figure indicates, pricing a straight life annuity is similar to pricing a temporary life annuity to age 115, the last age in many annuity mortality tables. To estimate the cost of annuity income benefits of a block of straight life annuities, the insurer estimates the cost of benefits for each year from the time of the first set of benefit payments until the members of the group reach age 115. The insurer would use an annuity mortality table to forecast how many annuitants would remain alive each year. Once again, to find the total of annuity income payments for each year, the insurer would multiply the number of annuitants remaining alive in that year by the annual benefit amount.

Estimating Benefit Costs for a Life Annuity with Period Certain

For a ***life annuity with period certain,*** the insurer pays the annuity benefit for at least a stated number of years—often called the *period*

Figure 8-20. Benefit payments for a straight life annuity.

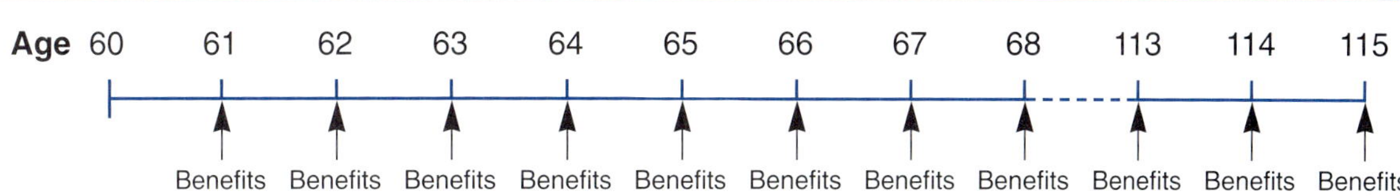

certain—whether the annuitant lives or dies. After the initial period certain, the insurer pays the annuity benefit only if the annuitant is still alive. To determine the benefit costs during the period certain, the insurer would follow the same process used to determine the benefit costs of an annuity certain. For example, for an annuity with a period certain of five years, the insurer will definitely have to pay an annuity benefit for the first five years, either to the annuitant, if the annuitant is still alive, or to the beneficiary. After the initial five years, the insurer would use a mortality table to estimate the cost of the remaining benefit payments.

Figure 8-21 compares the annual cost of benefits in the early years of a block of straight life annuities with those for a block of life annuities with period certain. As the figure shows, the benefit payments for the two annuities differ only in the first five years of the payout period. During the straight life annuity's first five years, the insurer pays a benefit only on those annuitants who remain alive. During the life annuity with period certain's first five years, the insurer pays a benefit on each of the 100,000 annuities that are part of the initial block of business, whether the annuitant lives or dies.

Estimating Benefit Costs for a Life Income with Refund Annuity

For a ***life income with refund annuity,*** the insurer makes the benefit payments so long as the annuitant remains alive, with the added condition that, if the annuitant dies before the insurer has made annuity payments at least equal to the amount of the premiums paid for the

Figure 8-21. Annual cost of benefits for straight life annuity compared to life annuity with period certain.

{1} Age	{2} Payout Year	{3} Number Surviving to End of Age (from Basic Table, Initial Sample =100,000)	{4} Benefits: Straight Life Annuity	{5} Benefits: Life Annuity with Period Certain
65	1	98,575	98,575(\$*x*)	100,000(\$*x*)
66	2	97,022	97,022(\$*x*)	100,000(\$*x*)
67	3	95,327	95,327(\$*x*)	100,000(\$*x*)
68	4	93,480	93,480(\$*x*)	100,000(\$*x*)
69	5	91,472	91,472(\$*x*)	100,000(\$*x*)
70	6	89,294	89,294(\$*x*)	89,294(\$*x*)
71	7	86,941	86,941(\$*x*)	86,941(\$*x*)

Figure 8-22. Benefit payments for life income with refund annuity.

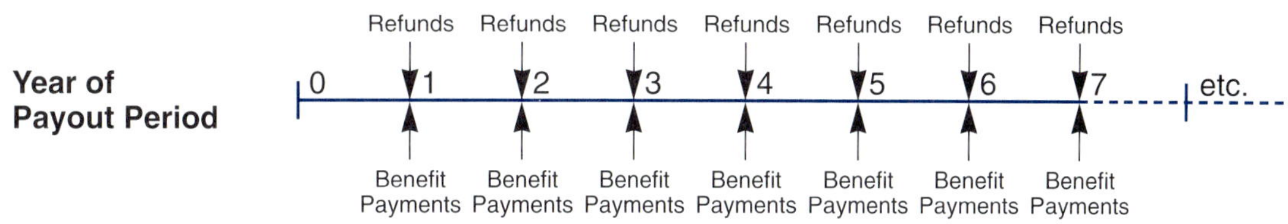

annuity, the insurer will pay a "refund" equal to the difference between the premiums paid for the contract and the benefits the annuitant received. Therefore, when estimating the cost of providing benefits for the early years of this type of product, the insurer must estimate the cost of any refunds. Suppose that for a specific product, \$52,000 of premium purchased a yearly benefit of \$10,000. The insurer would pay a refund for each annuitant who died during the first six years of the payout period. Figure 8-22 illustrates the refund and income benefits the insurer would have to pay for this product.

Benefits for Variable Annuities

Variable annuities are generally available with the same payout options as fixed annuities. In addition, a variable annuity's benefit amount may fluctuate during the payout period to reflect fluctuations in the value of the assets backing the annuity.

At the beginning of the payout period of a variable annuity, the customer purchases a certain number of annuity units. An ***annuity unit*** is a unit of ownership in a separate fund. The value of the annuity unit increases and decreases according to the fund's actual investment performance. The dollar amount of variable annuity benefit is determined by the value of an annuity unit at the time the benefit payment is made. For example, at the beginning of her variable annuity's payout period, Lisa Kady's account value purchases 40 annuity units. At the time of the first benefit payout, an annuity unit is worth \$100. Ms. Kady therefore receives an annuity benefit of \$4,000, calculated by multiplying 40 units by \$100. At the time of her second benefit payout, annuity units are worth \$103, so she receives \$4,120, calculated by multiplying 40 units by \$103. If annuity units were worth \$95, Ms. Kady would receive a yearly benefit amount of \$3,800, calculated by multiplying 40 units by \$95.

The table that follows restates the characteristics of the annuities we have described and summarizes some of the considerations related to pricing these annuities for the cost of benefits.

Type of annuity	Characteristics	Pricing considerations
Temporary life	The benefit is paid until the annuitant dies or until the end of the specified period, whichever occurs first.	Benefit costs are calculated using a mortality table to the end of specified period.
Certain	A specified number of benefit payments are made, whether the annuitant lives or dies.	A mortality table is not needed.
Straight life	The benefit is paid as long as the annuitant lives.	Benefit costs are calculated to the end of the mortality table.
Life with period certain	The benefit is paid as long as the annuitant lives and at least until the end of the specified period.	The benefit costs after the end of the period certain are calculated using a mortality table; the benefit costs during the period certain are calculated as an annuity certain—no mortality table is needed.
Life with refund	The benefit is paid as long as the annuitant lives, and a refund is paid if the customer does not recover at least the premiums paid.	Benefit costs are calculated using a mortality table and considering refunds in early years.
Variable	The benefit value varies.	The annuity benefit is calculated in annuity units, not dollars.

Setting Premiums for Health Insurance

To set premiums for health insurance, insurers use the same basic process as they use for life insurance, shown in Figure 8-16. However, the process is carried out differently for health insurance than for life insurance. In addition, the pricing process for medical expense insurance differs from the pricing process for disability income insurance. In this section, we first discuss some characteristics of the pricing process that are common to medical expense and disability insurance. Then we discuss separately the elements of the pricing process that differ for medical expense and disability insurance.

Estimating the Cost of Benefits for Health Insurance

The differences in the process of setting premiums for health insurance compared to the process for life insurance relate primarily to the first step in the process, calculating the cost of benefits. First, as we have discussed, insurers use *morbidity rates* rather than mortality rates to calculate the cost of benefits for health insurance. Whereas mortality rates are estimates of the proportion of people of certain ages who will die, morbidity rates are estimates of the proportion of people of certain ages who will suffer an illness or disability and also of how severe their illnesses or disabilities will be.

The second way that the process of calculating benefit costs for health insurance differs from that for life insurance relates to step 1b in Figure 8-16—estimating the average amount per claim. The amount of benefits paid under a health contract is more difficult to predict than the amount payable under a life contract. If a life insured dies, then the insurer generally pays the benefit amount stipulated by the contract. However, if an insured under a medical expense contract incurs a claim, the amount of the claim depends on the type of claim and the severity of the insured's illness. Similarly, the amount of a disability claim depends on the length of the insured's disability.

Because the amount of the benefits that will become payable under a health insurance contract is uncertain, insurers use morbidity data to forecast both the *number* of claims payable in a given year for a health insurance contract and the *cost* of each claim. To calculate the annual claim costs for a health insurance product, an insurer generally must forecast two figures: the number of claims, often called the *claim frequency;* and the average cost or *severity* of each claim. The annual claim costs are found by multiplying the two, as follows:

Annual Claim Costs = Number of Claims × Average Cost per Claim

For example, according to the morbidity table shown in Figure 8-5, a block of 55-year-old males covered under a hospital benefit policy would be expected to experience the following morbidity rates for each $1 unit of benefit:

Number of claims	Average claim
12.20 per 100 insureds	$9.31

According to this table, the expected annual claim costs for a hospital benefit policy issued to a 55-year-old insured would be

$$0.1220 \times \$9.31 = \$1.14$$

Note that this claim cost is for a $1 benefit, and can be used to derive annual claim costs for other benefit amounts. For example, if an insured purchased a policy with a $200 benefit amount, then the expected annual claim costs would equal $1.14 multiplied by 200, which equals $228.

For both disability and medical expense insurance, contract provisions strongly influence both the frequency and the average cost of covered claims. For example, consider the difference between a disability policy with a 30-day waiting period and one with a waiting period of 120 days. The insurer would have to pay many claims for relatively short disabilities on the policy with the shorter waiting period, whereas many of these short disabilities would terminate before any claim was payable under the policy with the longer waiting period. A continuance table, such as we discussed earlier in this chapter, can help an insurer forecast the lengths of disabilities.

Other contract provisions that can affect the cost of claims for disability or medical policies include maximum benefit provisions, stop-loss provisions, coinsurance or copayment provisions, deductibles, coordination of benefits provisions, exclusions, and contract provisions intended to help contain medical costs. Insurers must take into account the presence or absence of all these types of provisions when calculating the claim costs for a health product. Figure 8-23 details the effects of these contract provisions on benefit costs.

Pricing Medical Expense Insurance

For most medical expense insurance products—whether they are managed care or traditional indemnity products, group or individual products—the insurer guarantees the product's premium for only a limited period, often six months or a year. Although a specific policy may remain in force for a longer period, the insurer needs to price the product for only the time remaining until the next price revision.

Pricing a medical expense product is similar in many ways to pricing a six-month or a one-year term life product. The insurer forecasts the cost of benefits for the six-month or one-year period, uses this benefit cost to derive a net premium and, after addition of a loading or retention charge, derives a gross premium.

Because of the brief term of most medical expense products, investment income has a relatively small impact on the product's price. Frequently, the net premium is set so that it equals the full cost of benefits, rather than the present value of the cost of benefits. When the net premium is calculated in this way, the small amount of investment income the insurer earns may be accounted for in Step 5 of the pricing process—setting the gross premium. In such situations, the loading or retention charge is reduced by the amount of the estimated investment income.

An insurer can incorporate an expected underwriting margin into a health product's price by using higher morbidity rates to price the product than the insurer actually expects to experience, or by adding an amount to the premium calculated using expected claim costs.

Figure 8-23. How contract provisions influence the cost of benefits for health products.

Contract provision	Description of provision	Influence on benefit costs
Maximum benefit provision	Specifies the maximum benefit the insurer will pay on any single insured.	The lower the maximum benefit, the lower the potential cost of benefits.
Stop-loss provision	Specifies the insured's maximum out-of-pocket expense.	The lower the stop-loss limit, the higher benefit costs are likely to be.
Coinsurance/ copayment provision	Specifies the insured's share of the cost of any covered medical care.	As the insured's financial responsibility increases, the insurer's benefit costs generally decrease.
Deductible provision	Specifies the dollar value of medical care the insured must incur before the insurer will start paying benefits.	A high deductible generally decreases the insurer's benefit costs.
Coordination of benefits provision	Specifies the insurer's liability for benefits when the insured is also covered under another policy.	The greater the insurer's liability, the higher the insurer's cost of benefits is likely to be.
Cost-containment provision	Limits health-care costs through a variety of methods, including agreements with physicians and hospitals.	Cost-containment provisions generally decrease the cost of benefits.
Exclusion	Lists conditions and treatments that the policy does not cover.	The more conditions and treatments the policy excludes, the lower the cost of benefits.

Because of rising health care costs, intense competition, and the insurer's ability to alter prices on a frequent basis, traditional indemnity medical products are often low-margin products.

Because of the instability of health care costs, Step 6 of the pricing process—monitoring results and adjusting prices—is extremely important for medical expense insurance. Insurers pay close attention to how well their pricing assumptions mirror actual experience and price new and renewal policies based on this analysis.

Pricing Disability Income Insurance

The process of pricing disability income (DI) insurance is similar to the process for pricing level-premium term insurance. The reason is that insurers generally intend a DI policy's premium to remain level as long as the policy remains in force. Indeed, in the case of noncancellable DI, the insurer is obligated to offer a level premium for the life of the policy. In the case of guaranteed renewable and conditionally renewable DI, the insurer is permitted to raise the premium in certain circumstances; for example, if the product experiences higher claim costs than expected during pricing, the insurer can raise the premium for an entire block of policies, though not separately for individual policies. However, insurers generally price such policies as though the premium will remain level, while retaining the right to raise the premium if the insurer's experience is much worse than its pricing assumptions.

When pricing a DI product, the insurer forecasts the product's benefit costs for the entire life of the product. Many DI products can be kept in force until the insured reaches age 65. Some can even be kept in force for the insured's entire lifetime. The insurer then calculates the net single premium by finding the present value of the product's benefit costs. The insurer must take into account both the lapses and the deaths that will occur among its insureds. As with other products, a DI policy's gross premium is found by augmenting the net premium by an appropriate loading to account for expenses.

A DI policy's underwriting margin, and its net and gross premium, depend in large part on the product's renewal provisions. The more generous the renewal provision, the greater the product's underwriting margin is likely to be. For example, noncancellable DI includes greater margins than guaranteed renewable DI, whose margins are wider than conditionally renewable DI. The greater built-in margins reflect the greater risk to the insurer of the more generous guarantees.

As with life insurance, an insurer can incorporate an *expected* underwriting margin into a health insurance product's price, but the insurer cannot control the product's *actual* underwriting margin.

The list below summarizes some of the factors that relate to pricing health insurance for the cost of benefits.

- Morbidity data is used to calculate both the number of claims and the cost per claim.
- Calculating medical expense benefit costs is similar to calculating benefit costs for one-year term life.
- Calculating DI benefit costs is similar to calculating benefit costs for level-premium term policies.
- Traditional indemnity medical expense products often have thin margins.
- DI margins depend on whether the product is noncancellable, guaranteed renewable, or involves other premium or renewal guarantees.

Group Insurance Pricing

Estimating the cost of benefits for a group insurance product involves two considerations that do not apply to individual insurance:

1. Premiums for many group contracts are negotiated.
2. Premiums for many group contracts are expressed as a flat rate per unit of insurance that applies to each insured.

For group products marketed to medium-sized and large groups, premiums are generally negotiated, primarily for the following reasons:

- *Contract size.* A large or even a medium-sized group represents a large potential cash inflow for an insurer. An insurer has much to gain from satisfying such a customer's needs.
- *Competition.* Because the number of large groups is small, relative to the total number of groups, and because each large group represents a large potential cash inflow to the insurer, there is more competition among insurers for large-group business. Insurers must negotiate prices if they hope to win this business.
- *Custom-designed products.* The insurance needs of a large group are frequently unique and complex. Insurers can more readily fulfill those needs with a custom-designed and custom-priced product.

Although a large- or medium-size group covers a number of persons, the insurer generally charges the same premium rate per unit of insurance for each insured. Our next topic is how insurers use the pricing process in order to derive a uniform premium rate to apply to every member of an insured group.

Estimating Benefit Costs for Group Insurance

In order to estimate the overall benefit costs for a group product, the insurer estimates the cost of insuring each individual who is a member of the group at the beginning of the insurance period. For small groups, each member is usually underwritten as though each person were applying for an individual policy. However, underwriting a large or medium-sized group is much less exhaustive—the insurer generally does not consider as wide a range of individual characteristics as it does when underwriting an individual policy. Usually, the only personal characteristics an insurer uses to evaluate the cost of insuring group members are each individual's age, sex, amount of insurance, and, sometimes, the type of work that the individual does. A group's cost of insurance is also usually affected by several factors general to the group, such as the type of industry to which the group belongs and the geographic location of the group's members.

When underwriting a large or medium-sized group, the insurer generally uses the expected cost of insuring each individual group member to calculate an average premium rate for the entire group. The insurer then multiplies the average rate by the number of insureds or the total amount of insurance to calculate the group's total cost of insurance.

Figure 8-24 illustrates this process for a hypothetical group covered by a group life insurance policy. For simplicity, we have given our hypothetical group five members. Remember, however, that the members of a group this small would generally be underwritten individually. We have used a five-person group here to illustrate how the process would be carried out for a larger group.

Columns 2 and 3 in the figure show each insured's sex and age, and Column 4 shows the estimated monthly benefit cost for $1,000 of insurance coverage on a person of that age and sex. The monthly benefit cost for each insured group member is calculated using an appropriate mortality rate. In this case we have used 60 percent of the *1961 Standard Group Life Insurance Premium Rates.* These benefit costs are calculated by first dividing the annual mortality rate by 12 to find the monthly mortality rate, and then multiplying the monthly mortality rate by $1,000 to find the average benefit cost for each $1,000 of coverage.

Column 5 shows the amount of insurance coverage for each group member. In actual situations, the amount of a group member's insurance coverage is often a multiple of the insured's salary.

Figure 8-24. Calculating the net premium for a group life insurance product.

{1} Employee	{2} Sex	{3} Age	{4} Cost of Benefits per $1,000 of Insurance*	{5} Amount of Insurance	{6} Expected Cost of Claims (per Month) ({4} × {5})
A	F	25	$0.09	$ 60,000	$ 5.40
B	F	35	$0.12	$105,000	$ 12.60
C	M	45	$0.41	$180,000	$ 73.80
D	M	55	$0.99	$135,000	$133.65
E	F	60	$0.91	$300,000	$273.00
			Totals =	$780,000	$498.45

* Based on mortality data (approximately 60% of 1961 Standard Group Life Insurance Premium Rates)

Average Rate per $1,000 of Insurance = $498.45 ÷ 780 = $0.64

Columns 4 and 5 are used to calculate the monthly cost of insuring each group member. For example, Employee A is insured for $60,000 at a monthly cost of insurance of $0.09 per $1,000 of coverage. The total benefit cost per month of insuring Employee A can be calculated by multiplying the benefit cost per $1,000 of insurance ($0.09) by the number of $1,000s of coverage (60), or $0.09 × 60 = $5.40. The monthly cost of benefits for each group member is shown in Column 6.

The total benefit cost for the group is found by adding together the cost of benefits for each insured. As Figure 8-24 shows at the bottom of Column 6, the estimated monthly cost of benefits for this group is $498.45.

Calculating the Net Premium

The insurer uses the group's estimated monthly cost of benefits to calculate the net premium. First, the insurer divides the group's monthly cost of benefits by the total number of $1,000 units of insurance in the group in order to find the average cost of insurance per $1,000 of coverage. As the figure shows at the bottom of Column 5, the total amount of insurance for this group is $780,000, so there are 780 $1,000 units in the group. We calculate the average monthly cost of benefits for the entire group per $1,000 as follows:

$$\textbf{Average Monthly Cost per \$1,000} = \frac{\textbf{Monthly Cost of Benefits}}{\textbf{Number of \$1,000 Units}}$$

$$= \frac{\$498.45}{780}$$

$$= \$0.64$$

Subsequently, the group's net premium each month is found by multiplying this average cost of benefits by the total amount of insurance in force during the month. In this example, we are not considering investment income, because it is frequently a minor factor in group insurance pricing. During the first month, the total net premium would be $498.45, found by multiplying the net premium per $1,000 by the number of $1,000 units of insurance, in other words by multiplying $0.64 by 780.

If a new person were to join the group during the pricing period, then that same premium rate would be applied to the new person's coverage, regardless of the person's age and sex. For example, suppose that, six months into the year, Employee E, a 60-year-old female with $300,000 of coverage, were replaced by a 25-year-old male with $75,000 of coverage. In this situation, the group's total amount of insurance would be reduced by $300,000 – $75,000, or $225,000, to $555,000, but the net premium rate of $0.64 per $1,000 of insurance would remain the same. The group's new total monthly net premium would be the product of $0.64 and 555, which is $355.20. When the group's new net premium rate is calculated at the end of the year, the new employee's age and sex would be used to calculate the new net premium rate.

Net Premiums for Group Major Medical and Group Disability Insurance

To illustrate the process of calculating group insurance net premiums, we have been using an example featuring group life insurance. For life insurance, we have used mortality rates to calculate the "Cost of Benefits per $1,000 of Insurance." The same basic process is used to calculate premiums for group major medical and group disability insurance. However, benefit costs for health products are of course estimated using morbidity rates rather than mortality rates. In addition, the cost of benefits would be calculated for an appropriate unit of coverage. For example, the cost of disability benefits might be estimated for each $100 of monthly benefit. Medical expense benefits would most likely be estimated for each insured.

The following table reviews the process of calculating group net premium rates:

To calculate group net premium rates . . .	1. Calculate the expected benefit cost for each individual group member
	2. Add together the expected benefit cost for each member to find the benefit costs for the entire group
	3. Divide the total benefit costs by the amount of insurance in order to derive the cost per unit of insurance
	4. Use the net premium rate so calculated for all insureds until a new net premium rate is calculated at policy renewal

Incorporating the Underwriting Margin and Setting the Gross Premium

Insurers add an underwriting margin to a group product's price using the same methods we have described for individual insurance. Either (1) the insurer uses mortality or morbidity assumptions that are more conservative than those it expects to materialize, or (2) the insurer calculates the net premium using the mortality or morbidity assumptions it expects to materialize, and then adds a specified amount to this net premium.

As with individual insurance, the insurer calculates a group product's gross premium by adding an appropriate amount to the net premium to account for the insurer's expenses, contingencies, and an expense margin. In group insurance, this amount is generally called the ***retention charge.*** In addition, the portion of the retention charge that is an allowance for contingencies is called the ***risk charge.*** A product's overall risk charge is sometimes divided into two or more separate risk charges, designed to provide a cushion against various distinct risks. For example, in addition to a risk charge to recognize the possibility that the insurer might underestimate the cost of benefits or expenses, group products often also include a risk charge to account for the insurer's potential losses if the group terminates coverage prematurely.

As with most individual major medical insurance, the investment income an insurer earns on group insurance premiums is generally relatively small. Consequently, the net premium is often developed without consideration of investment income. When the net premium is calculated in this way, the retention charge, which otherwise would account for investment income, may be reduced to account for the absence of investment income.

In Conclusion

In this chapter, we concluded our discussion of product pricing by showing how insurers estimate their costs of providing a product's benefits and incorporate this cost into the product's price, along with an underwriting margin. We began by explaining how insurers calculate net premiums. Then we introduced various types of mortality and morbidity tables. We then explained how insurers incorporate benefit costs into the prices of various types of life insurance products and annuities. We then discussed benefit costs for health insurance and concluded by examining the distinctive benefit pricing methods used for group insurance.

In the next chapter we discuss reserves and cash values, which involve present value mathematical techniques that are similar to those used in pricing.

Key Terms and Concepts

net single premium
net annual premium
mortality table
mortality rate
tabular rate
statutory policy reserve
valuation mortality table
basic mortality table
sex-distinct mortality table
unisex mortality table
select mortality table
select period
ultimate mortality table
select and ultimate mortality table
aggregate mortality table
published mortality table
proprietary mortality table
projection method
setback method
morbidity
morbidity rate
continuance table
manual rating
manual rates
manual
experience rating
prospective experience rating
retrospective experience rating
dividend
experience rating refund
blended rating
credibility
block of insureds
block of policies
block of business
temporary life annuity
annuity certain
straight life annuity
life annuity with period certain
life income with refund annuity
annuity unit
retention charge
risk charge

CHAPTER

9

Reserves

LEARNING OBJECTIVES

After studying this chapter, you should be able to

- Distinguish between the prospective and retrospective methods of calculating policy reserves
- Interpret the differences between statutory policy reserves, GAAP policy reserves, and policy reserves calculated for tax purposes
- Recognize the different ways that reserves develop for different types of products
- Recognize surplus strain and how it can be alleviated by modified reserve methods
- Recognize how an insurer's reserving practices affect the insurer's solvency, growth, and profitability
- Identify several types of reserves that insurers maintain in addition to policy reserves
- Recognize how cash values are calculated and interpret how an insurer's approach to cash values can influence its financial results

OUTLINE

In this chapter we discuss reserves. ***Reserves*** are liabilities that an insurer maintains to meet future business obligations. Most reserves reflect an insurer's obligations to customers, though some reserves relate to an insurer's investments and others relate to taxes.

Reserves constitute the majority of an insurer's liabilities. As we know, the difference between an insurer's liabilities and its assets is the insurer's capital and surplus, and the amount of an insurer's capital is an important indicator of the insurer's solvency prospects. Insurers, regulators, investors, rating agencies, and customers can compare an insurer's assets to its reserves and other liabilities and can use this comparison to help evaluate an insurer's current solvency and profitability.

Policy reserves constitute the largest segment of most life insurer's reserves. ***Policy reserves*** are liabilities that identify the amount that, together with the future premiums to be received from an insurer's in-force policies and interest earned, is expected to be needed to pay future benefits on those in-force policies.

In this chapter, we initially discuss some of the differences between the reserves that insurers maintain for the different accounting systems. We then discuss the effects of an insurer's reserving practices on the insurer's solvency and profitability. After that, we examine several types of reserves that insurers maintain. We devote considerable attention to policy reserves and the other types of reserves that insurers must maintain to account for their obligations under life insurance, annuity, and health insurance policies. We describe these reserves in terms of their purpose, methods of calculation, and differences among policy types. We then discuss a number of other types of reserves. Finally, we describe surrender values, which are closely related to reserves.

Reserves for Different Accounting Systems

As we discussed earlier in this text, insurers generally maintain several sets of accounting records. In addition, insurers maintain several sets of reserves, each calculated in a different way and each one corresponding to a different accounting system. Most U.S. insurers calculate at least the following sets of reserves:

1. Statutory reserves
2. Generally Accepted Accounting Principles (GAAP) reserves
3. Internal management-basis reserves
4. Tax reserves

Guidelines for calculating statutory reserves in the United States are determined by each state based on NAIC model laws. Guidelines for GAAP reserves in the United States are determined by the Financial Accounting Standards Board (FASB). The guidelines for calculating U.S. GAAP reserves for nonparticipating traditional life and health insurance are described in Financial Accounting Standard (FAS) 60. The guidelines for determining U.S. GAAP reserves for universal life and most other interest-sensitive life and annuity products are specified in a different Financial Accounting Standard, FAS 97. Participating traditional products in the United States are covered by a third set of guidelines, set out in FAS 120. In this chapter we mainly discuss traditional, nonparticipating products—those covered by FAS 60. Occasionally, however, we touch upon the reserve requirements of interest-sensitive products covered by FAS 97 and the reserve requirements of participating traditional products covered by FAS 120.

Compared to statutory accounting, GAAP accounting for traditional life insurance products generally produces larger asset values and smaller net values for reserves and other liabilities. Because capital and surplus is equal to assets minus liabilities, GAAP generally produces larger capital and surplus values than does statutory accounting.

An insurer's internal accounting system often produces yet another value for reserves and other liabilities, and hence another value for capital and surplus. Most insurers believe that their internal accounting system produces the most realistic picture of their own financial situation. Nevertheless, insurers must always consider the status of their GAAP and statutory accounts, because these accounts are examined by regulators, rating agencies, potential customers, and potential investors.

In Canada, the statutory/GAAP dichotomy does not exist. The financial statements that insurers submit to Canadian regulators are prepared in accordance with Canadian GAAP, which differs in some ways from U.S. GAAP. Therefore, insurers need to identify one more set of reserves for their U.S. business than for their Canadian business.

In both countries, an insurer's reserves influence the insurer's income tax liability. Insurers are required to calculate yet another set of reserves for income tax purposes.

This chapter describes the differences between reserves calculated for GAAP and those calculated for statutory accounting, as well as various practices used only in Canada. We also touch upon the subject of tax reserves in the United States and Canada. Because each insurer uses its own internal accounting system, generalizing about the reserves calculated for these internal systems is impossible, except to say that many insurers use an internal accounting system that is a modified version of GAAP. For modified GAAP, reserve values calculated using the internal system are similar to those calculated according to true GAAP.

The Effects of Reserve Strength on Solvency and Profitability

Insurers have considerable latitude in determining the size of their reserves. For example, statutory requirements in the United States specify the minimum size of insurers' statutory policy reserves, but do not specify any maximum. In addition, U.S. GAAP policy reserves for traditional products, policy reserves in Canada, and some other types of reserves, such as claim reserves, are based on the insurer's projections of future conditions. Insurers have considerable discretion over these projections.

The degree of conservatism in an insurer's reserve valuation is an important business decision. Conservative reserving practices produce relatively large reserves. The relative conservatism of an insurer's reserving practices has important implications for the insurer's solvency, as well as for its profitability. The more conservative an insurer's reserves, the more protection they provide against insolvency.

However, conservative reserves can have different and conflicting effects on an insurer's profitability and growth. Conservative reserving typically improves an insurer's rating from the insurance rating agencies. A strong rating can have a positive impact on the insurer's competitive position, because many consumers prefer the perceived security of doing business with a highly rated insurer.

On the other hand, conservative reserving can damage an insurer's competitive position by forcing up prices for the insurer's products. If an insurer maintains conservative reserves, the insurer may need to charge a relatively high price in order to generate enough assets from premiums to cover its high reserve liability. In addition, conservative reserving can hurt an insurer's competitive position by increasing the insurer's level of *surplus strain*—a phenomenon we discuss later in this chapter.

Each insurer must adopt appropriate reserving practices based on its circumstances and its business objectives. The following table summarizes the potential benefits and drawbacks of maintaining conservative reserves.

Benefits	Drawbacks
• Conservative reserves provide greater protection against insolvency • Conservative reserves can lead to high ratings	• Conservative reserves can lead to higher prices • Conservative reserves may increase surplus strain

The following sections discuss the business decisions insurers make that determine the strength of their reserves. We begin by discussing the effect on reserve strength of the actuarial assumptions used to calculate reserves. We then explain how reserves can be strengthened or destrengthened by voluntary increases or reductions in reserves.

Actuarial Assumptions and Reserves

In the context of policy reserve valuation, ***actuarial assumptions*** include the interest rates, mortality or morbidity rates, withdrawal rates, and reserve methods on which an insurer bases its policy reserve calculations. The insurer's actuarial assumptions determine how conservative the insurer's reserves will be. Insurers must choose the actuarial assumptions to use in determining policy reserves.

Interest-Rate Assumptions

The higher the rate of interest used to compute reserves, the lower the reserves will be. For example, compare the reserve levels shown in Figure 9-1 for an ordinary life policy using different interest-rate assumptions. The reserve calculations are for $1,000 of coverage issued to the same person, and the calculations for each interest rate level are based on the same mortality rates. In this example, using a 3.5 percent interest rate instead of a 5.5 percent interest rate results in a policy reserve that is approximately 52.6 percent larger after 10 years, approximately 39.7 percent larger after 20 years, and approximately 28.8 percent larger after 30 years.

Assumed Mortality and Morbidity Rates

Reserve values are also affected by the mortality and morbidity assumptions selected. In most cases, the higher the mortality or morbidity rates used to calculate policy reserves for life and health insurance,

Figure 9-1. Effect of interest-rate assumption on reserve values.*

Interest rate	10th year reserve	20th year reserve	30th year reserve
3.5%	$92.98	$215.15	$362.64
4.0%	$83.60	$197.84	$340.47
4.5%	$75.19	$181.92	$319.58
5.0%	$67.65	$167.33	$299.98
5.5%	$60.93	$153.98	$281.64

**Based on $1,000 of coverage and identical mortality rates*

the larger the reserves will be. However, because of certain mathematical phenomena, higher mortality or morbidity rates *do not always* produce larger reserves.

Generally, for statutory purposes, companies use the mortality tables prescribed by the NAIC. Nevertheless, so long as insurers adhere to all statutory restrictions, they can use mortality or morbidity rates that produce the desired level of reserve strength. As an illustration, Figure 9-2 shows the results of calculating reserves using different mortality tables. All figures are for a $1,000 whole life policy issued to the same person, based on an interest rate of 5.5 percent. Note that, in this example, using the 1958 Commissioners Standard Ordinary (CSO) table rather than the 1980 CSO table produces a reserve that is 18 percent larger after 10 years, 18.9 percent larger after 20 years, and 17.8 percent larger after 30 years.

Assumptions as to Lapse Rates

In the United States, insurers are not generally permitted to consider lapses and withdrawals when calculating statutory policy or tax reserves. Therefore, withdrawal rates are an issue only for Canadian reserves and GAAP reserves in the United States. In most cases, a higher withdrawal rate assumption produces a lower reserve. In other cases, however, because of the way in which the product is designed, a higher withdrawal rate assumption produces a higher reserve. An insurer can value its GAAP or internal reserves assuming whatever withdrawal rates that produce the desired degree of conservatism.

Valuation Method

Later in the chapter, we discuss various methods insurers are permitted to use in calculating their statutory policy reserves, including the *net level premium* approach and the *full preliminary term* method. Using the same set of assumptions, the net level premium reserve valuation method will always result in higher reserves than the full

Figure 9-2. Effect of mortality assumption on reserve levels.*

Mortality table	10th reserve	20th reserve	30th reserve
American Experience	$108.51	$264.07	$453.09
1941 CSO	$117.63	$269.08	$442.49
1958 CSO	$109.67	$255.89	$427.36
1980 CSO	$ 92.98	$215.15	$362.64

All reserve figures based on insured of same age and sex, and $1,000 of coverage

preliminary term method. The full preliminary term method is used for tax reserves, and the net level premium approach is used for GAAP reserves. In many cases, the full preliminary term reserve method produces the lowest reserve amounts permitted for statutory purposes, but an insurance company may also use the net level premium approach, though most do not. Nevertheless, an insurer that wants to reserve conservatively may choose to use the net level premium approach.

Voluntary Strengthening and Destrengthening of Reserves

In some situations, an insurer may decide that its reserves are inadequate for a certain type of policy, block of policies, or product line. In such situations, the insurer may decide to engage in ***reserve strengthening,*** which is the process of increasing its reserves. In other situations, if an insurer decides that its reserves are too conservative, the insurer may undertake ***reserve destrengthening,*** which involves reducing the amount of its reserves.

Insurers generally strengthen or destrengthen their reserves by changing the assumptions used to calculate the value of the reserves. An insurer could strengthen its reserves by recalculating them using a lower interest-rate assumption or a more conservative mortality- or morbidity-rate assumption.

In order to strengthen or destrengthen statutory reserves in the United States, an insurer generally must obtain the permission of the state insurance commissioner. The minimum size of an insurer's statutory reserves is determined by law at the time the product is issued. Thereafter, if the insurer's statutory reserves are equal to the legal minimum, the insurer cannot destrengthen its reserves. However, if an insurer's reserves are larger than the law requires, then the insurer may be able to destrengthen its statutory reserves, so long as the reserves remain at least as large as those required by law.

Suppose an insurer has been calculating statutory policy reserves on a certain block of business using 4 percent interest and the *1980 CSO* mortality table. When the business was issued, the law specified minimum reserves based on 5.5 percent and the 1980 CSO but the insurer decided to use the more conservative 4 percent rate for this block of policies. If the insurance commissioner gave permission, the insurer could destrengthen the reserves on this business by recalculating them using any interest rate greater than 4 percent but not greater than 5.5 percent. Alternatively, the insurer could strengthen these reserves by using an interest rate lower than 4 percent.

In the United States, insurers cannot generally change the strength of the GAAP reserves related to their traditional products. Throughout the life of the policy, GAAP reserves must be calculated using the insurer's expectations at the time of issue. U.S. GAAP does not generally permit insurers to alter their assumptions later.

Insight 9-1 Rating Agencies Reserve Opinion on UNUM Corp.

Rating agencies are reacting cautiously to UNUM Corp.'s termination of a letter of intent it signed several weeks ago with a major reinsurer to reinsure its noncancellable block of individual disability business in the United States.

UNUM's move to reinsure its individual non-can disability business was a major component in its three-part plan to rid itself of that troublesome block of business.

Last month UNUM strengthened its reserves by $192 million for existing and anticipated claims in the non-can individual disability business and bought $60 million of excess-of-loss reinsurance.

A.M. Best Co. reaffirmed its A++ claims paying rating of UNUM Life Ins. Co. of America while Moody's has confirmed its Aa1 financial strength rating on the life unit.

Source: *Brian Cox, "Rating Agencies Reserve Opinion on UNUM Corp." Reprinted with permission from National Underwriter, Copyright © 1996, The National Underwriter Company* Life & Health/Financial Services Edition, *December 12, 1994, p.2.*

In Canada, an insurer may change its reserve assumptions from year to year without receiving regulatory permission. In addition, considerable judgment is required in reserve valuation in Canada. In Canada, insurers can influence the relative strength of their reserves by means of the way they carry out the valuation process.

Of course, a U.S. or Canadian insurer has full discretion over reserves calculated for its internal accounting system. The insurer can strengthen or destrengthen these reserves at will.

Reserve strengthening or destrengthening can serve a number of business purposes. For example, when an insurer decreases its liabilities by destrengthening its reserves, the insurer increases its capital. The insurer can then use that capital for other purposes, such as to support new business. On the other hand, an insurer may strengthen its reserves if its emerging experience with a product reveals that the assumptions the insurer used to calculate the reserves for the product were too optimistic. In such a situation, the insurer may decide to strengthen its reserves to protect its rating or its solvency. Insight 9-1 tells of an insurer that was able to keep its high rating, in part because it strengthened its reserves for a product line that had been experiencing poor results.

Policy Reserves for Life Insurance

The principal reserves relating to life insurance contracts are policy reserves. Policy reserves are also important for annuities and health insurance, as we will see later in the chapter.

Figure 9-3 illustrates the reasoning behind policy reserves. At most times in the life of a block of policies, the insurer has received more money in net premiums than it has paid out in benefits on the product. The insurer invests the excess of net premiums over benefits. As

Figure 9-3. Sources of funds for paying policy benefits.

	Policy Reserves
+	Future Net Premiums
−	Future Interest Earnings
	Total Future Benefits

Figure 9-3 shows, the insurer uses this excess, plus the interest earned from investing it, plus any net premiums it receives in the future, to pay the benefits that become due later in the life of the block of policies. At any time during the life of the block of policies, the policy reserve reflects the excess of the premiums received over benefits paid, plus the interest earned up to that time. Because the insurer must hold assets at least equal to the policy reserve, the policy reserve helps ensure that the insurer will have the assets it needs to pay benefits in the policy's later years.

Calculating Life Insurance Policy Reserves in the United States

This section illustrates the ***net level premium reserve valuation method,*** which assumes in its approach to calculating policy reserves that a policy's net premiums are level. As we discuss later in the chapter, U.S. insurers can also use other approaches, called *modified reserve methods.*

In the United States, insurers use two variations of the net level premium approach, called the prospective method and the retrospective method. In addition, policy reserves are calculated somewhat differently under GAAP than under statutory accounting, and both statutory and GAAP policy reserves may be calculated differently from those calculated under other accounting systems. In the following sections, we discuss policy reserves calculated by the prospective and retrospective methods and according to U.S. GAAP accounting and statutory accounting.

Prospective Method

In the United States, the ***prospective method*** looks ahead at a policy's future premiums and benefits and calculates policy reserves using the following equation:

Policy Reserve = **Present Value of Future Benefits** − **Present Value of Future Net Premiums**

Figure 9-4. Calculating the policy reserve for a block of policies using the prospective method.

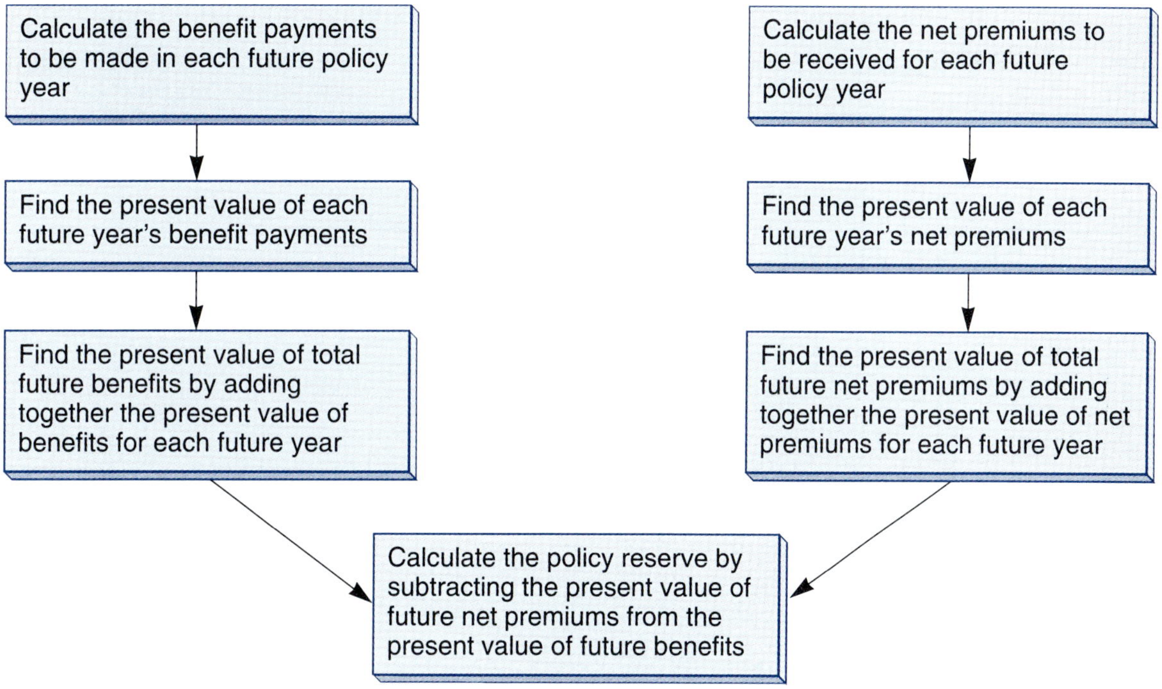

Figure 9-4 illustrates the process of calculating the policy reserve for a block of policies using the prospective method.

Figure 9-5 applies this process to a 10-year term life insurance product. Although we have chosen a specific product for this example, note that the policy reserve for any of an insurer's traditional products can be found using the basic approach of finding the present value of future benefits minus the present value of future net premiums.

Our calculation is for a block of 100,000 10-year term life insurance policies issued to males age 35. We have calculated the fifth-year reserve based on $1,000 of coverage per policy. The reserve per $1,000 of coverage can be used to calculate reserves for larger policies. The product's valuation net annual premium, calculated using the *1980 CSO* table and 4.5 percent interest, is $2.78994 per $1,000 of coverage. Figure 9-5 illustrates the policy's net premium income and the death benefits payable for each year of this product's term. In this example, we have assumed that no customers will withdraw or allow their policies to lapse. Our assumptions here as to lapse, mortality, and interest are similar to those that might be used to calculate a U.S. statutory reserve. We discuss statutory reserves in detail later in the chapter.

The first part of the process of calculating policy reserves involves calculating the net premiums and the benefits for each policy year.

Figure 9-5. Fifth-year policy reserve for 10-year term product—prospective method.

{1} Age	{2} Number living (Previous {2} – Previous {5})	{3} Net premium income ({2} × $2.78994)	{4} Present value of future net premiums (Interest Rate = 4.5%)	{5} Number dying ({2} × CSO mortality rate)	{6} Death benefits ({5} × $1,000)	{7} Present value of future death benefits (Interest Rate = 4.5%)
35	100,000	$278,994		211	$211,000	
36	99,789	$278,405		224	$224,000	
37	99,565	$277,780		239	$239,000	
38	99,326	$277,113		256	$256,000	
39	99,070	$276,399		276	$276,000	
40	**98,794**	**$275,629**	**$ 275,629**	**298**	**$298,000**	**$ 285,167**
41	**98,496**	**$274,794**	**$ 262,964**	**324**	**$324,000**	**$ 296,697**
42	**98,172**	**$273,894**	**$ 250,813**	**349**	**$349,000**	**$ 305,827**
43	**97,823**	**$272,920**	**$ 239,159**	**379**	**$379,000**	**$ 317,815**
44	**97,444**	**$271,863**	**$ 227,973**	**408**	**$408,000**	**$ 327,400**
			$1,256,538			**$1,532,906**

Present Value of Future Death Benefits – Present Value of Future Net Premiums = Policy Reserve

$1,532,906 – $1,256,538 = $276,368

The annual net premium income, shown in Column 3, is found by multiplying the number of living insureds at the beginning of each year by the net premium. The annual death benefits, shown in Column 6, are equal to the number of insureds who die each year multiplied by $1,000. The number dying is found by referring to a mortality table. Here we have used the *1980 CSO* table, a table intended for valuing statutory policy reserves in the United States.

In our example, we are calculating the insurer's policy reserve for this product at the end of the policy's fifth year. The next step in the process is to find the present value at the end of the fifth year of each future year's net premiums and benefits. Figure 9-5 shows, in Columns 4 and 7, the present values of each future year's net premiums and death benefits, discounted to the end of the product's fifth year. For this product, premiums are assumed to be paid at the beginning of each policy year, and death benefits paid at the end of each policy year. These assumptions explain the different discount factors applied to Columns 4 and 7.

The next step in the process involves calculating the total present value of future net premiums and the total present value of future death benefits. The figure shows the results of these calculations at the bottom of Columns 4 and 7.

The final step in calculating the policy reserve is subtracting the present value of future net premiums from the present value of future benefits. As the figure shows, the present value of future benefits is \$1,532,906, and the present value of future net premiums is equal to \$1,256,538. The insurer's total policy reserve liability for this product at this point in time is therefore equal to

$$\$1{,}532{,}906 - \$1{,}256{,}538 = \$276{,}368$$

The policy reserve per \$1,000 of coverage can then be found by dividing the total policy reserve by the number of \$1,000 units of coverage in force. Column 2 in Figure 9-5 shows that 98,794 policies remain in force at the beginning of Year 6. This is the same as the number that remain in force at the end of Year 5. Thus, we can find the fifth year reserve amount per \$1,000 of coverage as follows:

$$\$276{,}368 \div 98{,}794 = \$2.78$$

Retrospective Method

The ***retrospective method,*** summarized in Figure 9-6, looks back at a policy's past premiums and benefits to determine policy reserves and defines the policy reserve for a block of policies according to the following equation:

Policy Reserve	**=**	**Accumulated Value of Net Premiums**	**–**	**Accumulated Cost of Insurance**

The accumulated value of net premiums at any point during the life of a block of policies is equal to the amount received in net premiums since the beginning of the contract, plus interest. The ***accumulated cost of insurance*** at any time during the life of the block of policies is equal to the amount that the insurer has paid in benefits since the beginning of the contract, accumulated at interest.

In the absence of reserve strengthening or destrengthening, policy reserves are calculated using mortality and interest rate assumptions specified at policy issue, rather than the insurer's actual mortality and interest experience. In order to calculate the policy reserve for a product that has been in force for five years, the insurer must ordinarily use the mortality and interest rates assumed at issue, no matter what

Figure 9-6. Calculating the policy reserve for a block of policies using the retrospective method.

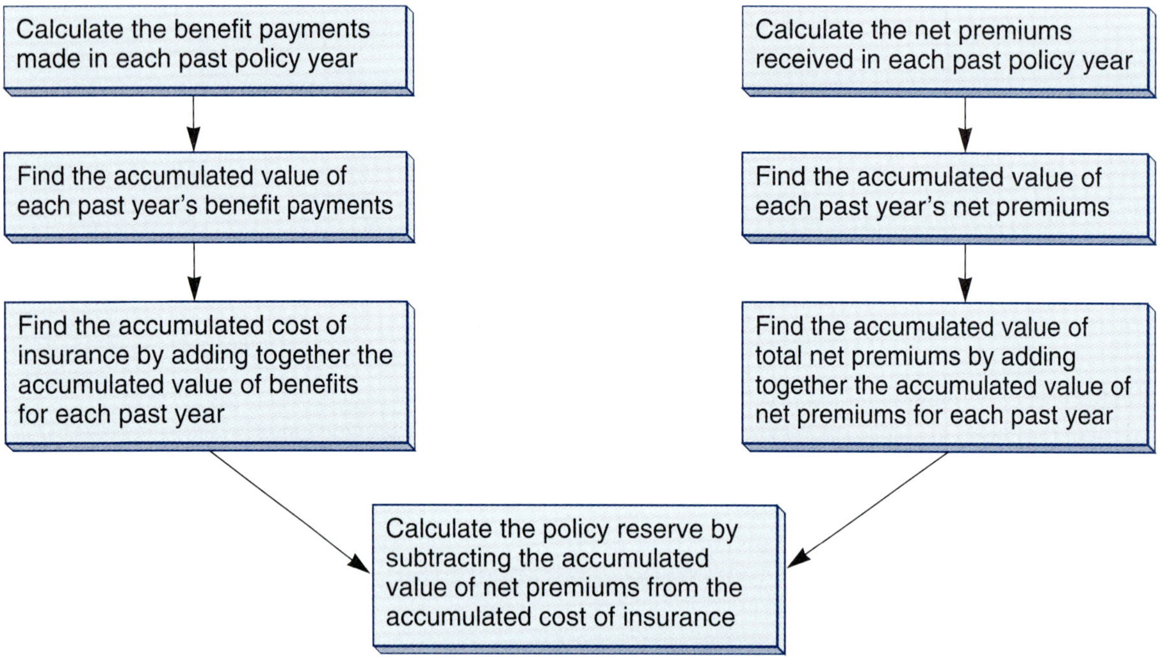

mortality and interest rates have actually been realized or what mortality and interest rates are currently being assumed for new policy issues.

The retrospective method and the prospective method, as they are used in the United States, always yield the same reserve amount, as long as the same actuarial assumptions are used.

The following table summarizes reserve calculation in the United States according to the prospective and retrospective approaches.

Prospective Policy Reserves	=	**Present Value of Future Benefits**	–	**Present Value of Future Net Premiums**
Retrospective Policy Reserves	=	**Accumulated Value of Net Premiums**	–	**Accumulated Cost of Insurance**

Calculating GAAP and Statutory Policy Reserves

The reserves reported in an insurer's U.S. statutory financial statements must be calculated based on criteria specified by state law. The state laws that specify how policy reserves must be calculated are based on the NAIC's Model ***Standard Valuation Law.*** The Standard Valuation Law specifies certain ***minimum reserve requirements***—

guidelines insurers must apply in calculating their statutory policy reserves. The minimum reserve requirements specify the mortality tables and other factors that insurers must use to calculate their minimum policy reserves. In addition, they specify a method that must be employed to calculate the interest rate to be used for calculating policy reserves.

Reserve requirements for flexible-premium or interest-sensitive life products are spelled out, not in the Standard Valuation Law, but in the NAIC's ***Universal Life Model Regulation.*** For flexible-premium products, insurers are required to follow specified criteria to estimate the future premium payments that customers will make, and to use those estimates when calculating reserves. Note that a number of states have not adopted the NAIC's Universal Life Model Regulation, and thus reserve practices may vary from one company to another.

Minimum reserve requirements are conservative. Consequently, statutory reserves for traditional life business in the United States are generally larger than net GAAP reserves* or reserves calculated according to an insurer's internal accounting system. Insurers are permitted to calculate statutory reserves using mortality and interest assumptions that create larger reserves than those produced by the minimum reserve requirements, but they cannot use assumptions which create policy reserves that are smaller than those calculated using the minimum requirements.

Three factors related to the minimum reserve requirements and the way statutory reserves are calculated generally contribute to the conservative nature of statutory policy reserves:

1. *Conservative mortality tables.* Statutory reserves for life insurance policies must be calculated using the NAIC's mandated valuation mortality tables, which are conservative and show higher mortality rates than insurers generally expect to experience.

2. *Low interest rates.* Statutory reserves must be calculated using conservative interest rates—rates that are lower than most insurers expect to earn. Lower interest rate assumptions result in higher present values and, thus, in higher reserves, generally speaking.

3. *No lapses or withdrawals.* Life insurance statutory reserves must be calculated assuming that no customers will withdraw from coverage. This requirement means that, often, the present value of benefits calculated by the insurer for statutory reserving purposes is considerably greater than the insurer's actual present value of benefits is likely to be, taking into account those customers who will withdraw or allow their coverage to lapse.

* Net GAAP reserves are equal to GAAP policy reserves minus deferred acquisition costs (DAC), as discussed later in this chapter.

The minimum reserve requirements of the Model Standard Valuation Law are revised frequently. Such revisions generally do not affect policy contracts that are already in force; the new minimum standards set forth in revised laws usually apply only to contracts issued after the date that a state adopts the revision. Policy reserves must be established and maintained based on the minimum standards in force when a product is issued.

Because all statutory reserves must be calculated in accordance with the legal requirements in effect when a product is issued, the task of calculating an insurer's overall statutory reserves can be highly complex. For example, a recent Annual Statement for a large insurer listed a total of 129 statutory valuation standards for life insurance alone. The mortality tables used in these standards ranged from the ***American Experience*** table, which was published in 1868, to the 1980 CSO table, and the standard interest rates ranged from 2.5 percent to 8.16 percent. These standards were for policies that were issued from before 1900 to the date of the Annual Statement.

Calculating U.S. GAAP policy reserves differs in several ways from calculating statutory policy reserves. For interest-sensitive life products covered by FAS 97, such as universal life products, GAAP policy reserves are equal to the policy's account value. For traditional life products, GAAP policy reserves are less conservative than statutory policy reserves. The following factors account for the less conservative nature of GAAP reserves for traditional life products compared to statutory reserves for such products:

1. *Mortality rate.* Under GAAP, insurers may use mortality rates they feel approximate their mortality expectations. Insurers generally base GAAP reserve mortality rates on basic tables, though they often use a higher percentage of the rate shown in the basic table than they use for pricing because they add a provision for adverse deviation.

2. *Interest rate.* Under GAAP, insurers may use interest rates that reflect their expectations, with a margin for conservatism.

3. *Lapses and withdrawals.* Insurers generally recognize that not all life insurance policies will remain in force until maturity. They may use withdrawal rates that approximate their expectations.

GAAP reserves for traditional fixed-premium products are calculated using the insurer's expectations for mortality, interest, and withdrawals, as determined at the time the policy is issued. The expectations determined at issue must generally then be used for the life of the policy. GAAP generally does not allow insurers to modify the basis on which reserves are calculated after the policy has been in force, even if the insurer's expectations at issue turn out to be wrong. In contrast, under certain conditions, insurers may be permitted to strengthen or destrengthen their statutory policy reserves after business has been in force by altering the assumptions used to calculate the reserves, as long as minimum standards are met.

Another important difference between the way GAAP and statutory reserves are calculated concerns their different definitions of the present value of future life insurance benefits. For statutory reserves, the present value of future benefits includes only one element: the present value of future death benefits. Under GAAP, the present value of future benefits for traditional products includes four elements: (1) the present value of future death benefits, (2) the present value of future surrender benefits, (3) the present value of all expected policy dividends, and (4) the present value of the insurer's expected maintenance expenses for the business. Of course, the present value of future surrender benefits is a factor only for products that offer a surrender benefit, and the present value of future policy dividends is only a factor for participating policies. In addition, because of the mathematics of policy reserve calculation, the present value of future level maintenance expenses generally influences the size of policy reserves only for limited-payment products, such as single-premium policies or 20-premium whole life plans.

Although GAAP reserve calculations for traditional, fixed-premium life insurance products are based primarily on the insurer's expected results for mortality, investment return, and withdrawals, GAAP reserves contain a *provision for adverse deviation*. The ***provision for adverse deviation*** can be defined as a safety margin to allow for unfavorable variations from actuarial assumptions. Nevertheless, GAAP reserves for traditional products are generally considerably smaller than statutory reserves. Figure 9-7 shows sample assumptions that might be used to calculate statutory and GAAP reserves, and the difference between the reserves calculated using the two sets of assumptions.

The following table summarizes the characteristics of statutory and GAAP policy reserves for traditional products in the United States.

Statutory policy reserves	GAAP policy reserves
• Calculated using valuation mortality tables, which contain a safety margin • Calculated using a low interest rate • Calculated assuming no withdrawals • Future benefits include death benefits only	• Calculated using basic mortality tables, which contain realistic mortality rates • Calculated using a realistic interest rate • Calculated assuming a realistic withdrawal rate • Future benefits include death benefits and, where appropriate, surrender benefits, dividends, and maintenance expenses • Reserves include a provision for adverse deviation

Figure 9-7. Comparison of statutory and GAAP reserves for a whole life product.

Product: $100,000 nonparticipating ordinary whole life insurance issued to males age 35*

Statutory and GAAP Policy Reserves for Selected Years

Policy reserves (U.S. basis)		
	Statutory	GAAP
Year 1	$ 835.21	$ 650.59
Year 5	$ 4,522.33	$ 3,908.81
Year 10	$ 9,909.36	$ 8,518.08
Year 15	$16,225.19	$14,025.75
Year 20	$23,503.23	$20,465.93

These Reserves Reflect the following Actuarial Assumptions

Annual premiums	
Statutory (net)	GAAP
$990.00	$527.14

Investment return (interest)	
Statutory	GAAP
4.5%	8.5%

Mortality assumptions per 1,000 lives		
Age	Statutory	GAAP
35	2.11	0.81
45	4.55	3.26
55	10.47	9.17

Surrender values	
Year 1	$ 0.00
Year 5	$ 2,382.87
Year 10	$ 7,890.61
Year 15	$14,347.97
Year 20	$21,789.09

Withdrawal rate (lapse)		
Year	Statutory	GAAP
1	0	25%
2	0	18%
3	0	15%
4	0	12%
> 4	0	10%

** The product is nonparticipating, so no future dividends are involved. The product is lifetime premium, so future maintenance expenses are a minimal concern. For statutory reserves, future benefits equal future death benefits. For GAAP reserves, future benefits include future death benefits and future surrender benefits.*

Calculating Life Insurance Policy Reserves in Canada

When calculating policy reserves, insurers in Canada must use the policy premium method. The ***policy premium method (PPM)*** is a version of the prospective method that uses gross premiums instead of net premiums. The retrospective method may not be used with the policy premium method because, when policy reserves are calculated using gross premiums, the retrospective method does not produce the same result as the prospective method.

According to the policy premium method, policy reserves are calculated using the following equation:

Policy Reserve	=	Present Value of Future Benefits	–	Present Value of Future *Gross* Premiums

Under Canadian GAAP, as under U.S. GAAP for traditional products, the value of future benefits includes estimated future dividends and maintenance expenses.

In Canada, insurers are required to base policy reserves for nonparticipating products on an analysis of a number of scenarios. We discussed scenario analysis in Chapter 3. Guidelines from the Canadian Institute of Actuaries (CIA) help actuaries choose which scenarios to use in their modeling. The guidelines help insurers select the appropriate interest rates, mortality or morbidity rates, and persistency rates to use in their scenario analysis.

By analyzing a number of scenarios, insurers can predict a range within which their future benefits and future premiums will most likely fall. Based on this range, they can calculate the reserves they need to maintain in order to safeguard their customers' interests. Insurers are expected to be relatively conservative in setting their reserves. In other words, given a range of possible values for their reserves, insurers are expected to select a value near the high end of the range.

Insurers in Canada are not required to perform scenario analysis when developing reserves for participating products. Instead, insurers calculate participating policy reserves based on their expected future experience, including their expected future policy dividend payments. This practice reflects the assumption that dividends will provide a buffer against adverse deviations. In the event of adverse deviations, insurers can simply reduce the amount of the dividends they pay to policyowners.

Unlike U.S. GAAP for traditional products, Canadian GAAP does not require insurers to continue to use the actuarial assumptions chosen at policy issue for the entire life of the product. Instead, insurers in Canada can change actuarial assumptions each year, based on their emerging experience and their new expectations for the future. For interest-sensitive products, future premiums are projected as part of the scenario analysis carried out to calculate policy reserves. These predicted future premiums are then used with the policy premium method to calculate policy reserves for these products.

Policy Reserves for Annuities

For the large majority of annuities, the policy reserve calculated using the prospective approach is equal to the present value of future benefits, because most annuities sold today are either flexible-premium deferred annuities (FPDAs) or single-premium annuities (single-premium deferred annuities or single-premium immediate annuities). In the case of single-premium annuities, no further premiums are paid after the initial premium. In the case of FPDAs, the insurer cannot know for certain what future premium payments the customer will make. Therefore, the policy reserve is calculated on the assumption that the customer will pay no further premiums. For the purposes of calculating policy reserves, future premiums for single premium and flexible premium annuities are equal to zero. For these types of annuities, the equation used to calculate policy reserves,

Policy Reserve = PV Future Benefits – PV Future Premiums

becomes

Policy Reserve = PV Future Benefits – 0

which, for annuities, can be reduced to

Policy Reserve = PV Future Benefits

Generally, a customer can receive a benefit under a deferred annuity contract in one of three ways: (1) the customer can surrender the contract during the accumulation period and receive the surrender value; (2) if the annuitant dies during the accumulation period, and the annuity provides a survivor benefit, the annuitant's beneficiary will receive the benefit; or (3) the customer can keep the contract in force until the annuity matures and receive the periodic annuity income benefit. Annuity reserving differs depending upon whether a contract is in its accumulation period or its payout period.

For both the accumulation period and the payout period, the Standard Valuation Law specifies the mortality and interest assumptions that insurers are required to use to calculate minimum statutory reserves. Insurers must hold annuity reserves at least as large as those calculated using these conservative minimum reserve requirements.

Statutory Reserves during the Annuity Accumulation Period

In the United States, the Standard Valuation Law requires insurers, during a deferred annuity's accumulation period, to calculate statutory reserves on a worst-case-scenario basis. In other words, during the accumulation period, the insurer must calculate the present value of future benefits for each possible benefit stream. Scenarios producing different benefit streams may include the following situations:

- The contract holder surrenders the contract in any year before the beginning of the benefit period
- The annuitant dies in any year before the beginning of the benefit period (for annuities which feature a survivor benefit)
- The annuity remains in force until it matures
- The contract holder annuitizes at some point other than the annuity's contractual maturity date
- The contract holder chooses any other option, such as free partial withdrawals followed by an early withdrawal of the remaining account balance

The insurer is then required by law to base the policy reserve on whichever of these calculations creates the largest reserve.

Statutory Reserves during the Annuity Payout Period

Once the accumulation period ends, annuity income benefits begin. During the payout period, the reserve is equal to the present value of future annuity benefits.

GAAP Annuity Reserves in the United States and Canada

For GAAP reserves in the United States, an annuity's reserve during the accumulation period is equal to the customer's account value. During the payout period, the reserve is equal to the present value of future benefits. Insurers may use mortality and interest assumptions that reflect their future expectations.

In Canada, an annuity's reserve during the accumulation period is not equal to the customer's account value, as with U.S. GAAP. Instead, insurers use scenario analysis to predict the nature and amount of future benefits. Insurers then use the scenario analysis results to calculate the present value of predicted future benefits.

Reserves for Health Insurance

Two important classes of health insurance are medical expense insurance and disability income insurance. The three types of reserves that are important for health insurance are (1) unearned premium reserves, (2) policy reserves, and (3) claim reserves. We discuss each of these types of reserve in the following sections.

Unearned Premium Reserves

For most group medical expense insurance, insurers generally maintain unearned premium reserves rather than policy reserves. An unearned premium reserve is reported on a financial statement when a medical expense contract provides coverage occurring partly in one accounting period and partly in the next. An ***unearned premium reserve*** is a liability account on a financial statement, and its value is equal to the portion of a premium that applies to coverage occurring in the accounting period following the period represented in the financial statement. Note that unearned premium reserves, rather than policy reserves, are also used for short-term group life and disability products. For industrial insurance and non-cancellable medical insurance products, insurers establish both unearned premium reserves and policy reserves.

Suppose the Westminster Company has a group insurance contract with the Edinburgh Insurance Company, and the Westminster Company pays an annual premium each year on January 31. Each year, on December 31, the insurer would still be in possession of one month's unearned premium from the Westminster Company. On its financial statements prepared as of December 31, the insurer would report an unearned premium reserve equal to one month's premium, or one twelfth of the company's annual premium.

If the policyholder pays premiums annually, and happens to pay the annual premium near the end of the year, the unearned premium reserve might be quite large, representing ten or eleven months of premium. If the policyholder pays a monthly premium, the reserve is likely to be relatively small, representing less than a month's premium. If the policyholder pays a monthly premium on the first day of each month, the insurer will not need to establish any unearned premium reserve for that policyholder for end-of-month financial statements.

Rather than calculate the precise unearned premium for each policy in force, most insurers approximate their total unearned premium reserve, using various assumptions. For example, insurers commonly assume that all annual premiums are paid on July 1, meaning that one-half of all annual premiums are unearned. Such approximations are generally considered to provide an adequate representation of an insurer's unearned premium liability.

Policy Reserves for Long-Term Health Insurance Products

For long-term health products that offer premium guarantees for a number of years, such as individual disability income (DI) products, long-term care (LTC) products, and hospital benefit products, insurers must establish policy reserves similar to those established for individual life products.

In the United States, statutory policy reserves for long-term health policies must be calculated using the prospective method. For this purpose, benefit costs are calculated using morbidity data. The law specifies which morbidity table to use to calculate minimum reserves for each type of policy. For policy reserve calculations, the law also specifies the maximum interest rate to use, which is equal to the maximum rate allowed for valuing the reserves of new life products. As is the case with statutory life reserves, statutory reserves for long-term health products must be valued according to the minimum reserve requirements in force when the policy was issued. A company's policy reserves for long-term health products may be set larger than the required reserves, but not smaller.

As with life reserves, U.S. insurers must base statutory long-term health reserves on the assumption that the plan will have no withdrawals. However, insurers must also assume that some insureds will die. To estimate the number of deaths, insurers may use any mortality table currently in use for valuing the reserves of new life products.

In the United States, GAAP reserves for long-term health products may be calculated using the insurer's realistic expectations for morbidity, mortality, persistency, and investment return. As with life products, insurers generally must use their expectations at the time of issue throughout the life of the product.

In Canada, insurers calculate long-term health product reserves using scenario analysis and the policy premium method.

Claim Reserves for Medical Expense and Disability Policies

Claim reserves are another significant type of reserve reflecting an insurer's liabilities to its health insurance customers. ***Claim reserves*** are liabilities reflecting amounts which an insurer expects to pay in the future on claims that have been incurred prior to the date of the financial statement, but which have not yet been paid in full by the insurer. Insurers must also set up claim reserves for their life business but, because of the frequency and sometimes long-term nature of health claims, claim reserves are a particularly significant factor in health insurance.

Claim reserves must be set up for all of the following types of pending claim payments:

- *Claims incurred, but not reported.** At any given time, insured events have occurred for which the claimants have not yet filed a claim. The claimant may simply not yet have found time to file the claim, or, in the case of a disability claim, the waiting period may not yet have ended. For disability insurance, no benefit is payable until the disability has continued past the end of the waiting period.

- *Pending claims.** At any given time, insurers have received a number of claims that they have not yet processed and approved. Time is required to investigate a claim and determine whether the claim is covered by the policy.

- *Claims in the course of settlement.** At any given time, insurers have approved a number of claims that they have not yet paid. The insurer may have difficulty determining the amount payable or the proper payee, or the claim may simply be going through the normal claim approval process, which takes time.

- *Present value of amounts not yet due.* At any given time, insurers are obligated for a number of claims requiring an ongoing series of payments. This reserve is typically established in connection with disability claims, which require payments that continue for a number of years.

The delays in reporting, processing, and paying claims vary widely with the practices of each insurer and the promptness of its customers in submitting claims. Most insurers must use their past experience to estimate claim reserves. For example, an insurer could base its estimate of the number of claims incurred but not yet reported on the number of such claims it has experienced in past years.

The Growth of Policy Reserves for Different Products

This section illustrates how policy reserves develop over the lifetime of various types of products. Figure 9-8 shows the growth, year by

* Similar types of reserves are also held for life insurance products.

Figure 9-8. The growth of the policy reserve for each $1,000 face value of a 10-year term life product.

{1} Policy year	{2} Number of insureds	{3} Premium income	{4} Interest income (4½%)	{5} Death Benefits	{6} Reserve at end of year [Previous {6} + {3} + {4} – {5}]
1	100,000	$278,994	$12,555	$211,000	$ 80,548
2	99,789	$278,405	$16,153	$224,000	$151,106
3	99,565	$277,780	$19,300	$239,000	$209,186
4	99,326	$277,113	$21,883	$256,000	$252,183
5	99,070	$276,399	$23,786	$276,000	$276,368
6	98,794	$275,629	$24,840	$298,000	$278,837
7	98,496	$274,798	$24,914	$324,000	$254,548
8	98,172	$273,894	$23,780	$349,000	$203,222
9	97,823	$272,920	$21,426	$379,000	$118,568
10	97,444	$271,863	$17,569	$408,000	$ 0

year, of the reserve for each $1,000 unit of a 10-year term life product. Notice that the reserve grows until it reaches a peak in Year 6, and then decreases to $0 at the end of the term. Year 7, the first year in which the reserve falls, is also the first year in which the benefits paid are greater than the sum of the net premiums and interest earned. The reserve at the end of Year 10 is $0, because then there are no future benefits to be paid nor future premiums to be received on the product.

The general pattern of policy reserve growth exhibited by this product is seen in most level-premium, level-benefit term life products. For example, the growth in the reserve for a 50-year term policy issued at age 35 with a face amount of $100,000 is represented by the graph shown in Figure 9-9. Note that this example illustrates the policy reserve of a single policy rather than that of an entire block of business. The reserve for a single policy is calculated by dividing the reserve for the block of policies by the number of policies remaining in force at any particular time.

As we can see from the illustration, the policy reserve for a term policy, even at its largest, is generally considerably smaller than the face amount of insurance coverage provided under the policy, because a term life plan often expires without a claim being paid. In contrast, the death benefit under a whole life policy always comes payable sooner or later, provided the policy is kept in force. Figure 9-10 illus-

Figure 9-9. Growth in policy reserve for a $100,000 50-year term life product issued at age 35.

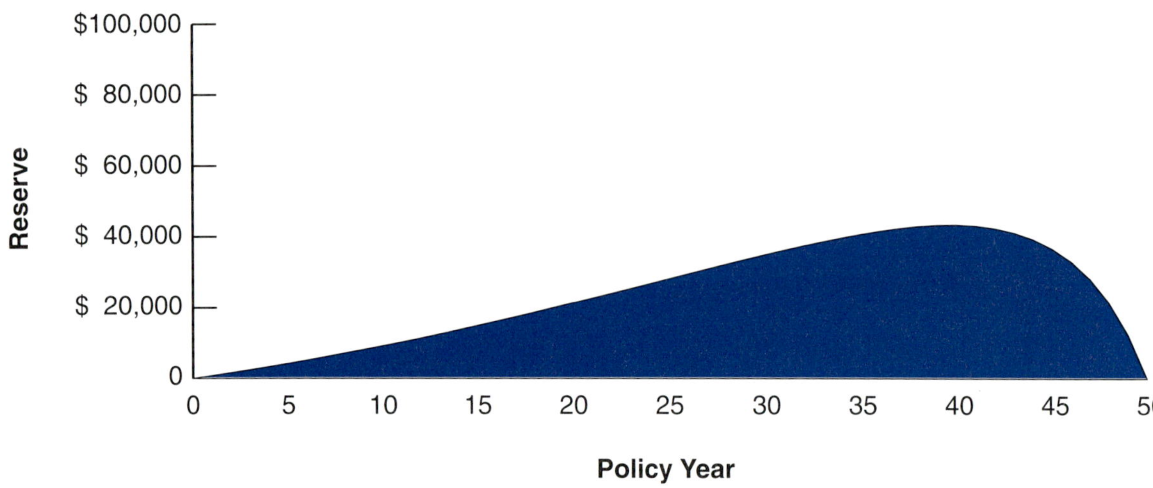

trates the growth of the policy reserve for a whole life policy with a $100,000 face amount. This policy reserve grows throughout the life of the policy. One year before the end of the mortality table, the present value of future benefits is very large—equal to the amount of insurance discounted just one year—and the present value of future premiums is small—equal to the amount of one year's premium. The mortality table assumes that all remaining insureds die in the last year of the table. At the end of the last year, the reserve equals the face value of the policy. At this time, the insurer pays the full death benefit for any insureds who remain alive, and the policy reserve falls to $0.

The premium payment schedule influences the growth of policy reserves. The reserves for a single- or limited-premium product will grow more quickly than those for an equivalent continuous-premium product. For example, the premium payments for a single-premium product cease after one year, and for a limited-payment product after 5 years, 10 years, or some other period of time. After premium payments cease, the reserve is equal to the present value of future benefits, because there are no future premiums. At this point, the reserve for a limited-payment product is greater than the reserve for an otherwise similar lifetime-payment product; the lifetime-payment product still has premiums to be paid.

Figure 9-11 shows that policy reserves grow more quickly for a limited-payment plan than for a continuous-payment plan. The only difference between the designs of the three products shown in the figure is their premium-payment schedules. The figure shows two limited-premium plans—a single-premium plan and a 10-payment plan—and a lifetime-payment plan. The benefits are the same for each

Figure 9-10. Growth in policy reserve for $100,000 of ordinary whole life issued at age 35.

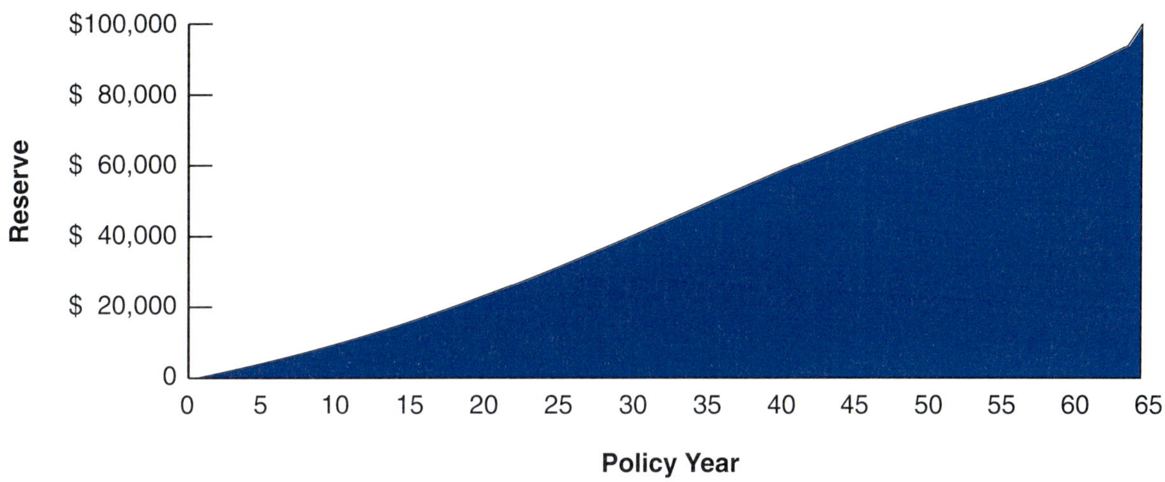

product. For the limited-payment plans, the amount of future premiums is always smaller than for the continuous-payment plan; therefore, the policy reserve is larger. Looked at another way, the amount the insurer has already received in premiums under limited-payment plans is always larger than for continuous-payment plans. From this point of view, also, it makes sense that the policy reserve is larger.

Surplus Strain

So far in this chapter, when illustrating the prospective and retrospective methods of calculating policy reserves as these methods are carried out in the United States, we have used the net level premium approach to calculating policy reserves. Using the net level premium approach to calculate policy reserves for such products as ordinary life, multi-year term life, and noncancellable and guaranteed renewable DI can create a phenomenon called surplus strain. *Surplus strain,* also known as *new business strain,* is the decrease in an insurer's capital and surplus caused by the high first-year costs and the reserving requirements associated with new products.

For many insurance products, the insurer's first-year expenses are substantial. In addition, in the product's first year, the insurer must establish reserves for the product. Consequently, the increase in a U.S. insurer's assets resulting from a product's first-year premium is often smaller than the increase in the insurer's liabilities created by the reserve the insurer must establish for the product. In such situations, the insurer's capital and surplus are reduced.

Figure 9-11. Reserve growth for a whole life product under single-premium, 10-payment, and lifetime-premium schedules.

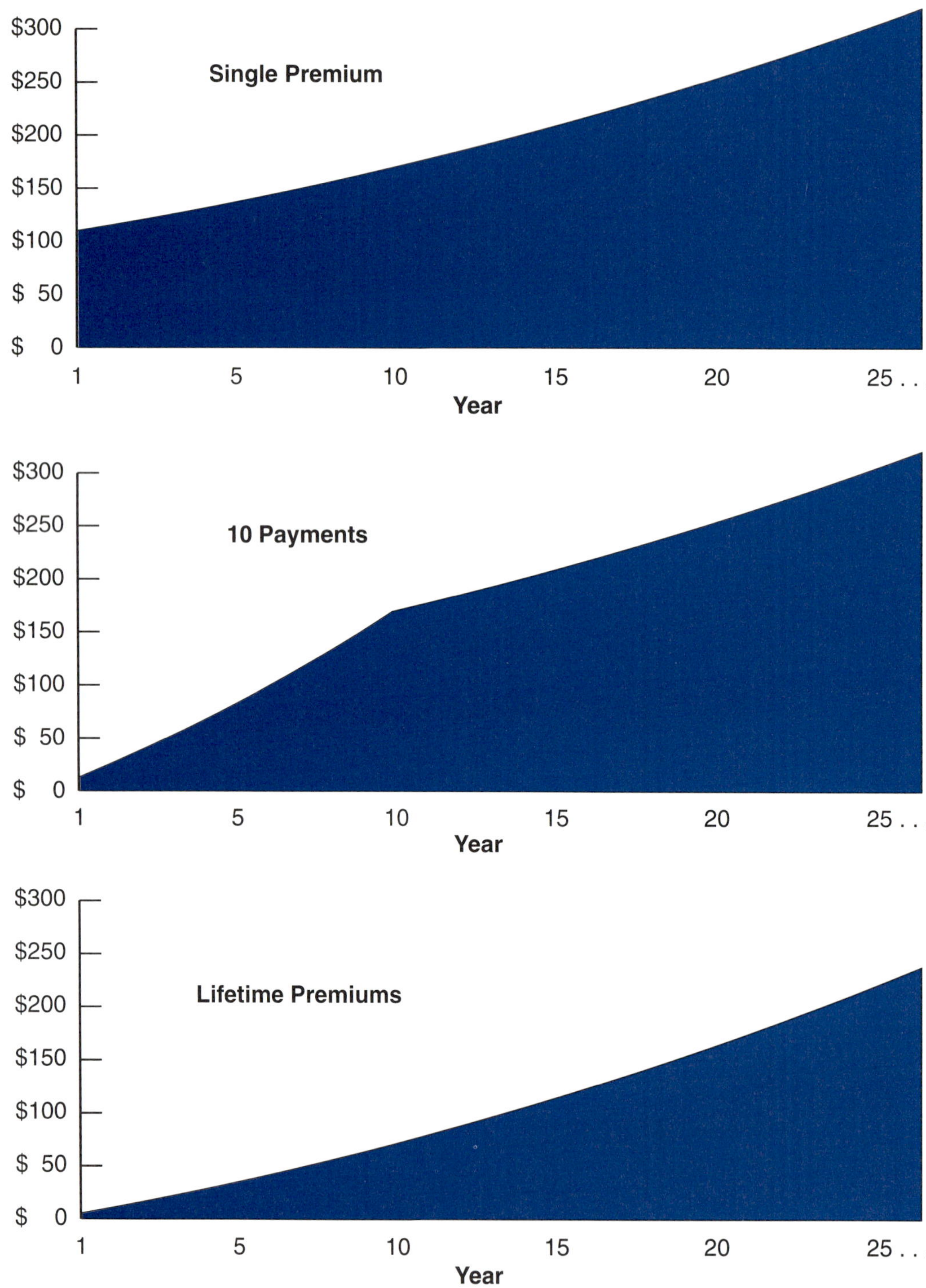

For example, suppose the Ventura Insurance Company sells a policy with a first-year premium of $150 and first-year expenses of $120. After paying its expenses, the insurer gains $30 in assets from this sale in the policy's first year. However, assume that the insurer, under the net level premium approach, must set up a first-year reserve liability of $100. Let's look at the effect of this transaction on the following simplified model of a balance sheet:

Balance Sheet	
Assets	**Liabilities**
+$30	+$100
	Capital and Surplus
	–$ 70

Because the insurer's assets increase by less than its liabilities, the insurer's capital and surplus must decrease to keep the equation in balance. Thus, the sale of this policy results in $70 of surplus strain.

For some insurers with strong capital and surplus accounts, surplus strain is easily managed. However, for insurers that are less well-capitalized, the decrease in capital and surplus created by their new business can cause their capital and surplus account to fall to an intolerably low level or prevent them from issuing as much new business as they would like. Even for well-capitalized companies, the decrease in capital and surplus caused by surplus strain can hinder the ability to carry out business plans. Therefore, surplus strain is an obstacle to new business.

Reserving Methods that Limit Statutory Surplus Strain

One way that insurers can reduce surplus strain is by using reinsurance. We discuss this use of reinsurance later in the text. Another way insurers can alleviate the potential problems of statutory surplus strain is to use a modified reserve method. A ***modified reserve method*** for calculating policy reserves is one that creates lower first-year statutory reserves than those calculated using the net level premium approach. Using a modified reserve method, the insurer experiences less surplus strain and can issue more new business without compromising its financial situation. Modified reserving methods are not used for any other products besides life and disability insurance.

As an illustration, refer again to our previous illustration concerning the Ventura Insurance Company. Suppose that the appropriate modified reserve method permits the insurer to establish a first-year reserve of $0 for the product. The contrasting changes in capital and surplus produced by the modified reserve method and the net level premium approach are illustrated below:

Net Level Premium Approach	
Assets	**Liabilities**
+$30	+$100
	Capital and Surplus
	–$ 70

Modified Method	
Assets	**Liabilities**
+$30	+$ 0
	Capital and Surplus
	+$30

In this illustration, whereas the net level premium approach reduces the insurer's capital and surplus by $70 in the first policy year, the modified reserve method causes capital and surplus to increase by $30 in the first year.

After a policy's first year, the modified reserve remains smaller than the net level reserve. However, as the years pass, the difference between the reserves calculated by the two methods grows smaller and the modified reserve approaches the net level reserve.

The modified reserving methods insurers may use for life products are outlined in the ***Commissioners' Reserve Valuation Method (CRVM),*** which is part of the Standard Valuation Law. Under CRVM, reserves for most life policies may be calculated using the full preliminary term method. The ***full preliminary term method*** is a modified reserving method according to which the reserve at the end of the first year is equal to the end-of-year reserve of a one-year term policy, which is $0. For certain life products with exceptionally high net level annual premiums, the CRVM requires a different modified reserve method, which creates a first-year reserve that is higher than $0, but lower than that created by the net level premium approach.

Health insurance reserving practices are guided by the NAIC's *Minimum Reserve Standards for Individual and Group Health Insurance Contracts,* rather than by the Standard Valuation Law. For noncancellable and guaranteed renewable DI and other long-term health products, insurers may use the two-year full preliminary term reserve, which allows the insurer to maintain a $0 reserve for the policy's first two years.

ExecuView Application 9-1 illustrates how using the net level method, rather than the full preliminary term approach, increases the surplus strain of the product illustrated in *ExecuView's* Whole Life Model.

Limiting Surplus Strain under GAAP

GAAP does not allow insurers to use modified reserve methods. Instead, GAAP limits surplus strain by permitting insurers to amortize (spread out) first-year expenses over several years. When an insurer

Application 9-1 Net Level and Full Preliminary Term Reserves

If you wish to demonstrate this example on your computer, start *ExecuView* and select the Whole Life Model. Be sure to select *Reset, All Models* from the Action menu to return *ExecuView* to its default settings. The default assumptions and profitability outcome for this model are shown in the following *ExecuView* screen:

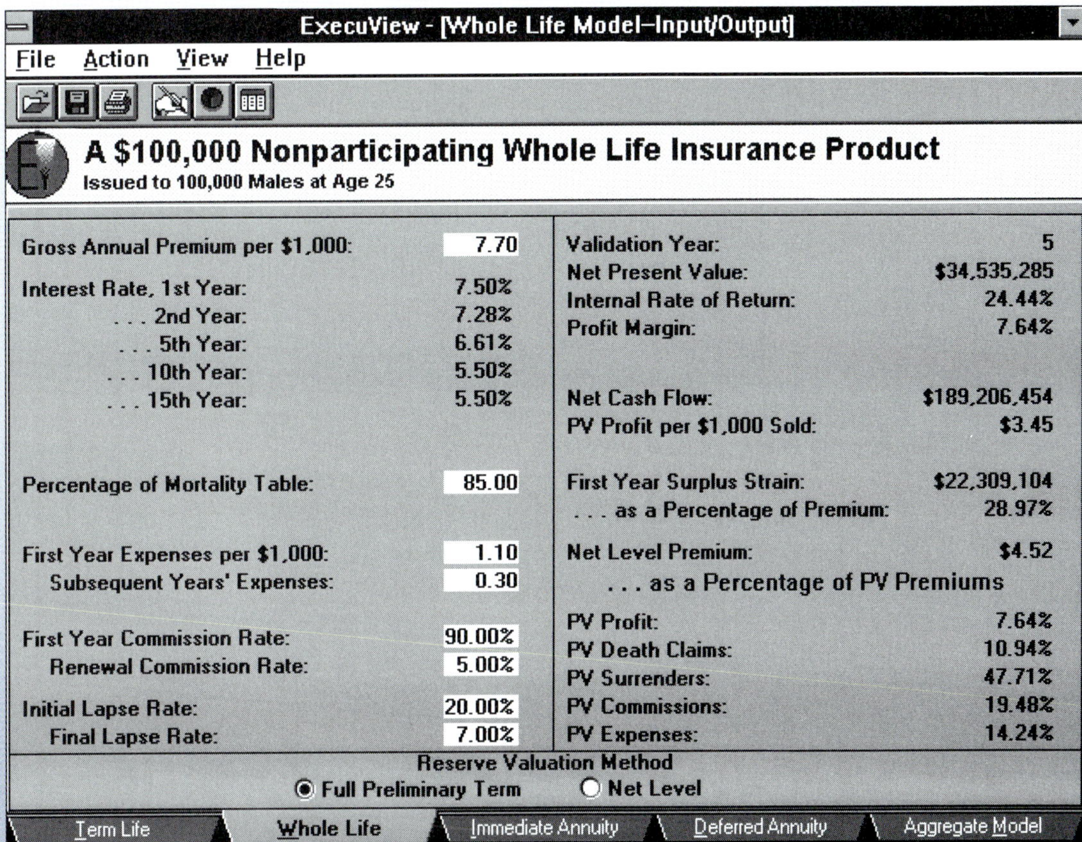

(*continued on next page*)

amortizes first-year expenses, only a portion of these expenses appears on the insurer's income statement for the year the expenses occur. In the next year, a further portion of the amortized expenses appears on the insurer's income statement, and so on in future years until all the expenses in question have been recognized. Note that the insurer must still pay all first-year expenses in the first year; however, the insurer need not recognize all the expenses in its income statement for that year.

When amortizing first-year expenses, in order to keep their accounts balanced, insurers create an asset account called ***deferred acquisition***

Application 9-1 Net Level and Full Preliminary Term Reserves (continued)

Insurers are required by law to hold a certain amount of policy reserves for every insurance product they sell. *ExecuView's* Whole Life Model offers a choice of two reserve valuation methods: the full preliminary term method and the net level method. Under its default settings, the Whole Life Model uses the full preliminary term reserve valuation method, which results in the reserve amounts per $1,000 of face value shown on the following table:

Full Preliminary Term Reserves

Year	Reserve per $1,000	Year	Reserve per $1,000
1	$ 0.00	16	$130.29
2	$ 6.44	17	$141.49
3	$ 13.19	18	$152.99
4	$ 20.27	19	$164.80
5	$ 27.68	20	$176.92
6	$ 35.41	21	$189.35
7	$ 43.45	22	$202.10
8	$ 51.83	23	$215.17
9	$ 60.52	24	$228.58
10	$ 69.54	25	$242.31
11	$ 78.88	26	$256.38
12	$ 88.54	27	$270.75
13	$ 98.51	28	$285.40
14	$108.80	29	$300.30
15	$119.39	30	$315.43

To see the full preliminary term reserve amounts in *ExecuView's* Whole Life Model, click on the *Results Table* icon. Now click on the *Totals per $1,000* tab. The annual reserve amounts per $1,000 for *ExecuView's* Whole Life Model appear in the second column from the right.

Notice that the reserve per $1,000 for the first year is $0.00. By allowing the insurers to maintain first-year reserves of $0, the full preliminary term reserve valuation method helps the product depicted in the model to keep first-year surplus strain relatively low—at 28.97 percent of first-year premium.

Using the net level reserve valuation method, the Whole Life Model maintains higher reserves, as shown in the following table:

(continued on next page)

costs (DAC). DAC is an accounting tool necessary for an insurer to amortize first-year expenses. The use of DAC in effect permits an insurer to defer the recognition of costs that the insurer has in fact already paid. In the year that the first-year expenses are incurred and paid, the DAC account is increased by an amount equal to the portion

Application 9-1 Net Level and Full Preliminary Term Reserves (continued)

Net Level Reserves

Year	Reserve per $1,000	Year	Reserve per $1,000
1	$ 6.07	16	$135.58
2	$ 12.47	17	$146.70
3	$ 19.18	18	$158.14
4	$ 26.22	19	$169.87
5	$ 33.58	20	$181.92
6	$ 41.27	21	$194.27
7	$ 49.26	22	$206.94
8	$ 57.59	23	$219.94
9	$ 66.22	24	$233.26
10	$ 75.19	25	$246.92
11	$ 84.47	26	$260.90
12	$ 94.07	27	$275.18
13	$103.99	28	$289.74
14	$114.21	29	$304.55
15	$124.74	30	$319.58

To see the net level reserve amounts in *ExecuView*'s Whole Life Model, first select *Net Level* from the reserve valuation methods at the bottom of the screen. Now click on the *Results Table* icon. Click on the *Totals per $1,000* tab. The annual reserve amounts per $1,000 for *ExecuView*'s Whole Life Model appear in the second-to-last column.

The higher reserve amounts calculated according to the net level method cause a number of changes in the model's profitability output. First-year surplus strain jumps to 107.78 percent, the validation year jumps to 9, and IRR falls more than 11 percentage points, but profit margin and net present value don't change at all. Using the net level reserve method as opposed to the full preliminary term method has a great effect on the timing of the product's profits, but over time has no effect on the *net amount* of these profits. Because the *ExecuView* models use the same interest rate to discount profits as is used to calculate investment income, this difference in timing should have no effect on the present value of profits, though its effect does show up in the validation year and internal rate of return.

The complete results of the change from full preliminary term to net level reserves in the Whole Life Model are shown on the following *ExecuView* screen:

(continued on next page)

of the expenses which is being deferred until a later year. In each succeeding year, the DAC account is reduced by the amount of deferred expenses recognized in that year. The effect of this process is that an insurer's first-year acquisition expenses are subtracted from an insurer's capital gradually, over a number of years, rather than all at once in the policy's first year. Thus, surplus strain is reduced or eliminated.

Application 9-1 Net Level and Full Preliminary Term Reserves (continued)

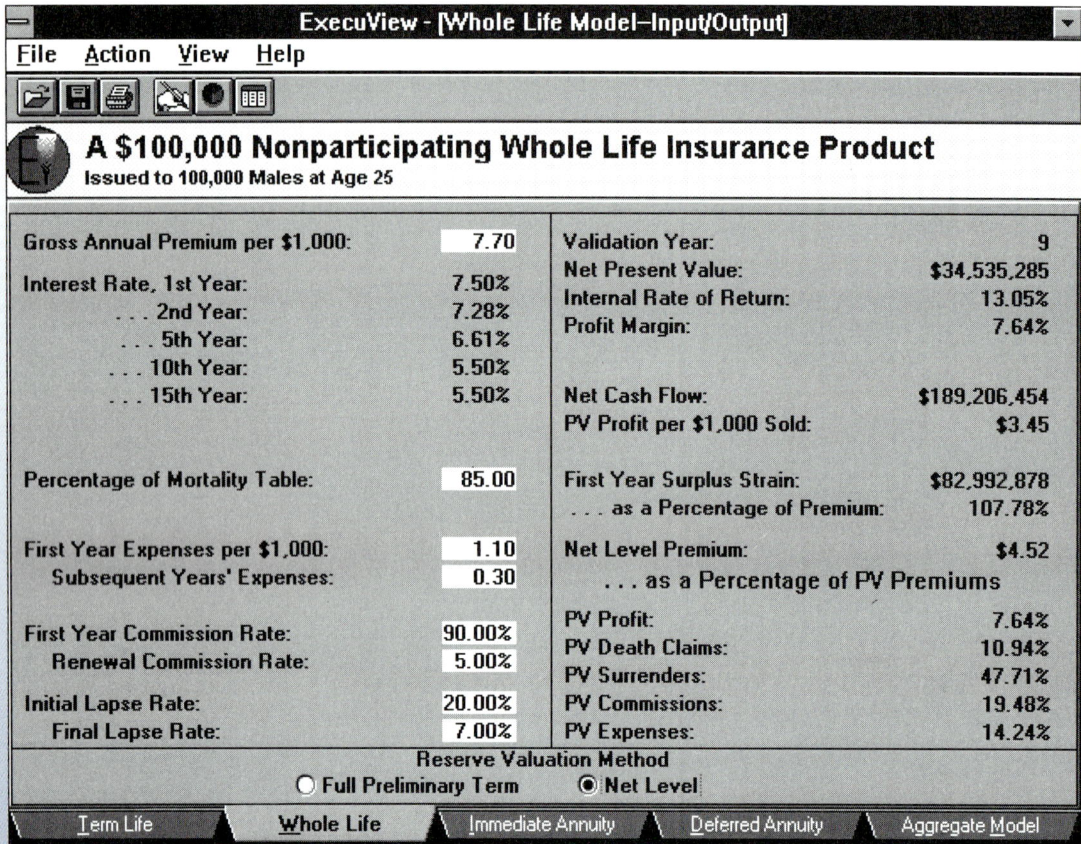

When analysts examine an insurer's GAAP reserves in order to evaluate the insurer's strength, they generally pay attention not only to the insurer's reserves, but also to its net GAAP reserves. ***Net GAAP reserves*** are equal to the insurer's policy reserves minus the insurer's deferred acquisition costs, as stated in the following equation:

Net GAAP Reserves = GAAP Policy Reserves – DAC

Net GAAP reserves are similar to modified statutory reserves in that both net GAAP reserves and modified statutory reserves represent the insurer's policy liabilities modified by an allowance for the high cost of first-year expenses.

To illustrate, let's return to the example we used previously of the Ventura Insurance Company. Recall that the first-year premium for the insurer's product was $150 and the first-year expenses were $120. Let's also say that the GAAP first-year reserve is $75 (recall that GAAP reserves for traditional business are generally smaller than statutory reserves).

Without the use of a DAC account, the sale of this policy would cause the following change in the insurer's assets:

Premium	+ $150
– Expenses	– 120
	= $ 30

Thus, the sale would result in surplus strain of $45, as illustrated below:

Balance Sheet	
Assets	**Liabilities**
+$30	+$75
	Capital and Surplus
	–$45

By establishing an asset account to identify the amount of first-year expenses that can be deferred to later years, insurers can avoid surplus strain. For example, assume that the Ventura Insurance Company can defer to later years $70 of its first-year expenses. The insurer would establish a DAC account of $70. The net change in the insurer's assets caused by the issue of this policy is shown in the following calculation:

Premium	+ $150
– Expenses	– 120
+ DAC	+ 70
Change in assets	= $100

As the calculation shows, the change in the insurer's assets is found by subtracting the first-year expenses from the first-year premium, then adding back the DAC. Therefore, in this example, the sale of the policy creates an increase in assets of $100.

The effect on the insurer's balance sheet of issuing this policy is shown in the following balance sheet:

Balance Sheet	
Assets	**Liabilities**
+$100	+$75
	Capital and Surplus
	+$25

The increase in assets is offset by an increase in the insurer's liabilities of $75, to create an increase in capital and surplus of $25.

The net GAAP reserve on this policy in its first year is equal to the GAAP policy reserve minus DAC. By subtracting $70 from $75, we calculate a net GAAP reserve of $5 for this policy.

Policy Reserves Calculated for Tax Purposes

In both the United States and Canada, an increase in an insurer's policy reserves is typically treated as a tax-deductible business expense for federal income tax purposes. In other words, an increase in an insurer's reserves reduces the insurer's income tax. However, both countries mandate specific methods for calculating reserves for federal income tax purposes which, in effect, set a ceiling on the insurer's income tax deduction for increases in reserves.

In the United States, federal tax law specifies the same mortality rates required to calculate statutory reserves, but a higher interest rate. The higher interest rate, in addition to other factors, causes the policy reserves calculated for tax purposes to be smaller than statutory reserves. Therefore, the insurer's tax liability is larger than if statutory reserves were used for this purpose. The insurer may use actual tax reserves that are less than or equal to the maximum allowable reserves.

In Canada, federal tax law specifies a set of assumptions that produce the maximum allowable value for policy reserves calculated for tax purposes. In Canada, the insurer may also use tax reserves that are equal to or less than this maximum allowable value.

Other Types of Reserves

In addition to reserves related to products, insurers maintain a number of other types of reserves in order to draw a more complete picture of their financial obligations. In this section, we discuss several of these types of reserves.

Reserves for Premiums Paid in Advance

An insurer reports a reserve for ***premiums paid in advance*** when an insured pays a premium in one accounting period for coverage that does not begin until the next period. This type of reserve differs from an unearned premium reserve in that premiums paid in advance are for coverage which does not begin until the next accounting period, whereas unearned premium reserves are for coverage that begins in an earlier accounting period and ends in a later period. The liability for premiums paid in advance appears on both U.S. and Canadian GAAP and U.S. statutory financial statements.

Suppose the Springdale Company pays monthly premiums for its group insurance to the Lullwater Insurance Company. On December 1, the Springdale Company pays for the next three months' coverage, thereby paying for January and February's coverage in advance. The insurer, on its December 31 Annual Statement, would establish a reserve for premiums paid in advance equal to the amount of the Springdale Company's premiums for January and February.

Dividend Liabilities

Insurers who sell participating individual life and health policies and experience-rated group policies are required to create ***dividend liabilities*** to account for policy dividends and experience rating refunds that they owe but have not yet paid. Dividends and experience rating refunds are based on the policy year, which does not necessarily coincide with the accounting year. When the policy year and the accounting year do not coincide, an insurer's accounting statement must show a dividend liability to account for dividends that will be paid in the next accounting period.

In order to establish this dividend reserve, the insurer must estimate the amount of the dividend that it will eventually pay on the policy. The statutory reserve is equal to the entire amount of the dividend which will eventually be paid. The GAAP reserve is equal to only that portion of the projected dividend that applies to the accounting year represented by the financial statement. The following example illustrates the difference between the statutory and the GAAP treatment of these kinds of reserves.

Suppose the Durand Company pays annual premiums for its group policy, and the policy's anniversary is March 31. On March 31, 1997, the insurer will pay a dividend. When preparing the statutory Annual Statement for the year 1996, the insurer must anticipate the amount of this dividend and report the entire amount as a dividend reserve on the Annual Statement.

Suppose the insurer creates GAAP statements for the year ending December 31, 1996. Three-quarters of the Durand Company's dividend applies to coverage that was provided in the year 1996. When preparing its GAAP statements for December 31, 1996, Durand would be required to report only three-quarters of the anticipated dividend as a dividend reserve liability.

As with unearned premium reserves, insurers are permitted to estimate their dividend reserves rather than calculating the reserve for each policy individually.

Premium Deficiency Reserves

In the United States, a policy's gross premium—the amount actually paid for the policy by customers—is sometimes less than the net annual premium used to calculate the statutory policy reserve. In this situation, statutory accounting requires the insurer to hold a separate reserve, known as a ***premium deficiency reserve,*** in addition to the policy's regular reserve. In Canada, premium deficiency reserves are not required, because policy reserves are calculated using gross premiums.

To understand why premium deficiency reserves are considered necessary, look again at the prospective formula for policy reserves.

Policy Reserve	=	Present Value of Future Benefits	–	Present Value of Future (Valuation) Net Premiums

If the valuation net premium is larger than the gross premium, then the policy reserve will be calculated by subtracting from the value of future benefits an amount that is larger than the present value of the premiums the insurer will actually receive. The resulting statutory policy reserve will be too small. Consequently, the insurer is required to maintain a premium deficiency reserve in addition to the policy reserve.

In the United States, gross premiums are sometimes smaller than valuation net premiums because of a significant mismatch between the mortality rates an insurer is required by law to use in the valuation of reserves, and the rates it expects to experience. When the mortality rates used for setting reserves are higher than those used for pricing, the statutory net premium may be larger than the gross premium. This situation may indicate that the statutory valuation mortality table has been in use for a considerable number of years, and is out of date.

Contingency Reserves

Contingency reserves are reserves created by insurers as a cushion against various special risks. Contingency reserves are not liabilities, but surplus accounts, so they also go by the names *special surplus, assigned surplus, appropriated surplus,* or *earmarked surplus.* Con-

Figure 9-12. Common types of contingency reserves.

Type of contingency reserve	Purpose
Group contingency reserve	To provide a reserve for greater-than-anticipated losses caused by an unusual concentration of risk under a group program. Group contingency reserves are required by some states
Claim fluctuation reserve	For small group coverage, serves as a cushion against future adverse experience, allowing the insurer to offer stable rates over a period of years
Group annuity contingency reserve	To absorb losses in the general account from increased longevity among group annuitants
Participation in separate accounts	For separate account variable annuities, to absorb increases in future actual expense relative to the expense charge assumed in the guarantees of these annuities
Guaranty fund	To fund covered claims against insolvent insurers. Most states have insolvency guaranty funds and require that solvent insurers pay assessments to guaranty funds. Some states require insurers to set aside a special surplus fund to provide for potential future guaranty fund assessments
Mortality fluctuation reserve	To absorb unusual deviations in assumed mortality or unusual losses from such causes as war or epidemics, usually for individual policies as opposed to group contracts. These reserves may be intended to cover fluctuations in the general account, separate accounts, or both
Contingency reserve for large risks	To absorb the effect of paying claims insured under large policies, if an insurer writes many policies with large face amounts and does not reinsure those policies
Special contingency reserve	To cover any unforeseen events

tingency reserves are intended to supplement liability reserve funds. Insurers set up some contingency reserves voluntarily, whereas others are mandatory. Contingency reserves are seen only in statutory accounting. GAAP specifically disallows contingency reserves.

Figure 9-12 describes several common types of contingency reserves.

Asset Fluctuation Reserves

The reserves we have discussed to this point relate to the insurer's obligations to its customers arising from its products in force. In the United States, insurers are also required to establish two statutory reserves to absorb gains and losses in the insurers' invested assets. These two reserves are called the interest maintenance reserve (IMR) and the asset valuation reserve (AVR).*

* The IMR and AVR supplanted the now-extinct *Mandatory Securities Valuation Reserve (MSVR)*.

An insurer recognizes a gain or loss on an asset when the insurer sells the asset at a higher or lower price than its purchase price. When an insurer sells an investment at a price higher than the asset's purchase price, the difference is said to be a ***realized capital gain.*** Selling an asset for less than its purchase price results in a ***realized capital loss.*** A capital gain or loss is *realized* when the insurer actually sells an investment. In contrast, at any point in time, an *unrealized* capital gain or loss is one which would occur *if* the insurer were to sell an investment at its market price at that moment. A capital gain or loss remains unrealized as long as the insurer holds the investment.

On an insurer's balance sheet, capital gains and losses either increase or decrease, respectively, the insurer's assets. A change in assets must, of course, be balanced by a change in either liabilities or capital and surplus. If capital gains and losses were allowed to directly affect an insurer's capital and surplus account, then under certain circumstances the insurer's capital and surplus might be subject to considerable short-term fluctuations, which most likely would not accurately represent the insurer's overall financial condition. Therefore, under U.S. statutory accounting conventions, capital gains and losses are instead reflected in the IMR and the AVR. These two reserves act as a buffer for the insurer's capital and surplus, causing capital and surplus to be affected only gradually by capital gains and losses. Thus, these two reserves help increase the stability of an insurer's capital account.

Although the IMR and AVR are liabilities, analysts often consider an insurer's AVR to be part of the insurer's adjusted capital and surplus for certain purposes. For example, when evaluating the strength of an insurer's capital and surplus in order to assess the insurer's financial strength, many analysts consider the insurer's AVR as part of capital and surplus. In this respect, the AVR is similar to a contingency reserve.

Interest Maintenance Reserve (IMR)

The ***interest maintenance reserve (IMR)*** absorbs *realized* capital gains and losses caused by changes in interest rates, as summarized in Figure 9-13. The IMR reflects only those interest-rate-related gains and losses realized on bonds, preferred stock, and mortgages, because these asset types are most directly influenced by changes in interest rates. When interest rates rise, the value of these asset types generally falls. When interest rates fall, the value of these asset types generally rises.

On the left side of the balance sheet, capital gains and losses cause an insurer's assets to increase or decrease. On the right side of the equation, capital gains and losses on these types of investments caused by interest rate changes must be reflected in the IMR. Capital gains cause an increase in the IMR. Capital losses cause a decrease in the IMR.

After they have been posted to the IMR, capital gains and losses are *amortized* to the insurer's capital over the remaining original term of the investment on which the gain or loss was realized. In other

Figure 9-13. How the IMR works.

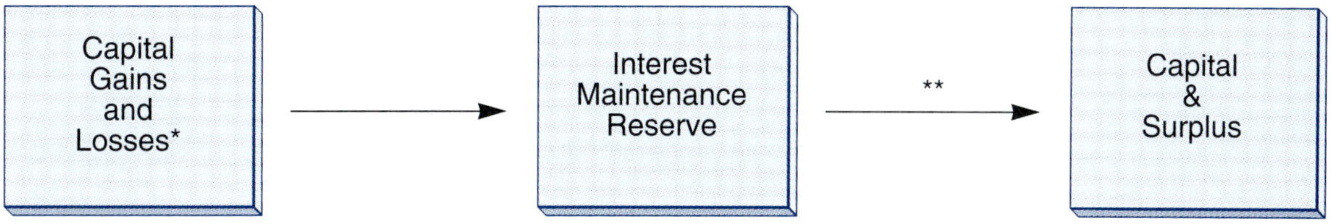

* *Must be realized; must be caused by interest-rate fluctuations; bonds, mortgages, preferred stock only*
** *All gains and losses transferred gradually (amortized) to capital and surplus over remaining life of original investment*

words, a portion of each capital gain or loss is transferred from the IMR to the insurer's capital each accounting year until, at the date the investment would have matured, the entire capital gain or loss has been transferred to capital and surplus. In this way, these types of capital gains and losses affect capital and surplus gradually, rather than all at once when the gain or loss is realized. The capital and surplus account is more stable with the IMR than it would be without.

In Canada, as in the United States, capital gains and losses caused by interest rate changes are amortized into capital and surplus rather than reflected in capital and surplus all at once. However, no formal reserve similar to the IMR exists. The amortization is carried out by other accounting methods. Under U.S. GAAP, realized capital gains and losses are generally recognized immediately in capital and surplus and not amortized.*

Asset Valuation Reserve (AVR)

In the United States, the ***asset valuation reserve (AVR)*** absorbs both realized *and* unrealized credit-related capital gains and losses. In Canada, there is no equivalent to the AVR. Whereas the IMR is intended to absorb capital gains and losses caused by interest rate changes, the AVR is intended to absorb changes in the value of assets caused by credit-related factors. Some common examples of credit-related factors that generally cause the value of an asset to fall are listed below:

- The issuer of a bond experiences financial difficulties and ceases paying interest or principal on the bond.
- A mortgage borrower stops making mortgage payments.
- Renters cannot be found for an office building held as a real estate investment.
- A stock issuer experiences unfavorable financial circumstances or goes bankrupt.

* For some unbundled products, a portion of capital gains and losses are amortized under U.S. GAAP.

Although these are all examples of how an asset can decline in value, the market value of assets may also increase for credit-related reasons. For example, a stock's value generally increases if the issuer achieves a favorable financial performance. Credit-related losses, however, are more common than credit-related gains.

U.S. statutory requirements mandate that credit-related capital gains and losses be reflected, on the right side of the accounting equation, in the AVR. Capital gains increase the AVR, while capital losses decrease the AVR. Certain catastrophic capital losses, however, are reflected directly in the insurer's capital and surplus. A severe loss of value of a real estate investment, for example, might bypass the AVR and be recognized directly in the insurer's capital and surplus. The AVR has two components—an *equity component* and a *default component.* The equity component reflects an insurer's capital gains and losses on equity investments, such as stocks and real estate. The default component reflects gains and losses on debt investments, such as bonds and mortgages.

At the end of every accounting year, an insurer may be required to increase its AVR by transferring an amount from its capital and surplus. The amount that the insurer must transfer from capital and surplus to the AVR depends on the perceived riskiness of the insurer's investments. The riskier the insurer's investments, the larger the AVR the insurer must maintain. Each year, the insurer is required to perform a calculation, based on the riskiness of the insurer's assets, to determine if the insurer must increase its AVR.

Because the AVR is a liability account, an insurer is not permitted to use the amount of its AVR to support new business, to purchase another company, to make dividend payments to stockholders or to policyholders, nor to accomplish any of the other purposes for which capital and surplus can be used. Some insurers seek to reduce the amount of their required AVR in order to increase the amount of their capital, and thus increase their strategic and operational flexibility. Because an insurer's maximum AVR depends on the riskiness of its investments, an insurer might decide to restructure its investment portfolio with a view to reducing the riskiness of its investment portfolio, thereby reducing the size of its required contributions to AVR and increasing its available capital and surplus.

Figure 9-14 summarizes some of the major characteristics of the types of reserves we have discussed in this section.

Surrender Values

In the last part of this chapter, we discuss cash surrender values, which are calculated in a similar manner to policy reserves. Many

Figure 9-14. Types of reserves, other than policy reserves.

Reserve for premiums paid in advance (U.S. statutory and GAAP)	• Reflects premiums paid for coverage that begins in following year
Dividend reserve (U.S. statutory and GAAP)	• Reflects dividends owed • When coverage period straddles Annual Statement date, reflects full amount of next year's estimated dividends (statutory), or reflects the portion of next year's estimated dividends that applies to past year (GAAP)
Premium deficiency reserve (U.S. statutory only)	• Must be established when valuation net premium exceeds pricing gross premium
Contingency reserve (U.S. statutory only)	• Established voluntarily • Serves as a cushion against future adverse experience • On balance sheet, part of capital and surplus
Interest maintenance reserve (IMR) (U.S. statutory only)	• Absorbs capital gains and losses on certain investments caused by interest rate changes • Gains and losses must be realized • Bonds, mortgages, preferred stock • Allows gains and losses to be reflected gradually in capital and surplus
Asset valuation reserve (AVR) (U.S. statutory only)	• Absorbs credit-related capital gains and losses • Absorbs realized *and* unrealized gains and losses • Each year, insurers must perform calculations in order to determine whether they must increase their AVR • Allows gains and losses to be reflected gradually in capital and surplus

years ago, insurers were not required to pay anything to a policyowner who surrendered a life insurance policy or allowed the policy to lapse. Today, for certain types of products, insurers are required in the United States to make a cash payment available to a policyowner whose policy lapses or is surrendered. The amount of this payment is called the ***cash value,*** *surrender value,* or *cash surrender value.* Most insurers also give the customer the option of using the cash value to purchase paid-up or extended term insurance.

Calculating Surrender Values

In the United States, just as methods of calculating statutory policy reserves are specified in the Standard Valuation Law, methods of calculating cash surrender values are described in the NAIC's ***Model***

Standard Nonforfeiture Law for Life Insurance and ***Model Standard Nonforfeiture Law for Individual Deferred Annuities.*** The model laws, which have been adopted with minor variations by most states, dictate the minimum nonforfeiture (surrender) values that insurers must pay for certain types of products. Insurers may pay higher surrender values than those derived from the model law, but not lower. Insurers must provide surrender benefit provisions in whole life policies and in deferred annuities during the accumulation period. Insurers are not required to pay surrender benefits for most term insurance policies, immediate annuities, or health insurance products.

The formula for calculating minimum cash values for life insurance is similar to the prospective method of calculating policy reserves.

Cash Value = Present Value of Future Benefits − Present Value of Future *Adjusted* Premiums

The only difference between this formula and the formula for calculating policy reserves is that cash values are calculated using *adjusted premiums,* rather than net premiums. The ***adjusted premium*** is equal to the valuation net annual premium plus an amount added to account for the insurer's expenses. Because the adjusted premium is larger than the net annual premium, the minimum cash value will be smaller than the policy reserve, assuming the same interest and mortality assumptions are used to calculate both.

The U.S. life insurance nonforfeiture law specifies the interest and mortality rates an insurer must use to calculate the minimum allowable cash value for a policy. This law also describes how to calculate the maximum expense allowance the insurer can add to the net premium to derive the adjusted premium. As we have discussed, the insurer is allowed to establish a larger cash value than the minimum prescribed by the model law. In a product's later years, many policies provide actual cash values that are equal to the policy reserve.

Annuity customers who surrender their annuities during the accumulation period are considered to have a right to their entire account value, less an amount intended to compensate the insurer for its expenses. The method for calculating an annuity's surrender value can be expressed by the following equation:

Surrender Value = Account Value – Expense Allowance

The annuity nonforfeiture law defines a method that must be used to calculate the maximum expense allowance. The insurer may pay a surrender value based on a smaller expense allowance, but not on a larger one. The nonforfeiture law also defines a minimum nonforfeiture interest rate for fixed annuities. For the purposes of calculating surrender values, an insurer must use an interest rate that is at least as large as this rate.

In Canada, insurers are not required by law to provide surrender values for any products. However, most insurers provide surrender benefits for whole life and deferred annuity products. Because surrender values are not required by law, Canadian law is silent on how surrender values should be calculated. Most Canadian insurers calculate surrender values based on principles similar to those used in the United States. Life insurance surrender values are generally calculated using an adjusted premium method, and annuity surrender values are generally equal to the account value minus an expense charge. Note that annuity surrender charges in Canada are often smaller than those common in the United States, because commissions paid to agents for annuity sales are considerably smaller in Canada than in the United States.

Minimum surrender values are calculated for ordinary life insurance and for annuities as follows:

Ordinary Life = PV Future Benefits – PV Future Adjusted Premiums
Annuities = Account Value – Expense Allowance

In Conclusion

This chapter discussed reserves and surrender values. We began by illustrating how policy reserves are calculated. Then we discussed policy reserves prepared according to different accounting principles and for different types of products. We also examined how policy reserves develop for products with different types of guarantees and how surplus strain can be reduced under GAAP and statutory reserving methods. We then discussed how different reserve practices can influence an insurer's profitability and solvency. We also described a number of reserves other than policy reserves. We ended the chapter by discussing how surrender values are calculated for ordinary life and deferred annuity products. This chapter concludes our discussion of product pricing and related issues.

The next five chapters of this textbook are about capital and surplus. Capital and surplus represents the owners' investment in the company, and also represents the company's last line of defense against financial risks. Actuarial assumptions for pricing and reserving are forecasts and virtually always differ somewhat from experience. If the deviations of experience from assumptions are *favorable* to the insurance company, then the actuarial assumptions were excessive, and the company realizes a larger-than-expected profit. Not all deviations are positive, however. *Adverse* deviations arise if the actuarial assumptions were inadequate. If adverse deviations materialize, then the insurer will not earn as large a profit as expected, and may even have to cover a loss. Whenever pricing is discovered to have been inadequate, the insurance company has failed to earn the expected profit and has failed to contribute to capital and surplus. Insurers must rely upon capital and surplus to cover the eventuality that their actuarial assumptions might inadequately reflect their experience. Chapter 10 provides an orientation to capital and surplus in life and health insurance companies.

Key Terms and Concepts

reserves
policy reserves
actuarial assumptions
reserve strengthening
reserve destrengthening
net level premium reserve valuation method
prospective method
retrospective method
accumulated cost of insurance
Standard Valuation Law
Universal Life Model Regulation
minimum reserve requirements
provision for adverse deviation
policy premium method (PPM)
unearned premium reserve
claim reserves
surplus strain
modified reserve method
Commissioners' Reserve Valuation Method (CRVM)
full preliminary term method
deferred acquisition costs (DAC)
net GAAP reserves
premiums paid in advance
dividend liabilities
premium deficiency reserve
contingency reserves
realized capital gain
realized capital loss
interest maintenance reserve (IMR)
asset valuation reserve (AVR)
cash value
Model Standard Nonforfeiture Law for Life Insurance
Model Standard Nonforfeiture Law for Individual Deferred Annuities
adjusted premium

PART 4

Managing Capital and Surplus

Part 4 consists of five chapters introducing the management of capital and surplus for insurance companies. Chapter 10 presents an overview of insurers' various needs for capital. Chapter 11 discusses how a multi-line insurer formulates strategies and tactics for meeting capital objectives. Chapter 12 shows ways insurers can strengthen their capital without raising funds from external sources. Chapter 13 tells how insurers can raise capital from external sources by issuing stock and surplus notes. Chapter 14 explains the strategic uses of reinsurance, including the role of reinsurance in reducing surplus strain.

CHAPTER

10

Introduction to Capital Management

LEARNING OBJECTIVES

After studying this chapter, you should be able to

- Determine the impact on reported capital arising from specified business transactions
- Recognize the different standards for minimum required (committed) capital, uncommitted (growth) capital, and target capital
- Demonstrate understanding of how an insurer's reported capital responds to changes in the insurer's exposures to the C-1 and C-2 risks
- Interpret how an insurer's return-on-capital ratio responds to changes in the level of either the insurer's earnings or its capital

OUTLINE

Capital and surplus are key to an insurance company's profitability and solvency. For an insurance company, capital and surplus represent the owners' investment in the company. Owners, whether they are policyholders or stockholders, expect to earn a fair return on their investments, and insurers must operate profitably in order to provide a fair return on those capital investments. Capital and surplus are also important to insurers because they are a company's ultimate defense against any solvency threat. Because of the crucial role of capital and surplus in an insurance company's success, insurers must maintain enough capital to support ongoing solvency and must find profitable ways to employ the capital and surplus on behalf of the company's owners.

In order to meet capital and surplus needs, insurance companies have developed capital management systems. In general, ***capital management*** involves planning for, obtaining, and controlling a company's long-term funds. The management of short-term funds, in contrast, is variously known as ***cash management,*** *treasury management,* or *working capital management.* Throughout this part of the text, we use the term *capital* in the broad sense of long-term funds, including both capital and surplus.

In approaching the task of capital management, insurance companies apply basic management activities to manage their long-term funds. An insurer must first analyze its capital needs, which requires it to analyze its financial risks. The insurer also must evaluate its current financial position—projected into the future by means of computerized financial simulation. Then, the insurer must develop and implement a plan to move from its current capital position to the desired capital position. Part 4 of the text is devoted to describing the capital management process as used by life and health insurance companies.

Chapter 10 introduces the topic of capital management by describing some aspects of that process. First, we show how the risk-return tradeoff affects the capital management process. Next, we describe how changes in an insurer's balance sheet produce changes in its reported capital. We then present the process insurers use for evaluating their capital needs and explain how insurers set their capital objectives.

How the Risk-Return Tradeoff Applies to Capital Management

We noted in Chapter 2 that the risk-return tradeoff is at the core of any financial decision an insurer makes. We also noted that insurers face a solvency-profitability tradeoff, a balancing act similar to the risk-return tradeoff. One of the most serious risks for insurers is the risk of insolvency; one of the most important goals is to generate adequate profits. An insurer can diminish its risk of insolvency by holding a large amount of capital relative to its financial commitments. The tradeoff is that holding a large amount of capital relative to the insurer's earnings diminishes the insurer's profitability as measured by return on capital. As we noted in Chapter 1, *return on capital* can be defined as the percentage return an insurer has earned on its capital; it is calculated by dividing a measure of *earnings*—usually earnings before interest, dividends, and taxes—by a measure of *total capital employed.* Thus, the basic risk-return tradeoff clearly applies to an insurer's capital management decisions. The insurer must hold enough capital to remain solvent, yet not so much that its profitability drops too low. An insurance company's solvency-profitability tradeoffs imply the following relationships between risk and capital:

- Whenever an insurer's exposure to risk increases while all other factors remain constant, the company's need for capital also increases. Conversely, whenever risk decreases while all other factors remain constant, the need for capital also decreases.
- Whenever the amount of an insurer's capital increases while all other factors remain constant, the company's exposure to risk decreases. Conversely, whenever capital decreases while all other factors remain constant, exposure to risk increases.
- Whenever an insurer's exposure to risk increases while all other factors remain constant, the company's potential profitability also increases. Conversely, whenever a company's risk exposure decreases while all other factors remain constant, potential profitability also decreases.
- Whenever the proportion of an insurer's capital relative to its earnings increases, the company's potential profitability decreases. Conversely, whenever the proportion of capital relative to earnings decreases, the company's potential profitability increases.

These relationships illustrate that, in order to evaluate its capital needs, an insurance company must also evaluate its risk exposure. Before we describe how insurers evaluate their capital needs and risk exposures for purposes of capital management, let's first look more closely at the basic balance sheet equation. Understanding how changes in the balance sheet affect the amount of an insurer's capital will help you understand the capital management process.

Capital in the Balance Sheet

Virtually all accounting changes recorded by an insurance company affect its reported capital and surplus either directly or indirectly. Various equivalent forms of the accounting equation—often given as Assets = Liabilities + Owners' Equity—are illustrated as follows:

U.S. statutory form:	U.S. GAAP form:	Canadian GAAP form:
Liabilities	Liabilities	Liabilities
+ Capital and Surplus	+ Owners' Equity	+ Equity
Assets	Assets	Assets

In this discussion, we use a simplified approach employing balance sheet models to illustrate the effect of various accounting changes on capital. Instead of showing the magnitude of the impact on an insurer's capital, however, we look only at the overall direction of the impact. In other words, we are interested only in whether an accounting change results in an increase or a decrease in capital.

Throughout this discussion, we make reference to specific statutory and GAAP account titles, even though we do not specifically adopt a statutory or GAAP outlook. Instead, our discussion generally takes the viewpoint of an internal financial reporting system. In the long-term view of capital management, the differences between statutory and GAAP are immaterial. By inspecting the relationships within the basic accounting equation, we can see that two fundamental types of accounting entries change the amount of an insurer's capital:

1. An increase in assets—while liabilities remain unchanged—results in an increase in capital. Conversely, a decrease in assets—while liabilities remain unchanged—results in a decrease in capital.

2. A decrease in liabilities—while assets remain unchanged—results in an increase in capital. Conversely, an increase in liabilities—while assets remain unchanged—results in a decrease in capital.

Effects of Changes in Assets

Let's consider an example to illustrate how changes in the amount of the company's assets result in changes in the amount of its capital. Suppose that Ergo Life Insurance Company's assets are $12 million; its liabilities are $8 million; and its capital and surplus are $4 million. The following balance sheet illustrates Ergo's position:

Balance Sheet	
Assets	**Liabilities**
$12 million	$8 million
	Capital and Surplus
	$4 million

Then, suppose that Ergo issues $1 million in common stock. The $1 million cash that Ergo receives in exchange for the stock increases Ergo's assets to $13 million. The $1 million represents an increase in the owners' investment in Ergo and increases the company's capital and surplus to $5 million. This issuance of stock would have no effect on Ergo's liabilities. We can illustrate this accounting change on Ergo's balance sheet as follows:

Balance Sheet	
Assets	**Liabilities**
Increase to $13 million	No change—$8 million
	Capital and Surplus
	Increase to $5 million

Remember: If Ergo's assets had decreased while its liabilities remained unchanged, the amount of its capital and surplus would also have decreased.

Another type of transaction that results in an increase or decrease in a company's assets—and a corresponding increase or decrease in capital—is a change in nonadmitted assets. You should recall from prior experience that ***nonadmitted assets*** are amounts that a U.S. insurer may not apply to back its statutory reserves, and that thus do not appear as asset values on the insurer's statutory balance sheet. When nonadmitted assets become admitted assets, total statutory assets increase and liabilities remain the same; therefore, statutory capital increases. The converse is also true—when admitted assets become nonadmitted assets, both statutory assets and statutory capital decrease.

Effects of Changes in Liabilities

A number of business activities affect the amount of a company's liabilities and, thus, the amount of its capital. For example, we saw in Chapter 9 that companies sometimes change the basis on which they value their reserves and, as a result, are able to decrease the amount of their reserves. Such a reduction in reserves results in an increase in the amount of the company's capital. Likewise, when a change in reserve valuation basis results in an increase in reserves, the company's capital decreases.

Let's look at an example to illustrate this accounting transaction. Suppose that Aria Life Insurance Company has assets of $20 million, liabilities of $13 million, and capital of $7 million, as illustrated in the following balance sheet:

Balance Sheet	
Assets	**Liabilities**
$20 million	$13 million
	Capital and Surplus
	$7 million

Following a change in its reserve valuation basis, Aria's reserves decrease by $1 million. As a result, Aria's liabilities decrease to $12 million and its capital increases to $8 million. Assets are unaffected. The following balance sheet illustrates how the change in reserve valuation basis affected Aria's capital:

Balance Sheet	
Assets	**Liabilities**
No change—$20 million	*Decrease to $12 million*
	Capital and Surplus
	Increase to $8 million

Figure 10-1 presents the important types of transactions that increase the amount of an insurer's capital.

Figure 10-1. Business transactions producing an increase in capital.

Type of account affected	Business activity that can increase capital
Asset accounts	**Rule:** An increase in an asset can produce an increase in capital.
Change in nonadmitted assets	When nonadmitted assets become admitted assets, statutory assets increase; as a result, statutory capital increases.
Liability accounts	**Rule:** A decrease in liabilities can produce an increase in capital.
Reserves	A decrease in reserves because of a change in reserve valuation basis increases capital.
Reserves on reinsured business	A reduction in policy reserves when business is reinsured can produce "surplus relief" and an increase in capital.
Liability for reinsurance in unauthorized companies	A reduction in the liability for reinsurance in unauthorized companies increases statutory capital. (Unauthorized companies are discussed in later chapters of this textbook.)

Because capital management decisions center on the solvency-profitability tradeoff, capital planning activities depend upon various approaches to evaluating capital and risk exposures. For the purposes of capital planning, these approaches are not particularly consistent from one organization to another. Nevertheless, we can provide a general description of many aspects of capital planning. We begin by describing the internal financial reporting systems insurers use in capital management.

Financial Reporting Systems for Capital Management

To this point in our discussion of capital management, we have referred to statutory and GAAP accounting. Statutory and GAAP approaches to financial reporting may not be the best financial reporting systems to apply for capital management purposes. Thus, for capital management purposes, life insurers typically employ special internal financial reporting systems. These internal financial reporting systems are designed to present a realistic view of capital for each insurer's product lines and other business units. The primary difference between these internal systems and statutory and GAAP approaches concerns the timing of their recognition of income, expenses, gains, and losses. Internal systems unique to a given insurer attempt to correct perceived inaccuracies in statutory and GAAP accounting and, thus, to produce financial measures that accurately depict an insurer's true financial status.

These internal financial reporting systems include, among others, *modified-GAAP accounting, economic-value-added (EVA) accounting, embedded-value accounting,* and *market-value accounting (MVA).* An insurer may apply one of these approaches to all of its lines of business, or it may apply one modified financial reporting system to one line of business and another system to another line of business. For example, an insurer may apply market-value accounting for lines of business in which the market values of assets and liabilities are straightforward, as is the case for short-term guaranteed investment contracts (GICs). In contrast, an insurer may apply a modified-GAAP system for lines of business in which the market values of assets and liabilities are less certain, as is the case for whole life insurance business. Our discussions of capital management presume some version of internal financial reporting, in contrast to a U.S. statutory or a true GAAP reporting basis.

These internal reporting systems allow the insurer to evaluate its current capital position and to establish a capital plan. As a first step in capital planning, insurers evaluate their needs for capital and use their findings to establish capital objectives.

FAST FACT

Life insurance industry holdings of capital and surplus amount to about 7 percent of total industry assets. In contrast, property and casualty industry holdings of capital and surplus amount to about 25 percent of industry assets. The level of life insurer capital and surplus is markedly lower because (1) life insurers require a relatively lesser provision for contingency risks and (2) laws limit the build-up of surplus by large mutual life insurers.[1]

Evaluating Capital Needs

Capital provides both a cushion against insolvency—ensuring an insurer can meet its existing obligations—and the financial basis for future growth. Insurers traditionally view their solvency risks and their resulting needs for a minimum amount of capital as relating to two distinct segments of their business obligations: existing commitments and future commitments. Accordingly, insurers often classify capital needs and capital objectives into the following two categories:

1. ***Required capital.*** Required capital supports financial obligations arising from an insurer's existing book of business and also allows the insurer to remain in business. Objectives for required capital, which is sometimes referred to as *committed capital,* are established by regulatory requirements, the recommendations of rating agencies, and the risk preferences of internal management. (Note that the term *required capital* does not suggest that the insurer has a capital shortfall.)

2. ***Uncommitted capital.*** Uncommitted capital supports financial obligations related to issuing and maintaining future business commitments. Insurers generally choose to hold an amount of uncommitted capital, which is sometimes referred to as *growth capital,* in order to support underwriting and issuing additional business. An insurer's target-level objectives for uncommitted capital are usually governed solely by internal management standards.

The total amount of capital the insurer chooses to hold in support of both existing and future business obligations is called ***target capital.*** In other words, target capital is the sum of an insurer's required and uncommitted capital. Note that target capital identifies the level of capital an insurer wants to maintain to support these objectives, and it is not necessarily the reported capital amount that the insurer has on hand at a given time. Figure 10-2 illustrates the relationship between the different needs for capital.

Next, we examine the external and internal standards that influence an insurance company's decisions about the minimum amount of capital it needs to hold and how much capital it ideally prefers to hold.

Standards for Required Capital

First, let's consider how insurers set a minimum amount of required capital to hold in view of their existing obligations. In setting internal objectives for minimum required capital, insurers consider the following sets of internal and external standards:

- Minimum capital requirements set by regulatory authorities
- Minimum capital guidelines set by various independent rating agencies
- Minimum capital standards set by internal management for prudent coverage of the risks in the company's overall operations

Let's look at each of these standards in greater detail.

Figure 10-2. Fundamental needs for target capital.

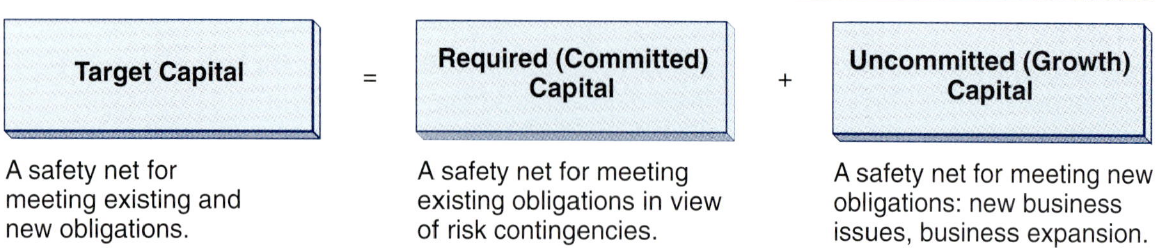

Minimum Capital Standards Set by Regulators

Regulators in Canada and the United States set a number of standards for minimum capital. The amount an insurer holds in order to comply with these standards for required capital may be referred to as ***regulatory capital.*** Generally, the consequence of failing to meet any one of the regulatory minimum standards would be a legal declaration of financial failure. Thus, these standards are completely mandatory. (We discuss these standards more fully in Chapter 18.)

As we noted in Chapter 2, in the United States, the NAIC-sponsored *Minimum Risk-Based Capital (RBC) Requirement* sets a minimum standard of regulatory capital that is calculated by using a specified formula. However, the NAIC's formula is not the only formula for deriving a risk-based capital ratio. Note that *risk-based capital* refers to a ratio derived using a specified approach to measurement, and not necessarily a regulatory standard for minimum capital. Specifically, ***risk-based capital ratios*** are ratios that compare a dollar amount of capital to a measure of risk. Risk-based capital ratios apply a risk-weighted formula for establishing the amount of capital needed to reflect specific risks in the insurer's business. For example, an insurer would multiply the amount of its stock investments by a specified percentage—called the ***risk-adjustment factor***—in order to identify the amount of capital needed to cover the risk that those stocks could lose value. Similarly, a company would multiply its revenues from individual life premiums by a specified risk-adjustment factor in order to evaluate the level of capital needed to cover the risk that its individual life products could be underpriced.

State laws set another type of minimum capital requirement, typically expressed as a flat dollar amount and derived without any attention to risk adjustment. State laws also set other requirements that affect required minimum capital and surplus. Insurers in Canada must meet a minimum level of risk-based (risk-adjusted) capital as dictated by the mandatory minimum continuing capital and surplus requirement (MCCSR). (Some additional solvency requirements are discussed in Chapters 15 and 18.)

Capital Required to Support a Target Quality Rating

Rating agencies in North America act as evaluators of insurers' financial positions. In this role, the rating agencies act independently of regulators and of the insurers themselves. Although each rating agency employs a proprietary rating system, rating agencies generally set a higher standard for minimum capital than do regulators. Most rating agencies assign a ***quality rating*** to insurers according to standards of *claims paying ability, credit worthiness,* or *financial strength*—all stricter standards than the minimum solvency standards applied by regulators.

For most large life and health insurance companies, the level of a quality rating can affect the insurer's success in several ways. An acceptable rating (1) facilitates an insurer's efforts to raise external capital by issuing financial instruments and selling policies, (2) secures a favorable cost of capital for the insurer, (3) enhances the security and loyalty of the insurer's sales force, and (4) enhances customer satisfaction. Thus, many large life and health insurers set for themselves a goal of earning a given target quality rating from rating agencies. This ***target quality rating*** represents the ideal level of quality rating that supports the insurance company's higher-level goals for making new sales and raising new capital.

Although achieving a target quality rating is optional from a legal standpoint, consumers and sales representatives often emphasize quality ratings. Thus, a company's target rating may be crucial to the company's business persistency and future sales. (Rating agencies are discussed at some length in Chapter 15.)

Internal Standards for Required Capital

For use within the company, each insurer sets its own standards for the minimum amount of capital necessary to support its unique risk profile. In the United States, an insurance company's internal management often bases these standards on the official RBC requirements, though internal standards typically are a multiple of the regulatory standard. The standards applied by a company's internal management typically result in a higher required capital amount than would the RBC standards.

The internal standards set by insurers are designed to provide enough capital to cover expected obligations and to provide a cushion against adverse deviations in pricing assumptions. An insurer's system of collecting fixed level premiums, investing premium income, and maintaining reserves to cover expected benefit costs is designed to cover the insurer's expected obligations. However, insurers sometimes encounter unexpectedly high product-related benefit payments or else poorer investment growth than they had applied for pricing purposes. Although the effects of adverse deviations—unexpected adverse events—generally smooth out over a long term, insurers need to hold capital and surplus as a cushion against any such adverse deviations in the short term. Any insurer needs to have enough capital and surplus to cover unexpected adverse events during a period long enough to allow the company's overall results to conform to the actuarial assumptions applied in the company's pricing.

Let's consider an example of an insurer's handling of a variance between actual benefit costs and expected benefit costs. Suppose Elmo

Insurance expected to pay benefit costs of $28 million in a given year, but its actual benefit costs for the year were $34 million. Thus, Elmo faced a benefit costs shortfall for the year of $6 million. We know that insurers generally cannot raise prices on existing business and cannot release reserves for business that remains in force. Assuming investment results were unable to cover the shortfall, where did Elmo find the funds to pay its claims and other benefits? The answer is that Elmo drew upon capital and surplus accumulated from positive operating results in prior years of operations.

In a different example, consider an insurer with claims results that meet expectations, but whose investment results are below expectations. Suppose that the Alma Assurance Company had expected to clear investment earnings of $24 million in a year when its actual investment earnings came to only $17 million. In that same year, Alma's claims expenses were on target. Thus, Alma faced a cash flow shortfall of $7 million for the year. We know that Alma's premium income and reserves are not available as sources of emergency cash, but Alma can cover the cash shortfall by drawing upon its capital and surplus.

Each insurer's management must evaluate its current book of business and establish the appropriate standards to apply in calculating the minimum amount of capital needed to cover the risks in its existing business. The specific capital standards a company establishes reflect both the insurer's existing risk profile and its current objectives for solvency, quality ratings, and profitability. A company's existing risk profile is the result of prior decisions by company management. For that reason, a company's current internal capital requirements are partially determined by prior managerial decisions. For example, a company that formerly included only a minimal safety margin in its pricing structure would now be subject to greater C-2 risk than would a company that had been using a more conservative approach. Similarly, a company that formerly followed an aggressive investment policy would now have a larger exposure to C-1 risk than would a company that had followed a conservative investment policy.

An example can demonstrate how capital needs are affected by different levels of risk exposure.[2] Consider two insurers, each having $100 million in assets and $10 million in capital. We will call these companies Abacus Life and Bedrock Life. In general, Abacus follows aggressive strategies, whereas Bedrock follows conservative strategies.

For both investments and products, Abacus Life has relatively high risk exposures. Abacus Life sells only group life and health products and GICs. As part of Abacus Life's effort to earn a higher return on the investment portfolio, the assets backing the GICs are concentrated in high-risk investments. In contrast, Bedrock Life has relatively low risk exposures from its investments and products. Bedrock Life sells only individual life and annuity products. Bedrock's investment portfolio is concentrated in high quality assets. Additionally, Bedrock has a highly effective asset/liability management program. Worksheet 1 presents some measures of C-risk exposures for Abacus and Bedrock.

Worksheet 1
Hypothetical Risk Exposures for Abacus Life and Bedrock Life

Assets	**Abacus Life**	**Bedrock Life**
Bonds: • Government bonds	$ 3,000,000	$ 6,000,000
• High-grade corporate bonds	35,000,000	70,000,000
• Junk corporate bonds	30,000,000	-0-
Mortgage loans	20,000,000	20,000,000
Real estate	8,000,000	2,000,000
Common stocks	4,000,000	2,000,000
Total Assets	**$100,000,000**	**$100,000,000**
Premiums	**Abacus Life**	**Bedrock Life**
Individual life	$ -0-	$ 10,000,000
Individual annuity	-0-	10,000,000
Group life and health	25,000,000	-0-
Group annuity	15,000,000	-0-
Total Premiums	**$ 40,000,000**	**$ 20,000,000**
Reserves	**Abacus Life**	**Bedrock Life**
Individual life reserves	$ -0-	$ 30,000,000
Individual annuity reserves	-0-	60,000,000
Group life and health reserves	10,000,000	-0-
Group annuity reserves	80,000,000	-0-
Total Reserves	**$ 90,000,000**	**$ 90,000,000**
Capital	**$ 10,000,000**	**$ 10,000,000**

For internal decision-making, both companies use the same C-1 and C-2 risk-adjustment factors. These C-1 and C-2 risk-adjustment factors are set at a value that these companies believe represents a median for the industry. Bedrock Life uses standard industry risk-adjustment factors for C-3 risk. However, because of its aggressive investment strategy, Abacus Life's C-3 risk-adjustment factors are set higher than the industry standard. Because of Bedrock's conservative management, strong operating controls, and strict underwriting standards, Bedrock uses a C-4 risk-adjustment factor that is 50 percent lower than the industry median.

Worksheet 2 shows the risk-adjustment factors adopted by each company.

Worksheet 2
Hypothetical Risk-Adjustment Factors for Abacus Life and Bedrock Life

Risk Exposures	C-1 Risk-Adjustment Factors	
	Abacus	**Bedrock**
Bonds: • Government bonds	0.0%	0.0%
• Other investment-grade bonds	1.0%	1.0%
• Below-investment-grade bonds	5.0%	5.0%
Mortgage loans	1.5%	1.5%
Real estate	5.0%	5.0%
Common stocks	30.0%	30.0%
	C-2 Risk-Adjustment Factors	
	Abacus	**Bedrock**
Individual life tabular cost of mortality	20.0%	20.0%
Annuity reserves	1.0%	1.0%
Group life and health premiums	20.0%	20.0%
	C-3 Risk-Adjustment Factors	
	Abacus	**Bedrock**
Individual life reserves	4.0%	2.0%
Annuity reserves	3.0%	1.5%
	C-4 Risk-Adjustment Factors	
	Abacus	**Bedrock**
Applied to total assets	2.0%	1.0%

To find the level of capital need implied by these risk-adjustment factors, the risk factors in Worksheet 2 must be multiplied by the associated measures of risk exposure from Worksheet 1.

Next we need to find risk-based capital requirement for each risk category and the total risk-based capital requirement for each company. This calculation requires multiplying the risk-adjustment factors in Worksheet 2 by the associated financial statement values in Worksheet 1, as shown in Worksheet 3.

Worksheet 3
Risk Capital Calculation for Abacus Life and Bedrock Life

	Abacus Life	Bedrock Life
C-1 Risk		
Bonds: • Governments	$ -0-	$ -0-
• High-grade corporate bonds	350,000	700,000
• Low-grade bonds	1,500,000	-0-
Mortgage loans	300,000	300,000
Real estate	400,000	100,000
Common stocks	1,200,000	600,000
Total C-1 Risk-Capital Requirement	**$ 3,750,000**	**$ 1,700,000**
C-2 Risk		
Individual life tabular cost of mortality	$ -0-	$ 1,000,000
Annuity reserves	800,000	600,000
Group life and health premiums	5,000,000	-0-
Total C-2 Risk-Capital Requirement	**$ 5,800,000**	**$ 1,600,000**
C-3 Risk		
Individual life reserves	$ -0-	$ 600,000
Annuity reserves	2,400,000	900,000
Total C-3 Risk-Capital Requirement	**$ 2,400,000**	**$ 1,500,000**
C-4 Risk		
Total Assets	**$ 2,000,000**	**$ 1,000,000**
Total Risk Capital		
Total Risk-Capital Requirement	**$13,950,000**	**$ 5,800,000**

The results of this calculation show that Abacus Life has a much higher risk-capital requirement than Bedrock Life. This difference reflects the companies' different product types and investment strategies. Abacus Life sells riskier products (e.g., group health), which produces a higher C-2 risk capital component. Likewise, Abacus Life has a riskier investment strategy and therefore has higher C-1 and C-3 risk capital requirements. Although both companies have the same total assets, Abacus Life's risk-capital requirement is more than twice that of Bedrock Life. In this example, $10 million of capital is more than adequate to cover the risk needs of Bedrock Life but is not enough for Abacus Life.

Three Views of Required Capital

In theory, the minimum capital standards set by the three groups—regulators, rating agencies, and internal management—are independent of each other. In general, though, the standards for regulatory capital would be the lowest, because the regulatory standards represent a borderline test for a legal declaration of financial failure. Rating agencies and internal management tend to set considerably higher targets than do regulators. Thus, the higher of the standards set by rating agencies and internal management usually determines the minimum level for required capital. In recent years in the United States and Canada, rating agencies have tended to set the highest minimum standards.

Let's consider an example of how the various standards for required capital relate to each other. Suppose that the management of Orca Insurance estimates that Orca needs to hold $10 million in capital to cover deviations of actual cash flows from expected cash flows, $8 million for minimum regulatory capital, and $12 million in capital to meet its need for a prestigious quality rating. In this situation, Orca's overall need for required capital would be $12 million, because $12 million is the highest of these various standards for required capital.

Standards for Uncommitted Capital

The capital an insurer elects to hold in support of new business is often referred to as *uncommitted (growth) capital.* As we saw in Figure 10-2, uncommitted capital is the difference between target capital and required capital. The level of the uncommitted capital component of an insurer's target *capital* is set at the discretion of the insurer's internal management and, in general, is intended to provide funds to meet the insurer's capital requirements.

Plans to issue new insurance and annuity business require a commitment of surplus because simply issuing new life insurance and annuity business places a strain on an insurer's capital. (Specifically, new business places a strain on statutory surplus.) Insurers usually must establish new reserves whenever they issue new business, even though the first-year revenue from the new business is often less than even the expenses associated with selling and issuing the new business. As we saw in *ExecuView* applications in earlier chapters, start-up expenses associated with new business often are not recovered until several years after the new business is issued. As noted in Chapter 9, these high start-up expenses can draw down an insurer's surplus, creating *surplus strain* or *new business strain.* (Chapter 14 illustrates how some insurers obtain reinsurance coverage to address the problem of surplus strain.)

In addition to providing funds to relieve surplus strain, uncommitted capital provides funds for

- Providing returns to stockholders, either by enhancing the growth of the business and thus driving up stock price, or by paying a dividend;
- Paying off debts or retiring outstanding stock; and
- Paying policy dividends on participating policies.

Maximum Limits on Capital

FAST FACT

Confederation Life, which failed in 1995, followed a classic prescription for insolvency: high returns and low capitalization. In 1984, Confed had no debt and had surplus equal to 14 percent of liabilities. By 1990, Confed had $1.5 billion in debt, and surplus equal to 6.7 percent of liabilities. Between 1982 and 1992, Confed averaged 23 percent annual growth.[3]

Because of the risk-return tradeoff, insurance companies must guard against the dangers of holding too much capital just as they guard against the danger of having too little capital. One danger of holding too much capital is that the insurer might not be employing its capital to earn a rate of return that is acceptable to all of its various stakeholders—owners, employees, rating agencies, policyholders and contractholders, and participants in the capital markets. An insurer that holds excessive capital will find it difficult to earn a satisfactory rate of return for the company's owners. For a stock company, the behavior of the company's stock price provides clues as to the insurer's effectiveness in employing capital. We return to our discussion of this aspect of the risk-return tradeoff later in the chapter.

For both U.S. and Canadian insurers, rating agencies set yet another constraint on the amount of capital insurers hold. These rating agencies look unfavorably upon a rated company's maintaining any more than some maximum level of capital, which the rating agencies usually express in terms of a multiple of the NAIC's required minimum RBC. If an insurer exceeded that maximum level of capital, then some rating agencies would be likely to downgrade the insurer's quality rating below the level that the company's management would prefer to maintain. The rating agencies reason that an insurer has a responsibility to earn a reasonable level of return, and taking too little risk implies that a company might not be aggressive enough in seeking returns.

It should be no surprise that another maximum limitation on capital and surplus is a statutory limitation. Insurance regulations in many states limit the amount of surplus held by companies that issue participating policies. These states require the insurer to distribute in the form of policy dividends any surplus in excess of the limit to holders of participating insurance policies. However, there is no similar requirement for insurers to distribute their surplus to their stockholders.

Analyzing Capital Investments

Before leaving our discussion of insurers' capital needs, we describe capital budgeting, which is an important component of the capital management process. As we noted first in Chapter 1 and again in later chapters, long-term investment projects are sometimes called *capital investment projects* or *capital expenditures.* In insurance companies, new financial products are major capital investment projects. As we have noted, new financial products, like business development opportunities in any other business, require a capital investment. Insurers' other business development activities, such as acquiring another company or obtaining a new information management system, also require a long-term investment. Capital budgeting is the analysis of investments in such opportunities.

We have noted that uncommitted capital provides funds to allow the company to issue new business and provide for future growth. An insurance company that has plenty of uncommitted capital can afford the strain of issuing new business. In turn, the new business, if written on a sound basis, forms a new profit stream that continues to increase the company's capital. Figure 10-3 shows a representative earnings stream for a profitable life insurance company product.

An insurance company that cannot easily afford the capital strain of issuing new business faces a different problem—the insurer cannot expect to collect the future ongoing earnings streams that profitable

Figure 10-3. Bar graph of a representative earnings stream from a profitable product.

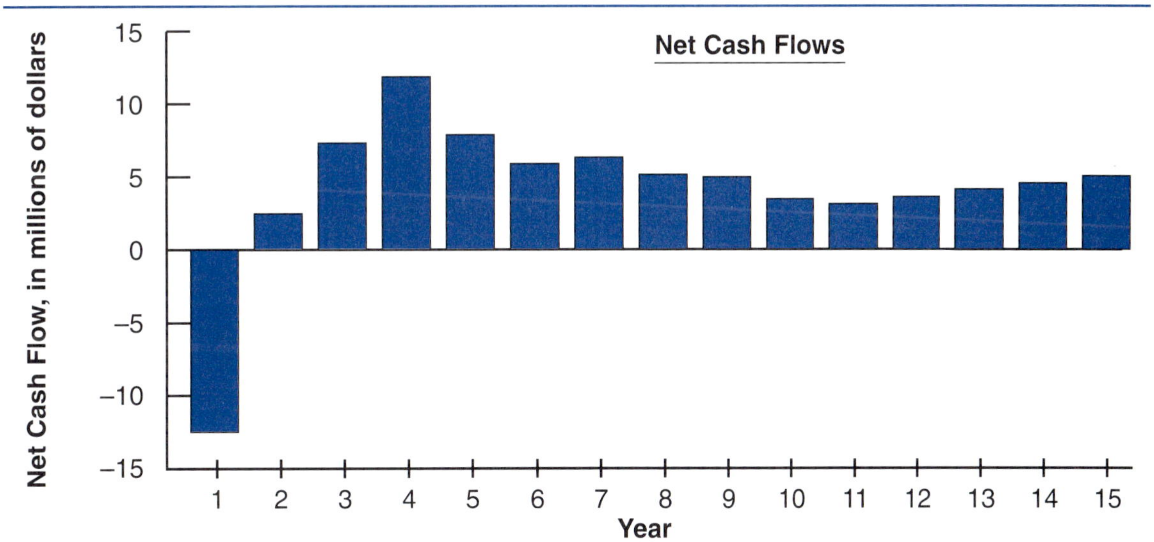

business would have provided. In this regard, we can apply the old adage: *It takes money to make money.* Let's look now at how insurers analyze the expected profitability of capital investments.

In order for an insurance company to grow and prosper, two conditions are necessary: (1) the insurance company must continue to generate new business and (2) the new business must be issued on a profitable basis. The need to have capital available for investment in order to eventually generate new capital is a key to understanding the momentum driving the capital management process in an insurance company.

Insurers use a number of methods to evaluate the profitability of proposed capital investments and current operations. Earlier in the chapter, we mentioned one profitability measure—return on capital—which can be calculated as follows:

$$\text{Return on Capital} = \frac{\text{Earnings}}{\text{Capital and Surplus}}$$

Another important influence of long-term corporate profitability is known as cost of capital. ***Cost of capital*** can be defined as the overall rate of interest the company pays for the funds it employs. Estimating an accurate cost of capital is guesswork for insurers, and particularly for mutual insurers. As we demonstrate when we discuss weighted averages in Chapter 15, cost of capital is often calculated by taking a weighted average of the various interest costs, transaction costs, or opportunity costs the organization pays for funds obtained from various sources, such as its various sources of debt and equity capital. The result of such a calculation is known as the *weighted average cost of capital (WACC).*

A corporation's cost of capital is important because it often serves as the organization's hurdle rate for capital investment projects. A ***hurdle rate,*** also sometimes known as *required return,* is a minimum percentage rate of return on capital—or other profitability measure—that a company must earn in order to recoup its cost of capital. At some extreme, a company could hold more capital than it needs to cover its planned capital investments. In such a situation, the company may not be able to generate on the excess capital returns that exceed its hurdle rate. Of course, the solution to that problem would be to either find new and profitable investment opportunities for the capital or else to return the capital to owners. Owners then would be free to seek higher investment returns through alternative investment opportunities.

Another profitability measurement, sometimes known as a company's ***profit margin (spread),*** can be found as the difference between the company's return on capital and its cost of capital.* A positive profit margin represents a desirable outcome. A larger spread is generally more desirable than a small spread, so long as earning the larger spread does not violate the investors' risk tolerances. The risk-return tradeoff suggests that as profitability increases, the level of risk-taking generally increases.

Example: Sensitivity of Return on Capital

By looking at an example, we can see how the amount of capital a company holds and the amount of its earnings affect the company's profitability. Assume that at year end the Cyber Insurance Company had capital of $100 million, earnings of $15 million, and a cost of capital of 6 percent. Cyber's return on capital for that year was 15 percent ($15 million divided by $100 million), and its spread was 9 percent (15 percent minus 6 percent).

Now, let's adjust first (1) the amount of Cyber's earnings and then (2) the amount of its capital. In this way, we illustrate how those changes would affect the company's profitability.

Change in Earnings. Suppose that during the second year Cyber earned only $8 million, but its capital remained at $100 million and its cost of capital remained at 6 percent. The reduction in earnings reduces Cyber's return on capital from 15 percent to 8 percent and reduces its spread from 9 percent to 2 percent. This conclusion is demonstrated in Worksheet 4.

Worksheet 4
Effect of Decreasing Cyber's Earnings

Cyber Example 1	End of Year 1	End of Year 2	Change
Total capital	$100 million	$100 million	No change
Earnings	$ 15 million	$ 8 million	–$7 million
Cost of capital	6%	6%	No change
Return on capital	15%	8%	–7%
Spread	9%	2%	–7%

Conversely, suppose that during the second year Cyber's earnings had increased to $20 million, while its capital remained at $100 million and its cost of capital remained at 6 percent. In this case, Cyber's

* In terms of the micro-pricing approach to product pricing employed in this textbook, the spread or margin associated with a product would be expressed in slightly different terms, although the general concept is similar.

return on capital would increase to 20 percent and its spread would increase to 14 percent. This conclusion is demonstrated in Worksheet 5.

Worksheet 5
Effect of Increasing Cyber's Earnings

Cyber Example 2	End of Year 1	End of Year 2	Change
Total capital	$100 million	$100 million	-0-
Earnings	$ 15 million	$ 20 million	+$5 million
Cost of capital	6%	6%	-0-
Return on capital	15%	20%	+5%
Spread	9%	14%	+5%

These examples illustrate that if earnings drop and capital remains level, then profitability (represented by return on capital) will drop; however, if earnings increase while capital remains level, then profitability also increases.

Change in Capital. Finally, what happens to Cyber's profitability if the amount of its capital changes? Let's assume that Cyber's second-year earnings remained at the first-year level of $15 million and its cost of capital remained at 6 percent but that its capital increased from $100 million to $150 million. In this case, Cyber's return on capital would diminish from 15 percent to 10 percent, and its spread would drop to 4 percent. This conclusion is demonstrated in Worksheet 6.

Worksheet 6
Effect of Increasing Cyber's Capital

Cyber Example 3	End of Year 1	End of Year 2	Change
Total capital	$100 million	$150 million	+$50 million
Earnings	$ 15 million	$ 15 million	-0-
Cost of capital	6%	6%	-0-
Return on capital	15%	10%	–5%
Spread	9%	4%	–5%

Conversely, suppose that Cyber's capital was reduced to $75 million, but its earnings remained at $15 million and its cost of capital remained at 6 percent. By reducing its capital, Cyber would increase its return on capital to 20 percent and would increase its spread to 14 percent. This conclusion is demonstrated in Worksheet 7.

Worksheet 7 Effect of Decreasing Cyber's Capital			
Cyber Example 4	**End of Year 1**	**End of Year 2**	**Change**
Total capital	$100 million	$75 million	–$25 million
Earnings	$ 15 million	$15 million	-0-
Cost of capital	6%	6%	-0-
Return on capital	15%	20%	+5%
Spread	9%	14%	+5%

As we have illustrated, when the amount of a company's capital increases and its earnings remain level, the company's return on capital and the spread are reduced. Conversely, when a company's capital decreases while its earnings remain level, the company's return on capital and the spread are increased. (If both earnings and capital were to change at once, the effects would interact to a degree that would depend upon how dramatically each dimension had changed. Those effects are beyond the scope of our present discussion.) Figure 10-4 summarizes the outcomes of the relationships that we illustrated.

Note that the Cyber example highlights the effects of the risk-return tradeoff. A very well-capitalized insurer is probably a very low-risk insurer; such a company is also likely to be highly solvent but is not necessarily highly profitable. Alternatively, an insurer that is highly profitable is possibly a risky insurer; such a company also

Figure 10-4. Sensitivity of return on capital to changes in capital and earnings.

	Return on capital percentage	**Spread percentage**
If **capital increases,** but earnings remain level, then ...	Decreases	Decreases
If **capital decreases,** but earnings remain level, then ...	Increases	Increases
If **earnings increase,** but capital remains level ...	Increases	Increases
If **earnings decrease,** but capital remains level ...	Decreases	Decreases

could be poorly capitalized and unstable financially. Insurers must carefully balance these effects of the risk-return tradeoff when making capital management decisions. Let's turn our attention now to how insurance companies evaluate their risk exposure for purposes of capital management.

Evaluating Risk Exposures

Insurers can experience unexpected needs for capital and surplus as a result of unexpected fluctuations in underwriting experience, investment values, interest rates, and other business results. These unexpected fluctuations or risks can result in actual and immediate effects on capital and surplus, or they can represent only unrealized potential effects. As noted in Chapter 2, the Society of Actuaries in the United States developed a classification system for the financial risks insurers face. This system consists of four categories of *contingency risk*, labeled C-1 through C-4. (Experts have noted that this risk classification system fails to include *all* of the financial risks insurers face.)

All of these C risks represent major areas of a life and health insurer's exposure to losses in value and decreases in returns. Each insurer's profile of exposure to the C risks influences that insurer's level of need for a safety cushion of capital and surplus beyond the legally required minimum capital amount. An insurance company's financial managers must decide how much safety cushion is enough, but not too much. In the remainder of this section, we describe how the various types of C risks can act to reduce an insurer's capital and surplus. The C risks are summarized in Figure 10-5, repeated from Chapter 2.

C-1 Risk Exposure

Once again, *C-1 risk* or *asset risk* is the risk that assets could lose value, although C-1 does not include the risk of losses in asset value related to interest-rate movements. C-1 risk affects asset values, but not the values of product liabilities. Managing and controlling C-1 risk is the province of the insurer's portfolio managers and its investments staff. Careful credit analysis and investment analysis is the best defense against C-1 risk. Market-value data concerning C-1 risk are readily available for many stocks and bonds. Many of the assets life and health insurers hold are relatively easily valued. This aspect of the life and health insurer's business, thus, is well suited to quantitative analysis.

In the simplest of terms, the negative impact of C-1 risk arises from a decrease in the value of assets. If we assume that the insurer's liability values remain unchanged, then the decrease in the value of *assets* is necessarily accompanied by an equal decrease in the value

Figure 10-5. C risks for life and health insurers, and examples of each.

C-1 Asset Risks	• Loss in assets' market value, except if caused by interest rate movements • Borrower's default in payment of interest • Borrower's default in payment of principal
C-2 Pricing Risks	• Adverse change in mortality or morbidity experience • Increase in cost of providing health care • Increase in company's operating expenses • Pricing deficiencies
C-3 Interest-rate Risks	• Assets' loss of value because of interest-rate increases; loss on forced sales of assets when interest rates rise • Withdrawals by customers when interest rates rise • Loss on bond calls and mortgage prepayments when interest rates fall • Losses due to asset/liability mismatches
C-4 General Management Risks	• Market risk from expansion into new lines of business • Market risk from geographic expansion • Changes in tax law • Fraud • Mismanagement • Lawsuits • Guaranty fund assessments • Runs on assets caused by fear of insolvency

of the insurer's capital and surplus. For example, suppose that Aurora Mutual's assets were originally valued at $100 million, its liabilities at $65 million, and its capital and surplus at $35 million. If Aurora's real estate investments perform so poorly that they must be written down, and consequently its investments drop in value to $95 million, then Aurora's capital and surplus diminish to $30 million.

C-2 Risk Exposure

C-2 risk or *pricing risk* is the risk that an insurer's liabilities might increase in value. When the value of an insurer's liabilities increases, and the insurer's asset values remain unchanged, then the insurer's capital and surplus would necessarily decrease in value. C-2 risk affects the insurer's product liabilities, but not its assets. Managing

C-2 risk is the job of the insurer's product development and pricing actuaries because of the importance of careful product design.

One difficulty inherent in managing C-2 risk is achieving reliable valuation of product liabilities. The major difficulty in setting a valuation of liabilities is that an objective basis for market valuation of insurance products is not readily available and thus cannot be applied to this process. (For product liabilities, market valuation data is available only from sales of comparable blocks of policies in the reinsurance markets.) Another reason is that the timing of changes in cash flows cannot be derived from market valuation data.

C-3 Risk Exposure

C-3 risk is variously labeled *mismatch risk, asset/liability matching risk, interest-rate risk,* and *asset/liability management risk.* In this textbook, we refer to it as *interest-rate risk.* C-3 risk exposure arises from changes in interest rates and can affect both the insurer's assets and the insurer's liabilities at once. You should note that when assets lose value or liabilities gain value because of interest-rate movements, these risk exposures are classified as C-3 risks, and not as C-1 or C-2 risks.

Interest-rate changes have more complex effects than the effects of a simple change in the value of assets alone or liabilities alone. As these complex effects occur, an ultimate threat to the insurer's solvency is that current cash obligations for liabilities could exceed the insurer's currently available cash and liquid assets. The exact impact of the C-3 risk exposure depends upon whether interest rates are rising or falling.

C-3 Risk Exposure When Interest Rates Rise. The C-3 risk associated with an increase in market interest rates arises because an insurer's assets and liabilities both will ordinarily decrease in value under these conditions. (An additional aspect of C-3 risk is the chance of unexpected fluctuations in cash outflows associated with assets and liabilities.) The risk exposure for insurers is that the value of the assets will decrease by a greater factor than will the value of the liabilities. When assets lose value at a faster rate than liabilities, the insurer's capital and surplus necessarily decrease in value. Thus, the ultimate effect of this change is similar to the effect of either a simple increase in the value of liabilities alone or a simple decrease in the value of assets alone.

C-3 Risk Exposure When Interest Rates Fall. The C-3 risk associated with a *decrease* in interest rates arises because, under these conditions, an insurer's assets and liabilities can both *increase* in value. Unfortunately, the value of the liabilities can increase by a greater factor

Figure 10-6. The C risks and decreases in capital.

<table>
<tr><th>Capital and surplus decrease if . . .</th><th>C-1 risk</th><th>C-2 risk</th><th>C-3 risk only</th></tr>
<tr><td rowspan="2">Assets . . .</td><td rowspan="2">Decrease</td><td rowspan="2">Remain unchanged</td><td>Increase</td></tr>
<tr><td>Decrease</td></tr>
<tr><td rowspan="2">While liabilities . . .</td><td rowspan="2">Remain unchanged</td><td rowspan="2">Increase</td><td>Increase</td></tr>
<tr><td>Decrease</td></tr>
</table>

than does the value of the assets. The ultimate effect of such a change is similar to the effect of a simple increase in the value of liabilities—the insurer's capital and surplus necessarily decrease in value.

Insurers have a relatively precise way of measuring the magnitude of expected change in these values in response to interest rate changes. As we will see later, insurers predict the magnitude of these changes by using measures of interest-rate sensitivity known as *duration* and *convexity statistics.* We discuss duration and convexity in Chapter 17.

Figure 10-6 shows in summary form how the C-1 through C-3 risks can produce a decrease in a life insurer's actual capital and surplus.

Addressing C-4 Risk Exposure

The *C-4 risks* (general management risks) of social, political, accounting, and legal losses are varied. C-4 risks include the risk of a run on assets if consumers as a group lose confidence in the organization's quality and choose to withdraw their funds. As a group, C-4 risks are less susceptible to the analysis we have applied here to risks C-1 through C-3. Insurance executives employ a variety of decision-support tools and devise strategies and programs to avoid or respond to these varied C-4 risks.

Identifying Additional Contingency Risks

The C-1 through C-4 system of contingency risks encompasses all risks officially recognized by the Society of Actuaries. For internal management purposes, however, some insurers employ an additional unofficial "C-5" risk classification for risks not acknowledged among the Society of Actuaries' original contingency risks. One example of a C-5 risk is the risk of loss from fluctuations in foreign exchange rates for insurers doing business in more than one currency. The uses for added categories of risk are numerous, and discussion of them is beyond the scope of this textbook. The purpose of adding special risk categories would be to specify risks for which the insurer would like to allocate a portion of its capital.

In Conclusion

Chapter 10 served as our orientation to capital management. In this chapter, our focus was defining capital and explaining why insurance companies need it. We saw that an insurance company's minimum need for capital is subject to a number of external and internal standards. In discussing the reason for holding risk capital, we examined the C risks and the nature of their impact on target capital. Next, in Chapter 11, we turn our attention to describing strategies that insurers use to manage capital.

Key Terms and Concepts

capital management
cash management
required capital
nonadmitted assets
uncommitted capital
target capital
regulatory capital
risk-based capital ratios
risk-adjustment factor
quality rating
target quality rating
cost of capital
hurdle rate
profit margin (spread)

References

1. Alan Gart, Ph.D.; David J. Nye, Ph.D.; Connor M. Harrison, CPCU, AU, ARP, AIAF; Robert J. Gibbons, Ph.D., CPCU, and CLU, Coordinating Author; *Insurance Company Finance and Investments,* Third Edition (Malvern, PA: Insurance Institute of America, 1994), pp. 20–21.

2. *Capital Management in the Life Insurance Industry,* 1995 Edition (Atlanta, GA: LOMA, 1995), pp. 38–41.

3. James Daw and Jonathan Ferguson, "The Collapse of Confederation Life: How and Why It Happened," *The Canadian Journal of Life Insurance,* Vol. 11, No. 62/63 (1995), pp. 27–28. Reprinted there with permission of the Toronto Star Syndicate.

CHAPTER

Capital Planning

11

LEARNING OBJECTIVES

After studying this chapter, you should be able to

- Identify a number of basic strategies that an insurer can use to increase its capital
- Identify basic strategies that an insurer can use for deploying uncommitted capital for business development
- Recognize that multiple product lines within one organization may have interrelated needs for capital
- Recognize the term *cash-flow-based surplus*

OUTLINE

In Chapter 10, we explored the reasons for insurers to hold at least a minimum level of capital and surplus, and the reasons that they might also want to limit any excessive accumulation of capital and surplus. Now, in Chapter 11, we review the capital planning process to show how insurers establish their capital objectives. We also describe the fundamental strategies that insurance companies employ for meeting their capital objectives. As we noted in Chapter 10, the term *capital* refers to long-term funds, including capital and surplus. The long-term view is important to insurers, because the financial outcomes from a company's initial investment in insurance products—whether profits or unforeseen losses—emerge slowly, over a period of several years.

Before we discuss the complex processes used to establish strategies for meeting capital objectives, we must first establish a common vocabulary to use in reference to the various organizational units within insurance companies.

Note about Organizational Structures

For the purposes of our present discussion, we would find it convenient if insurance companies were organized according to a uniform structural plan. Unfortunately, insurance companies seldom organize or operate in a manner designed to make textbooks easier. Not only do insurance companies take a variety of organizational forms, but insurance companies tend to periodically restructure their organizational form. Further, each insurance company consists of many organizational units. We could label these units profit centers, divisions, strategic business units (SBUs), subsidiaries, product lines, teams, or lines of business, but none of these labels would accurately reflect the usage in all organizations. In general, though, we can observe that many insurance companies are divided into units—such as divisions, profit centers, or SBUs—on the basis of the company's product lines or lines of business. Because these different organizational units go by a variety of names, we need to agree upon a system for labeling them.

For the purposes of our discussion, we must take into account at least three levels within a typical organizational structure for insurance providers. These organizational levels are as follows:

- *Corporate level.* The very broadest executive view of corporate headquarters, having command over all operations of all units of the organization

- *Line-of-business level.* The relatively broad view that represents command over all operations of a single product line, division, or other profit center of an organization
- *Single-product level.* A relatively narrow view associated with managing a single financial product

In many insurance companies, technical functions such as marketing, actuarial, and financial are represented at both the corporate level and at a divisional or product-line level.

Corporate Planning

Insurance companies, like all organizations, must engage in planning in order to be successful. ***Planning*** is the process of establishing goals and objectives and then formulating the strategies, tactics, and other supporting activities needed to achieve those goals and objectives. ***Goals*** and ***objectives*** are the results that the business activity is designed to achieve.* The target capital objective and the other supporting capital objectives are examples of objectives developed as part of a formal process of capital planning. ***Strategies*** are broad plans or methods for achieving goals and objectives. ***Tactics*** are specific action plans for accomplishing strategies. Later, Chapter 11 describes the strategies and tactics that life and health insurance companies use to meet their capital objectives.

An organization's planning process can be quite complex, encompassing much more than simply capital planning. Formal corporate plans exist within a ***planning hierarchy,*** which consists of at least the following three levels of plans:

1. At the top of the planning hierarchy is the ***corporate strategic plan,*** which is a comprehensive long-term plan created by the corporation's senior executives and board members. These individuals make far-reaching decisions on the basis of vast supporting analysis from a corporate planning staff and from senior managers in charge of product lines, divisions, or major functional areas of a company.
2. The next level down in the planning hierarchy includes ***functional-area plans,*** which are long-term plans created for the various functional areas of the organization. For example, a cor-

* Although some textbooks distinguish between *goals* and *objectives,* no such distinction is maintained in common usage, and none will be maintained in this textbook. The distinction in some management literature revolves around the connection of measurable results to some outcomes but not to others. For example, the label *goal* is sometimes assigned to an outcome with measurability of results and the label *objective* to outcomes without measurability of results. Management literature is not consistent in the assignment of these labels to one concept or the other.

porate capital plan is essentially a long-term functional-area plan for the organization's financial function. Likewise, a corporate marketing plan is a long-term plan for the organization's marketing function.

3. The bottom level in this hierarchy consists of ***tactical (operational) plans,*** which are plans developed at the profit-center level for the day-to-day implementation of the corporation's strategic plan.

In order for an organization to be successful, all functional-area plans and tactical plans must support the organization's strategic plan. In other words, planning at all levels of the corporation is designed to enable the corporation to carry out its strategic plan and to meet its corporate strategic goals and objectives. Many companies approach strategic planning through a top-down, bottom-up approach. A ***top-down, bottom-up approach*** to strategic planning involves first sending a proposed strategic plan down through the levels of the organizational hierarchy, from the corporate level to the lowest operating levels of management, and then back up again to the corporate level. At every step along the way, the plan is refined and revised.

In addition, corporate planners must blend the various functional-area plans into a corporate plan that supports the strategic plan. We describe this process of blending various lower-level capital plans into a corporate capital plan later in the chapter. Figure 11-1 summarizes the process of blending corporate plans from various levels in the organization.

To improve your understanding of the interrelationships among strategic planning, marketing strategy and objectives, and financial strategy and objectives, see Insight 11-1.

Capital Planning

Like strategic planning, capital planning often proceeds according to a top-down, bottom-up approach. Thus, capital planning begins with developing a proposed capital plan at the corporate level, then moves down through the organizational hierarchy to the various product-lines. Then, information developed at all levels moves back up through the organizational hierarchy.

Here, we consider the capital planning process in the context of a multi-line company, partly because the vast majority of insurance providers operate in multiple lines of business, and also because the planning process for a multi-line company is broader in scope than is the process for a single-line company. First we briefly review capital planning at the single-product level, then examine it in more detail at the line-of-business (LOB) level and the broader corporate level.

Figure 11-1. The blending of corporate plans from various organizational levels.

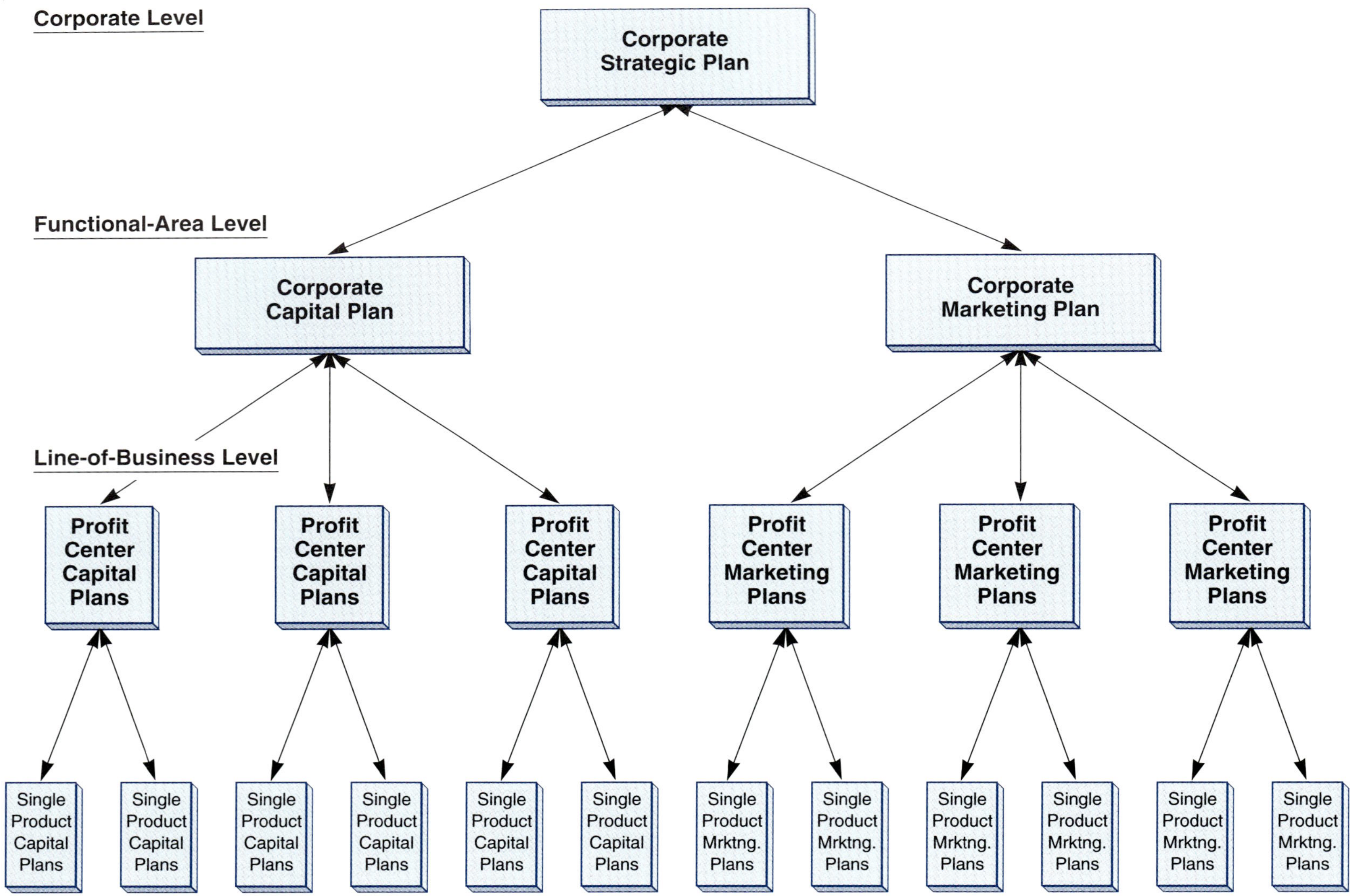

Insight 11-1 Surplus Management and Corporate Strategy at Mass Mutual

The remarks that follow are from an address by James McKeon, then CEO and President, Massachusetts Mutual Insurance Company.

Two perspectives must be balanced before becoming strategically managed: strategic decisions which involve decisions concerning markets, products and distribution; and the financial consequences of these decisions.

At Mass Mutual, we have chosen to measure our success in financial terms along three dimensions: (1) size as measured by statutory assets under management; (2) profitability as measured by return on equity; and (3) capital adequacy. These three financial measures must be kept in balance. Accelerated growth in statutory assets can put pressure on profitability and capital adequacy. Likewise, the need to build surplus has implications for profit requirements and growth.

Capital adequacy is extremely important. At Mass Mutual total capital is the sum of required surplus and corporate capital which we retain to fund growth and to provide flexibility and additional protection. Required surplus is that needed to cover the three normal risks: asset default, insurance risk, and asset/liability mismatch.

In measuring these risks, we use similar techniques to other companies in the industry. We measure capital adequacy as the ratio of total capital to required capital. We call this ratio our benchmark surplus ratio. It is similar to Moody's capitalization ratio.

Strategies must be affordable. Strategies which call for accelerated growth may have to be tempered in light of their financial implications for profitability and capital adequacy. So, in the final stages of developing our corporate and line-of-business plans, we balance our strategies and financials. Under our approach, strategies are completed before financials. In this way, strategies drive financials. We do not want to back into our strategies based on what we can afford, although the financial implications may lead to a tempering of our strategies or their timing.

Source: *James C. McKeon, "Strategic Management: The Key to Operational Excellence,"* Resource, *July 1991, p. 21.*

Capital Planning for Single Products

We described the product-design process and how it relates to capital planning in some detail in earlier chapters, and thus this chapter does not go into detail about capital planning for single products. The techniques of financial analysis employed in evaluating a single product include all of the techniques presented in our *ExecuView* Asset-Share Model, including

- Validation point (breakeven point) (payback period)
- Surplus strain (new business strain)
- Net present value (NPV), also known as *present value of profits*
- Internal rate of return (IRR or return on investment)
- Present value of profits divided by present value of premiums, also known as *profit margin*

These financial analysis techniques are an important component of product planning and design, enabling an insurer to analyze individual products in order to establish capital budgeting standards—such as target capital and target return on capital—for each proposed new product. In order for a product to break even, the product's expected rate of return must at least equal the percentage cost of capital associated with that product. For example, when the cost of capital associated with offering a life insurance product is 8 percent, then the product must earn a return on capital of at least 8 percent, or the insurer would have a loss on the product.

If the initial analysis of a product's pricing structure indicates that the product's rate of return would not equal or exceed the cost of capital, then one approach to correcting the problem would be to set a higher price for the product. In a profit-testing model, such a higher price would result in an increased expected return on the product and a short-term improvement in predicted capital position. However, in the real world, increasing prices can have negative as well as positive effects. Product prices that are too high can shorten the product's payback period or validation period, but can also reduce the product's persistency and depress its total sales. These actions have both long-term and short-term effects on the insurer's capital position. In turn, shortening the product's payback period would have the effect of improving the insurer's capital position in the short term. Reducing the product's persistency and total sales would have the effect of weakening the insurer's capital position in the long term.

Capital Planning for a Line of Business

As part of capital planning for each line of business, the line-of-business staff studies the capital budgeting analyses of all proposed new products as well as all existing products. The capital budgeting data used is similar to the output of the *ExecuView* Asset-Share Model provided along with this text. Line-of-business executives use capital budgeting information in the process of selecting the most promising new business opportunities, and they propose the best of these opportunities to the corporate planning staff.

The line-of-business staff also must project each product line's target capital and target return on capital. In order to estimate these amounts, the line-of-business staff must obtain forecasts of the following factors with respect to their product line:

- Return on capital
- Cost of capital
- Rate of growth in sales
- Reported capital
- Expenses

- Profit margin
- Surplus strain

The results of the planning and estimation processes from various product lines are then turned over to the corporate staff for coordination with the capital plans submitted by the company's other lines of business. A single-line company would obviously not need to blend planning information from several product lines. After obtaining the needed forecasts for the single product line, executives in single-line companies would proceed to analyzing corporate capital needs.

Capital Planning at the Corporate Level

In a multi-line company, corporate planners must consolidate the separate capital management reports and projections prepared by the various line-of-business staffs. Corporate planners begin this process by analyzing the capital planning reports from the various lines of business, as illustrated in *ExecuView* Application 11-1. This analysis allows corporate planners to identify such factors as

- The combined effect of these capital plans on projected future corporate financial results
- Interaction of risk exposures among a number of lines of business; the fit between various lines of business could act to increase or diminish the corporation's overall risk exposures
- Opportunities to invest capital in the existing lines of business that are highly profitable
- Needs for capital that do not arise from current product lines: for example, a need for capital to invest in a new information system or a need for capital to support entering a new line of business
- A need to exit unprofitable or otherwise undesirable lines of business
- The corporation's current capacity and expected future capacity to raise capital from external sources

Once an insurance company's corporate staff has assembled and analyzed line-of-business data, they can begin to establish a corporate-level financial plan. We can summarize and assemble the elements of the capital planning process into a fairly straightforward three-step procedure, as follows:

1. The first step is to set a target capital objective. We can view the process of setting target capital, as described in Chapter 10, as a process of estimating the company's capital needs.

Application 11-1 The Importance of an Appropriate Product Mix

If you wish to demonstrate this example on your computer, start *ExecuView* and select the Aggregate Model. Be sure to select *Reset, All Models* from the Action menu to return *ExecuView* to its default settings. The default assumptions and profitability outcome for this model are shown on the following *ExecuView* screen.

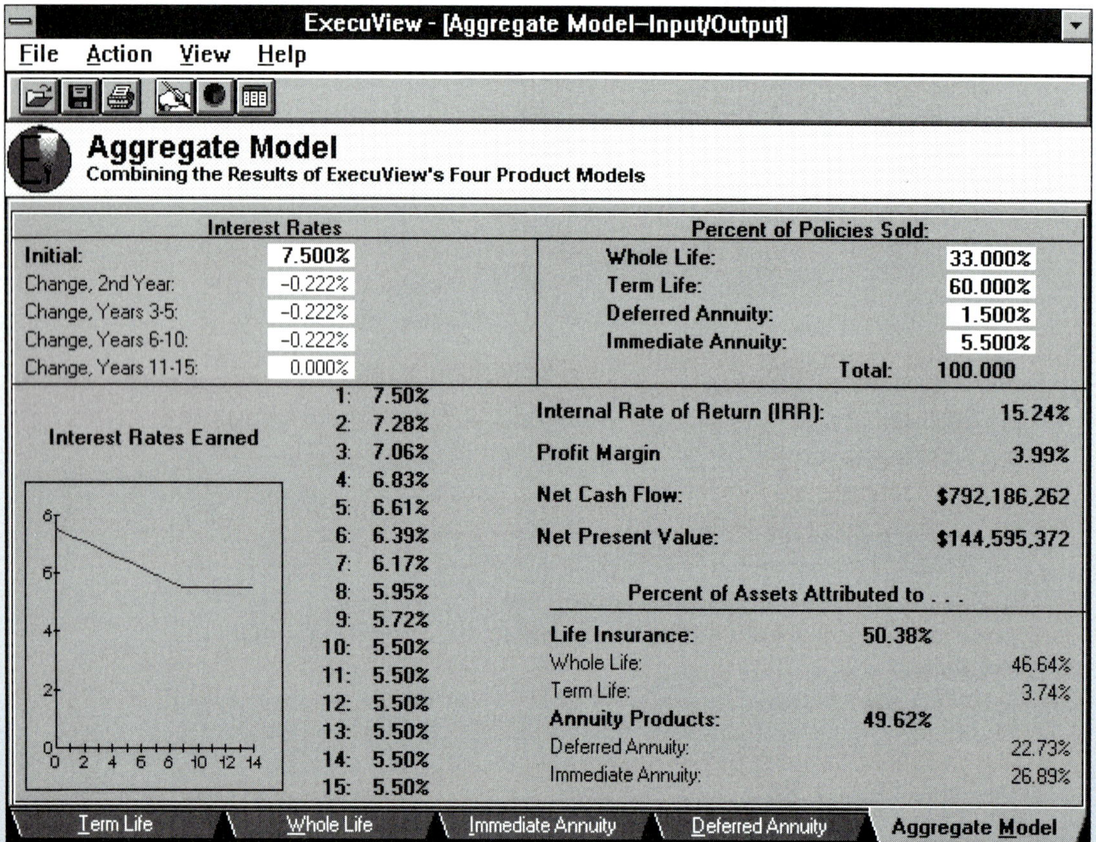

Different types of insurance products exhibit differing degrees of susceptibility to each of the four C risks. One of the reasons insurers must pay careful attention to their product mix is in order to avoid excessively exposing the company to a single C risk. Suppose the EV Life Insurance Company maintains the following product mix, reflecting—by product type—the number of policies sold:

Whole Life	33.00%
Term Life	60.00%
SPDA	1.50%
Immediate Annuity	5.50%

(continued on next page)

Application 11-1 The Importance of an Appropriate Product Mix (*continued*)

Assuming this product mix, EV Life used its pricing models to forecast profitability if the company were to experience tremendous fluctuations in the interest it earns on its asset portfolio. EV Life tested the performance of its products under an initial interest rate of 7.5% that decreases 0.5 percentage points per year for 10 years, and then increases 1 percentage point per year for 5 years.

> In the Aggregate Model, under *Interest Rates,* set *Change, 2nd Year; Change, Years 3–5;* and *Change, Years 6–10* to -0.5%. Set *Change, Years 11–15* to 1.0%. Press the <enter> key to see the results of these changes.

EV Life's models demonstrate that the present product mix shows moderate profitability under these fluctuating interest rates, earning an IRR of 7.85 percent, a profit margin of 1.35 percent, and a net present value of around $50 million, as shown in the following *ExecuView* screen. However, at the end of the model's profit test period, the immediate annuity product accounts for a negative portion of total assets, indicating that the immediate annuity product suffered a net loss.

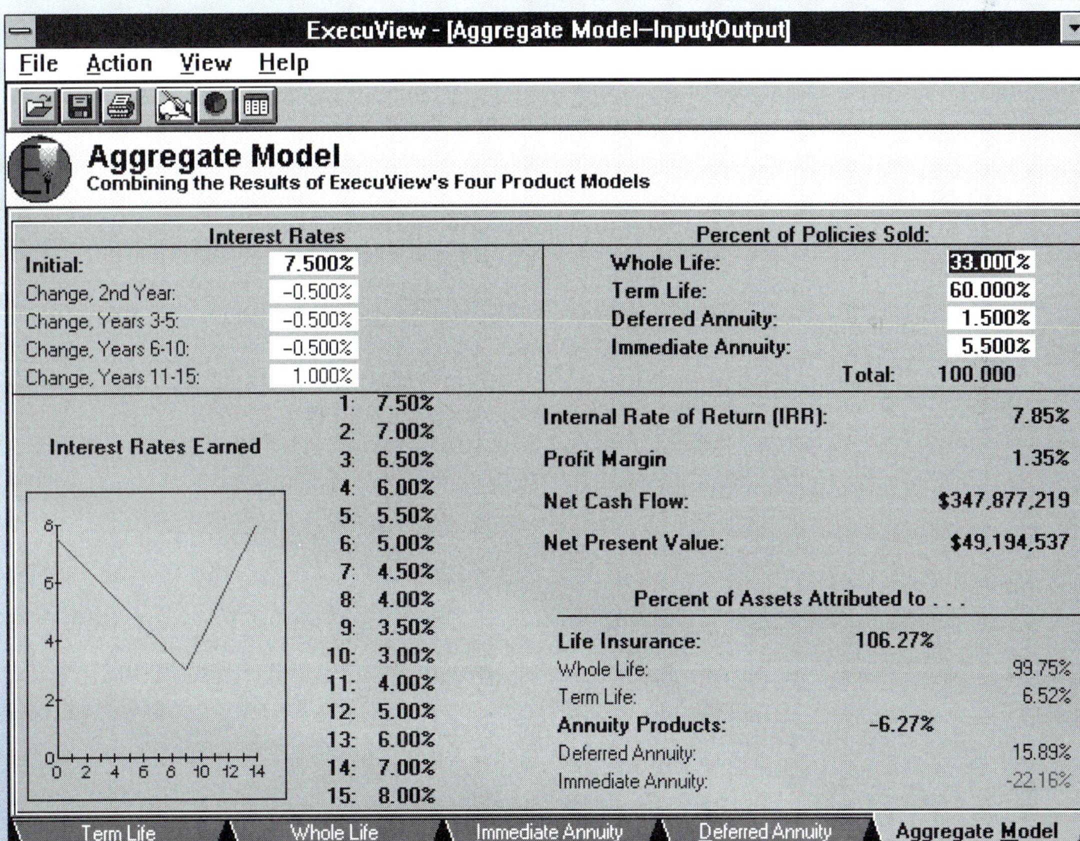

(*continued on next page*)

Application 11-1 The Importance of an Appropriate Product Mix *(continued)*

EV Life's immediate annuity product offers a crediting rate that becomes fixed in the first policy year. This feature makes the profitability of the immediate annuity especially sensitive to fluctuations in interest rates. Because EV Life wishes to test, under the same interest rate conditions described earlier in this application, the profitability of a product mix including a larger share of immediate annuities, EV Life tested the following product mix:

Whole Life	28.00%
Term Life	58.00%
SPDA	1.50%
Immediate Annuity	12.50%

➢ Adjust the *Product Mix* so that *Whole Life = 28%, Term Life = 58%, SPDA = 1.5%,* and *Immediate Annuity = 12.5%.* Press the <enter> key to see the results of these changes.

This product mix, combined with fluctuating interest rates, produces an aggregate net loss on EV Life's four products. If this scenario were to actually occur, EV Life's financial position might be seriously damaged. The results of these changes in the product mix are displayed on the following *ExecuView* screen:

(continued on next page)

2. The second step is to compare the amount of target capital with the amount of capital that the company currently expects to have. This step allows planners to discover whether the company is facing a projected shortfall or a projected excess.

3. The final step is to develop and adopt appropriate capital management strategies that will enable the organization to meet its target capital objective. A company having projected excess capital must find profitable new ways to invest or reinvest the available capital. A company having a projected shortfall must find additional capital.

Although the basic capital planning procedure described here can be viewed as having many more intermediate phases than the ones we presented, the capital planning process always must include at least these steps. This three-step capital planning procedure is summarized in Figure 11-2.

Now let's examine each of these steps in more detail.

Setting a Corporate-Level Objective for Target Capital

The first step in blending the capital plans from several lines of business is to tentatively set a corporate-level target capital objective.

Application 11-1 The Importance of an Appropriate Product Mix *(continued)*

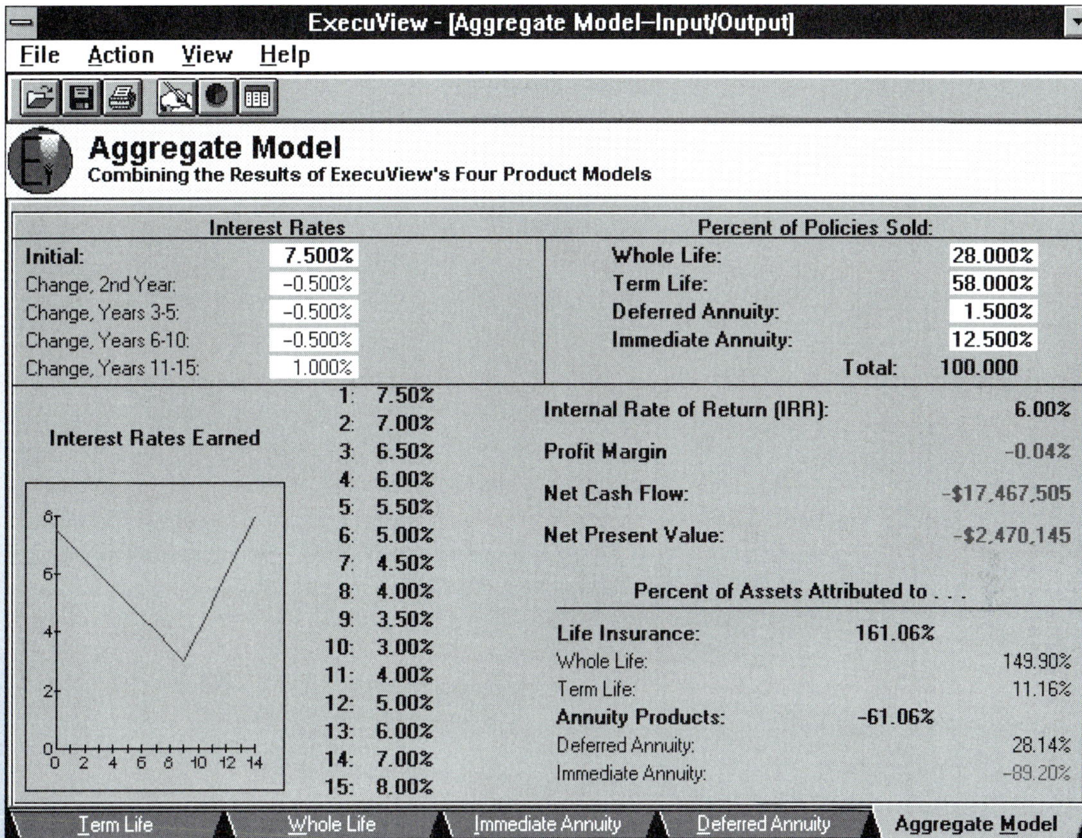

This illustration shows that annuity products—more specifically, immediate annuity products—can be particularly sensitive to C-3 (interest rate) risk. Annuity products are particularly sensitive to fluctuations in interest rates because the profits earned on annuity products are largely the result of interest margins—the difference between the interest rate the insurer is earning and the rate it is crediting to its customers. If an annuity product's crediting rate is fixed, as in *ExecuView*'s Immediate Annuity Model, then as interest rates fall, the product's interest margin—and therefore its profit margin—will also decline. Insurers can use many techniques for controlling the exposure to C-3 risk. One of these techniques is to control the share of annuities in the product mix.

In order to produce an initial estimate of a corporate target capital objective, corporate planners sum the target capital objective amounts for all the lines of business. They then consider the various components of target capital, making sure that all required (committed) capital will be available at all times and evaluating whether all uncommitted (growth) capital can be supplied at all times. Then, they

Figure 11-2. A capital planning process for insurers.

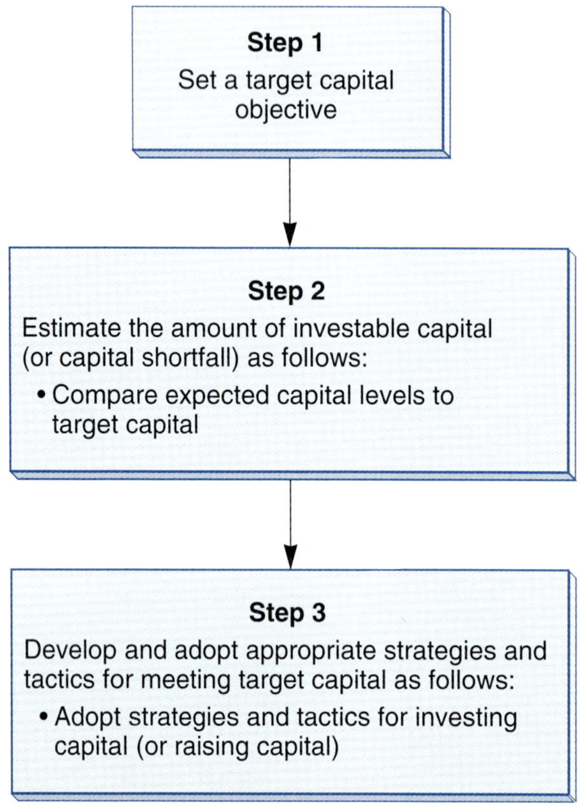

must adjust this first tentative estimate to reflect any interactions between risk exposures for the various lines of business.

Adjustments for the Combination of Risk Exposures

An interaction between risk exposures for lines of business can act either to increase or decrease the corporation's overall risk exposures. Two primary effects may result from the interaction of risk exposures: (1) risk augmentation and (2) risk offset.

An interaction between risk exposures produces an effect known as ***risk augmentation*** if the interaction produces a corporate risk exposure *greater* than the sum of the line-of-business risk exposures. Risk augmentation effects are likely to be associated with C-3 risk and are generally limited to the insurer's investment operations. If capital planners at the corporate level discover an instance of a risk augmentation effect, they must increase the corporation's required capital objective to reflect the added risk exposure.

In contrast, an interaction between risk exposures produces an effect known as ***risk offset*** if the interaction produces an overall corporate risk exposure *smaller* than the sum of the separate line-of-business risk exposures. If capital planners at the corporate level discover an instance of a risk offset effect, they must adjust the corporation's capital objectives to reflect the diminished risk exposure.

A common source of a risk offset arises from the interaction of contingency risks between a life insurance product line and an immediate annuity product line. In this combination of product lines, the relevant mortality risks take opposite directions. In the case of an immediate annuity product, the relevant contingency risk is the possibility that the covered population will live longer than expected. In the opposing case of a life insurance product, the relevant contingency risk is the possibility that the covered population will die sooner than expected. Thus, in evaluating the combination of mortality risks for both lines, insurers must recognize that both of these adverse contingencies are unlikely to materialize at the same time. A company offering both product lines would have no reason to hold capital equal to the sum of the capital needed for both of these opposing contingencies.

According to research by the Society of Actuaries, any number that insurers might assign for the combination of risk exposures is highly subjective, and planners cannot place a high degree of confidence on any single number chosen to account for the combination of risks.[1] The assignment of a dollar amount to the net effect of combined risk offsets or risk augmentations requires complex computer modeling techniques.

In order to set a number for the combination of risk exposures, insurers prepare long-term forecasts of both net cash flows and statutory capital positions. The financial simulation processes employed in this effort are *cash-flow testing* and *dynamic solvency testing*, discussed in Chapter 3. The year-by-year patterns of net cash flows and capital positions can reveal potential cash-flow shortfalls or capital shortfalls that might arise under given sets of adverse conditions. The value of the information derived from these financial simulation processes does not come from their providing a single "right answer;" instead, the value comes from providing management with insight into the relative long-term impact of key variables on net cash flows and capital. Accordingly, actuarial and technical reports to senior management must emphasize these insights; it is not enough for reports to simply present the numerical output from the simulations.

In any event, the risk adjustments to account for the combination of risk exposures can result in an estimate for corporate-level target capital (or required capital) that differs substantially from the sum of the capital objectives for the separate lines of business. The phases of analysis in this step of capital planning are depicted in Figure 11-3. The final output of this effort is a level of target capital needed at the

Figure 11-3. Summing and adjusting the line-of-businesses' (LOB) capital plans.

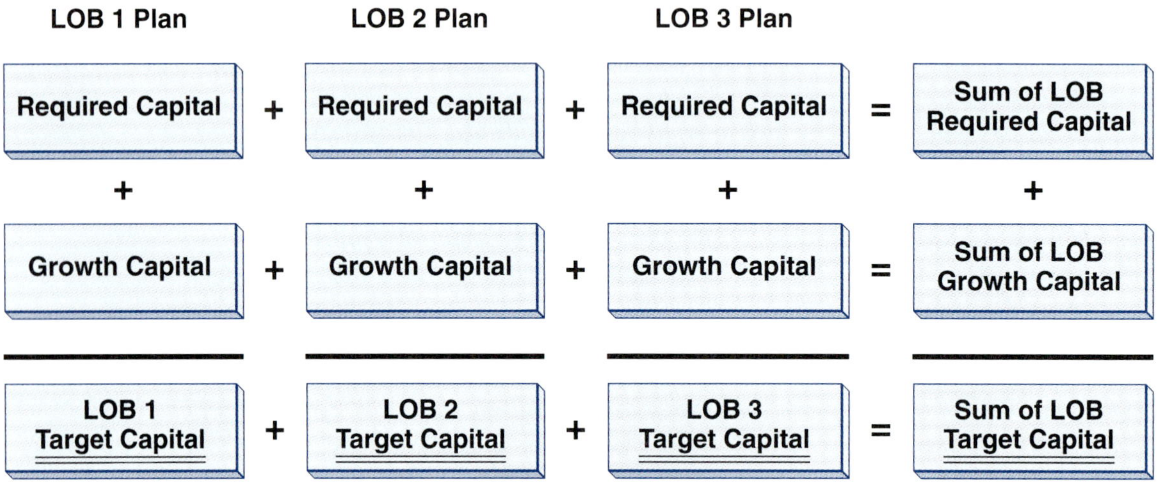

Step 1: Sum the target capital estimates from all lines of business, as shown for LOB 1, LOB 2, and LOB 3 above.

Step 2: Analyze interaction of LOB risks. Identify need for augmentations or offsets of risks.

Step 3: Adjust *Sum of LOB* capital estimates to account for augmentations or offsets.

Step 4: Sum the risk-adjusted amounts for LOB capital. The result is corporate target capital, after adjustment for the combination of risks.

corporate level to ensure that all of the line-of-business capital objectives can be met.

Evaluating an Organization's Capital Position

Capital planners next evaluate the adequacy of the organization's present capital position for meeting the organization's predicted capital needs. The effort of evaluating the present capital position is not limited to balance sheets and a traditional accounting perspective. Instead, this effort requires simulation modeling. In this effort, although planners look at the organization's current net worth as a starting point for evaluating the company's financial position, they actually use accounting figures as only a basis for simulation modeling. Under this approach, capital planners use various input factors, such as expected interest rates and sometimes expected rates of growth in business, for producing forecasts of the company's future financial position or net worth.

One useful output from such a forecasting process is a measure of current net worth called cash-flow based surplus. An insurance company's ***cash-flow based surplus (CFS)*** is the present value of expected cash flows for existing assets minus the present value of expected cash flows for existing liabilities, all discounted at a specified interest rate.[2] Additionally, CFS can be thought of as representing the amount of cash that would remain in the business if all existing contractual benefits were paid now at their discounted present value. (The interest rate used for discounting would probably be an estimate of the insurer's cost of capital.)

The value of an insurer's cash-flow based surplus is predicated on discounted cash-flow concepts instead of statutory accounting or traditional GAAP accounting concepts. Because a dollar value for cash-flow based surplus is calculated using data from an internal financial reporting system, the dollar amount of cash-flow based surplus ordinarily differs substantially from the dollar amount of *statutory* capital and surplus. Although the mechanics of calculating a dollar value for CFS are not simple and straightforward, this concept can be expressed symbolically in the following terms:

Cash-Flow Based Surplus, Given Interest Rate *i*%	=	Present Value of Asset Cash Flows Discounted at *i*%	–	Present Value of Liability Cash Flows Discounted at *i*%

Beyond a single forecast of CFS or any other forecasted value, a more useful output of simulation modeling is an array of forecasts for a value such as CFS. An array of CFS values reflecting a variety of interest-rate scenarios is far more useful for indicating a company's inherent financial strength than would be a single CFS value. Once they have produced an array of values, analysts can attach probabilities to the various potential outcomes in the array. Thus, although the analytical process of assigning probabilities to these outcomes makes liberal use of numbers and mathematics, the process is highly subjective. For the sake of simplicity, here we can think of this process as if planners were simply comparing one number to another, but the reality is far more complex.

The results of CFS analysis and other similar analyses allow capital planners to compare the organization's present capital position to its target capital position. If the planners identify any gaps between these positions, they can identify and adopt capital management strategies for appropriately bridging the gaps. This final step in the capital planning process is the subject of the remainder of this chapter. The strategies are chosen on the basis of their appropriateness to the nature of the insurer's own perceived gap between its actual capital resources and needed resources, as well as to their fit with the company's risk preferences.

Capital Management Strategies

We noted earlier in this chapter that *strategies* are broad plans or approaches for achieving goals and objectives and *tactics* are specific action plans for carrying out strategies. An insurer's goals are necessarily related to keeping the company's risks and returns within a range that is comfortable for all concerned—including regulators, policyowners, stockholders, employees, and creditors.

When an insurer finishes assessing its current capital position, any action must focus upon correcting one of two undesirable conditions: (1) not having enough capital to support the insurer's identified needs for capital or (2) having more capital than the insurer has made plans to employ. As illustrated in Figure 11-4, we can identify four basic strategies for addressing these imbalances between an insurer's capital position and its risk exposures.

For convenience, we can classify into two basic categories the strategies available to insurers for achieving their capital targets:

1. Strengthening the company's capital position, by either (*a*) raising new capital or (*b*) reducing the company's need for capital by reducing its exposure to risk
2. Making use of excess capital, by either (*a*) increasing profitable capital investment or (*b*) accepting greater exposure to risk

Although later chapters of this textbook elaborate upon the many tactics available for supporting these basic strategies, here in Chapter 11 we review only these tactics. In addition, here we evaluate the potential effects of these strategies relative to the risk-return tradeoff.

Strengthening an Insurer's Capital Position

Although not every shortfall between target capital and actual capital would be dire, an insurer facing a shortfall would usually take

Figure 11-4. Strategies for addressing imbalances between capital holdings and risk-taking.

Not enough capital	More than enough capital
Approaches for correcting the imbalance:	
1. Raise new capital	1. Increase profitable capital investment
2. Reduce the need for capital by limiting risk-taking	2. Assume greater risk, thus increasing the employment of capital

action. Even a small shortfall of capital resources might trigger such unwanted consequences as lower quality ratings, policyowner concerns, difficulty in selling new insurance contracts, difficulty in attracting and retaining a sales force, and an increase in the company's cost of capital. (Keep in mind also that financial modeling involves a high degree of subjectivity, so that a predicted shortfall could represent merely a conservative bias in the modeling process.)

In Chapter 10, we addressed the distinctions between required (committed) capital and uncommitted (growth) capital. An insurance company may be motivated to strengthen its capital position when it has more than enough *required capital,* but not enough *uncommitted capital* to fund all of the profitable investment opportunities the company has identified. In such a situation, a company would fall short of its *target capital* objective. However, a company that at least meets its required capital objective would not be facing a real threat to its continued solvency. In more serious situations, an insurer's motivation for strengthening its capital may arise from its needing a capital infusion to fund even the company's *required capital* objective.

In any case, to strengthen its capital position, an insurance company could raise capital, reduce its need for capital, or both. Next we present numerous tactics for accomplishing these strategies. As you review these tactics, you should keep in mind that raising new capital without increasing earnings acts to reduce return on capital, and, because of the effects of the risk-return tradeoff, decreasing risk can bring about a reduction in profitability.

Tactics for Raising Capital

During the period 1988 to 1993, statutory capital and surplus for the life insurance industry increased by $40 billion. Of this increase, the greatest share of the overall growth resulted from gains from operations. Of this $40 billion, $13 billion was attributable to paid-in capital and surplus, and $20 billion was paid out in dividends to stockholders.[3] In Chapter 10, we presented the basic forms of accounting entries that would accompany an increase in capital. There we saw that increases in capital arose from any transaction producing either a net increase in assets or a net decrease in liabilities.

As in any corporate financing problem, the basic sources of additions to a life insurer's capital can be classified as internal or external sources. The capital that a company earns from its operations is considered to come from *internal* sources. A company can create new capital from internal sources, or else it can obtain capital from outside investors such as a parent company, affiliated corporations, partners in a strategic alliance or joint venture, or the public capital markets. The capital that a company obtains from partners, investors, or the public capital markets is considered to come from *external* sources. In Chapters 12 through 15, we identify and describe some internal and

Insight 11-2 Ways for Insurers to Raise Capital

When the financial managers of life and health insurance companies want to increase the company's capital, what actions can they take? More choices are available to stock companies than to mutual companies. To obtain the same flexibility that stock companies have in raising capital, mutual companies can elect to demutualize. All of the following choices are available to stock companies for increasing statutory capital, and a few of these choices are also available to mutual insurers:

- Reduce dividends and retain the earnings that would otherwise have been paid as dividends (stock and mutual companies)
- Slow the growth of new business (stock and mutual companies)
- Obtain reinsurance and thereby transfer insurance liabilities to another carrier (stock and mutual companies)
- Sell any subsidiaries or blocks of business that are sources of capital strain (stock and mutual companies)
- Raise money through traditional external channels of financing: issue common stock, preferred stock, surplus notes, or corporate debt (mutuals cannot directly issue stock, but they can issue bonds and surplus notes)
- Sell investments that can bring a capital gain (stock and mutual companies)
- Merge with another company (stock and mutual companies)
- Obtain capital from an existing parent company (stock companies only)
- Sell a controlling interest in the company (stock companies only)

Source: *Adapted from Paul Reardon, "Marketing Discipline and the Financial Strength of Life Insurance Companies,"* Journal of CLU and ChFC *(January 1993), pp. 44–45.*

external sources of capital. For now, Insight 11-2 discusses a few specific transactions that have the effect of increasing reported capital.

Tactics for Reducing Risk Exposures

Although insurers are generally conservative in their risk taking, insurers must nevertheless take enough risk to be able to earn an adequate profit on behalf of their owners. For an insurer needing more capital, one alternative to raising new capital is to reduce the need for capital by reducing the company's overall exposure to risks. Reducing the company's risk effectively reduces the amount of capital required to support risks; reducing required capital without reducing total capital effectively increases the amount of uncommitted capital that can be used to fund investment opportunities. The following tactics have the effect of diminishing an insurer's risk exposures:

- Reducing sales of new business, thus reducing new business strain
- Selling off unprofitable or risky lines of business
- Obtaining more reinsurance, which reduces new business strain
- Imposing stricter underwriting standards, thus rejecting more applicants for insurance

- Designing new products with features that limit the insurer's new exposures to various financial risks
- Controlling product pricing—probably by effectively increasing prices
- Adopting a stricter claim adjudication policy by scrutinizing claims more closely for errors, fraud, or other problems
- Reducing incentives offered to sales agents and brokers
- Limiting investment portfolio risk exposures
- Investing in only the most highly rated bonds
- Limiting investment in real estate
- Employing hedging strategies in portfolio management programs

When an insurer reduces its risk exposures, the risk-return tradeoff indicates that the company will suffer a penalty: it will become less profitable. However, becoming less profitable may be an indication of increased prudence, solvency, and safety. Interpreting the attractiveness of becoming less profitable requires deciding whether the present level of risk exposures (and profitability) is unacceptably high or already low.

This discussion emphasizes the positive actions an insurance company can take in order to increase capital. However, increasing capital is not the only potential objective of an insurer's capital management processes. In the interest of efficient and profitable operations, a well-capitalized insurer might be more greatly challenged by the need to find profitable employment for capital on hand. Today's insurance companies by and large are well capitalized. In many cases, then, an important objective of capital management is to reduce the insurer's level of capitalization so as to improve the operation's potential returns.

Strategies for Investing Capital

We noted earlier that an insurer might find that its current capital position exceeds its target capital objective. This excess capital represents investable capital. On the surface, having "too much" capital does not seem to be an urgent problem. Although the problem might not be *urgent* in every instance, corporations face a penalty for having too much capital: their profitability declines. Thus, an insurer with investable capital would take steps to put that capital to profitable use. Insight 11-3 presents one view of how insurance companies should use their excess capital. Next we review a number of tactics that would support the strategy of investing excess capital.

Insight 11-3 Excerpt from *The Dangerous Leap to Maximizing Returns*

Investing insurance companies' excess capital for total return has become an idea worth considering even though it rocks a precept of Western culture that is central to most strategic business planning: The belief that growth is good. We assume that business growth will lead to profit growth and enhanced shareholder value, and that managers' tasks are to identify the growth segments on which the companies can capitalize. Even downsizing is done with the belief that it makes companies leaner and therefore better able to take advantage of growth opportunities.

However, while business growth will generally lead to profit growth, all businesses cannot be growth companies and, in a mature industry, most can't. Thinking growth in a no-growth industry can lead to irrational pricing behavior and create more damage than defensive planning or redeployment of assets.

Although there clearly are growth opportunities within the life/health insurance industry, the fact is that our core markets are stagnant and the growth markets have limited profit potential. The outlook for the life/health industry is mixed.

Fortunately, the industry starts with a strong financial footing. Data from A.M. Best Co. indicates that capital and surplus for the life/health industry exceeds 8 percent of its total assets. More than half of the companies in the A.M. Best data base have capital and surplus in excess of 20 percent of assets, with a disproportionate number of these well-capitalized companies belonging to so-called small insurers—companies with less than $500 million in total assets. For most companies, insurance is an industry of excess capital.

The strategic question which needs to be addressed is what to do with this excess, or discretionary, capital. The business decision most companies focus on is whether to use discretionary capital to grow the company internally, to acquire blocks of business, or to buy new companies. The default option, which the numbers suggest is followed by most companies, is to just sit on the excess. This strategy will keep capital-to-assets ratios high and will keep regulators happy, but it may not make the most business sense.

Industry return on equity could be improved significantly by a strategy of discretionary investment of excess capital, with the most dramatic improvement possible for smaller companies with up to $500 million in assets. Whether this makes sense for individual companies will depend on a host of variables, including expected product profit margins and the company's efficiency in converting capital into sales.

Yet for an industry with excess capital and limited growth opportunities, this is a strategy well worth considering for the short term or long term. To do so requires a change in investment philosophy to discriminate between investment assets hedging product liabilities and those which are excess to product requirements. It also requires a re-thinking of our instinctive belief that growth is always good.

Source: *Excerpted from Michael Fasano, "The Dangerous Leap to Maximizing Returns,"* Best's Review, *Life/Health Edition (August 1994), pp. 40–42. Reprinted with permission of the publisher.*

Tactics for Investing More Capital

A number of tactics are available to insurers that need to employ their resources more profitably. An insurance company can increase its investment in capital-intensive business projects, particularly in issuing or assuming insurance and annuity contracts. We have repeatedly noted that issuing new insurance or annuity business involves a large initial capital investment that is expected to eventually return a profit. Some activities that reflect this general approach of investing capital to improve profitability include

- Writing new insurance and annuity business
- Writing reinsurance for other insurers

- Entering a new line of business, possibly using an approach involving greater risk-taking
- Purchasing (acquiring) a capital-poor insurance company
- Funding an existing capital-hungry subsidiary or other affiliate

Yet another approach that would effectively permit a U.S. insurance company to profitably invest an accumulation of capital and surplus would be to undertake transactions having statutory accounting effects that serve to employ the excess capital. These approaches actually involve acknowledging or taking on greater risk. Some examples of activities that support this approach include

- Spending cash for nonadmitted operating assets—for example, some types of computer systems and office space for administrative operations
- Engaging in reserve strengthening as appropriate
- Writing down the value of invested assets as appropriate
- Investing in riskier assets and asset classes

Another approach to investing excess capital is to pay off or retire corporate equity issues. For example, excess capital can be used to buy back equity instruments issued by the company, particularly those instruments that carry a high cost of capital. Examples of activities supporting this general approach include

- Retiring surplus notes
- Retiring capital stock
- Increasing treasury stock

If the corporation cannot invest its capital in profitable opportunities, it can exercise its option to return the capital to the company's owners. An insurer might return surplus funds to its owners in the form of dividends. In general, an organization would declare extra dividends in the event that it had not identified adequately profitable investment opportunities for the available funds.

Tactics That Involve Taking Greater Risk

Insurers sometimes choose to take on a greater exposure to risk not for the sake of the risk itself, but for the sake of improving their profitability at a time when their solvency needs for capital are more than adequately covered. We have already looked at the reasoning behind this tactic of improving profitability by taking on an increased exposure to risk. As we have discussed previously, the risk-return tradeoff implies that taking greater risk and having a chance of earning more profits generally go hand in hand. As we also discussed previously, for a given amount of earnings, the rate of return on capital increases when the amount of capital decreases. The following tactics have the effect of increasing an insurer's risk exposures:

- Increasing sales of new business, thus producing new business strain
- Increasing the amount of insurance the company carries at its own risk, thus reducing the amount of reinsurance it purchases
- Liberalizing underwriting standards, thus accepting more applicants for insurance
- Controlling design of new products so as to increase new exposures to various financial risks
- Controlling product pricing—by in effect decreasing product prices
- Adopting a more liberal claim adjudication policy
- Offering more generous incentives to sales agents and brokers
- Increasing portfolio investment in relatively riskier assets, particularly those involving a greater risk-capital adjustment factor within the NAIC's Risk-Based Capital calculation. For example, a company could increase its investments in assets such as junk bonds or real estate, both of which are riskier than most of the assets in a typical insurer's asset portfolio.

In Conclusion

This chapter described how the capital planning process relates to corporate strategic planning. This chapter also explained how the capital planning process enables insurers to establish their capital objectives. Finally, we reviewed common strategies and tactics for capital management in insurance companies. In Chapter 12, we turn our attention to internal sources for additional capital. Then in Chapters 13 and 14, we review some specific ways of raising capital from external sources—for example by issuing securities and using reinsurance.

Key Terms and Concepts

planning
goals
objectives
strategies
tactics
planning hierarchy
corporate strategic plan
functional-area plans
tactical (operational) plans
top-down, bottom-up approach
risk augmentation
risk offset
cash-flow based surplus (CFS)

References

1. *Capital Management in the Life Insurance Industry* (Atlanta, GA: LOMA, 1995), pp. 22–23, 42–43.

2. James A. Geyer and Michael E. Mateja, "Appendix C-1: Cash-Flow Based Surplus, TSA 1991–92 Reports of Mortality, Morbidity, and Other Experience," *COVARA: Combination of Risks,* pp. 503–504. Transactions of the Society of Actuaries, Copyright © 1993.

3. *Life & Health Reinsurance: Pockets of Opportunity* (Hartford, CT: Conning & Company, 1995), p. 52.

CHAPTER

Internal Sources of Capital

12

LEARNING OBJECTIVES

After studying this chapter, you should be able to

- Identify and interpret several internal sources of capital
- Demonstrate understanding of sale-leaseback transactions and their benefits to insurers
- Recognize several forms of asset-backed securities and the benefits of issuing these securities
- Interpret how sales of receivables might increase statutory capital for U.S. insurers

OUTLINE

In the early 1990s, the life and health insurance industry undertook an intensive round of capital growth. The $12.8 billion of new capital U.S. life insurers raised during the period from 1991 through 1994 effectively demonstrates life and health insurers' ability to raise capital, as illustrated in Figure 12-1. This chapter discusses a variety of approaches for improving a life and health insurer's capital position.

First, let's consider what we mean by *improving a life and health insurer's capital position.* Insurers' efforts to strengthen their capital positions can take one of two basic approaches:

1. Directly increasing the total amount of capital, or

2. Decreasing the level of risk relative to capital, thus decreasing the insurer's need for capital

Stated another way, *improving an insurer's capital position* can mean more than simply increasing the insurer's total dollar amount of capital and surplus. Although one valid approach to improving an insurer's capital position is to increase its total capital base, that's not the only valid approach. Another approach would be to decrease the insurer's need for capital by decreasing the company's overall level of risk exposure. When a company's overall risk decreases, the company's required capital also decreases.

FAST FACT

During the period 1988 to 1993, statutory capital and surplus for the life insurance industry increased by 63 percent, an increase of $40 billion.[1]

The advisability of applying any given tactic for improving capital depends upon each insurer's unique situation. An insurer's action to obtain new capital should above all be consistent with that insurer's strategic objectives. Although this textbook does not undertake to judge the value of any given financial action, it is also important to note here that not all means of increasing capital are equally desirable for every situation. In other words, the validity of employing any given tactic would depend upon its appropriateness for addressing a given situation, and not upon any intrinsic merit of the tactic.

Some of the available means for increasing capital through internal sources are based upon achieving fundamental improvements in operations, whereas other tactics produce increases that are at least partly cosmetic. Making capital appear on a balance sheet as a result of cosmetic changes is often referred to as ***uncovering hidden capital.*** Specifically, tactics for uncovering hidden capital rely upon reclassifications of assets or liabilities for valid accounting, regulatory, and tax purposes. Collectively, the tactics for uncovering hidden capital are often referred to as ***financial engineering, financial reengineering,*** or ***financial restructuring.*** The alternative tactics that are based upon

Figure 12-1. Capital strengthening by the 100 largest stock life insurers in the early 1990s.

Year	Percent increase, entire industry	Amount of increase, 100 largest stock insurers only	Historical reason for increasing capital
1991	18.0%	$ 4.0 billion	Solvency scare, S&L scandal
1992	13.4%	$ 3.7 billion	Rating agencies' requirements
1993	19.4%	$ 4.7 billion	Risk-Based Capital requirements
1994	2.7%	$ 1.6 billion	Voluntary improvements

Source: *Reprinted with permission of Townsend & Schupp, from a presentation by Fred Townsend on March 11, 1995.*

fundamental improvements in managing the business are likely to produce long-term improvements, and thus are fundamentally stronger than the more cosmetic tactics. However, both approaches may be valid.

To understand how insurers can take action to increase their capital and surplus, we look briefly at various business transactions producing changes in an insurer's capital and surplus account. By examining the U.S. Annual Statement blank, we find that the amount of an insurance company's statutory capital and surplus changes in response to the following transactions:

FAST FACT

At the end of 1993, the insurance industry's average level of RBC was 464 percent as compared to a minimum NAIC standard of 200 percent.[2]

- Net gains or losses from operations
- Asset revaluation reflecting either unrealized capital gains and losses on invested assets or changes in admissibility of asset values
- Changes in a liability for reinsurance in unauthorized companies
- Changes in the valuation basis of reserves
- Changes in separate accounts
- Transactions in treasury stock
- Adjustments to surplus, including increases or decreases in special contingency reserves
- Payments of dividends to stockholders or to holders of participating policies
- Miscellaneous write-in items

Because of the surplus strain associated with issuing new policies, insurance companies that are steadily issuing new business need to be able to obtain new capital somehow. Insurers can employ a variety of approaches for obtaining new capital from internal or external sources. Insurers often choose to rely upon the gains generated by established blocks of life, health, and annuity business as their primary internal source of capital. New capital is available to insurers from other internal sources, however.

Although we can see that the alternative internal sources of capital are numerous, we cannot see at first glance how the transactions we have mentioned might bring about an increase in an insurer's capital and surplus. In some cases, *how* these various actions produce increases in capital (or decreases in risk) is immediately apparent only to experts in insurance company finance. These various tactics for obtaining capital enable insurers to improve their capital ratios and/or their total capital.

Let's consider now how the topic of raising new capital fits into the overall capital management process. In Chapter 11, we explored the capital management activities related to establishing the amount of an insurer's capital needs. We have already said that *capital management* concerns planning for, obtaining, and controlling long-term financing. As we noted in Chapter 11, the *capital management process* in insurance companies focuses on three main activities:

1. Setting a target capital objective
2. Analyzing needed adjustments in the organization's present capital position in order to meet the target capital objective
3. Adopting appropriate strategies for meeting the target capital objective

Here in Chapter 12 we consider how insurers implement their capital plans by finding internal sources of capital.

Overview of Internal Sources of Capital

First we can take a broad look at the array of options for raising capital. We know that capital and surplus can be increased without going outside of the company by one of two basic approaches: (1) earning it from sales or (2) making changes in holdings of assets or liabilities that enable the insurer to increase reportable capital in a manner that does not diminish the risk-return profile of the business.

Insurance companies generally have the following basic internal sources for capital and surplus:

Gains from operations (earnings)	Uncovering hidden capital
• Maintaining product profitability • Reducing dividend payouts	• Change in reserve valuation • Change in asset valuation • Change in asset classification

The main source of increase in an insurer's capital is likely to be earnings from profitable business activities, an internal source of capital. Certainly, an increase in earnings has by far the strongest positive effects of any source of changes in capital. Selling any type of asset at a capital gain produces a net addition to cash in the amount of the capital gain, and an addition to reportable capital.

Maintaining Profitable Business

Maintaining or improving the profitability of the insurance company's operations is an insurer's strongest source of capital strengthening. The initial financial effect of issuing new business is a major drain on statutory capital. An insurance company that has plenty of excess capital can afford the so-called strain of issuing new business. The initial capital strain associated with new products consists mainly of acquisition expenses and new reserves. After a product breaks even, though, the new product provides an ongoing stream of new profits that continues to build the company's capital. Once the insurer recovers from the initial effects of new business strain, the new product could for several years generate a stream of unencumbered earnings. Figure 12-2 shows a representative earnings stream for a profitable life insurance company product based on the product in *ExecuView*'s Whole Life Model.

Product profitability is an important source of additions to capital and surplus. Whenever product operations produce a realized gain, then the insurance company earns profit that increases capital and surplus. For now we consider the basic components of a net gain from

Figure 12-2. Earnings stream profile.

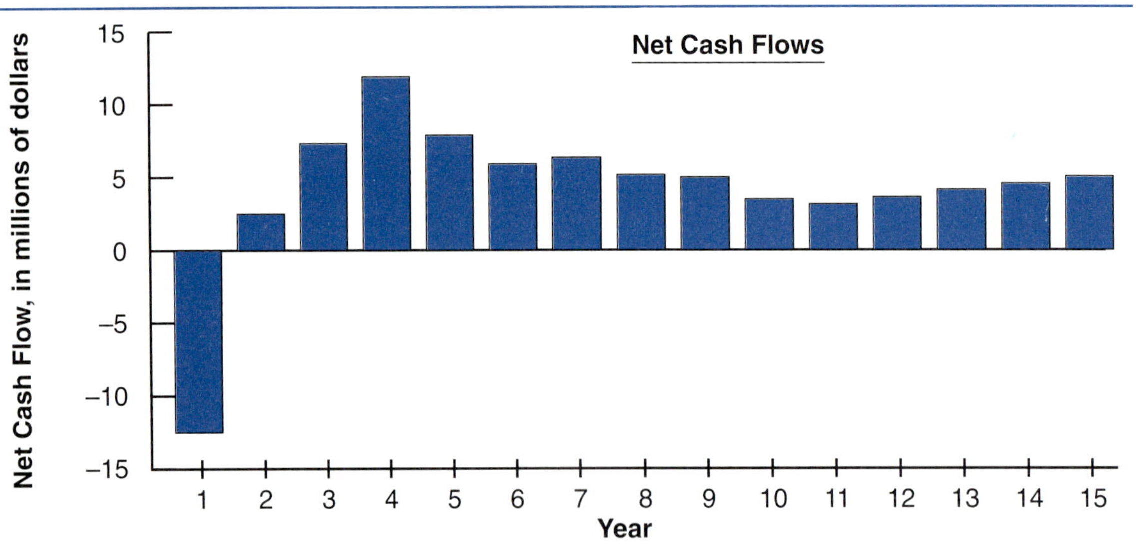

insurance operations. A net gain can consist of positive results from (1) investments, (2) insurance risks such as mortality or morbidity, and (3) expenses, as follows:

1. *The margin from investments.* To the extent that a company's investment returns remain positive, the insurer will realize a net gain from its investment activities.
2. *The margin on insurance risks.* To the extent that an insurer's actual experience with respect to claims and benefit payments is favorable, the insurer will realize a net gain from its insurance risks.
3. *The expense margin.* To the extent that an insurer's actual experience with respect to its operating expenses is favorable, the insurer will realize a net gain from its premium loading for operating expenses. Expense management is crucial because of the role it plays in contributing to product profitability.

You should note, of course, that a company's experience with investment returns, insurance risks, and expenses can also be unfavorable. In the case of unfavorable experience, the insurer would be forced to rely upon its capital and surplus to cover the amount of the unexpected loss.

Product profitability is a powerful component of overall profitability, solvency, liquidity, and general financial success for insurers. Well-designed financial products have to have a profit margin built in. Setting a new product's prices high enough to permit the company to realize a profit is sometimes referred to as *discipline in pricing.* The gains from well-designed products eventually lead to capital enhancement.

As we noted in Chapter 1, we can additionally relate these pricing components to an income statement form of worksheet. In an income statement format, expense items are subtracted from revenue items. The main revenue items considered for the purpose of finding the insurer's net income are (1) premium income and (2) net investment income. The main expense items taken into account for the purpose of finding the net gain (or loss) from operations include payments of contractual benefits, acquisition expenses, administrative expenses, and the like.

The following simplified balance sheet illustrates how a net gain from operations affects surplus on the balance sheet:

Balance Sheet	
Assets	**Liabilities**
Increase	No change
	Capital and Surplus
	Increase

FAST FACT

. . . while AIDS deaths in the 1980s were not sufficient in number to seriously affect the solvency of the life insurance industry, they did produce higher than expected mortality rates in some geographic regions and age categories, particularly for group insurance. These increased death rates, combined with generally declining interest rates in the early 1990s, made it much harder for life insurance companies to earn the profits anticipated.[3]

Another key to the profitability of insurance operations is for the insurer to have and follow a well-developed strategic plan. The strategic plan should ensure that the product portfolio is appropriate, and that the product strategies chosen are well matched to the insurance company's strategic strengths. If a company's business mix is not suited to the insurer's overall strategy, a good strategic plan might call for (1) entering new lines of business and/or (2) exiting old and unprofitable lines of business by selling the block of business. Any profit realized from selling an existing block of business at a profit would be a source of new capital. In addition, the existing capital that had been allocated to supporting the block of business would be freed for use in other opportunities.

Reducing Payments of Dividends to Stockholders

We discussed in an earlier chapter that insurers need capital for funding the payment of a fair investment return to the insurance company's stockholders. The business must pay the cost of employing the equity capital provided by stockholders. The likely consequences of not paying a fair return to stockholders would be a reduced stock price and a higher cost of capital. For their part, stockholders expect to obtain a fair return on their stock investment.

The return a company provides to stockholders can take the form of either dividend payments or increases in the stock price. Dividend payments provide a return in the form of current income. Increases in stock price provide a return in the form of a capital gain. The business organization can choose either (1) to pay out dividends or else (2) to retain the earnings, and reinvest them in the business in the expectation that the stock price will improve enough to fairly compensate the stockholders for the use of their capital.

Let's look at the balance sheet effects of paying cash dividends to stockholders. Dividends paid to stockholders are withdrawn from the unassigned surplus account, and dividend payments are recorded by a decrease in unassigned surplus along with a decrease in assets (cash). The following balance sheet model shows the balance sheet effects associated with a typical dividend payout transaction for dividends to common stockholders:

Balance Sheet	
Assets	**Liabilities**
Decrease	No change
	Capital and Surplus
	Decrease

Two ways for stock insurers to continue to hold some of the capital that they already have would be to (1) pay out as dividends a smaller-than-usual share of their current earnings or (2) reduce the growth rate of their dividend payments. When the company retains earnings to fund the company's growth, the action may be viewed as a reinvestment of the profits in the company. Retaining earnings can have a positive impact on stock price, and increases in stock price are satisfying to stockholders.

Retaining earnings would generally have a positive impact on stock price if the financial markets expect that the company can earn a higher return by reinvesting the earnings than the stockholders could earn by collecting dividends and then reinvesting the dividends on their own behalf. Thus, high-growth, high-earnings companies may pay small or no dividends.

However, not every decision to retain earnings is assured of a positive interpretation in the financial markets. A negative reaction in financial markets could produce a decrease in the insurer's stock price, and in such cases the withholding of a dividend would not necessarily bring about any lasting increase in capital and surplus.

The internal sources of capital discussed so far in this chapter are based on the most basic principles of business success: earning gains from effective sales and efficient administration of the business, and sometimes reinvesting those earnings in the business. These business fundamentals, however, are not the only internal sources of capital for insurers. The remaining internal sources are sometimes referred to as sources of hidden capital.

Uncovering Hidden Capital

Insurers face a complex set of regulations and other external restrictions on many fronts—from laws, insurance regulators, statutory accounting practices, and rating agencies. Sometimes, while working within these restrictions, insurers are able to reclassify assets or liabilities in a manner that increases the insurer's capital. *Hidden capital* appears when an insurance company in some manner increases reportable capital by recharacterizing assets or liabilities that it already possesses. Many, but not all, reasons for reclassifying so-called hidden capital represent good business practice. The validity of a given transaction depends upon the soundness of the business reasons for the transaction and upon the transaction's impact upon the business's future earning power. Three basic types of transactions often result in unlocking hidden capital:

1. Actions to change reserve valuations and thus to directly reduce—or *destrengthen*—the amount of policy reserve liabilities, thus in-

creasing surplus. So long as the original reserves were established on a conservative basis, and so long as experience is favorable relative to the assumptions employed in designing a product, actuaries are granted the professional discretion to change the original statutory reserve valuation on a block of business.

2. Environmental events that increase the market value of investments in common stock or other assets carried at market value would also increase the value of capital for insurance companies.

3. Transactions that increase the admitted value of existing assets would also increase the value of statutory surplus for U.S. insurance companies. Insurance companies often own assets for which the full value is not admitted on the statutory balance sheet. However, insurers can often take steps to qualify the value of nonadmitted assets as admitted on the statutory balance sheet. For example, cash is an admitted asset; if the value of a given noncash asset is nonadmitted and if an insurer can sell the nonadmitted asset for cash, then the cash obtained from selling the asset would be an admitted asset.

Our next topic of discussion is how a change in the amount of reserves affects capital and surplus. Whereas the variety of transactions that can result in changes in the admitted value of assets is broad, the concept behind the change in the amount of reserves is relatively straightforward. For that reason, we begin by considering the effect of a change in reserve valuation.

Change in Reserve Valuation

From Chapter 9 you should recall that, to some extent, insurers have discretion in the amount they establish as a reserve for any given contractual obligation. When the amount of a statutory policy reserve changes in response to a change in the basis for the reserve valuation, there is usually a related change in the insurer's statutory surplus. Policy reserves are a liability. Whenever a liability amount increases, the increase is generally matched by a corresponding decrease in the insurer's surplus. When a liability amount decreases, the decrease is generally matched by a corresponding increase in the insurer's surplus.

A ***reserve valuation*** can be defined for our present purpose as either (1) the process of establishing a value for an insurer's required policy reserves or (2) the value that is established by actuarial methods for an insurer's required policy reserves. To some extent, the methods of setting a statutory reserve valuation are prescribed by law. However, the prescribed reserve valuation methods allow for the professional discretion of actuaries to influence—to a limited extent—the amount of statutory reserves for U.S. insurers. Sometimes an insurance company's actuaries find a reason for making a correction in a reserve valuation. For example, actuaries might find that the valuation basis no longer reflects the insurer's direct experience with mortality, morbidity, or investments. A change in the reserve valuation could potentially result in either increasing or decreasing the amount of the reserve liabilities. In any event, though, the reserve valuation could not be diminished below the minimum levels prescribed by law. In many cases, an insurer must obtain approval from the appropriate state insurance commissioner before implementing a reduction in statutory reserves.

Whenever the reserve liability amount is increased, the action is termed ***reserve strengthening.*** An increase in reserve amounts because of a change in the reserve valuation basis produces a decrease in the insurer's surplus. When permissible, a decrease in the reserve liability for this reason produces an increase in the insurer's surplus. Whenever the reserve liability amount is decreased, the action is termed ***reserve destrengthening.*** As shown in the balance sheet model below, when policy reserves decrease and there is no accompanying change in asset values, then capital and surplus increase.

Balance Sheet	
Assets	**Liabilities**
No change	*Decrease in policy reserves*
	Capital and Surplus
	Increase

Increase in Valuation of Assets

In any environment, the values of some assets—for example, art or collectibles—are customarily determined on a subjective basis. In some cases, asset values are determined partly or wholly by expert opinion. Additionally, in the United States, asset values can be admitted or nonadmitted for statutory accounting purposes. Admitted and nonadmitted asset categories do not apply under Canadian accounting rules.

Logic tells us that an increase in an insurer's statutory capital and surplus would result from any transaction that increased the value of the insurer's existing assets. Likewise, reclassifying asset values from nonadmitted to admitted increases statutory capital and surplus. As shown in the balance sheet model below, when assets increase and there is no accompanying change in liabilities, then capital and surplus increase.

Balance Sheet	
Assets	**Liabilities**
Increase	No change
	Capital and Surplus
	Increase

For statutory accounting purposes, insurers could achieve higher admitted asset values by transactions that involve (1) converting partially nonadmitted assets to wholly admitted assets, (2) recording a higher book value for an admitted asset, or (3) recording an increase in the market value of assets that are carried on the books at market value.

Important examples of wholly nonadmitted assets for U.S. life and health insurers are the home office building, furniture, office equipment, stationery and office supplies, sales agents' balances due, and some receivables due from reinsurers. An insurer's capital and surplus balance would ordinarily *increase* upon a conversion of a nonadmitted asset to admitted status. When a nonadmitted asset is sold for cash, the transaction would be accounted for by a decrease in a nonadmitted asset, an increase in cash, and an increase in surplus. An example of converting a nonadmitted asset to an admitted asset arises when the insurer sells its office building or perhaps its computer equipment, whereupon the nonadmitted asset is replaced with cash, a fully admitted asset. As shown in the balance sheet model below, assets would increase as a result of the sale, there would be no accompanying change in liabilities, and capital and surplus would increase.

Balance Sheet (U.S. statutory only)	
Admitted Assets	**Liabilities**
Increase	No change
	Capital and Surplus
	Increase

Next we review some techniques for modifying the reportable values of assets so that reportable capital will be increased, although the basic economic condition of the insurance company will not automatically be improved. These techniques include sale-leaseback transactions, asset securitization, and reverse mergers.

Sale-Leaseback Transactions

Sale-leaseback transactions are a common and long-accepted means at the disposal of U.S. insurers for increasing reported capital without necessarily making any fundamental change in the risk-return profile of the business. A ***sale-leaseback transaction*** is a lease arrangement wherein the original owner of an asset—for example, a home office building or operating equipment—sells the asset to another party in exchange for cash; then, the asset's original owner leases the sold asset from the new owner. The original owner of the asset—in this case, the insurance company—retains uninterrupted use of the asset. For the purpose outlined here, the typical sale-leaseback transaction involves two steps:

1. A building owner sells a building for cash or other liquid assets.
2. The original owner of the building leases the building from its new owner.

Insurance companies have long participated in sale-leaseback transactions for a number of purposes, at some times acting as buyers and at other times acting as sellers in these transactions. For U.S. companies, a sale-leaseback transaction can produce the advantages of increasing reportable capital plus providing federal tax savings.

A sale-leaseback transaction can present drawbacks for the asset's original owner. For instance, the original owner's tax situation could be changed for the worse in that (1) any capital gain on the sale of the asset would be taxable and (2) any depreciation on the building would be a tax-deductible expense to an owner but would not carry a deduction for a lessee. Moreover, a lessee undertakes the new expense of paying a series of lease payments.

How Sale-Leaseback Transactions Improve Reportable Capital

Sale-leaseback transactions offer a most obvious benefit when applied to the insurer's office building or operating equipment. In statutory accounting, a home office building and home office operating equipment are treated as nonadmitted assets. Thus, for Annual Statement filings, the home office building ordinarily has no value, even though such an office building often in fact does have considerable market value. When the insurer undertakes a sale-leaseback of its office building, the first step of the process is to sell the building for cash or other liquid assets. Selling the office building for cash creates the effect of substituting an admitted asset—cash—in place of a nonadmitted asset—the office building. When the insurer undertakes a sale-leaseback of its office building, the second step of the process is to lease the premises for its business use, so that the insurer must make lease payments. In the United States, the leasing portion of the arrangement gives the insurer a distinct bonus for federal income tax purposes: any lease of premises or equipment for business operations is generally tax-deductible as a business expense.

Sale-Leaseback Example

The Onyx Insurance Group owns its home office building, worth $20 million. Onyx has entered into an agreement with Acreage Properties wherein Acreage Properties will purchase Onyx's home office building for a cash price of $20 million. Thus, Onyx will benefit by obtaining an increase of $20 million in admitted assets, and an increase of $20 million in capital and surplus. Onyx will not have to undergo the effort and expense of moving out of the building, because Onyx plans to retain use of the home office building and to lease it from Acreage Properties for a regular monthly payment. For Onyx, that monthly payment will be accompanied by a tax benefit in that the lease payment is a business expense, which Onyx will be able to deduct for federal income tax purposes. This income tax deduction will increase Onyx's net income for the year and thus will increase Onyx's contribution to surplus for the year. Figure 12-3 illustrates the transactions between Onyx and Acreage.

FAST FACT

Insurers at times have participated in sale-leaseback transactions from the other side of the transaction—as investors. An insurer might purchase commercial real estate from a developer and lease the property back to the developer. In this case, the real estate would likely be an admitted asset on the insurer's books, and statutory capital would be unaffected.

Creating Asset-Backed Securities

Life and health insurers have been able to improve their capital positions by creating asset-backed securities, an action sometimes known as *securitization.* In this context, ***securitization*** refers to the formation of a pool or portfolio of assets, often debt securities, and the subsequent creation of new securities representing shares in the portfolio. Whenever the new securities are secured by the values of other assets, the new securities are known as ***asset-backed securities.*** Ownership of the newly created securities represents ownership in the principal of and any returns from the pool of assets.

Here's how securitization works: suppose an insurer is holding assets (which could be partially or wholly nonadmitted for U.S. statutory purposes), often in the form of bonds, mortgages, receivables, or some other form of debt that other parties owe to the insurer.* The insurer can create a pool of these debt instruments or other assets, can issue securities based on shares in this pool, and can then sell these new shares to other investors. These shares give their investors a pro-rata portion of the principal plus any returns from the assets supporting the pool.

By creating asset-backed securities from assets an insurer already holds, the insurers can obtain benefits whether the insurer sells the new securities or continues to hold them. By *selling* the newly created securities, then from a U.S. statutory accounting viewpoint, the

* This is also done with real estate assets in the form of real estate investment trusts.

Figure 12-3. Illustration of a sale-leaseback transaction.

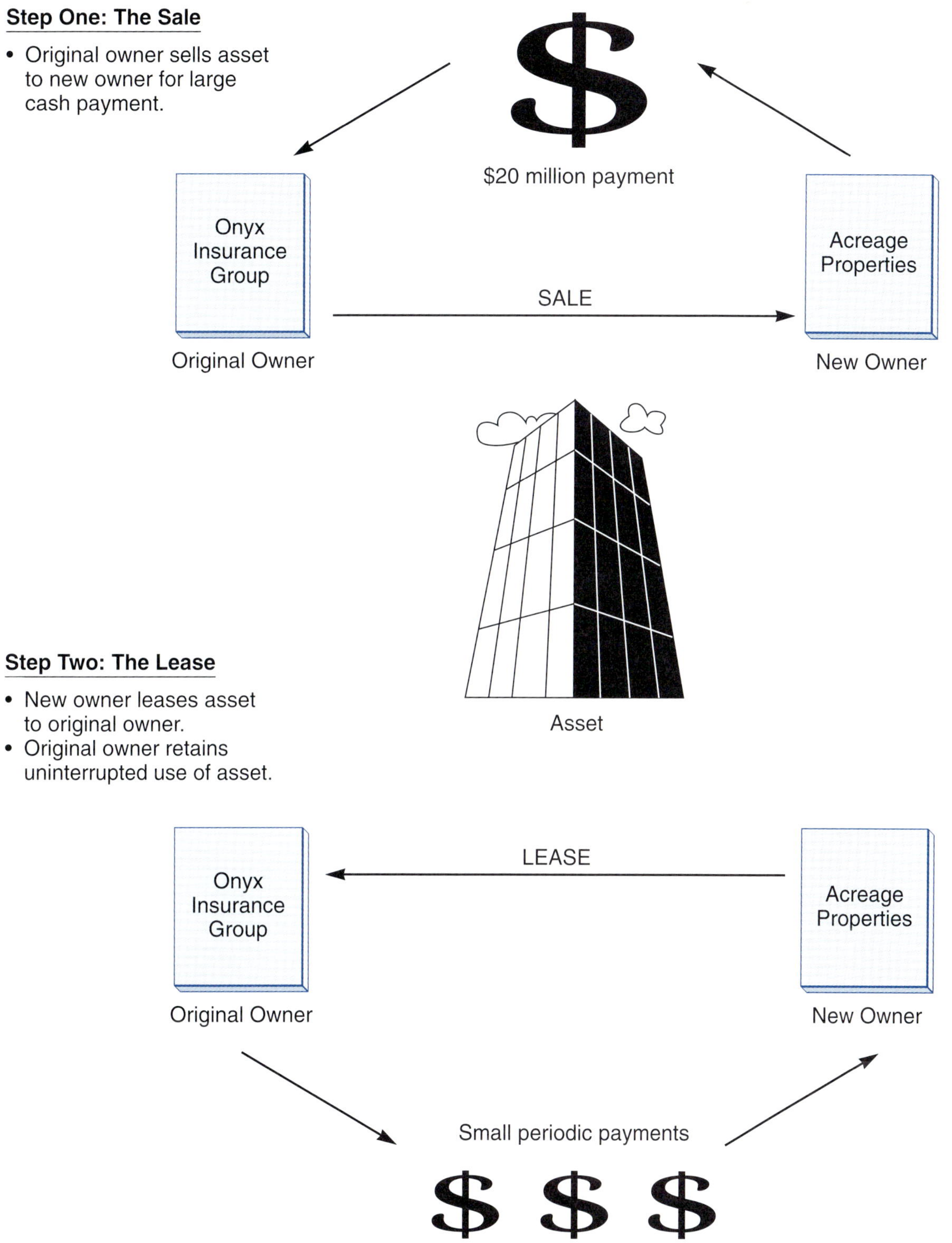

insurer can improve its liquidity and can exchange a nonadmitted or partially admitted asset for cash, a fully admitted asset. Instead of selling the asset-backed securities, the insurer might continue to hold them in its investment portfolio. If the insurer continues to *hold* the newly created securities, then the insurer can benefit because the admitted value of these new securities would in all likelihood be greater than the admitted value of the former securities. The admitted value of the new securities is greater than for the old (underlying) securities because the new securities are overcollateralized with respect to the underlying assets. In other words, the new issues are secured by better collateral.

Here's how an insurer can win by holding the new securities: for U.S. statutory reporting purposes, some assets are admitted, and some assets are not. Securitization can permit converting some of an insurer's assets from an asset classification wherein relatively less of the value is admitted—such as commercial real estate, commercial mortgages, or junk bonds—and into a classification of high-quality secured debt (bonds), wherein more of the asset's value is admitted. The establishment of these assets also permits the insurer to obtain cash by selling investments that were previously not marketable and whose value had fallen. If insurers value securitization for no other reason, they value it because it can reestablish the marketability of investments whose marketability had diminished.

Various insurers have applied forms of asset securitization to address several common problems that faced the insurance industry's investments, and thus its capital, in the early 1990s. For some insurers, these problems were

- Excessive investment in poorly performing junk bonds
- Excessive investment in poorly performing mortgages, particularly in mortgages on commercial real estate
- Excessive investment in overvalued commercial real estate

Poor performance of these asset categories was reflected in the assignment of a high NAIC risk-adjustment factor to these asset categories.

CMOs and CBOs

Two examples of asset-backed securities that a number of life insurers issued in the early 1990s were *collateralized mortgage obligations (CMOs)* and *collateralized bond obligations (CBOs).* Because these securities are founded upon other securities, CMOs and CBOs are sometimes classified as *pass-through* securities, *derivative* financial instruments, or *derivatives.*

In the insurance industry, one typical success story about securitization features the ***collateralized mortgage obligation (CMO).*** A

CMO can be defined as a type of bond that is secured by a pool of mortgages. The issuer of CMOs assembles a portfolio or pool of mortgages, divides the portfolio into maturity classes known as *tranches,* and then creates bonds within each of the tranches. The insurer then typically sells the newly created CMOs. Principal and interest on the bonds is secured by the principal and interest on the portfolio of mortgages. Because the supporting portfolio of mortgages is put up as security or collateral for the new CMO bonds, the bonds are said to be *collateralized.*

The resulting CMO securities are typically highly rated by independent bond rating agencies because the CMOs are secured by collateral having a value considerably greater than the principal and debt service promised by the CMOs themselves. When this condition applies, the CMOs are said to be *overcollateralized.*

For insurers, secured and highly rated debt instruments carry a much more desirable official RBC risk factor than do mortgages. Once mortgages are packaged as CMOs, even if the insurer continues to hold most of the CMOs in its portfolio, a far greater share of their value becomes admitted.

A second and similar pass-through security is the ***collateralized bond obligation (CBO).*** As the name suggests, CBOs are secured by a pool of *bond* investments. The bonds securing the CBO are often high-yield (junk) bonds. An issue of CBOs is divided, on the basis of quality—representing relative *likelihood of default*—into classes called *tiers.* The issuer of the CBO assembles a portfolio of bonds, divides the portfolio into *tiers,* and then typically sells the CBOs. (The insurer may instead choose to hold the new CBO bonds.)

The principal and interest for the new CBOs are secured by the principal and interest on the supporting portfolio of bonds. Because this portfolio of bonds serves as security or collateral for the new CBO bonds, the CBO bonds are said to be *collateralized.* In fact, because the face values of the junk bonds typically exceed the level of security needed to meet the insurer's obligations under the CBO bonds, the CBO bonds are said to be *overcollateralized.* Because the resulting CBOs are secured bonds, they are typically rated higher than the underlying junk bonds. For insurers in the United States, the better-rated secured class of bonds incurs a much lower, and thus better, RBC risk-adjustment factor than do junk bonds. In addition, CBOs secured by junk bonds are readily marketable, whereas the junk bonds themselves may not be.

Selling Agents' Debit Balances and Other Receivables

Most insurers with an agency force have an account receivable for ***debit balances.*** In this context, debit balances reflect amounts that the sales agents have collected from customers and now owe to the company. A ***receivable*** is a type of asset based upon an outside party's promise to pay cash to the holder of the receivable. The holder of a receivable can sell to a third party the right to the monies due. In exchange for obtaining immediate cash, the holder of the receivable in effect pays a fee by selling the receivable at a discount from its face amount.

Receivables for agents' debit balances are one type of receivable that is particular to insurers. These agents' debit balances are nonadmitted for U.S. statutory accounting purposes. Agents' debit balances can be sold at a discount in exchange for cash. The buyers of these receivables are sometimes a parent company or another affiliated company, sometimes banks or other financial institutions. By selling these receivables for cash, insurers can obtain an admitted asset and thus can raise capital. The balance sheet model below shows the U.S. statutory accounting effect of selling this nonadmitted asset for immediate cash, which is an admitted asset.

Balance Sheet (U.S. statutory)	
Admitted Assets	**Liabilities**
Increase	No change
	Capital and Surplus
	Increase

Selling Reinsurance Recoverables

A transaction similar to selling agents' debit balances is selling *amounts recoverable from reinsurers,* another form of receivable. ***Reinsurance recoverable*** is recorded in an account titled *amounts recoverable from reinsurers.* This receivable represents a balance that a reinsurer owes to the insurer. Insurance companies sometimes sell these balances in order to raise immediate cash. The buyers of these contracts sometimes are banks, a parent company, or an affiliate of the insurance company. These receivables (or recoverables) are sold for cash through a contract of agreement known as a ***receivables purchase agreement.*** The practice of selling reinsurance recoverables is far more prevalent in indemnity lines of insurance than in life and annuity lines of business.

Amounts recoverable from reinsurers are ordinarily an admitted asset. For U.S. statutory accounting purposes, the insurer obtains the benefit of replacing a nonadmitted asset with an admitted asset only if the reinsurance recoverable is a nonadmitted asset. If a reinsurer is not properly authorized to do business in a given jurisdiction, recoverables from that reinsurer are nonadmitted assets. Reinsurance recoverables that remain outstanding longer than the period during which they can qualify as admitted assets are also nonadmitted.

Thus, the benefit of replacing a nonadmitted asset with an admitted asset—and thus improving statutory capital—would be available in the case of amounts recoverable from *unauthorized* reinsurers or in the case of recoverables aged more than 90 days.

Selling Policy Loans and Business Operations

Insurers can sell virtually any asset in exchange for cash or other assets. Insurers sometimes sell to another party their policy loan balances due from policyholders. In addition, insurers sometimes sell an internal business operation such as their investment department, their information processing department, or their broker-dealer marketing operation. Often, a sale of an internal operation is accomplished by means of a ***spin-off,*** a transaction wherein an internal operation is "taken public." In a spin-off, the internal operation, such as the investment department, is legally incorporated as a separate business entity, and shares of its stock then are sold to the public for cash. The offering of the new company's stock for sale to the public is known as an ***initial public offering (IPO).*** In these cases, the new stock shares sold represent new capital. Either stock or mutual insurers may spin off an internal business operation in this manner.

Finally, it is worth mentioning here that insurers sometimes sell a product line, such as all of their disability income business, usually through a reinsurance transaction. Generally, the sale of a product line would benefit the insurer more by removing the burden of an uncertain package of future risks than by any actual cash proceeds or any profit on the sale.

Reverse Merger Transactions

Reverse merger transactions are another technique that some mutual insurers have used for unlocking hidden capital. A simple business ***merger*** is a transaction joining two business corporations. A ***reverse merger*** transaction is a complex merger procedure for spinning off a business operation and then reabsorbing the same business operation. A reverse merger transaction can be used for establishing a valid basis for permitting mutuals to take credit for the business operation's market value that would otherwise remain hidden by virtue of statutory accounting principles. The reverse merger technique has occasionally been applied by mutual insurers as a way of taking credit for asset appreciation in instances wherein assets have risen vastly in terms of market value, but not in terms of book value.

Statutory accounting requires carrying the majority of assets at their historical or book value, rather than at market value. Although stock insurers can take advantage of increases in market value by issuing stock to raise new capital, mutuals cannot do so. Reverse merger transactions are costly and somewhat complicated, but their expense may be justified if the resulting increase in surplus promises to be appropriately large. A procedure outlining one way to accomplish a reverse merger transaction follows:

1. The insurer begins by identifying an undervalued product line or an undervalued investment operation. The operation is *undervalued* in the sense that its statutory book value is lower than its hypothetical market value. The insurer would ordinarily apply a discounting technique to the operation's expected future cash flows in order to develop an estimated value of the business.

2. The insurer next creates a downstream stock subsidiary. (We define a downstream holding company in Chapter 19.)

3. In order to capitalize the new stock subsidiary, the insurer donates the undervalued product or investment operation to the new subsidiary. (Thus the new stock subsidiary represents a spin-off of the insurer's undervalued operation—the one the insurer identified in Step 1 above.)

4. The newly created subsidiary then merges with another unrelated company—a merger partner. The merger partner must be a public company with a publicly verifiable basis for its share price. The merger transaction may be accomplished by means of a stock swap, or by selling for cash a portion of the new subsidiary's stock to the merger partner. Briefly, a ***stock swap*** is a transaction wherein two companies exchange shares of stock. The result of a stock swap is that each company then owns a portion of the other.

5. If a stock swap is used, then the mutual's stock subsidiary exchanges its stock shares for publicly traded stock in the merger partner's company. This stock swap establishes the new basis for valuation: the value of the new subsidiary's stock can be expressed as a multiple of the value of the publicly traded stock.

6. For accounting purposes, the stock swap transaction sets a value for the shares of the mutual insurer's stock subsidiary. Assets previously valued at book value can be revalued on a more favorable basis. The insurer can then record the assets of this new subsidiary on the statutory books at a newly established and higher value. The insurer's admitted assets and capital and surplus would increase accordingly.

7. The amount of the increase in the parent company's capital and surplus is roughly the difference between the stock subsidiary's new market value and its old book value as an undervalued in-

ternal operation. For example, if the old business had a book value of $35 million, and the new shares had a market value of $75 million, the increase achievable in surplus would be, on a pre-tax basis, roughly equal to $40 million, the difference between $75 million and $35 million.

8. ***Transaction costs*** generally are the legal and administrative costs associated with planning and executing a financial exchange. For a reverse merger, the magnitude of the gain in reportable capital and surplus can be well worth the expense of substantial transaction costs.

Example of a Reverse Merger Transaction

Behemoth Mutual has an investment subsidiary with assets and cash flows having a net present value of $100 million. On Behemoth Mutual's books, the value of the subsidiary is recorded at $50 million. Behemoth Mutual undertakes a reverse merger transaction and swaps stock on a one-for-one basis with Acme Business Products, whose blue-chip shares are listed on the New York Stock Exchange (NYSE). The Acme stock exchanged has an established public market value of $100 million. Because the swap was executed on a one-for-one basis, the stock of the Behemoth Mutual subsidiary must also have a market value of $100 million.

This reverse merger transaction between Behemoth and Acme succeeds in creating an identifiable market value for the Behemoth assets. The gross pre-tax amount of the statutory surplus that Behemoth could stand to gain through this transaction is $50 million. In this example, the transaction costs necessary to accomplish the reverse merger would be on the order of $500,000 to $750,000.

Figure 12-4 illustrates the transaction between Behemoth and Acme.

In Conclusion

In Chapter 12, our focus has been on ways of strengthening an insurer's capital and surplus from managing the company's internal resources. Once the insurance company's financial management team has completed its capital planning processes, the company's financial plans must be implemented. Implementing a capital plan can mean raising new capital. In order to approach the topic of obtaining new capital financing, we reviewed the accounting basics associated with the statutory capital and surplus accounts. We reviewed the fundamental types of accounting transactions that would result in an increase to these accounts.

Figure 12-4. Illustration of a reverse merger.

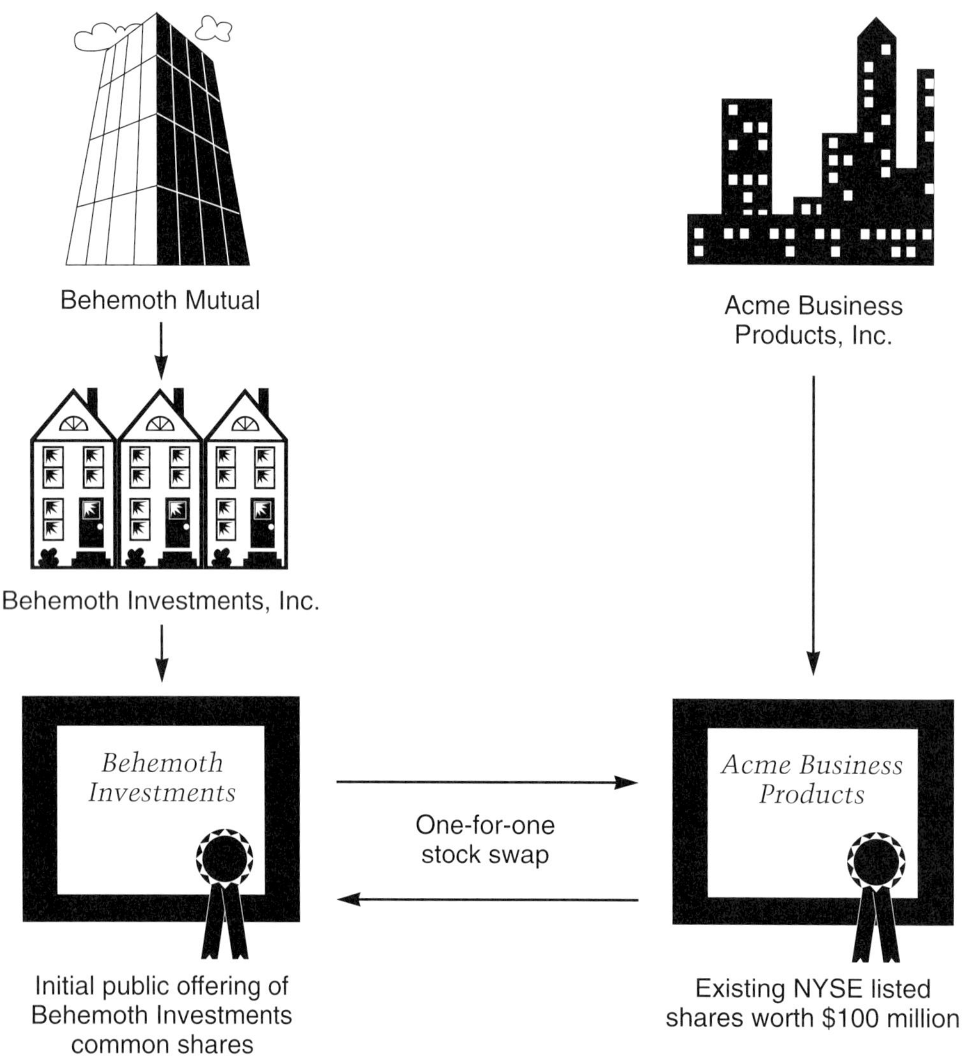

Within the broad category of internal sources of capital, we then reviewed a number of specific techniques for strengthening capital: maintaining profitable operations, selling investments to collect capital gains, converting nonadmitted assets to admitted assets, and repackaging lackluster investments by issuing asset-backed securities.

Implementing a capital plan can mean raising new capital. Now that we have seen how insurers can generate new capital internally, we will turn our attention to how insurers can strengthen capital using external sources. Chapter 13 will present a number of financial instruments (common stock, preferred stock, and surplus notes) that insurers can issue and thereby strengthen capital.

Key Terms and Concepts

uncovering hidden capital
financial engineering
financial reengineering
financial restructuring
reserve valuation
reserve strengthening
reserve destrengthening
sale-leaseback transaction
securitization
asset-backed securities
collateralized bond obligation (CBO)
collateralized mortgage obligation (CMO)
debit balances
receivable
receivables for agents' debit balances
reinsurance recoverable
receivables purchase agreement
spin-off
initial public offering (IPO)
merger
reverse merger
stock swap
transaction costs

References

1. *Life & Health Reinsurance: Pockets of Opportunity* (Hartford, CT: Conning & Company, 1995), p. 52.

2. *Life & Health Reinsurance: Pockets of Opportunity* (Hartford, CT: Conning & Company, 1995), pp. 24–25.

3. Edward E. Graves, editor, *McGill's Life Insurance,* (Bryn Mawr, PA: The American College, 1994), p. 424.

CHAPTER

Issuing Financial Instruments

13

LEARNING OBJECTIVES

After studying this chapter, you should be able to

- Identify the benefits and limitations of issuing various financial instruments in order to obtain capital
- Demonstrate understanding of the solvency-profitability tradeoffs of issuing common and preferred stock
- Contrast issuing common stock with issuing corporate bonds
- Demonstrate understanding of surplus notes and their uses

OUTLINE

When we discussed the capital management process in Chapter 11, we saw that insurers make plans for their capital development and then proceed to implement their capital plans. In order to implement its capital plan, an insurer must identify how it will obtain any needed capital. Recall that, for purposes of this discussion, we use the term *capital* in the broad sense of long-term funds so that it refers to the combination of capital and surplus.

In Chapter 12, we reviewed the internal sources that an insurance company may employ to increase its capital. Insurers also may take advantage of external sources for obtaining capital. When a corporation—insurance or noninsurance—needs to obtain long-term financing from external sources, the corporation typically considers the possibility of issuing financial instruments, such as stocks and bonds. Our focus in this chapter is to describe how insurers can increase their capital and surplus by issuing certain types of financial instruments.

The financial instruments that an insurance company issues depend greatly upon whether the company is a stock or a mutual insurer. Stock insurance companies, unlike mutual companies, are able to issue common stock and preferred stock. Although both stock and mutual insurers are able to issue bonds, insurance companies rarely issue bonds. In order to understand why insurers do not often issue bonds, you need to understand the difference between debt financing and equity financing. We begin our discussion with that topic. Then we describe the three primary financial instruments insurance companies use to increase their capital: (1) common stock, (2) preferred stock, and (3) surplus notes, which are a special type of financial instrument issued only by insurance companies.

Equity Financing versus Debt Financing

Equity financing is a process by which a corporation raises funds by issuing financial instruments—known as ***equity instruments***—that represent an ownership (equity) interest in the issuing corporation. Common and preferred stock are equity instruments; the stockholders own the issuing corporation. The shares of stock sold are classified as equities (capital and surplus) on the issuing company's balance sheet.

By contrast, secured bonds and unsecured bonds (debentures) are classified as ***debt instruments*** because they represent debts that the issuing corporation owes to the bondholders. Raising funds by issuing debt instruments is known as ***debt financing.*** The debt instruments are classified as liabilities on the issuing company's balance sheet.

For purposes of our discussion, it is important to note the distinction between equity financing and debt financing because equity financing is a source of capital whereas debt financing is a form of borrowing and is NOT a source of capital. We can demonstrate this point in basic terms by considering the accounting entries connected with issuing and selling common stock (an equity instrument)—and conventional long-term bonds (a debt instrument). When an insurance company issues and sells shares of common stock, the transaction is accounted for on the company's balance sheet as an increase to cash (an asset account) and an increase to the company's capital and surplus. The balance-sheet effects of issuing and selling common stock are illustrated in the following figure:

Balance Sheet 1	
Assets *Increase in cash from sale of common stock*	**Liabilities** No change **Capital and Surplus** *Increase*

When a corporation issues and sells bonds, the transaction is accounted for on the company's balance sheet as an increase to cash (an asset account) and an increase to bonds payable (a liability account). The balance-sheet effects of issuing and selling long-term bonds are illustrated in the following figure:

Balance Sheet 2	
Assets *Increase in cash from sale of bonds*	**Liabilities** *Increase in debt from issuance of bonds* **Capital and Surplus** No change

The examples show that, although bond issuances are a source of cash, bond issuances are not a source of equity capital. In addition, while proceeds from the sale of bonds improve the issuer's liquidity, the added liability can operate to the detriment of the issuer's solvency.

In the interest of maintaining a prudent balance of types of financing in their balance sheets, insurers avoid securing a great deal of long-term financing through conventional borrowing. As we noted in an earlier chapter, insurers have substantial long-term liability positions in the form of their contractual reserves. The contractual liabilities associated with insurance products have many characteristics of conventional debt financing. For example, life insurance and annuity reserves, like conventional debt, have long-term maturities and guaranteed principal amounts that the insurer must pay out in the future. As a result, insurance companies tend to avoid issuing bonds or other financial instruments that would increase their long-term debt obligations.

Common Stock

The general characteristics of common stock as a source of financing are the same for stock insurance companies as they are for any other stock corporation. Shares of a company's own common stock are classified as equity and represent a share of ownership in the company. For life and health insurers, sales of new shares of their own common stock directly increase the capital accounts. Increasing the balance of the capital accounts generally represents an improvement in the company's solvency position. However, the familiar risk-return tradeoff is always in effect. The issuer must hope that the costs associated with issuing stock and increasing the amount of stock in circulation will be more than offset by the benefit of substantial inflows of capital to fund the company's business activities. In order to illustrate the risk-return tradeoff, we first describe the costs involved in issuing securities and then describe how issuing common stock affects an insurance company's profitability.

Costs of Issuing Common Stock

In making an offering of securities, insurers typically incur a number of expenses, including the expense of using an investment banker. ***Investment banking companies*** are a type of financial intermediary whose business is to take new issues of securities to market. Frequently, the investment banking company purchases the securities from the issuing company at one price and then resells the securities to the public at another price. The expenses associated with issuing securities, including stock, are known as ***flotation costs.*** Flotation costs include costs of compliance with securities laws, fees paid to an investment banker, and internal administrative expenses. These costs reduce the net proceeds that the issuer receives from the sale of stock. For the issuer's U.S. federal income taxes, these flotation costs are the only tax-deductible business expenses associated with issuing common stock.

In addition, insurance companies that issue stock incur administrative costs associated with the need to maintain communication with stockholders, often through an *investor relations* function. In comparison to flotation costs, the amount of these administrative costs is relatively low.

Another potential cost of raising capital by issuing common stock relates to an effect described as market signaling. ***Market signaling*** is any action on the part of company insiders that informs participants in public financial markets about the level of management's overall confidence in the company. Researchers have found evidence that a company's stock price often decreases dramatically on the day the company makes a public announcement of a new stock issue. Moreover, a company's stock price often increases dramatically on the day the company announces a ***stock repurchase,*** a transaction whereby a company in effect invests in its own stock. The popular explanation for these effects is that, by issuing stock, the company's management is signaling to the financial markets a belief that its stock is overvalued in the market, plus a lack of confidence in the company's ability to service new debt. On the other hand, by repurchasing stock, management is publicly signaling confidence in the company's financial position. A stock repurchase signals that the company views its stock as a good investment.

The need to provide a financial return to shareholders is the main cost or limitation to having stock financing on the company's books. Although the cash collected from the sale of common stock does not have to be repaid to the purchasers of the stock, the stockholders do expect to obtain a return on their investments. Part of the return that an issuer of stock provides to stockholders takes the form of dividends on common stock. A ***dividend*** on common stock is a payment of a share of the company's profits to corporate shareholders. Dividends on common stock are paid only if the issuing corporation's board of directors declares the payment of dividends; the corporation has no legal obligation to pay dividends on common stock. To some extent, a dividend payment is supported by a company's financial well being. Most states impose ***capital impairment restrictions*** that prohibit stock companies from paying out as cash dividends any portion of the company's ***legal capital,*** which is often defined as the total par value of outstanding stock.

FAST FACT

For large public stock offerings, the total cost—administrative cost plus underwriting cost—ranges between 5 and 10 percent of the amount of funds raised. The total cost can rise as high as 20 percent or more on a small company common stock issue.[1]

For life insurers' U.S. statutory accounting purposes, dividends paid on common stock are deducted from the insurer's unassigned surplus and, thus, directly diminish unassigned surplus. Although the insurer must bear the cost of paying dividends on common stock, in the United States, dividend payments are not tax deductible to the insurer.

Figure 13-1. Example of dilution of earnings, Easton Assurance Company.

	Without new issue	With new issue	Differences resulting from the new issue
Total capital	$4,000,000.00	$4,400,000.00	+$400,000.00
Earnings	$ 440,000.00	$ 440,000.00	No change
Shares outstanding	125,000	160,000	+35,000 shares
Earnings per share	$ 3.52	$ 2.75	–$ 0.77
Return on capital	11%	10%	–1%

Effects of Common Stock on Profitability

Although issuing common stock typically increases an insurer's capital it also may reduce the company's profitability. When an insurance company increases its capital and surplus by issuing stock, the company must also increase the dollar amount of its earnings in order to maintain its current rate of return on capital. Likewise, when more shares of stock have a claim on the same amount of earnings, earnings per share are lowered. In relation to new issues of common stock, this effect is referred to as ***dilution of earnings.***

We can examine these effects on an insurer's profitability by means of the example illustrated in Figure 13-1. Suppose that the Easton Assurance Company's total earnings for the year ended in December were $440,000. At the beginning of the year, Easton had 125,000 shares of common stock outstanding. In October, Easton issued and sold 35,000 new shares of common stock, thus increasing the number of shares outstanding to 160,000. Easton's CEO, an Easton shareholder, is dismayed upon comparing Easton's actual earnings per share and return on capital to the numbers that could have been if the additional stock had not been sold. For Easton, the result of issuing the new shares was to reduce earnings per share from $3.52 to $2.75 and to reduce return on capital from 11 percent to 10 percent.

Preferred Stock

A second type of equity instrument that stock insurers sometimes issue is ***preferred stock.*** The general characteristics of preferred stock as a source of financing are the same for stock insurance companies as they are for any stock corporation and, in many ways, are the same as the characteristics of common stock. Proceeds from the sale of preferred stock increase the issuing corporation's capital and surplus accounts just as do proceeds from the sale of common stock. The balance-sheet effects of issuing preferred stock are illustrated in the following simplified balance-sheet figure:

Balance Sheet	
Assets	**Liabilities**
Increase in cash from sale of preferred stock	No change
	Capital and Surplus
	Increase

Preferred and common stock have many other similarities. Issuing either preferred or common stock requires the issuing corporation to pay flotation costs that reduce the corporation's net proceeds from the sale of stock. Owners of both preferred and common stock expect to obtain a return on their investments in the form of dividends. Dividends on common or preferred stock are payable only upon the approval of the issuing corporation's board of directors. The board may choose not to declare the payment of a scheduled dividend on preferred stock if the company's circumstances—such as extreme financial distress—warrant such a choice. Because preferred stocks are equity securities, a failure to make a scheduled payment of dividends on preferred stock is not construed as a default. Recall that issuers of debt instruments, such as bonds, are considered to have defaulted if they miss an interest payment. This is because debt instruments carry a legal obligation for the issuer to make interest payments. On the other hand, issuers of equity securities are not said to default on the securities if they fail to pay a dividend. Companies are not legally obligated to pay dividends on equity securities. In addition, dividend payments—whether paid on preferred or common stock—are not tax deductible to the issuing company. By contrast, in the United States, interest payments on debt are tax deductible.

Despite these similarities between preferred and common stock, preferred stock is sometimes referred to as a hybrid type of corporate security because it has some of the characteristics of debt instruments and some of the characteristics of equity instruments. Preferred stock differs from common stock—and is correspondingly similar to debt instruments—in two notable respects:

1. As with debt instruments, which have interest payment schedules, dividends on preferred stock have a set payment schedule. Unlike debt, preferred stock generally has no fixed maturity date.

2. Unlike dividend payments on common stock, dividend payments on preferred stock are characterized as ***fixed dividends***

because those payments are often fixed in both schedule and amount. The holders of preferred stock expect to be paid dividends on a set payment schedule. Usually, dividends on preferred stock are ***cumulative*** because unpaid dividends amass and must be paid in full before any dividends may be paid on the company's common stock. Recall, however, that a failure to pay preferred stock dividends is not construed as a default.

Figure 13-2 summarizes the similarities and differences between common stock, preferred stock, and corporate bonds from the issuer's perspective.

Because preferred stock has some characteristics of debt financing, life and health insurance companies tend to issue common stock more often than preferred stock. Nevertheless, many stock insurance companies do issue preferred stock.

Surplus Notes

The third type of financial instrument commonly issued by insurance companies is a hybrid instrument known as a surplus note. A

Figure 13-2. Comparison of common stock, preferred stock, and corporate bonds.

Common stock	Preferred stock	Corporate bonds
• Classified as equity or capital. • Proceeds increase capital. • Dividend payments diminish surplus directly. • Contributed capital is never repaid to the investor; to recover any of the investment, investors can sell shares. • Proceeds improve liquidity and solvency. • Dividend payments are NOT tax deductible. • Failure to pay dividends is NOT construed as a default; declaration of dividends is optional.	• Classified as equity or capital. • Proceeds increase capital. • Dividend payments diminish surplus directly. • Contributed capital may have to be repaid to investors, although this is rare. • Proceeds improve liquidity and solvency. • Dividend payments are NOT tax deductible. • Failure to pay dividends is NOT construed as a default.	• Classified as debt or liabilities. • Proceeds do NOT increase capital. • Interest and principal payments diminish earnings directly, surplus indirectly. • Proceeds must be repaid to the investor. • Proceeds improve liquidity, NOT solvency. • Interest payments are tax deductible. • Failure to pay interest or principal is construed as a default.

surplus note, or *surplus debenture,* is a special type of unsecured debt instrument that is issued only by insurance companies and that has characteristics of both traditional equity instruments and traditional debt instruments.

Surplus notes are issued with a fixed schedule of payments of principal and interest. Typically, the insurer is permitted to make scheduled payments of interest and principal on a surplus note only with the approval of the insurance commissioner in the insurer's state of domicile. Payment of claims on the insurer's product liabilities specifically takes priority over the disbursement of scheduled payments of interest and principal on surplus notes. In financial terminology, the surplus notes are thus said to be ***subordinated*** to the insurer's contractual liabilities. The insurance commissioner has a right to disallow disbursement of a scheduled principal or interest payment if the disbursement would harm the insurer's financial position. In contrast to the case of debt financing, though, the insurer's failure to make a payment to holders of surplus notes cannot be construed as an act of default. Thus, the surplus notes technically may never have to be repaid because they could be renewable indefinitely—a fact that has produced some controversy.

For statutory accounting purposes in the United States, a surplus note is treated as a part of surplus. In other words, for statutory reporting purposes the surplus note is treated as equity. In Canada and the United States, for tax purposes and for purposes of GAAP accounting, though, surplus notes are treated as debt instruments. These differing treatments under the three accounting systems can be summarized as follows:

Accounting system	Surplus notes are treated as . . .
Statutory	Equity capital
GAAP	Debt liabilities
Tax	Debt liabilities with deductible expenses

How does issuing surplus notes strengthen the insurer's statutory surplus account? The entire proceeds from surplus notes constitute new surplus. The proceeds from a sale of surplus notes are recorded by one entry that increases the issuing company's surplus account and another entry that increases the cash account. As illustrated in the following simplified statutory balance sheet, accounting entries to record the receipt of proceeds include an increase in cash and a corresponding increase in contributed surplus. There is no change in liabilities.

Balance Sheet	
Admitted Assets	**Liabilities**
Increase	No change
	Capital and Surplus
	Increase

The increase in surplus is an important benefit of issuing surplus notes, but its not the only benefit. As one bonus, an issuer includes the surplus notes' proceeds in its adjusted capital for the purposes of calculating the RBC (Risk-Based Capital) ratio requirement. In essence, the proceeds from surplus notes directly improve the issuer's RBC ratio. In contrast, issuance of traditional debt would weaken the issuer's RBC ratio. As yet another bonus, interest payments on surplus notes are tax deductible as a business expense, just as would be the interest on debt. Finally, the presence on an issuing company's balance sheet of the added capital from surplus notes is often—but within some limitations—viewed favorably by rating agencies. If the percentage of capital attributable to surplus notes is within any maximum guidelines imposed by the rating agencies, issuing surplus notes would be likely to enhance an insurer's claims-paying rating if the rating agency analysts were suitably impressed. However, one rating agency limits the percentage of total capital from surplus notes that it will acknowledge.

Between March 1993 and March 1994, the 11 large and already financially strong insurers named in Figure 13-3 issued surplus notes worth $3.337 billion.[2] A number of large mutual insurers, and also

Figure 13-3. Issuers of surplus notes, 1993–94.

- General American Life
- John Hancock Mutual Life
- Mass Mutual
- Metropolitan Life
- National Life of Vermont
- Nationwide Mutual
- New England Mutual
- New York Life
- Pacific Mutual Life
- Principal Mutual Life
- Prudential

some stock insurers, issued surplus notes during the initial application of the risk-based capital (RBC) rules in the United States during the early 1990s. In issuing surplus notes, these companies were generally motivated by an interest in improving their surplus positions in order to present a better financial profile with respect to the RBC rules.

Upon the institution of the RBC rules, insurers regarded the issuance of surplus notes as an attractive option for the purpose of raising additional capital. Until the application of the RBC rules in 1993, however, insurers commonly issued surplus notes for only a few limited purposes. These purposes historically included the following:

1. To provide the initial capitalization of a mutual insurance company
2. To finance in part the issuer's purchase of another insurance company
3. To improve a troubled financial position

Surplus Notes Compared to Debt and Equity Financing

Although a mutual insurer cannot issue traditional stock and does not usually issue conventional bonds, the option to issue surplus notes provides the mutual insurer with the most appealing features of the traditional debt and equity financial instruments. Even though stock companies have the options of issuing stock or bonds rather than surplus notes, surplus notes are uniquely attractive. The advantages of surplus notes over traditional bonds arise from the hybrid nature of the surplus notes. Surplus notes are said to have a hybrid nature because they offer the issuer some of the advantages of both debt (bond) and equity (stock) issues.

As we have already noted, one attractive feature of ordinary debt issues is that, in the United States, the issuer's interest payments on a debt issue are deductible for federal income tax purposes. Likewise, interest payments on surplus notes are deductible for federal income tax purposes. Ordinary equity financing by issuing stock appeals to prospective issuers because a stock issue directly increases the issuer's capital or surplus. For most purposes where capitalization is a matter of concern—for instance, minimum capitalization requirements and quality ratings—the proceeds of a surplus note count as surplus, a type of equity. The points of comparison between common stock and surplus notes are summarized in Figure 13-4.

Issuing surplus notes is an attractive but limited option for raising needed capital. The advantageous treatment of surplus notes arises from the insurance regulatory environment. However, the regulatory environment is subject to ongoing change and is beyond the

Figure 13-4. Features of raising capital through surplus notes and common stock.

Surplus notes

- Classified as debt in GAAP treatment, as equity in statutory treatment.
- Proceeds increase capital and surplus for statutory purposes.
- Interest payments diminish *earnings* directly, capital and surplus indirectly.
- Principal amount is not necessarily repaid to the investor.
- Proceeds improve liquidity and solvency.
- Interest payments are tax deductible.
- Failure to pay interest or principal is not construed as a default.
- Payment of interest is subject to regulatory approval.
- Both stock and mutual insurers can issue surplus notes.

Common stock

- Classified for accounting purposes as equity (capital).
- Proceeds increase capital and surplus.
- Dividend payments diminish *capital* and surplus directly.
- Contributed capital is not repaid to the investor; to recover any invested funds, the investor must sell the stock.
- Proceeds improve liquidity and solvency.
- Dividend payments are NOT tax deductible in the United States.
- Failure to pay dividends is not construed as a default.
- Declaration of dividends is optional to the board.
- Stock insurers can issue stock; mutual insurers cannot.

direct control of insurers themselves. Insurance regulators, accountants, and tax authorities could act at any time and on relatively short notice to change the favorable regulatory treatment of surplus notes.

In Conclusion

Implementing a capital plan can mean raising new capital. We know that insurers can generate new capital internally, or they can attract capital infusions from external sources. Chapter 13 presented a number of financial instruments that insurers can issue and thereby strengthen capital: common stock, preferred stock, and surplus notes—a special type of obligation issued only by insurers. We also learned why life and health insurers do not issue bonds to strengthen capital and why life and health insurers do not typically issue conventional corporate bonds.

Our discussion of ways of obtaining capital infusions from external sources continues in Chapters 14 and 15. Chapter 14 is devoted to discussing the financial benefits that life and health insurers can derive by participating in reinsurance transactions. Then, Chapter 15 presents an overview of mergers, acquisitions, and demutualization for life and health insurance companies.

Key Terms and Concepts

equity financing
equity instruments
debt instruments
debt financing
investment banking company
flotation costs
market signaling
stock repurchase
dividend
capital impairment restrictions
legal capital
dilution of earnings
preferred stock
fixed dividends
cumulative (dividends)
surplus note
subordinated

References

1. Lawrence J. Gitman, *Principles of Managerial Finance,* Seventh Edition (HarperCollins, 1994), p. 533.

2. Arthur Fliegelman, CFA, *Surplus Notes: Prospects and Uncertainties* (Salomon Brothers, July 26), 1994.

CHAPTER

Uses of Reinsurance

14

LEARNING OBJECTIVES

After studying this chapter, you should be able to

- Distinguish between assumption reinsurance and indemnity reinsurance
- Demonstrate understanding of surplus strain and surplus relief from reinsurance
- Interpret some issues regarding regulation and taxation that affect reinsurance in the United States
- Contrast the effects of an insurer ceding traditional indemnity reinsurance versus issuing surplus notes or stock

OUTLINE

To many, reinsurance is a mysterious and obscure realm of the insurance industry. ***Reinsurance*** can be viewed as insurance on insurance policies; as such, it is an important tool for both risk management and financial management. With regard to risk management, reinsurance can protect an insurer against the insurance risks it has assumed—that is, against the possibility that its products will not perform as well as expected. With regard to financial management, reinsurance can enable an insurer to manage its statutory earnings and surplus in any given year and, thus, can strongly impact profitability and solvency.

As this chapter describes, the uses of reinsurance are varied and are not limited to financial management. Reinsurance virtually always helps to stabilize financial risks and also can provide a variety of other benefits. For example, a single reinsurance agreement can enable an insurer to launch a chosen marketing strategy, limit its insurance risk, and obtain external capital.

Before we see the effects of reinsurance, we review some reinsurance basics. We identify the parties to a reinsurance transaction and describe the various types of reinsurance agreements. Then we cover the financial applications of reinsurance transactions for primary insurers. Later, our discussion compares indemnity reinsurance to an insurer's potential external sources of capital. Then, we describe two other important uses of reinsurance: (1) to achieve market objectives and (2) to manage underwriting capacity and business volumes. Chapter 14 concludes by briefly covering how reinsurance is regulated in the United States.

Introduction to Life and Health Reinsurance

The reinsurance mechanism serves to redistribute risks among insurers and, thus, is crucial to the smooth functioning of the insurance markets. Reinsurance activity in the aggregate can be viewed as a wholesale or secondary market for insurance, with the retail market for insurance constituting the retail or primary insurance market. Some companies specialize in the reinsurance market and are known as ***professional reinsurers.*** Other insurance companies participate in both the primary insurance market and the secondary reinsurance market. An insurance company that provides reinsurance to a reinsurer is known as a ***retrocessionaire.*** As illustrated in Figure 14-1, the chain of risk transfers involving insurance and reinsurance can be arranged so that a consumer buys risk protection

Figure 14-1. Chain of participants in a reinsurance transaction.

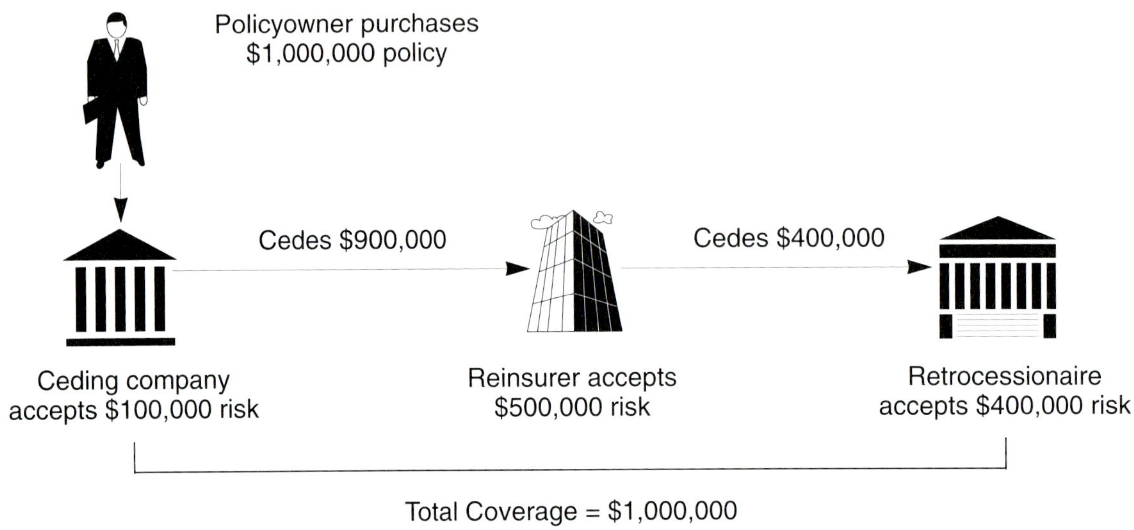

from a retail insurance company; the retail insurer buys risk protection from a reinsurer; and the reinsurer buys risk protection from one or more retrocessionaires. An insurance company may assume any or all of these roles. For example, one insurance company may assume the role of the primary (or retail) insurer in some transactions and also may act as a reinsurer or retrocessionaire in other transactions.

Typically, a reinsurance agreement is formed by two parties—the *ceding company* and the *assuming company.** The company that transfers risk to another company is called the ***ceding company,*** the *primary insurer,* or the *direct writing company.* From the ceding company's viewpoint, the transfer of risk is a transaction known as a ***cession.*** The company that reinsures risk on contracts issued by another insurance company is termed the ***assuming company*** or the *reinsurer.* From the assuming company's viewpoint, the transfer or acceptance of risk is a transaction known as an ***assumption.*****

A Typical Life Reinsurance Transaction

In order to introduce some concepts and basic terminology of the reinsurance business, let's consider a typical reinsurance transaction

* In indemnity reinsurance, only the insurers are parties to the contract. In assumption reinsurance, the policyholder may also be a party to a reinsurance agreement.

** This application of the term *assumption* in opposition to the term *cession* is not to be confused with the distinction between *assumption reinsurance* and *indemnity reinsurance.*

connected with a large life insurance policy. The cast of characters in this case study includes a life insurance consumer, Mr. Dexter Alcott, the Neptune Insurance Company, and Atlas Reinsurance.

Mr. Alcott applied for a $3 million whole life policy from the Neptune Insurance Company.[1] Very few insurance companies are large enough to issue a $3 million life policy without reinsurance, and Neptune was no exception. In the event of Mr. Alcott's early death, the $3 million benefit payment would have seriously weakened Neptune's financial condition.

Long before Mr. Alcott's purchase, however, Neptune Insurance had entered into a contractual agreement for Atlas Reinsurance Company to reinsure part of the mortality risk of very large policies. Such a contract for reinsurance is known as a ***reinsurance treaty.*** This treaty contained two typical provisions setting lower and upper limits upon the amounts of the risks to be reinsured. Under one such provision, known as a ***scheduled retention limit,*** Neptune agreed that whenever it issued life insurance in an amount of at least $50,000, Neptune would reinsure with Atlas Re the amount greater than $50,000. Thus, in this example, $50,000 is Neptune's *scheduled retention limit.*

By means of another provision known as an ***automatic binding limit,*** the reinsurance treaty also limited the maximum amount that Neptune could automatically cede to Atlas Re on any one policy. This treaty set this maximum at four times the amount that Neptune retained on the policy—in other words, four times $50,000, which amounts to $200,000. For a policy amount of $250,000 or less, the reinsurance treaty permitted Neptune to automatically cede the entire amount above its retention limit ($200,000). Any such automatic cession is a type of ***automatic reinsurance,*** because Atlas Re agreed to automatically accept the risk upon Neptune's issuance of a policy.

FAST FACT

During 1993, reinsurers assumed a face amount of $19 trillion of ordinary life insurance—24 percent of the total in force. In 1993, $18 billion in life insurance premiums were ceded between nonaffiliated companies, as compared to $16 billion in property/casualty premiums.[2]

However, Mr. Alcott's policy amount exceeded the automatic binding limit. In this situation, the reinsurance treaty required Neptune to submit the application and all pertinent underwriting documentation to the reinsurer. Atlas Re could then independently make underwriting decisions about (1) whether to approve the case as a standard risk and (2) whether to assume the major part of the risk. A reinsurance treaty giving the reinsurer the option of accepting or declining a risk based on its own underwriting evaluation is classified as ***facultative reinsurance.*** Because Mr. Alcott's policy was subject to an independent underwriting decision by the reinsurance company, it was reinsured under a facultative and not an automatic reinsurance arrangement.

In our example, when the underwriting documentation reached Neptune Life's underwriter, she classified Mr. Alcott as a standard mortality risk and also provided the underwriting documentation to Atlas Re. Because the proposed amount of insurance exceeded the reinsurance treaty's automatic binding limit, the underwriter also officially informed Atlas Re that Neptune was prepared to assume $50,000 of the risk. She asked Atlas Re to cover the remaining $2,950,000 of the risk.

Atlas Re's underwriters decided not to retain the entire $2,950,000 risk, and so they passed along, or ***retroceded,*** a portion of the risk to other reinsurers, who in this situation were acting as retrocessionaires. Only after Atlas Re notified Neptune that reinsurance coverage for the remaining $2,950,000 had been arranged at a standard rating did Neptune's underwriter give approval for issuing the policy. Atlas Re provided Neptune with administrative data on the policy. The form containing this data is the reinsurance ***cession.***

In this example, as with many reinsurance situations, the chosen method of premium payment for the shared risk was the ***yearly renewable term (YRT) reinsurance method.*** According to this method, on the anniversary date of each policy reinsured, Neptune was required to pay Atlas Re a one-year term premium in an amount based on the amount reinsured. Thus, for Mr. Alcott's policy, Neptune paid Atlas Re a premium for the amount reinsured. The amount of that premium was calculated as if for one-year term life insurance, even though Mr. Alcott had a whole life policy. Whereas reinsurance premiums are typically remitted monthly, the amount of the premiums is calculated for a period of one year in advance.

Upon Mr. Alcott's death, Atlas Re collected from its retrocessionaires the amounts that they had reinsured for his policy. Atlas in turn paid Neptune the total amount of the death benefit that was reinsured. Then, Neptune paid the beneficiary the full amount due. The insured and the beneficiary were never aware that a reinsurance situation existed, nor did they need to know. By using reinsurance, the Neptune Insurance Company was able to issue a single policy large enough to cover Mr. Alcott's insurance needs.

Types of Reinsurance Agreements

Reinsurance is offered under a variety of arrangements, and every reinsurance arrangement can be classified as either an *assumption reinsurance agreement* or an *indemnity reinsurance agreement.* The distinction between these two broad classifications depends on whether the purpose of the reinsurance is to effect a permanent transfer or a temporary transfer of all or part of the various risks and income associated with a specified block of insurance business. Unlike assumption reinsurance agreements, indemnity reinsurance agreements typically specify a *recapture* procedure to be followed in order to transfer the reinsured business back to the issuing company. Let's look at these two broad classifications of reinsurance agreements.

Assumption Reinsurance

The broad type of reinsurance employed to effect a complete, permanent, and total transfer of in-force business—not newly written business—is ***assumption reinsurance.*** Under an assumption reinsurance agreement, the ceding company makes no provision for recapturing the ceded business. As a result, assumption reinsurance can be viewed as the reinsurer's purchase of the business ceded. Once business is ceded, the reinsurance agreement is completed and the parties have no further contractual obligations under the agreement.

In assumption reinsurance, the original carrier's obligations under the ceded insurance contracts are generally fully extinguished; the assuming company becomes totally and directly liable to all policyholders. The assuming company becomes a direct party to the insurance contracts that were ceded and is said to "stand in the place" of the original carrier. The assuming company must issue new insurance certificates, known as ***assumption certificates,*** to all policyholders, thus indicating that the assuming company has assumed all of the risk under the policies.

Assumption reinsurance transactions, which must be approved by the state insurance department, are the most common method of buying and selling blocks of insurance business. Assumption reinsurance transactions can be used to effect the sale of an entire insurance company. Assumption reinsurance transactions permit licensed insurers to *exit* a line of business rather easily by ceding or transferring an entire line of business to a reinsurer. Assumption reinsurance transactions also permit licensed insurers to *enter* a new line of business rather easily by assuming or reinsuring an entire line of business from another insurer. (Chapter 19 presents more information about the use of assumption reinsurance in merger transactions.) Also, the financial distress of a ceding company can lead to a total reinsurance assumption of the company's in-force business.

Indemnity Reinsurance

Indemnity reinsurance is the broad type of reinsurance employed to effect a usually partial transfer of business and to form a basis for sharing the risks of the insurance business—whether insurance or financial risks. In contrast to assumption reinsurance agreements, indemnity reinsurance agreements create an ongoing contractual relationship between the parties to the agreement. While an agreement is in effect and business is reinsured, the ceding company pays periodic ***reinsurance premiums*** to the assuming company. In exchange, the reinsurer agrees to reimburse the ceding company for some stated portion of claims that are incurred under the reinsured business. Under some types of agreements, the reinsurer also reimburses the ceding company for surrender values, taxes, commissions, and other reimbursable expenses. As we mentioned earlier, indemnity reinsurance agreements—unlike assumption reinsurance agreements—typically contain a *recapture provision* that allows the ceding company to take back the reinsured business. A ***recapture provision*** is a contractual clause specifying a procedure that would allow the ceding company to end the reinsurance arrangement on a given block of reinsured business.

The parties to a reinsurance agreement have a great deal of flexibility in negotiating the terms of their agreement. As a result, reinsurance contracts may contain a variety of terms. For example, some types of reinsurance agreements provide for the reinsurer to pay commissions, known as either *reinsurance commissions, expense allowances,* or *ceding commissions,* to the ceding company. A ***reinsurance (ceding) commission*** can be defined as an allowance that the reinsurer grants to the ceding company and that is intended to cover part or all of the ceding company's acquisition costs and other costs related to the reinsured business. The reinsurance commission is usually calculated as a percentage of the reinsurance premium paid and reduces the amount of the reinsurance premium the ceding company must pay. In some reinsurance coverages, the reinsurance or ceding commission may also include a profit factor for the ceding company.[3] This profit factor is equal to any excess of the reinsurance commission over the actual costs the ceding company incurred in originating the business.

There are three basic types of indemnity reinsurance agreements: traditional indemnity reinsurance, nontraditional financial reinsurance, and joint ventures. In this chapter, references to indemnity reinsurance generally include all three types of indemnity reinsurance.

Traditional Indemnity Reinsurance

Traditional indemnity reinsurance is used to effect a partial and permanent, but recapturable, transfer of newly written business—not in-force business. Under a traditional indemnity reinsurance agreement, the ceding company underwrites and issues insurance contracts, which are then reinsured. The ceding company administers the insurance contracts and remains a party to those contracts. Thus, the ceding company remains liable for paying all incurred claims on the reinsured portion of the business, but will be reimbursed for all or part of those claims by the reinsurer. Typically, the reinsurer is responsible for establishing and maintaining the reserves for the reinsured portion of the business. However, the ceding company retains responsibility for maintaining reserves for the retained portion of the business. As we describe later in the chapter, this shifting of responsibility for reserves from the ceding company to the reinsurer can greatly benefit the ceding company.

Many different plans of traditional indemnity reinsurance are available for life, health, and annuity lines of business. Typically, insurance companies use traditional indemnity reinsurance to enable them to share their insurance risk and financial risk with a reinsurer. For example, most insurers establish a ***retention limit,*** which is a stated maximum amount of insurance that the company will assume on any one risk. Any amounts that exceed the retention limit are reinsured. An insurer is using reinsurance to share insurance risk if the insurer sets a retention limit and reinsures amounts exceeding that limit. Later in the chapter, we describe how insurers also use reinsurance to share financial risk.

Nontraditional Financial Reinsurance

Nontraditional financial reinsurance is employed to effect a partial and *temporary* transfer of in-force business—not newly written business. Although financial reinsurance involves a transfer of insurance risk, the primary purpose of financial reinsurance is to allow the ceding company to adjust the timing of its expenses and profits, and not to transfer insurance risk. By adjusting the timing of expenses and profits, insurers are able to obtain surplus relief and to manage their tax burden. The role of reinsurance in surplus relief and tax management is discussed later in this chapter. In many other respects, financial reinsurance agreements resemble traditional indemnity reinsurance agreements.

Reinsurance Joint Ventures

In general, a ***joint venture*** is a type of partnership arrangement between two otherwise independent businesses, providing for the two businesses to undertake a specific project for a specified time period. A venture involving more than two businesses is called a ***consortium.*** Insurers sometimes enter into a joint venture and include reinsurance as a part of the arrangement. Reinsurance joint ventures typically are employed to effect a permanent, but recapturable, transfer of newly written business.

Although reinsurance joint ventures typically employ indemnity reinsurance coverage, these partnerships are entered into for marketing purposes rather than for the purpose of transferring insurance or financial risk. In reinsurance joint ventures, unlike in traditional indemnity reinsurance, the underwriting and administrative burdens associated with the ceded business may be transferred to the reinsurer. We will describe in more detail how insurers use reinsurance—particularly reinsurance joint ventures—to achieve market objectives.

Now that we have examined the major classifications of reinsurance coverages, we can see how they relate to each other. Figure 14-2 illustrates the contrasting features of the various broad classifications of life, health, and annuity reinsurance.

Figure 14-2. Classifications of reinsurance.

	Assumption Reinsurance	Indemnity Reinsurance		
		Traditional indemnity reinsurance	Financial reinsurance	Reinsurance joint ventures
Is the arrangement temporary or permanent?	Permanent; no recapture provision	Permanent, but the issuer has the right to recapture the business	Temporary, and the issuer has the right to recapture the business	Permanent, but the issuer has the right to recapture the business
Is the reinsurer a party to the primary contract?	The reinsurer becomes a party to the primary insurance contract	The reinsurer never becomes a party to the primary insurance contract	The reinsurer never becomes a party to the primary insurance contract	The reinsurer never becomes a party to the primary insurance contract
New or in-force business?	In-force business	New business	Usually in-force business	New business
Main purposes?	Total risk transfer	Risk sharing	Shifting expense and profit	Marketing
Who administers the contracts?	The reinsurer	The primary insurer	The primary insurer	The reinsurer, usually

The Variety of Uses for Reinsurance

As we just described, the type of reinsurance agreement that an insurance company enters into typically depends on the business purpose that the insurer hopes to achieve. In addition, a decision to cede or assume reinsurance is accompanied by a predictable set of marketing, tax, accounting, and administrative effects that can enable insurers to achieve a number of business purposes. We can view the uses of reinsurance as addressing the concerns of each of an insurance operation's three main functional areas: marketing, insurance administration, and finance. Note, however, that the specific impact of any given reinsurance transaction depends in part upon whether the transaction is seen from the viewpoint of the ceding company or the assuming company.

We describe three broad categories of strategic business purposes for reinsurance, including financial management objectives, marketing objectives, and insurance administration objectives. Because our focus in this section of the text is on capital and surplus management, we begin by describing how insurers use reinsurance to manage their financial capacity. Figure 14-3 summarizes the strategic business purposes that we describe in this chapter.

Figure 14-3. Business objectives achievable through reinsurance transactions.

Objectives	By ceding reinsurance, an insurer can	By assuming reinsurance, an insurer can
1. Managing capital and surplus	• Relieve surplus strain by transferring liabilities or obtaining assets	• Employ excess financial capacity by transferring assets or accepting liabilities
2. Managing reserves	• Decrease reserves allocated to any given block of business	• Increase total reserves
3. Managing taxes	• Manage timing of income and expenses reporting • Manage insurer's tax filing status	• Manage timing of income and expenses reporting • Manage insurer's tax filing status
4. Implementing market strategies	• Exit a current market • Reduce presence in a current market	• Enter a new market • Increase presence in a current market
5. Managing underwriting capacity	• Relieve strain on internal underwriting capacity • Outsource underwriting to other insurers	• Employ excess underwriting capacity • "In-source" underwriting for other insurers
6. Gaining expertise in a new line of business	• Gain access to expert underwriting advice from reinsurers by ceding business in an unfamiliar line	• Gain underwriting experience by reinsuring business in an unfamiliar line

Using Reinsurance to Manage Financial Capacity

Financial capacity relates to the strength of an insurer's financial resources—its capital and surplus—to issue new business. The basic problem of financial capacity is one of capital and surplus management—that is, an insurer can have either *too little* capital and surplus relative to its insurance obligations, or it can have *too much.* To some degree, having too little capital presents a solvency problem, whereas having too much capital represents a profitability or an efficiency problem. (We discussed this latter problem near the end of Chapter 10.)

The Challenge: Surplus Strain

When an insurer issues new insurance contracts, it incurs acquisition expenses and moreover must establish new reserves for those contracts. As a result, issuing new business decreases the insurer's capital and surplus. This effect is commonly called *new business strain* or *surplus strain.* The strain arises partly because of U.S. statutory accounting principles, which require using cash-basis accounting for acquisition expenses for new business. Under cash-basis accounting, all acquisition expenses are allocated to the year in which the insurance contract is issued. However, the insurance company records premium revenue from an insurance contract for only one year of coverage at a time. Thus, in statutory accounting, all of the acquisition expenses for the life of the policy can be offset by the revenue for only the first policy year. In addition to covering acquisition expenses, insurers must establish a reserve for every new policy—even though the first-year revenue from the policy is typically insufficient to cover even the acquisition expenses. Taken in isolation from the rest of a company's operations, these difficulties of issuing new insurance contracts result in surplus strain.

When a company's financial capacity diminishes, the company might decide to adjust its underwriting practices so as to take on less risk. Two actions underwriters can take to reduce the amount of risk they accept are (1) to toughen the insurer's underwriting standards so as to reject some riskier applications that formerly would have been approved and (2) to lower the insurer's retention limit so that a greater portion of each risk is passed along to a reinsurer. In real terms, reduced financial capacity would require the insurance company's underwriting staff to take action to accept a smaller total amount of risk than the insurer would previously have accepted.

Addressing Surplus Strain: Surplus Relief

Any action that an insurer takes to relieve the effects of surplus strain is referred to as seeking ***surplus relief.*** In the United States, traditional indemnity reinsurance has historically been used to cede new insurance business in order to relieve the effects of surplus strain. Thus, the use of reinsurance for the purpose of offsetting surplus strain is referred to as *surplus relief.* The NAIC defines surplus relief as the net effect of income received from reinsurance ceded minus payments disbursed for reinsurance assumed.

How does reinsurance actually work to relieve surplus strain? The exact form of surplus relief provided through any reinsurance agreement depends to some extent upon the nature of the reinsurance coverage, but also upon the unique needs of the parties to the agreement. Two elements of a traditional indemnity reinsurance agreement work to offset surplus strain. These elements are the *reserve credit* and the *reinsurance (ceding) commission* or *expense allowance.*

- A primary insurer can transfer to the reinsurer the responsibility for holding reserves on reinsured business. The primary insurer thus can avoid establishing and maintaining a reserve liability that would otherwise be its responsibility. The accounting treatment for recording such a transfer of reserves on the books of the ceding company is known as a ***reserve credit.*** Thus, when it issues a policy, the primary insurer establishes a reserve on its books and then reduces the amount of that reserve by recording a reserve credit to reflect the reinsurance transaction.

- For business ceded to a reinsurer, direct writing insurers often collect commissions, known as *reinsurance commissions, ceding commissions,* or *expense allowances.* Reinsurance or ceding commissions constitute current income to the direct writing insurer.

Example: Surplus Relief in Group Health Business

Suppose that the Luxor Life and Health Insurance Company is facing a decision about whether to obtain traditional indemnity reinsurance on a group health case for which Luxor receives annual premium income of $600,000. Luxor's financial people must project how this case would help or harm the company's overall financial position for the year. Thus, they must analyze how reinsuring the case would provide surplus relief.

Figure 14-4 illustrates the effect of an indemnity reinsurance transaction on Luxor's first-year income attributable to new group health

Figure 14-4. Luxor's surplus relief obtained from indemnity reinsurance.

Business effects for the primary insurer	New business strain without reinsurance	Surplus relief with reinsurance
1. Premiums written	$600,000	$ 600,000
2. Premiums reinsured	-0-	(600,000)
3. Unearned premium reserve	(400,000)	-0-
4. Premiums earned	200,000	-0-
5. Reinsurance commissions earned	-0-	150,000
6. Claims incurred	(100,000)	-0-
7. Acquisition expenses (stat)	(150,000)	(120,000)
Primary insurer's 1st-year gain/(strain)	$ (50,000)	$ 30,000

Surplus relief obtained from this reinsurance transaction:

Net Loss without Coverage	plus	Net Gain with Coverage	equals	Surplus Relief Amount
$50,000	+	$30,000	=	$80,000

business. The column on the left shows the effect of new business strain without any relief; the column on the right shows the effect of new business strain with reinsurance as surplus relief.

Without reinsurance, Luxor would earn premium income of \$600,000 on the case, but that income would be more than offset by establishing an unearned premium reserve, paying claims, and paying acquisition expenses. After subtracting the total of \$650,000 in costs, then without reinsurance, Luxor would have a net loss of \$50,000 on the case.

With reinsurance, Luxor would pass along all \$600,000 of premium income to the reinsurer, but the reinsurer would then pay Luxor a ceding commission of \$150,000, including an expense allowance of \$30,000; this commission would partially offset Luxor's acquisition expenses. Luxor would not be required to establish a reserve, and the reinsurer would pay all claims that arise and a part of Luxor's acquisition expenses. With reinsurance on the case, Luxor would earn positive net income of \$30,000. The sum of the absolute values of these two amounts—(\$50,000 + \$30,000 = \$80,000)—is the total amount of surplus relief that Luxor can achieve by ceding the case.

The well-being of the life and health insurance industry relies in part upon the reinsurance mechanism to appropriately and effectively redistribute the risks assumed by direct writing insurance companies. Although reinsurance is a commonly accepted practice among insurers, industry analysts recognize that insurers must practice moderation in obtaining surplus relief through reinsurance. Why? An insurance company's excessive reliance on reinsurance for surplus relief may indicate to external parties that the company's surplus is inadequate for the volume of business that it is writing. Also, external parties recognize that the profit the reinsurer expects to earn on the reinsurance transaction represents an opportunity cost to the ceding company.

Business Effects of Reinsurance Transactions

The variety of possible arrangements involving reinsurance of life, health, and annuity contracts renders it difficult to generalize about any one pattern of broad financial outcomes (i.e., in capital or net gain) that typically result on the balance sheets of the ceding and assuming companies. Instead, we can look at separate business effects of various transfers of assets, liabilities, income, and expenses that arise regularly in connection with life, health, and annuity reinsurance. These effects are summarized in Figure 14-5.

Next we consider the effects of reinsurance cessions on the ceding company's financial picture. Then we review the accounting effects of reinsurance assumptions on the balance sheet of the reinsurer.

Figure 14-5. Business effects of ceding and assuming reinsurance.

By ceding reinsurance, a direct insurer . . .	By assuming reinsurance, a reinsurer . . .
• Obtains reinsurance reserve credits, thus reducing its liabilities • Incurs the expense of paying reinsurance premiums • May obtain business expense reimbursements for expenses including incurred claims, surrenders, reserve adjustments, and taxes • May earn a ceding commission • Obtains tax effects, as desired	• Establishes and maintains new reserves for reinsurance assumed, thus increasing its liabilities • Earns premium income on reinsurance assumed • Incurs the expense of reimbursing the ceding company for business expenses including incurred claims, surrenders, reserve adjustments (under modified coinsurance only), and taxes • May pay a ceding commission • Obtains tax effects, as desired

Balance-Sheet Effects of Ceding Reinsurance

When assets, liabilities, income, and expenses are transferred as part of a reinsurance agreement, reinsurance *cessions* typically affect the ceding company's financial picture in a number of ways. We describe these transfers of assets, liabilities, income, and expenses in a reinsurance transaction.

Depending on the terms of the reinsurance agreement, the ceding company's assets (usually cash) may increase or decrease as a result of a reinsurance transaction. The payment of reinsurance premiums decreases the insurer's assets, but this decrease may be more than offset by the amount of premiums the ceding company receives on the reinsured business. In addition, the ceding company may earn ceding commissions, which are considered to be current income and reduce the amount of reinsurance premiums payable.

The ceding company is reimbursed by the reinsurer for incurred claims and, under some types of reinsurance agreements, for surrender values, modified coinsurance reserve adjustments, taxes, commissions, experience refunds, and other reimbursable expenses. To record this reimbursement, the ceding company records an increase in assets. These expenses that the reinsurer covers are generally known as *amounts recoverable from reinsurers.* The terms of some reinsurance agreements might provide for the reinsurer to reimburse a variety of disbursements by the primary insurer. One example of expenses that are often reimbursable is claim payments. The net effect of the transfers between a reinsurer and a ceding company may be an increase or a decrease in the ceding company's assets.

The reinsurer usually becomes responsible for establishing reserves on the reinsured business, and then the ceding company is entitled to a *reserve credit.* (The amount of the reserve credit depends upon the method of reinsurance used.) Reinsurance reserve credits typically decrease the ceding company's reserve liabilities on its balance sheet. Note that this reinsurance application of the word *credit* is inconsistent with the usual accounting application of the term, where a credit would ordinarily represent a decrease in a liability.

The reinsurance premiums, net of ceding commissions, that the ceding company must pay on reinsured risks are recorded as an expense of the ceding company. An expense tends to decrease the company's net gain. To the extent that any net gain would eventually have the effect of increasing capital and surplus, one might say that an expense tends to draw down surplus. The ceding company takes credit for the reinsurer's obligation to pay a ceding commission by reducing the total reinsurance premium and other consideration that the ceding company pays to the reinsurer.

Generally, ceding reinsurance produces immediate relief to the new business strain on a company's capital and surplus. We already know that the issuance of new business generates a decrease in capital and surplus. We also know that reinsuring the business generally can relieve surplus strain. However, the exact level of surplus relief depends upon the provisions of a specific reinsurance agreement; thus, we cannot say whether using reinsurance would in all situations counteract all of an insurer's new business strain.

An insurer is motivated to issue more business and reinsure the excess risk when by so doing the insurer will be able to earn more money than it could have earned without issuing and reinsuring the added business. Because ceding reinsurance typically results in an immediate increase in capital and surplus, why wouldn't an insurer always want to reinsure all of its business? Once again, we can refer to the risk-return tradeoff for our answer. Upon transferring risk to a reinsurer, the ceding company gives up potential long-term profits.

The insurer gives up profits in three respects:

1. For this risk coverage, the ceding company incurs a cost equal to the difference between the reinsurance premiums it pays and the amounts expected to be reimbursed by the reinsurer. This cost diminishes the insurer's potential net income from the reinsured business.

2. Reinsurance in effect allows the ceding company to substitute a commitment for the known timing and amount of the reinsurance premium in exchange for the risk of bearing other expenses of unknown timing and amount, such as claims. By substituting known expenses for unknown expenses, the ceding company avoids the risk that it might not have enough resources to cover unexpectedly high expenses, and the insurer also avoids the po-

tential added profits that might arise from unexpectedly low expenses.

3. The ceding company must transfer cash or perhaps other non-cash assets to a reinsurer as payment of reinsurance premiums. Thus, the ceding company loses the opportunity to benefit from the compound growth of investment income that the insurer otherwise could have earned on these assets.

Balance-Sheet Effects of Assuming Reinsurance

Just as with ceding reinsurance, reinsurance *assumptions* typically affect the assuming company's financial picture in a number of ways. The reinsurer typically experiences an increase in assets (usually cash) that reflects the amount of reinsurance premiums received, net of ceding commissions. The reinsurer typically experiences a decrease in assets (an increase in an expense), reflecting amounts payable to reimburse the ceding company for incurred claims, surrender values, modified coinsurance reserve adjustments, taxes, commissions, and other reimbursable expenses. To the extent that the ceding company transfers assets to the reinsurer through premiums, the reinsurer benefits from any investment income in excess of the statutory increase in reserve liabilities. The burden of new reserves for reinsurance assumed is typically reflected by an increase in the reinsurer's liabilities and by a decrease in the reinsurer's capital and surplus.

A reinsurer is motivated to assume reinsurance when assuming business will enable the reinsurer to earn more money than it could have earned without assuming the added business. Because assuming reinsurance generally results in an initial decrease in the reinsurer's capital and surplus, why would a company want to assume reinsurance? Not surprisingly, the risk-return tradeoff can provide our answer. By assuming added risk from an outside firm, the reinsurer is able to enhance its return on its capital. This is partly because assuming reinsurance can generate income for the reinsurer. It is also partly because (as we saw at the end of Chapter 10) the probable outcome of decreasing capital without otherwise diminishing the inherent riskiness of the business would be to increase the rate of return on the business as a whole.

Tax Effects of Ceding Reinsurance

One function of financial managers in any industry is to identify reasonable ways to control taxes. The federal income tax laws affecting life and health insurers and reinsurers in the United States are complex and subject to constant change and reinterpretation. Although the specifics of achieving these tax effects are beyond the scope of this textbook, we can identify two approaches financial managers use to influence the magnitude of the company's taxes: (1) timing the reporting of taxable income or losses and (2) qualifying for special tax filing status.

Reinsurance transactions afford insurers an opportunity to employ these fundamental approaches to tax management. Because reinsurance arrangements are negotiated contracts, the parties to the contract have reasonable flexibility in tailoring contract provisions to suit their tax needs. Thus, many reinsurance arrangements are carefully structured to secure tax advantages. However, the Internal Revenue Service (IRS) exercises considerable authority in its interpretation of the tax effects of any given arrangement.

Timing the Reporting of Taxable Income or Losses

Insurers and reinsurers have frequently used reinsurance to *decrease current taxable income* and, thus, to manage their total tax bills. For instance, suppose that an insurance company's taxable income for the year would be $1,200,000 without reinsurance, but $900,000 with reinsurance. At any given tax rate, the tax for that year would be greater on the higher amount than on the lower amount.

In other circumstances, an insurer or reinsurer can diminish its total tax bill by *increasing its taxable income* for the current year. Suppose an insurer has carried forward previous years' tax-loss credits that the insurer now wishes to offset against current income. These tax-loss credits expire if they are not used within a specified number of years. In such circumstances, the insurer or reinsurer would want to increase its current taxable income sufficiently to offset any tax credits that are about to expire and could accomplish this effect through reinsurance.

Qualifying for Special Tax-Filing Status as a Life, Non-Life, or Small Company

A U.S. insurance company can use reinsurance to qualify with the Internal Revenue Service (IRS) for treatment as a *life company* or as a *non-life company*—whichever status is more advantageous for tax purposes. In Canada, insurers are taxed as regular corporations, and no special tax benefits are associated with being classified as a life company.

In order to qualify as a life company for U.S. tax purposes, an insurer must meet all of the following tests:

- The majority of the insurer's business must be insurance.
- The insurer must be engaged in the issuance or reinsurance of life insurance policies or annuities.

- The insurer must hold more than half of its reserves as coverage for the types of liabilities that the IRS classifies for this purpose as *life insurance.* For this IRS purpose, *life insurance* also includes annuities and noncancellable accident and health policies.

Because a given insurer might derive greater tax benefit from one status or the other, the insurer might want to take steps to qualify as a life company, or it might act to avoid life company status. In order to qualify for ***life insurance company tax status*** in the United States, an insurer might need to increase its life insurance reserves to meet the IRS requirement. The insurer could increase its life insurance reserves by either assuming life business or ceding non-life business. In contrast, in order to qualify for ***non-life company tax status,*** an insurer could take action either to cede life business or to assume non-life business.

Additionally, the IRS offers tax-favored treatment to small insurance companies. For this IRS purpose, ***small insurance company tax status*** is available to an insurance company that has less than $15 million of taxable income and less than $500 million of assets. Using reinsurance to reduce overall taxable income has enabled some U.S. insurers to qualify for small company tax status.

Indemnity Reinsurance Compared to Other Capital Sources

Once an insurance company's financial planners have determined that they want to obtain new external financing, they need to choose how to obtain that financing. Ceding reinsurance will generally be a more complex choice than a choice of issuing financial instruments, because reinsurance affects both insurance risk and financial risk, whereas financial instruments affect only financial outcomes. Now that we have seen how reinsurance can affect an insurance company's financial outcomes, we look at the insurance company's considerations for deciding whether to obtain (1) permanent capital from issuing stock (if that is an option), (2) temporary capital by ceding indemnity reinsurance, or (3) temporary capital by issuing surplus notes.

Indemnity Reinsurance Compared to Stock Financing

Most of the *similarities* between the financial effects of obtaining indemnity reinsurance and issuing common stock arise because both mechanisms can strengthen a company's capital position. However, as summarized in Figure 14-6, the differences between these mechanisms may be more pronounced than the similarities. The following

Figure 14-6. Comparison of financing sources: indemnity reinsurance and common stock.

Obtaining indemnity reinsurance	Issuing common stock
• Available to both stock and mutual insurers • Provides surplus relief • Provides temporary improvement in capital • Improves liquidity and solvency position • Impacts underwriting results because reinsurer accepts excess risk • Ceding company *must* compensate reinsurer • Requires state-level authorization of reinsurer • Insurer must perform a due diligence inquiry • Generates some tax-deductible business expense • Reinsurer must perform a due diligence inquiry • Price and terms negotiated privately, often by means of competitive bidding • Results in no dilution of ownership	• Available to stock insurers but not mutuals • Provides surplus relief • Provides new permanent capital • Improves liquidity and solvency position • No impact upon underwriting results, because no risk is transferred • No requirement to repay stockholders • Regulatory approval required for issuing stock • Need to comply with securities laws • Minimal tax-deductible business expenses (flotation expenses only) • No due diligence inquiry is required • Price determined in an open market for common stocks • Results in dilution of ownership

points compare and contrast the option of ceding indemnity reinsurance to the option of issuing common stock:

1. Both stock and mutual insurers can obtain indemnity reinsurance, but only stock insurers can issue common stock.

2. Because issuing stock and ceding insurance both serve to attract new capital, both also provide surplus relief.

3. Issuing stock provides surplus relief by permanently increasing the issuing company's capital. In contrast, ceding reinsurance does not directly increase an insurer's capital. Instead, reinsurance can provide capital indirectly by reducing the ceding company's liabilities by more than it reduces the company's assets.

4. Both issuing stock and ceding reinsurance increase an insurer's capital. Thus, both transactions improve the insurer's liquidity and solvency positions.

5. Because both stock issuances and reinsurance cessions increase an insurer's capital, once the insurer undertakes either transaction, the insurer must then work harder to maintain the rate of return on capital that it had been earning. Why? When capital increases, a greater dollar amount of net gain is required in order for the company to maintain its historical percentage rate of return on capital. (This principle was illustrated in Chapter 10.)

6. An insurance company's issuance of stock has no impact whatsoever on the insurer's underwriting results. However, ceding indemnity reinsurance limits the ceding insurer's exposure to underwriting risks, and sets an upper limit on the ceding insurer's potential losses. Reinsurance limits the ceding insurer's overall risk exposures.

7. In obtaining indemnity reinsurance, the insurer commits to a series of future transactions that will affect the company's future income. In issuing common stock, a company undertakes no obligation to repay the stockholders' investment—although the issuer does have a responsibility to attempt to provide a fair return on that investment.

8. Issuing stock requires the insurer to comply with federal securities laws, a process involving some effort and expense. Reinsurance does not invoke any need to comply with federal securities laws, but generally requires that the reinsurer be authorized by the appropriate state insurance department.

9. Obtaining indemnity reinsurance or issuing common stock can generate business expenses that would be tax-deductible to an insurer for U.S. income tax purposes. Flotation costs, discussed in Chapter 13, are the only tax-deductible business expenses of issuing common stock.

10. In order to enter into a reinsurance arrangement in good faith, the insurance company and the reinsurer must each thoroughly investigate the financial stability of the other party to the contract. This required investigation process is known as ***due diligence,*** and usually includes evaluating whether (*a*) the other party's reserves are adequate, (*b*) its current pricing techniques are sound, and (*c*) its products are likely to be profitable. In order to issue common stock, the insurer is not required to perform a due diligence investigation, but the insurer is subject to the investment banker's fiduciary duty of due diligence. (Due diligence is discussed in another context in Chapter 19.)

11. In a reinsurance transaction, the price and other terms of the agreement are negotiated directly between the insurer and the reinsurer. Often, available business is submitted for competitive bidding from reinsurers. In a stock issuance, the stock price is set by a bidding process in the open market.

12. Stock issuances increase capital by increasing the company's ownership base. A larger ownership base represents dilution in the power of each share of voting stock. In contrast, through ceding reinsurance a company can improve its capital position without increasing its ownership base.

Note that the similarities between the financial effects of indemnity reinsurance and the effects of common stock financing mostly reflect the fact that both mechanisms strengthen capital. The many differences between the two mechanisms reflect the fact that stock provides capital through an increase in equity, whereas reinsurance provides capital by means of asset and liability transfers.

Ceding Indemnity Reinsurance Compared to Issuing Surplus Notes

A comparison between ceding indemnity reinsurance and issuing surplus notes reveals many contrasts, summarized in Figure 14-7. As we noted in Chapter 13, mutual insurers tend to obtain financing from either reinsurance or surplus notes, reflecting the options most readily available to them. Thus, although this analysis relates to both stock and mutual companies, it particularly reflects a mutual company's decision process.

Companies comparing the options of obtaining reinsurance or issuing surplus notes generally perform a detailed analysis that carefully models the unique characteristics of their situations. Additionally, the relative merits of the two options are largely derived from the ever-changing regulatory environment. In a given situation, companies select the option that has the better merit for their situation. The following points compare and contrast the usual effects of ceding either traditional indemnity reinsurance or financial reinsurance against the usual effects of issuing surplus notes:

1. Either reinsurance or surplus notes can strengthen the insurer's statutory capital and surplus position, thus providing surplus relief.

2. For stock companies, ceding reinsurance can increase capital without increasing the company's ownership base of stockholders. Surplus notes increase statutory capital without diluting ownership.

3. The transfer of excess risks through indemnity reinsurance can set limits upon the insurer's underwriting results, but issues of surplus notes—or any financial instruments—do not affect the insurer's underwriting results.

4. For indemnity reinsurance, the business reinsured usually generates the income that the insurer applies toward compensating the reinsurer. In contrast, payments on surplus notes are not directly tied to income from any specific block of business or other asset, although scheduled payments on surplus notes are due only when earnings can fund the payments and state approval is received.

Figure 14-7. Comparison of financing sources: indemnity reinsurance and surplus notes.

Obtaining indemnity reinsurance	Issuing surplus notes
• Both stock and mutual insurers can obtain reinsurance • Reinsurance provides temporary capital, thus improving liquidity and solvency position • No dilution of ownership • Obtaining reinsurance affects underwriting results because reinsurer accepts insurer's excess risk • Reinsured business generates the income for paying the reinsurer • Reinsurer must be compensated, generally by sharing in the direct insurer's potential profits • Reinsurance generates tax-deductible business expenses • Reinsurer and primary insurer both must perform due diligence inquiry • Obtaining reinsurance generally has a higher percentage cost of capital than issuing surplus notes • The insurer cedes a share of the product risks and investment risks. The insurer also transfers the requirement of holding reserves and capital on those risks • Reinsurance transactions must be approved by state regulators • Proceeds may be taken in the form of cash or noncash credits • Terms of a reinsurance treaty are easily renegotiated • Recapture of insurance permitted • No high fixed transaction cost, no minimum transaction size	• Both stock and mutual insurers can issue surplus notes • Surplus notes provide long-term, potentially permanent capital, thus improving liquidity and solvency position • No dilution of ownership • Surplus notes have no effect upon underwriting results • Surplus notes have a fixed repayment schedule, fixed maturity date; payments are due when earnings are available from which to pay them • Interest must be paid and principal repaid on schedule, subject to regulatory approval, although notes may be renewable indefinitely • Surplus notes generate tax-deductible business expenses • Investment bankers and institutional purchasers must exercise fiduciary duty of due diligence • Issuing surplus notes generally has a lower percentage cost of capital than ceding reinsurance • All risks remain on the books of the ceding company. The insurer must maintain all required reserves and capital • Surplus notes must be approved by state regulators • Proceeds are necessarily in cash • Renegotiating terms of surplus notes is impractical if an issue is widely held • Prepayment not permitted • High fixed transaction cost, high minimum transaction size

5. Both reinsurance and surplus notes require the insurer to pay an expense to the company providing the financing. In both cases, the net business expense for obtaining the financing may be deducted for U.S. federal income tax purposes.

6. In order to use reinsurance, the ceding company must perform due diligence on the financial position of the reinsurer. Likewise, the reinsurer must perform due diligence on the ceding company. An insurer is not required to perform a due diligence

investigation on anyone else when the insurer issues surplus notes. However, an investment banker generally conducts a due diligence investigation of the insurer in connection with the insurer's issuing surplus notes.* (Due diligence is discussed in Chaper 19.)

7. The cost of capital for issuing surplus notes is generally less expensive than it is for ceding reinsurance. However, studies show that under various conditions either option could offer a lower percentage cost of capital.[4]

8. Surplus notes necessarily provide proceeds in the form of cash, which is generally an unimportant concern to insurers, because insurers generally receive substantial and regular cash from premiums. Reinsurance can be structured so that it provides (a) cash or (b) an increase in capital and surplus.

9. Because surplus notes are generally widely distributed among buyers, it would be difficult to renegotiate the terms of an outstanding surplus note. On the other hand, reinsurance treaties usually involve only one or two other companies, and thus their terms are relatively simply renegotiated.

10. Surplus notes generally limit the insurer's option to prepay the note, but indemnity reinsurance treaties generally have flexible recapture provisions. Thus, a surplus note stays on the issuer's books until it is paid off, with few options for paying it off ahead of schedule, whereas indemnity reinsurance generally is reversible.

11. The fixed flotation costs of issuing surplus notes in effect set a relatively high practical minimum size for an issue of surplus notes. Reinsurance transactions are practical for very small amounts of surplus relief.

As we noted earlier in the chapter, reinsurance can allow an insurance company to achieve a number of objectives in addition to the financial objectives we have described. The next part of this chapter describes how insurers use reinsurance to achieve market objectives and to manage underwriting capacity and business volumes.

Using Reinsurance to Achieve Market Objectives

For strategic reasons, an insurer might choose to enter a new market or to exit a market it currently serves. Through the use of reinsurance, an insurer can accomplish a strategic goal of entering a new

* The exception would arise whenever an affiliated company had purchased the issue.

Insight 14-1 What Ingredients Establish Success in a Joint Venture?

A *strategic alliance* is a substitute for a merger or an acquisition and in U.S. law is treated as such for antitrust and other legal purposes. The most common strategic alliance is the *joint venture (JV)*, in which two different corporations set up a third, jointly owned enterprise in the corporate form. Many JVs fail to produce results. Why? Research has shown that successful JVs are those in which the corporate owners have complementary skills or resources (e.g., one of the partners supplies the technology while the other supplies the marketing). The most successful JVs seem to be those in which one of the partners owns a controlling interest. If more than two corporations are involved in a venture, it is called a *consortium* rather than a joint venture. Consortia are quite common in Europe, with as many as five and six corporations combining to set up new permanent corporations.

Source: *Stanley Foster Reed and Alexandra Reed LaJoux,* The Art of M&A, A Merger Acquisition Buyout Guide, *Second Edition, (Burr Ridge, IL: Richard D. Irwin, Inc. 1995), pp. 15–16.*

market by assuming new risk on policies issued by another company. Also, through the use of reinsurance, an insurer can exit a market by ceding risk on policies the insurer itself issued.

When an insurer's strategic plans call for expanding its markets by entering a new territory, the insurer ordinarily might obtain approval to do business in the new territory or else might acquire an insurance company that is already licensed to sell insurance in the state. A third option for entering a new territory is through a *joint venture* or strategic alliance arrangement with another insurer.

An insurer can enter a territory where it has no product distribution outlet by first manufacturing and then reinsuring insurance sold by another insurer that does have a distribution system operating in the chosen territory. To effect such a marketing partnership, a direct writer and a reinsurer typically employ indemnity reinsurance to partially transfer the risks under newly written business—not in-force business—on a permanent, but recapturable basis. Insight 14-1 presents the reasons that joint ventures and strategic alliances have enjoyed popularity in the 1990s.

Example of a Joint Venture: Shield and Armor

For example, consider the case of Shield Insurance and Armor Assurance. Suppose that Shield Insurance has an agency distribution system in the state of Illinois and is licensed to sell insurance there. Armor Assurance is licensed to sell insurance in Illinois, but it has no distribution outlet there. Armor would nonetheless like to market universal life in Illinois. For its part, Shield does not write universal life coverage, although Shield's distribution system would like to be able to offer universal life coverage to its clients. To address their common needs, Shield and Armor enter into a marketing joint venture.

Under the terms of the joint venture agreement, Armor will manufacture, underwrite, service, and administer a type of universal life (UL) coverage. Shield will issue the UL coverage in its own name, and Shield's sales force will market the policies. Shield's sales force will collect sales commissions from Armor, and Shield will collect a ceding commission from Armor. Immediately upon issuing the UL policies, Shield will cede the entire risk to Armor. Armor, however, will not become a party to the primary UL insurance contract.

Fronting Arrangements in Reinsurance

Another type of joint venture between a reinsurer and an insurer is sometimes known as fronting. ***Fronting*** is an arrangement wherein one insurer, known as the ***fronting company,*** acts as a primary insurer and issues policies that another company, the reinsurer, has underwritten; then, the primary insurer immediately cedes most of the risk to the same reinsurer. The parties to a fronting arrangement are often affiliated companies. Fronting arrangements permit a reinsurer to in effect sell business in a jurisdiction where the reinsurer is not licensed to do business. An ***unauthorized reinsurer*** is not *authorized* as a reinsurer by the regulatory authorities in the direct writing insurer's state of domicile. Note that a reinsurance company can be *authorized* as a reinsurer but not *licensed* as a direct writer.

The most common situations in which a reinsurer enters into a fronting arrangement are when (1) the reinsurer's anticipated business volume is too small to justify the cost of obtaining a license as a direct writer in a given state or (2) the reinsurer does not have an agency force. The reinsurer that obtains business in this manner may even have been rejected for licensing in the jurisdiction where the policies are being fronted. The unauthorized reinsurer may be licensed in other states, or it may even be a foreign corporation that is not licensed anywhere in the United States. In a fronting arrangement, the reinsurer is not licensed as a direct writer and may or may not be authorized as a reinsurer.

Some fronting arrangements have been the focus of regulatory attention, because regulators have a duty to protect the public against the activities of reinsurers indirectly doing business in territories where the local insurance commissioner lacks jurisdiction over them. Not surprisingly, some jurisdictions prohibit fronting. In the United States, most states have adopted regulations designed to discourage the practice. These limitations include (1) limiting the volume of fronting business permitted, (2) limiting the percentage that an originating company may cede in a fronting arrangement, and (3) requiring audits and other monitoring designed to detect any illegal applications of fronting. In addition, under some circumstances, insurers are required to establish an extra reserve related to transactions with unauthorized reinsurers. Despite the existence of limiting regulation, some insurers go ahead and enter into an agreement with an unauthorized reinsurer, particularly a reinsurer that has a corporate affiliation with the primary insurer.

Example of Fronting: Motown and Phantom

In order to pursue its chosen strategy for geographic diversification, Phantom Life wants to insure residents of the state of Michigan. Phantom Life encountered an obstacle to implementing its strategic plan when Phantom found that the likely business volume would not support the costs of obtaining a license to do business in Michigan. Phantom Life must use its backup plan and employ a fronting arrangement with Motown Security Assurance, an insurer domiciled and licensed in Michigan. Now, whenever an application is submitted on the Phantom products sold in Michigan through Motown Security Assurance, Motown will issue the contract to the applicant and will immediately cede most of the risk to Phantom Life. Phantom pays Motown a fee for the service of issuing the policy. (This situation differs from our earlier example of the joint venture between Armor and Shield in that Armor and Shield were both licensed to operate in the state where they did business, but Phantom is not.)

Using Reinsurance to Manage Underwriting Capacity and Business Volumes

In any industry, having a mismatch between the volume of orders from customers and the business's capacity to process those orders presents an efficiency problem. ***Business volume*** generally refers to the amount of an insurer's new sales. For insurance companies, business volume is sometimes measured in terms of number of applications, amount of insurance sold, amount of annual premiums, or amount of reserves. Insurance companies can have too much or too little business volume relative to their available processing capacity.

An insurer can be said to have excess business volume or inadequate processing capacity if it has more new business than it can process. Conversely, an insurer has too little business volume or idle processing capacity if it has less new business than it can process. Fortunately, reinsurance transactions can be used to address either of these potential problems associated with business volume.

Excess business volume represents one type of operating inefficiency that an insurer would probably choose to correct. Likewise, excess business capacity represents an inefficiency. For instance, if an insurance company has excess administrative resources for processing its new business volume, the company can put that excess capacity to work by assuming reinsurance. An insurer needing to obtain more business could address the problem by assuming reinsurance. Unfortunately, the converse is NOT true. If an insurance company's administrative resources are insufficient for administering its current business volume, ceding reinsurance on an indemnity basis would not solve the problem, because ceding reinsurance involves an added burden of recordkeeping and communication.

The facet of administrative capacity that is most readily addressed by the use of reinsurance is underwriting depth and experience. In this context, ***underwriting depth and experience*** refers to the adequacy of an insurer's underwriting staff and other resources to process applications. When an insurer's internal underwriting resources are inadequate relative to its business volume, obtaining reinsurance can relieve strain on the internal underwriting staff. By ceding traditional indemnity reinsurance, an insurer can in effect gain ancillary underwriting resources, because the reinsurer takes an advisory role in the underwriting of business reinsured under traditional plans of indemnity reinsurance. By reinsuring, the ceding company is likely to gain access to broader underwriting expertise than it has on its staff. Obtaining access to underwriting expertise in an unfamiliar line of business could also be a primary motivation in seeking a reinsurance arrangement such as a reinsurance joint venture, because joint ventures can allow for all underwriting to be performed by the reinsurer.

On the other hand, an insurer can employ excess underwriting capacity by assuming business in a joint venture or fronting arrangement. When a company assumes business, in effect the reinsurer accepts responsibility for some aspect of underwriting for another insurer. A company can choose to reinsure business primarily in markets where the company has expertise, but a company also can choose to gain underwriting experience in an unfamiliar line by entering into a joint venture to reinsure that new type of business.

Regulation Affecting Reinsurance

In the United States, the regulation of reinsurance comes from rulings by (1) state insurance departments, often in conjunction with the NAIC, or (2) the Internal Revenue Service (IRS). Reinsurance transactions themselves are subject to far less regulatory scrutiny than are primary insurance transactions. However, U.S. insurance regulators closely monitor insurers' use of reinsurance for surplus relief. One of the NAIC's 12 IRIS (Insurance Regulatory Information

System) ratios in effect sets a limit on the recommended level of surplus relief obtained through reinsurance. The IRIS ***surplus relief ratio*** can be expressed as follows:

$$\text{Surplus Relief Ratio} = \frac{\text{Net Commissions and Expense Allowance on Reinsurance}}{\text{Capital and Surplus}}$$

The acceptable range for results for this ratio depends upon the size of a company. An insurer's having a result outside of the acceptable range for the IRIS surplus relief ratio could trigger a detailed regulatory examination of the insurer's reinsurance programs. Most insurers make every effort to structure their reinsurance agreements and programs so as to avoid violating the IRIS limits.*

In Conclusion

Reinsurance is yet another mechanism for enhancing an insurer's capital and surplus by attracting and employing resources external to the insurance company. In our overview of reinsurance options, we examined how reinsurance can relieve the strain that new business puts on capital and how reinsurance can in effect be a source of external financing. In our overview of the financial applications of reinsurance, we learned that the financial benefits of reinsurance come in a package with many other business benefits.

Insurers have not yet exhausted the versatility of the reinsurance mechanism, nor have insurers exhausted their creativity in finding specially tailored mechanisms for enhancing their capital and surplus positions. The area of reinsurance is complex, and we are not able to fully explore here the many accommodations that reinsurers are able to offer primary insurers.

* The NAIC's ratio for evaluating an insurer's net amount for all reinsurance activities should not be confused with the surplus relief effect from a single reinsurance transaction. The annual surplus relief amount on a single reinsurance transaction can be calculated as the sum of the absolute value of any net surplus strain for the year had the product not been reinsured AND the amount of any net gain for the year including the effects of the reinsurance.

Key Terms and Concepts

reinsurance
professional reinsurers
retrocessionaire
ceding company
cession
assuming company
assumption
reinsurance treaty
scheduled retention limit
automatic binding limit
automatic reinsurance
facultative reinsurance
retroceded
yearly renewable term (YRT) reinsurance method
assumption reinsurance
assumption certificates
indemnity reinsurance
reinsurance premiums
recapture provision
reinsurance (ceding) commission
traditional indemnity reinsurance
retention limit
joint venture
consortium
surplus relief
reserve credit
life insurance company tax status
non-life company tax status
small insurance company tax status
due diligence
fronting
fronting company
unauthorized reinsurer
business volume
underwriting depth and experience
surplus relief ratio

References

1. Excerpted and adapted with permission of the publisher from Eli A. Grossman, *Life Reinsurance* (Atlanta, GA: LOMA, 1980), pp. 3–5.
2. *Life & Health Reinsurance: Pockets of Opportunity* (Hartford, CT: Conning & Company, 1995), p. 5.
3. Robert W. Strain, editor, *Reinsurance Contract Wording* (Tanglewood, TX: Strain Publishing, 1992), p. 763.
4. Marc Slutzsky, Hank Sulikowski, and Mel Young, "A Comparison of Reinsurance and Surplus Notes for Raising Capital," *Reinsurance Section News* (Society of Actuaries Newsletter), March 1994, pp. 11–12.

PART 5

Managing and Monitoring Solvency and Profitability

In Part 5, Chapters 15 through 18 are about the monitoring of insurance companies' financial strength by internal and external parties. To begin, Chapter 15 discusses nonregulatory monitoring of insurers' financial strength—by the company's own staff, its customers, its investors, and the rating agencies that assign quality ratings. Chapter 15 also introduces the financial analysis tools that are commonly used to monitor insurers' financial strength and describes quality ratings and the function of rating agencies in the insurance industry.

Various types of financial institutions, including commercial banks and life and health insurance companies, place strong emphasis on managing the organization's cash flows. Toward the effort of managing their cash flows, financial institutions now apply a set of sophisticated management approaches that are collectively known as *asset/liability management (ALM).* Chapters 16 and 17 introduce asset/liability management, a program that involves internal and regulatory monitoring of insurers. First, Chapter 16 presents the main objectives of asset/liability management and shows how the regulatory climate in Canada and the United States encouraged the adoption of ALM practices. Chapter 16 also discusses some pitfalls for insurance companies to avoid in the practice of ALM. Next, Chapter 17 surveys some of the technical approaches that insurers use for analyzing the interactions between their asset and liability portfolios. Additionally, Chapter 17 introduces the typical internal system of formal reports that insurance companies employ for asset/liability management reporting.

Chapter 18 takes an outsider's view of an insurance company by focusing on regulatory monitoring of insurers' financial strength. Chapter 18 shows how regulators routinely monitor insurers' solvency and describes the actions regulators take upon identifying that an insurer is having financial difficulty. Chapter 18 concludes with a discussion of the role of guaranty associations in protecting the public in the event of an insurance company's solvency crisis.

CHAPTER

15

Monitoring Financial Strength

LEARNING OBJECTIVES

After studying this chapter, you should be able to

- Identify one published source of financial information about insurers
- Distinguish among the purposes of horizontal, vertical, and cross-sectional types of financial analysis
- Recognize some common pitfalls encountered in comparing financial information
- Distinguish among and recognize capital, leverage, liquidity, and profitability ratios for life and health insurers
- Recognize the role of insurance industry rating agencies, the activities that rating agencies undertake in order to analyze insurance companies, and the reasons that these quality ratings are important to insurers and insurance consumers

OUTLINE

As we have seen throughout this text, an insurance company's financial activities can be viewed as a continuing balancing act between two related but sometimes conflicting goals: maximizing returns and ensuring financial solvency. We first encountered this concept of the balancing act in Chapter 2, and we have discussed it in various chapters throughout the text. Here we introduce the financial analysis tools used to monitor financial performance, and we describe the activities and functions of insurance company rating agencies.

Financial ratio analysis is a diagnostic tool used by financial analysts. ***Financial ratio analysis*** consists of calculating the relationships between various financial statement values for the purpose of assessing a company's financial performance and financial condition. Ratio analysis is an important aspect of any financial analysis, whether the analysis is conducted by a company's internal management, an outside rating agency, a regulatory group, or an interested potential investor. In this chapter, we discuss the sources of information for financial analysis, the importance of both quantitative and qualitative analysis, and some of the most important financial ratios, including capital ratios, leverage ratios, liquidity ratios, and profitability ratios. But, before discussing the actual financial tools for monitoring the financial strength of insurers, we examine (1) who needs this monitoring and why, (2) the type of financial information that is analyzed, and (3) where analysts find needed information.

Who Uses Financial Analysis?

Many different people and organizations, each with their own goals and needs, use financial analysis. Among the parties applying or taking an interest in financial analysis of insurers are (1) the companies themselves, (2) investors and potential investors, (3) consumers of financial products, (4) marketers such as independent agents and brokers, (5) regulators, and (6) rating agencies. These parties have differing interests, which may be described as follows:

- *Insurance companies* conduct financial analysis of their own financial condition for the purpose of making sure that they continue to operate on a financially sound basis and that they remain competitive with other financial institutions. Insurance companies also analyze the financial condition of competing financial institutions.

- *Investors and potential investors in insurance companies* conduct financial analysis for the purpose of learning whether an insurer's securities, such as its common stock, are a suitable investment for them. Few individual investors have the financial expertise, time, or technology needed to conduct full-scale financial analysis of insurance companies, but institutional investors either have or can hire the expertise. Individual investors rely largely on the opinions of rating agencies and other professional financial analysts.

- *Consumers* of insurance and other financial products look for assurance that an insurance company is financially sound and will be a reliable provider of financial protection. Like individual investors, individual consumers seldom have the expertise, technology, or time to conduct their own sophisticated financial analysis. On behalf of individual consumers, *consumer watchdog groups,* such as Belth's *Insurance Forum,* monitor the financial conditions of insurance companies and make the results available to consumers.
- *Insurance brokers, independent insurance agents,* and *marketers of insurance products* use financial reporting when deciding which insurance companies' products to market to their clients.
- *Regulators* work on behalf of the public good by making sure that the insurance industry remains a reliable provider of financial protection for consumers. Regulators conduct financial studies of insurance companies mainly to identify insurers with potential financial problems and to make sure that any problems are addressed. In identifying problems, state regulators have access to the NAIC's ***Insurance Regulatory Information System (IRIS)*** and ***Financial Analysis and Solvency Tracking (FAST)*** system, which we discuss briefly in this chapter and more extensively in Chapter 18.
- *Rating agencies* produce quality ratings and summary financial information for consumers and investors. Insurers in turn use these quality ratings both for comparing themselves with other insurers and, when the ratings are favorable, for promoting their products and services to consumers, investors, and agents.

This chapter discusses financial analysis and solvency monitoring primarily as they are conducted internally and by rating agencies.

Sources of Information for Financial Analysis

The individuals and organizations monitoring the financial strength of insurance companies obtain information from a number of sources.

The financial information available to them ranges from fairly raw financial data in an insurer's internal reports to summarized financial information and financial ratio results published by rating agencies and regulators. Some financial information about the industry is published and made available to the general public; other information is not published and is difficult for just anyone to obtain because it is considered private.

Private financial information includes the various internal financial reports that an insurance company produces for its own use—for example, monthly budget reports and monthly sales figures. Private internal information also includes the raw financial data that insurers maintain in their databases. Insurance company staff members who conduct internal financial monitoring for their own company have extensive access to the company's raw data and internal reports. Outside organizations, such as regulators and rating agencies, may also gain access to some of this internal information, but only on a need-to-know basis. Insurers sometimes invite a rating agency to analyze the insurer's solvency or its claims paying ability. When rating agencies are conducting a rating analysis, they gain access to reports and financial data that the insurer would not normally share with an outside party. Similarly, insurance regulatory agencies periodically conduct on-site examinations of insurers and gain access to private information.

Two sources of readily available financial information about an insurance company are the company's statutory financial statements and, if required, its GAAP-based annual report to the company's owners. In the United States, all insurers must file a statutory-basis Annual Statement with the insurance authorities in every state in which they do business. Most states require insurers to file these statements on a quarterly basis. Most insurers must also file the Annual Statement with the National Association of Insurance Commissioners (NAIC). These filings with the state authorities and the NAIC form the basis for much of the solvency surveillance carried out by the states and the NAIC.

In Canada, all insurers must file a GAAP-based Annual Return with the federal Office of the Superintendent of Financial Institutions (OSFI). Although the Annual Return required of insurers in Canada is similar in many respects to the Annual Statement in the United States, the Annual Return is prepared according to Canadian GAAP accounting standards.

Further, in the United States, all stock insurers are required to file GAAP-based annual reports and quarterly 10-Q reports with the Securities and Exchange Commission (SEC). These annual reports are published and distributed to all of a company's stockholders and to others interested in the company.

Publication of Financial Data about Insurers

Most of the financial information in U.S. statutory filings is stored in the NAIC's financial database. This database contains annual and quarterly financial information for approximately 5,000 insurance companies—property/casualty as well as life/health. All of the state insurance regulatory departments are linked to the NAIC's database by computer. The NAIC and the various rating agencies additionally publish summary financial information about insurance companies. Such summary information typically includes financial ratio results. For example, the NAIC, the A.M. Best Company, and TRAC Insurance Services, Ltd., all publish ratio results for insurance companies.

Comparing Financial Data

Although a variety of published financial data about insurance companies is readily accessible to a researcher, we must caution that correctly using the data requires special knowledge. Correctly interpreting published financial data—particularly financial data describing financial institutions—requires insurance-specific financial expertise. When considering the published sources of financial information, the inexperienced reader must keep in mind that financial information should be compared only if it was developed on the same accounting basis. Further, information may appear to the novice to have been developed on a comparable basis when it actually was not. Consider the following examples of potential pitfalls in evaluating the comparability of financial statement data:

- U.S. statutory and GAAP balance sheets show amounts for assets and liabilities. However, statutory and GAAP requirements apply different sets of assumptions to arrive at the reported amounts of balance sheet assets and liabilities. One company's GAAP statements are thus not comparable with another company's statutory statements.

- Further, generally accepted accounting principles themselves permit some variation in the assumptions used to arrive at various reported amounts. When comparing values from two apparently similar GAAP statements, the analyst must be aware of the assumptions used for arriving at those values and make appropriate adjustments to ensure that the comparisons are valid. For example, U.S. GAAP allows for several *depreciation methods*—methods of calculating the depreciated value of assets. The GAAP-based financial statements of companies using different depreciation methods would not be strictly comparable. Each method can produce a different reported amount for the depreciated assets.

- Likewise, statutory accounting permits some variation in the assumptions underlying reported amounts. For example, this textbook has already mentioned that companies employ differing degrees of conservatism in setting the amounts of reserves for life insurance or annuities. When comparing values from two apparently similar statutory statements, the analyst must make any adjustments needed for ensuring that the comparisons are valid.
- Similarly, the results of published financial ratios depend upon the assumptions used in developing those ratio values. For example, the *quick liquidity ratio* presented later in this chapter measures the relationship between an insurance company's liquid assets and its reserves. However, in developing the results for the quick liquidity ratio, one financial analyst may employ the book value of the insurer's assets, while another analyst states the assets at market value.
- Comparisons of two insurance companies having dissimilar mixes of products may not be valid. A company with a concentration of business in group health would have financial ratio results very different from those of another company with a concentration of business in life insurance and annuities.
- Comparisons of two companies operating in different jurisdictions may not be valid. For instance, a comparison of data taken from the U.S. Annual Statement of one company to data taken from the Canadian Annual Return of another company would be useless.

Quantitative and Qualitative Information

A complete understanding of an insurer's financial condition requires both quantitative and qualitative information and analysis. While the mathematical examination of financial figures makes up an extensive part of any financial analysis, experienced financial analysts also seek other sources of information that may provide additional insights into a company's condition. Qualitative information may appear less concrete and more ambiguous than numbers, but qualitative information is often essential for gaining a balanced understanding of a company's financial data. Sources of qualitative information include public financial statements, internal company records, interviews with company management, press coverage of the company, and the company's notes to its financial statements. These sources provide the following types of information:

- Public financial statements provide information about the quality of a company's assets, not just the amounts of the assets. Public financial filings can also show evidence of burdensome obligations resulting from holding company relationships.

- Internal records, available only to analysts inside a company, provide valuable information about the quality of a company's earnings and the sources of its profits. An analyst could need to know whether a life company's profits arise from its traditional whole life business or its universal life business.

- Interviews with management are used to inform analysts about the ability and qualifications of a company's management as well as management's intentions for the company's future.

- News coverage may indicate financial and nonfinancial developments—such as the passage of new legislation, a filing of a lawsuit, an adverse court ruling, or a natural disaster—that could affect the company.

- Notes to a company's financial statements often provide crucial information that is not otherwise apparent. These notes typically describe major developments affecting either the company's financial condition or the reporting of it. For example, the ***accounting policies note*** typically included in an annual report describes the accounting conventions used during the past year. This accounting policies note also states whether the company has changed its accounting policies since the prior reporting period. Any such change cautions analysts against directly comparing the current financial statement with previous statements. Other notes identify large one-time losses and gains, or unusual and important events—such as a lawsuit or a natural disaster—that could damage the company's financial outlook.

By obtaining a variety of qualitative and quantitative information, analysts hope to find not just the obvious financial figures but also less apparent information that may help them gauge a company's potential. Insight 15-1 presents the qualitative factors that the A.M. Best Company applied to its evaluation of every life and health insurer's overall financial strength for 1993.

Financial Statement Analysis

Financial statement analysis is the evaluation of information presented in financial statements. The major financial statements are informally known as the *balance sheet*, the *income statement*, the *statement of cash flows*, and the *statement of retained earnings*.

Insight 15-1 Best's Qualitative Factors

The A.M. Best Company, a rating service specializing in the insurance industry, assigns ratings of financial stability to insurers based on quantitative and qualitative criteria. Best's quantitative criteria generally compare an insurer's performance to industry norms, whereas Best's qualitative criteria are based on the evaluator's judgment of more abstract elements to measure the company's current and future financial strength. Factors considered are size of contracts issued, surrender charges or market value adjustments, withdrawal systems, distribution systems, financial disincentives for replacement of policies, liquidity of assets, cash flows, and insurer's media profile. Best's qualitative criteria include the following:

- **Spread of risk.** Company's stability based on geographic base, product lines, and distribution systems; exposure to regulatory or residual market risks; distribution and performance of company's assets.
- **Quality and appropriateness of reinsurance.** Appropriateness of company's reinsurance program relative to policy limits and underwriting risks involved, amount of business written, and the financial capacity and credit-worthiness of its reinsurers.
- **Quality and diversification of assets.** Company's invested assets (e.g., stocks, bonds, real estate, mortgage loans) in terms of their diversification, liquidity, stability, and potential effect on policyholders' security in the event of unfavorable changes in underwriting and/or economic conditions.
- **Adequacy of policy and loss reserves.** Insurer's profitability, leverage (capitalization), and liquidity, specifically net income and policyholders' surplus, relative to its policy reserves. For life/health companies, also valuation basis, interest assumptions, and degree of conservatism in establishing reserves.
- **Adequacy of surplus.** Adequacy of insurer's surplus in providing margin of safety against the unexpected, given the company's underwriting, investment, and reinsurance exposure.
- **Capital structure/holding company.** Overall quality of insurer's capital structure, focusing on any financial instruments requiring debt service which might place demands on future earnings, surplus accumulation, and cash flows. Level of operating leverage employed against insurer's capital base and potential volatility of its business. A company's rating can be affected by its parent's financial flexibility.
- **Management experience and objectives.** Experience and integrity of insurer's management team, management's ability to enhance security of company's policyholders.
- **Market presence.** Insurer's strategies for responding to competitive challenges, regulatory pressures, and changing demographics of marketplace.
- **Policyholders' confidence.** Insurer's ability to satisfy obligations to policyholders under adverse conditions.

Source: *Preface, 1995 Best's Insurance Reports—Life/Health Edition (Oldwick, NJ: A.M. Best Company, 1996), pp. x–xi.*

These statements can be analyzed in a number of different ways. Three of the most important approaches to financial statement analysis are cross-sectional analysis, horizontal analysis, and vertical analysis.

- ***Cross-sectional analysis*** is a type of financial analysis designed for comparing one company's financial performance to the performance of one or more similar firms or else to industry-wide norms. Cross-sectional analysis involves examining the financial figures of more than one company at the same point in time. Cross-sectional analysis can employ either the dollar amounts that appear in financial statements or ratio values. Moreover, cross-sectional analysis can be used to compare overall results or only the results of selected operations.

- ***Horizontal analysis***—also called *trend analysis* and *time-series analysis*—is a type of financial analysis designed for identifying changes in one company's financial statement values over the course of several financial reporting periods. Horizontal analysis can also employ flat dollar amounts or ratio values. Horizontal analysis is not typically used to compare the performance of two or more firms.
- ***Vertical analysis*** is a type of financial analysis designed for examining the financial structure of one company at one point in time. Vertical analysis involves comparing various account values to one key account value on the same financial statement. For example, vertical analysis could be used to compare each line item from a company's income statement (statement of operations) to the company's total revenue. Each line item then would be expressed as a percentage of total revenue. Similarly, vertical analysis could be used to compare all line items from the balance sheet to a company's total liabilities.

Horizontal analysis and vertical analysis are similar in that they can both be used to evaluate a single company. They differ in that *horizontal analysis* is used to compare sets of data from different accounting periods, while *vertical analysis* compares data within one accounting period. Note, however, that the financial ratios created for vertical analysis can later be employed in cross-sectional analysis or horizontal analysis. Cross-sectional applications of ratio analysis enable an analyst to compare data from more than one company.

Using Ratios to Measure Financial Strength

A ***ratio*** is a comparison of two numeric values that results in a measurement expressed as a percentage or a fraction. When the ratio is expressed as a fraction, the number or expression in the top part of the fraction is known as the ***numerator;*** the number or expression in the bottom part of the fraction is known as the ***denominator.*** Ratios are typically presented as mathematical formulas. For example, the basic capital ratio formula is

$$\text{Capital Ratio} = \frac{\text{Capital and Surplus}}{\text{Liabilities}}$$

Suppose Argyle Insurance Company has capital (which includes *capital and surplus*) worth \$5 million and liabilities worth \$50 million. Here is the result of plugging these numbers into the capital ratio formula.

$$\$5{,}000{,}000 \div \$50{,}000{,}000 = .10, \text{ or } 10\%$$

This result shows that Argyle's liabilities are 10 times larger than its capital, which is typically an acceptable ratio result.

Figure 15-1 shows the basic or "generic" versions of the capital ratio, profitability ratio, leverage ratio, and liquidity ratio. In the sections that follow, we present the modified versions of these ratios that are typically applied to the financial data of insurance companies.

Modified Financial Ratios for Insurers

After years of observing the relationship between an insurer's financial condition and its financial ratios, analysts have learned that generic versions of financial ratios—such as the ones presented in Figure 15-1—are rarely suitable for a thorough financial analysis of an insurer. To take into account the unique aspects of insurers' financial statements, analysts have developed specialized versions of capital ratios, leverage ratios, liquidity ratios, and profitability ratios. In some instances, analysts have developed entirely new types of ratios.

So that the ratios designed for companies other than financial institutions will be accurate when used for insurers, analysts also often

Figure 15-1. Some non-industry-specific basic financial ratios.

Capital Ratio

$$\text{Capital Ratio} = \frac{\text{Capital}}{\text{Liabilities}}$$

Profitability Ratio

$$\text{Profitability Ratio} = \frac{\text{Earnings}}{\text{Sales}}$$

Leverage Ratio

$$\text{Leverage Ratio} = \frac{\text{Liabilities}}{\text{Capital}}$$

Liquidity Ratio

$$\text{Liquidity Ratio} = \frac{\text{Assets}}{\text{Liabilities}}$$

modify the forms of those ratios. The basic financial ratios generally can be modified by means of employing either (1) *adjusted measures* of traditional financial data or (2) *weighted values.*

To create an *adjusted measure* of financial performance, analysts take financial statement amounts and then modify the amounts for use in a ratio formula. Analysts make such modifications whenever they believe that, for the purpose of their analysis, using the adjusted amounts in a ratio calculation will provide a more accurate picture of an insurer's financial condition than would the unadjusted numbers. Balance sheet amounts that are often adjusted for financial ratio analysis of insurance company statements include (1) capital and surplus, (2) liabilities, and (3) assets.

Adjusted Capital and Surplus

One common adjustment to the reported statutory amounts of capital and surplus for insurance companies in the United States is to add the *asset valuation reserve (AVR)* and the *interest maintenance reserve (IMR)* back into capital and surplus. As we saw in Chapter 9, because the AVR and IMR do not represent obligations to pay money to any outside party, the AVR and IMR are not viewed as being "true liabilities." Another common adjustment includes adding other reserves that are optional and thus do not represent true liabilities. The amount of capital and surplus that results after a series of these adjustments is called an insurer's ***adjusted capital and surplus.*** One formula for finding adjusted capital and surplus is

$$\text{Adjusted Capital and Surplus} = \text{Capital and Surplus} + \text{AVR} + \text{IMR} + \text{Other Optional Reserves}$$

Adjusted Liabilities

A similar adjustment can be made to the liabilities side of the capital ratio. The AVR, IMR, and other optional reserves can be *subtracted* from a company's statutory liabilities, resulting in a measure of obligations called ***adjusted liabilities.*** A life and health insurance company's obligations can be defined as contractual reserves alone or contractual reserves along with other miscellaneous reserves and other liabilities. When developing a capital ratio, an analyst attempts to find the most appropriate measure of liabilities for the purpose at hand. One formula for finding adjusted liabilities is as follows:

$$\text{Adjusted Liabilities} = \text{Statutory Liabilities} - \text{AVR} - \text{IMR} + \text{Other Optional Reserves}$$

Adjusted Assets

Just as analysts sometimes adjust the measures of an insurer's capital and liabilities, analysts also sometimes adjust the reported amounts for assets. One important fact to note in connection with assets is that, for U.S. statutory accounting purposes, bonds are reported at book value whereas common stocks are reported at market value. For various purposes of financial analysis, however, a life and health insurance company's asset values can be reported in any of the following variations:

- All assets reported at *market* value
- All assets reported at *book* value
- All assets reported at a mix of book values and market values
- All assets reported at a diminished *risk-adjusted* value
- Only liquid assets reported—that is, only assets that can be converted to cash quickly and without loss of value

A financial analyst may also include or exclude specific categories of assets to suit the purpose of a given analysis. The purpose of each of these adjustments is to make each ratio calculation as sensitive as possible to a particular purpose for conducting financial analysis.

Weighted Values

A ***weighted value*** is an amount that has been multiplied by a percentage. The two most common reasons for weighting a value are (1) to indicate the effect risk may have on the value or (2) sometimes to indicate the proportion of a total amount that the value represents. Ratios that use weighted values are called *weighted ratios.* As with adjusted ratios, the purpose of weighted ratios is to provide analysts with a more complete or accurate measure of a company's financial condition. By using a risk-weighted element in calculating a capital ratio, an analyst is introducing a qualitative element to a quantitative formula. In this way, the analyst is considering the level of risk represented by the insurer's particular assets and liabilities. The NAIC's Risk-Based Capital formula, discussed in Chapters 2 and 10, is an example of a weighted ratio formula.

One important financial example of a weighted ratio is the calculation of a company's ***weighted average cost of capital (WACC),*** which is the overall cost that the company pays to obtain new funds from all sources. Calculating the WACC requires the following steps:

1. Finding the proportions of each source of a company's financing
2. Finding the cost of funds from each source

3. Weighting the costs to reflect the proportion of the firm's total capital associated with each cost, done by multiplying the percentage cost of each type of financing by its proportion in the company's capital structure
4. Summing the weighted costs

For example, suppose the Astro Corporation has capital from three sources, as follows:

1. 50 percent of its financing is common stock obtained at a cost of 10 percent
2. 20 percent of its financing is preferred stock obtained at a cost of 6 percent
3. 30 percent of its financing is long-term bonds obtained at a cost of 8 percent

Figure 15-2 shows how we calculate that Astro's weighted average cost of capital is 8.6 percent.

The capital ratio presented earlier in this chapter is an example of an unweighted capital ratio. Unweighted ratios may not provide a sound basis for comparing the performance of different insurers, partly because unweighted ratios bypass consideration of the different levels of risk inherent in different insurers' reserving practices and in their investments. The relative conservatism or riskiness of an insurer's management philosophy are reflected in an insurer's decisions about reserving practices, the asset mix of its investment portfolio, and its asset valuation practices. Reserving practices establish the amount of liabilities that an insurer reports; the asset mix influences the level of liquid assets available to pay an insurer's obligations; and asset valuation practices establish the amount of assets an insurer reports. Figure 15-3 summarizes these options reflecting the conservatism or aggressiveness of management philosophy.

An insurer's practices with regard to each of these three key decisions can be interpreted as conservative or aggressive. As we mentioned in Chapters 1 and 9, reserving practices are considered

Figure 15-2. Calculating the Astro Corporation's weighted average cost of capital (WACC).

	Cost	×	Weighting		
Common stock	10%	×	50%	=	0.050
Preferred stock	6%	×	20%	=	0.012
Long-term bonds	8%	×	30%	=	0.024
Weighted average cost of capital (WACC)				**=**	**0.086**

Figure 15-3. How conservatism or aggressiveness can affect financial condition.

Reserving practices	→	Amount of reported liabilities
Asset mix decisions	→	Availability of cash and liquid assets
Asset valuation decisions	→	Amount of reported assets

relatively *conservative* if reserves are set at a level greater than needed to cover the insurer's benefit obligations, and relatively *aggressive* if reserves are set at a level that is just enough to cover the insurer's benefit obligations. Many factors contribute to determining whether an insurer's investment practices are conservative or aggressive, and we reviewed some of these factors in Chapter 2. Although asset mix decisions are not a focus of this textbook, we can note here that asset mix decisions are relatively conservative if an insurer's portfolio is invested in a low-risk manner. For instance, a conservative asset mix would be appropriately diversified, and would consist mostly of moderate-risk and moderate-return assets. As we noted in Chapter 10, asset valuation practices are considered relatively *conservative* if asset values are set at a low level, and relatively *aggressive* if asset values are set at a high level. Figure 15-4 summarizes the effects of an insurer's conservative or aggressive practices on its overall risk profile. Next we review the modified forms of financial ratios that analysts typically use for evaluating insurance companies.

Capital Ratios for Insurers

We have noted already that capital ratios are a measure of an insurer's financial strength. In general, the greater the value of the capital ratio, the stronger the insurer's financial position. However, as we

Figure 15-4. How some key choices affect an insurer's overall risk profile.

Reserving practices . . .	Asset mix decisions . . .	Asset valuation practices . . .
. . . are considered to be relatively **conservative** if . . .		
Reserves (values of liabilities) are set at a high level.	Asset mix is well diversified and reflects moderate-risk, moderate-return choices.	Asset values are set at a low level.
. . . are considered to be relatively **aggressive** if . . .		
Reserves (values of liabilities) are set at a low level.	Asset mix is poorly diversified or reflects high-risk, high-return choices.	Asset values are set at a high level.

also noted earlier in this text, a number of factors can significantly affect a company's capital position, and no two insurance companies have the same risk exposures. Therefore, the same unweighted capital ratio value that would be acceptable for one insurer would be too low for another insurer that has more exposure to capital risk. Likewise, comparing the unweighted capital ratios of two insurers would not be informative.

To account for different levels of risk exposure, analysts typically employ risk-weighted ratios and adjusted values to measure a company's capital strength. For this reason, the NAIC developed an official Risk-Based Capital (RBC) ratio requirement for regulators to use in identifying potentially impaired insurers. In Canada, regulators rely on the somewhat similar *minimum continuing capital and surplus requirements (MCCSR),* which also involve a risk-weighted capital calculation. Further, as we noted in Chapter 10, internal management and rating agencies use risk-weighted capital formulas for evaluating desirable—rather than minimum—levels of capital. We return to the topic of the NAIC's Risk-Based Capital (RBC) requirement and Canada's MCCSR in more detail in Chapter 18.

Leverage Ratios for Insurers

Capital and surplus ratios are only one approach to comparing an insurance company's assets to its obligations. Leverage ratios are also used for comparing an insurer's obligations to its ability to meet those obligations. Leverage is a key concept in the field of finance. ***Leverage*** (the ***leverage effect***) can be defined as a financial effect in which incurring fixed costs—either operating costs or financing costs—usually in order to gain access to greater resources, automatically magnifies risks and potential returns to the company's owners. In finance, the presence of fixed costs, such as the cost of debt repayment, automatically magnifies both risks and returns. The leverage effect applies to all types of firms, including insurance companies. As a company's leverage increases, the company's exposure to risk of loss increases, and the company's potential for earnings also increases. Conversely, as the company's leverage decreases, the company's risk of loss decreases, and the company's potential for earnings also decreases. In other words, the leverage effect magnifies the risk-return tradeoff.

For example, suppose that Ratchet Assurance can borrow money for 8 percent interest. If Ratchet can invest the borrowed money to earn a return of 10 percent, then Ratchet's owners will be able to keep a marginal return of 2 percent on the borrowed funds. Upon borrowing the money at 8 percent, though, Ratchet establishes an obligation to meet a fixed interest expense. Thus, leverage also magnifies the risk to Ratchet's owners: If Ratchet's management cannot find a way to invest the money to earn at least 8 percent, Ratchet's owners will lose money every time Ratchet pays loan interest.

We can distinguish among three types of leverage: total leverage, operating leverage, and financial leverage. Briefly, ***operating leverage*** can be defined as the effect whereby incurring fixed operating costs automatically magnifies a company's risks and potential returns. Similarly, ***financial leverage*** is defined as the effect whereby incurring fixed financing costs—usually borrowed funds—automatically magnifies a company's risks and potential returns. ***Total leverage*** is the combined effect of operating and financial leverage, and total leverage represents the effect whereby incurring fixed costs automatically magnifies both risks and potential returns to the company's owners. Financial leverage, operating leverage, and total leverage can be either positive or negative.

If a company can employ fixed operating costs to generate a return greater than the cost of employing the fixed operating costs, it is taking advantage of positive operating leverage. If a company takes on increased fixed operating costs but then fails to earn enough of a return from operations to cover the added costs, then the company is experiencing negative operating leverage and is in a worse position than if it had not taken on the fixed costs in the first place. The hope of gaining positive operating leverage may be the motive behind insurers' undertaking such efforts as reengineering and mergers, discussed in Chapter 20.

Although insurers do not typically have significant amounts of traditional debt, insurers must in effect "repay" the premiums that the customers in essence "loaned" to them. Thus, an insurer's contractual obligations to its customers are sometimes viewed as being similar to debt. If any company borrows funds, invests the funds, and earns a return greater than the interest expense the company must pay to the lender, then the company earns a return that it would not otherwise have earned. The difference between the cost of borrowing money and the return earned by using the borrowed money is variously called the *margin, spread, marginal return,* or *profit margin.* (This notion echoes our discussions of profit margins in earlier chapters.) Any such profit margin represents a higher overall level of returns to the company's owners than if the company had not borrowed funds. This effect of earning an enhanced return due to the presence of leverage is termed a ***positive leverage effect.***

As you probably suspect, whenever investors identify an increased potential for returns, the company also has an increased risk of loss. If a company borrows funds, invests the funds, and earns a return lower than the interest expense the company must pay to the lender, then the company is in a worse position than if it had not taken on the leverage. This diminished return because of the presence of leverage is termed a ***negative leverage effect.***

Figure 15-5. Examples of positive leverage and negative leverage.

	With debt	Positive leverage if earnings rise in Period 2	Negative leverage if earnings drop in Period 2
	Period 1	**Positive Period 2**	**Negative Period 2**
Earnings before interest and taxes	$100,000	$200,000	$ 50,000
Period 2: Percent change in earnings	N/A	**up 100.0%**	**down 50.0%**
Interest paid on fixed-cost debt	$ 20,000	$ 20,000	$ 20,000
Net earnings before taxes	$ 80,000	$180,000	$ 30,000
Taxes (40%)	$ 32,000	$ 72,000	$ 12,000
Net earnings after taxes	$ 48,000	$108,000	$ 18,000
Period 2: Percent change in earnings	N/A	**up 125.0%**	**down 62.5%**
Capital and surplus	$1 million	$1 million	$1 million
Percent Return on Capital = Net Earnings / Capital and Surplus	4.8%	10.8%	1.8%

Let's consider a couple of brief examples to see how, with existing debt, a company's increase or decrease in earnings is magnified. In Figure 15-5, we present examples of earnings calculations for two scenarios involving a company with fixed debt charges: one in which the company experiences a dramatic increase in earnings, and another in which the same company experiences a dramatic decrease in earnings.

In our scenario illustrating positive financial leverage, when the company's gross earnings (or EBIT) went up 100.0 percent, net earnings went up 125.0 percent. In the scenario illustrating negative financial leverage, when gross earnings (or EBIT) went down 50.0 percent, net earnings went down 62.5 percent.

The purpose of leverage ratios is to measure an organization's debt burden relative to the resources available to support the debt burden. The basic leverage ratio for insurers is the inverse of the basic capital ratio for insurers. Thus, this basic leverage ratio for insurers is

$$\textbf{Leverage Ratio} = \frac{\textbf{Liabilities}}{\textbf{Capital}}$$

For insurance leverage ratios, liabilities can be measured in terms of contractual reserves alone or contractual reserves plus other miscellaneous reserves and other liabilities. This section presents two leverage ratios: (1) the insurance leverage ratio and (2) the surplus relief ratio.

The Insurance Leverage Ratio

One leverage ratio for noninsurance businesses, the *debt-equity* ratio, is the ratio of long-term debt to total equity. A somewhat comparable leverage ratio for life and health insurance companies, called the ***insurance leverage ratio,*** is the ratio of contractual reserves to capital and surplus. Note that this insurance leverage ratio—also sometimes known as the *gross leverage ratio*—focuses on contractual insurance obligations, and not *all* liabilities. The insurance leverage ratio is

$$\text{Insurance Leverage Ratio} = \frac{\text{Contractual Reserves}}{\text{Capital and Surplus}}$$

The Surplus Relief Ratio

One ratio mentioned in Chapter 14 examines the insurer's use of reinsurance, whether providing reinsurance to other insurance companies or obtaining reinsurance for its own liabilities. This ratio is known as the surplus relief ratio. *Surplus relief* generally refers to the effect that reinsurance can have on improving an insurer's capital and surplus position. As we noted in Chapter 14, ceding reinsurance can be viewed as an alternative source of financing for insurers, and thus reinsurance affects leverage.

The ***surplus relief ratio*** compares the insurer's net cost for or net earnings from ceding and assuming reinsurance to the insurer's capital and surplus. Thus, a surplus relief ratio generally has a *positive* value whenever an insurer ceded more reinsurance coverage than the insurer assumed. Conversely, a surplus relief ratio generally has a *negative* value whenever an insurer assumed more reinsurance than it ceded. The surplus relief ratio is as follows:

$$\text{Surplus Relief Ratio} = \frac{\text{Net Cost for or Net Income from Reinsurance}}{\text{Capital and Surplus}}$$

An accurate interpretation of a company's results for the surplus relief ratio is relative to each company's absolute level of capital and surplus, its lines of business, and many other factors. We can nevertheless make some generalizations about the meaning of high or low values for the surplus relief ratio. A very large *positive* value for the surplus relief ratio can sometimes indicate that the company's own management believes that its capital and surplus is too low, and thus has obtained an extraordinary amount of reinsurance. Conversely, a very large *negative* value for the surplus relief ratio can indicate that an insurer is straining its capital and surplus by assuming large amounts of reinsurance.

Liquidity Ratios for Insurers

Liquidity of assets refers to the ease with which assets can be converted to cash without loss in value. ***Liquid assets*** include cash and other readily marketable assets. Traditional liquidity ratios compare some measure of a company's liquid assets to a measure of the company's short-term liabilities. Not surprisingly, measures of an insurer's liquidity focus on whether the insurance company can meet its cash commitments. Thus, any type of insurance liquidity ratio compares the value of some measure of liquid assets to some measure of total reserves. Liquidity ratios for insurers generally take the following form:

$$\text{Generic Insurance Liquidity Ratio} = \frac{\text{Liquid Assets}}{\text{Total Reserves}}$$

The exact level of liquidity that any insurer needs depends primarily on the lines of insurance business being evaluated. In general, however, a relatively high value for a liquidity ratio indicates that the company has plenty of ready cash for meeting its immediate obligations. On the other hand, excessively high values for a liquidity ratio can indicate inefficient deployment of assets, and can raise concerns about the company's having adequate yields to support products.

Analysts of life and health insurers employ a number of ratios specifically designed to measure the liquidity positions of life and health insurers. The liquidity ratios we discuss are known as quick liquidity, current liquidity, and the insurance liquidity ratio. Because these ratios can be formulated in a number of ways, depending upon the purpose of a given analytical exercise, the formulas given here should be regarded as representative ways of expressing these formulas.

- ***Quick liquidity*** compares an insurer's liquid assets to *contractual reserves*—not to total liabilities. This ratio indicates a company's ability to meet maturing obligations without selling its long-term investments or borrowing money. The quick liquidity ratio is calculated as follows:

$$\text{Quick Liquidity Ratio} = \frac{\text{Liquid Assets at Statutory Value}}{\text{Contractual Reserves}}$$

- ***Current liquidity*** compares all of an insurer's short-term and long-term assets not invested in affiliates with all of the insurer's *liabilities*—not reserves alone. This ratio measures an insurer's ability to meet all of its financial obligations without borrowing money. The formula for the *current liquidity* ratio is

$$\text{Current Liquidity Ratio} = \frac{\text{Market Values of Total Short- and Long-Term Assets Not Invested in Affiliates}}{\text{Total Liabilities}}$$

- The ***insurance liquidity ratio*** compares the market value of liquid assets to some measure of total reserves. Thus, an insurance liquidity ratio would take the following form:

$$\text{Insurance Liquidity Ratio} = \frac{\text{Liquid Assets at Market Value}}{\text{Total Reserves}}$$

Profitability Ratios for Insurers

Profitability ratios measure the success of an insurer's growth effort and focus on whether a company is prospering. Profitability ratios typically compare a measure of gain from operations (the ratio's numerator) to a measure of the resources employed or invested to earn the gain (in the ratio's denominator). In general, the higher the value of a profitability ratio, the better. (At some very high levels, though, a high value could indicate extreme riskiness.) The adequacy of a company's profits, as reflected in its profitability ratios, can provide useful insights into the company's financial strength. To measure an insurer's efficiency of operations, the A.M. Best Company and IRIS both employ a number of ratios that compare some measure of the insurer's business activity to the insurer's premium income and other product-related income. In all of these premium income ratios, the denominator (bottom) of the ratio is net premiums written. ***Net premiums written*** refers to premiums written adjusted to exclude reinsurance effects.

One premium-based profitability ratio compares *net gain from operations* to net premiums written. Another such ratio compares *benefits paid* to net premiums written. Yet another ratio compares *commissions paid* to net premiums written. Within a normal range of results for these ratios, an insurer would like for premiums to be high in relation to benefits and commissions paid. Also, an insurer would prefer for the net gain from operations to be high in relation to net premiums written.

For life and health insurance companies, inadequate profits can result from any of the following circumstances:[1]

- Adverse mortality and morbidity experience relative to product pricing assumptions
- Inadequacy of investment income relative to crediting rates and other product design elements
- High commissions, loose control of expenses, and excessive spending in general
- A mismatch between statutory reserve requirements, current market interest rates, and premium rates for new business, and crediting rates for interest-sensitive business

Analysts also use profitability ratios when performing a horizontal or cross-sectional analysis. However, expert analysts typically do not use companywide profitability ratios in intercompany comparisons (cross-sectional analysis) of insurance companies. Instead, intercompany comparisons focus on comparing the companies' profitability results from the same line of business, and not their corporatewide profitability. For example, it makes sense to compare the profitability ratios of Eucalyptus Life and Health's group life and health line to similar ratio results for Archer Assurance's group life and health line. It does not make sense to compare the results of Eucalyptus Life and Health's group life and health line to Archer Assurance's property and casualty lines.

Selecting Appropriate Measures of Profits Earned and Resources Employed

Before analysts can develop viable profitability ratios, they need to choose the appropriate measures of both (1) profits earned and (2) resources employed. In choosing an appropriate measure of profit, an analyst can choose between profit *before taxes* and profit *after taxes.* Choosing a measure of the resources employed depends on the analyst's purpose in seeking the profitability information. An analyst may be seeking an overall measure of the insurer's profitability. Another analyst may seek to identify the sources of the insurer's profits. To find these sources, analysts typically look in detail at an insurer's two main sources of cash inflows: *investment income* and *premium income.* In the next few pages we present profitability ratios that measure gross profit, net profit, and investment profit. We then look at a number of profitability ratios that compare profits to premiums.

- The ***gross profit ratio,*** in the version employed by the A.M. Best Company, provides an uncomplicated measure of the growth in an insurance company's capital and surplus. This gross profit ratio compares the insurer's contributions to capital and surplus for one period to the insurer's beginning capital and surplus for the period. Contributions to capital and surplus are calculated as ending capital and surplus minus beginning capital and surplus. The gross profit ratio for insurers is expressed as

$$\text{Gross Profit Ratio} = \frac{\text{Gross Contributions to Capital and Surplus}}{\text{Beginning Capital and Surplus}}$$

- As we noted in Chapter 1, *return on capital,* similar to the standard *return on equity (ROE),* can be defined as the percentage return an insurer has earned on its capital. The ratio employs a measure of earnings taken from the end of a period and a measure of capital and surplus from the beginning of the same period. Return on capital is calculated by dividing some measure of earnings by some measure of *total capital employed.* Two measures of *earnings* sometimes used in this ratio are earnings before interest, dividends, and taxes and *net gain from operations.* The result of this return on capital ratio shows how efficiently the company has used capital and surplus to earn a return. The return on capital ratio for insurers can be expressed as

$$\text{Return on Capital Ratio} = \frac{\text{Ending Earnings}}{\text{Beginning Capital and Surplus}}$$

- The ***return on invested assets (ROIA) ratio*** for insurers takes into account the net gain from all sources of income—including premiums and investments. The ratio then compares this earnings amount to the investment portfolio assets to show how efficiently the company used the investment portfolio to earn a return. The return on invested assets for insurers can be expressed as

$$\text{Return on Invested Assets Ratio} = \frac{\text{Net Gain from Operations}}{\text{Average Invested Assets}}$$

- The ***investment yield ratio*** for insurers measures the effectiveness of the insurer's investment managers in earning returns on the investment portfolio. The result of this ratio shows how efficiently the company used the investment portfolio to earn a return. This variation on traditional ROA compares the insurer's investment income to the insurer's average invested assets for the period. The investment yield ratio for insurers can be expressed as

$$\text{Investment Yield Ratio} = \frac{\text{Investment Income}}{\text{Average Invested Assets}}$$

- To measure an insurer's ***net gain to total income,*** financial analysts apply the formula

$$\text{Net Gain to Total Income Ratio} = \frac{\text{Net Gain from Operations}}{\text{Total Income + Realized Capital Gains and Losses}}$$

This relationship highlights the share of an insurer's operating income that represents a profit. Viewed in another way, this ratio also represents the share of the insurer's revenue that is NOT used to cover expenses. This is one of the NAIC's IRIS ratios. In IRIS, any result greater than zero is considered to be within the normal range. Any negative value for this test is not within the normal range.

Before finalizing our discussion of financial measurement of insurance companies, we must discuss one additional measure of profitability. This measure of profitability differs from the profitability ratios we have already discussed in that it is a dollar amount.

Economic Value Added Analysis

Economic value added (EVA), sometimes called *value added, embedded value,* or even *residual income,* is an approach to evaluating the profitability of a business entity. EVA involves comparing the business entity's return to its overall cost of capital. We discussed cost of capital in several earlier chapters, including Chapters 1 and 10, and we discussed the weighted average cost of capital (WACC) earlier in this chapter. In theory, the measure of profitability derived using EVA is more precise than are such traditional profitability measures as GAAP-based return on capital. Thus, EVA is theoretically the methodology of choice for comparing a business's return on capital with its cost of capital. One reason for the preference is that traditional return on capital, return on assets, and return on equity do not take into consideration the cost of capital, whereas EVA does.

For example, suppose that the Sycamore Company is earning 15 percent return on capital and the Glendale Company is earning 10 percent return on capital. Taken alone, these return on capital figures seem to indicate that Sycamore is more profitable than Glendale. However, we also need to know that Sycamore's cost of capital is 18 percent and Glendale's is 8 percent. As illustrated in the table below, when cost of capital is also considered, Glendale is more profitable than Sycamore.

	Sycamore	Glendale
Return on capital	15%	10%
Cost of capital	18%	8%
Profit margin (loss)	(3%)	2%

Because Sycamore is paying a higher percentage cost of capital than the percentage return it is earning on that capital, Sycamore's capital is actually diminishing. On the other hand, Glendale is earning a higher percentage return on capital than the percentage cost it is paying for the use of that capital, and therefore Glendale is *adding value*—increasing its capital.

The numerical result for EVA represents the dollar amount by which a given business venture is expected to increase (or decrease) the company's value, considering the cost of capital. For a given venture, if an EVA result is positive, then the venture's return on capital is greater than its cost of capital, and the venture is *adding value,* or increasing capital. Similarly, if an EVA result is negative, the venture is *destroying value,* or decreasing the company's capital.

The EVA calculation requires first developing a dollar-amount estimate of a business entity's net operating cash flows and subtracting from that figure a capital charge that is equal to a dollar-amount estimate of the cost of capital employed to earn the operating cash flows. Thus, EVA parallels the familiar formula *profit equals income minus expenses.* Calculating EVA utilizes the net present value (NPV) calculation discussed in Chapter 6. For EVA calculations, the discount rate used is the cost of capital, expressed as a percentage. The EVA formula for one period can be summarized in the following form:

EVA for One Period = Operating Cash Flows – Capital Charge

EVA for a project extending over several years can be calculated using a procedure involving taking the present value of each period's EVA and then summing the results, as follows:

Step 1: Find annual net operating cash flows and an annual capital charge. The capital charge is calculated as

Capital Charge = Capital Employed that Year × WACC Percentage

Step 2: Subtract the annual capital charge from the annual net operating cash flows, and then discount each annual amount at the WACC percentage. Upon completing Step 2, you will have a series of annual EVA amounts.

Step 3: Sum the annual results from Step 2. Upon completing Step 3, you will have a lifetime EVA amount.

This procedure is summarized in the following worksheet:

+ [Year 1 Net Operating Cash Flows – Year 1 Capital Charge] discounted at the WACC rate
+ [Year 2 Net Operating Cash Flows – Year 2 Capital Charge] discounted at the WACC rate
. . . + [Year *n* Net Operating Cash Flows – Year *n* Capital Charge] discounted at the WACC rate
= EVA

Proper interpretation and application of EVA can be used to identify sources of a company's profitability. In addition to taking into account the cost of capital, EVA can be contrasted with traditional profitability ratios—such as ROA, ROE, and ROI—in several other respects:

- Traditional profitability measures are based on accounting returns and, thus, reflect a variety of accounting conventions and include noncash transactions, whereas EVA is based on the cash flows related to a business venture.
- Traditional profitability measures are based on comparing expected results to actual results, whereas EVA calculations may incorporate highly subjective estimates of future streams of revenues, sales, and costs. Moreover, this subjectivity presents a means for managerial manipulation of EVA results.
- Traditional profitability measures are based on a single accounting period, whereas EVA is based on the entire lifetime of cash flows related to a business venture.
- Traditional profitability measures may not automatically take into account the time value of money, whereas EVA takes into account the time value of money by discounting cash flows.
- EVA behaves differently from traditional profitability measures in that small changes in EVA assumptions can produce large changes in EVA results, and, thus, it can be tough to understand changes in EVA results from one year to another.
- EVA produces a dollar amount figure that is a function of the investment project's size, whereas traditional profitability measures produce a percentage. Percentages are useful for comparing investment projects of different sizes.

Organizations often have difficulty in gaining acceptance for EVA. Traditional accounting measures of profitability are strongly entrenched in many organizations. In addition, traditional accounting measures are easier for many people to understand than are discounted cash flow techniques such as EVA. For convenience, insurers frequently substitute statutory cash flows in place of net operating cash flows. Although insurers in the United States and Canada already routinely forecast their future cash flows for other purposes, implementing EVA can be costly, even for insurers. Insight 15-2 discusses some keys to successful implementation of EVA.

Insight 15-2 EVA Works—But Not If You Make These Mistakes

Scores of companies have turned to economic value added (EVA) over the past few years as a new way to gauge financial performance. Highly regarded corporations like Coca-Cola, AT&T, Quaker Oats, and Briggs & Stratton have set up EVA measurement systems throughout their organizations. These have provided financial discipline, encouraged managers to act like owners, and, most important, have boosted shareholders' fortunes.

But despite these widely reported successes, only a handful of companies today are getting EVA right. What we've seen in the rush toward EVA is that many companies don't know how to implement it and therefore aren't getting nearly its full benefits.

Here are five main ways business people err in applying EVA:

• **They don't make it a way of life.** The most common mistake is to think that all you need to do is calculate EVA. If a company tells me that's what they're doing, I say, "Excuse me, but you're only calculating EVA. You're not adopting it." EVA is really the centerpiece of a comprehensive financial management system. That means all the policies, procedures, measures, and methods companies use to guide and control their operations and strategy. It has to do with how they set overall financial goals, how they communicate those goals inside the organization and outside to the investment community, and how they evaluate opportunities to build the business and invest capital, whether it's for the purchase of a single piece of equipment or the acquisition of a company.

Example: Many companies fail to tie compensation to changes in EVA. Say you have a CEO whose bonus and pension are linked to earnings and who will be retiring in three years. A rational CEO might slash R&D to get short-term profits up; five years down the road profits will be hurt with no new products coming onstream. But what you spend on R&D doesn't affect EVA in the year you spend it, so the CEO has nothing to gain by squeezing R&D. In other words, once EVA is adapted to a given system, it's difficult for managers to play games with the budget at shareholders' expense.

• **Most managers try to implement EVA too fast.** You can't implement EVA overnight. For an enterprise with sales under $250 million, becoming an EVA company takes four to five months. For companies with up to $1 billion in sales, it could take six to nine months. And for a very large company, it could take a couple of years.

Start with top management using it day to day, then gradually push it down through the ranks. Some companies make the mistake of trying to implement it all at once, but they'll probably have too many people to train and too much disruption. And if top managers don't understand EVA deeply, how can they explain it to those working for them?

While EVA should be fully integrated into your company, don't overdo it by trying to apply it to every nook and cranny. That makes it too complicated and expensive to administer. Engine maker Briggs & Stratton found the right balance for EVA. Previously managed as one big company, it was highly vertically integrated

Insight 15-2 EVA Works—But Not If You Make These Mistakes (continued)

and made many different engine lines. Top management first considered figuring just one overall EVA measurement, but they recognized that a single calculation wouldn't show what was really going on in different parts of the company. So they decided to divide the company by types of engine and by critical functions (manufacturing, distribution, and so forth) and measure EVA in those areas. Carving the company up into finer pieces would have made information gathering too expensive and given people too much incentive to maximize locally at the expense of the company.

• **The boss lacks conviction.** Too often the CEO or division or department head abrogates his responsibility to force the implementation of EVA from the top down. This is necessary because EVA is not always something operating people will want to do. Say you have mediocre managers who have been overpaid, who have a bonus plan that pays them to meet their budget, and who can easily meet their budget. Life is good. What incentive do they have to make a change to EVA, under which they will suddenly be held accountable for creating value? They may well resist it. Yes, there's a process of selling EVA, but it should be sold with the idea that it's going to be bought.

Also, if the boss is not totally committed, staffs can form fiefdoms and war among themselves. Say the CFO (chief financial officer) is leading the EVA charge, and the head of human resources, who is also very powerful, sees the EVA incentive plan as poaching on his territory. The human resources people have incentives to undermine EVA, or they let the CFO develop EVA while they keep the old incentive program in place and simply call it an EVA program. That blows the whole thing. You lose about 50 percent of the power of EVA if the incentive plan is not truly driven by it.

• **Managers fuss too much.** When implementing EVA, companies tend to make it a big philosophical issue. Managers try to convince everyone that, by George, we've got to create shareholder value. And they get into a big debate about what it means to create value for the shareholder as opposed to the employee or the community. This becomes terribly distracting and ultimately meaningless. You should put the philosophizing aside and say to your people something like: "What if we found a measure of financial performance that really captures all the things a person can do to run the business more efficiently, to satisfy customers, to reward shareholders? Wouldn't it make sense to use that to shape our financial decision-making?" And leave it at that. If you integrate EVA well enough, all your stakeholders will be taken care of.

• **Training gets short shrift.** Companies sometimes don't disseminate EVA knowledge widely enough through the organization. Those that understand EVA know how important it is to train everyone in the organization because even those with the smallest jobs can help create value. This means linking EVA to key operating metrics like cycle time or inventory turns and making sure the people involved understand how EVA fits in. For instance, inventory turns have an EVA payoff because if you're turning your inventory faster, you have reduced the amount of capital you need and thus have raised EVA.

Varity, a farm equipment manufacturer based in Buffalo, gave EVA training to all 3,500 of its European employees, including the guys who tighten bolts on tractors. One man who managed its inventory stockroom told his boss one day, "My suggestion, now that I understand EVA, is that you put a lock on the warehouse door and throw the key away. We're filling up this warehouse with inventory just because it's there. If you gave us a football field, we would fill up a football field. If you gave us a broom closet, we'd fill a broom closet. So give us a broom closet. Make inventory the responsibility of the dispatchers on line." When his boss asked him why he didn't say this before, he said, "Nobody asked."

Done right, EVA precipitates a major cultural change without requiring people to be aware of it and go on camping trips together or beat drums. What you're doing is very quietly weaving into your culture a new financial management, measurement, and incentive system. Before you know it, what jumps out is a new culture that's right for times of rapid change and turmoil. People put the creation of shareholder value at the top of the pyramid, and when that happens, chances are your business will end up on top too.

Source: *G. Bennett Stewart III, "EVA Works—But Not If You Make These Mistakes,"* Fortune *(May 5, 1995), pp. 117–118. Reprinted with permission of the publisher.*

Rating Agency Monitoring of Insurers

A number of rating agencies analyze and provide reports on the financial strength of insurance companies. ***Rating agencies*** are organizations, owned independently of any insurer or government body, that evaluate the financial condition of insurers and provide information to potential customers of and investors in insurance companies.

The Rating Agencies

Some rating agencies are better known than others. Each rating agency independently decides what types of information it will publish and what sources of information it will use. The following rating agencies are among the most active: (1) A.M. Best Company, (2) Conning & Company, (3) Duff & Phelps, (4) Fitch Investors Service, (5) Moody's Investors Service, (6) Standard & Poor's, (7) Thomson BankWatch, (8) Townsend & Schupp, (9) TRAC Insurance Services, Ltd., (10) Ward Financial Group, and (11) Weiss Research.

For more in-depth descriptions of the activities of a few of these agencies, see Insight 15-3.

Insight 15-3 Introduction to the Rating Agencies

Here we describe five large and well-known rating agencies: A.M. Best, Standard & Poor's, Moody's, Duff & Phelps, and Weiss.

A.M. Best

A.M. Best Company is the oldest insurance company rating agency, having reported on the financial conditions of life and health insurers since 1906. In fact, until the mid-1980s, Best had a virtual monopoly on the insurance company rating business. Until 1989, Best evaluated practically all insurers at no cost to the insurer. In 1989, Best started charging insurers a small, flat fee for their rating. In 1993, Best instituted a fee system based on the size of the insurer. Today, the large majority of insurers are still evaluated by Best, though a few choose not to pay Best's rating fee.

Standard & Poor's

Standard & Poor's (S&P) provides two types of ratings. The first type of rating is a *claims paying ability rating.* This type of rating is provided to insurers who request a rating and pay the appropriate fee. The second type of rating provided by S&P is a *qualified solvency rating.* S&P formulates a qualified solvency rating for a large portion of the insurers that do not have an S&P claims paying ability rating. Qualified solvency ratings are less detailed than claims paying ability ratings. If S&P decides to formulate a qualified solvency rating of a particular insurer, S&P will go ahead with the rating regardless of the desires of the insurer. (In contrast, some agencies permit an insurer to withdraw the request for a rating if an unfavorable rating is expected.)

Moody's and Duff & Phelps

Moody's Investors Service and Duff & Phelps both rate insurers who request a rating and pay the required fee. In addition, both agencies in the past have rated insurers that did not request a rating.

Weiss Research

Weiss Research evaluates practically all U.S. insurers over a certain minimum size, regardless of the desires of the insurer. Therefore, Weiss rates more insurers than any of the other rating agencies, including even Best. Weiss receives no money from the insurers it rates, deriving all its revenues from sales of its rating reports and directories. Because it receives no money from insurers, Weiss claims to be the most independent of the rating agencies.

Source: *Adapted with permission of the publisher,* Life Insurance Industry Rating Agencies *(Atlanta, GA: LOMA, 1992), pp. 29–45.*

How Rating Agencies Evaluate Insurers

All of the rating agencies named above rate insurers by assigning a grade within their proprietary system of alphabetical or numerical ratings. Each rating agency has a slightly different rating system. The rating systems of the agencies we mentioned earlier are described in Figure 15-6. No one agency's categories precisely correspond to any other agency's categories.

Figure 15-6. Rating systems of the rating agencies.

A.M. Best	S&P's Claims Paying Ratings	Moody's	Duff & Phelps	Weiss Research
A++ (Superior)	AAA (Superior)	Aaa (Exceptional)	AAA (Highest)	A+ (Excellent)
A+	AA+ (Excellent)	Aa1 (Excellent)	AA+ (Very high)	A
A (Excellent)	AA	Aa2	AA	A–
A–	AA–	Aa3	AA–	B+ (Good)
B++ (Very good)	A+ (Good)	A1 (Good)	A+ (High)	B
B+	A	A2	A	B–
B (Adequate)	A–	A3	A–	C+ (Fair)
B–	BBB+ (Adequate)	Baa1 (Adequate)	BBB+ (Below average)	C
C++ (Fair)	BBB	Baa2	BBB	C–
C+	BBB–	Baa3	BBB–	D+ (Weak)
C (Marginal)	BB+	Ba1 (Questionable)	BB+	D
C–	BB	Ba2	BB	D–
D (Very vulnerable)	BB–	Ba3	BB–	E+ (Very weak)
E (Under state supervision)	B+ (Vulnerable)	B1 (Poor)	B+	E
	B	B2	B	E–
F (In liquidation)	B–	B3	B–	F (Failed)
	CCC	Caa (Very poor)	CCC	U (Unrated)
	R (Regulatory action)	Ca (Extremely poor)	DD	
		C (Lowest)		

Source: *Adapted with permission of the publisher,* Life Insurance Industry Rating Agencies *(Atlanta, GA: LOMA, 1992), p. 8.*

The A.M. Best Company evaluates a number of insurers to which it does not assign one of its usual letter ratings. Instead, Best assigns one of several possible "NA" (for "not assigned") ratings. These NA ratings are also numbered NA-1, NA-2, NA-3, etc., producing a code that indicates why Best did not assign a rating. For example, Best would assign an NA rating to indicate that an insurer was "of less than minimum size," or that an insurer had "insufficient operating experience."

In addition to assigning the rating itself, the rating agencies also produce a written evaluation of the company and often give the rationale behind their rating. While the rating itself provides a quick and easy idea of an insurer's financial strength, some critics charge that the rating grade system is too simplistic. These critics usually recommend that users of rating agency data also read the rating agency's narrative report about an insurer rather than relying entirely on the rating grade.

Rating Methodologies

Among the various rating agencies, the range of rating methodologies and criteria applied includes the following:

- Some agencies apply only quantitative analysis, whereas others use both quantitative and qualitative analysis.
- Some agencies obtain and use data only from statutory accounting reports, whereas other agencies also consult other sources.
- Some agencies obtain information directly from the insurer's management, whereas others do not.
- Some agencies publicly disclose their ratings methodologies, whereas others do not.
- Some agencies focus their evaluation mainly on the insurer's solvency, whereas others focus mainly on the insurer's claims paying ability; some do both.

For many of the rating agencies, quantitative analysis of statutory data is only the starting point of the evaluation. Besides statutory financial statement data, agencies might use quantitative information from sources such as GAAP-basis accounting statements; statements created for internal management purposes and prepared on a "modified GAAP" basis; reports from regulatory examinations; audit reports from public accountants; or results of the company's required cash-flow testing.

In a rating agency's view, probably the most important quantitative factor to be evaluated is the level and adequacy of an insurer's capital. Rating agencies compare the absolute dollar amount of an insurer's capital (plus the asset valuation reserve and any voluntary reserves or liabilities) to the level of risk the agency sees in the insurer's business. The agencies generally evaluate an insurer's risk in a fashion similar to the NAIC's Risk-Based Capital (RBC) process, by considering the insurer's levels of C risks (as discussed in Chapter 2). Several of the rating agencies use a *target capital approach* to evaluating an insurer's capital. Each rating agency has its own methods of evaluating an insurer's risk profile and, where applicable, setting a target level of capital. The rating agencies' methods generally differ somewhat from the methods set by the NAIC's RBC requirement.

Different rating agencies place different amounts of emphasis on each of the important quantitative factors. In addition to an insurer's capital, some other important quantitative factors rating agencies consider are as follows:

- *Mix of business by product line.* The rating agencies find the shares of the insurer's total reserves for each product line, the shares of new and renewal premium from each product line, and the insurer's net amount at risk for each product line. The rating agencies note whether a large share of an insurer's business is in risky or thin-margin product lines.

- *Risk diversification* in the insurer's asset and liability portfolios.

- *Profitability and profit margins.* The insurer's overall returns, represented by such measures as ROE and ROA, should be adequate. The insurer's underwriting and interest margins should also be adequate.

- *Levels of operating expenses.*

- *Persistency rates* for the insurer's products.

- *Reinsurance.* The agencies note the amount of any reinsurance ceded or assumed by the insurer, and the importance of the use of reinsurance to the insurer's financial profile.

- *Investments.* The rating agencies note the insurer's investment return and the asset quality of the investment portfolio. To evaluate asset quality, the agencies find the amount of the insurer's holdings of risky assets and assets in default; they then take these as a percentage of the insurer's total assets and of the insurer's adjusted capital. The types of assets that agencies sometimes consider risky include junk bonds, commercial real estate, commercial mortgages, and investments in affiliated companies. The types of assets that agencies generally consider to be of high quality include investment-grade bonds and U.S. government securities.

- *Liquidity.* The agencies consider whether the insurer might have too large a share of its assets invested in relatively illiquid investments, such as private placements or real estate.
- *Match of assets and liabilities.* The agencies consider whether the insurer's match of assets and liabilities reduces the insurer's exposure to interest-rate risk.
- *Financial leverage.* For an insurer controlled by a holding company, the agencies also evaluate the levels of the holding company's debt.

Except for the Weiss ratings, TRAC's ratings, and S&P's qualified solvency ratings, the ratings methodologies typically require the raters to interpret the quantitative findings in light of other qualitative factors. Important qualitative factors typically considered are sales growth and stability. The rating agencies obtain much of their information about these qualitative factors from their communications with an insurance company's management. The most important qualitative factors include the following:

- Explanations of quantitative factors
- Plans to correct circumstances that appear undesirable
- The experience and competence of the insurer's key executives
- The insurer's mission, strategic objectives, and business plans
- The insurer's asset/liability management policies
- The insurer's investment philosophy
- Characteristics of the insurer's distribution system
- The insurer's product strategies
- The insurer's underwriting and reinsurance policies and practices
- The insurer's marketing strategies, whether the company has a profitable market niche, and the insurer's competitive situation
- The nature of the insurer's parent company and the insurer's relationship to its parent (if applicable)

Rating agencies regularly make public announcements of their decisions. To illustrate how the agencies explain a rating assignment, Figure 15-7 explains the rationale behind two of A.M. Best's decisions about ratings.

Some rating agencies—including A.M. Best, Standard & Poor's with respect to its claims paying ability rating, and Duff & Phelps—permit an insurer to request that the rating be withheld from publication.

Figure 15-7. How A.M. Best explained one rating downgrade and one initial rating assignment.[2]

Protected Home Mutual Life Downgraded Over Low Capitalization, CMO Investment

A.M. Best Co. lowered the Best's Rating of Protected Home Mutual Life Insurance Co., Sharon, Pa., to B from B+.

The action reflects the insurer's relatively low capitalization, its heavy reliance upon annuity and interest-sensitive life business, and its proportionally large exposure to some of the accrual classes of mortgage-backed securities. Offsetting these negatives to some extent are the company's consistent profitability over the past five years and its relatively conservative practice for its interest-sensitive products.

Protected Home's capital position (4.3 percent of liabilities as of June 30) is a result of its rapid growth in recent years. This is a matter of some concern given the company's relatively high level of investment in certain classes of mortgage-backed securities whose market value can change rapidly in a rising interest-rate environment. More than 80 percent of the insurer's reserves are for annuity and interest-sensitive life products, with 67 percent of these resources protected by surrender charges at year-end 1993.

Profitability has been strong, with net operating income of $1.2 million for 1993, and $1.3 million for the first half of 1994. In addition, it is important to note that Protected Home reserves on full account value for its annuity business, which is a very conservative reserving method that slightly understates surplus.

According to A.M. Best Co. data for the first six months of 1994, Protected Home had net premiums written of $13.8 million and capital and surplus of $8.5 million.

Maritime Life Gets Initial A+ Rating; Growing Business, Investments Cited[3]

A.M. Best Co. has assigned an initial rating of A+ to Canada's Maritime Life Insurance Co.

The rating acknowledges the Halifax, Nova Scotia-based company's established individual insurance division, good and growing market share in the group and investment markets, sound risk-adjusted capitalization and well managed investment portfolio.

The rating also recognizes the inherent strength the company receives through its ownership by John Hancock Mutual Life Insurance Co., Boston.

Maritime Life is recognized as the largest company in Canada exclusively operating through an independent distribution channel, which is being supplemented by the development of complementary personal distribution channels to capitalize on emerging markets. The company sells a full range of individual life, investment and group insurance products that provide for virtually all client needs and afford the company diverse sources of income.

A.M. Best believes that Maritime Life will continue to grow in its various lines of business and increase its national presence through its established and growing number of independent distributors. New business growth is expected to be supplemented by acquisitions as opportunities arise.

Risk-adjusted capitalization remains strong and is augmented by the implicit support of the ultimate parent, John Hancock. The overall performance of the investment portfolio compares well with industry averages, despite the considerable concentration in mortgage loans. Although the overall mortgage portfolio represents nearly two-thirds of invested assets, nearly 40 percent of the portfolio is comprised of National Housing Act (NHA) guaranteed loans.

Conventional commercial loans have historically been stringently underwritten, resulting in overall performance that is well within acceptable guidelines in comparison to industry averages. Although A.M. Best believes that more defaults will continue to adversely impact near-term profitability, earnings are expected to improve as a result of expenses and adherence to stringent asset/liability techniques inherited through the expertise of the parent.

Earnings for the first six months are ahead of management expectations, with reported net after-tax income of more than C$7.9 million (US$5.9 million), compared with C$7 million in the prior year's period.

Other rating agencies—including Weiss, TRAC, and Moody's—publish an insurer's rating regardless of the insurer's wishes. In addition, Standard & Poor's does not give an insurer the option of withholding from publication its qualified solvency rating.

Effects of Quality Ratings on Profitability

The purpose of the ratings given by the rating agencies is to *reflect* an insurer's financial condition. However, ratings can also *affect* an insurer's financial condition. An insurer's rating affects the ability to attract new business. Some customers may choose only to do business with an insurer with the very highest rating, and many others would prefer to do business with an insurer that has a rating at least near the top. Consumer preference for higher-rated companies has increased recently because of the phenomenon called flight to quality. ***Flight to quality*** is the common term for the tendency of many consumers and sales agents, made wary by several highly publicized insolvencies during the late 1980s and early 1990s, who now choose to do business only with highly rated insurers.

Second, an insurer's persistency can be seriously damaged by one or more ratings downgrades. A ***ratings downgrade*** is a reduction in an insurer's quality rating. A downgrade often leads to disintermediation, in which a portion of an insurer's customers, concerned about the company's financial stability, withdraw their account or policy values. In the worst-case scenario, ratings actions can lead to a run on assets. A ***run on assets***—also sometimes called a *run on the bank*—is a sustained outflow of funds that occurs when many customers request to withdraw their funds within a short period of time. Customers generally do this because they fear that if they don't withdraw their money quickly, then they won't be able to withdraw it at all. When a run on assets occurs, an insurer may not be able to convert enough investments to cash to meet the demands of customers, or may have to absorb damaging investment losses in order to meet its cash needs. An extreme run on assets can threaten an insurer's solvency. In fact, it is generally believed that a run on assets in the aftermath of rating downgrades was partially responsible for at least one insurance company insolvency, that of Mutual Benefit Life in 1991.

An insurer must make a number of strategic decisions relative to its ratings and the rating agencies. The insurer must decide if it should take any specific actions to improve its ratings. For many insurers, good ratings are an important strategic objective. At times, however, the objective of "pleasing" the rating agencies conflicts with an insurer's other objectives. For example, partly in response to the flight to quality by customers, many insurers undertook or are undertaking their own flight to quality: these insurers sold off the majority of their risky investments and reinvested those assets into highly conservative investments so as to improve their ratings or obtain the very highest ratings. In the process, these insurers sacrificed a certain amount of potential investment return. These insurers decided that a higher rating was more important to their financial future than the additional investment return that they might have earned by keeping some of their riskier assets.

If excellent quality ratings are one of an insurers' top strategic priorities, the following questions remain: How many ratings should the insurer obtain? What target quality rating do they plan to achieve? On the following pages, Insight 15-4, "On Measuring Financial Strength: Coping with a Downgrade," and Insight 15-5, "Zephyr Mutual Obtains Two New Ratings: A Case Study," tell some of the ins and outs of obtaining ratings.

In Conclusion

In this chapter, we focused on the quantitative tools used by analysts. However, quantitative information is not the only basis on which an insurer is evaluated. Judgment plays an important role in financial analysis and financial decision making. Evaluating an organization's financial performance is not simply a matter of entering numbers into a spreadsheet or calculator and then having finalized decisions appear automatically as the output of the process.

Evaluating an organization's financial performance requires gathering information about the organization and its external environment, organizing that information in a useful manner, and then interpreting the meaning of the information. Even when all the correct numbers are available, prudent human judgment is needed to understand what the information means.

Key Terms and Concepts

financial ratio analysis
Insurance Regulatory Information System (IRIS)
Financial Analysis and Solvency Tracking (FAST)
accounting policies note
financial statement analysis
cross-sectional analysis
horizontal analysis
vertical analysis
ratio
numerator
denominator
adjusted capital and surplus
adjusted liabilities
weighted value
weighted average cost of capital (WACC)
leverage
leverage effect
operating leverage
financial leverage

total leverage
positive leverage effect
negative leverage effect
insurance leverage ratio
surplus relief ratio
liquidity
liquid assets
quick liquidity
current liquidity
insurance liquidity ratio
net premiums written
gross profit ratio
return on invested assets (ROIA) ratio
investment yield ratio
net gain to total income
economic value added (EVA)
rating agencies
flight to quality
ratings downgrade
run on assets

References

1. *IRIS Ratio Results* (Washington D.C.: National Association of Insurance Commissioners, 1994), pp. 35–36.

2. "Protected Home Mutual Life Downgraded Over Low Capitalization, CMO Investment," *BestWeek* Life/Health Edition, September 19, 1994, pp. 1–2. Reprinted by permission of the publisher.

3. "Maritime Life Gets an Initial A+ Rating; Growing Business, Investments Cited," *BestWeek* Life/Health Edition, September 26, 1994, pp. 1–2. Reprinted by permission of the publisher.

Insight 15-4 On Measuring Financial Strength: Coping with a Downgrade

Is there life after a rating downgrade? Some might say that having a rating downgrade is sort of like becoming a parent—your life will never be the same again. The year 1991 was one in which many companies were faced with rating downgrades in the wake of Executive Life, Mutual Benefit Life, and First Capital Life failures. Out of these experiences came a heightened awareness and concern about financial strength.

At a LOMA EMaP conference in Seattle, Marilee Roller, president and chief operating officer of Pacific Corinthian Life—the company Pacific Mutual formed from the remains of First Capital Life in 1992—discussed ratings, rating agencies, and the steps her company takes to analyze and ensure its own financial strength.

Said Ms. Roller, "Our ratings are important to us because of the sophistication of our client base, and thankfully we have maintained strong double A+ ratings with our other rating agencies. As have most companies, however, recently we've focused a lot of attention on monitoring and reporting on the key elements to good ratings—asset quality, liquidity, diversification, and adequate surplus.

"We've been using financial analysis tools for many years, so we are quite sophisticated in how we analyze surplus and how we track and manage it," Roller pointed out. "We have a good system. We know how much surplus we have and how much we need," she explained. Roller believes the solvency crisis has helped the industry as a whole, because it increased the focus on financial strength and asset quality.

What drives rating agencies?

The 1991 downgrades caused the industry to become much more aware of what rating agencies are looking at and worrying about when they evaluate companies. Pacific Mutual compiled and analyzed information from many available sources—e.g., from discussions with rating agencies, from public statements, from studying competitors' ratings, etc.—and came up with a list of rating agency concerns, as Ms. Roller notes below.

• Profitability. "Profitability is a key factor in assessing financial strength and something I would argue should be emphasized more."

• Liquidity. "When Executive Life's problems became public, the news triggered a run on First Capital. A liquidity crisis caused the ultimate downfall and state take-over of both these companies. The acid test for liquidity is the question, 'How would your company survive a run on the bank?' In other words, what could you reasonably expect to sell within 10 days, 30 days? At Pacific Mutual we track liquidity, and we look great. We compare highly marketable assets to liabilities which can be surrendered, taking into account surrender charges and market values of the assets. We ask ourselves, 'What would happen if we really were to sell everything?' We'd actually realize gains. It is very gratifying for us to figure out that we really could survive a run on the bank. This is a strong selling tool, and we tell our story annually in a brochure on our investments. Our liquidity model is doubly useful, both to show to whoever is concerned about it (rating agencies, clients, brokers, etc.) and as a very high level macro look at our own company. If you do this regularly, you can track whether your liquidity is improving, declining, or not changing."

• Leverage. "Leverage has a lot to do with ratios—of assets-to-surplus, liabilities - to - surplus, etc.—but this is a faulty or inadequate measure, as becomes obvious when the new RBC formula is used. You cannot use a simple surplus-to-asset ratio, and I'm sure everyone understands that by now. We were able to argue this position because we had been using a version of RBC calculations for a long time. In my view, even though your ratio looks pretty good, you have to be concerned with quality—of your surplus and your assets, for instance. This is one of our bragging points at Pacific Mutual. We have clean surplus. We have no surplus relief; we have not done sale-leasebacks of our assets; and we have adequate reserves for any real estate losses. The story was different with First Capital, though, and that was one of its problems. First Capital had a great deal of surplus relief on the books and maintained a long battle with California about whether or not it was all right."

• Real estate. "Real estate is a big concern with rating agencies because the real estate markets have been in trouble for a long time and because mortgages and real estate played a significant role in Mutual Benefit Life's downfall. We have been asked a lot of questions about real estate holdings and have prepared extensive analyses of our portfolio for the rating agencies. Important rating agency concerns are diversification in property types and avoiding over-concentration in geographical areas."

• Junk bonds. "Junk bonds are obvious concerns for rating agencies, because junk bonds are what brought down Executive Life

Insight 15-4 Coping with a Downgrade (continued)

and First Capital Life, and many of these bonds are not readily marketable. Because of the perception the public now has of junk bonds and the history of First Capital, our five-year rehabilitation plan for Pacific Corinthian includes a commitment to reduce the junk bonds down to 5 percent by the end of 1997."

• Management of parent companies. "This is a very valid concern for rating agencies. It was a major cause of First Capital Life's problems, stemming from risky investments and high management fees. First Capital holdings leveraged the purchase of the life company and tried to finance it with fees and dividends."

• Franchise value. "If you have a niche market, that's great for rating agencies."

• Surplus is supreme. "If you have a lot of it, you're probably okay. In my view, you have too much of it for the rating agencies. but because the perception of the industry is still uncertain and the rating agencies are still worried, I think we may have to be overcapitalized for a while. So you probably need to carry more surplus now than you think you really need to run your business."

Is the tail wagging the dog?

The increased awareness of financial strength has been a benefit for rating agencies, Roller observed. But it can also cause companies to take non-economic actions in order to play the rating game. Because of the public perception of junk bonds and troubled real estate, companies are forced to make more conservative investments in order to improve asset quality. This is good, because there is less risk. But it's bad, too, because companies give up yield and potential.

Asset quality is a critical factor in evaluating financial strength, but the measurement and reporting of asset statistics can be very misleading. "I don't know how we can get away from focusing on percentages," Roller said. "Percentages are available on a company for whatever you want to look at—junk bonds to total bonds, junk bonds to total assets, troubled real estate or troubled assets as a percentage of surplus. Anyone doing ratings can pull your numbers out of the Annual Statement and compare them with any other company and publish these comparisons. But straight percentages don't always tell the whole story because they don't allow for lengthy footnote explanations of quality."

Watching percentages is causing companies to react to the depressed real estate market. "Because it's depressed," she pointed out, "the industry is encouraged to disinvest. But because we're disinvesting it gets more depressed. And it isn't necessarily a good idea to get rid of real estate mortgage loan portfolios, although it may make the rating agencies more comfortable. A lot of companies have good real estate and don't get into trouble with their real estate. A company may have generally good real estate and foreclose early on any troubled mortgages, for economic reasons. This would be better in the long run because of the company's expertise in managing mortgages. But foreclosures hurt in the percentage games, even though there's more economic value to getting out of mortgage problems by foreclosing and managing the property through its problems."

One thing Roller mentioned some companies are doing to improve asset quality in relation to bonds is restructuring their mortgage portfolios. "They are scrutinizing mortgages and turning them into bonds or buying CMO-backed (collateralized mortgage obligation) bonds instead of buying mortgages themselves. This way," she explained, "they have the advantages of a real estate investment, but the real estate is characterized as a bond."

One mistake Mutual Benefit and Executive Life made was putting all their eggs in one basket, so to speak, in Roller's view. "They both had huge concentrations of assets. Executive Life had a few very large, very questionable bonds as a large percentage of their surplus. Mutual Benefit was devastated by about four real estate projects. So diversification is very important."

She has similar views about junk bonds. "As I noted, we have very few high yield bonds, but I wouldn't necessarily want to have to get rid of them just for the sake of the numbers. That's exactly what happens, though."

The effect on the consumer is circular, also. "The policyholder can feel more confidence in the industry's more conservative investment approach, but the yields are lower and so the payouts will be lower," she explained.

Source: *Lucy Barnes McDowell, "On Measuring Financial Strength,"* Resource, *October 1993, pp. 9–12. Adapted with permission of the publisher.*

Insight 15-5 Zephyr Mutual Obtains Two New Ratings: A Case Study

This case study of Zephyr Mutual Life Insurance Company's successful efforts to obtain two new ratings during 1991 is a true story, with all names disguised. Zephyr Mutual had never before been rated except by agencies, such as A.M. Best Company, which routinely rate very nearly everyone. The dates given here accurately reflect the time frame of events, but are not the actual dates on which the events occurred.

Zephyr Life Insurance Company is a medium-to-large size mutual company. Zephyr had a strong surplus position in relation to its assets, exceeding the surplus positions of 90 percent or more of all U.S. life insurance companies; it had a high quality investment portfolio; it had a mature management with the ability to maintain and carefully build upon this solid foundation. The company had obtained the top rating from A.M. Best year after year, and this rating was all it ever needed. Because of Zephyr's plans to expand into a new market, however, the company decided to obtain a rating from Periscope Rating Agency, which enjoyed an established reputation in that market. Two other factors influencing Zephyr's decision were the financial turbulence within the life insurance industry and the opinion of some observers that Best had given its top ratings to too many companies. So in early May 1991, Zephyr contacted Periscope, and the two parties set a meeting for July 26th at the insurer's home office.

Immediately after this contact, Zephyr Mutual sent Periscope the last five years of statutory Annual Statements for Zephyr and for its two largest subsidiaries. Then, the following staff of Zephyr Mutual took part in four preparatory meetings lasting about two hours each:

- Chairman of the board
- President
- Executive vice president
- Chief marketing officer
- Chief investment officer
- Chief actuary
- Insurance operations officer
- Tax officer
- Comptroller
- Two investment department managers, acting as coordinators for the project

The main topic of discussion at these meetings was the "presentation book." A presentation book, although not required by Periscope, seemed a convenient form for summarizing the needed information in one document. Periscope had provided a list of data not available from the Annual Statement that it was likely to request. In addition, Zephyr wanted to volunteer a number of additional facts about itself. The resulting presentation book contained about 100 pages, and included the following items:

- Biographical data on the company executives
- Company history
- Organization chart
- Consolidated income statements and balance sheets (necessary because the principal subsidiaries had filed their statutory Annual Statements as separate entities)
- Breakdown of investments by type and quality, including those in default, also on a consolidated basis
- Detailed listings and analysis of investments in stocks, mortgages and real estate (by industry group, geographical area, and so forth)
- Book value versus market value comparisons of investments
- Gross investment income (dollar amount and yield rate) by asset type
- Actual surplus plus MSVR plus hidden surplus in conservative statutory life insurance reserves
- Home office payroll
- Policyowner service turnaround times compared to industry averages
- Distribution systems, major products and target markets of the parent and subsidiaries
- Underwriting and reinsurance practices

On July 26th, four representatives from Periscope arrived for an all-day meeting in which Zephyr's committee made presentations about such varied items as the company's philosophy, history, present status and future direction. The agenda was at least partially determined by the presentation book, and each of the participating Zephyr executives spoke. Some executives were present the entire time, while others attended only as needed. Several times after the July 26th meeting, Periscope requested additional data, which Zephyr promptly supplied. Then, in early October, Zephyr learned that

Insight 15-5 Zephyr Mutual Obtains Two New Ratings: A Case Study (cont'd)

it had been assigned Periscope's highest ratings.

During the summer, an increasing number of experts and consumer advocates said that an insurer ought to have a financial strength or claims paying ability rating from at least two of the "big four" raters. Although Periscope was well known, Periscope was not one of the "big four." A.M. Best Company was, though, so Zephyr needed only one more "big four" rating. Therefore, shortly after the July 26th meeting, Zephyr contacted one of the other "big four" raters, which we'll call Protractor, about getting a claims paying ability rating. Zephyr set up a meeting with Protractor for September 26th at Zephyr's home office.

The Protractor Agency requested the following information:

- The last five years of statutory Annual Statements
- The last five audited statements (i.e., the outside auditor's restatement of statutory results)
- The results of the most recent NAIC triennial examination

In addition, the Protractor Agency required Zephyr to complete surveys asking for considerable disclosure about investments (especially real estate, mortgages, and joint ventures) and investment policy. The questions that the Protractor Agency asked included: (1) Were investments determined by a committee? (2) Were established investment guidelines used? (3) Did Zephyr maintain a watch list of problem loans and problem real estate?

Zephyr's committee of executives and coordinators met two additional times to prepare for the September 26th meeting. They decided to add the following information to the presentation book:

- Corporate mission statement and strategic plans
- Cost control measures that had recently been adopted or were planned for the near future
- Age, sex, and family income breakdown of the in-force business
- Sales results per agent as compared to similar companies
- Actual-to-expected mortality
- More information on Zephyr's health insurance subsidiary, such as its role within the family of companies and its underwriting and claim payment philosophy
- Asset concentration showing those bond issuers in whom the investment was more than a certain percentage of surplus and MSVR

The committee made the following other improvements to the original presentation book:

- Much of the investment data previously shown on a consolidated basis was broken down between Zephyr and its two largest subsidiaries.
- Certain items were deleted so that the presentation book was only slightly larger than it formerly had been.

September 26th arrived and another all-day meeting took place. This meeting proceeded similarly to July 26th. In addition to discussing the presentation book and answering questions raised by the two rating agency representatives, Zephyr furnished a forecast of product profitability, cash flows, and balance sheets.

After several weeks, Zephyr visited Protractor for the purpose of presenting even more information. Zephyr prepared additional statistical data comparing Zephyr to other companies of similar size. On November 15th, some of Zephyr's officers visited Protractor's headquarters with the new data. After this meeting, Protractor asked for still more data. About three weeks later, Protractor assigned Zephyr its highest rating.

Although Zephyr did not keep track of the exact cost of staff time for this entire project's cost, it is possible to come up with a rough estimate. Staff spent a grand total of almost 700 hours on the project. Assuming, for illustration purposes only, that the average salary (including fringes) of everyone involved was $50 per hour, then the total estimated soft-dollar cost was nearly $35,000. Of course, this figure does not include the fees paid directly to the rating agencies.

Having obtained the top ratings from three agencies, Zephyr now must constantly strive to keep them. One wonders: Would it have been better to aim for the second highest rating and not sweat so much? Will the investment department feel that its hands are tied? Will the amount of extra business generated make it all worthwhile?

Source: *Adapted with permission of the publisher,* Life Insurance Industry Rating Agencies *(Atlanta, GA: LOMA, 1992), pp. 23–27.*

CHAPTER

Orientation to Asset/Liability Management

16

LEARNING OBJECTIVES

After studying this chapter, you should be able to

- Recognize the main objectives of asset/liability management (ALM) for insurance companies
- Recognize important model laws requiring ALM practices in the United States
- Recognize important features of the regulatory environment requiring ALM practices in Canada
- Distinguish actual solvency from technical solvency for insurance companies
- Interpret how movements in market interest rates affect life insurers
- Interpret the roles of the ALM team and the ALM steering committee
- Recognize the different types of expertise that actuaries and financial analysts contribute to ALM applications
- Identify some potential pitfalls associated with operating an ALM program

OUTLINE

In a financial environment involving regular movements in market interest rates, profitability and solvency concerns require each insurer to successfully coordinate the patterns of net cash flows from both its investment and its product portfolios. During the late 1980s and early 1990s, while facing competitive pressure to promise customers higher crediting rates than the insurers' investment portfolios could support, a few insurers took the risk of mismatching the cash flows of their product and investment portfolios. In 1991, four insurance companies—Executive Life (California and New York), First Capital Life of California, Mutual Benefit (New Jersey), and Fidelity Bankers Life (Virginia)—failed partly as a result of breaking the rules of good asset/liability management. Fortunately, the historical mistakes of a few financial institutions were instructive to those that survive.

To avoid making similar mistakes, various types of financial institutions, including commercial banks and life and health insurance companies, are applying a set of sophisticated management approaches that are collectively known as asset/liability management. For life and health insurers, ***asset/liability management (ALM)*** can be defined as a management program for coordinating the financial effects from the insurer's portfolio of product liabilities on the one hand and its investment portfolio on the other hand. (ALM for banks is approached quite differently from ALM for insurance companies.) ALM is designed to support an insurer's strategic objectives concerning solvency and profitability. This management approach focuses upon managing net cash flows and the risks associated with them so as to ensure the insurer's ongoing technical solvency. For some life and health insurance companies in the United States and Canada, some ALM activities are legally mandated—not voluntary.

From an ALM viewpoint, insurers can be viewed as managing two portfolios of financial instruments: their investment portfolio and their product portfolio. A ***portfolio*** is simply a collection of financial assets. For life insurance companies, the *investment* portfolio can also be called the *asset* portfolio. An insurer's *product* portfolio can also be called the *liability* portfolio.* Insurers must manage the asset and the liability portfolios each on its own terms. Additionally, insurers must coordinate the management of the two portfolios so as to earn an acceptable return for their efforts.

---

* Because a portfolio is a collection of assets, it might appear inconsistent to refer to a liability portfolio. However, from the perspectives of ALM and capital budgeting, an insurance company's products are business ventures on which the company expects to earn a profit.

What are the basic challenges of managing a portfolio of financial instruments? In an abstract view, managing these portfolios involves (1) managing risks at an acceptable level and (2) taking advantage of opportunities to earn a return. The product or liability portfolio poses one distinctive set of risks and opportunities, and the asset or investment portfolio poses another. The insurer must manage the distinct risks and opportunities facing each of these major portfolios. In addition, the insurer must manage a third distinctive set of risks and opportunities attendant upon the interaction between the asset and liability portfolios. In summary, the risks and opportunities that insurers face in managing the cash flows from their two main portfolios can be divided into the following categories:*

- Challenges and opportunities for the investment portfolio
- Challenges and opportunities for the insurance product portfolio
- Challenges and opportunities arising from interaction between cash flows of the investment portfolio and the product portfolio

Chapter 16 provides an orientation to the nature of ALM programs for life and health insurers. First in Chapter 16, we consider the main source of instability in insurers' cash flows: interest-rate fluctuations. Next we review how regulation in the United States encouraged widespread adoption of ALM practices for life and health insurance companies. Our review of the laws that instituted ALM practices gives us a glimpse of those practices.

While ALM in insurance companies was evolving into a full-fledged management system, insurers applied the maxim that *structure follows strategy,* and accordingly they adapted their organizational form to better support effective ALM. Two organizational adaptations that insurers today find supportive of effective ALM are (1) formally adding ALM functions to the organization—usually by creating an ALM technical team and an ALM steering committee, and (2) adopting a formal system of internal financial reports for communicating ALM information to the decision makers who need it. The information conveyed through these ALM reports is very technical. Accordingly, an unusually high level of expertise is required for effective ALM, and a number of pitfalls lurk within ALM's unusual level of complexity. Thus, even many large and well-managed insurers have taken only the first fledgling steps into ALM practices. Also, many use consultants to help with advanced ALM applications.

The complexity of ALM arises from several of its characteristics. One is that ALM requires integrating decision making about two

* This classification scheme parallels the C-1 through C-3 contingency risks but differs by including opportunities in addition to risks.

separate areas of insurance operations: (1) investments and (2) product design and pricing. Thus, ALM requires teamwork among groups with diverse financial expertise. ALM requires incorporating expertise from at least two different technical fields—actuarial analysis and investment analysis, and thus it is said to be a *cross-disciplinary* undertaking. Additionally, ALM requires using computers and sophisticated mathematical modeling to develop financial forecasts. In this activity, ALM requires unusual skill and technical expertise in the area of financial modeling.

Major Objectives of Asset/Liability Management

For life and health insurance companies, what are the broad objectives of asset/liability management? We can identify three main objectives as follows:

1. Insurance companies use asset/liability management to gain a better understanding of the company's ongoing technical solvency by managing the company's day-to-day net cash flows and their associated risks. (We discuss technical solvency later in this chapter.)

2. Insurance companies use ALM to manage their risk exposures arising from variations in market interest rates. In order to support this objective of ALM, the insurance company's actuaries and investment professionals must apply a set of integrated strategies for product design, product pricing, and investment management—all with the goal of matching the relatively more controllable cash flows of the company's investments with the relatively less controllable cash flows of the products those investments support.

3. At a minimum, insurance companies practice asset/liability management in order to comply with the regulatory requirements discussed later in this chapter.

Of these three main objectives for ALM, compliance and the need to remain technically solvent are necessary in order for the company to continue operating at all. In contrast, managing the risks from changing market interest rates supports a company's strategic objectives of ensuring solvency and enhancing profitability.

Insurers approach the second ALM objective by trying to control the net cash flows from the product portfolio and the investment portfolio. However, the company's actions taken to support this ALM objective should not undermine the company's main objectives for its product portfolio and its investment portfolio. An insurer's main

Figure 16-1. Financial management objectives and their priority for insurers.

FIRST:	**Corporate-level objectives**	
	• Target growth in capital and surplus • Target return on equity • Target capital and surplus	
NEXT:	**Product portfolio objectives**	**Investment portfolio objectives**
	• Marketability of products	• High return on invested assets
	• Actuarially sound pricing	• Limited investment risk
THEN:	**ALM objectives**	
	• To prevent technical insolvency and attempt to ensure technical solvency	
	• To manage net cash flows, thus limiting the C-3 risks from a cash-flow mismatch between the product portfolio and the investment portfolio	
	• To comply with regulations requiring specified ALM practices	

objectives for the product portfolio often would be (1) to enhance the consumer appeal and marketability of the product and (2) to price the product on an actuarially sound basis. For the investment portfolio, an insurer's main objectives often would be (1) to earn a high return on investments (measured by the return on invested assets ratio, discussed in Chapter 15) and (2) to limit investment risk to a level within the company's comfort zone. In turn, actions taken to achieve product portfolio and investment portfolio objectives must not undermine the insurance company's corporate-level strategic objectives relating to solvency and profitability, such as (1) earning a given level of corporate return on equity, (2) achieving a stated level of growth in capital and surplus, and (3) maintaining a stated target level of capital and surplus.

Figure 16-1 summarizes the relationships among these four sets of management objectives.

In the next section we take a closer look at two of the main objectives of ALM for insurance companies. First, we review how ALM supports technical solvency, and then we discuss why managing C-3 risk is a driving force behind ALM.

Ensuring Technical Solvency through Asset/Liability Management

We noted that one important objective of ALM is to support the company's day-to-day solvency. The objectives of ALM can be viewed either from a proactive viewpoint that focuses upon goal achievement from a defensive viewpoint that emphasizes managing risks. From the proactive viewpoint, the overriding goal of managing cash flows would be to maintain a condition wherein cash inflows would always *exceed or equal* cash outflows. This condition is known as a ***positive net cash flow (net cash inflow).*** This condition is equivalent to maintaining a positive value for cash-flow based surplus (CFS), as defined in Chapter 11. A positive net cash flow equates to the idea of maintaining adequate liquidity (as discussed in Chapter 2 of this text), as well as to the idea of maintaining technical solvency. In order to ensure positive cash flows, ALM experts first predict and then closely analyze the insurer's expected cash flow patterns in order to identify the profitable opportunities embedded within those patterns.

From thc defensive viewpoint, a primary objective would be to avoid any risk that cash outflows might ever exceed cash inflows. A condition wherein cash outflows exceed cash inflows is known as a ***negative net cash flow.*** This undesirable condition is equivalent to having a negative value for cash-flow based surplus (CFS), which we discussed in Chapter 11. A negative net cash flow relates to the idea of inadequate liquidity (also discussed in Chapters 2 and 15), and could possibly lead to technical insolvency, for instance if liquidity needs forced an insurer to sell assets at a loss. In order to avoid the risk of having a negative net cash flow, ALM experts first predict and then closely analyze the insurer's expected cash flow patterns in order to identify sources of risk within those patterns. Also from the defensive viewpoint, a secondary objective would be to have adequate liquidity to cover negative net cash flows if they materialize.

The concept of maintaining a positive net cash flow is equivalent to the concept of remaining *technically* solvent. Previously in this text we have concentrated our attention to solvency on concepts such as wealth, capital and surplus, net worth, and cash-flow based surplus—measures reflecting a long-term view of solvency. When we consider solvency in the context of ALM, we need to understand two views of solvency, which are referred to as actual solvency and technical solvency.

- ***Actual solvency*** is the condition of having a positive net worth. A company is actually solvent so long as the company's total assets equal or exceed its total liabilities. In insurance, the viewpoint of actual solvency corresponds to a focus upon adequate capitalization. Actual solvency reflects the long-term view of solvency that is closely aligned with the primary concerns of stockholders, strategic planners, and individuals involved in the capital management process. Because appraising the overall wealth of a company requires addressing many theoretical issues, actual solvency is more difficult to measure than is technical solvency. Analysis of CFS, first presented in Chapter 11, can improve understanding of actual solvency.

- ***Technical solvency*** refers to a company's ability to pay its obligations as they come due. In order for a company to be technically solvent, the company's cash and other current assets must equal or exceed the company's current liabilities. (In this case, a market valuation basis is the pertinent valuation basis for assets and liabilities.) Technical solvency is the aspect of solvency that is most urgent in managing day-to-day operations. Technical solvency is ordinarily more readily measured than actual solvency, because for most businesses determining technical solvency relies upon a factual, market-valuation basis rather than a theoretical basis. ALM for insurance companies focuses on technical solvency. A company can be technically insolvent while it remains actually solvent; current assets can fall below current liabilities even while total assets (current assets plus long-term assets) exceed total liabilities (current liabilities plus long-term liabilities).

In ALM, an ideal condition is known as cash-flow matching. For insurers, ***cash-flow matching*** can be defined as a condition wherein the insurer's cash inflows exactly match in timing and amount the insurer's needs for meeting its cash obligations. True cash-flow matching is achievable only in strictly limited circumstances. An example of true cash-flow matching could be established by creating a portfolio of bond investments that produces the exact pattern of cash inflows needed to meet the insurer's cash requirements for making the guaranteed payments under a guaranteed investment contract (GIC). True matching can be achieved in such a strictly limited application because a GIC's cash flows are perfectly predictable and are not subject to interest-rate fluctuations.

However, most insurance company products have unpredictable cash-flow patterns. Therefore, insurers cannot realistically expect to achieve and sustain perfect cash-flow matching in connection with their more complex products, such as interest-sensitive products. The effects of interest-rate movements and other risk factors render perfect cash-flow matching an elusive ideal.

Nonetheless, insurers use many tactics in the attempt to employ ALM on a broad scale and over a long period. Some techniques of ALM that many life and health insurers use are portfolio segmentation, cash-flow testing, dynamic-solvency testing, and duration matching. The ALM applications of these techniques are presented in Chapter 17.

In managing cash flows, what challenges arise from the interaction between an insurance organization's asset and liability portfolios? For life and health insurers, the asset portfolio consists mainly of fixed-income and long-term financial instruments—corporate bonds, government bonds, and mortgages. The expected cash inflows from the insurer's investments are not guaranteed. On the other hand, insurers' liability portfolios consist mainly of the company's products, which guarantee payment by the insurer. Thus, insurers rely upon a nonguaranteed source of funds to pay guaranteed obligations.

Because the asset management process is more or less determined by the liability portfolios, the ALM process is sometimes said to be ***liability-driven.*** An ALM process is liability-driven when it is guided by the belief that asset management activities should adjust the asset portfolio to fit the nature of the liability portfolios. In addition, a liability-driven process acknowledges that insurance companies are above all ***customer-driven*** or ***market-driven.*** However, product design and pricing can and should also be ***asset-driven,*** meaning that product design should take into account the nature of the financial assets available in financial markets. Figure 16-2 presents a glossary of the expressions describing these various driving forces. Figure 16-3 illustrates in flowchart form how ALM considerations are incorporated into product planning and design.

If insurers were able to accurately predict the timing and amount of their cash flows, insurers would face only a relatively simple management problem in matching the cash flows of their assets and liabilities. We know this because, until the 1970s, insurers and other financial institutions *were* able to predict their cash flows with a relatively high degree of certainty. Beginning in the 1970s, however, interest rates began to fluctuate over a wider range of values than before. An ability to predict interest-rate movements with relative accuracy is fundamental to predicting cash flows. Today, the cash flows of financial institutions are more difficult to predict than they once were when interest rates stayed within a narrower range of values. Even the basis for estimating these cash flows now undergoes constant change.

Because interest-rate changes are central to an insurer's financial experience, next we look specifically at how changes in interest rates affect insurance companies and, consequently, are at the heart of the ALM process.

Figure 16-2. Glossary of different motivating forces for ALM.

- **Asset-driven ALM.** An approach to ALM guided by the belief that product design should take into account the nature of the financial assets available in financial markets
- **Customer-driven management.** An approach to management guided by the belief that management processes should focus foremost on meeting customers' needs
- **Liability-driven ALM.** An approach to ALM guided by the belief that the asset management process should be driven by the nature of the liability portfolios
- **Market-driven management.** An approach to management guided by the belief that all management processes should focus foremost on market imperatives such as competitive forces, the economic environments, and meeting customers' needs

Figure 16-3. Flowchart for evaluating cash-flow characteristics of a planned product.

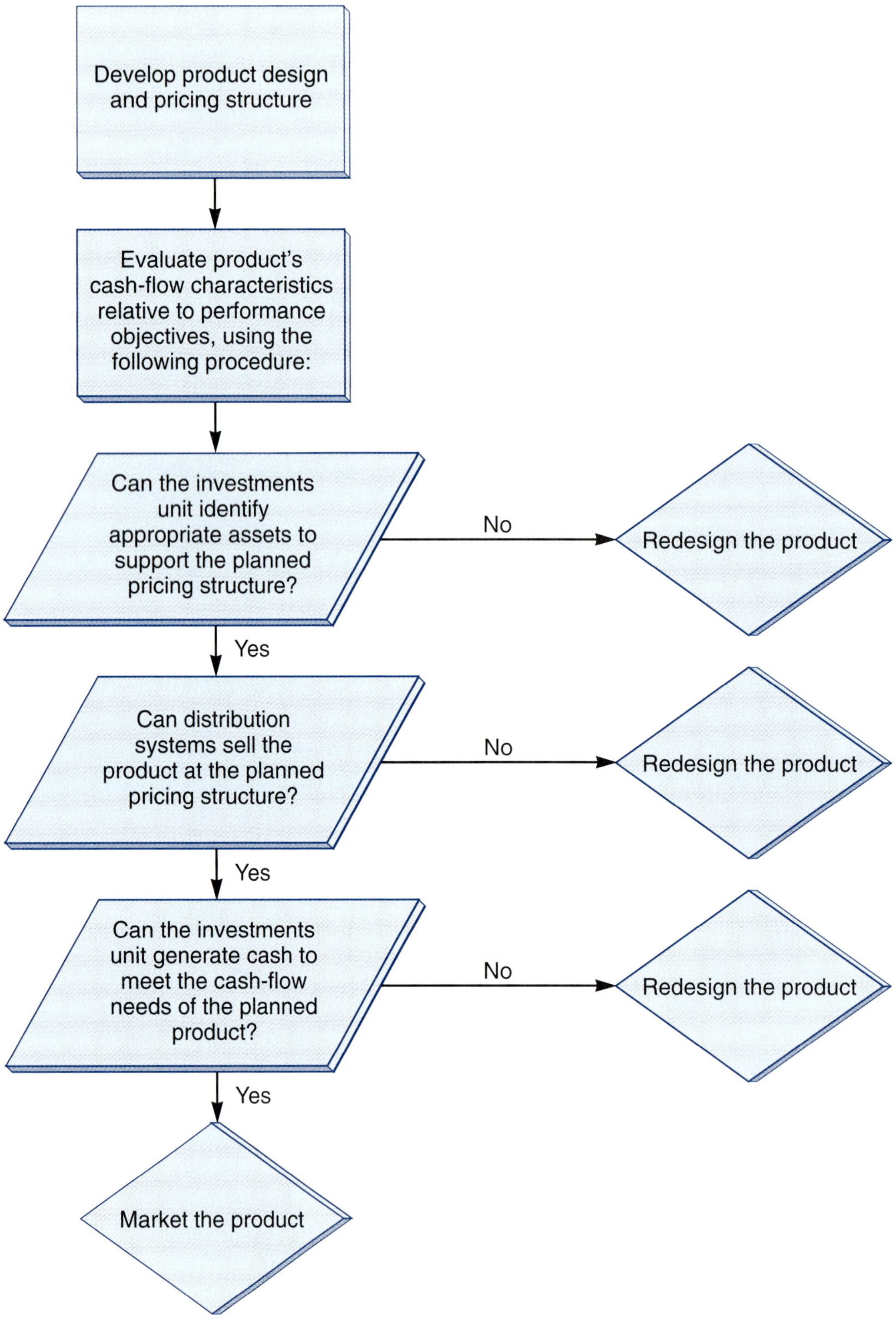

Figure 16-4. Examples of how C risk exposures can produce decreases in capital and surplus.

Accounting Equation: **Assets – Liabilities = Capital and Surplus**

	Capital and surplus can DECREASE if	
	Assets . . .	**While interest-sensitive liabilities . . .**
C-1 Risk decrease in assets	• Decrease	• Remain unchanged
C-2 Risk increase in liabilities	• Remain unchanged	• Increase
C-3 Risk interest-rate changes	• *Increase* • *Decrease*	• *Increase* • *Decrease*

Interest-Rate Changes and Capital and Surplus

Life insurance companies traditionally analyze their risk exposures by applying the system of contingency risks, which we discussed at some length in Chapter 2. This approach involves systematically evaluating the company's exposure to various categories of risk, anticipating how the company's risk exposures would affect the company's cash flows, and eventually predicting how the changes in cash flows would affect capital and surplus. As we discussed in Chapter 3, insurers typically approach cash-flow forecasting by applying simulation models to demonstrate how their financial performance would turn out after several years under specified standardized sets of favorable, neutral, and adverse conditions. Refer to Figure 16-4, which is repeated from Chapter 10, to review how the C-1 through C-3 risks can produce a decrease in a life insurer's capital and surplus.

Interest-Rate Changes and Net Cash Flows

The crux of the need for ALM is interest-rate fluctuations. Movements in market interest rates are the single most important source of insurers' exposure to losses. As described in Insight 16-1, interest-rate changes present financial managers in the life insurance industry with a never-ending stream of new challenges.

Market interest rates are constantly in motion. As investors, insurers must accept the market rates of return arising from the auction processes in the financial markets. In turn, market rates of return are

Insight 16-1 Sudden Drop in Interest Rates Keeps Insurers Guessing

For insurers return on investment and crediting rates are linked to market rates. The interest rate issue with life insurers is the spread between the rates credited to policyholders and the rate of return on the insurers' portfolios. The investment income they earn compared with interest credited is their profit margin.

When rates suddenly fall, insurers can widen their spreads because they are able to lower policyholders' crediting rates faster than the average yield on their portfolio declines. This occurs because policyholders typically expect and are willing to accept the new money rates immediately, while the average portfolio yield changes much more slowly. Meanwhile, the average yield on insurers' portfolios may still be rising, a phenomenon called spread expansion.

When interest rates rise, the opposite scenario, called spread compression, occurs. Policyholders expect to get the higher rate credited immediately and for competitive reasons, insurers are forced to do this, but the average yield on the portfolio is rising very slowly.

On the other hand, a sudden shift to lower interest rates makes new business more difficult to come by, depending on how quickly banks follow suit in their interest rate structure and what rates banks are crediting on their certificates of deposit. If insurance companies are reducing their crediting rates and banks maintain or adjust rates at different levels, this encourages individuals to look to the higher-yielding investment CDs. "Insurers who previously were growing their fixed annuity business when interest rates were at higher levels have found that now they are losing some to the banks," notes Larry G. Mayewski, senior vice president of the life/health division at A.M. Best Co.

The area where falling rates can impose a squeeze is on traditional life insurance, particularly dividends on whole life insurance, depending on how quickly insurers ratchet down their dividend scales. Many times insurers don't lower dividend scales, and if the new money rates of return are lower, margins are squeezed for companies writing traditional, dividend-paying life insurance, says Mayewski.

For holders of mortgage-backed securities, falling interest rates increase the risk of prepayments as mortgage holders refinance or pay off their existing debt. Many insurance companies target specific levels of interest sensitivity to match their investments to their obligations. Rising prepayments would cut into insurer's margins, because they would be forced to compensate for the decline in interest sensitivity in their portfolios.

Asset/liability management has become increasingly difficult for life insurers because of the high level of volatility in the financial markets. Insurers' interest-sensitive portfolios and products, dealings in derivatives and mortgage-backed securities create additional challenges with interest rates moving around significantly and unpredictably.

"It is a very challenging environment to manage insurance company assets in," says Arthur Fliegelman, vice president of bond portfolio analysis at Salomon Brothers. "In an environment where markets are volatile with rates moving rapidly, the volatility is more of the challenge than the actual rate level."

Source: *Michael A. Farinella, "Sudden Drop in Interest Rates Keeps Insurers Guessing,"* BestWeek *Life/Health Edition, May 15, 1995, p.5*

influenced by other forces in the socioeconomic environment—forces that are beyond the control of insurers. Insurers must nevertheless respond to the market forces influencing market rates of return. For instance, customers of insurance companies expect the insurers to *credit* them with fair market interest rates on their "deposits" into the insurance company, and insurers must satisfy these expectations. Otherwise, the customers would be likely to remove their money from the insurer's management.

In order to understand more precisely how changes in market interest rates directly affect insurers, we examine the effects that life and health insurers experience as a result of (1) *increases* in interest rates and (2) *decreases* in interest rates. Note that these changes in market interest rates translate into operating gains or losses for insurers, and, as discussed in Chapter 15, these operating gains or losses in turn produce increases or decreases in insurers' capital.

Effects of Interest-Rate Increases

When market interest rates *rise,* life insurers may experience the following financial effects:

- Customers may demand a greater return or crediting rate to match comparable returns available in other financial products. Otherwise, customers may exercise their options to withdraw their funds and invest the funds in higher-yielding opportunities. Customers can withdraw their funds by (1) surrendering their policies, (2) taking policy loans, or (3) withdrawing money from various accumulation products, such as deferred annuities.

- If excessive surrenders occur, insurers may need to liquidate assets unexpectedly or to borrow short-term funds when interest rates are high. When interest rates are high, customers are more likely to withdraw their funds so that the funds can be placed in higher-yield investments, and the insurer may have to liquidate assets or borrow funds to meet these withdrawals.

- In order to attract new premiums and keep old deposits, the insurance company may need to promise a return consistent with the new higher market interest rate. In order to support the increased rate, the insurer, in turn, would need to earn a greater return on investments.

- When interest rates rise, insurers are subject to a phenomenon known as spread compression. ***Spread compression*** occurs when insurers are forced to take a smaller spread because customers demand to get the higher market rate credited immediately, even though the average yield on the insurer's investment portfolio rises only very slowly.

- New investments earn the new higher prevailing rate. Money that is being invested at the new higher rate comes from two main sources: (1) premium income and (2) funds from investments already in the insurer's portfolio. However, assets in the portfolio continue to earn yields reflecting the market at the time they were purchased.

- Briefly, a ***duration statistic*** measures the responsiveness of asset or liability values to changes in interest rates. This responsiveness of financial values to changes in interest rates is also known as *interest-rate sensitivity.* Although duration is not discussed fully until Chapter 17, it bears noting here that a *duration mismatch* between an insurer's asset and liability portfolios can magnify an economic loss when interest rates change in either direction. In theory, the interest-rate sensitivity values for an insurer's asset and liability portfolios should ideally be perfectly equal or *matched.* In that case, whenever interest rates increase, the values of assets and liabilities would both decrease by an equal amount. However, if the asset and liability portfolios were not well matched and the assets were longer-term than the liabilities, then the values of the assets would decrease more than the values of the liabilities.

Effects of Interest-Rate Decreases

Insurers generally can expect to have excess cash available for investment only when interest rates are low. When market interest rates decrease, life insurers may experience the following financial effects:

- Bonds held in the insurer's portfolio, if purchased earlier at higher market interest rates, gain market value.
- When market interest rates fall, then insurers can lower customers' crediting rates immediately, whereas the average rate of return on their investment portfolio declines only slowly. As a result, insurers experience a phenomenon called spread expansion—as opposed to *spread compression.* ***Spread expansion*** is the widening of an insurer's spread that occurs when market interest rates fall, and insurers are able to reduce crediting rates to the current market level while they continue to earn an average portfolio rate of return that is higher than the current market rates.
- Whenever interest rates fall, callable bonds become more likely to be called, and mortgages become more likely to be prepaid. Issuers of debt that the insurance company holds, if those issuers are paying older and higher interest rates, are likely to ***refinance***—repay the debt and make new borrowing arrangements at the new lower prevailing rates. The insurer thus would lose the higher-yielding older investments and would have to reinvest the proceeds at the prevailing lower interest rates.
- New investments will earn only the new lower interest rate. When fixed-period and fixed-income investments mature, the proceeds must be reinvested. The new investment will reflect current market conditions and will earn only the prevailing lower interest rate.

- A mismatch between asset and liability interest-rate sensitivities can magnify an economic loss when interest rates change in either direction. (Later in this textbook we explain more about interest-rate sensitivities.)

For another view of the effects insurers experience when interest rates are low, see Insight 16-2.

This concludes our consideration of why interest-rate fluctuations strongly affect an insurance company's financial environment. Next, we review the features of the regulatory environments affecting ALM practices in the United States and Canada.

Insight 16-2 A Low Interest-Rate Environment Has Had at Least Six Separate Effects on the Life Insurance Industry

The impact of interest-rate swings on life insurance companies is both broad and deep. Probably the most important factor shaping life and health insurers' actions in 1995 was the fact that long-term interest rates were falling throughout 1995.

1. Low interest rates in 1995 exposed insurers to reinvestment risk in their asset portfolio. That means they received a lower yield than they had planned when investing in an interest-sensitive asset. They may have counted on these assets to fund a liability with a guaranteed crediting rate.

2. Volatile behavior of interest rates has increased uncertainty about future market interest rates. The importance of the investment officer's role in risk management has changed so that investment officers now must apply sophisticated quantitative methods and must productively manage the yield, duration, options risk, and liquidity on assets backing the larger share of interest-sensitive products many companies now have.

3. Low interest rates in 1995 raised the market value of life insurance companies and reduced their cost of capital. Therefore, low interest rates have made it much easier to raise capital for badly needed expansion in critical product lines and in company size.

4. Low interest rates intensified the pace of merger and acquisition activity involving life insurance companies. An insurer's average cost of capital includes not only the interest rate costs of borrowing but also the opportunity costs of committed capital within the company. For stock companies, the cost to raise funds by issuing common stock also fell. To achieve the same expansion objective, acquiring a going concern is less costly than starting up a new business line.

5. Low interest rates raised the annual contribution that some pension plan sponsors paid to life insurers in order to fund qualified defined benefit plan liabilities.

6. Low interest rates can increase a financial product's competitive advantage. Life insurance and its rival industries—commercial banking, mutual funds, and retail securities brokerages, for example—are intensely competitive. For products having interest-sensitive crediting rates, many life insurance companies have a competitive advantage over their competitors in a low interest rate environment following a period of higher interest rates as in 1995. Because life insurers' net investment yield is based on a portfolio of securities purchased when interest rates were higher, those insurers can credit higher rates on some products than rivals in other industries can when current market interest rates are low. Of course, not all insurers had this situation.

Source: *Excerpted and adapted with permission. Paul A. Reardon, Ph.D., Chief Investment Officer, "A Review of Life Insurance Industry Financial and Investment Trends Through 1995,"* Investment Topics *(Washington, D.C.: American Council of Life Insurance), pp. 2–3.*

ALM and the Regulatory Environments in the United States and Canada

The historical change in the financial environment from an era of relatively stable interest rates (before the 1970s) to an era of less stable interest rates (during and after the 1970s) required financial institutions either to adapt or to fail. As some financial institutions stumbled in their scurry to adapt, regulators in the United States and Canada began requiring responsible behavior suited to the new broader range of fluctuations in interest rates. Regulators thus encouraged a conscious practice of ALM approaches.

Regulatory requirements describe the approaches that insurers must follow in order to provide a minimum level of responsible monitoring of asset/liability mismatch (C-3) risks. Various regulations require specified minimum levels of cash-flow forecasting, dictate investment behaviors, and dictate product-design behaviors.

The regulatory environment in Canada is substantially different from that in the United States. In general, specific ALM practices in Canada are dictated by the Canadian Institute of Actuaries (CIA), rather than by federal and provincial regulations. The governmental authorities in turn support the CIA's standards of practice by requiring companies to follow those standards. In Canada, the regulatory environment for asset/liability management has the following characteristics:[1]

- A strong federal regulatory system
- A history of financial reporting for insurance companies based on a GAAP or near-GAAP standard
- For the appointed actuary, legally supported professional standards of actuarial practice developed through the CIA, combined with a strong statutory role
- The Insurance Companies Act (1992), a federal regulation that modernized insurance regulation by (1) strengthening the discretionary powers of company management while also (2) increasing the discretionary action and enforcement of regulators

Most of the U.S. laws promoting ALM were developed as model laws through the National Association of Insurance Commissioners (NAIC). Specifically, we review the

- ***Amendments to the Standard Valuation Law*** in 1980
- ***Policy Loan Interest Rate Model Law*** in 1980
- ***Investment Limitation Model Law*** in 1989

- NAIC's ***Actuarial Opinion and Memorandum (AOM)*** model law in 1991
- ***Asset Valuation Reserve and the Interest Maintenance Reserve (AVR/IMR)*** in 1992—replacing the Mandatory Securities Valuation Reserve (MSVR)

Amendments to the Standard Valuation Law (1980)

In 1980, the NAIC published model amendments to the older Standard Valuation Law. Insurers formerly were required to establish fixed interest-rate assumptions for reserves and nonforfeiture values at the outset of a contract, and were not permitted to make any change thereafter. For contracts having their inception after the amendments, these amendments permitted changing every 12 months the maximum interest rates permitted for valuations of reserves and nonforfeiture values for use with new business. This change gave insurers a mechanism for managing risks by adjusting policy reserves and nonforfeiture values to reflect changes in market interest rates.

Policy Loan Interest Rate Model Law (1980)

This model law was a response to a need to control policy loan activity during periods of rising interest rates. When policyholders withdraw funds through policy loans, the insurer's investment earnings on those funds are limited to the policy loan interest rate. Additionally, in order to meet an unexpected demand for new loans, the insurer may have to unexpectedly sell assets at a loss.

Before the law, a contract's policy loan interest rate had to be specified in the contract when it was issued, and the rate remained fixed thereafter. This model law permits insurers to increase the policy loan interest rate up to four times annually, within specified limits, and to decrease the interest rate under some circumstances. Through this law, insurers gained a mechanism for adjusting policy loan interest rates to reflect changes in market interest rates, and thus they gained a mechanism for managing some interest-rate mismatching (C-3) risks.

Investment Limitation Model Law (1989)

The 1989 Investment Limitation Model Law limits an insurer's concentration of asset holdings in various classes of assets and also limits an insurer's concentration of investments in the securities of any single issuer. The intention behind this law was to essentially require insurers to exhibit responsible behavior with respect to prudent diversification of their investment portfolios. In finance, ***diversification*** can be defined as the use of a variety of asset types in an effort to limit exposure to risk. When a portfolio consists of a variety of different assets, each with a different risk profile, any losses in one asset can be offset by gains in another asset.

Actuarial Opinion and Memorandum Model Law (1991)

The NAIC's Actuarial Opinion and Memorandum (AOM) model law requires many life insurers to appoint a valuation actuary to perform cash-flow testing. The intention of this law is to mandate responsible asset/liability management behavior for companies issuing interest-sensitive products. You should recall from Chapter 3 that *cash-flow testing* (CFT) can be defined as a process of projecting and comparing, as of a given valuation date, the timing and amount of asset and liability cash flows after the valuation date. The required ***actuarial opinion statement*** is a public document that must be filed along with the U.S. Annual Statement. This law requires all large life insurers to perform cash-flow testing.

For the purpose of meeting this requirement in the United States and a similar requirement in Canada, the appointed actuary must certify that the insurer's reserves and related items are adequate to provide for "the anticipated cash flows required by the contractual obligations and related expenses of the company."

The NAIC's model bill specifies

- Rules for appointing an actuary
- Liabilities to be covered by the actuarial opinion
- Seven interest-rate scenarios required for use in cash-flow testing. These scenarios were described in Chapter 3 (see Figure 3-5)
- Formal reporting approaches for presenting the results of cash-flow testing. The language the NAIC suggests for use in the statement of actuarial opinion is as follows:

  The reserves and related items, when considered in light of the assets held by the company with respect to such reserves and related actuarial items including, but not limited to, investment earnings on such assets, and the considerations anticipated to be received and retained under such policies and contracts, make adequate provision, according to presently accepted actuarial standards of practice, for the anticipated cash flows required by the contractual obligations and related expenses of the company.

Investment Reserves: the AVR/IMR (1992)

As discussed in Chapter 9, investment reserves are designed to cushion the insurer's financial position against the effects of short-term fluctuations in investment values. Investment reserves are not true reserves in that they do not represent a debt owed to any external party.

Beginning in 1992, life insurance companies in the United States were required to establish an Asset Valuation Reserve (AVR) and an Interest Maintenance Reserve (IMR). These reserves supplanted the now-defunct Mandatory Securities Valuation Reserve (MSVR), and they are often referred to jointly as the *AVR/ IMR*. The AVR and IMR require holding investment reserves for a broader spectrum of assets than did the MSVR. Canadian regulations have no counterpart to these investment reserves.

Organizing for ALM

Fitting ALM comfortably into a company's organizational structure is a complex effort, and many insurers have not yet fully created their planned ALM structures, mechanisms, and processes. In addition, as new ALM techniques develop and as the financial environment changes, the spectrum of an insurer's planned ALM applications and adaptations also changes. Any ALM program must advance along two dimensions:

1. Sophistication in using quantitative analysis techniques
2. Sophistication in integrating ALM into corporate communication and corporate strategy

Along these two dimensions, four phases of ALM adoption can be identified from the four possible combinations of beginning or advanced levels of advancement. Figure 16-5 shows these phases. We have labeled these Phase I through Phase IV, as follows:

Figure 16-5. Phases of ALM adoption by insurance companies.

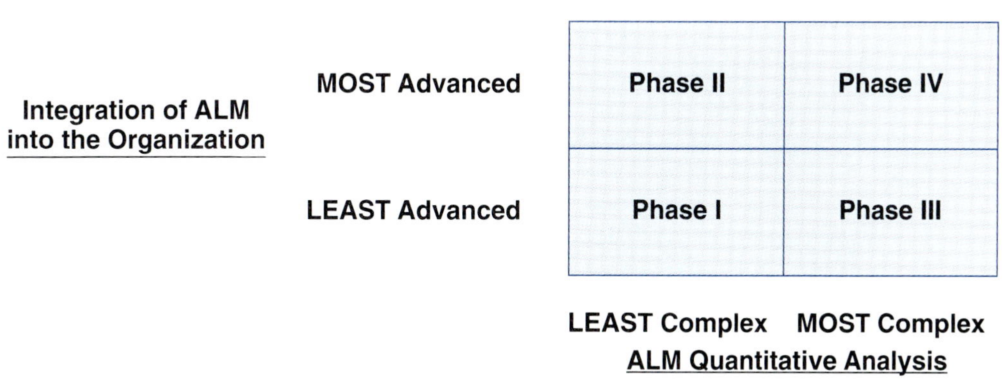

Phase I of ALM Adoption

Companies that have few interest-rate sensitive product offerings or that are just beginning an ALM program tend to perform minimal quantitative analysis, and also tend to have only limited communication in place between the product management team and the investments management team. These companies may have only loose investment guidelines, and their investment portfolios may not be segmented even though the company has many types of liabilities. (Segmentation of investments is discussed in Chapter 17.)

Phase II of ALM Adoption

Some insurance companies have attempted to improve their organizational integration and communication, but they fall short on the technical applications and tend to perform only a minimum of quantitative analysis. These companies probably have an ALM team, an ALM steering committee, and a system of formal ALM reporting. However, in this stage, limitations related to analytical capabilities represent an important roadblock against effective ALM. These companies may or may not have purchased specialized ALM software and they may or may not use consultants to move them along the path of ALM adoption. As a result, Phase II companies use ALM once a year or as needed for compliance, but do not routinely use it for decision support.

Phase III of ALM Adoption

Some companies have purchased commercial ALM software packages and have the technical ability and expertise to analyze data for ALM purposes, but they are behind in establishing the appropriate organizational structures and communication. These companies may have an ALM team, an ALM steering committee, and a system of formal ALM reporting. However, in this stage, limitations related to communication represent an important roadblock against fully using the output from their analysis. As a result, Phase III companies use ALM once a year or as needed for compliance, but do not routinely use it for decision support.

Phase IV of ALM Adoption

Insurance companies at the forefront of implementing an ALM program tend to perform sophisticated quantitative modeling; have integrated investment strategies into product design and product characteristics into investment objectives; have an ALM technical team or teams and an ALM steering committee; and tend to have extensive communication in place between the product management team and the investments management team. Phase IV requires having the information, being able to communicate it, and using it appropriately. Large companies with plentiful resources would tend to reach a Phase IV condition first. Companies in Phase IV of ALM adoption segment their investment portfolios, and manage these portfolio segments appropriately for the liability portfolios that are matched with them. Phase IV companies use ALM output on a daily basis as support for routine decision making related to asset purchase and sale decisions, marketing decisions, and crediting-rate decisions.

Because ALM programs are still evolving, many companies are still phasing in some non-mandatory aspects of ALM systems, according to LOMA research. A life and health insurance company must adapt its organizational structure to ensure the effectiveness of its ALM program. For ALM, each insurer would find it useful to make the following adaptations:[2]

- Incorporating ALM into the organization's formal financial reporting systems of written reports.
- Providing for effective communication across departmental lines—among marketing officers, actuaries, and investment experts. Communication across departmental lines is sometimes termed ***horizontal communication*** (or ***lateral communication***).
- Providing for effective vertical communication between technical experts and top executives. Communication up and down the lines of the organizational hierarchy is sometimes termed ***vertical communication.*** Effective vertical communication partly depends upon clear definition of authority and responsibility.
- Segmenting asset and liability portfolios. Usually, insurers group their liabilities into product lines, segment their asset portfolios, and then match specified asset segments with the various product lines.
- Obtaining any needed technological support, including the financial software needed for simulation modeling and duration analysis.
- Ensuring that incentive-based compensation systems work to align the staff's personal goals with the goals of the ALM program.

Next we examine the actions insurers take in order to integrate ALM communications into the formal organizational structure. For a successful ALM effort, the organizational design must give the ALM function a reporting relationship to a standing committee of the company's board of directors and also must give the ALM effort appropriate technical decision support from a team of actuarial and investment experts.

Organizational Structures and Processes for ALM

Typically, ALM programs supersede the traditional vertical lines of communication within an organizational hierarchy. In other words, companies rarely establish any permanent ALM department as an isolated unit within the traditional organizational hierarchy. Instead, the ALM process is usually carried out by task teams and standing committees. In this context, a ***task team*** can be defined as a work group assigned with fulfilling a long-term or permanent mission, and having a membership chosen on the basis of individual expertise and ability to carry out the team's mission. A ***standing committee*** can be defined as a work group formed on a permanent basis to meet a more or less permanent organizational need, and often having the authority to make decisions for the organization within a limited area of responsibility. Standing committees usually have a membership selected on the basis of organizational title or position. Moreover, interactions between the task team and standing committee are often organized in a nontraditional *matrix organizational form.* A ***matrix organization*** is one in which *ad hoc* committees or teams of experts from various disciplines work to support a single project or program.

Additionally, the ALM process establishes nontraditional lines of communication that cross the formal boundaries provided within a traditional hierarchy. ALM provides the meeting ground where product actuaries, valuation actuaries, and investment analysts compare their technical findings. Without any integrating force from a cross-disciplinary effort such as ALM, these actuarial and investment functions might operate independently in their pursuit of strategic goals, each potentially undermining the efforts of the others.

A large insurance company has at least a high-level steering committee overseeing ALM processes, and at least one technical task team to perform the necessary hands-on analysis and recommend action on the basis of that analysis. In a small company, the same group of individuals might perform all of these functions. In a large and diversified company, many teams might perform these functions: each product line would likely have at least one task team of its own, and each subsidiary would likely have its own steering committee. Our discussion will proceed according to the assumption that an insurance company would have one ALM steering committee and one ALM technical team. In Figure 16-6, an organizational diagram depicts this structure.

An ALM Steering Committee

A high-level committee of financial decision makers ordinarily serves as a steering committee for ALM activities. A steering committee relationship of this sort exists regardless of the insurer's level of implementation of an ALM program. The steering committee is

Figure 16-6. Organization of the ALM function.

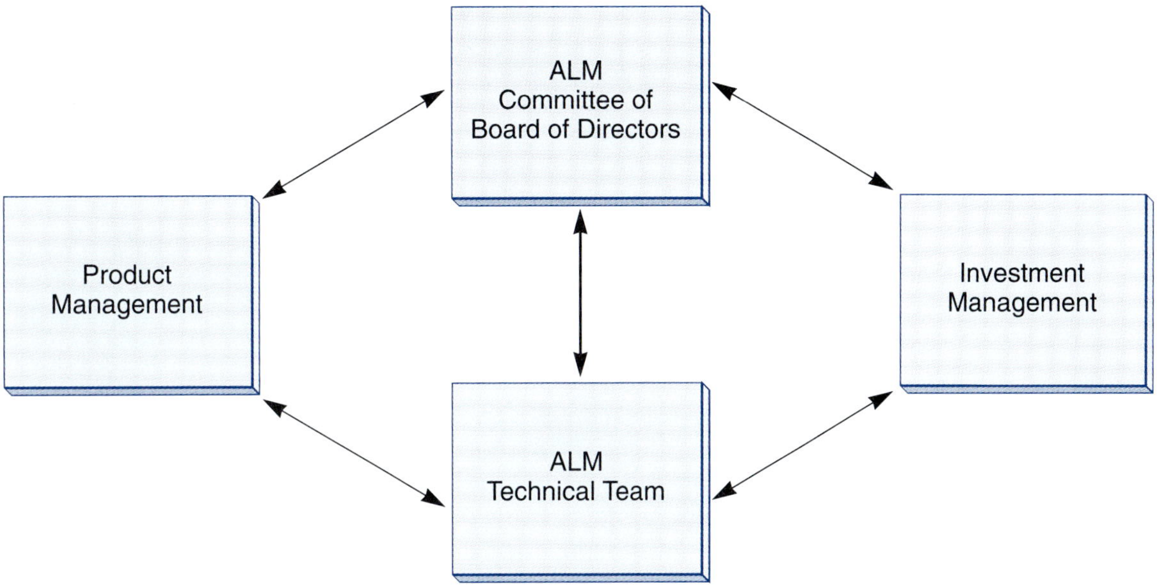

Source: *Adapted from* Asset-Liability Management in the Life Insurance Industry *(Atlanta, GA: LOMA, 1993), p. 44.*

ordinarily a standing committee of the company's board of directors. Such a steering committee would likely include participation by the insurance company's chief executive officer, general counsel, chief financial officer or chief investment officer, chief actuary, and sometimes the chief marketing officer. In many companies, the standing committee that oversees ALM programs is known as the *finance committee*, the *investment committee*, or the *executive committee*. Because the names and duties of board committees are not standardized throughout the industry, in our present discussion we will refer to the board committee that oversees the ALM program as the ***ALM steering committee.*** This steering committee sets investment and other financial policies, and also oversees the company's ALM programs. Primary responsibilities of this steering committee include

- Setting policy for investment activities and empowering staff or consultants acting on behalf of the company to undertake transactions as needed to carry out those policies
- Setting limits on transaction amounts
- Declaring interest-crediting rates on all interest-sensitive lines of business
- Setting general investment policy and overall financial objectives for the insurance company

- Approving every purchase of private placement securities
- Reviewing reports and recommendations from the ALM technical working group and setting ALM policies and strategies

Steering committees obtain advice on technical matters from highly expert technical working groups, often referred to as *ALM teams.* An ALM technical team reporting to the ALM steering committee provides technical analysis, technical interpretation, and recommendations for action. The steering committee takes action by ratifying, modifying, or rejecting recommendations from the ALM technical team, and takes into consideration decision-making information obtained from other sources.

An ALM Technical Team

An insurance company's financial management activities rely upon many areas of specialized expertise, particularly in a large life and health insurance organization. The need for a sophisticated approach to ALM requires bringing together a working group of technical experts from diverse areas of the insurance organization. The team is sometimes known as an asset/liability management team (ALM team). Titles for the asset/liability management function, however, are different from one company to the next. For convenience, we use the title ***ALM team*** in reference to any ALM technical working group.

For effective ALM, life and health insurers must coordinate their financial expertise in the areas of

- Investment policy and operations
- Product design and pricing
- Insurance risk management, including underwriting, product/market diversification, claims management, and reinsurance programs
- Operating expenses, including information systems costs, legal costs, and employee compensation costs

Once again, recall that the purpose of an ALM team is to coordinate the timing of the insurance company's cash-flow patterns. ALM team members approach their tasks by working in consultation with one another for purposes of coordinating product prices, product features, product crediting rates, investment portfolios, product lines, and corporate support expenditures. Generally, an insurer's actuarial staff and investment staff—working separately and together—are responsible for accomplishing most of the analytical work of an ALM team. The insurer's marketing staff and information systems staff are involved to a lesser degree.

Although some work of the ALM team requires the expertise of both actuaries and investment experts, some ALM tasks can be identified with one area of expertise more so than with the other. We discuss first the ALM tasks that are performed mostly by product actuaries, and then the ALM tasks that rely mostly upon the work of other financial and investment experts.

ALM Tasks Performed by Actuarial Experts

An insurer's actuarial staff contributes expertise on a formal, regular basis as well as on an *ad hoc* basis. The actuarial staff makes *ad hoc* contributions to the ALM process by performing studies that assist other actuarial staff in setting product prices and designing new products. For example, these *ad hoc* duties might include finding the costs of including various optional contract provisions, providing formulas for setting target surplus for a proposed product, and setting reasonable profit objectives for a proposed product. The actuarial staff makes formal contributions to the ALM process by preparing regular periodic reports and submitting the reports through the technical team and then up to the steering committee and sometimes also up to the company's full board of directors.

Contributions that actuarial experts make to the ALM team's duties include regularly preparing

- A *liability duration* report to the investment department, showing policy reserve amounts, measures of liability durations, and target investment yields for new and existing investments as needed to support each product line;
- Recommendations which if adopted by the board of directors are called ***crediting-rate resolutions.*** These resolutions declare the crediting rates to be awarded on interest-sensitive products.
- C*ash-flow testing analysis* for the appointed (valuation) actuary in support of the Actuarial Opinion and Memorandum (AOM) to accompany the Annual Statement (We first encountered cash-flow testing in Chapter 3); and
- *Dynamic solvency testing* to project earnings by lines of business under various economic scenarios, and for use in setting target surplus levels as part of capital and surplus management (We first encountered dynamic solvency testing in Chapter 3).

ALM Tasks Performed by Investment Experts

An insurance company's investment experts are equal partners with the product actuaries on the ALM team. Investment experts make at least the following contributions to the ALM team:

- Reporting to senior management and the steering committee about the current performance of investment portfolios;
- Managing asset acquisitions and sales by selecting assets, purchasing assets, selling assets, and assigning asset purchases to appropriate portfolio segments;
- Developing investment strategies for each product line, often implemented by developing specially defined portfolio segments for different product lines;
- Projecting asset maturities, asset prepayments, and rates of return on reinvestments, and finally forecasting future portfolio yields;
- Consulting with actuarial staff in the setting of interest-crediting rates based on investment opportunities currently available in financial markets; and
- Informing product design actuaries of investment opportunities, asset innovations, and the potential uses of these opportunities in support of future insurance products.

The work of an ALM team may be poorly understood by many employees in a company. Thus, one of the ALM team's communication duties is educating non-experts about ALM work. Technical experts can and should undertake to promote understanding of and interest in ALM as appropriate throughout the organization. For their part, non-experts should pursue education about issues connected with ALM.

Pitfalls Arising from the Complexity of ALM

Ordinarily, the level of detail a managerial decision maker requires is lower at the top of the organization and greater at the bottom of the organization. In other words, top-level managers focus mainly on the "big picture" while lower-level managers require more "nitty-gritty" detail. This rule of thumb is best not applied rigorously to ALM reporting. In insurance companies, members of the ALM steering committee need some technical understanding of the company's ALM team and processes, and of how effectively those people and processes are performing. Effective ALM requires top-level decision makers to make ongoing commitments to the following activities:

- Pursuing their education regarding ALM processes
- Improving their understanding of ALM issues
- Requesting and absorbing ALM reporting in greater detail than is customary for top-level decision makers for most purposes

Members of an insurance company's board of directors, including inside directors who are officers of the company, need to understand and be able to identify which sets of external circumstances would threaten the insurance company's survival. These people should be able to respond to the following four questions about their company's financial condition:

1. What are the likely market interest-rate movements that would cause our company to lose money? What interest-rate movements would cause our company to make money?
2. How likely are those interest-rate changes to occur soon?
3. How much GAAP and statutory capital would the company have remaining after absorbing those losses or gains?
4. What strategies can our company use to reduce our unwanted exposure to interest-rate movements?

Pitfalls in Implementing ALM

The truly unusual complexity of several of the analytical techniques employed for ALM purposes gives rise to a few pitfalls in implementing ALM. In general, these pitfalls are related to insufficient awareness of risk-taking, insufficient motivation to undertake educational activities to keep up with ALM technical developments, misinterpretation of ALM data, and even misapplication of ALM techniques. These pitfalls can be summarized as follows:

- So long as a company's profits appear to continue at an acceptable pace, some decision makers can fail to recognize that those profits might be in some sense connected to the company's risk-taking. Remember, one lesson from the risk-return tradeoff is that unusually high returns can indicate that the investor has taken a big risk.
- So long as profit measures continue to look acceptable, some crucial decision makers are not sufficiently motivated to go through the necessary learning processes and to learn to interpret data developed using the more complex ALM techniques.
- Caution is required in interpreting ALM output. Because ALM reports can be complex, top-level decision makers might misinterpret the data and make ill-suited decisions on a mistaken basis. Even technical specialists might incorrectly interpret ALM outputs, and could thus misinterpret data in reporting to top-level decision makers. Because some analytical techniques employed in ALM are not widely understood, even large-scale mistakes in analysis, interpretation, or application can escape

Insight 16-3 Nothing Is So Frightening as Ignorance in Action

Recently I was examining the investment strategy of a large life insurer that had a small book of traditional life products, a modest amount of universal life insurance, and a huge business in single premium deferred annuities (SPDAs). In light of its highly leveraged balance sheet, I was comforted to read in the annual report that the firm pursued a careful, disciplined policy of matching the durations of assets to liabilities in an effort to minimize any exposure to interest rate risk. However, I became suspicious when, upon reading further, it purported to have an asset portfolio with an aggregate duration of 6.5 and a liability portfolio with a 7.0 duration. The asset portfolio was invested largely in junk bonds and mortgage-backed securities, both of which often have shorter durations than many corporate bonds due to the prevalence of aggressive call features and prepayment provisions. My own analysis showed that the duration of assets, adjusted for the interest sensitivity of cash flows, was 3.5.

I was also suspicious that the liability duration had been badly estimated, as I have never seen an SPDA portfolio with such a long duration. Further, the company required low or no surrender charges on its annuities, distributed its products via Wall Street brokers, and had a clientele that exhibited characteristics of "hot money." Given that they had erred so badly on the asset duration calculations, I decided to check their liability duration estimates. Using their own actuarial projections for interest-sensitive lapses, I found the aggregate liability duration to be 1.2. Taking into account their leverage ratio, I estimated the company's surplus duration to be 61.7, a far cry from "minimal interest rate risk exposure." In further checking, I found that the company had been focusing on Macaulay duration measures which, in an interest-sensitive cash flow context, have virtually nothing to do with exposure to interest rate risk. This was all the more surprising to me when I learned that the company's Chief Investment Officer was a candidate for the Ph.D. in finance, and the board of directors included several individuals with a background in finance that would be hard to surpass. If they wanted to "bet the bank" on interest rates, it would have been hard to assume a more aggressive posture.

If a little knowledge is dangerous, where is the man who has so much as to be out of danger?

—On Elemental Instruction in Physiology [1877]

Source: *David F. Babel, "Asset/Liability Matching in the Life Insurance Industry,"* The Financial Dynamics of the Insurance Industry, *Edward I. Altman and Irwin T. Vanderhoof, editors. Irwin and New York University, 1995, pp. 250, 254–255. Reprinted with permission of Irwin Professional Publishing.*

notice. Insight 16-3 describes how an outside analyst found some large mistakes in an insurer's interpretation of its asset/liability matching. Even technical specialists might improperly employ ALM techniques, and could thus present the wrong data in reporting to top-level decision makers.

In Conclusion

Chapter 16 has presented an orientation to asset/liability management for life and health insurance companies. Here we reviewed the reasons for employing ALM and considered the main source of instability affecting insurers' cash flows: interest-rate fluctuations. Next we reviewed the history of regulatory encouragement of ALM practices for life and health insurance companies.

As the practice of asset/liability management in insurance companies emerged, insurers adapted an organizational form that would better support effective ALM. Two important adaptations were adding a new ALM unit to the organization and adopting a new formal system of ALM reports for communicating ALM information to staff who need it. Our attention turned to the roles of the ALM team and the ALM steering committee. We examined the variety of technical reports used for conveying ALM information to the decision makers who must rely upon it. Because the information conveyed through these reports is uncommonly technical, we reviewed a number of the pitfalls lurking within that unusual level of complexity.

ALM continues to evolve on at least two frontiers: (1) integration into the organization and (2) technical sophistication. On one frontier, ALM is becoming integrated into insurers' financial operations. On the second frontier, the improving power of personal computers renders it possible for analysts to produce multiple scenarios of 20-year cash-flow projections daily or weekly. Analysts have gained expertise with existing ALM techniques, and are continually developing new techniques and applications.

Chapter 17 presents the technical approaches that product man-agers and asset managers have at their disposal for supporting asset/liability management efforts.

Key Terms and Concepts

- asset/liability management (ALM)
- portfolio
- positive net cash flow (net cash inflow)
- negative net cash flow
- actual solvency
- technical solvency
- cash-flow matching
- liability-driven
- customer-driven
- market-driven
- asset-driven
- spread compression
- duration statistic
- spread expansion
- refinance
- Amendments to the Standard Valuation Law
- Policy Loan Interest Rate Model Law
- Investment Limitation Model Law
- Actuarial Opinion and Memorandum (AOM) model law
- actuarial opinion statement
- Asset Valuation Reserve and the Interest Maintenance Reserve (AVR/IMR)
- diversification
- horizontal (lateral) communication
- vertical communication
- task team
- standing committee
- matrix organization
- ALM steering committee
- ALM team
- crediting-rate resolution

References

1. *Asset-Liability Management in the Life Insurance Industry,* (Atlanta, GA: LOMA, 1993), p. 73.
2. *Ibid,* p. 2.

CHAPTER

Approaches to Asset/Liability Management

17

LEARNING OBJECTIVES

After studying this chapter, you should be able to

- Recognize how ALM programs support insurers' profitability objectives
- Determine how interest-rate movements expose insurers to specific financial risks in their asset and liability portfolios
- Identify the benefits of portfolio segmentation and portfolio gap (mismatch) analysis
- Recognize the purposes of analyzing interest-rate sensitivities of asset and liability portfolios
- Analyze the effects of mismatched interest-rate sensitivities, once given the direction of an interest-rate movement
- Identify the purposes of typical reports within a formal ALM reporting system
- Recognize several investment strategies and product design strategies that insurers apply for correcting a gap or mismatch

OUTLINE

In Chapter 16, we noted that a primary objective of ALM is to help insurers balance the financial behaviors of their asset and their liability portfolios—both of which are exposed to risks arising from constantly changing market interest rates. In pursuit of this objective, financial experts develop elaborate financial theories, devise mathematical descriptions of financial instruments and the financial environment, and turn these theories and models into computer-based applications. Many of these applications are designed to enable insurers to create a match of some sort between the characteristics of the assets and the liabilities.

Mastery of several technical specialties is required in order to carry out the usual types of ALM analysis. The techniques applied for implementing an ALM program can be so complex that more than one Nobel Prize in mathematics has been awarded for the development of these techniques. For more information about the history of asset/liability management techniques, see Figure 17-1.

In addition, ALM techniques and ALM applications continually evolve, generally reflecting advances in the capacity of computers and in mathematical theory. Teaching how to apply these techniques is not a goal of this book. Because ALM analysis provides valuable support for managerial decision making, this chapter identifies some widely used ALM applications and presents the general purposes of some important ALM techniques.

ALM and Asset/Liability Spread

As we have established, an effective asset/liability management program supports both a proactive and a defensive view of managing an insurance business. From a proactive viewpoint, ALM focuses on making senior decision makers conscious of managing the spread or profit margin between the investment portfolio and the product portfolio. An important precept of ALM is that an insurance company's asset and liability portfolios comprise a single system. Insurance companies earn a spread—or *profit margin*—by lending money to borrowers at one rate and obtaining money from customers at another rate. From a holistic view of an insurance operation, an insurer's product portfolio activity represents the company's obtaining money from customers, whereas its asset portfolio activity represents the insurer's lending money to borrowers. The profit margin represents the difference between the interest rates for lending and for borrowing. The concept of a profit margin also conveniently summarizes the results of the two portfolios in a single performance measure.

Figure 17-1. Timeline of advances in mathematics and financial applications supporting ALM.

Year	Name	Contribution toward present-day ALM techniques
1800	William Morgan, Equitable Life Assurance Society (London)	First professional actuary in modern sense. First to recognize need for maintaining adequate reserves to cover future liabilities, the need to carry forward a margin of surplus, and the need for classifying and measuring sources of profit.
1893	George J. Lidstone, British actuary	Anticipated the concept of mean term, which is equivalent to the duration.
1938	Frederick R. Macauley	Generally acknowledged to have introduced concept of *duration,* which is standard terminology today (later presented by Redington as *mean term*). Duration was also discovered independently by several others.
1939	Sir John Hicks, Nobel Laureate	Independently proposed concept of duration.
1942	Tjalling C. Koopmans, mathematical economist	Suggested cash-flow matching or dedication for insulating a fixed-income portfolio against shifts in the term structure of interest rates. With Leonid Kantorovich, awarded Nobel Memorial Prize in 1975 for application of linear programming to cash-flow matching and to resource allocation problems.
1945	Paul A. Samuelson, Nobel Laureate	Independently proposed concept of duration.
1952	Frank M. Redington, Chief Actuary, Prudential Assurance Company	Introduced the idea of portfolio immunization in "Review of the Principles of Life-Office Valuations," expressing concepts of (1) equal and parallel treatment in valuation of assets and liabilities and (2) a version of duration matching—equating *mean terms* of assets and liabilities while requiring assets to be more spread out than liabilities. Gold Medal, British Institute of Actuaries, 1968.
1952	Harry Markowitz	Introduced modern portfolio theory (MPT), the basis for present-day practices of managing investment portfolios.
1973	Fischer Black and Myron Scholes	Derived option-pricing theory (OPT), using a formula to price stock options by the *principle of no arbitrage* to earn interest at exactly the risk-free rate. OPT can also be applied to pricing debt options and valuing interest-sensitive cash flows. Considered the most important advance in financial and economic theory of the 1970s.

Source: *Elias S. W. Shiu, "Asset/Liability Management: From Immunization to Option-Pricing Theory,"* Financial Management of Life Insurance Companies, *J. David Cummins and Joan Lamm-Tennant, editors (Boston, MA: Kluwer Academic Publishers, 1991), pp. 151–158.*

For example, if the Azure Assurance Corporation earned 8 percent on its entire asset portfolio and paid 6 percent to customers on its entire product portfolio, then the Azure Assurance Corporation's spread would be 2 percent. This model applies equally to an insurance organization's entire operation or to a product line within a broader operation. Accordingly, if the Cadmium Insurance Company earned 10 percent on the assets associated with its guaranteed investment contract (GIC) business while crediting GIC customers a rate of 9 percent for the use of their funds, Cadmium's spread on its GIC business would be 1 percent.

From a defensive view of insurance company operations, ALM reporting makes senior decision makers conscious of the link between their choices and various acceptable and unacceptable effects of the risk-return tradeoff. Through ALM, decision makers become aware of the need to limit risks to reflect management's and the owners' risk tolerances. Insurance companies use ALM for managing their asset and liability risk exposures from changes in market interest rates (C-3 risk). ALM is designed to enable an insurance company's actuaries and investment professionals to coordinate their strategies for product design, product pricing, and investment management.

In accordance with both the proactive and the defensive fronts of insurance company management, the main approach to ALM over the years has been to create mathematical models of both the products and of the assets associated with those products. In this effort, insurers typically classify their broad product offerings into distinct lines of products having similar cash-flow patterns and risk characteristics, a process referred to as ***portfolio segmentation.*** Once analysts have identified and described the characteristics of a given product, then they go about selecting a portfolio of assets suited to that product. Generally, the goal is to select assets that will provide cash inflows that match in timing and amount the insurance company's needs to (1) fund the company's cash obligations arising from the products and (2) achieve a target profit margin. As financial theory and technology have improved, greater levels of sophistication in analysis have become possible, although different companies achieve different degrees of sophistication in the effort to match cash flows.

The discussion of C-3 risk in Chapter 10 demonstrated that changes in market interest rates can produce a decrease in the capital and surplus of life and health insurers. In Chapter 16, we remarked that one important objective of ALM is to manage the insurer's interest-rate (C-3) risk. Managing financial risks from changing market interest rates supports a company's strategic objectives relating to both solvency and profitability.

Using ALM for Managing C-3 Risks

Most insurance companies approach ALM from at least two fronts—the asset side and the liability side. On the asset side, ALM programs focus on portfolio management policies, strategies, and tactics suited to the needs of the liabilities those assets are intended to support. Investment portfolio management must respond defensively to any unfavorable mismatch between (1) actuarial assumptions underlying the insurer's products and (2) changes in the business environment. On the liability side, ALM programs usually focus on designing and pricing contracts so that the behavior of their cash flows will be predictable and supportable. Specifically, the product design actuaries model potential events in the financial markets and the economy, and then incorporate into the products features designed for protecting the insurer from such risks as (1) disintermediation (withdrawals) and (2) underpricing. From the assets side, the investment staff can protect the insurer by using portfolio insurance techniques such as hedging strategies, which we discuss later in this chapter.

Approaching ALM by Matching Cash-Flow Patterns

Some financial instruments naturally have readily predictable cash flows. Predictability of cash flows permits the company to directly and reliably *match* the cash flows of a specified asset portfolio with the cash-flow needs of a specified liability portfolio. Unfortunately, as we noted last chapter, direct *matching* of life insurers' cash flows is feasible for only a few product lines, because most insurance company liabilities have unpredictable cash flows. Instead, life and health insurers generally must use more complex approaches to asset/liability management. This chapter reviews some of the added complexities.

Although the practice of ALM can be quite technical, the basic idea of *matching* cash flows is deceptively simple to understand. Indeed, a practice of matching asset and liability cash flows can be viewed as a simplified approximation of the more complex asset/liability *management* processes. For that reason, it is useful for us to review the general procedure for managing the cash flows of a matched pair of portfolios. This procedure is summarized in Figure 17-2.

If insurers' forecasting abilities were perfect, companies could simply provide for meeting the net cash *outflows* associated with a given product liability by purchasing assets expected to produce a "mirror image" pattern of net cash *inflows.* In simple terms, cash-flow matching requires an insurance company's investments to provide net cash inflows that match in timing and amount the net cash outflows for the insurer's products. Matching these streams of cash inflows and cash outflows requires making forecasts. Before an insur-

Figure 17-2. A procedure for cash-flow management.

1. Segment product lines and predict cash flow patterns of various liability types
2. Predict cash flow patterns of various asset types
3. Establish pairings of assets with liabilities
4. Predict financial outcomes resulting from pairings of specified assets and liabilities
5. Attach probabilities or risk levels to predicted financial outcomes
6. Interpret uncertainties in predicted financial outcomes as types of mismatch risks, using cash-flow testing, dynamic solvency testing, and other analytical techniques

ance company can match the patterns of its products' net cash outflows, however, it must describe and predict those patterns. For examples of the types of cash flows connected with the asset portfolio and the liability portfolio, see Figure 17-3.

An insurer can construct a portfolio of assets that will in theory produce a chosen pattern of cash flows. However, before a company can begin constructing a precisely engineered portfolio, first it must identify assets having the desired payment patterns. Insurance companies approach this effort by developing forecasts of the behavior of various assets. Forecasts are by their very nature uncertain. Because any supposed match between a liability portfolio and an asset portfolio is based on the expected behavior of their cash flows, the effectiveness of the match is limited by the accuracy of the underlying forecasts.

Despite this uncertainty, insurers make good use of forecasts. Investment experts generally can know the probable timing and amount of net cash inflows from various asset types, based on a given interest-rate scenario. Product-side experts generally can predict, based on a

Figure 17-3. Examples of asset and liability cash flows.

Examples of cash flows of the asset portfolio		Examples of cash flows of the liability portfolio	
Net inflows	**Net outflows**	**Net inflows**	**Net outflows**
• Interest income • Loan repayments • Dividend income • Gain on sales of assets	• Capital losses • Asset purchases • Transaction costs • Operating expenses	• Premium income • Annuity income	• Claims, settlements • Surrenders • Operating expenses • Guaranty-fund assessments

given interest-rate scenario, the timing and amount of cash demands related to various product types. Furthermore, insurers can predict the financial-statement effects of the cash-flow interactions between assets and liabilities. These cash-flow results from a pairing of assets and liabilities would be reflected on the income statement and possibly on the balance sheet. On the income statement, the effects would appear as an operating gain (or loss), whereas on the balance sheet they could even produce changes in capital and surplus. (In Chapter 10 we saw that a net gain from operations can have an effect of increasing capital and surplus, whereas a net loss can have an effect of diminishing capital and surplus.)

Because insurers recognize that their ability to predict the timing and amount of cash flows is imperfect, they additionally employ techniques for attaching confidence levels to their predictions. In this context, ***confidence levels*** can be thought of as probabilities of achieving predicted outcomes. Probabilities of not achieving a desired outcome can alternatively be viewed as *risks.* For example, an insurer might attach a 95 percent confidence level to a prediction that the cash inflows from one product will be between $10 million and $12 million a year. This 95 percent confidence level also implies a 5 percent risk that the predicted outcome will be less than $10 million or greater than $12 million.

For a pairing of asset and liability portfolios, the risks of not achieving expected patterns of cash flows are sometimes classified as ***mismatch risks.*** These mismatch risks are at the crux of the challenge that the ALM process takes on. As additional foundation for considering how life insurers approach ALM, we next review the risk components that insurers must manage.

Risks from Mismatching Asset and Liability Cash Flows

Certain types of financial risks are magnified by a poor matching of assets and liabilities. These financial risks can be divided into four categories:

1. ***Default risk,*** part of the C-1 risk in the system of C risks, is the risk of incurring capital losses from defaults on investments. (The other part of C-1 risk is the risk of a loss in market value.)
2. ***Income risk*** is the risk associated with the level and timing of income.
3. ***Disintermediation risk,*** which includes lapse risk and withdrawal risk, is the risk of unexpectedly high levels of customer withdrawals of funds from the financial institution, including the risk of a run on assets.

4. ***Reinvestment risk*** is the risk that funds generated from the asset portfolio will be invested at market interest rates lower than the rates they had been earning.

Figure 17-4 presents examples of events that are associated with each of the four mismatch risk categories. Figure 17-5 summarizes how these categories of financial risks relate to the insurer's asset and liability portfolios.

The uncertainties in the cash flows are not the only uncertainties hampering the ALM effort. In addition to the specific financial risks affecting cash flows, uncertainty is inherent in any chosen match between assets and liabilities because any given match is based on a selected interest-rate scenario or range of scenarios. If the match is based on a scenario that turns out to be incorrect, then even if you had perfect foreknowledge of the cash flows, the assets and liabilities could be seriously mismatched anyway.

The complexities of these risks and the uncertainties in the matching process render a direct cash-flow matching process too imprecise for practical application to asset/liability management. Nevertheless,

Figure 17-4. Cash-flow risks for life insurers, with examples.

Default Risk	• Borrowers' default in payment of principal • Overall decrease in credit quality of assets due to financial antiselection when interest rates fall
Income Risk	• Borrowers' default in payment of interest • Loss of interest income when interest rates fall and callable bonds are retired • Loss of interest income due to mortgage prepayment when interest rates fall • Adverse change in mortality or morbidity experience • Increased cost of insured health care • Increased company operating expenses • Pricing deficiencies
Disintermediation Risk	• Increased policy surrenders when interest rates rise • Increased policy loans when interest rates rise • Increased bond calls when interest rates fall • Increased mortgage prepayments when interest rates fall
Reinvestment Risk	• After interest rates fall, insurer's inability to secure investment returns equal to those assumed in product design • Increased policy loan repayments when interest rates fall

Figure 17-5. Financial risks and how they affect insurance assets and liabilities.

Types of financial risk magnified by A/L mismatch	Cyclical conditions driving each type of financial risk	How each financial risk affects asset and liability portfolios	
		Insurer's liabilities	**Insurer's assets**
Default risk	In a recession, risk of defaults increases.	Insurer *guarantees* return of principal on some products. In recession, withdrawals and policy loans could increase.	Insurer cannot always obtain a guarantee of return of principal on its investments. In a recession, borrowers may default, market values of assets could drop.
Income risk	In a recession, asset earnings may decrease. In prosperity, insurer may invest in riskier assets, and competitive forces encourage making stronger product guarantees.	Insurer's products usually pay out constant annual amounts, or else large single sums. If product pricing assumptions are not realized, insurers could face difficulty in making contractual payments.	Earnings patterns from insurer's investments are not constant. (The resulting mixed cash inflow patterns may not match the constant payouts.)
Disintermediation risk	When market interest rates are high, customer withdrawals and policy loan payouts increase.	When rates are high, withdrawals and policy loan payouts increase. Withdrawals reflect book values, although market values would be low while interest rates are high.	Policy loans depress return on assets. When interest rates are high, market values are low. In order to fund withdrawals, insurer must sell assets while asset values are depressed.
Reinvestment risk	When market interest rates are low, insurers must commit to reinvest at current low rates.		When rates are low, bond values go up. Then, the insurer must reinvest while promised returns are low. Loan prepayments increase.

these risks are the crucial issues that the ALM process must manage. Thus, ALM must focus on either predicting the uncertainties with greater precision or else reducing exposure to the risks.

Proper application of ALM techniques is designed to permit decision makers to select (1) the lowest possible risk level for a chosen level of profitability or (2) the greatest possible return for a chosen level of risk.

Technical Approaches Used in ALM Programs

Although the quantitative tools insurers use for ALM are not generally regarded as being simple, we can understand their general purposes. Here we provide an overview of the following important technical tools and approaches used in ALM:

- Portfolio segmentation by product line
- Cash-flow management
- Portfolio gap analysis, including maturity analysis and interest-rate sensitivity analysis
- Simulation analysis, including cash-flow testing and dynamic solvency testing
- Optimization analysis
- Hedging strategies for investing

Portfolio Segmentation and Cash-Flow Management

As we mentioned at the outset of this chapter, *portfolio segmentation* involves designating portions of the insurer's asset or liability portfolios as separate units for convenience in managing those units. These units are known as ***portfolio segments.*** For example, an asset portfolio segment might consist of only mortgages and bonds with maturities ranging from seven to ten years. A liability portfolio segment might be a specified product line such as individual annuities. Insight 17-1 describes how one insurance company approached portfolio segmentation.

An insurer's approaches to subdividing its asset and liability portfolios for ease of management can take the following forms:

- Creating separately incorporated subsidiaries for different product lines
- Formally creating separate-account portfolios within one corporate entity
- Informally dividing into portfolio segments the recordkeeping for the company's general-account portfolio

Establishing a portfolio segment requires keeping distinct records of the segment's performance, so that the segment is then readily moni-

Insight 17-1 Product Segmentation at Kansas City Life

In the late 1970s, Kansas City Life (KCL) began successfully marketing deferred annuity contracts and in the early 1980s introduced its first universal life policy with a crediting rate that was indexed to 13-week Treasury bills. These products clearly required investment management beyond what had been done in the past. In 1984, Kansas City Life completed a segmentation of its general account by primary product lines. The purpose of this segmentation was to help manage the assets in line with the characteristics of the company's products. For each product segment, KCL allocates an amount of general account assets equal to the book value of the segment's statutory reserves. The only asset types allocated to the product segments are policy loans, bonds, mortgages, preferred stocks, and cash. As shown in the following table, KCL's system employs seven main product segments plus a corporate account. The following pie charts also show the relative size of each product segment. A brief description of each product segment follows the pie charts.

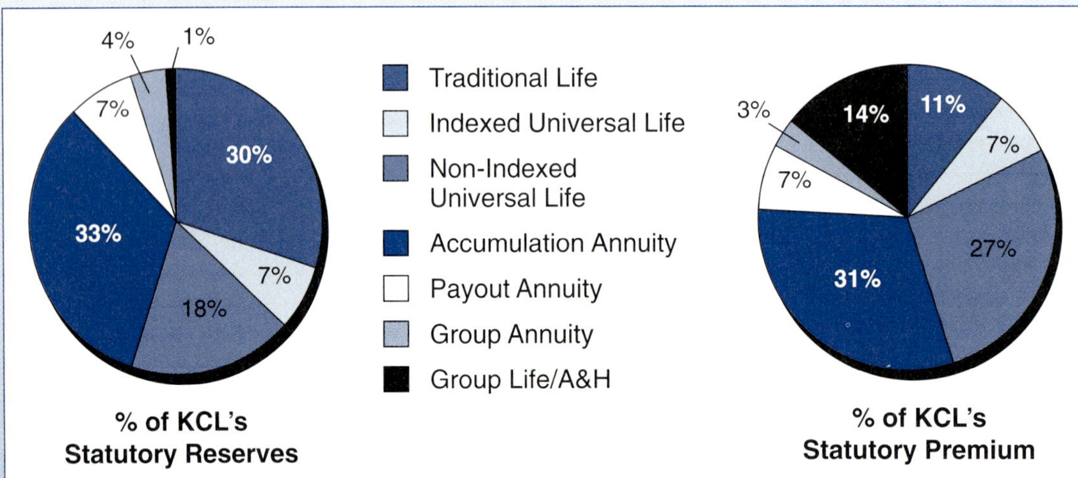

tored as a unit. Typically, a portfolio segment's composition reflects an effort to obtain desired outcomes as to the portfolio's (1) interest-rate sensitivity, (2) market-value volatility, (3) term remaining to maturity, (4) credit quality, and perhaps other characteristics. The specified set of desired outcomes for a portfolio segment is that segment's ***performance profile,*** or *portfolio performance specifications.*

After establishing portfolio segments, then in an ALM technique known as ***interest-rate sensitivity matching,*** insurers establish a pairing between an asset portfolio segment and a liability portfolio segment. In such a pairing, the asset portfolio is regarded as a funding source for the liability portfolio. The pairing of the portfolio segments is based upon the effort to pair assets and liabilities having complementary performance profiles.

Once an asset and a liability portfolio segment are paired, each segment is monitored closely. One purpose of the monitoring is to ensure that each portfolio segment continues to fit its performance profile.

Insight 17-1 Product Segmentation at Kansas City Life (continued)

- **Traditional life.** This product line includes all individual life business except interest-sensitive individual life products. The traditional life liabilities are primarily long-term, nonpar products with low interest-crediting guarantees. For these products, policy loans and lapses are sensitive to market interest rates.
- **Indexed universal life.** The interest-crediting rate is guaranteed to never be less than 3 percent or the 90-day T-Bill discount rate, whichever is greater.
- **Non-indexed universal life.** For these products, interest is credited using the Investment Year Method.
- **Accumulation annuity.** This product segment consists of all individual deferred annuities. Interest is credited using the Investment Year Method. Funds are available for withdrawal on a book-value basis. Most funds have a surrender charge that grades to zero sometime between 7 and 20 years from policy issue.
- **Payout annuity.** This line contains all immediate annuities and supplementary contracts arising from life or annuity contracts. These products are characterized by an established income payment stream that may or may not include life contingencies. Typically, these contracts do not allow surrenders.
- **Group annuity.** This is a closed block of funds accumulating for the pension plans of small employers. Withdrawals for benefit payments are available without penalty while other withdrawals may be subject to a surrender charge and possible market value adjustments.
- **Group life/A&H.** This segment consists of group life and A&H products. Most of the reserves allocated to this fund support short- and long-term disability coverages.

Source: *Reprinted with permission of the publisher from* Asset-Liability Management in the Life Insurance Industry *(Atlanta, GA: LOMA, 1993), p. 106.*

Comparing performance outcomes to performance specifications may take the form of gap analysis, our next topic of discussion. Any mismatches with respect to the assigned performance profiles may be corrected by adjusting the asset portfolio segment through actions such as investment trades or hedging strategies.

Portfolio Gap Analysis

Gap analysis is a technique for evaluating the paired asset and liability portfolio segments relative to measures such as their weighted-average maturities or their sensitivity to interest-rate changes. Within the portfolio segments that have been matched according to weighted-average maturity, funding analysts can predict unfavorable gaps. In the context of ALM, a ***gap*** is a mismatch between the asset and liability portfolio. Such gaps are important because they indicate the presence of a cash-flow surplus or deficit arising from the pairing between the two portfolios. Figure 17-6 summarizes the conditions identifying an interest-rate sensitivity match or mismatch between the weighted average maturities of an insurance company's asset and liability portfolios.

Keep in mind that the institution's assets must produce the cash flows needed to fund the institution's liability payments. Whenever the cash inflows from an asset portfolio exceed the cash outflows from the associated liability portfolio, the gap represents a net cash inflow. However, whenever the cash outflows from a liability portfolio exceed the cash inflows from the associated asset portfolio, the institution has a net cash outflow on those portfolio segments.

Some financial institutions are interested in analyzing portfolios according to their ***weighted-average maturity***—that is, according to the dollar-weighted average time period remaining until the instruments held in the portfolio expire or reach full value. (Dollar-weighted measures of average portfolio maturity are sometimes known as *Macauley durations.*) Although dollar-weighted measures of average portfolio maturity are inadequate to meet the needs of some life and health insurance companies, the application of this measure follows the same procedure that insurers use in applying measures that are more useful to them: interest-rate sensitivity measures such as option-adjusted duration and convexity.

A ***maturity gap formula*** can be used for finding the gap between the weighted-average maturities of an asset portfolio and a liability portfolio. The general statement of a gap formula applied to weighted-average maturities (Macauley durations) is *the dollar value of assets weighted by maturity minus the dollar value of liabilities weighted by maturity.* The dollar-value difference between the weighted-average maturity of the assets and that of the liabilities is the ***maturity gap,*** also known as a *maturity mismatch.* Figure 17-7 shows a procedure for finding the maturity gap between an asset portfolio and a liability portfolio. Note that this procedure applies equally to finding the *interest-rate sensitivity gap (the duration and convexity gap)* between an asset portfolio and a liability portfolio, as we see in the next section.

Figure 17-6. Maturity match and maturity gap (mismatch) conditions for paired asset and liability portfolio segments.

A maturity match exists if . . .		
The Asset Portfolio's Average Maturity	=	The Liability Portfolio's Average Maturity
A maturity gap (mismatch) exists if . . .		
The Asset Portfolio's Average Maturity	>	The Liability Portfolio's Average Maturity
The Asset Portfolio's Average Maturity	<	The Liability Portfolio's Average Maturity

Figure 17-7. Asset/liability gap analysis procedure for dollar weighted-average maturities (Macauley durations).

$$\text{Maturity Gap} = \left(\begin{array}{c}\text{Value of}\\ \text{Portfolio}\\ \text{Assets}\end{array} \times \begin{array}{c}\text{Maturity}\\ \text{Weighting}\\ \text{Factor}\end{array}\right) - \left(\begin{array}{c}\text{Value of}\\ \text{Portfolio}\\ \text{Liabilities}\end{array} \times \begin{array}{c}\text{Maturity}\\ \text{Weighting}\\ \text{Factor}\end{array}\right)$$

$$\begin{array}{c}\text{Expected Cash-Flow}\\ \text{Surplus (or Deficit)}\end{array} = \begin{array}{c}\text{Weighted Asset}\\ \text{Values}\end{array} - \begin{array}{c}\text{Weighted Liability}\\ \text{Values}\end{array}$$

Gap Analysis of Interest-Rate Sensitivities

An ***option-adjusted duration statistic*** is a measure that insurance companies use for expressing the relationship between interest-rate changes and changes in the market valuation of an asset or a portfolio. For a given asset, the estimate of the change in the asset's market value in response to a given change in market interest rates is known as a *duration statistic.* (Hereafter, whenever we refer to duration we are making reference to the option-adjusted type of duration and not to the Macauley type of duration.) The higher the duration statistic, the more sensitive the asset's market value is to interest-rate fluctuations. In general, as market interest rates increase, the market value of most assets decreases.

Analysis of option-adjusted durations can be applied to portfolio analysis and portfolio matching. When this type of duration analysis is applied to an asset portfolio, investment analysts can estimate the portfolio's overall sensitivity to changes in interest rates. Armed with this information, insurers can take action to protect (or "immunize") their asset portfolios against the various aspects of interest-rate risk (C-3 risk).

In practice, insurance companies generally employ analysis of duration and convexity statistics. In this context, a ***convexity statistic*** is a measure indicating the stability of the duration statistic. ***Duration and convexity matching*** refers to the effort to construct asset portfolios that match specified blocks of liabilities in terms of duration and convexity. The fine points of convexity analysis are beyond the scope of this textbook. On the subject of convexity, let it suffice that *duration and convexity matching* provides a more refined standard than duration matching alone. Together, duration and convexity statistics measure the sensitivity of a financial value to interest-rate movements.

Insurers apply duration matching of portfolios in an effort to select portfolio assets in terms of their overall sensitivity to fluctuations in market interest rates, and to match the overall sensitivities of the assets to those of the associated liabilities. In this context, *sensitivity* refers to the magnitude of change in asset or liability values in response to a given change in interest rates. For instance, one portfolio worth $16 million when the market interest rate is 6.00 percent might decrease in value to $15.5 million after interest rates increase to 6.25 percent. However, another portfolio worth $16 million when the market interest rates are 6.00 percent might decrease in value to $15 million after interest rates increase to 6.25 percent. This second portfolio then would be considered more sensitive to interest-rate changes than would the first portfolio.

A simplified procedure for duration matching can be expressed as follows:

1. Estimate the interest-rate sensitivity of a specified block of liabilities.

2. Select a portfolio of assets designed to have duration and convexity statistics that match those of the associated liabilities.

In duration matching, in theory the ideal condition would be for the duration of the assets to equal the duration of the liabilities. In practice, though, some companies intentionally mismatch durations in order to better suit the company's conservative or aggressive philosophy. The perfectly matched condition is described as a *duration match.* If a perfect match is not achieved, then the assets and liabilities are described as having a *duration mismatch* or a *duration gap.*

The procedure shown in Figure 17-8 for finding the composite duration gap between an asset and a liability portfolio is similar to the procedure for finding the weighted-average maturity gap. As this figure illustrates, the dollar-value difference between the weighted-average duration of the assets and that of the liabilities is the ***duration gap,*** also known as a *duration mismatch.*

Figure 17-9 summarizes the conditions describing a duration and convexity match or mismatch of an insurance company's asset and liability portfolios.

Henceforth, we can use the expression *interest-rate sensitivity* to refer to duration and convexity. Now we discuss why insurers seek a matched condition and avoid a mismatched condition.

Figure 17-8. Asset/liability duration gap analysis procedure.

Duration Gap = (**Value of Portfolio Assets** × **Duration Weighting Factor**) – (**Value of Portfolio Liabilities** × **Duration Weighting Factor**)

Funding Surplus or Deficit = **Duration-Weighted Asset Values** – **Duration-Weighted Liability Values**

Figure 17-9. Duration and convexity match or gap conditions between asset and liability portfolios.

An interest-rate sensitivity match exists if . . .		
Asset Portfolio Duration and Convexity	=	Liability Portfolio Duration and Convexity
An interest-rate sensitivity gap exists if . . .		
Asset Portfolio Duration and Convexity	>	Liability Portfolio Duration and Convexity
Asset Portfolio Duration and Convexity	<	Liability Portfolio Duration and Convexity

The Ideal of Matching Interest-Rate Sensitivities

The ideal condition that managers hope to achieve is an interest-rate sensitivity match between assets and liabilities. An ***interest-rate sensitivity match*** is a condition in which the duration and convexity of assets equals the duration and convexity of liabilities, reflecting the relative sensitivities of the asset or liability values to movements in the market interest rate. The meaning of an *interest-rate sensitivity match* between assets and liabilities is that when market interest rates move, the values of the matched assets and liabilities will move together. In more specific terms, the values of the assets and liabilities will move in the same direction and at the same rate. In the end, if the interest-rate sensitivity of assets perfectly equals the interest-rate sensitivity of the liabilities, then whenever market interest rates move, the resulting impact on assets will match the resulting impact on liabilities. Thus, in the presence of a perfect duration and convexity match, interest-rate movements will theoretically not produce any net change in capital and surplus.* This perfect match, however, is the only condition that consistently "insures" the insurer against losses arising from interest-rate movements.

Unfortunately, interest-rate sensitivity calculations are only estimates, and perfect duration and convexity matches are rarely, if ever, achieved. Further, if a perfect match could be achieved, the matched condition would not last. After even a slight change in interest rates, the previously established values for duration and convexity become obsolete, and must be recalculated. The new duration and convexity statistics could be drastically different from the former ones. This phenomenon has been called ***duration creep.*** Finally, as we noted earlier in this chapter, insurers sometimes intentionally choose to have a mismatch, with the idea of taking a calculated risk and hoping to be rewarded with more return.

* Note that this condition is true for a duration and convexity match. Although this textbook does not discuss convexity in any great detail, the optimal condition requires a convexity match in addition to a duration match.

The Meaning of an Interest-Rate Sensitivity Gap

The condition that insurance companies want to avoid is a significant undesirable interest-rate sensitivity gap between associated portfolios of assets and liabilities. An *interest-rate sensitivity gap (duration gap)* describes a condition in which the interest-rate sensitivity of assets does not equal the interest-rate sensitivity of liabilities. Recall from Chapter 10 that when interest rates move in a given direction, market values of the asset and liability portfolios typically will both change in the opposite direction from the interest-rate movement. However, if the portfolio interest-rate sensitivities are mismatched, then the value of the asset portfolio will change at a different rate than the value of the liability portfolio.

Such unequal changes in market value produce a net reduction in the market value of the company's capital and surplus in either of two possible circumstances:

1. Whenever interest rates are *increasing*, a reduction will occur if asset duration exceeds liability duration.
2. Whenever interest rates are *decreasing*, a reduction will occur if liability duration exceeds asset duration.

Figure 17-10 identifies which conditions of duration and convexity mismatching will automatically produce losses of market value of capital and surplus under given interest-rate conditions. (Note that this value change does not refer to U.S. statutory accounting values.)

Gap Conditions Whenever Interest Rates Increase

Recall that duration and convexity statistics describe the magnitude of change in a portfolio's value in response to any given interest-rate change. If the duration and convexity statistics for an asset portfolio have higher values than those for the associated liability portfolio, these statistics indicate that, upon a shift in market interest rates, the value of the asset portfolio will change by a greater magnitude or faster than will the value of the liability portfolio. Thus, whenever interest rates are increasing, asset values would decrease faster than

Figure 17-10. Interest-rate sensitivity gap conditions that automatically produce losses.

Direction of interest-rate changes	Duration and convexity gap conditions			Net effect
Increasing	Asset Portfolio Duration and Convexity	>	Liability Portfolio Duration and Convexity	Decrease
Decreasing	Asset Portfolio Duration and Convexity	<	Liability Portfolio Duration and Convexity	Decrease

liability values. In consequence, the market value of capital and surplus would suffer a decrease.

Gap Conditions Whenever Interest Rates Decrease

Whenever market interest rates are decreasing, the dollar value of financial instruments would be increasing. Thus, asset and liability values would both be increasing. However, if the liability values increased faster than the asset values, then the market value of capital and surplus would suffer a decrease. (By comparing this discussion with our earlier discussion of C-3 risk, you will see that here we have restated the notion of C-3 risk in terms of the duration and convexity measures.)

Safety Margins in Gap Analysis

The attempt to match asset and liability portfolio characteristics forms a complex puzzle. The solution to this puzzle is to use models to test the effects of changes in the direction of interest-rate movements, estimate the interest-rate sensitivity of the product portfolio, and then adjust the holdings in the asset portfolio so that its composite interest-rate sensitivity will change in an acceptable manner. Because the duration and convexity statistics used in modeling are necessarily estimates or forecasts, an insurer might take a conservative approach by building a safety margin. Some mismatch conditions are consistent with the effort to set a safety margin.

The acceptable mismatch conditions are the reverse of those in which the insurer would certainly lose. When market interest rates are falling, it is better for asset values to increase faster or more than liability values increase. When market interest rates are rising, it is better for liability values to fall more or faster than asset values fall. As summarized in Figure 17-11, the more desired duration mismatch conditions are as follows:

1. Whenever market interest rates are known to be *decreasing,* a safety margin exists if asset duration somewhat exceeds *liability* duration.
2. Whenever market interest rates are known to be *increasing,* a safety margin exists if liability duration somewhat exceeds *asset* duration.

Figure 17-11. Interest-rate sensitivity gaps that do NOT automatically produce losses.

Direction of interest-rate changes	Duration and convexity mismatch (gap) conditions
Decreasing	Asset Portfolio Duration and Convexity > Liability Portfolio Duration and Convexity
Increasing	Asset Portfolio Duration and Convexity < Liability Portfolio Duration and Convexity

Figure 17-12. Illustration of price curves showing the convexity of an asset and a liability.

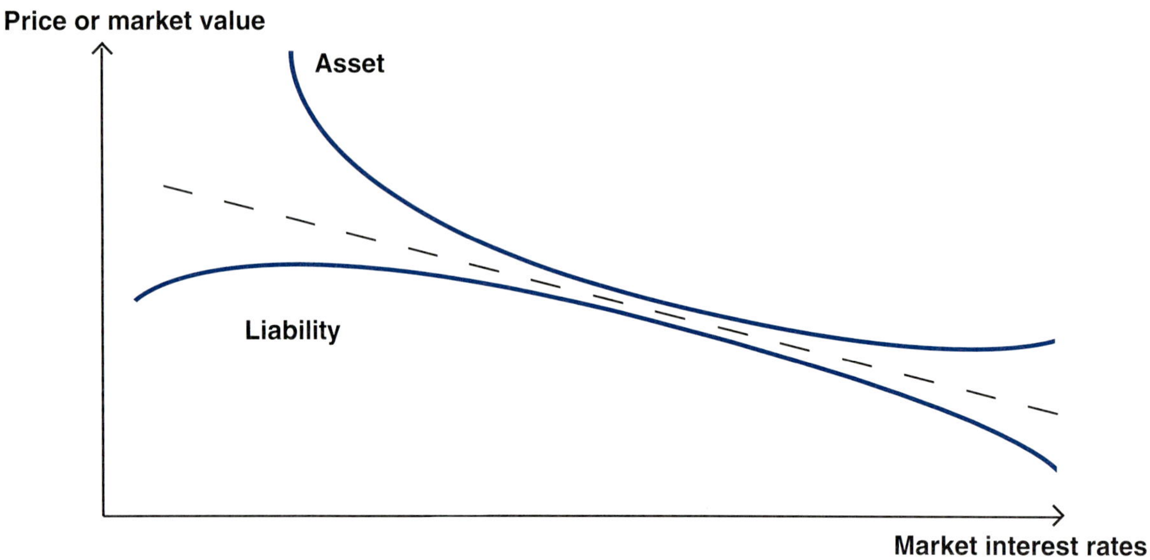

A model builder could identify the "safe" side of a duration mismatch only if the model builder could accurately predict the *direction* of market interest-rate movements. Unfortunately, even the basic direction—up or down—of interest-rate movements can be difficult to predict. Therefore, the only consistently safe position an insurer can adopt with respect to durations is a perfect duration match. It is not possible for an insurer to compensate for the risk exposure of a gap by permanently setting the duration of assets higher than the duration of liabilities, or *vice versa.*

Positive convexity is a good attribute for an asset to have, because the asset will gain more value when interest rates fall than it will lose if rates increase by the same amount. Just as assets benefit from positive convexity, so do liabilities benefit from negative convexity. Figure 17-12 depicts price curves for a positively convex asset and a negatively convex liability.

To summarize our discussion of duration gaps, Figure 17-13 shows all of the potential loss or gain conditions connected with interest-rate sensitivity gaps under specified interest-rate scenarios.

Now our discussion will turn to how insurers use techniques such as cash-flow testing in order to set probabilities on estimated asset/liability matches.

Cash-Flow Testing and Dynamic Solvency Testing

Throughout this book, we have noted that insurers employ many assumptions as a basis for making financial decisions. These assump-

Figure 17-13. Gain or loss conditions resulting from different types of mismatches (gaps).

Direction of interest-rate changes	Direction of the mismatch			Effect of the gap
Increasing	Asset Portfolio Duration and Convexity	>	Liability Portfolio Duration and Convexity	Loss in value
Decreasing	Asset Portfolio Duration and Convexity	<	Liability Portfolio Duration and Convexity	Loss in value
Decreasing	Asset Portfolio Duration and Convexity	>	Liability Portfolio Duration and Convexity	Gain in value
Increasing	Asset Portfolio Duration and Convexity	<	Liability Portfolio Duration and Convexity	Gain in value

tions are typically based on forecasts, and insurers must attempt to reduce the possibility that an inaccurate forecast might end in financial disaster. In this effort, insurers use simulation models and sensitivity testing to predict how altering various assumptions will affect results. Simulation modeling and sensitivity analysis make insurers aware of the potential effect that inaccurate assumptions could have on the company's financial condition. In this way, insurers can minimize negative consequences and reduce the risk inherent in a business that operates under conditions of uncertainty about the future.

As we saw in Chapter 3, simulation employs mathematical modeling that simulates the behavior of the elements affecting the outcome. The same mathematical model is then applied to a set of known or hypothetical data inputs. The results can be viewed as likely future outcomes of present-day decisions. Scenario analysis generally requires examining multiple simulation trials. The duration and convexity gap analysis that we have just described is accomplished using simulation modeling and scenario analysis. Two important applications of simulation modeling and scenario analysis for insurers are the two types of interest-sensitive cash-flow analysis that we described in Chapter 3: *cash-flow testing (CFT)* and *dynamic solvency testing (DST)*.

Cash-Flow Testing

As discussed in Chapter 3, cash-flow testing (CFT) uses simulation modeling for projecting into a future period an insurance company's existing business in terms of assets, liabilities, and owners' equity. Ordinarily, analysts start the CFT process by setting assets equal to reserves, and then project future income and cash flows under about 40 to 100 different interest-rate scenarios. (Cash-flow testing of a product is illustrated in Insight 3-5.) Cash-flow tests incorporate many types of internal and external forecasts. Insurers use cash-flow testing to analyze how departures from their forecasts and assumptions could produce changes in their expected cash flows. Insurers use CFT to analyze cash inflows and outflows under a variety of conditions that depart from the company's forecasts and expectations. One primary function of CFT is to identify interest-rate scenarios that would threaten a company's financial results. In the United States and Canada, insurers use CFT to model the company's future financial results under a number of interest-rate scenarios.

Because cash-flow testing requires developing models based on a number of forecasting scenarios, cash-flow testing is a type of dynamic modeling. However, cash-flow testing is not what actuaries mean when they make reference to *dynamic solvency testing.*

Dynamic-Solvency Testing

Dynamic solvency testing (DST)—sometimes known as *dynamic analysis of financial condition* or *dynamic financial condition analysis*—uses simulation modeling to project into a future period an insurance company's existing and future business in terms of assets, liabilities, and owners' equity. Ordinarily, analysts set assets to a level greater than liabilities, thus acknowledging capital and surplus, and then they project cash flows into the future under various interest-rate scenarios. Insurers undertake dynamic solvency testing for the purpose of understanding the risks to the company's financial position under different interest-rate scenarios.

As the term is applied in the United States and Canada, DST involves modeling the company's future financial condition under a number of business-growth scenarios and a number of interest-rate scenarios. One function of DST is to identify scenarios that would threaten a company's long-term financial results.

Dynamic solvency testing represents an advance over CFT in that DST examines the company's financial risks with regard to business not yet issued, whereas CFT focuses upon risks connected with business already in force. For any company that plans to continue to issue new business, DST offers a much more realistic view of future risks than does CFT.

Insight 17-2 is a Society of Actuaries case study evaluating the potential effectiveness of DST in predicting the threat of insolvency in the historical case of a failed company. The study concluded that this company's failure could have been averted by timely application of DST analysis.

Insight 17-2 Post-Mortem Dynamic Solvency Testing of Fidelity Bankers' Life

Company Data

Date of regulatory intervention: May 13, 1991

Best Study's diagnosis of primary cause of failure: Overstated assets*

History of A.M. Best Ratings:	
3 years before financial impairment	A + c
2 years before financial impairment	A + c
1 year before financial impairment	A + c
At the time of financial impairment	B+

Formation/ownership: Formed in 1967; purchased in 1976 by Monarch Life Insurance Company; sold to a wholly owned subsidiary of First Capital Holdings Corp. in 1985. 44 percent of the outstanding common stock was acquired by Shearson-Lehman Holdings, Inc., in 1988. (First Capital Life Insurance Company, domiciled in California, was another subsidiary of First Capital Holdings Corp.; it became financially impaired on May 14, 1991.)

Domicile: Virginia

Territory: The District of Columbia and all states except New York

Major lines of business: Individual life and annuity business; traditional (non-interest-sensitive) block of life business was sold in 1990. Business was distributed through insurance brokerage agencies, personal-producing general agents, and other financial institutions.

Distribution of selected assets by asset type as a % of admitted assets (12/31/90):

Bonds	54.0%
Stocks	1.0%
Mortgages	1.0%
Real Estate	0.1%
Short-term assets	39.0%

40% of long-term bonds were below investment grade; the average maturity of the entire bond portfolio was 7 years.

Other 1986-1990 statutory financial data (amounts shown in thousands):

Year	Admitted assets	Capital and surplus (C&S)+	Surplus ratio++	Net gain from operations	Common stock & real estate as % of C&S
1986	$ 393,109	$ 30,517	7.8%	$ 7,102	33.2%
1987	$1,214,169	$ 39,809	3.3%	$ 7,979	21.6%
1988	$2,318,642	$ 67,059	2.9%	$18,643	42.9%
1989	$3,568,614	$ 74,285	2.1%	$14,588	45.3%
1990	$4,069,081	$121,985	3.0%	$33,416	22.4%

+ *Includes a $50 million surplus note, assumed in the 1985 acquisition of the company*

++ *Capital and surplus as a % of admitted assets*

* Defined as asset problems with an insurer's own investments, whereby a significant decline in market value, large holdings of inappropriate or unauthorized assets, or lack of asset diversification results in financial impairment.

Insight 17-2 Post-Mortem DST of Fidelity Bankers' Life (continued)

Apparent strategic deficiencies: Limited diversification by line of business, reliance on surplus notes rather than equity capital; affiliation with another highly leveraged company also heavily investing in non-investment grade bonds with rapid growth in interest-sensitive business.

General Accounting Office commentary on reasons for company failure: In congressional testimony concerning the failures of Executive Life Insurance Company, First Executive Life Insurance Company of New York, First Capital Life Insurance Company, and Fidelity Bankers' Richard Fogel, the Assistant Comptroller General, observed in his concluding remarks that the growth of these companies was supported by questionable business strategies and their reliance on surplus notes, questionable financial reinsurance transactions, and investments in high-risk assets.

News media commentary on reasons for failure: The May 14, 1991, *Los Angeles Times* reported that the company had been seized by Virginia state regulators, quoting regulators as saying the company was fundamentally sound, but because of the California regulator's intervention with its sister company, First Capital Life Insurance Company, policyholders seeking to cash out their policies might cause it to run out of cash.

Causes of Failure

The Best Study identified this company's primary cause of failure as its overstated assets, (particularly with regard to its investments in below-investment-grade bonds. Another important cause was too-rapid growth relative to available capital and surplus.

Potential Value of DST

Timeliness: At year-end 1986, the company had a 7.8 percent surplus ratio and reported earnings representing a return on equity of 23.4 percent. The data available does not suggest it was too late then to take advantage of DST in planning actions necessary to ensure its continued financial health.

Resource constraints: As a member of the First Capital Holdings Group including First Capital Life Insurance Company—a company with several billion dollars in assets—this company was by far the best-resourced of those studied. However, though not constrained by resources from performing DST, it probably would have been difficult at year-end 1986 for management to have viewed allocating resources to DST as worthwhile.

Validity of assumptions: While ideally DST would have been done for the parent company's insurance operations as a whole, this study has not investigated Fidelity Bankers' affiliates. The conclusion drawn assumes DST was performed for Fidelity Bankers' alone. Although what might at year-end 1986 have been seen as plausible stress scenarios regarding the deterioration in non-investment grade bond values, the company's new business and asset growth, and policyholder withdrawals could have produced results much more favorable than those actually experienced, and it is reasonable to expect that they would have signaled potential liquidity problems. Had DST been done for the parent's insurance operation as a whole, the modeled threat of liquidity problems might have been more pronounced.

Relevance: Had DST been done as of year-end 1986, expected results would have been related to the company's identified cause of failure. It is less clear whether DST would have indicated the fall-off in surplus ratios because the extremely rapid growth in assets (increasing more than ten-fold between 1986 and 1990) would have been very difficult to credibly forecast.

Insight 17-2 Post-Mortem DST of Fidelity Bankers' Life (continued)

Addition to other information: The company's concentration in interest-sensitive markets with potentially volatile policyholder withdrawal rates, combined with its aggressive pursuit of new business and asset growth and relatively modest capital to support that growth, was a distinctly high-risk strategy. The risk that this strategy would lead to failure was not sufficiently clear from the other information available. DST would have provided valuable additional information to help the company judge that risk and prevent its failure.

Overall conclusion: As measured in this study, DST would have had a significant potential role in preventing its failure.

Source: *Reprinted, with permission, from Fillingham, Robert S., "The Potential Role of Dynamic Solvency Testing in Preventing Insolvencies of Insurance Companies: A Historical Perspective,"* Transactions, Society of Actuaries, 1993–94 Reports, *356–58. Copyright © 1995 by the Society of Actuaries.*

Optimization Modeling

Optimization modeling is a form of mathematical modeling that involves finding an optimum simultaneous solution to several equations. The numerical solution found by using an optimization model will be the maximum possible result or the minimum possible result for a chosen objective. These maximum or minimum results are known as ***optimum results.*** Optimization modeling was intimidatingly complex to apply in the early days of computer technology. However, with present-day computer technology, many variations of optimization modeling have become feasible, including quadratic programming, dynamic programming, and multidimensional programming. In ALM applications, optimization models permit analysts to analyze the risk-return tradeoff and to select either (1) the lowest possible risk level for a chosen level of profitability, or (2) the greatest possible return for a chosen level of risk.

Portfolio Insurance

Asset portfolio management activities that set absolute limits upon potential investment losses are collectively referred to as ***portfolio insurance.*** One important approach to achieving portfolio insurance is through a variety of tactics to carry out a strategy known as hedging. ***Hedging*** refers to a strategy of investing in a given asset in order to reduce the overall riskiness of a given portfolio's asset mix. For insurers, hedging is often achieved by purchasing various types of options contracts. By holding suitable types of option contracts for their assets, insurers can limit their potential investment losses arising from unexpected changes in the value of the assets.

For insurers, assets commonly purchased for hedging purposes include various types of derivative contracts. ***Derivative financial instruments*** are financial assets based on other securities. Most derivative instruments expire within nine months after they are issued. Types of derivative contracts that are important to insurers include *options, forwards, futures,* and *swaps.* **Options** are defined as limited-time contracts giving the owner the right to either buy or sell a specified asset for a stated price. ***Forward contracts*** and ***futures contracts*** are limited-time agreements to buy or sell an asset in the future for a stated price. A ***swap contract*** is a limited-time agreement to exchange the cash flow from one asset for the cash flow from another asset. Interest-rate swap contracts can take the forms of caps or floors.

Because the values of futures and options change with interest-rate movements, futures and options can be used for increasing or decreasing a portfolio's duration or convexity. Buying or selling futures is generally used for increasing or lowering the duration of a portfolio. Options, on the other hand, are used for correcting a portfolio's convexity.

One example of a hedge using an option would be a put option on a bond. An insurer owning both a bond and a put option on that bond would be protected against declines in the bond's market value. If the put option specified a striking price of $900, then even if the bond's market price fell to $700, the insurer could avoid any portion of the loss in market value below the $900 striking price. That is because, during the life of the put, the insurer can sell the bond for $900 to the writer of the put option.

Interest-rate swaps are agreements between two parties to exchange a set of cash flows, typically with one based on a fixed interest rate and the other based on a floating interest rate. Interest-rate swaps permit an insurer to, in effect, convert an existing fixed-rate asset into a "simulated" floating-rate asset, or vice versa. Even though the original asset remains in the portfolio, the combination of the asset and the swap will have all the yield, duration, and convexity features of the simulated asset. (Any accounting differences between a true bond and a simulated one are beyond the scope of this book.)

Caps and ***floors*** are special forms of interest-rate swaps. Both caps and floors are used for fine tuning a portfolio's duration and convexity. Here's how a cap works: The buyer of a cap typically pays a purchase price in the form of an up-front single premium. In return the buyer receives the *notional amount* times the excess, if any, of a current index interest rate over a specified *strike-level* interest rate (for example, 6 percent), with payments being made regularly over the life of the cap. A floor works in a similar manner, but the amounts of payments to the buyer of a floor are instead based on any excess of the strike level rate over the current designated index rate. Because many of the approaches to ALM analysis are the domain of skilled professionals, the meaning of the analysis must be communicated to top decision makers in a form that qualifies as usable decision-support information. Next, we present the typical reports used for communicating ALM within a company.

The Formal ALM Reporting System

One important challenge insurers face in successfully implementing an ALM program is that of communicating highly technical decision-support information among a variety of financial professionals and top-level decision makers. In Chapter 16, we noted that this challenge is generally overcome by an effort at cooperative communication on the part of experts and non-experts alike. Specifically, companies develop formal ALM reporting systems to help technical experts and non-experts work together to implement ALM strategies.

The work of the actuarial and investment experts on the ALM team is documented and communicated through a formal reporting system. These ALM reports, although less commonplace than balance sheets and income statements, are certainly as important to the company's success as most of the commonplace accounting reports.

Technical experts in insurance companies use a system of ALM summary reports for communicating to the ALM steering committee and to regulators the results of technical ALM analysis. These reports should support effective decision making by the ALM steering committee and any other board members who receive the reports. Even though members of the ALM technical team generally are experts, the technical analysis they produce must be summarized and interpreted for communication to others—including decision makers—who are not technical experts. A subject-area expert from a functional area—usually the investment or the actuarial area—first would share the results of a given analytical exercise with the full ALM team, and then with the ALM steering committee.

Figure 17-14 presents each of the report types considered here, and gives a general idea of how often insurance companies develop each type of report. (Keep in mind that both the title of the report and its frequency are likely to vary from one company to another.)

Investment Activity Report

The ***investment activity report*** is possibly the most detailed of any report in a formal ALM reporting system. This report, typically the most frequent of any in the ALM system, presents the specifics about

Figure 17-14. Types of ALM reports.

Report title	Frequency
1. Investment Activity Report	Weekly
2. Crediting-Rate Resolutions	Monthly*
3. Investment Portfolio Performance Review	Quarterly
4. Duration Gap Report	Quarterly
5. Actuarial Opinion and Memorandum	Qnnually
6. Dynamic-Solvency Testing Report	Annually

** New money rates may be established monthly or more often, whereas old money rates may be established quarterly or annually.*

all investment portfolio transactions, including all asset purchases and all dispositions of assets from the portfolio through sales, prepayments (redemptions), or repayment at maturity. For each newly acquired asset, the report typically presents the asset's yield, term to maturity, duration, and quality rating.

Crediting-Rate Resolutions

To insurance companies, a crediting rate is the interest rate the insurer pays its clients on interest-sensitive products. Although companies decide how often they can reset their crediting rates, in general, companies reset new money rates more often than old money rates. Thus, crediting rates for ***new money***—initial deposits—may be set monthly, whereas crediting rates for ***old money***—money already on deposit—may be set annually. ***Crediting-rate resolutions,*** when adopted, represent the formal declaration by the board of directors of the rate of interest the insurer will credit (pay) on clients' money held in interest-sensitive products. The actuarial staff drafts these crediting-rate resolutions, one for each product. Then, the drafts are presented for approval and adoption by the ALM steering committee on behalf of the board of directors. An *annual* crediting-rate resolution report typically presents great detail about the company's ***interest crediting strategies,*** also known as interest crediting formulas. An example of an interest crediting strategy for a given product would be a decision to generally credit that product with interest at a rate equal to the investment portfolio earnings rate minus 1.50 percent.

Investment Portfolio Performance Review

Regularly, the ALM team submits to the board of directors and steering committee a comprehensive written review of the company's investment performance, known as an ***investment portfolio performance review.*** This report is probably the most comprehensive of any report in an ALM reports system, but is not the most detailed, because it covers much of the information in summary form. The range of information covered in the investment portfolio performance review includes quarterly and year-to-date information about the following aspects of investment performance:

- Overall investment growth, broken down by asset growth and income growth; analysis of capital gains and losses; analysis of changes in the market value of assets
- Summary of investment acquisitions and dispositions by asset type; analysis of the effect on yields of all acquisitions and dispositions
- Summary of distribution of assets and comparison of the company's asset distribution against the asset distribution of the industry as a whole
- Summary explanations of key events in the external environment and discussion of strategic responses to those events
- Reports on special topics such as real estate investments, problem assets, and investments in foreign securities

Duration Gap Report

Many insurance companies prepare a report describing the results of duration analysis of their investment portfolios. The ***duration gap report*** provides a "snapshot" of the insurer's asset/liability match at the time of the report. As we discussed earlier in this chapter, a duration statistic typically measures the insurer's current exposure to portfolio cash flow mismatches caused by changes in market interest rates. A company's duration analysis for purposes of this report could be of the weighted average maturity (Macauley duration) type or the option-adjusted duration type along with convexity analysis.

Information in these reports is highly perishable because even small changes in market interest rates and other economic factors can produce dramatic changes in the asset/liability gap. A duration gap report is submitted quarterly to the steering committee and the Board of Directors. The information in a duration gap report includes but is not limited to duration and convexity statistics. The information typically provided in a duration gap report can be divided into the following categories:

- Duration and convexity statistics for assets and liabilities
- The book value of the assets allocated to each portfolio segment or line of business, the current market value of the assets, and the book value of the liabilities in each product line

- Actual investment portfolio yields compared to target investment portfolio yields

Documentation of the Actuarial Opinion and Memorandum

As discussed in Chapter 16, the Actuarial Opinion and Memorandum (AOM) is a statement that many U.S. insurance companies are required to prepare annually. The AOM consists of two distinct documents, (1) the opinion and (2) the memorandum. Whereas the memorandum is lengthy, the opinion is brief and must be submitted with every Annual Statement. Canadian companies must submit a similar statement to Canadian authorities. The opinion must then be signed by a qualified and duly assigned actuary acting in the role of *appointed actuary.* The official actuarial opinion simply states that the company's reserves are adequate given the assets supporting them. (The suggested wording of the opinion appeared in Chapter 16.)

Although the opinion statement itself is brief, it must be supported by extensive analysis. In the United States, this analysis consists mainly of cash-flow testing (CFT) using all required CFT scenarios and perhaps a number of elective CFT scenarios. In Canada, the actuarial opinion must be supported by dynamic solvency testing (DST), and many U.S. companies elect to employ DST. The supporting analysis is formally recorded in a document that many insurers develop annually. This analysis generally is prepared by the insurer's inhouse actuarial staff.

The analysis of reserves and assets in the report supporting the actuarial opinion includes the following information:

- Descriptions of product characteristics
- Descriptions of assets' characteristics by asset class, term to maturity, and yield
- Descriptions of the methodology employed in the analysis, including key assumptions employed in modeling
- The modeling results themselves
- An explanation of how the modeling results support the conclusion that reserves are adequate

Documenting the memorandum requires looking at the insurer's current book of business, as of the latest Annual Statement, but not its projected future book of business. The cash-flow analysis performed for the purposes of the AOM tests whether current reserves are adequate to support future benefit and expense payments for current business, given the assets backing the reserves. The CFT performed for the purpose of the tests the insurer's current financial position.

In the context of actuarial modeling, the terms *financial position* and *financial condition* refer to different concepts. Specifically, ***financial position*** refers to an insurer's current financial situation, with no thought for future business that the insurer is likely to issue. In contrast, ***financial condition*** refers to the insurer's prospects for surviving and prospering long into the future, taking into account both its current financial position and its future business.

The requirements do not give any guidance in interpreting the results of the testing and they do not specify any follow-up action to be taken if the results of the CFT analysis are not satisfactory. In other words, the requirements make no specific provision that a company must strengthen its reserves if it fails at least two of the required scenarios.

Using data obtained from investment experts, actuaries simulate the elective and required cash-flow testing scenarios. The actuaries interpret the output from the modeling, and then report the results and the interpretation of the results in both technical and non-technical terms. The report of these CFT results typically shows the following information:

- Several projections of statutory earnings for each line of business under various interest-rate scenarios; the report also identifies which of the projected interest-rate scenarios would be favorable and which would be unfavorable
- A summary of the projected book and market values of the insurer's surplus for every year of projection, and accumulated surplus after 20 to 30 years
- Additional reserves established as a result of CFT
- Projections of cash flows from assets and of future yields on assets
- Projections of annual net cash flows

In Conclusion

In this chapter, we have described the fundamental problems that can arise because of an asset/liability mismatch. We then discussed some of the analytical tools that insurers use to identify potential mismatches. Finally, we discussed how insurers apply these tools as part of their ALM process and how valuable ALM information is communicated to relevant parties.

Key Terms and Concepts

portfolio segmentation
confidence level
mismatch risk
default risk
income risk
disintermediation risk
reinvestment risk
portfolio segment
performance profile
interest-rate sensitivity matching
gap analysis
gap
weighted-average maturity
maturity gap formula
maturity gap
option-adjusted duration statistic
convexity statistic
duration and convexity matching
duration gap
interest-rate sensitivity match
duration creep
optimization modeling
optimum results
portfolio insurance
hedging
derivative financial instrument
options
forward contract
futures contract
swap contract
interest-rate swap
cap
floor
investment activity report
new money
old money
crediting-rate resolution
interest crediting strategy
investment portfolio performance review
duration gap report
financial position
financial condition

CHAPTER 18

Regulatory Monitoring of Solvency

LEARNING OBJECTIVES

After studying this chapter, you should be able to

- Recognize and distinguish among various mechanisms that regulators use for monitoring insurers' solvency
- Interpret the minimum risk-adjusted capital requirements imposed under the NAIC-sponsored RBC system in the United States and the MCCSR system in Canada
- Identify the alternative actions regulators can apply to a financially impaired insurer
- Interpret the roles of guaranty associations in the United States and CompCorp in Canada

OUTLINE

In Chapter 15, we described some of the financial tools that insurers and rating agencies use to evaluate the financial strength of insurance companies. In this chapter, we focus on the ways regulators monitor the solvency of insurers. We also discuss the events that take place if an insurer becomes insolvent, as well as ways in which regulators deal with a financially impaired insurer. Finally, we discuss ***guaranty associations***—agencies responsible for ensuring that the customers of an insolvent insurer are treated equitably when the insurer is closed down and its assets are distributed.

Monitoring of Solvency in the United States

In the United States, insurance regulators in the separate states—assisted and guided by the NAIC—use a number of tools to monitor the financial condition of insurers with a view to preventing insolvencies. These tools include the Insurance Regulatory Information System (IRIS), the Financial Analysis and Solvency Tracking (FAST) system, required risk-based capital (RBC) monitoring, and routine and non-routine on-site examinations.

IRIS Ratios

As we mentioned in Chapter 15, the NAIC applies 12 financial ratio tests, called ***IRIS ratios,*** to the information reported in an insurer's statutory Annual Statement. The purpose of the IRIS system is to help insurance commissioners identify insurers requiring the most scrutiny. The process of applying these 12 ratio tests is known as the ***statistical phase of IRIS.***

Every year every U.S. insurer's financial statements are subjected to the ratio tests in the statistical phase of IRIS. If an insurer's results for a given year pass the statistical phase, then the insurer is usually finished with IRIS for that year. If an insurer's results do not pass the statistical phase, then NAIC examiners proceed to a second phase of analysis wherein they apply qualitative and quantitative standards to further analyze the insurer's Annual Statement data. This second phase of IRIS analysis is called the ***analytical phase of IRIS.***

If IRIS results show significantly unusual results for a given insurer, the NAIC reports these findings first to the insurer's state of domicile, and then to the other states where the insurer does business. Unfavorable results from the IRIS system are intended to indicate that further investigation by the states might be warranted. The NAIC recommends that states not use IRIS results as the sole basis for evaluating an insurer's financial prospects.

The Statistical Phase of IRIS

The statistical phase of IRIS consists of applying 12 standard financial ratios to data from an insurance company's statutory Annual Statement. As illustrated in Figure 18-1, the NAIC publishes the normal range for the results of each ratio and discloses the industry's mean and median results for each ratio.

Generally, a company either "passes" or "fails" the statistical phase. Any of the following conditions discovered during the statistical phase would represent a company's failing the statistical phase, and the company's financial data would then be required to undergo the analytical phase of IRIS:

- Four or more of the 12 basic ratios having values outside of the normal range
- Significant increases or decreases in the insurer's surplus relief ratio
- The insurer's investing in an affiliate operation an amount greater than the parent company's total surplus

In addition, the NAIC's examining team may also add a given insurer to the analytical phase examination even though that insurer officially passed the statistical phase.[1]

The Analytical Phase of IRIS

During the analytical phase, NAIC examiners perform qualitative analysis of a company's Annual Statement data. Each insurer examined is assigned one of four priority ratings: *first priority, second priority, third priority,* and *no priority.* The *first priority* category represents the worst results, whereas *no priority* represents the best. Insurers can sometimes also be rated *no priority* if the examiners know that unusual statistical-phase results arise from an insignificant event or circumstance such as a one-time transaction or a one-time peculiarity in accounting practices. The examination results of the analytical phase pertaining to specific companies are not made public. By contrast, the results of each insurer's ratio tests during the statistical phase are published.

FAST System

Although small insurers account for a sizable majority of insurer insolvencies, the insolvencies of large insurers—such as Executive Life

Figure 18-1. IRIS ratios applied in the statistical phase.

Number	Name	Ratio explanation	1994 Mean value	1994 Normal range
Ratio 1	Net change in capital and surplus	Measures growth in capital and surplus (excluding new paid-in capital and surplus)	8.4	–10% to 50%
Ratio 1A	Gross change in capital and surplus	Measures growth in capital and surplus	15.3	–10% to 50%
Ratio 2	Net gain to total income	Measures profitability (ratio of net gain to total income, including capital gains and losses)	13.9	> 0%
Ratio 3	Discontinued	Discontinued	NA	NA
Ratio 4	Adequacy of investment income	Compares investment income to interest income needed to support products	498.1	125% to 900%
Ratio 5	Nonadmitted to admitted assets	Measures quality of assets	4.2	< 10%
Ratio 6	Real estate to capital and surplus	Shows assets invested in real estate as percentage of capital and surplus	5.7	< 200%* < 100%**
Ratio 7	Investment in affiliates to capital and surplus	Shows investment in affiliated companies as percentage of capital and surplus	16.5	< 100%
Ratio 8	Surplus relief	Measures reinsurance effects on capital and surplus	3.7	–99% to 30%* –10% to 10%**
Ratio 9	Change in premium	Measures annual growth in premium income	40.2	–10% to 50%
Ratio 10	Change in product mix	Measures change in percentage of total premiums from each product line	1.8	< 5%
Ratio 11	Change in asset mix	Measures change in allocation of investment portfolio to various asset classes	1.9	< 5%
Ratio 12	Change in reserving ratio	Shows ratio of aggregate increase in reserves to single and renewal premiums (individual life)	14.6	–20% to 20%

**For companies with capital and surplus greater than $5 million.*
***For companies with capital and surplus equal to or less than $5 million.*

Source: Insurance Regulatory Information System Ratio Results—1994, *Revised Edition (Washington, D.C.: National Association of Insurance Commissioners, June 1995), p. 78.*

and Mutual Benefit Life—account for most of the total cost of insolvencies. Because the NAIC places emphasis on preventing insolvencies of large companies, the NAIC treats the financial statements of some larger insurers to an additional analysis within the ***Financial Analysis and Solvency Tracking (FAST) system.*** Insurers are subject to being analyzed under the FAST system if they write business in at least 17 states and have gross premiums greater than $50 million.

The FAST system uses two types of analysis to examine an insurer's financial statement information:

1. Ratio analysis of the insurer's most recent financial statements
2. Analysis of the five-year history of specific aspects of the insurer's financial statement. The aspects to be analyzed are chosen by NAIC analysts on a case-by-case basis.

The analysis carried out under FAST differs from the statistical phase of IRIS in the following ways:

- FAST assigns different point values to different ratio results, whereas IRIS designates an insurer's ratio results only as either normal or not normal.
- FAST analysis takes into account the five-year progression of an insurer's financial situation, in addition to its present status, whereas IRIS takes into account only the present status of an insurer's financial condition.
- Whereas how IRIS ratios are calculated is public information, the NAIC keeps confidential the details of the calculations undertaken for purposes of the FAST system.
- All results of a FAST system analysis and the examination results of the analytical phase of IRIS are kept confidential, whereas IRIS ratio results are published.

If the examiners find unusual results during the FAST analysis, the NAIC contacts the insurer's state of domicile for further information about the insurer's financial condition and to learn about any regulatory action the state has taken against the insurer. If the NAIC determines that the state has taken appropriate action toward the insurer, then the NAIC may either end its involvement in the case or continue to monitor the insurer. If the NAIC finds that the state's regulatory action toward the insurer is inadequate, then the NAIC will recommend further action. If the state does not follow the NAIC's recommendation, then the NAIC notifies the other states in which the insurer does business and coordinates all the states' actions toward the insurer.

Risk-Based Capital Monitoring

Another NAIC-sponsored tool for monitoring insurance company solvency, adopted by most states, is the system of *Risk-Based Capital (RBC) requirements.* (We introduced the NAIC-sponsored RBC requirements in Chapter 2 and mentioned them briefly again in Chapter 15.)

These requirements provide a means for evaluating the adequacy of an insurer's capital relative to the riskiness of the insurer's operations.

The NAIC's RBC requirements have four components: (1) an RBC calculation formula, (2) mandatory RBC reporting requirements, (3) a set of RBC standards, and (4) a prescribed set of follow-up procedures for the insurance commissioners to undertake in the event that any insurer's RBC results fall below the RBC standards. The ***NAIC's RBC ratio calculation*** is based upon dividing the insurer's reported *capital* by the risk-weighted *minimum (required) capital* that regulators regard as being sufficient. (Chapter 10 discussed calculating risk-adjusted values for an insurer's reported capital.) The NAIC's very complex RBC ratio calculation can be expressed in the following simplified form:

$$\text{Insurer's NAIC RBC \%} = \frac{\text{Insurer's Reported Capital in Dollars}}{\text{Insurer's Risk-Based Minimum Capital in Dollars}}$$

Thus, when an insurer's reportable capital is $270 million and its risk-based minimum capital is $100 million, then its NAIC RBC percentage result would be 270 percent. If an insurer's result for this ratio falls below one of the specified minimum standards, then regulators must begin regulatory action. The nature of the regulatory action to be taken is related to the exact value of that ratio result. Figure 18-2 shows the cut-off points and the regulatory actions required if an insurer's RBC ratio falls below the given standard.

How the NAIC's RBC Ratio Accounts for an Insurer's Unique Levels of Risk

The minimum level of capital used in the denominator of the NAIC's RBC ratio takes into account the unique risk characteristics of each insurer's business. In this formula, as in many non-NAIC RBC formulas, an insurer's total risk is analyzed relative to the four C risks. For regulatory reporting, an insurer must adjust its statutory financial statement values by applying NAIC-prescribed risk-adjustment factors, thus reducing reported capital to represent the insurer's level of exposure to each C risk.

As we saw in Chapter 10, where we applied risk-adjustment factors to the financial statements of Abacus Life and Bedrock Life, these risk-adjustment factors are percentage values that are applied to values in the insurer's statutory financial statements and used to find the insurer's minimum risk-based capital. A larger percentage value for a risk-adjustment factor produces a higher value for minimum risk-based capital and surplus. The higher the insurer's risk, the lower will be the insurer's Risk-Based Capital ratio result. The higher

Figure 18-2. Required regulatory actions under the RBC monitoring system.

Level	Range of ratio results	Prescribed regulatory action
1. Trend test corridor	Less than 250% and at least 200%	Life insurers having results in this range must submit a confidential plan of action to state of domicile.
2. Company action level	Less than 200% and at least 150%	Life insurers having results in this range must submit a confidential plan of action to state of domicile.
3. Regulatory action level	Less than 150% and at least 100%	Life insurers having results in this range become subject to confidential investigation by state of domicile.
4. Authorized control level	Less than 100% and at least 70%	State of domicile is authorized to take into receivership insurers having results in this range.
5. Mandatory control level	Less than 70%	State of domicile is mandated to take into receivership insurers having results in this range.

Source: *Adapted with permission from the publisher,* Capital Management in the Life and Health Insurance Industry, *Updated Edition (Atlanta, GA: LOMA, 1995), p. 23.*

the insurer's risk, the higher will be the dollar amount of minimum required capital in the denominator of the formula.

To take C-1 risk into consideration, for instance, the statutory dollar value of an insurer's assets is multiplied by an *NAIC-prescribed risk-adjustment factor.* This risk-adjustment factor in effect reduces the value of the assets in a manner that reflects the riskiness of the insurer's investment in that asset. The method used to calculate asset risk is similar to that used to calculate an insurer's maximum asset valuation reserve (AVR), discussed in Chapter 8. An insurer's C-2 component of risk-based capital is found by applying risk-adjustment factors to the company's premium income and its net amount at risk. Similarly, the C-3 component of risk-based capital is found by multiplying the insurer's reserves for each product by a risk-adjustment factor. Because C-4 (general management) risk is difficult to quantify, the NAIC's RBC calculation requires making only one risk adjustment in order to find the C-4 component of risk-based capital. This adjustment reflects the risk of guaranty-fund assessments. A ***guaranty-fund assessment*** is a charge payable by sound insurers as a contribution toward the customer obligations of a failed insurer. For purposes of the NAIC's RBC calculation, the formula for finding C-4 risk is 2 percent of the insurer's life and annuity premiums plus 0.5 percent of any health insurance premiums that are potentially subject to guaranty-fund assessments.

Once the insurer's financial statement values have been adjusted to reflect the effects of the C risks, these values are entered into a formula for deriving the insurer's risk-weighted minimum capital and surplus. For RBC purposes, and with reference to the C risks as C1, C2, C3, and C4, an insurer's risk-based minimum capital and surplus is calculated as follows:

$$\text{Insurer's NAIC Risk-Based Minimum Capital and Surplus} = \frac{C4 + \sqrt{(C1 + C3)^2 + (C2)^2}}{2}$$

On-Site Regulatory Examinations

Another tool that insurance regulators use to monitor the solvency of insurers is routine ***on-site regulatory examinations.*** In order to carry out such an examination, representatives of a state's insurance department, called ***examiners,*** visit the insurer's home office and examine the soundness of the insurer's financial accounts and records, operating procedures, business plans, and management.

On-site regulatory examinations usually consist of two parts: (1) a financial condition examination and (2) a market conduct examination. The ***financial condition examination*** is intended to identify and monitor any threats to the insurer's solvency. The ***market conduct examination*** is intended to verify that, in its dealings with customers, the insurer is complying with all applicable statutes and regulations regarding sales, advertising, underwriting, and claims. Our focus here is on the financial condition examination.

Each state's statutes specify the requirements for routine on-site regulatory examinations of insurers. In most states, each insurer domiciled in the state must be examined routinely once every three to five years. In addition, the insurance commissioner has the discretion to have an insurer examined at shorter intervals.

Each insurance company is domiciled within one of the NAIC's four zones. These zones are shown in Figure 18-3. Examinations are generally initiated by an insurer's state of domicile. However, in some specified circumstances, examiners from other jurisdictions where the insurer operates are sometimes invited to participate in an examination. For example, if an insurer domiciled in the Midwestern Zone receives over $5 million of premiums annually or more than 30 percent of its premiums from the West Zone, then according to NAIC guidelines, the West Zone must be invited to participate in any examination of that insurer.

For any insurer operating in more than one zone or in more than three states, the NAIC recommends that the insurer receive an association examination. Almost all insurer examinations are association examinations. An ***association examination*** is an on-site regulatory

Figure 18-3. NAIC Zone Map.

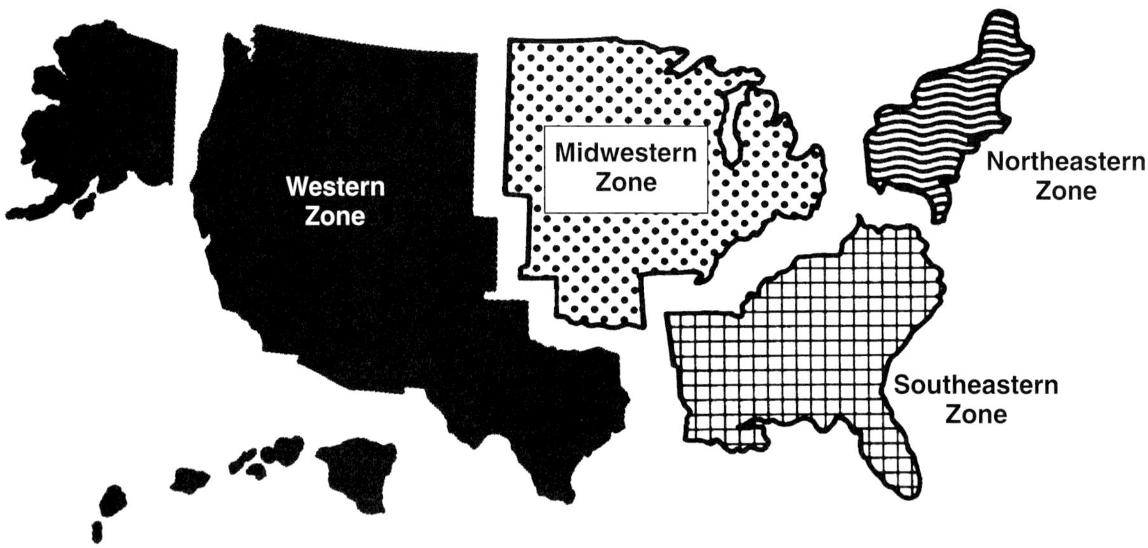

Source: *National Association of Insurance Commissioners.*

examination that conforms to the procedures outlined in the NAIC's *Examiners Handbook.* The ***Examiners Handbook***[2] outlines standard procedures for performing either a financial condition examination or a market conduct examination. The *Examiners Handbook* contains separate sets of guidelines for conducting examinations of (1) life and health insurers or property and casualty insurers, (2) rating and statistical organizations, and (3) health maintenance organizations (HMOs).

As we have discussed, most states require a regular on-site regulatory examination for each insurer once every three to five years, but also permit regulators to require examinations more frequently than scheduled. The *Examiners Handbook* suggests requiring an earlier-than-scheduled examination in the following situations:

- After a change in a company's management control
- After significant changes in operating results
- After the insurer significantly changes its mix of business
- When triggered by unusual IRIS results or unusual findings in other NAIC analyses
- When the previous examination report recommends an earlier-than-scheduled examination
- When adverse information is received from another state or some other outside source

- If the insurer's assets are concentrated in high-risk investments
- If the insurer's liabilities are concentrated in high-risk lines of business
- If an audit of the insurer by an independent accountant or actuary reveals unusual developments
- If the insurer's financial statements include unusual footnotes that cause the regulators to suspect impending financial problems
- If the insurer enters into agreements with an affiliated company or other organization to artificially boost the insurer's reported capital and surplus
- After any development in the external business environment that could adversely affect the insurer's solvency. For example, an insurer's solvency could become impaired in the wake of a downturn in a regional real estate market where the insurer is heavily invested or in the wake of the insolvency of a reinsurer.

Financial Condition Examinations

In the United States, financial condition examinations serve the purposes of ensuring that every insurer is financially sound in two broad respects: (1) that the insurer's accounting records are accurate and that the insurer is being operated on a sound and lawful basis and (2) that the insurer's financial and business profiles do not contain any hazards to the insurer's solvency. Historically, examinations emphasized the first of these two purposes, because fraud and unsound business practices caused most of the insolvencies of prior decades. However, a growing number of insolvencies in recent years were attributed to unwise financial and operating decisions. Thus, regulatory examinations have begun to concentrate more on insurers' financial profiles.

Examiners verify the accuracy of an insurer's financial records in order to corroborate the operating results reported in the insurer's Annual Statement. Inaccurate financial records may conceal financial problems or unlawful activities, which have the potential to threaten the insurer's solvency. An entire section of the *Examiners Handbook* is devoted to procedures designed to test the accuracy of an insurer's financial recordkeeping.

In addition to the insurer's financial records, the examiners also review numerous other factors that help them evaluate whether the insurer is being operated soundly and in compliance with the law, such as

- *Internal security and controls.* The examiners verify that the insurer follows appropriate procedures to ensure that the insurer's assets are secure and that its accounting records are accurate.

- *Management competence.* Examiners consider management competence as an indication of whether the examiners can rely upon the company's internal accounting control system.
- *Relationships with affiliates.* The examiners must ensure that transactions between the insurer and any affiliated companies do not conceal potential financial difficulties.
- *Computer-based operations.* The examiners must make sure that the insurer's information systems produce accurate information, that the information contained in the insurer's information systems is properly secured, and that the insurer has a workable contingency plan for use in case the insurer's systems are incapacitated by a disaster.
- *Reinsurance.* The examiners review reinsurance agreements to make sure that these agreements do not compromise the financial condition of either a ceding company or an assuming company. Also, when examining a ceding company, they analyze the quality of the company's reinsurers in order to verify that the ceding company should reasonably expect to be able to collect the amounts recoverable from its reinsurers.

In examining the insurer's business and financial profiles, examiners might perform a broad-based analysis of the insurer's financial accounts and lines of business, or they might focus their analysis on specified problem areas, as identified from the insurer's Annual Statement, IRIS, the FAST system, previous examinations, or any other source. For example, examiners may suspect a problem with the quality of the insurer's asset portfolio. They might therefore scrutinize any substantial holdings of such potentially risky assets as real estate or CMOs. Alternatively, if claims against the insurer's health products seem unreasonably high, examiners might check the insurer's underwriting standards and procedures. Some of the other factors that examiners review include

- The nature, riskiness, and diversification of the insurer's in-force business
- The adequacy of the insurer's reserves
- The insurer's expenses, particularly distribution expenses
- Other aspects of the insurer's asset portfolio, such as liquidity and diversification
- The insurer's capital position

The Examination Report. The results of any NAIC examination are routinely summarized in a document called an ***examination report.***

Figure 18-4. *Examiners Handbook:* Minimum contents of the examination report.

- Company history
- Management control
- Corporate records
- Fidelity bonds and other insurance
- Officers', employees', and agents' welfare and pension plans
- Territory and plan of operation
- Growth of company
- Business in force by states
- Mortality and morbidity experience
- Reinsurance
- Accounts and records
- Financial statements
  1. Statement of assets and liabilities
  2. Statement of operations
  3. Supporting schedules and exhibits to the extent deemed desirable
  4. Reconciliation of surplus for the period since the last examination
  5. Analysis of changes in financial statements resulting from the examination

Source: Examiners Handbook: Financial Condition Examiners Handbook, *Volume I, Revised Edition (Kansas City, MO: National Association of Insurance Commissioners, 1988, 1995), p. 1-61. Reprinted with permission of the publisher.*

The examination report is submitted to regulators in each state in which an insurer is licensed and also to the insurance company's officers. The examination report emphasizes any adverse conditions the examiners discover and any significant changes in the insurer's operations or financial condition since the last report. The examination report must at least identify and report any problems uncovered during the most recent examination. The report may also offer explanations of the causes of problems and suggestions for how the insurer might correct the problems. As shown in Figure 18-4, the *Examiners Handbook* lists a selection of topics that may be discussed in the examination report.

Promoting Efficiency in NAIC Examinations

Two approaches that promote efficiency in completing regulatory examinations are (1) relying upon the statutory audit results of independent auditors and (2) conducting *limited-scope examinations* for non-routine investigations. Performing routine regulatory examinations often duplicates work already performed by external auditors.

Accordingly, as a basis for identifying problem areas, the NAIC encourages regulatory examiners to review the work performed by the company's external auditor's relative to the company's statutory accounting records. This arrangement permits regulatory examiners to devote their resources to problem areas within a company.

In contrast to a full-scope regulatory examination, a ***limited-scope regulatory examination*** focuses on one or more areas requiring immediate attention, rather than covering the full extent of the insurer's operations and financial situation. Limited-scope regulatory examinations are useful for undertaking non-routine examinations. However, many states require mandatory routine examination to be full in scope.

Regulatory Monitoring of Solvency in Canada

In Canada, the ***Office of the Superintendent of Financial Institutions (OSFI),*** a branch of the federal government, is responsible for monitoring federally licensed insurers. Provincially licensed insurers are monitored by their province's department of insurance. At least once every three years, each Canadian insurer must submit its Annual Return to a routine regulatory examination by OSFI or the provincial department of insurance. Although federally licensed insurers are examined by OSFI and provincially licensed insurers are generally examined by their province, some provinces have an arrangement with OSFI whereby OSFI examines insurers licensed in those provinces. The examinations administered in Canada differ somewhat from their U.S. counterparts. Before discussing the nature of the examinations, however, we examine another tool Canadian regulators employ for safeguarding insurers' solvency: the Minimum Continuing Capital and Surplus Requirements (MCCSR).

Minimum Continuing Capital and Surplus Requirements

The ***Minimum Continuing Capital and Surplus Requirements (MCCSR)*** are similar to the NAIC's RBC requirements in the United States. MCCSR was created by the Canadian Life and Health Insurance Association (CLHIA). All federally licensed companies must meet the requirements. Quebec-licensed companies must meet a slightly different set of requirements that are similar to the federal MCCSR.

Like RBC, the MCCSR formula requires insurers to calculate adjusted financial statement values for four categories of risks. The four MCCSR risk categories are

- Asset risk
- Pricing risk

- Interest-margin pricing risk
- Interest-rate risk

The MCCSR ratio requirement is similar in form to the NAIC-sponsored RBC ratio requirement in that both represent a ratio of *reported* capital to risk-adjusted *minimum* capital, as follows:

$$\text{Insurer's MCCSR Result} = \frac{\text{Insurer's Reported Capital in Dollars}}{\text{Insurer's Risk-Based Minimum Capital in Dollars}}$$

In Canada, if an insurer's ratio of reported capital to minimum capital falls below 120 percent, then the insurer becomes subject to closer regulatory scrutiny. For MCCSR purposes, an insurer's total minimum capital requirement is calculated by simply adding together the amounts calculated for the four risk factors. Although these procedures for calculating MCCSR are somewhat similar to the procedures for calculating the NAIC's RBC ratio, an MCCSR ratio result of 120 percent is distinctly *not* equivalent to an NAIC RBC result of 120 percent. One important factor contributing to the differences between these results is that the methods of calculating minimum capital amounts differ substantially between MCCSR and NAIC-sponsored RBC.

Risk Adjustments under the MCCSR Calculation

Let's consider some important differences between the MCCSR and the RBC risk adjustments used in finding each insurer's minimum capital. Even though three of the MCCSR risks—asset risk, pricing risk, and interest-rate risk—roughly correspond to three of the C risks used for the NAIC's RBC purposes, the fourth risk category is quite different. Additionally, the two systems specify different risk-adjustment factors for use in the calculations related to the similar risk factors.

The methods used to calculate asset risk and pricing risk under MCCSR are roughly similar to the methods used in applying the C-1 and C-2 risk factors for the RBC calculation. However, many of the risk-adjustment factors used for MCCSR calculations differ from the exact percentages applied for RBC calculations.

Interest-rate risk for the MCCSR risk-adjustment calculation corresponds to C-3 risk in the RBC risk-adjustment calculation. The MCCSR risk adjustment for interest-rate risk is calculated using the same procedure as for RBC risk adjustments, though the MCCSR risk-adjustment percentages are different. Under MCCSR, the value of the risk-adjustment factor applied for each product is tied to the withdrawal provisions featured by the products. For some products, the values of the risk-adjustment factors can be as high as 10 percent of policy reserves.

In the U.S. system, the fourth contingency risk (C-4) is general management risk. MCCSR does not explicitly account for general management risk. However, the MCCSR system includes a fourth risk category that is not taken into account in the U.S. RBC system. This fourth MCCSR category is interest-margin pricing risk. This MCCSR risk-adjustment factor differs substantially from any of the C risks. ***Interest-margin pricing risk*** can be defined as the risk that, in the aftermath of changes in interest rates, an insurer's realized interest margins could be smaller than expected, and the insurer's product-related cash outflows would then exceed its product reserves. The risk-adjustment factor for interest-margin pricing risk is intended to account for this risk. *Interest margin* is another term for *investment margin,* defined earlier, in Chapter 8. For this purpose, ***interest margin*** is defined as the difference between the amount of investment income the insurer earns and the investment income the insurer either (1) credits to the product or else (2) assumed when pricing the product.

Regulatory Examinations in Canada

Although Canadian examinations of insurers are similar to U.S. examinations of financial condition, there are some differences. Notably, unlike regulatory examinations of financial condition in the United States, Canadian regulatory examinations do not verify the accuracy of the insurer's financial records. Instead, Canadian examinations rely completely on the insurer's external auditors for financial verification, and then concentrate on evaluating any solvency risks. Also, Canadian examinations begin well in advance of the on-site visit. Canadian examiners use a set of *early-warning* ratios similar to the ratio tests used in IRIS and the FAST system. In advance of an examination, Canadian examiners analyze an insurer's financial statements, apply these early warning ratios, and take note of any other information available. Examiners then create a customized examination plan that is designed to focus the on-site examination on the risks identified from the insurer's financial information. During the examination, the examiners follow the customized examination plan and analyze any or all of the factors that are frequently mentioned as potential threats to an insurer's solvency: capital and surplus adequacy, asset quality, asset liquidity, reserve sufficiency, the match of assets to liabilities, and the insurer's corresponding interest-rate risk.

Examiners in Canada may also analyze areas of concern beyond simply solvency—for example, examiners may also review the adequacy of the insurer's margins. In addition, examiners in Canada identify any problems suggested by the insurer's reported dynamic

Figure 18-7. Routine solvency monitoring by regulators in the United States and Canada.

United States	Canada
• *Annual Statement* information • IRIS ratios • FAST system • Risk-Based Capital (RBC) requirements • On-site examinations	• *Annual Return* information • Early-warning financial ratio tests • Minimum continuing capital and surplus requirements • On-site examinations

solvency testing (DST) results. For example, suppose a company's DST results suggest the following scenario: an insurer intends to issue new business in a stated amount, but the new business has inadequate margins, and the insurer has insufficient capital and surplus to support the underpriced new business. The examiners would discuss this plan with company representatives. By using DST, examiners can analyze an insurer's present financial condition, plus identify potential problems in the insurer's future plans.

Figure 18-7 recaps our discussion of regulatory solvency surveillance tools in the United States and Canada.

Regulatory Action in the Event of Insolvency

Despite reserve and surplus requirements, despite cash-flow testing and dynamic solvency testing, despite the close monitoring of insurers by rating agencies and government regulators, and despite the best efforts of management and employees, some insurers do become insolvent. When this happens, regulators can take several actions to safeguard the interests of the insurer's customers and other stakeholders. Here, we describe the array of actions regulators can take when an insurer becomes insolvent.

As we have discussed, the RBC model law in the United States prescribes specific actions that regulators are expected to take when an insurer's RBC ratio falls below specified threshold levels. However, regulators have the authority to intervene in an insurer's operations based on their judgment that the insurer's financial situation is hazardous, even if the insurer's RBC ratio does not dictate any regulatory action.

When regulators in the United States decide that an insurer's financial situation requires regulatory intervention, the law provides for four levels of regulatory action. U.S. regulators can

1. Order the insurer to take specified corrective actions
2. Place the insurer under administrative supervision
3. Place the insurer in rehabilitation
4. Place the insurer in liquidation

Note that, in Canada, liquidation is currently the only action specifically authorized by legislation. The OSFI or provincial insurance departments can apply ***moral suasion***—defined in this context as the regulators' application of informal pressure in an effort to encourage voluntary actions by financial institutions. Although Canadian regulators can politely request that insurers take corrective action, the regulators cannot force a financially troubled insurer into rehabilitation nor can they require the insurer to undertake any specified corrective actions. However, at the time of this writing, legislation is pending in Canada that would grant regulators options in addition to liquidation. Figure 18-8 summarizes the levels of regulatory intervention available to regulators in the United States and Canada.

In the United States, three NAIC model acts, adopted by the states with variations, prescribe the actions regulators can take. The three model acts are

1. The *Model Regulation to Define Standards and Commissioner's Authority for Companies Deemed to be in Hazardous Financial Condition,* known for short as the ***model Hazardous Condition Regulation***
2. The *Administrative Supervision Model Act,* known for short as the ***model Supervision Act***
3. The *Model Rehabilitation and Liquidation Act,* known for short as the ***model Rehabilitation Act.*** Instead of the rehabilitation act, an older law, called the ***Uniform Insurers Liquidation Act,*** governs rehabilitations and liquidations in some states.

Figure 18-8. Levels of regulatory intervention in the United States and Canada.

United States	Canada
1. Specified mandatory corrective action	1. Moral suasion
2. Administrative supervision	2. Receivership and liquidation
3. Receivership and rehabilitation	
4. Receivership and liquidation	

Regulators in the United States will choose which level of intervention to pursue, depending on the nature and seriousness of the insurer's financial condition. The regulators' actions are generally subject to review by the courts and can be challenged in court by the insurer's management or other interested parties.

Mandatory Corrective Action

The *model Hazardous Condition Regulation* authorizes the insurance commissioner of an insurer's state of domicile to order the insurer to take specified actions to improve its financial condition. Under this regulation, the commissioner can order the insurer to

- Cede reinsurance to reduce its liabilities and obtain surplus relief
- Limit its new or renewal business on products that are not guaranteed renewable
- Reduce its general and commission expenses by specified methods
- Increase its capital and surplus
- Suspend or limit dividend payments to stockholders and/or policyholders
- Limit or withdraw from specified investments
- File reports concerning the value of its assets
- Document the adequacy of its premium rates

Administrative Supervision

The *Supervision Act* authorizes the insurance commissioner to place an insurer under administrative supervision. When an insurer is under ***administrative supervision,*** the commissioner can require the insurer to gain permission from the commissioner before taking any of a variety of specified actions. The law specifies that the commissioner may require the insurer to obtain permission before taking any of the following actions:

- Selling or transferring assets or in-force business or using them as collateral
- Withdrawing, lending, or investing its funds
- Incurring debt
- Accepting new premiums

- Renewing policies that are not guaranteed renewable
- Merging with another company
- Entering into a reinsurance agreement
- Paying specified policy or account values
- Making any management change
- Increasing the compensation of its officers or directors

Receivership and Rehabilitation or Liquidation

When an insurance commissioner judges that an insurer's financial difficulties are so severe that more serious action is warranted than placing the insurer under supervision, then the commissioner may choose to place the insurer in receivership. When an insurer is placed in ***receivership*** (sometimes known as *conservatorship*), the state insurance commissioner, acting for the state court, takes control of and administers the insurer's assets and liabilities. The commissioner, or someone acting on the commissioner's behalf, acts as the ***receiver (conservator)***—the person responsible for formulating a plan to distribute the insurer's assets and for making sure that the insurer's obligations to customers are fulfilled to the extent possible.

In the United States, an insurance receivership can have two possible outcomes: rehabilitation or liquidation. In the case of a ***rehabilitation,*** the impaired insurer continues to exist after the receivership. In the case of a ***liquidation,*** the receiver either transfers all of the insurer's business and assets to other insurers, or sells the insurer's assets and terminates its business. In either case, a liquidated insurer ceases to exist. Recall that in Canada, liquidation is currently the only possible result of an insurer's insolvency.

Usually, state authorities in the United States first place an impaired insurer in rehabilitation, with the hope that the insurer can be saved. The damage to an insurer's reputation caused by being placed in rehabilitation can make it difficult for the insurer to continue to do business successfully. Consequently, many insurers initially placed in rehabilitation end up in liquidation.

Regulators use the rehabilitation period to assess more precisely the financial situation of the insurer by comparing the insurer's assets to its liabilities. If rehabilitation seems feasible, then regulators may find an investor to infuse capital into the impaired insurer.

Although liquidation marks the end of an insurance company's existence, insurance regulators make every effort to continue coverage for a liquidated insurer's customers. Because the underwriting profile of some customers of the failed insurer may have worsened since they first obtained coverage, these policyowners could be unable to obtain equivalent replacement coverage from another insurer.

When regulators arrange to transfer a liquidated insurer's business to one or more other insurers or to continue coverage by some other means, policyowners generally have the right to opt out of the arrangement. Generally, the policyowners have one of two choices in this regard:

- Continue coverage and be credited with a specified percentage of their account value with a new carrier or
- Discontinue coverage and receive in cash a specified smaller percentage of their account value.

For example, in the settlement offered to customers of Executive Life, a large insurer that was liquidated in the early 1990s, policyowners had the choice of continuing coverage at 100 percent of their account values or discontinuing coverage and receiving 85 percent of their account values in cash.

When an insurer is liquidated, one or more other insurers often purchase the failed insurer's assets and liabilities. For example, Confederation Life's Canadian individual life and health business was sold to Maritime Life, its U.S. group life and health business was sold to Great-West Life, its subsidiary in the United Kingdom was sold to Sun Life of Canada, and so on. When no other insurer can be found to take over the defunct insurer's business, a guaranty association generally provides substitute coverage for the remaining policyowners. (We discuss guaranty associations later in this chapter.) If the value of a liquidated insurer's assets is extremely inadequate, the liquidator can terminate all insurance coverage, sell the insurer's assets, and distribute the proceeds as equitably as possible among the policyowners.

Regulators liquidate an insolvent insurer with the help of one or more guaranty associations. In the next section, we discuss guaranty associations and their role in insurer insolvencies.

The Role of Guaranty Associations in Insolvencies

A *guaranty association* is an agency responsible for ensuring that the customers of an insolvent insurer are treated equitably when the insurer is closed down and its assets are distributed. Once regulators have decided to liquidate a troubled insurer, then at least one guaranty association becomes involved in the liquidation process. Ideally, a guaranty association should ensure that policyowners receive their policy benefits and policy values—subject to specified limits—in accordance with the provisions of their policies. Because guaranty associations function somewhat differently in the United States and Canada, we discuss them separately.

Guaranty Associations in the United States

Each state in the United States has established a state guaranty association. Most of the state guaranty association laws conform substantially to the NAIC's Life and Health Insurance Guaranty Association Model Act. However, the guaranty association laws of a few states differ considerably from the model act.

FAST FACT

In 1941, the first guaranty association mechanism in the United States for life and health insurance companies was formed in New York. By 1990, all 50 states had life and health insurance company guaranty association mechanisms.[3]

Insurers are required to participate in a state's guaranty association in order to be licensed in that state. A state guaranty association's members include all the insurers licensed to do business in that state. State guaranty associations are generally governed by a ***board of representatives*** of the insurers doing the most business in the state. A state's guaranty association has the right to assess the solvent insurers licensed in that state to help pay an insolvency insurer's product-related obligations to residents of the state.

An ***assessment*** is a charge imposed by a public authority for the public good. A *guaranty-fund assessment* is a charge payable by sound insurers as a contribution toward the unsupported customer obligations of a failed insurer that had operated in a jurisdiction where the surviving insurer does business. Each state may suspend or revoke the license of any insurance company that fails to pay guaranty-fund assessments.

In the event of an insolvency, when regulators begin to explore ways to continue coverage for an insolvent insurer's policyowners, the guaranty association also begins to plan to replace the shortfall between the insolvent insurer's assets and its obligations to customers. A guaranty association provides no relief for the insolvent insurer's general creditors. The guaranty association is responsible for funding only the insurer's obligations to policyholders, and reviews only the company's product-related liabilities.

After determining the difference between the insurer's assets and its product-related liabilities, the guaranty association assesses the other insurers licensed in its state in the amount necessary to cover its responsibilities to customers under the state's guaranty fund act. The guaranty association also assesses a small amount to recover its administrative expenses. Each insurer's share of the total assessment is set according to the insurer's percentage share of the total premiums written in that state.

For example, suppose the Careless Insurance Company is insolvent and, as a consequence, the guaranty fund needs to collect $100 million. Suppose also that the Conscientious Insurance Company writes 20 percent of the business by premium volume in the state. The Conscientious Company will be assessed 20 percent of $100 million, or $20 million, to help pay for the Careless Company's insolvency.

Once the guaranty associations involved in an insolvency have collected assessments, the assessments are used to help continue coverage to the insolvent insurer's customers. In Chapter 14 we noted that assumption reinsurance is often used to permanently transfer contractual obligations from an insolvent insurer to a solvent one. Upon liquidation of the insolvent company, if the liquidation settlement provides for the coverage to be transferred to a solvent insurer, then some of the assets collected through guaranty-fund assessments may be transferred to the assuming insurer. The total amount of assets transferred to the assuming insurer is negotiated as part of the agreement between regulators and the assuming insurer. Sometimes policyholders are furnished with continuation coverage directly by the guaranty association. In such cases, the guaranty association itself uses the assessment funds to help continue the coverage.

Figure 18-9 illustrates the guaranty-fund assessment process.

In the event of an insolvency, most guaranty associations come to the aid of residents of their state who are insured by an insurer licensed in the state. If a customer purchases insurance in one state and then moves to a state in which the insurer is not licensed, then

Figure 18-9. The guaranty-fund assessment process.

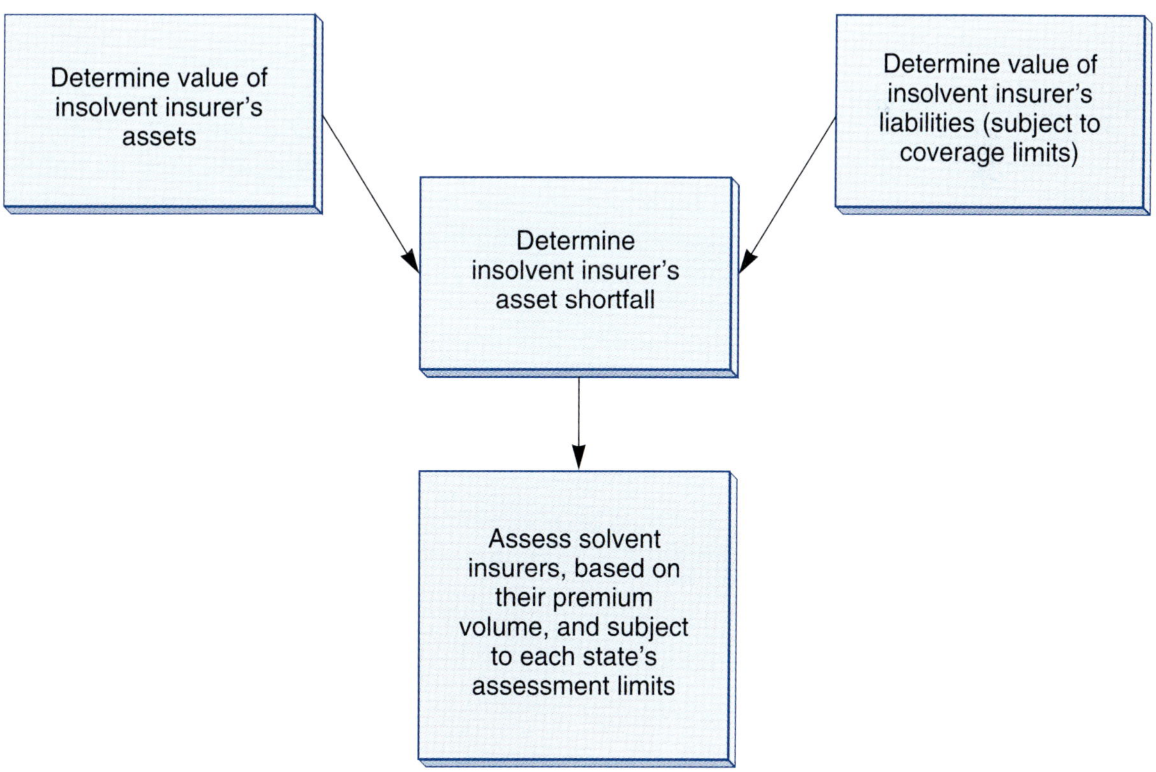

that person is usually covered by the state in which the insurer is domiciled.

An insolvency involving an insurer doing business in a number of states can be highly complicated. For example, each state guaranty association must decide how much to assess for the policyowners living in its state. Also, although the insurer's state of domicile has the primary authority to arrange to resolve the insolvency, each state involved must then approve any proposed arrangement. In addition, because guaranty association coverages, laws, and processes differ considerably from state to state, establishing a single settlement plan for an insolvency involving many states can be an exceedingly complex task.

The problems of insolvencies involving large, multi-state insurers are brokered through an association of guaranty associations. The ***National Organization of Life and Health Guaranty Associations (NOLHGA)*** is an organization created by the state guaranty associations to coordinate multi-state insolvencies. Among other things, NOLHGA coordinates communication between the state guaranty associations, acts as a clearinghouse of information, and helps calculate the obligations of and coordinate the participation of the guaranty associations involved in an insolvency. NOLHGA has a ***disposition committee,*** which works with multi-state insolvencies to arrange an equitable settlement.

Limitation on Guaranty-Fund Assessments

The guaranty association's assessment power is subject to an important limitation. According to the model law, in a given year no insurer can be assessed more than 2 percent of its total premiums written in the state in that year, although different states set the limit as low as 1 percent or as high as 4 percent. Many states have a premium tax, usually also set at 2 percent of an insurer's total premiums written in the state in that year. In states having a premium tax, guaranty-fund assessments are offset against the premium tax. For a large insolvency, a guaranty association could have to assess the insurers in its state each year for several years before fully recovering the insolvent insurer's asset shortfall.

Limitation on Guaranty-Fund Coverage of Account Values

The amount of a failed insurer's liabilities that guaranty associations will fund is also limited. Although the model law suggests maximum limits for the liability of a guaranty fund on any one life, state coverages vary considerably. For example, maximum coverages for death benefits range from a low of $100,000 in Kansas to a high of $500,000 in New Jersey.

CompCorp in Canada

Whereas the United States features a guaranty association for each state, Canada has only one: the ***Canadian Life and Health Insurance Compensation Corporation (CompCorp).*** The overwhelming majority of Canadian insurers are members of CompCorp. Because Canada has only one guaranty association, an association like NOLHGA is not necessary.

In many ways, CompCorp operates in a similar fashion to the state guaranty associations in the United States. The primary differences between CompCorp and the U.S. system are the assessment limits and the coverage limits. CompCorp can assess an insurer only up to 0.5 percent of the insurer's premium volume in any one year, although an extra 0.35 percent can be assessed if a majority of the member companies agree that circumstances warrant an additional assessment. In addition, CompCorp has the ability to borrow a limited amount from each of its members, the loan payable at the end of 10 years.

CompCorp's coverage limits are as follows:

For life insurance death benefits	$200,000 per individual
For life insurance cash values	$60,000 per individual
For life annuity and disability contracts	$2,000 per individual per month
For all health benefits other than disability income	$60,000 per individual

In Conclusion

This chapter provided an overview of the activities undertaken by regulators to monitor the solvency of life and health insurers. We described the major tools that regulators use to conduct solvency surveillance, and also discussed the procedures undertaken when an insurer becomes financially weakened or insolvent. Finally, we discussed guaranty associations: organizations that try to ensure that the policyowners of an insolvent insurer receive their policy benefits and policy values in accordance with the provisions of their policies and within the limits of guaranty-fund assessments.

Key Terms and Concepts

guaranty association
IRIS ratios
statistical phase of IRIS
analytical phase of IRIS
Financial Analysis and Solvency Tracking (FAST) system
NAIC's RBC ratio calculation
guaranty-fund assessment
on-site regulatory examinations
examiners
financial condition examination
market conduct examination
association examination
Examiners Handbook
examination report
limited-scope regulatory examination
Office of the Superintendent of Financial Institutions (OSFI)
Minimum Continuing Capital and Surplus Requirements (MCCSR)
interest-margin pricing risk
interest margin
moral suasion
model Hazardous Condition Regulation
model Supervision Act
model Rehabilitation Act
Uniform Insurers Liquidation Act
administrative supervision
receivership
receiver (conservator)
rehabilitation
liquidation
Life and Health Insurance Guaranty Association Model Act
board of representatives
assessment
National Organization of Life and Health Guaranty Associations (NOLHGA)
disposition committee
Canadian Life and Health Insurance Compensation Corporation (CompCorp)

References

1. *Life Insurance Industry Rating Agencies* (Atlanta, GA: LOMA, 1992), pp. 73–74.
2. *Examiners Handbook: Financial Condition Examiners Handbook,* Volume I, Revised Edition (Kansas City, Mo: National Association of Insurance Commissioners, 1976, 1994).
3. ACLI *1994 Life Insurance Fact Book,* p. 132.

PART 6

Seeking Profitability through Organizational Change

At times, insurance companies need to step back from specific solvency and profitability issues and look at more structural aspects of their operations. Such an analysis of corporate structure can often lead companies to make fundamental changes in their entire operations. In the final two chapters of this text, we look at some structural changes that insurance companies sometimes make in order to further their profitability and solvency objectives.

Specifically, in Chapter 19, we examine why and how an insurance company can alter its entire organizational form, either through merging with another company, acquiring another company, establishing a holding company, or even changing from a mutual company to a stock company. Then, in Chapter 20, we look at the types of fundamental changes insurers are making in their various operational areas to ensure that they are (1) operating in the most economical manner and (2) seeking and retaining profitable sources of revenue.

CHAPTER

Restructuring the Corporate Form

19

LEARNING OBJECTIVES

After studying this chapter, you should be able to

- Interpret how mergers and acquisitions permit insurers to achieve relatively rapid growth
- Identify the financial benefits insurers can achieve through mergers, acquisitions, divestitures, spin-offs, and demutualization
- Recognize the steps in the merger process
- Interpret how holding company arrangements can aid an insurer's growth

OUTLINE

Often, insurance companies that are attempting to grow and prosper need to look outside their own boundaries to find those growth prospects. By looking outside its existing structure, a company can often find new sources of capital or new, profitable uses for existing capital. Once it has stepped outside its current boundaries, a company could even decide that the boundaries themselves—the current organizational form—should be altered to improve the company's capital position and future prospects. In this chapter, we describe how an insurer can improve its capital position by restructuring its corporate form. Insurers and their lawyers exhibit considerable creativity in legally restructuring the corporate form for the purpose of finding capital that they either want for the company's growth or need for the company's survival.

Our discussion focuses on three ways insurers can grow capital by restructuring their corporate form. First, we describe how an insurer can restructure—and obtain new capital sources—by means of mergers, acquisitions, divestitures, and the like. *Mergers* and *acquisitions* have the effect of combining formerly independent corporations. A transaction that is an acquisition for the purchasing company can be viewed as a *divestiture* or a *takeover* from the viewpoint of the target company. For a review of the distinctions among these various transactions, see Figure 19-1, which contains a glossary of terms related to corporate legal structure.

FAST FACT

U.S. life insurers announced a record 56 merger and acquisition transactions in 1995, totaling $8.8 billion. U.S. health and managed care companies announced 35 merger and acquisition transactions, having aggregate value of $6.0 billion, more than twice the value for 1994.[1]

Next, we discuss how insurers use holding company relationships to enter into various types of corporate affiliations. As noted in the glossary in Figure 19-1, a ***holding company*** is a corporation that owns another corporation or other corporations, known as subsidiaries. These subsidiaries continue to maintain a separate identity from the holding company.

The third structural change we describe in this chapter is ***demutualization,*** the process by which a mutual insurer changes its corporate form to that of a stock insurer. By demutualizing, a mutual insurer can gain access to all of the growth options and capital sources that are available to stock insurers.

Our purpose at hand is to explore why an insurance company would make changes in its corporate form. Insurers can achieve several goals by restructuring their corporate forms, and we describe many of these goals in this chapter. Keep in mind, however, that our overriding purpose is to describe how restructuring the legal form of the corporation enables an insurer to accelerate its growth.

Figure 19-1. Glossary of terms related to corporate form.

Terms related to mergers and acquisitions

- **Acquisition.** A transaction wherein one corporation purchases a controlling interest in another so-called *target corporation,* resulting in a linkage between formerly independent corporations.
- **Affiliation.** A relationship between corporations based upon common elements of ownership between corporations.
- **Conglomerate.** A group of corporations in unrelated businesses, all under the control of one holding company.
- **Consolidation.** A transaction wherein two corporations combine to form a distinct new corporation (also called a merger).
- **Divestiture.** A corporation's disposition of an asset, investment, or operation by any means, including outright sale, sale to employees, or liquidation.
- **Merger.** A transaction wherein two corporations combine to form a distinct new corporation (commonly called a consolidation in Canada).
- **Parent corporation.** A corporation that creates another corporation. The parent corporation may either own the subsidiaries itself or it may create a holding company that owns the subsidiaries.
- **Spin-off.** A transaction wherein an existing corporation identifies a discrete internal operating unit and reorganizes that operating unit into an independently operating subsidiary company.
- **Subsidiary.** A corporation that is owned by another corporation.
- **Takeover.** A transaction wherein one corporation purchases a controlling interest in another so-called *target* corporation. If the purchase takes place against the will of the target company, the transaction is called a ***hostile takeover.***
- **Target corporation.** A corporation that is the focus of another corporation's efforts to acquire it.
- **Holding company.** A company that owns another corporation or other corporations, which continue to exist as separate entities. The companies owned by a holding company are known as its *subsidiaries.*
- **Downstream holding company.** A company created by a parent corporation and owned or controlled by the corporation that formed it; the downstream holding company in turn owns or controls subsidiary corporations, which continue to exist as separate entities.
- **Upstream holding company.** A type of holding company that owns the parent company, and was created to control corporate subsidiaries, which continue to exist as separate entities.

Growth through Mergers and Acquisitions

Mergers have become increasingly frequent in the insurance industry. Many companies in the life and health insurance industry are now in some way affiliated with at least one other corporation. Insight 19-1 describes some of the forces driving recent merger and consolidation activity.

Insight 19-1 Merger Mania Tide Engulfs Life and Health Insurers

Merger and acquisition activity in the insurance industry again rose sharply in 1994, principally because of a significant jump in life and health insurer deals. A record number and dollar volume of life and accident and health mergers took place, and nothing seems to be on the horizon to slow the momentum of insurance industry consolidations. The forces driving insurance industry consolidations are broad, deep-seated, and show no signs of slowing. Some of these forces, which tend to be interrelated and to reinforce each other, are as follows:

• Competition is putting pressure on insurers to become more efficient, cut overhead and distribution costs, and look to economies of scale and increased market share.

• Entry of banks into annuities and insurance is causing changes in distribution channels, product innovation, and competitive pressures. Financial institutions are acquiring insurers, and insurers are acquiring banking firms, and the pace of such acquisitions will accelerate as legislative and regulatory barriers fall.

• Inadequate operating margins and rates of return for many insurers are functions of management deficiencies as well as competitive disadvantages. This, in turn, is contributing to shareholder dissatisfaction and forced sales.

• Capital redeployment is an ongoing process. In a relatively free economy, capital gravitates to higher-return opportunities from low-return disappointments. More divestitures of insurance operations are certainly anticipated, especially by non-financial holding companies and conglomerate owners.

• Government regulation and taxes are expected to result in an increasing need for surplus growth, which can be obtained from an outside investor group or acquirer. Mutual companies are being pressed to merge with each other or to liquidate assets to meet surplus needs. Greater capital adequacy thresholds are adding to the pressures to consolidate.

• Increasing globalization of insurance and financial markets is expected to stimulate a greater level of cross-border mergers, joint ventures, and partnerships. The trend of more U.S. buyers of foreign insurance firms is now strongly in place and expected to expand. The return of European buyers to U.S. insurance markets is believed to be just a matter of time.

• Financing tends to be readily available for industry mergers that are economically justifiable.

It is estimated that the number of life and health insurance company mergers more than doubled in 1994 from the 39 recorded in 1993. Below are some of the trends that emerged in 1993 and 1994:

• Mutual fund management companies became popular targets for life insurers seeking to broaden product offerings and distribution channels.

• Managed care companies were involved in a wave of consolidations on the part of purchasers seeking to improve market penetration and economies of scale.

• Mutual insurance companies continued to seek ways to meet growing capital demands.

• Sales of blocks of business blossomed as insurers realigned their operations.

• Divestitures were common.

Longer term, the number of industry deals—including all industry sectors—could approach 300 per year by the end of the decade, versus 221 in 1994, with dollar volume exceeding $15 billion by then, compared with $12 billion in 1994.

Source: *Adapted from* Mergers and Acquisitions 1995 Edition: The Thinning of the Herd *(Hartford, CT: Conning & Company, 1995), pp. 5, 8–9, 12–13, 75–77. Reprinted with permission of the pubisher.*

As we explore the topic of mergers, we see that the rationale for insurers to undertake mergers is strong. We also see that their successful implementation is difficult and expensive.

Corporate mergers are in essence transactions involving a change in the ownership of an asset. In the case of corporate acquisitions, the asset being purchased and sold is a controlling interest in a corporation. Although a merger is one distinct form of an acquisition, for simplicity we use the term *merger* throughout this chapter to refer to all transactions in which a controlling interest in a corporation is purchased or sold.

Alternative Growth Strategies

FAST FACT

In 1993, by means of a $4.1 billion stock swap, Primerica Corporation acquired the 73 percent of the Travelers Corporation that it did not already own. The pact created one of the largest U.S. financial services companies, with total assets of $100 billion.[2]

We have already made reference to the alternative paths available to a company as it seeks growth. Two paths that interest us in the discussion at hand are (1) growth from internally generated return on capital and (2) growth generated by merging with other companies. By reference to examples using our simplified balance sheet models, we can demonstrate the differing effects of growth from return on capital and surplus on one path versus growth by restructuring on the other path. Our examples refer to one slowly growing and successful company, called the Refuge Insurance Company, and one more rapidly growing company, called the Vigor Insurance Group.

Growth from Return on Capital: Refuge Insurance Company

Suppose the Refuge Insurance Company has a beginning net worth (statutory capital and surplus) of $20 million. Refuge's balance sheet is as follows:

Refuge Balance Sheet 1	
Admitted Assets	**Liabilities**
$90 million	$70 million
	Capital and Surplus
	$20 million

If Refuge earns a 10 percent annual after-tax return on *equity,* then in one year its capital and surplus would increase by $2 million. We can show the growth from earnings on our simplified balance sheet as follows:

Refuge Balance Sheet 2	
Admitted Assets	**Liabilities**
$93 million	$71 million
	Capital and Surplus
	$22 million

In one year of reasonably successful operations, Refuge can grow its capital and surplus from $20 million to $22 million. This level of annual growth is respectable by industry standards. Suppose, though, that Refuge's decision makers believe that the company will not have attained critical mass for its current markets until it amasses capital and surplus of at least $30 million. In that case, the historical 10 percent growth rate would be inadequate. The crucial message here is that growing capital internally by compounding the company's growth in capital and surplus generated entirely by internal operations can be a relatively slow process.

Growth by Merger: Vigor Insurance Group

Suppose that the Vigor Insurance Group has the same beginning balance sheet that Refuge had.

Vigor Balance Sheet 1

Admitted Assets	Liabilities
$90 million	$70 million
	Capital and Surplus
	$20 million

Vigor, however, has chosen to pursue a more aggressive growth strategy than Refuge and, thus, purchases another insurance company in consideration for the issuance of Vigor's common stock. The target company has capital and surplus of $10 million, and Vigor's transaction costs are $1.5 million. On the next annual balance sheet, Vigor's aggressive strategy of growth by takeover might permit Vigor to record a *net increase* in capital and surplus in the amount of $8.5 million and to show a total net worth of $28.5 million.

Vigor Balance Sheet 2

Admitted Assets	Liabilities
$98.5 million	$70 million
	Capital and Surplus
	$28.5 million

By undertaking such an aggressive growth strategy, Vigor may realize a much larger increase in capital and surplus than Refuge realized. Although the foregoing examples were simplified, they illustrate that alternative growth strategies can result in significant differences in growth rates. Although mergers can be expensive and arduous, insurers undertake the merger process in the hope of gaining some benefit

FAST FACT

In 1994, Metropolitan Life and the Travelers, two of the largest U.S. insurers, jointly formed a health maintenance organization (HMO) known as MetraHealth. In 1995, about one year after forming MetraHealth, the parent companies announced the sale of MetraHealth to United HealthCare Corporation for a package of fixed and contingent consideration: a fixed basic consideration of $1.65 billion in cash and stock, plus a potential additional consideration of up to $700 million, contingent upon MetraHealth's meeting its earnings projections.

Insight 19-2 Consolidation among Health Insurers: The Drive to Operational Excellence

Several recent events in the health care arena indicate that acquisition activity will continue and could intensify in 1996. The first of these was Aetna's announced sale of its property-casualty unit for $4 billion and its plan to invest a significant portion of these proceeds in a large HMO. Another major story has been the unfolding of Wellpoint's attempted acquisition of HSI. And the acquisition of MetraHealth by United HealthCare is still regarded as a watershed event; it's the first time that a regional managed care company has crossed over to compete effectively on a national scale.

This sudden interest in consolidation is driven by: (1) the opportunity for increased margins through more administrative efficiency and economies of scale; (2) the desire for new markets or products, especially through joint ventures; (3) improving claims management capacity by acquiring better systems and/or staff; and (4) leveraging the two parties' comparative advantages, such as available capital or market segment.

Acquisition represents the evolution of the marketplace, where the stronger managed care companies acquire and assimilate smaller or perhaps less-efficient managed care organizations, to bring some local markets towards oligopoly and/or expand breadth. Acquisitions or joint ventures also can expand the traditional HMO product offering (e.g., indemnity and specialty coverages), distribution system and geographic scope. The addition of these products allows HMOs to become "one-stop shopping centers" for larger, national employers. Traditionally, HMOs have not been major players in providing the primary health plan for employers, because they lacked the geographic breadth to serve a national account. Conversely, health insurers have served the national market with indemnity and PPO plans, but have lacked the managed care expertise of the HMOs. Integrating these structures will build stronger health insurance/HMO companies with both national and regional scope. The acquisition of MetraHealth by United HealthCare and the Healthsource acquisition of the Provident health line are examples of this strategy. Converting ASO and/or indemnity lines to managed care is also the strategy for several commercial carriers, such as CIGNA and Aetna.

Additionally, demographic and legislative forces are aligning to encourage managed care companies to enter new markets and offer new products. Recent reform initiatives involving Medicare are specifically geared to enrolling recipients in managed care plans. Because the target population is fundamentally different from the traditional commercial membership base, HMO networks that administer Medicare benefits differ from commercial HMOs, focusing more on geriatric delivery. While there may be some physician overlap, Medicare HMOs generally are developed separately.

From Conning's HMO database, we illustrate the current concentration of the managed care industry in the accompanying table and chart. These numbers assume managed care includes HMO and POS products only. The inclusion of PPOs would impact the traditional indemnity carriers such as Aetna and CIGNA, boosting their market share to the top five. However, for POS and HMO delivery alone, and when considering all Blue Cross/Blue Shield entities as one, just six managed care organizations deliver 40 percent of all managed health care. Currently, 16 organizations deliver 75 percent of all HMO/POS-related care. We expect consolidation to continue. It is possible that in five to ten years, 25 super organizations will control 90 percent of the market.

related to their strategic or operating objectives. Insight 19-2 explains the motives driving some recent merger activity.

Why Undertake Mergers?

As the foregoing examples illustrated, mergers can be an important tool of capital management. Nevertheless, the reasons for undertaking

Insight 19-2 Consolidation among Health Insurers: The Drive to Operational Excellence (continued)

Concentration of HMO-Insured Lives	
Selected organizations	**Market share**
Kaiser Permanente	12.3%
United HealthCare Corp.	6.9%
Healthsource	5.6%
Blue Cross/Blue Shield	5.0%
Prudential	4.8%
CIGNA	4.7%
Humana, Inc.	4.2%
U.S. Healthcare, Inc.	4.2%
Aetna	2.9%

16 HMOs Control 75% of the Care Delivered*

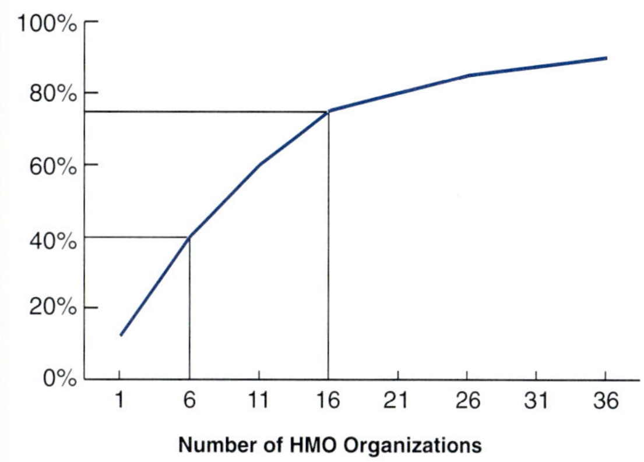

* Does not include unaffiliated category (10%), which would bring the total to 100%

Source: *"Consolidation among Health Insurers: The Drive to Operational Excellence,"* The Conning Commentary, *Vol. 5, No. 1 (Hartford, CT: Conning & Company, January 1996), pp. 4–5. Reprinted with permission of the publisher.*

mergers go beyond the focus of capital management and encompass areas that are more closely associated with strategic management. Insurance companies merge to achieve a variety of strategic purposes. Common motives that insurers have for undertaking mergers include the following:

- An insurer might seek a merger partner in order for both companies to improve the economies of scale achievable in their operations. In this case, ***economies of scale*** refers to the savings expected to be achievable while maintaining the combined company's growth. Economists tell us that the relationship between size and cost savings is such that, within some normal range of sizes, as an operation's size increases, the operation's unit costs decrease. Thus, by virtue of increasing its scale, an insurer might be able to reduce its expenses as a percentage of sales, thus increasing its profitability. For example, an insurer with a superior technological base might benefit from economies of scale after merging with another company and thereby spreading over a larger revenue base the cost of supporting the technology. Clearly, economies of scale from a variety of sources can enhance the insurer's competitiveness and capital position.
- An insurer that is relatively small may seek a merger partner in order to increase the size of its operations. Generally, quality

insurers that enjoy a strong capital and surplus base benefit from a general bias in favor of large company size. Specifically, insurers benefit from a larger net worth by attracting capital at a lower cost, earning higher financial and claims paying ratings, appealing to more conservative customers, and broadening distribution systems.

- An insurer that lacks uncommitted (growth) capital might choose to join with a partner that has a strong capital position. In such an arrangement, the strong partner has excess capital and is searching for safe, profitable, and efficient ways to employ that capital. One insurer with too little capital and another insurer with too much capital can be ideal partners, particularly if the companies are also well matched in terms of their strategic objectives. Such a pairing provides both partners with an opportunity to improve their position with respect to the ongoing balancing act required by the risk-return tradeoff.
- An insurer that has weak capital might seek a strong partner simply to counteract its own weakness in capitalization and, thus, to avoid or reduce the potential for either a financial failure or a hostile takeover.
- An insurer that wants to expand by offering new products and services or adding new distribution systems might choose to join forces with an insurer that is experienced in those areas.
- An insurer that wants to increase its dominance within a chosen market segment might choose to join forces with another insurer that also operates within that market segment.
- An insurer that wants to expand by entering new geographic and/or target markets might choose to join forces with an insurer that is authorized to operate in, and is already experienced in, those markets.

FAST FACT

During 1994, Travelers entered into a joint venture for its health care business, then sold it; spun off Transport Life Insurance Company to shareholders; purchased the property and casualty business of Aetna; and sold its real estate developer.

Why Sell in a Merger or Divestiture?

In order for one company to make an acquisition, another company—referred to as the *target company*—must generally at the very least give up a portion of its operations or even entirely lose its separate identity. What benefits do mergers typically provide to the target company? Some of these benefits are as follows:

- An insurer might make a strategic decision to pursue a focused marketing strategy. In such a case, the insurer must divest itself of the lines of its business that are not consistent with its chosen area of focus. For example, an insurance company that has traditionally sold both life and health insurance might decide to focus on life insurance and sell or transfer all of its health insurance business to another company.

- An insurer might make a strategic decision to cut mounting losses on a line of business in which the insurer's operations have been inefficient.
- An insurer might want to collect the profits on the sale of an asset—such as a business operation or a block of business—that has a high market value, but a low statutory-basis book value. In such a case, the asset can be sold at a premium. For example, suppose one of an insurer's business operations has a book value of $50 million, but a market value of $150 million. By selling that asset for its market value, the insurer can realize a pre-tax increase in capital and surplus of $100 million.
- An insurer having poor returns might choose to sell a profitable block of business in order to "buy time" until management either can find a suitable partner for a full merger or can come up with a strategy to renew the company's profitability in its remaining book of business.
- Owners of a small and closely held stock company might simply want to cash in on the value of the business whenever a good offer appears.

Why Hesitate to Merge?

The parties to a merger expect that the benefits of the undertaking will outweigh the drawbacks of the undertaking. These drawbacks generally revolve around three issues: (1) high costs, (2) corporate cultural diversities, and (3) uncertainties as to outcomes. Some likely drawbacks of mergers are as follows:

- The parties to a merger often incur considerable expenses for legal, accounting, investment, and actuarial services.
- When two companies merge, they almost always consolidate some of their operations. In such a case, both companies face the disruption and initial expense of combining operations. For example, one company's operations typically must move to a new location. If such a consolidation requires one company to move its operations across state lines, those operations must comply with state laws and regulations of the new jurisdiction.
- During the merger negotiations and during any changeover period, the morale of employees is understandably likely to be adversely

affected, particularly when employees face unpleasant prospects such as job loss or relocation.

- During the period of consolidation, the organization must resolve cultural clashes on many fronts, including differences of management philosophies, incompatibility of distribution systems, redundancy of management staffs, and incompatibilities between administrative systems.
- One or both parties may need to review and re-establish business relationships with suppliers and distributors.
- Reinsurance relations and treaties must be examined for determining whether the new company would have redundant relationships and whether the existing agreements would be invalidated by automatic termination provisions upon a change in control.
- Both parties to a merger face the risk that some hoped-for benefits may not be fully realized.

Despite the potential pitfalls to a successful insurance company merger, the process has been undertaken repeatedly and successfully.

How Mergers Are Accomplished

The procedure for a merger of insurance companies in the United States involves several essential, though not simple, steps on the part of the parties to the merger. For convenience in this discussion, we refer to these parties as the "purchaser" and the "target company." With the help of a great deal of advice from the legal, actuarial, investment, and accounting professions, the exact proceedings of any given merger transaction are tailored to the situations of the merging parties. Regardless, we can generalize about the processes involved. Figure 19-2 summarizes the eight steps for implementing a merger of insurance companies.

Identify a Target Company

First, the prospective purchaser must perform preliminary research and screening to identify one or more potential target companies. For each target company, the prospective purchaser must identify owners of any important concentrations of stock.

Enter into Negotiations

The purchaser then must contact the target company and begin informal negotiations. The negotiation process progresses from an informal to a formal stage after the purchaser typically provides the target company with a formal document known as a letter of intent. A ***letter of intent*** is usually a nonbinding letter from the prospective

Figure 19-2. Purchaser's basic steps to a merger.

1. Perform research and screening to identify a target company or several target companies. For each target company, identify any concentrations of stock holdings.
2. Make initial approach to target company, informally begin negotiations. Open formal negotiations with a letter of intent.
3. Perform due diligence investigation.
4. Set a value for the target company. Come to an agreement with sellers as to the purchase price and the form of consideration that purchaser will deliver to sellers.
5. Enter into a contract, secured by earnest money. To establish a formal agreement, parties must first obtain approval from their boards of directors and, sometimes, stockholders and policyowners.
6. Secure all regulatory approvals and tax rulings, if applicable.
7. Close transaction and pay purchase price.
8. Consolidate business operations.

purchaser to the target company outlining the understandings of both parties prior to the beginning of contractual negotiations. Usually some provisions of a letter of intent are binding, such as a confidentiality agreement and a lock-up provision specifying that the target company cannot negotiate with anyone else for a defined period of time. Figure 19-3 shows a sample letter of intent.

Conduct a Due Diligence Investigation

When two insurers are considering a merger, the parties must complete a due diligence investigation. Generally, such a ***due diligence investigation*** is a thorough analysis of each party's assets, liabilities, and future prospects.* A due diligence investigation in the context of a merger is especially important because the purchaser assumes *all* liabilities of the target company, known or unknown. Accordingly, great care is generally used in evaluating the adequacy of the target company's reserves, examining potential tax liabilities, identifying any adverse business trends, examining pending litigation, confirming the adequacy of reinsurance, evaluating product pricing, and reviewing the value of in-force business.

Obtain a Valuation of Assets and Liabilities

The purchaser usually undertakes a formal analysis of the assets and liabilities of the target company. Generally, the purchaser hires

* Note that this perspective on due diligence differs from the use of the term relative to public offerings of securities, where *due diligence* refers to a legally defined duty of care and review to be exercised by officers, directors, and underwriters.

Figure 19-3. Sample letter of intent.

STRICTLY PRIVATE AND CONFIDENTIAL
January 1, 199X

Target Corporation
Corporate Office Park
New York, New York

To the Board of Directors:

This letter of intent sets forth the basic terms and conditions under which Acquisition, Inc. (The "Purchaser") will enter into a definitive merger agreement (the "Merger Agreement") with Target Corporation (the "Company") for the merger of the Purchaser with and into the Company (the "Merger"). It is anticipated that the consummation of the Merger will occur on or before ____________________,199__, or on such other date to which the parties may agree.

Purchase Price

Pursuant to the Merger Agreement, upon consummation of the Merger, the selling stockholders of the Company will receive in exchange for each share of the Company's common stock and preferred stock (the "Stock") outstanding as of the date of this letter:

(5) ____________________ Dollars ($____________) in cash; and

(6) One share of preferred stock ("Preferred Stock") of the surviving corporation of the Merger with a liquidation preference in the amount of ____________________ Dollars (____________) and containing the terms set forth on Exhibit A hereto.

Conditions to Closing

The consummation of the Merger shall be subject to the satisfaction of the following conditions:

General

After executing this letter and until ______________________________, 199__, the Company agrees, and shall use its best efforts to cause its officers, directors, employees, agents, and stockholders, not to solicit or encourage, directly or indirectly, in any manner any discussion with, or furnish or cause to be furnished by any information to, any person other than Purchaser in connection with, or negotiate for or otherwise pursue, the sale of the Stock of the Company or the capital stock of its subsidiaries, all or substantially all of the assets of the Company or its subsidiaries, or any business combination or Merger of the Company or its subsidiaries with any other party. You will promptly inform Purchaser of any inquiries or proposals with respect to

Figure 19-3. Sample letter of intent (continued).

the foregoing. [In the event that the agreements in this paragraph are violated by the Company or its officers, directors, employees, agents, or stockholders, and Purchaser does not consummate the Merger, then, in addition to other remedies available to Purchaser, Purchaser shall be entitled to receive from the Company all out-of-pocket expenses (including reasonable attorneys' fees and expenses relating to the financing), which Purchaser has incurred.

Neither of the parties to this letter shall disclose to the public or to any third party the existence of this letter or the proposed sale described herein other than with the express prior written consent of the other party, except as may be required by law.

From and after the date hereof, upon reasonable prior notice and during normal business hours, the Company will grant to each of Purchaser and its agents, employees and designees full and complete access to the books and records and personnel of the Company and its subsidiaries. Except as may be required by law or court order, all information so obtained, not otherwise already public, will be held in confidence.

[Except as provided herein,] each party will be responsible for its own expenses in connection with all matters relating to the transaction herein proposed. If the proposed transaction shall not be consummated for any reason other than a violation of the agreement not to solicit other offers or negotiate with other purchasers, neither party will be responsible for any of the other's expenses.

Each party will indemnify, defend and hold harmless the other against the claims of any brokers or finders claiming by, through or under the indemnifying party.

Except for matters relating to (i) the confidentiality of this proposal and the business operations of the Company and its subsidiary, (ii) the agreement not to negotiate with others for or otherwise pursue the sale of the Company or its subsidiary, and (iii) the agreement that each party will bear its own expenses in connection herewith, this letter does not create a binding, legal obligation on any party but merely represents the present intentions of the parties.

In the event that for any reason the definitive Merger Agreement is not executed by ______________,199__, any party may discontinue negotiations and terminate this letter without liability to any other party.

Source: *Stanley Foster Reed and Alex Reed Lajoux,* The Art of M&A: A Merger Acquisition Buyout Guide, *2nd Edition (Richard D. Irwin, 1996), pp. 511–514. Reprinted with permission by the publisher.*

professionals to provide an actuarial valuation of the in-force business, a market value of assets, and an estimated value of liabilities, including contingent liabilities. The purchaser uses these valuations for establishing a purchase price. If the consideration paid to the target company shareholders includes stock of the purchaser, then similar valuations of the purchaser are important to the target company.

Enter into a Binding Contract

Each company's boards of directors and, sometimes, shareholders must formally approve any merger transaction. After both companies have obtained their approval, the purchaser and the target company enter into a binding contract, usually secured by payment of earnest money. The binding contract is likely to be known as a *merger agreement* or a definitive *acquisition agreement.* According to statutes in most states, the purchaser must arrange to buy the shares of any target company shareholders who vote against the transaction and must properly protect their rights as dissenting shareholders.

Obtain Necessary Regulatory Approvals and Tax Rulings

As the undertaking progresses, both parties must accomplish various tasks in order to obtain regulatory approval of the merger. The term ***compliance*** generally refers to all activities undertaken in order to fulfill regulatory requirements. For insurers involved in merger transactions, legal compliance encompasses such activities as announcement of the agreement (if a public company is involved), financial reporting, continuation of business in the ordinary course, federal antitrust filings (if the transaction is large enough), and approval of the transaction by the appropriate insurance regulatory authorities. For U.S. federal income tax purposes, insurance companies often obtain an advance determination from the IRS to learn what tax treatment will be accorded the proposed transaction.

Perform the Closing

At the closing of a merger transaction, formal articles of merger are filed with the appropriate regulatory agencies and the merger consideration (less any earnest money) is paid. Thus, the parties to a merger conclude the transaction in a formal ***closing*** process by exchanging legal documents, at which time the purchaser pays the purchase price. If stock is issued to target company shareholders, new shares must be issued.

Implement Merger of Business Operations

Once the legal aspects of merging have been completed, the insurers get on with the operational aspects of a merger. These operational activities typically include: renegotiating contracts with agents and suppliers, physically relocating operations, instituting uniform compensation and employment practices, integrating marketing plans and product lines, and merging and eliminating redundant information management systems. Now, we look in more detail at the various forms mergers and acquisitions can take.

Acquisition Methods

Insurers use a variety of methods to acquire another insurer or the business of another insurer. The specific method used depends on such factors as the organizational form of the target and the tax consequences of the acquisition or merger, among other factors.

At times, an insurer purchases the assets of another company. Such a transaction is known as an ***asset purchase.*** Figure 19-4 shows how an asset-purchase transaction is accomplished. Using this approach, none of the target company's capital stock is transferred to the purchaser. Consequently, such an asset purchase can be used to purchase some or all of the assets from both stock and mutual insurance companies. Often, such an asset purchase takes the form of an assumption reinsurance agreement.

Under the terms of an assumption reinsurance agreement, the purchasing company assumes part or all of the target company's in-force insurance business. (See Chapter 13 for a description of assumption reinsurance.) Insight 19-3 shows how an assumption reinsurance arrange-

Figure 19-4. Diagram of an asset-purchase acquisition.

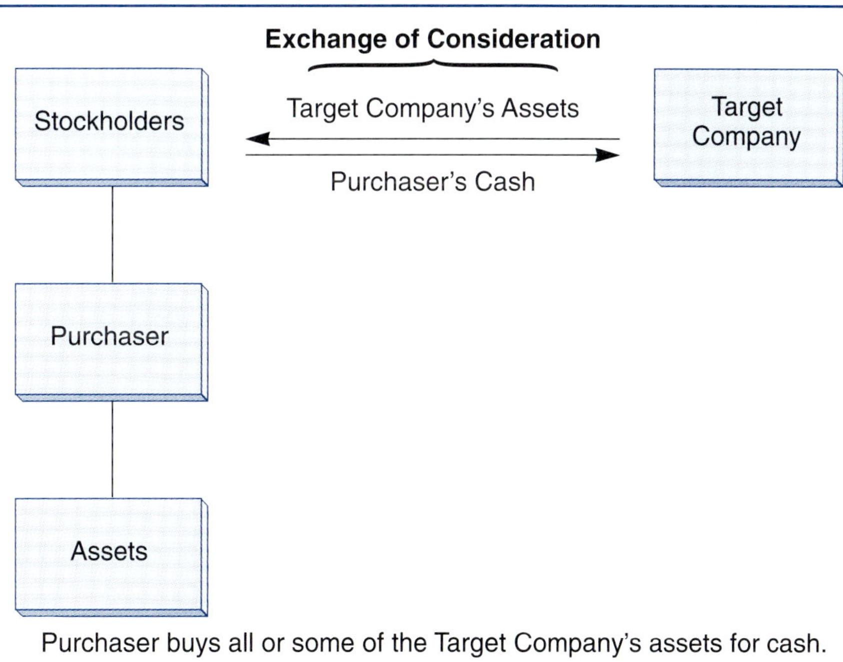

Insight 19-3 Limited Buys Lobo's Individual Life Business

Limited Life and Annuity Insurance Company is well-capitalized and thriving. Limited's management would like for the company to grow rapidly, and thus Limited plans to acquire all of the individual life business on the books of the Lobo Insurance Company. For its part, Lobo needs to strengthen its capitalization, and Lobo's management has decided that individual life business will not be part of the company's future. Thus, Lobo's management is agreeable to selling the individual life business to Limited.

Limited's acquisition consultants recommend undertaking the acquisition of the block of life business by means of assumption reinsurance. To effect the purchase transaction, Limited must obtain permission for the acquisition from the state insurance department regulators in Limited's home state and Lobo's home state. Also, because the transaction involves assumption reinsurance, Limited must obtain any approval required from state insurance regulators. Then, Limited and Lobo must agree upon the terms of the reinsurance contract, including the amount and payment method of the ceding commission.

Limited must arrange to pay Lobo for the individual life business. Because this transaction uses assumption reinsurance, the type of consideration that Limited and Lobo will exchange is fairly narrowly prescribed. For its part, Lobo must provide consideration by transferring to Limited an amount of assets equal to all reserve liabilities supporting Lobo's individual life business, less the amount of the reinsurance ceding commission Lobo has agreed to pay to Limited. Finally, Limited must issue assumption certificates to all of the affected policyholders, thus indicating to policyholders that Limited has assumed all of the risk under the policies. At this point, Limited becomes totally and directly liable to all of the affected policyholders and "stands in the place" of Lobo for all contractual obligations under the assumed individual life business. Under emerging assumption reinsurance laws, policyholders would have the right to object to the transfer to Limited and stay with Lobo.

ment can be used to help one company (the target) to exit a line of insurance business and another company (the purchaser) to grow rapidly.

Another means for acquiring an insurer is to purchase the target insurer's stock. Such an arrangement is known as a ***stock purchase.*** In such an arrangement, the purchaser pays for the target company's stock using cash, notes of indebtedness, or its own stock. A diagram in Figure 19-5 shows how a stock-purchase acquisition is accomplished. Because mutual companies do not issue stock, a mutual insurer cannot be purchased in such a manner. However, a mutual insurer can purchase other insurers by purchasing their stock. Note that several forms of stock-purchase acquisitions are used, each of which takes advantage of a specific portion of the tax code. Distinctions among these forms go beyond the scope of this text.

An insurance company can also acquire another insurance company by means of a statutory merger. Although statutory mergers can take several forms, all share certain common characteristics. We first discuss the general characteristics of a statutory merger, and then describe the most common forms such mergers take.

Statutory Mergers

In the United States, a ***statutory merger*** is defined as a merger that meets state legal requirements for a merger between two corpora-

Figure 19-5. Diagram of a stock-purchase acquisition.

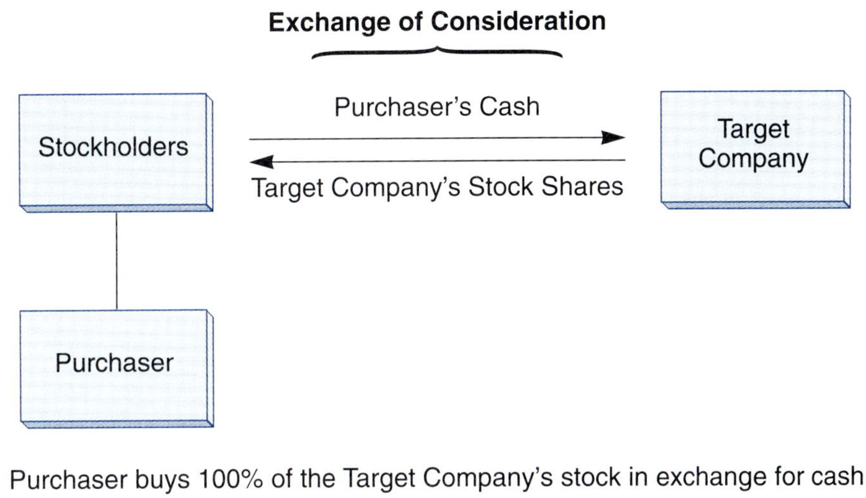

tions. Generally, an insurance company can be merged only with another insurance company. That is, an insurance company cannot be merged with a non-insurance corporation, and vice-versa.

Many state merger laws are quite flexible in the consideration that can be delivered to the owners of the target company and in the combinations that can be achieved through statutory mergers. A stock insurer can be merged into another stock insurer. In a typical transaction, the stockholders of the target company are compensated in the form of cash, stock of the acquiring company or its parent company, or a combination of some cash and some stock. The arrangements for making payment usually turn on the desires of the target company's stockholders and whether the transaction is taxable.

A mutual insurance company can be merged into another mutual insurance company. Here, the policyowners of the target mutual insurer become mutual owners of the acquiring mutual insurer. Moreover, in many states, a mutual insurance company can be merged into a stock insurance company. In essence, the mutual insurer becomes "demutualized" and the policyowners of the target insurer receive as consideration for the merger cash or stock of the acquiring insurer, or its parent company, or a combination.

Stockholders or policyowners of a target company that is being merged must be given the right to vote on the transaction. Most corporate mergers require a *simple-majority vote,* requiring only that the supporting vote exceed 50 percent. However, some insurance company mergers require a *super-majority vote,* such as a supporting vote of at least two-thirds. Shareholders of the target company, and in some instances policyholders, are given *dissenters' rights* to vote against the merger and to take action to block the merger.

Figure 19-6. Before and after diagrams of a basic statutory merger.

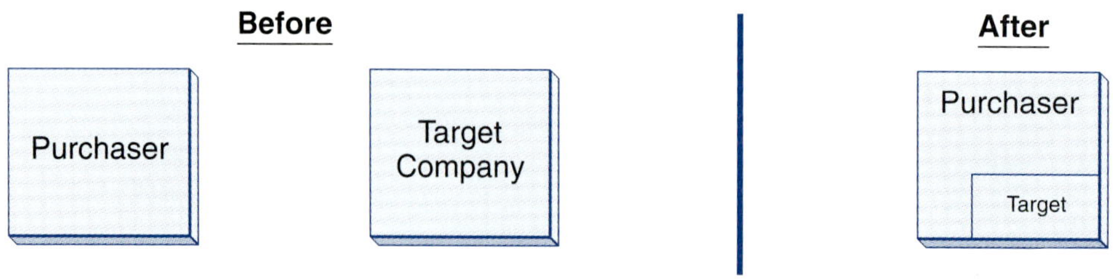

Target Company is completely absorbed by Purchaser.

In the United States, a statutory merger can take a number of different forms. In the following sections, we describe two of these forms: the basic statutory merger and the triangular merger.

Basic Statutory Merger. A ***basic statutory merger*** involves the merger of one corporate entity into another. As illustrated in Figure 19-6, the purchaser (or acquiring company) in a basic statutory merger absorbs the target company. The acquiring company assumes all the target company's liabilities and gains ownership of all the target company's assets. Consequently, all subsidiaries of the target company also will be owned by the acquiring company after the merger, because the stock of a subsidiary is an asset of the target company.

After the merger, the target company ceases to exist and loses its separate identity. Upon losing its identity, the target company also loses its corporate charter and its authority to transact insurance business. This authority to transact insurance business is *not* among the assets the acquiring company gains; all state insurance licenses owned by the target are lost when the target is absorbed. Thus, if the target company were licensed to conduct business in 50 states and the acquiring company were licensed to conduct business in 10 states, then after a basic statutory merger of the companies, the surviving company would remain licensed only in 10 states.

Because of the potential loss of valuable state licenses, a basic statutory merger of insurance companies is often not the best method for one insurer to use to acquire another. An acquiring insurer would be more likely to simply purchase the target company's stock, if possible, or take another approach to merging.

Triangular Mergers. A ***triangular merger*** is a corporate reorganization involving three corporate entities: (1) the purchaser, (2) a subsidiary of the purchaser, and (3) the target company. A triangular merger may involve a forward merger or a reverse merger. As illustrated in Figure 19-7, the ***forward triangular merger*** is designed so that the target

Figure 19-7. Forward triangular merger.

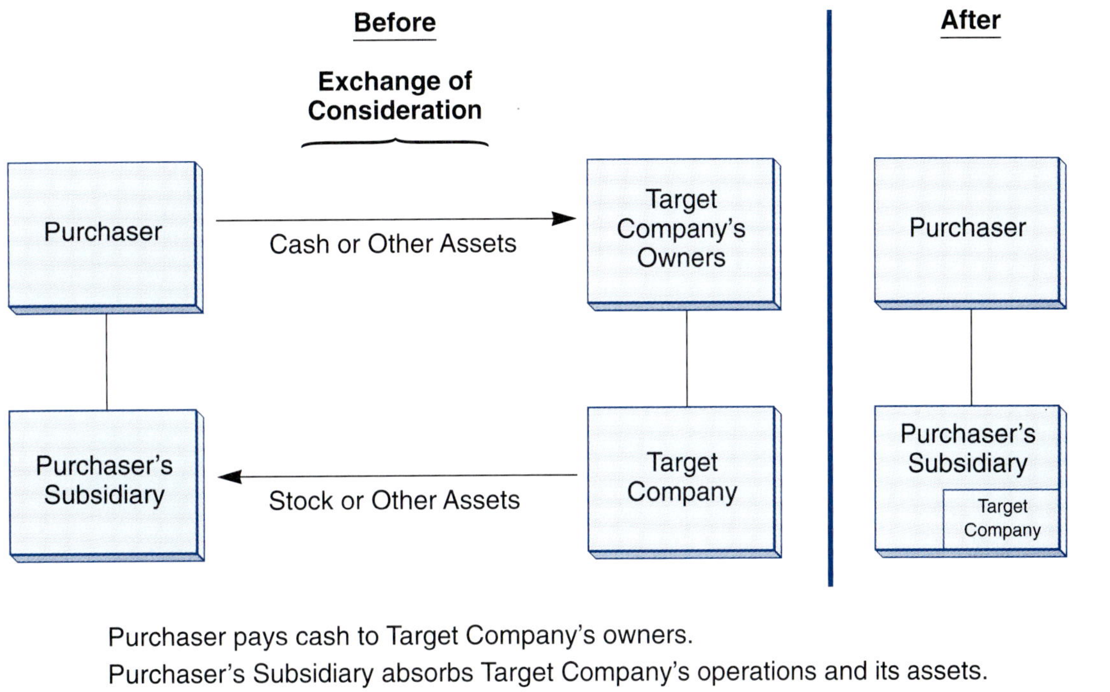

company merges into a subsidiary of the purchaser—not the purchaser itself. Consideration for the merger may be stock of the parent company, which is important if the stock of the parent is registered and traded on an exchange. Note that for a target insurer to be merged into a subsidiary of the parent, that subsidiary must also be an insurer.

A ***reverse triangular merger,*** as you might imagine, is just the opposite of the forward triangular merger. Here the subsidiary company of the purchaser is merged into the target company. After the merger, the target becomes the subsidiary of the purchaser. A reverse triangular merger is illustrated in Figure 19-8.

Which Type of Merger Is Most Appropriate?

When considering how to structure a specific merger transaction, an insurer considers a wide variety of factors. The insurer would generally base the choice of how to structure a specific merger transaction on factors such as whether it is incorporated as a stock or mutual company, the tax consequences of the transaction, the accounting consequences of the transaction, the legal compliance costs associated with a given arrangement, and the fit between the consequences of the arrangement and the company's objectives in entering into the transaction.

Figure 19-8. Reverse triangular merger.

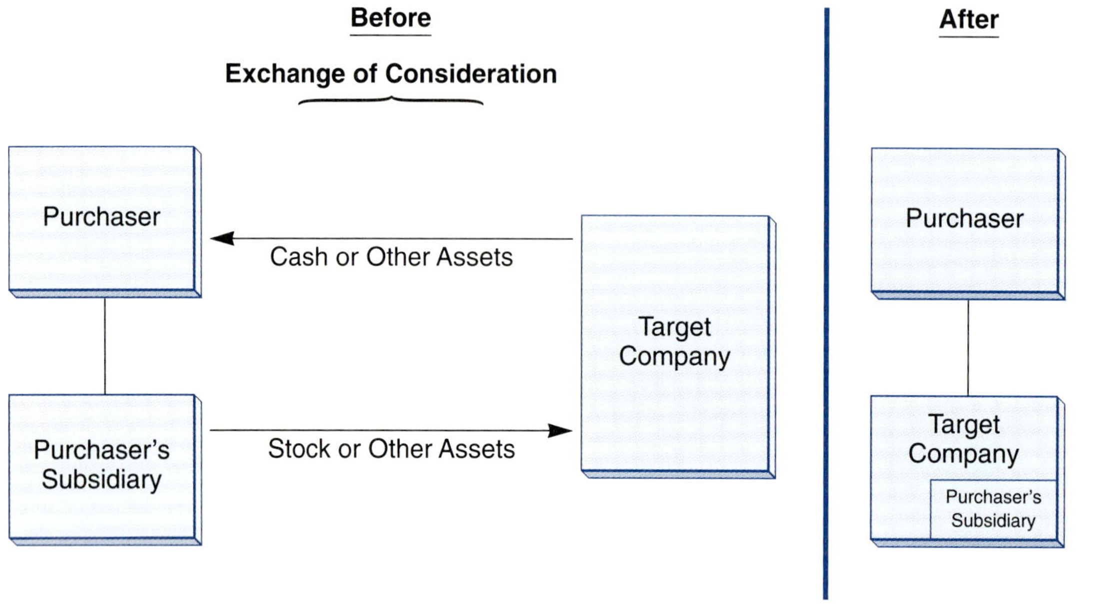

Purchaser's Subsidiary merges into the Target Company.
Purchaser's Subsidiary is dissolved.
Purchaser owns stock in Target Company.

Establishing Holding Companies to Facilitate Growth

The mechanism that corporations often employ when they wish to maintain an affiliation among a pair or a group of separate corporate entities is the formation of a holding company structure. For example, when a stock insurance company is acquired, a holding company affiliation may arise as a consequence of the acquisition. By *holding company structure,* we mean an arrangement wherein one company owns and controls another company or companies, which continue to exist as separate entities. (The glossary in Figure 19-1 includes a review of terminology relating to holding companies.)

In the insurance industry, the distinction between *downstream* and *upstream* holding companies is important. Upstream and downstream holding company relationships are illustrated in Figure 19-9. A *downstream holding company* is said to be downstream because it is owned or controlled by the corporation that forms it; the downstream holding company is said to be a holding company because it in turn owns

Figure 19-9. Upstream and downstream holding companies.

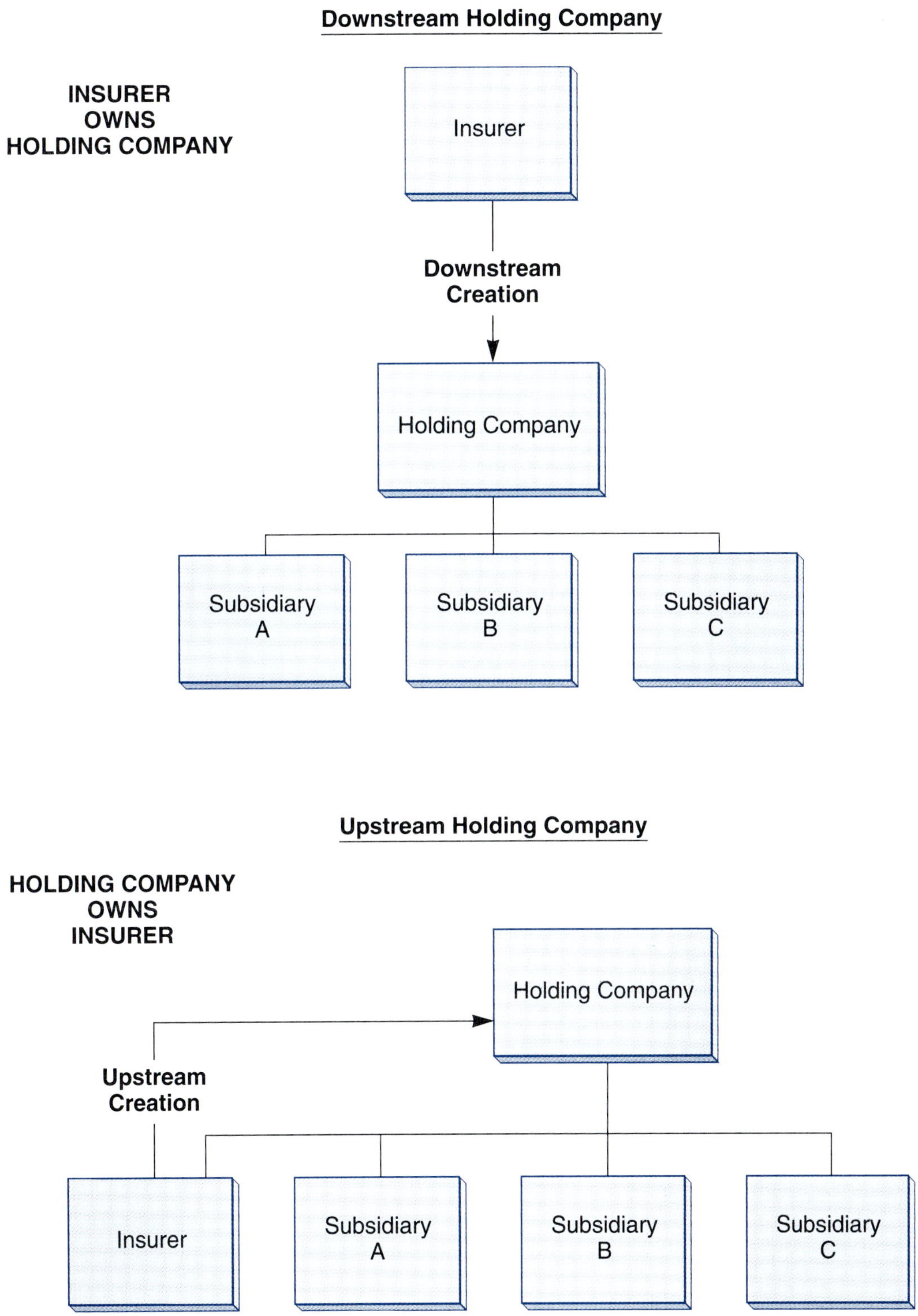

or controls another company or companies. In a downstream holding company arrangement, the parent corporation remains independent and continues to control the entire holding company structure. Both stock and mutual insurers can own other companies, which would then be downstream from the insurer. We have already seen in this chapter that a stock subsidiary can be useful to a mutual insurance company, which can use the subsidiary to issue stock and to enter into triangular mergers.

An *upstream holding company* is said to be upstream from its parent because the holding company owns the parent company. In the insurance industry, upstream holding companies can come into being in at least two ways. A stock insurer can form a holding company that thereafter controls the insurer. Additionally, upon being purchased by an existing corporation, a stock insurer can become controlled by that corporation in an upstream holding company relationship. By contrast, a mutual insurer cannot form an upstream holding company, nor can a mutual insurer be purchased by an upstream holding company.

In order to deliberately set up and maintain a holding company structure, an insurer incurs two types of expenses: (1) the legal expenses of incorporating the new company and (2) the ongoing expense of maintaining a separate corporate structure. Nevertheless, the benefits insurers can enjoy from participating in a holding company structure often outweigh the costs. Some of these benefits apply regardless of whether the holding company is upstream or downstream from the insurer. Examples of such benefits include the ability of the holding company to gather talented asset managers, investment staff, accountants, and actuaries so that these resources can be shared among various subsidiaries. Holding company stock can also be issued and used as consideration for further growth.

Either version of a holding company structure can also (1) allow insurers to realize some tax advantages and (2) facilitate mergers. In the following sections, we look at these benefits, and then we describe the benefits that are applicable only to stock companies that are downstream from a holding company. (A mutual insurance company cannot be downstream from a holding company.)

Consolidated Tax Returns for U.S. Income Taxes

A significant benefit of being affiliated with other companies is that, under some circumstances,* affiliated companies can file consolidated tax returns and, thus, may be able to enjoy a lower overall tax bill than if they had filed separately.** Note that this benefit is inseparable from

* There are limitations on how long a holding company must own life and non-life companies before the group can file consolidated tax returns.

** One exception is that companies eligible for a small company tax rate might lose the deduction by filing a consolidated return.

Insight 19-4 The Maximum Group

A holding company known as the Maximum Group owns two subsidiaries, Argo Life Insurance Company and Boggs Health Insurance Company. The Maximum Group's only assets and operations are those of Argo and Boggs. For a given tax year, Argo had much better operating results than Boggs. In fact, Argo had a before-tax gain of $800,000; at a tax rate of 35 percent, Argo, if filing alone, would have faced an income tax bill of $280,000. Boggs had an operating loss of $200,000 and, thus, owed no income taxes for the year. Because Argo and Boggs are affiliates owned by a holding company, Maximum must consolidate the income tax returns for Argo and Boggs within its own tax reporting system. On Maximum's consolidated return, the amount of Argo's gain is reduced by the amount of Boggs's loss, so that for these two subsidiaries, Maximum reports a total operating gain of only $600,000 for the year. At the 35 percent tax rate, Maximum owes $210,000 in income taxes. By comparing Argo's corporate tax liability against the separate tax bills for Argo and Boggs (see below), we can see that the consolidation resulted in a current-year tax savings of $70,000. Note that the consolidated tax filing may offer an advantage only as to the timing of the tax payment, as Boggs would otherwise carry a loss forward to apply to future years' gains.

Tax Savings from Combined Tax Returns

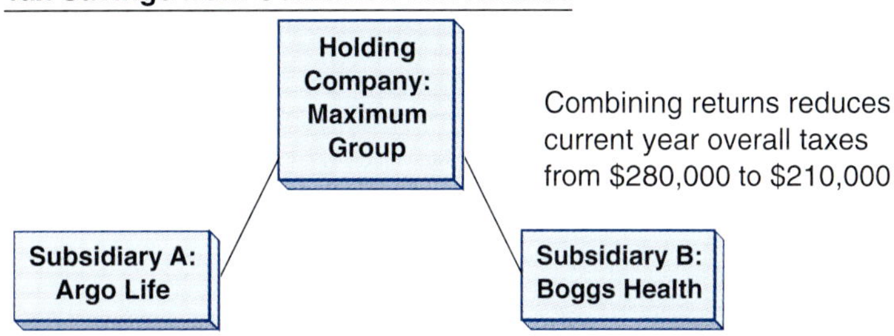

Tax situation: Separate filings	Earns $800,000 profits and owes $280,000 for income taxes	Loses $200,000 and owes no income taxes
Tax situation: Consolidated	Maximum Group earns a before-tax profit of $600,000 and owes income tax of $210,000. Tax savings amounts to $70,000.	

the holding company structure in that, once two companies are both owned by a holding company and qualify to file a consolidated tax return, they must file a consolidated return. The benefits of a consolidated tax return arise when one company's gains in a given tax period can be offset by an affiliated company's losses in the same tax period. Insight 19-4 provides an example of how a consolidated tax return can result in a lower total tax bill for a group of affiliated companies.

Holding Company Structures Can Facilitate Mergers

A holding company structure can also help an insurance company that wants to become affiliated with another company. The holding company structure facilitates mergers in three primary ways:

1. A holding company structure provides flexibility in the insurer's ability to obtain financing for an acquisition.

2. Some types of statutory mergers between insurers can be accomplished only by using holding companies.

3. A holding company structure allows some assets and operations to be shielded from the limitations normally placed on insurance companies.

The last point applies whenever an insurance company is affiliated with a non-insurance company. In the absence of a holding company arrangement, the non-insurance company could be subject to the same rules applied to insurers. With a holding company structure, a non-insurance company that is affiliated with a life company can invest in assets not permitted for a life company. In addition, the non-insurance company is exempt from many other regulations that apply specifically to life insurers.

Benefits of Having an Upstream Holding Company

Another potential benefit of holding company relationships relates to the opportunity for corporations to transfer assets between a parent and a subsidiary. An upstream holding company has great flexibility in borrowing funds and raising capital that can be transferred to a downstream insurer without limitation, thus allowing the insurer to relieve deficiencies in its capital and surplus. On the other hand, states set limitations on the amount of funds an insurance company can transfer to an upstream holding company. The limitations are based upon the insurance subsidiary's prior year's statutory earnings and surplus.* In contrast, an insurer's ability to contribute funds to a downstream holding company is less restricted.

A second benefit may arise if an insurer's upstream holding company issues debt or equity, with the proceeds being used to benefit the insurer. This arrangement strengthens the life insurer financially. In the case of debt issuance, it supports more favorable ratings than if the insurer had directly incurred the debt. Through an upstream holding company, an insurer can finance purchases of other companies by using holding company debt, and thus would avoid showing the debt on the insurer's own balance sheet. In such an arrangement, the debt is sometimes called *off-balance-sheet financing.*

Demutualization as a Growth Strategy

In the past decade, many insurers have made growth a strategic imperative. Sometimes, insurers measure growth in terms of admitted

* The maximum limits vary by state, but they are generally based upon 10 percent of statutory surplus, or the insurer's prior year's net income or gain from operations.

assets, insurance in force, or reserves. For the purposes of this discussion, when we refer to *growth,* we mean ability to raise new capital. When finding more funding is the objective, stock insurance companies have many options, not all of which are available to mutual insurers. Options available only to stock companies include issuing stock and creating upstream holding companies.

Some insurers have felt so constrained by the limitations of the mutual form of ownership that they have undergone the complex and expensive process of converting from the mutual form to the stock form. Other mutual insurers have resorted to increasingly creative ways of overcoming the drawbacks of the mutual form. For a profile of an actual demutualization that took place between 1989 and 1991, see Insight 19-5.

The usual reasons for undertaking a demutualization are related to the mutual insurer's desire to overcome the disadvantages connected with not having capital stock for sale in public markets. The ability to issue stock provides the following potential benefits:

- The insurer gains an additional way to raise capital externally by issuing stock and an opportunity to obtain access to the broader capital sources needed in order to pursue a strategy calling for rapid growth through mergers and acquisition transactions.
- The insurer gains the opportunity to form an upstream holding company structure, which in turn supports new opportunities for obtaining off-balance-sheet financing and facilitates diversification in financial services.
- The insurer gains the opportunity to later be acquired by means of an acquisition of its stock.
- The insurer is able to employ stock shares and stock options as incentive compensation for top management. For more data about this approach, see the Fast Fact in this section.

FAST FACT

CEOs who own large amounts of company stock outperform CEOs who have small stock holdings, according to a study of 105 large companies by the Wyatt Company. The study finds that companies with above-median CEO stock ownership had an annual average return to shareholders of 11.4 percent, compared to 7.3 percent at companies with below-median CEO stock ownership.[3]

Why Hesitate to Demutualize?

Many of the same issues that make mergers complex are also present in the effort for a mutual company to convert to the stock form. The drawbacks of demutualization, like the drawbacks of mergers and acquisitions, generally revolve around the issues of (1) high costs and (2) uncertainties as to outcomes. Some likely drawbacks of demutualization are as follows:

- Conversion is accomplished at considerable expense for legal, accounting, and actuarial advice. This expense could seriously deplete capital and thus impair the company's future operations. In the United States, ease of conversion from mutual to stock form varies from one state to another, but in no case is it easy.

Insight 19-5 Demutualization at NWNL

The possibility of demutualization first arose as part of NWNL's strategic planning process. As part of strategic planning, the company identified the need for capital and the cost of capital as one of the major issues facing us in the 1990s. We also identified the need for more flexibility in acquiring and growing businesses outside of life insurance and the need to use debt as part of our permanent capital structure—but not on the balance sheet of the life insurance companies. This required an upstream holding company, which was not possible under our hybrid structure.

The conversion process is really about trips to the capital markets. These trips may not be pleasant or affordable unless a company can become a viable stock enterprise, able to compete in the capital markets as well as in the insurance marketplace.

Unlike most insurers, NWNL was a hybrid stock and mutual company before its conversion, a situation made possible by Minnesota law. The company's profits and revenues were generated separately by the stock department and the mutual department, which were owned respectively by shareholders and policyholders. On an economic basis, the stock department accounted for about two-thirds of the enterprise, but voting control actually rested in the hands of mutual policyholders by about a nine-to-one margin. Because of our unique structure, our greatest challenge in demutualizing was balancing the interests of existing shareholders with the interests of existing mutual policyholders and designing a plan that was fair to both parties.

Major Policyholder Issues

The key issues from the policyholder standpoint were

- Who would share in the distribution?
- How much would policyholders receive in the aggregate?
- How would the aggregate amount be split among eligible policyholders?
- What form would the distribution take—cash, stock, or other assets?
- How would participation rights be maintained for mutual policyholders?

Although the detailed answers to these questions are beyond the scope of this article, a few points are worth noting in this regard:

- Applicable Minnesota statutes provided little direction regarding issues of fairness to policyholders.
- The dollar amount of the aggregate distribution was set on a market-value basis.
- The Society of Actuaries "Report of the Task Force on Mutual Life Company Conversion" was helpful to us in the resolution of these policyholder issues.

The Major Stockholder Issue

- The one main shareholder concern was related to the dilution of shareholders' existing ownership interest and the impact of demutualization on the company's earning power.

In the final analysis, the biggest surprise to management was that the response from shareholders and policyholders alike was overwhelmingly accepting.

Source: *Adapted with permission of the publisher from John H. Flittie, "NWNL Looks at Life after Demutualization,"* Resource *(July/August 1989), pp. 21–22, 24–25.*

- Educating policyholders and securing a policyowner vote is costly, as is the process of valuing the company.
- The hoped-for benefits of becoming a stock company may not be fully achieved.
- In undergoing conversion, a company faces new administrative burdens in establishing and maintaining communication with stockholders.
- Because mutual companies cannot issue stock, for mutual companies any risk of unwanted takeover is minimal. Upon an issuance of stock, an insurance company becomes available for takeover, whether wanted or unwanted.

Compliance Required for Altering an Insurer's Legal Form

Insurers are required to meet extensive regulatory requirements connected with changes in the company's legal structure. These requirements for changing the legal form of an organization cause the company to incur transaction costs that the insurer must take into consideration before undertaking any change in legal form. In effect, these legal requirements discourage such undertakings. Companies move ahead with mergers only after extensive deliberation and only in the confident expectation that substantial benefits will accrue as a result of the merger.

Insurers make an effort to be aware of the legal requirements associated with any given strategic or investment decision. In the effort to ensure compliance in all areas of their operations, many insurers have appointed a permanent senior-level officer to oversee compliance issues. When properly advised of the legal implications of financial decisions, insurance executives can make an informed choice about

- Planning and budgeting for the delay and expense of compliance
- Structuring transactions so as to avoid triggering legal requirements
- Rejecting a potential transaction

Compliance with the many requirements affecting mergers can be costly. Keep in mind, however, that compliance is not nearly so costly as a failure to comply. Such a failure can trigger significant fines and other penalties. Because the cost and effort involved in compliance can materially affect the feasibility of a transaction, it seems appropriate here to survey the breadth of potential compliance issues. First we review the bodies of law that affect mergers in the United States and Canada, including U.S. federal laws that affect an insurer's restructuring; the applicable state laws; and, finally, Canadian regulation of mergers, acquisitions, and demutualizations.

U.S. Federal Laws Affecting Mergers

Although insurance companies have generally been exempt from federal jurisdiction, insurers are not completely beyond the reach of these laws, and their general exemption from these laws has long faced at least rhetorical attack. The major areas of federal law that affect mergers, acquisitions, and demutualizations involving insurance companies are antitrust laws, securities laws, and tax laws.

Federal ***antitrust laws*** are designed to prevent monopolies, restraint of trade, and any ownership changes that could materially diminish

Figure 19-10. Landmark U.S. antitrust legislation.

Sherman Anti-Trust Act	1890	Prohibits business dealings tending to create a monopoly
Clayton Anti-Trust Act (Holding Company Act)	1914	Regulates local price discrimination, interlocking directorates, holding company structures, and other issues directed toward maintaining competitive forces
Federal Trade Commission Act	1914	Created the Federal Trade Commission to oversee interstate commerce

competition in the marketplace. Antitrust laws can affect mergers because, by definition, mergers involve ownership changes. As shown in Figure 19-10, landmark U.S. federal antitrust laws include the ***Sherman Anti-Trust Act of 1890,*** the ***Clayton Anti-Trust Act of 1914,*** and the ***Federal Trade Commission Act of 1914.***

U.S. federal ***securities laws*** are designed to ensure full disclosure of needed information to interested investors. Securities laws affect mergers because mergers are frequently structured so that large blocks of stock change ownership or so that new stock must be issued. As shown in Figure 19-11, the important federal securities laws are the ***Securities Act of 1933,*** the ***Securities Exchange Act of 1934,*** and the ***National Exchange Market System Act of 1975.***

U.S. federal tax laws are designed to ensure revenues for the support of the federal government. As we noted earlier in the chapter, companies carefully structure a merger so that the exchange of legal consideration takes the form that offers them the best possible tax consequences for their situation.

State Regulation of Insurance Company Mergers

Both state and federal regulation of insurance company purchases focus on ensuring that purchasers will respect the insurance company's fiduciary obligation to protect the rights of policyowners and beneficiaries. In the United States, state insurance regulations are particularly concerned with preventing a holding company structure from separating an insurer's assets and liabilities from that insurer's control. Insurance regulators are fully aware that a holding company could "raid" the capital and surplus of an insurance subsidiary for the purpose of funding either the holding company or another subsidiary. Almost all states have thus passed holding company laws to protect insurance companies and their policyholders and beneficiaries from any such eventuality.

Insurance regulators exercise holding company laws to control and monitor activities between holding companies in two major ways.

Figure 19-11. Landmark U.S. securities legislation.

Securities Act (Truth in Securities Act)	1933	Regulated disclosure concerning sales of securities; Requires registration of securities, public disclosure, and publication of a prospectus
Securities Exchange Act	1934	Created the Securities and Exchange Commission to enforce compliance with securities laws
National Exchange Market System Act	1975	Established a nationwide system for the clearance and settlement of securities transactions; prohibited the fixing of sales commission rates

First, under the ***Insurance Holding Company Acts*** in the various states, any company proposing to acquire control of a domestic insurer must first file with the domestic insurer's home state a comprehensive application for approval in order to take control of its insurer. Usually, *control* means the ability to vote 10 percent or more of the voting securities of the insurer. In some states, the control threshold is 5 percent. Generally, the state regulator wants to know the background of those proposing to acquire the insurer, which would include all members of the board of directors of the ultimate parent company, as well as its principal officers. The regulator also must be informed of any debt being used to finance the acquisition and how the acquiring party proposes to repay the debt. If the regulator believes that the debt incurred at the holding company level to buy the insurer will put too much pressure on the insurer to generate dividends after acquisition, the regulator is likely not to approve the acquisition.

Regulators also control insurance company holding arrangements by monitoring certain dealings between the insurer and its holding company. Typically, if a holding company has any means to "siphon" funds from an insurer, the regulator wants to be aware of the potential transfer of funds so that inappropriate transfers of funds can then be prevented.

Canadian Regulation of Insurance Company Mergers

In Canada, regulation affecting insurance company mergers is mostly federal. The main Canadian antitrust law is the federal ***Competition Act of 1986,*** which applies equally to all Canadian business activity, not only to insurance companies. The Competition Act is designed to prevent undesirable monopolies, price-fixing, and other anticompetitive or deceptive trade practices. In Canada, federally incorporated companies are subject to federal regulation, and provincially incorporated companies are subject to provincial regulation.

The general approach of Canadian laws governing insurance company mergers focuses upon limiting the level of ownership of a holding company in any Canadian life and health insurance company. Under Canadian law, companies incorporated in Canada are referred to as ***resident corporations;*** companies incorporated outside of Canada are referred to as ***nonresident corporations.*** A Canadian resident life and health insurer is not permitted to own more than 30 percent of the shares of another resident insurer. Canadian law further restricts non-resident ownership of Canadian insurance company stock.

In Conclusion

This concludes our discussion of the considerations influencing decisions related to changes in the corporate structure. Our discussion mentioned repeatedly that burdensome and expensive legal compliance is a drawback to such activity. Nevertheless, mergers, acquisitions, holding company arrangements, and demutualization are all vehicles an insurance company can use to strengthen its financial position and grow safely.

Key Terms and Concepts

holding company
demutualization
acquisition
affiliation
conglomerate
consolidation
divestiture
merger
parent corporation
spin-off
subsidiary
takeover
target corporation
downstream holding company
upstream holding company
economies of scale
letter of intent
due diligence investigation
compliance
closing
asset purchase
stock purchase
statutory merger
basic statutory merger
triangular merger
forward triangular merger
reverse triangular merger
antitrust laws
Sherman Anti-Trust Act of 1890
Clayton Anti-Trust Act of 1914
Federal Trade Commission Act of 1914
securities laws
Securities Act of 1933
Securities Exchange Act of 1934
National Exchange Market System Act of 1975
Insurance Holding Company Acts
Competition Act of 1986
resident corporation
nonresident corporation

References

1. "Mergers and Acquisitions and Public Equity Offerings: Some Like It Hot!" *Strategic Study Series* (Hartford, CT: Conning & Company, 1996), p. 16.

2. "Travelers, Primerica Ratings Affirmed after Merger Pact," *Best's Insurance Management Reports,* Life/Health Edition (September 27, 1993), Release 39, p. 1.

3. "Fast Forward," *Across the Board* (April 1995), p. 8.

CHAPTER

20

Keys to Profitability

LEARNING OBJECTIVES

After studying this chapter, you should be able to

- Recognize ways insurers can reduce their administration and distribution expenses
- Identify distinctions among reengineering, downsizing, outsourcing, and continuous process improvement
- Identify types of fraud against insurers, and approaches for preventing fraud
- Recognize how insurers use technology to improve profitability
- Interpret how the concept of core competencies applies to long-term growth
- Identify the factors that affect the potential for revenue growth from global markets
- Recognize the value of ethical standards in the insurance industry

OUTLINE

Until fairly recently, the insurance industry was stable and predictable, and the majority of insurers maintained profitable operations by continuing traditional industry practices. The industry was heavily regulated and faced little competition from the other providers of financial services. However, the last quarter century has brought accelerating change in the form of deregulation, technological innovation, economic volatility, and an increasingly sophisticated consumer.

The inflation and interest-rate fluctuations of the 1970s and 1980s proved that the business environment for insurers can be quite unstable. As a result of deregulation of the financial services industry, insurers now face competition from banks and other financial institutions. Computer technology both requires and enables insurers to totally rethink the way they do business. The average financial consumer has a greater understanding of financial matters is computer literate, and is comfortable with new technology. When it comes to purchasing insurance, consumers are more choosy than in the past. Accordingly, insurers now offer a greater variety of financial services than ever before.[1]

Insurers are responding to the challenges in this business environment by searching for new approaches to profitability.

In this chapter we discuss several of the approaches insurers are applying to increase profitability. First, we consider efforts designed to control administrative and distribution expenses. Administrative expenses can be controlled by means of downsizing, reengineering, and outsourcing. New information systems technology can affect administrative expenses, distribution expenses, or both. Similarly, approaching consumers through non-traditional distribution systems can help insurers to reduce distribution expenses or to reach a larger market.

Then we consider other approaches to insurance company expense control and revenue growth. Specifically, we discuss

- The growing importance of mergers and consolidations
- The benefits of combating fraud
- The need for new technologies
- Understanding and exploiting *core competencies*
- The role of loyalty—on the part of customers, sales representatives, employees, and investors—in company profitability
- The potential of the global marketplace in expenses and generate new sales
- The role of ethics in supporting profitability and the effort to control solvency

Controlling Administrative Expenses

On average, in the United States, administrative expenses—including home and field office expenses, but excluding non-commission expenses—make up about 6.7 percent of an insurer's total yearly expenditures.[2] Particularly when profit margins are slim, reducing these expenses can considerably improve profitability. Now we consider several initiatives that insurers and other businesses have employed with an eye toward controlling expenses: downsizing, reengineering, and outsourcing.

Downsizing

Downsizing is a reduction in the size of a company's work force. In theory, downsizing should be used for eliminating non-essential employees or positions, thus reducing the company's expenses without damaging the company's operating effectiveness. The following three techniques are often used for downsizing:

1. *Attrition.* ***Attrition*** can be defined as a naturally occurring and gradual reduction in membership. When a company downsizes by attrition, the company purposefully elects to not replace employees who leave their jobs for reasons of retirement, resignation, death, or disability.
2. *Early retirement programs.* An ***early retirement program*** can be defined as a systematic effort on the part of a company's management to force or encourage employees who are nearing retirement age but have not yet reached it to retire immediately. Early retirement programs may be voluntary or mandatory.
3. *Layoffs.* A ***layoff*** is a permanent dismissal or temporary suspension of employees.

As an alternative to downsizing, many companies are pursuing an approach that attempts to match a company's business volume with the present size of its workforce. Under this approach, a company with redundant employees attempts to increase its sales volume, revenue, and wealth without increasing or decreasing its staff size. In this way, instead of reducing the size of its workforce, a company can grow until a proper balance is achieved.

Unintended Effects of Downsizing

In practice, downsizing can involve eliminating key positions or employees, and thus can damage the company's operating effectiveness. According to one popular surgical metaphor, downsizing is intended to cut out fat, but often it cuts out muscle. An important drawback to downsizing is the potential for harm to the morale of remaining staff. Upon seeing many of their co-workers terminated, staff develop concern about their own job security. Remaining employees also experience greater workloads and sometimes find that they must work longer hours. Many companies have found that downsizing does not achieve its desired results unless it is accompanied by genuine reengineering.

For more information about the possible negative consequences of corporate downsizing, read Insight 20-1.

Reengineering

Reengineering is sometimes confused with downsizing. Many companies have used the term *reengineering* to try to put a positive face on their efforts to downsize. In fact, reengineering need not involve any downsizing at all. ***Reengineering*** can be defined as the comprehensive and systematic analysis and redesign of an organization's work processes with a goal of dramatically increasing customer satisfaction and dramatically improving efficiency. By improving its work processes, an insurer generally improves operating efficiency, thus increasing the revenue that can be generated with a given level of resources. Improving business processes generally enables an insurer to provide superior service to its customers, which in turn helps persistency and the generation of sales to new and existing customers, resulting in improved revenues.

Implementing a Reengineering Program

A reengineering program attempts to create the ideal work process for a company. Implementing a reengineering program generally involves the following steps:

1. Analyze the organization's existing work processes
2. Identify inefficiencies in the existing work processes
3. Identify performance standards for the reengineered work processes
4. Design new, more efficient, and more effective work processes
5. Identify the human and systems resources that will be needed to complete the reengineered work processes
6. Identify the organizational changes necessary for supporting the new work processes
7. Implement necessary changes

Insight 20-1 Corporate Anorexia

In a nation where diets and diet metaphors abound, U.S. companies have been obsessed for the past few years with trimming away the fat, getting lean and mean, shedding the weight in order to compete in the new global economy. But in their obsession to cut costs—and people—have some companies perhaps cut too close to the bone, leaving themselves with insufficient human resources to serve existing customers—or to generate new customers and new revenue? Some people think so, and they invoke a new, more worrisome metaphor to describe the state that the most fanatical cost-cutters have gotten themselves into: corporate anorexia.

No one disputes that some companies needed to reduce staff and cut costs. But the consensus emerging among critics is that much of the downsizing has been driven by a shortsighted, bean-counting mentality rather than the sort of strategic, long-term vision required to reshape a company into a smaller, but healthier, organization.

In his book *Corporate Executions,* Alan Downs, a former corporate hatchet man who helped orchestrate Black Friday-style massive firings at several companies in the early '90s but who today is critical of downsizing practices, argues that the only explanation for the kinds of monstrous layoffs we've seen is that management has either become greedily obsessed with short-term profit or else it has been asleep at the switch—or both. "How do you wake up one day and suddenly realize that you have 2,000 too many workers? That's what we pay management for. If that kind of miscalculation happened in inventory, the person responsible would be out the door that afternoon," he says in an interview. "We show more respect for materials in this country than we do for humans."

While Downs may be the most strident of the downsizing critics, he's not alone in suggesting that many large-scale work force reductions have been little more than a quick and dirty attempt to shore up a sagging bottom line—and to curry favor with Wall Street, which unfailingly rewards large-scale layoffs with an impulsive jump in a company's stock price. In the most odious cases, top executives have been able to cash in on million-dollar bonuses written into their contracts when Wall Street rewarded "cutting away the fat" with hefty stock-price jumps.

But while senior management may walk away from a downsized company with wads of cash, the rewards for the company are often short-lived. A study by New York-based Mitchell & Co. of 16 firms that cut more than 10 percent of their work force in the mid-'80s found that although Wall Street initially applauded the cuts with higher stock prices, two years later 10 of the 16 were trading below the stock market average and 12 were trading lower than comparable firms in their industries.

The American Management Association's (AMA) statistics on downsizing raise more than a hint of suggestion that the mad rush to cut costs at many U.S. firms has been shortsighted—if not downright foolish. Only 47 percent of the companies reporting work force reductions since 1990 realized any increase in operating profits within a year following the reductions. Long-term (more than one year after the cuts) only 46 percent reported increased profits. Only one-third of the cost-cutting firms reported an increase in worker productivity within a year after the cuts. "You certainly have to wonder why the success rate has been so low," says Eric Greenberg, director of research for the AMA in New York.

Some analysts point to the banking industry as an example of how cutting back on critical support staff damages the core business. Few banks have actually cut salespeople, but many have either cut or stopped growing their support staff, says Terence Parker of the Globecon Group, a New York financial consulting firm specializing in wholesale banking. As banks add new products, the sales staff has to take on the responsibility for marketing a broader range of services. "The problem is, corporate clients are continually looking for added value," says Parker.

Parker agrees with banking analysts who have suggested that the inability to offer new products and generate new revenue has been a factor that's driven some banks to seek mergers with healthier players. "You can't have it both ways," says Parker. "The banks that are 'managing expenses' are in the second tier of also-rans."

Axing crucial support functions is one way downsizing hurts a company's ability to grow, but it's not the only flaw in the downsizing formula. Some critics charge that too heavy an emphasis on cost-cutting eventually transforms a corporate culture. Risk-taking be-

Insight 20-1 Corporate Anorexia (continued)

comes . . . well, riskier. People who once may have led a charge into a new market are loath to take such chances when every decision is held under the cost accountant's microscope.

"I've talked with CEOs who wonder if their managers would know what to do with a growth opportunity if one should come their way," says Dwight Gertz of Mercer Management Consulting in Boston. In a book published last year called *Grow to be Great,* which exhorts managers to focus on business growth rather than cost-cutting, Gertz uses the term "managerial tunnel vision" to describe the tendency to focus solely on the cost side of the coin. "A whole generation of managers has devoted their attention to continuous improvement, quality control, making companies smaller and more efficient at what they do," says Gertz. "The problem is, they've riveted their thinking and energy on ways of gaining efficiencies in existing businesses while obscuring their vision of new possibilities for future growth."

Another unintended and counterproductive effect of downsizing is that, contrary to what management often believes, a lean staff is not necessarily more entrepreneurial; cutting workers does not reduce bureaucracy or open up the lines of communication. "Quite the opposite, downsizing erects more barriers than it eliminates," says Charles Heckscher, chair of the Labor Studies and Employment Relations Department at Rutgers University in New Brunswick, N.J. Managers are just too pressed for time these days to pay attention to things outside their department. "You end up with a more bureaucratic company because everyone is focused on his own little piece," says Heckscher.

Although the number of companies that eliminate jobs is increasing, downsizing is no longer a linear slide toward an ever-shrinking work force. Last year, many companies created new jobs even as they eliminated existing jobs. In fact, only 27 percent of the companies in the AMA survey ended the year with a net reduction in their work force.

Alan Downs brands it a symptom of the "binge-purge" management mentality that keeps an eye on quarterly profits rather than long-term strategy. "Management opens and closes the hiring gate according to short-term financials, not long-term business needs," he says.

In the face of mounting criticism leveled at downsizing mania, is there any sign of a pendulum swing back in the other direction?

"Frankly, I don't see it," says Downs. "Many people are speaking out against layoffs, but the message still doesn't sell. I can go to a company and try to sell an alternative to layoffs, but it involves retraining workers and restructuring the company. How do you sell that against someone who says, 'I can get rid of 5,000 workers and get your bottom line up in two months?'"

Source: *David Stamps, "Corporate Anorexia,"* Training *(February 1996), pp. 24–30. Adapted with permission from the FEB 1996 issue of* TRAINING *Magazine.*

Insight 20-2 tells how one insurer improved a crucial business process. The insight describes the inefficiencies of the process before the reengineering, and shows how the reengineering effort eliminated these inefficiencies.

Process Inefficiencies Addressed by Reengineering

A number of problems typically contribute to inefficiencies in a process. The major problems commonly addressed by reengineering are the following:

- *Multiple hand-offs.* Different steps in a business process are performed by different employees. Once Employee A has finished

Insight 20-2 Reengineering at General American Life[3]

In 1986, General American Life conducted a major reorganization of its group life and health line and reengineered its case installation process. Systems development also accompanied this effort. The objective of these changes was to increase the company's ability to compete for new business on the basis of speedy service. During the typical case installation process, a company loads the case into its administrative and claims processing systems and generates claims kits, employee identification cards, plan booklets, broker's commission payments, and legal documents. These changes allowed General American to make major improvements in service speed. Before then, General American took 17 weeks to install a new case. Afterward, it took 6.5 weeks to do so. In a 1993 LOMA benchmark survey of the new business service times of 38 insurance companies, General American came in second, behind an insurer that sells highly standardized products.

Catalysts for Reengineering

Two factors were largely responsible for General American's decision to reorganize and reengineer its group lines: intense competition in the group health market and the field force's discontent with the existing case installation process.

The Reengineering Team

To address these problems, General American established a cross-functional project team (which today would very likely be called a reengineering team) to interview group customers about their expectations with respect to the case installation process. The team found a significant gap between what these customers expected and what they received. The team also conducted an analysis of the existing process, identifying process steps and the organizational units responsible for them and mapping the typical flow of work.

Problems with the Existing Process

The team identified three reasons the existing process did not work well:

- Organizational barriers increased processing time and created too many opportunities for errors. In 1985, General American's group lines were structured on a functional basis. Thirteen departments in three corporate divisions in three separate locations performed case installation functions.
- Work flow occurred in a rigid, sequential manner. Many steps were not performed until underwriting was completed, a practice that caused significant delays.
- Each manager's concern was limited to the functions performed in his or her unit. No single manager had overall responsibility for a particular customer case. Case tracking was difficult. There were no performance standards. Performance reporting was nonexistent.

Team Recommendations

To correct these problems, the project team recommended three changes: functional consolidation, the creation of a case manager position (called a new business coordinator), and workflow reengineering. The company implemented these recommendations.

Functional Consolidation

The company consolidated all administrative functions associated with new business processing into a single unit called Group Case Installation and Administration (GCIA). This consolidation eliminated redundant activities, realized economies in technical expertise, and brought authority and responsibility for case installation under a single manager. It was accompanied by a service quality improvement initiative that encouraged employees to become customer-oriented and that established performance standards for them to meet. By themselves, however, these moves cut case installation time by only 2 percent.

Creation of Case Managers

The company created what it calls new business coordinators (NBCs) that report to the executive in charge of Group Case Installation and Administration. The company assigns each new large case to a particular new business coordinator, who becomes responsible for the case and for ensuring that case-specific time standards are met. NBCs make sure all case information necessary to processing is assembled, and they coordinate the work flow of various specialists who perform specific process functions. On the organization chart, the NBCs appear as peers to these specialists, who also report to the head of Group Case Installation and Administration. The creation of NBCs cut case installation time by only two weeks.

Business Process Reengineering

The company reengineered the case installation business process and, in so doing, cut case installation time in half, a significantly greater improvement than it achieved through functional consolidation or the creation of the

Insight 20-2 Reengineering at General American Life (continued)

case manager position. Under the old process, the company's field force submitted sold case information to the underwriter for risk assessment and approval. Because the underwriters were not concerned about the information needs of other administrative functions, each functional area that received the case after the underwriter often received a case that was already several weeks old and missing key information. To get this information, these functional areas would bombard field offices with requests. One functional area might request the same information another area would request. This practice caused major time delays, annoyed the field force, and generated errors. Business process reengineering resulted in the creation of a new critical path for work and cut the case installation time by nine weeks. Under the new approach, the field submits sold case information directly to a new business coordinator assigned to handle cases from it. The NBC then examines the case for missing data and supplies information needed by all functional areas (contracts, administration, claims, underwriting, etc.). When all of the information is complete, the NBC releases the case to all functional areas, which then perform process steps concurrently—instead of sequentially as they had done before.

Systems Development

General American designed a new case management tracking system, run on a mainframe computer and accessed by terminal, to support its reengineered case installation process. When the new case arrives, it is entered into the system. The system assigns case-specific deadlines for deliverables and generates summary progress reports for new business coordinators. In 1993, the company introduced a PC-based electronic mail system called LINK that allows field offices to submit new cases electronically.

Source: *Lawrence K. Connor, "Case Study of Time-Based Competition,"* Reengineering the Life Insurance Company: Integrating Technology, People, and Work *(Atlanta, GA: LOMA, 1994), p. 91.*

his part of a process, he hands it off to Employee B, who does her part and hands it off to Employee C. Often, employees from more than one department are involved in a single process. Each hand-off increases the time required to complete the process. One goal of reengineering is to involve as few employees as possible in a process.

- *Unnecessary process steps.* Many processes include steps that contribute no value for the customer. In other words, from a customer's perspective, these steps do not improve the quality of the product or service. Conducting file searches and obtaining approvals for routine transactions that could be better handled at lower organizational levels are examples of steps in a process that add no value. Reengineering attempts to reduce or remove non-essential steps.

- *High error rates.* An inefficient and ineffective process often causes errors in the performance of the process. For example, the more steps in a process, the more likely that an error will be made during one of those steps. When errors occur, the insurer must devote time and resources to correcting the errors. Reengineering seeks to reduce error rates.

- *Slack time in the process.* Slack time results when a process is halted because an action that needs to be taken cannot be performed promptly. For example, a company policy might dictate that one step may not be started until another step is completed. If the first step is delayed, the second step (and all subsequent steps) will be delayed as well, producing slack time. Reengineering attempts to remove slack time in processes.

Results of Reengineering

To eliminate process inefficiencies, insurers often need to introduce new work processes, expanded training, enhanced information systems support, and changes in organizational structure.

After reengineering, insurance company employees generally find that they have greater responsibilities at work. Instead of being asked to perform one or two steps in a process, employees may be asked to complete most or all of the steps in a process. Generally, employees also must make more decisions than before. In order to fulfill their new responsibilities, the employees generally need additional training, and access to enhanced information systems. Though employees are uncomfortable with the changed nature of their work, many enjoy their new-found autonomy and responsibility.

Reengineering may require changes in an insurer's organizational structure. In particular, because front-line employees are entrusted with greater decision-making responsibilities, a number of supervisory positions are no longer needed. Thus, reengineering often leads to a flatter organizational structure. In addition, because process activities are redesigned and streamlined, some employees who used to perform obsolete processes are no longer needed. In such situations, insurers must decide whether to reassign or release these employees.

Reengineering can also involve launching a continuous process improvement program. Like reengineering, ***continuous process improvement*** involves the analysis and redesign of a company's work processes. Unlike reengineering, continuous process improvement requires analyzing only one or a few processes at a time. Continuous process improvement also requires analyzing the same processes repeatedly: after a process has been redesigned, the new process should later be analyzed to ensure its continued suitability in changing circumstances.

Outsourcing

Outsourcing is another example of an approach for reducing expenses, as well as for concentrating on core competencies. ***Outsourcing*** is the practice of hiring an outside vendor to perform a business function. Examples of functions that insurers have outsourced are

- Information systems (IS)
- Investment management
- Administrative services
- Distribution of products
- Manufacture of products

The main benefit to be derived from outsourcing is cost savings. In many cases, an insurer can pay less for an outside organization to perform a function than the insurer would pay for performing the function itself. In such situations, outsourcing makes economic sense. A vendor may be able to perform a function more cheaply than the insurer if the vendor

- Specializes in a specific function and has greater expertise in that function than does the insurer
- Can achieve economies of scale in its area of specialization because the vendor does a greater amount of such work than does the insurer

Either or both of these factors can help the vendor to perform such functions at lower cost than could the insurer.

Sometimes, rather than outsourcing, an insurer may want to sell its services to outside organizations. If an insurer has excess capacity and strong expertise in a given area, and if its own business volume permits, it makes sense for the insurer to sell its services to other organizations.

Benefits of Outsourcing

A reduction in expenses is only one possible advantage of outsourcing. Other benefits insurers often seek from outsourcing include the following:

- *Improved service.* An outside organization with considerable expertise in a certain area should be able to provide superior customer service in that area. Plus, an insurer can change vendors if the service is unsatisfactory.
- *Access to new technologies.* A specialized provider generally has access to emerging technologies that can improve operations in its specialization.
- *Greater organizational flexibility.* Outsourcing can simplify an organization's structure.
- *Greater emphasis on core competencies.* Outsourcing can allow an organization to devote more of its efforts and resources to its

core competencies—those functions that are most crucial to the organization's success. We discuss the relationship between outsourcing and core competencies later in this chapter.

- *More effective use of capital.* When a company outsources a function, capital that would have been required to fund an internal unit can be deployed for other, more profitable uses.

Drawbacks to Outsourcing

Use of outsourcing also presents some potential drawbacks, such as the following:

- *Diminished control.* A company typically loses some control over a process that is outsourced. An outside vendor may not always act in the same manner as the company that hired it.
- *Drain of expertise.* Outsourcing may deprive an organization of expertise that is important to the management of the organization. For example, if an organization outsources its information systems (IS) functions, then the company loses IS resources that would be valuable for other purposes, such as strategic planning.
- *Limited vendor understanding of the organization's business.* A vendor may lack important knowledge of the outsourcing organization's operations. For example, if an insurer outsources IS, the vendor needs to have a certain level of understanding of insurance and of the insurer's specific situation. To address this drawback, the insurer can transfer out some of its employees to the vendor.

New Approaches to Distribution

In this section, we discuss some methods of reducing expenses within the context of the traditional agent/broker system. Then we discuss alternative approaches to distribution. In some situations, insurers are exploring these alternatives in an effort to reduce distribution expenses. In other situations, insurers are exploring these alternatives in order to reach additional segments of the market and thus to expand their revenue base.

Modifying the Agency System

Many insurers have concluded that, to compete effectively in the evolving marketplace, they need to reduce the cost and increase the effectiveness of their distribution systems. Insurers wishing to modify their distribution systems can either make changes within the agency system or develop additional distribution channels. One typical approach to changing the agency system is modifying the traditional mode of agent compensation.

Levelized Commissions and Other Approaches to Modifying Agent Compensation

The most talked-about approach to modifying agent compensation is through the use of *levelized commissions.* Traditional commission schedules—sometimes known as *front-loaded commissions*—feature high first-year commissions and relatively low renewal commissions. For example, a traditional life insurance commission schedule might pay the agent 90 percent of the policy's annual premium in Year 1, and 3 percent in all subsequent years that the policy remains in force. By contrast, a ***levelized commission schedule*** pays a smaller first-year commission and more substantial renewal commissions. For example, a typical levelized commission schedule for life insurance might pay a 15 percent commission for 10 years, followed by 2 percent for the remainder of the life of the policy.

ExecuView Application 20-1 illustrates the effect that a switch to levelized commissions might have on the cash flows generated by a life insurance product.

Proponents claim that levelized commissions benefit all parties involved in the insurance purchase. Customers can benefit from high renewal commissions, which encourage the agent to provide quality customer service after the sale. The increased emphasis on renewal commissions also increases the incentive for an agent to keep the business on the books, which benefits the insurance company. Persistent business is typically more profitable business. Levelized commissions can benefit an insurer's expense profile because insurers are relieved of the burden of paying high first-year commissions, which reduces first-year surplus strain. In addition, because of the steady and higher commission rates that they typically pay in later years, levelized commissions are likely to increase the length of time that agents remain with an insurer. Better agent retention reduces an insurer's costs of recruiting and training new agents, which are often substantial.

Proponents of levelized commissions also claim advantages for agents. Levelized commissions can be designed so that they are actuarially equivalent, or actuarially more valuable, than front-loaded commissions. In other words, the present value of the levelized commissions, taking into account forecasted withdrawal rates, is equal to or greater than the present value of front-loaded commissions. In addition, levelized commissions can provide agents with a more stable and predictable income stream than can front-loaded commissions.

Nonetheless, many agents oppose levelized commissions for the following reasons:

Application 20-1 Levelized Commission Rates

Start *ExecuView* and select the Whole Life Model. Be sure to select *Reset, All Models* from the Action menu to return *ExecuView* to its default settings. The default values for this model are shown on the following *ExecuView* screen.

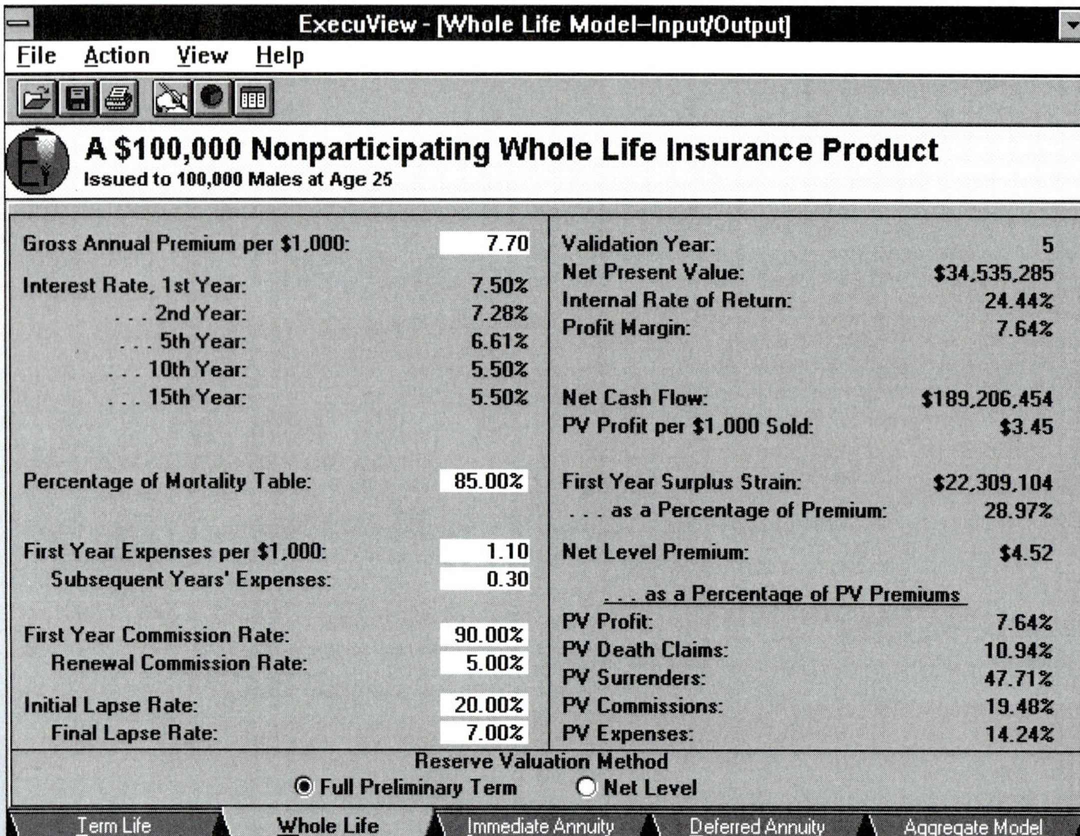

The EV Life Insurance Company is considering of introducing levelized commissions to one of its whole life products. By doing so, EV Life hopes to reduce its acquisition costs and retain more of its agents, and, as a consequence, more of its customers. However, EV Life will not introduce levelized commissions if doing so would significantly decrease either agent compensation or profitability.

The whole life product EV Life currently offers a first year commission of 90 percent of premium and renewal commissions of 5 percent of premium per year. Under this commission schedule, EV pays as commissions 19.48 percent of all premiums collected and earns a profit margin of 7.64 percent. To see how a different commission schedule would affect total agent compensation and profitability, EV Life tries several scenarios on its asset-share model. EV Life's actuaries have recommended changing the first year commission to 25 percent of premium and renewal commissions to 15 percent of premium, changes they estimate will result in 2 percent fewer lapses throughout the life of this product.

(*continued on next page*)

Application 20-1 Levelized Commission Rates (continued)

➤ Change the *First Year Commission Rate* to 25%. Change the *Renewal Commission Rate* to 15%. Change the *Initial Lapse Rate* to *18%,* and the *Final Lapse Rate* to 5%. Press <enter> to view the results of these changes.

The asset-share model indicates that this commission schedule results in reduced compensation for EV's agents. The graphs below show that, using this particular schedule, commission expenses have been reduced to approximately 16.5 percent of premiums collected.

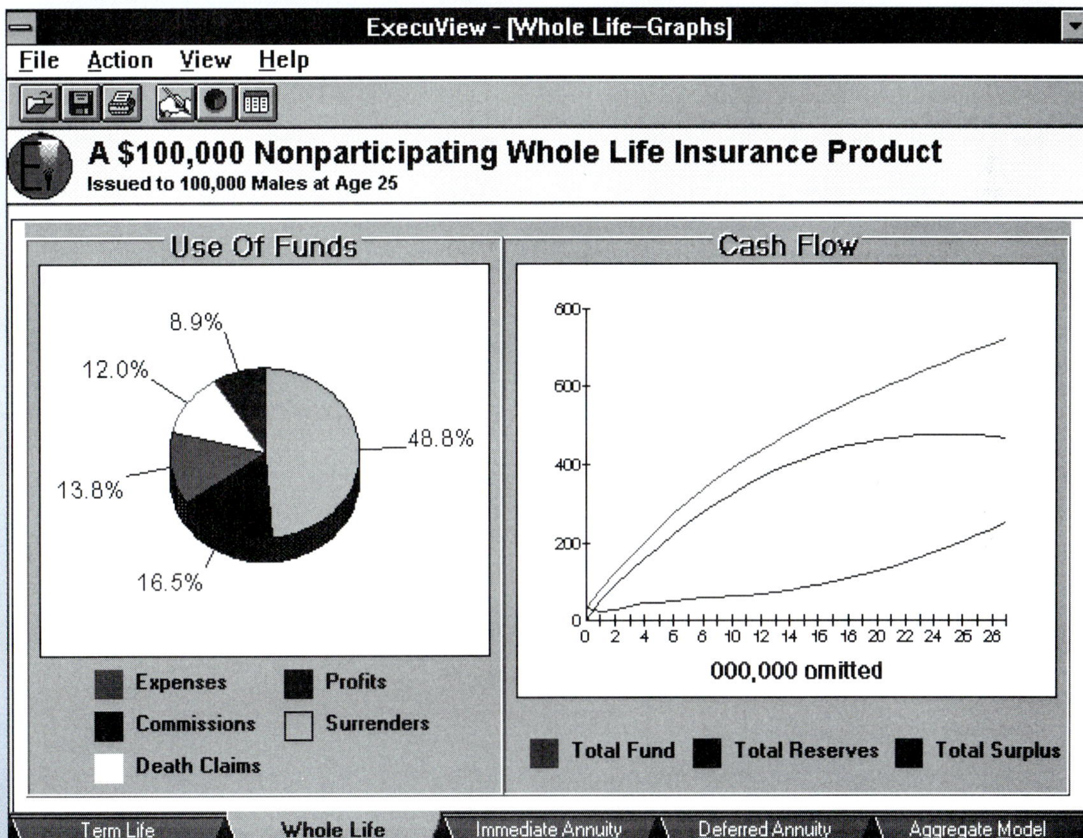

If EV Life wants to keep its sales force satisfied, it needs to offer higher commission rates on this product. This time, EV Life's actuarial staff recommends a first year rate of 30 percent and a renewal rate of 18 percent.

➤ Change the *First Year Commission Rate* to 30%. Change the *Renewal Commission Rate* to 18%. Press <enter> to view the results of these changes.

(*continued on next page*)

Application 20-1 Levelized Commission Rates (continued)

The result of this latest commission schedule is a product that pays 19.77 percent of premiums collected as commissions, almost precisely the percentage paid out under EV Life's current, non-levelized commission schedule. The levelized commission rates cause a slight reduction in the profitability of the product, but EV Life has decided to accept the smaller profit margin in return for the reduction in risk it achieves by reducing its acquisition costs. The *ExecuView* screen below summarizes the performance of this whole life product in EV Life's asset-share model.

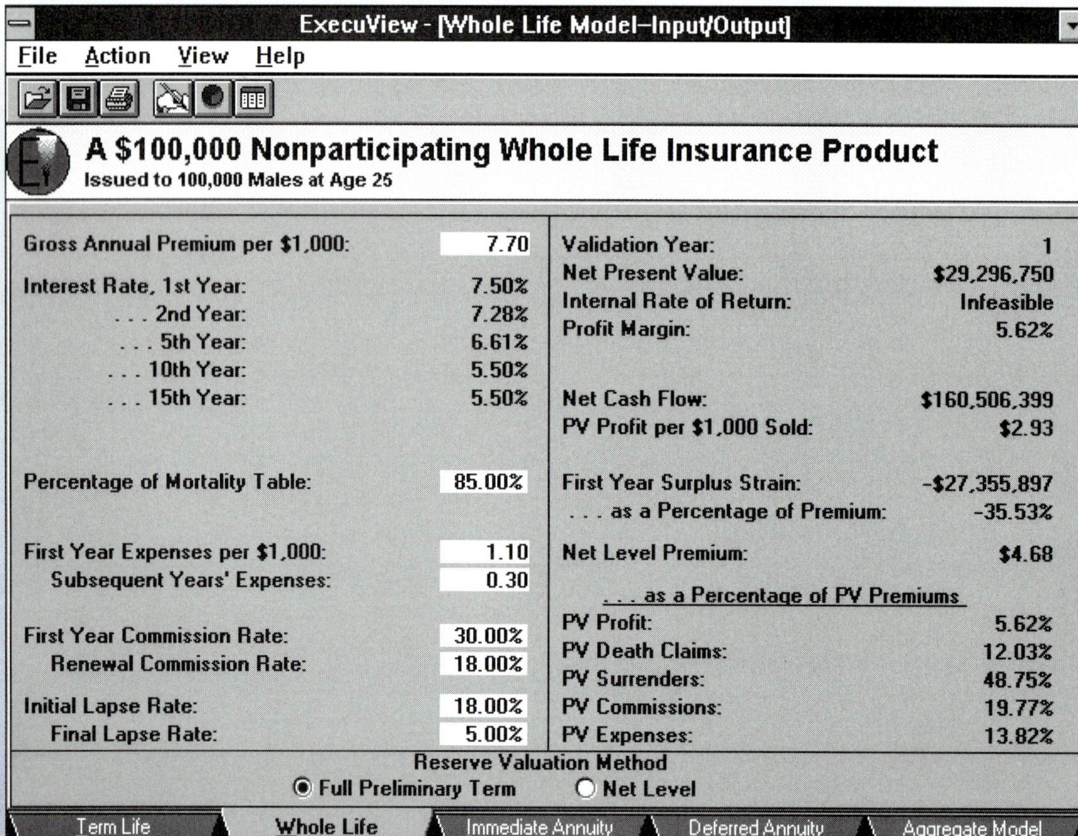

Note that, under the new commission schedule, the IRR is "infeasible." The reason for this change is that the product's acquisition costs are so low as a result of the levelized commission schedule that the product does not experience a loss in its first year. Recall from Chapter 6 that, unless there is a loss in at least one year, it is impossible to calculate an IRR. The fact that the product does not experience a loss in its first year is also reflected in the product's surplus strain, which is *negative* $26,173,398 under the levelized schedule. A negative surplus strain indicates that the product begins to earn a profit in its first policy year.

- Many agents expect levelized commissions not simply to restructure agent compensation, but to reduce it.
- Most of an agent's product-related expenses occur during the year in which the product is sold.
- If a policy lapses early or the insured dies in the early years of the policy, the agent's compensation would be considerably reduced under a levelized commission schedule, even though the agent may have expended considerable time, money, and effort making the sale.
- New agents, without additional financial support, would probably have a difficult time earning an acceptable living on levelized commissions. New agents lack an established book of business generating renewal commissions and, under levelized compensation, would earn smaller first-year commissions.

Because of agent skepticism, and because the majority of insurers continue to employ traditional commission schedules, an insurer contemplating a switch to levelized commissions face the following possibilities:

- Are agent-brokers likely to stop distributing that insurer's products if it switches to levelized commissions?
- Are the insurer's efforts to recruit agents likely to become more difficult under levelized commissions?
- Will career agents begin to leave the company to work for other insurers if the company switches to levelized commissions?

Although the subject is frequently discussed, only a few insurers in the United States and Canada have adopted a levelized commission schedule. Those that do most often use a levelized commission schedule for some products and a traditional commission schedule for other products. For example, an insurer may use a levelized commission schedule for term products but a traditional schedule for whole life products. Insight 20-3 tells of one insurer's early results with a levelized commission schedule.

In addition to levelized commissions, insurers use several other alternatives to the traditional compensation structure. Several of these alternatives are summarized in Figure 20-1.

Alternatives to the Agency System

Rather than modifying their agency distribution channel, a few insurers are replacing, and many others are supplementing, their tradi-

Insight 20-3 Prudential Edges toward Level Commissions with Launch of New Universal Life Insurer

Prudential Insurance Co. of America's decision to form a universal life subsidiary marks a departure from traditional commission structures and shows where the insurer sees its future growth.

The new company, Prudential Select Life Insurance Co. of America, is expected to complement Prudential's existing brokerage operations by offering universal life policies, which aren't otherwise available through the company.

Universal life, which accounts for about 35 percent of the sales in the life industry, represents a significant growth area for Prudential.

Prudential Select Life, a Minnesota-based company capitalized at $30 million, will cater to the upscale brokerage market. It is introducing four universal life products: a term alternative universal life policy, a cash accumulation universal life policy, a last survivor universal life policy, and a first-to-die life policy.

All four products are also unusual in that Prudential Select Life is paying levelized commissions for the first 10 years of the policy. Levelized commissions have been gaining acceptance among insurance companies as a way to avoid encouraging their agents to replace policies. Most other life insurance policies pay hefty commissions up front, which tail off significantly in succeeding years. This traditional structure has been faulted for encouraging agents to replace old policies with new ones to increase their commissions, a practice known as churning.

Ira Kleinman, Prudential Select Life's president and chief executive officer, said, "These products offer several significant advantages. They are designed specifically for the high-end market with a minimum of $1 million face amount. . . . They offer up to $30 million single life maximum face amount and $50 million survivorship-maximum subject to Prudential aggregate maximums and age/rating limits. They also will be issued to people up to 85 years old."

Kleinman said Prudential Select Life expects to write about 1,000 policies at an average premium of $21,000 in its first year, which equates to revenue of about $21 million. It also has a ten-year goal of $100 million.

Under the levelized commission structure, Kleinman said Prudential Select Life's policies will pay a 15 percent commission in the first through tenth years and 2 percent after that, along with an up-front expense reimbursement allowance. Prudential's usual commission structure pays as much as a 50 percent commission in the first year and much less in succeeding years.

The new commission structure was driven by market forces rather than compliance issues, Kleinman said. Over the past few years, regulators increasingly have targeted insurers and their agents for alleged churning.

Kleinman said a level commission structure is more appropriate for the upscale market, which Prudential Select Life is targeting, than for the middle market. He said products sold to the middle market are less complicated and don't require the same level of sophistication of service by producers. Prudential Select Life, through its level commissions and expense reimbursement allowance, recognizes the importance of its producers' cooperation with clients' financial and legal advisers, he said.

The level commission structure also will put Prudential in a position to meet possible commission disclosure requirements in the future, Kleinman said.

Source: *Dan Lonkevich, "Prudential Edges toward Level Commissions with Launch of New Universal Life Insurer,"* BestWeek, *Life/Health Edition, October 16, 1995, p.1. Reprinted by permission of the publisher.*

tional agency business with other distribution channels. In cultivating these alternative distribution channels, insurers are seeking either reduced distribution expenses, increased revenues by reaching untapped market segments, or both. The alternative distribution channels we discuss are banks, direct marketing, interactive electronic media, worksite marketing, and fee-based financial planners.

Figure 20-1. Additional alternative modes of compensation.

- **Persistency bonuses.** Agents receive a bonus based on the persistency of the business they sell.
- **Profit-sharing and stock ownership plans.** Agents share in the success of the insurer by earning stock as part of their compensation.
- **Deferred commission.** A portion of the agent's commission is deferred until the agent's retirement, or until vested.
- **Reduced commissions on replacements or internal replacements.** Reduced commissions on either internal replacements or all replacements discourage churning (an agent's unnecessary replacement of insurance products in order to earn new first-year commissions) and encourage agents to sell more profitable non-replacement business.
- **Trailers.** A trailer is a percentage of the assets under the insurer's management. For annuities, some insurers are replacing all or part of the front-end commission with a trailer. Thus, if an insurer pays a 1 percent yearly trailer, and a customer has $100,000 in a variable annuity in a given year, then the agent receives a $1,000 trailer. The trailer is paid yearly as long as the insurer holds the customer's funds.

Bank Distribution

Many insurers see banks as an attractive distribution system. Bank distribution is generally less expensive than agent distribution. Although insurers generally pay banks commissions similar to those they pay agents, with bank distribution the insurer is relieved of the expenses of agent recruiting and training and of the concerns of agent retention. Bank customers represent a sizable market, and banks generally already possess the customer information they need to target specific markets. In addition, banks help insurers reach certain middle-income consumers who may not currently be well served by the agency system.

Direct Marketing

Direct response marketing is the sale of products through direct contact between the customer and the company selling the product. Direct marketing cuts out the distributor's role; no commissioned agents or brokers are used in the direct marketing of insurance products. If sales staff are needed, they are usually paid significantly less than an insurer would pay to an agent or broker. Common media for direct marketing include the mail, print and broadcast advertising, and telephone solicitation. Direct marketing is potentially a lower-cost method of distributing certain products, and is primarily used to market simple, easy-to-understand coverages.

A number of insurers distribute their products entirely through direct marketing rather than through agents. Some insurers who market primarily through an agency force have diversified into direct marketing for certain products in order to compete with direct marketing insurers and other low-cost providers. However, most such insurers still rely on agents for the majority of their revenues, and must be careful not to antagonize agents by putting their direct marketing operations into competition with their agency force.

Electronic Distribution

A number of insurers and insurance brokers are beginning to explore marketing products through various new interactive electronic media, including the Internet, electronic kiosks, and interactive television. For insurers who market directly through these channels, electronic distribution offers a potential lower-cost distribution method. Electronic distribution also offers the possibility of enhancing revenues by reaching customers that might not otherwise be reached.

The *Internet* is a vast electronic network that can be accessed from a personal computer over an ordinary telephone line. People and businesses place information on the Internet, and those who wish to access that information need simply find the appropriate electronic address. Both the quantity of information available on the Internet and the number of people with access to the Internet are growing exponentially. Insurance companies and insurance agents and brokers have begun using the Internet to provide consumers with policy applications and thus to make sales. Others are using Internet sites to identify potential customers who may then be contacted by agents or brokers. The full marketing potential of the Internet is still emerging. The near future will likely see the development of huge electronic markets where customers can select from the products of many different insurance companies all in a single electronic forum.[4] Insight 20-4 tells of an insurance brokerage service that operates over the Internet.

Electronic kiosks are unstaffed stations that provide customers with an electronic means to interact with and sometimes see and talk to sales representatives who are in another location. The salesperson can send the customer information or an electronic or paper application, and the customer can send a signed paper copy of the application back to the salesperson or insurance company.

Interactive television is an emerging technology that permits people to communicate with remote sites through their television sets. One predicted application of interactive television is immediate response to television commercial messages. Interactive television may be an effective channel for insurance distribution in the future.

Worksite Marketing

Worksite marketing is the marketing of insurance products to people at their place of work. The cooperation of employers is required before any

Insight 20-4 Real-Time Access to Personalized Insurance Quotes

Real-time access to personalized quotes showing the best buys in term life and fixed annuity products is available to insurance producers and consumers alike via a new service on the Internet created by a Nevada insurance agent.

The service, called QuickQuote, debuted last spring with a home page on the Internet's World Wide Web, said Daniel P. Wager, president and founder of QuickQuote Insurance Agency Inc. in Incline Village, Nevada.

Initially, requests for quotes were fulfilled manually via e-mail from the agency to Internet shoppers, he said, adding that instantaneous quotes on the shopper's computer screen began in mid-July for term and mid-August for fixed annuities.

Currently, Mr. Wager said about 180 term life carriers are in QuickQuote's database.

He said another 22 term carriers will be added over the next couple of months.

All term insurers are rated A– or better by A.M. Best Co. and the 60 fixed annuity writers in the QuickQuote database are all rated A+ by A.M. Best, said Mr. Wager.

That number may be expanded in the future by including annuity writers with Best rating of A and A–, he said.

Mr. Wager said QuickQuote Insurance agency has either general agent or managing general agent contracts with all insurers that participate in QuickQuote.

Independent agents who aren't appointed with all the carriers on the service "can become appointed through us by becoming a member of the QuickQuote Preferred Network," he said.

Mike Loffa, executive vice president at Midland Life (formerly Midland Mutual Life), told the National Underwriter that being on QuickQuote "gives us the opportunity to expand our product delivery to another group of clients."

Mr. Loffa said, "We think there's a significant number of people who prefer to shop for insurance through the Internet or other electronic malls rather than the more traditional channels."

He said since QuickQuote is so new, no data is available on the number of policies Midland Life may have sold through the electronic service.

Activity on the Internet quote service, said Mr. Wager, is running about 1,500 "hits" per day.

Of that number, he said, "about 500 people are actually requesting quotes."

Mr. Wager said, "completed sales are running at about 2 percent of quotes requested."

The biggest sale so far has been a term policy with a face amount of $750,000, he said.

Anyone with access to the World Wide Web can reach the service by pointing their browsers to http://www.quickquote.com, he said.

A shopper who logs onto the QuickQuote home page and requests either a term or annuity quote fills out a brief questionnaire and the five least expensive term products or the five best-performing annuities pop onto the screen.

The questionnaire asks for basic underwriting data such as name, age, height, weight, smoking habits, etc., said Mr. Wager.

If the shopper decides to make a purchase, he said, "all they do is highlight the company shown at the bottom of the quote report, click, and an insurance application comes to the screen."

The app is filled out directly on the shopper's computer screen, and when completed "the consumer hits a button and the application is electronically sent to QuickQuote Insurance Agency," said Mr. Wager.

At that point, if a medical workup is necessary the app is electronically routed to a paramedical company in the consumer's area which e-mails the applicant to set up an appointment.

The paramedical firm sends the results of the medical examination directly to the carrier, said Mr. Wager.

The electronic application acquired over the Internet is immediately printed out at the agency and sent to the consumer for their signature, he said, noting that electronic apps are not permitted by state insurance regulators.

The signed app is picked up by the paramedical firm which "routes it back to the agency which forwards it directly to the insurance carrier," said Mr. Wager.

While anyone with Internet access can reach QuickQuote's home page, Mr. Wager said his agency can only "transact business in states where it is licensed."

The agency has applied for approval in all states, and has so far been licensed in 30, he said, adding, "We expect to be able to do business in the rest by the end of September."

Source: *David C. Jones, "Real-Time Access to Personalized Insurance Quotes." Reprinted with permission from* National Underwriter, *copyright © 1996, The National Underwriter Company* Life & Health/Financial Services Edition, *September 4, 1995, p. 14.*

such worksite marketing efforts may begin. Employees are free to accept or decline the offered products, and the employees typically must pay all or, when employer contributions are involved at least part of the product's premium. The products are generally sold on either a guaranteed-issue or simplified underwriting basis, and premiums are often deducted from the employee's paycheck. This form of distribution is used for all types of life insurance, hospital indemnity insurance, short- and long-term disability insurance, dental insurance, vision care insurance, dread disease insurance, and some annuity products.

Depending on the insurer, products sold under a worksite marketing arrangement may be priced on a group or an individual basis. In most situations, products sold through worksite marketing supplement the employee benefits already offered by the employer. An employer typically enters into a worksite marketing arrangement because it allows the employer to offer additional benefits to employees at little cost to the employer. Many employees appreciate the convenience associated with purchasing and paying for such products through payroll deductions.

Many insurers believe worksite marketing has the potential to increase revenues by providing access to middle- and lower-income markets. In addition, worksite marketing has the potential to reduce an insurer's expenses per policy sold by spreading out marketing expenses over a number of policies.

Distribution through Fee-Based Financial Planners and Consultants

A number of financial planners, consultants, and accountants provide financial advice to customers in return for a fee based on the amount of time the planner spends working for the customer. Customers are responsible for paying this fee regardless of whether they purchase the recommended product; the consultants are not permitted to receive compensation from the business that issues the product.

Some insurers have designed products for distribution through this type of planner. Most of the products insurers sell through fee-based planners are unbundled products, such as universal life and fixed and variable annuities. Because the planners do not receive commissions, the products are generally low-load products. ***Low-load products*** are those whose front-end loads or other expense charges are relatively small.

Fee-based planners are another distribution alternative that allows insurers to keep distribution costs low and to offer competitive products. However, to avoid distribution conflict, insurers that rely primarily on agency distribution generally must avoid putting their low-load products in direct competition with their agent-sold products.

Mergers and Consolidations

One of the more notable responses by insurance companies to changes in the business environment within the past ten years has been an increase in the number of insurance company mergers and consolidations. We discussed mergers and consolidations in detail in Chapter 19. This section discusses two factors that drive insurance-industry consolidation: (1) the desire to reduce costs through improved administrative efficiency and (2) the need to increase revenues.

Reducing Costs through Economies of Scale

We have already discussed that a large scale of operations is important in the life and health insurance industry. One way an insurer can quickly increase its size so that it can achieve economies of scale is by merging or consolidating with another company.

Economies of scale are cost efficiencies that can be achieved in large-scale operations. ***Cost efficiencies*** refers to an organization's reducing its unit costs by spending less money to achieve a specified level of production. A ***unit cost*** can be defined as the incurred expense that can be attributed to a single measured unit of work. A unit cost can be calculated as follows:

$$\text{Unit Cost} = \frac{\text{Fixed Costs} + (\text{Total Variable Costs})}{\text{Number of Units}}$$

Fixed costs are those costs incurred regardless of the number of units produced or processed. ***Total variable costs,*** which equal variable cost per unit times the number of units produced, are those costs that can be directly attributed to the production or processing of the units produced. Economies of scale reduce unit costs by increasing the number of units processed. As the number of units increases, total variable costs will increase, but fixed costs remain unchanged, and unit costs decrease.

For example, suppose the Sandhill Insurance Company issues 500 disability insurance policies per month. Fixed costs are \$2,000 per month, and variable cost per policy issued is \$15. We can calculate the unit cost of each disability policy that Sandhill issues as follows:

$$\textbf{Unit Cost} = \frac{\$2{,}000 + (\$15 \times 500)}{500}$$

$$\textbf{Unit Cost} = \$19$$

If Sandhill were able to issue 1,000 policies per month, its unit costs would decrease as follows:

$$\textbf{Unit Cost} = \frac{\$2{,}000 + (\$15 \times 1{,}000)}{1{,}000}$$

$$\textbf{Unit Cost} = \$17$$

Although there are limits to economies of increasing scale, economies of scale exist as long as an increase in output causes the unit cost to decrease. Another possibility is *diseconomies of scale,* in which an increase in output causes unit costs to increase. Sandhill could experience diseconomies of scale by continuing to increase the number of polices it issues to the point at which employees are so overwhelmed with policy issues that efficiency actually decreased.

When mergers and consolidations take place, fixed costs generally increase, though unit costs can often be reduced. For example, a merger might cause a doubling of fixed costs, but a tripling of the number of units produced or processed. In general, we can identify two types of cost efficiencies that help to contain costs in a merged or consolidated insurance company: (1) operating and administrative efficiencies and (2) financial efficiencies.

For insurers, two readily observable sources of *operating* efficiencies that can be gained from a merger are: (1) the experience and expertise of the employees of the acquired or acquiring company and (2) the strength of the pooled technological resources of the two companies. Sources of *financial* efficiencies resulting from a merger can include (1) access to quantity discounts on purchases because of the increased scale of operations and (2) improved terms—such as lower brokerage fees and higher rates of return—on investments because of the increase in the amount of money and assets under management. The types of efficiencies that insurers can gain from mergers and consolidations are summarized in Figure 20-2.

Increasing Revenues through Mergers

An insurance company that wants to enter a new market—for example, in another state or in another country—may wish to do so by

Figure 20-2. Efficiencies from economies of scale.

Operating efficiencies	Financial efficiencies
• Gains from pooling employees' expertise • Gains from pooling technology	• Access to quantity discounts • Access to improved investment terms

merging with or acquiring a company already established in that market. Similarly, an insurer wishing to offer a product with which it has no experience may decide to merge with an insurer that already offers the product. Entering new markets and offering new products through mergers can help insurers avoid many of the costs of product design and implementation. Moreover, after a merger, a company can often attract a great deal of new business. The following list describes a number of reasons that newly merged corporations attract new business and generate additional revenue:

- Merged companies can cross-sell their products to each other's customers.
- Combining the products or markets of one company with the marketing and distribution capacity of another company can generate an increase market share.
- Mergers can generate public interest and thus build name recognition among potential insurance buyers.
- Customers, employees, providers, and distributors are generally attracted to large and growing companies.

Improving Profitability by Leveraging Technology

Many insurers are improving their profitability by taking advantage of the technological innovations that characterize the modern business environment. Some benefits of applying technological innovation to an insurer's business operations are familiar to most of us. For example, the use of technology to reduce costs and improve customer service has been well-documented in many publications. In recent years, insurers who invested heavily in new technologies have found that, in order to realize cost savings from their new technological capabilities, they need to increase their volume of business.

Excess Capacity

Technology is credited with driving a number of mergers and acquisitions because of the excess capacity possessed by a number of insurers. When an insurer invests in technological improvements, these improvements often increase the insurer's fixed costs. Upon increasing its fixed costs, then, in order to realize potential cost savings from the investment, the insurer needs to increase the volume (the number of units) of business handled by the new technology so that its unit costs will decrease. When an insurer's fixed costs are high and the insurer needs to increase the volume of its business to reduce its unit costs, the insurer is said to have excess capacity.

We saw in the previous section how an increase in the number of units processed or produced can reduce unit costs. Many insurers with excess capacity are turning to mergers in order to increase the volume of business processed by their systems and thus realize potential cost savings. An insurer that has invested a significant portion of its capital in technology might do well to merge with an insurer that has not yet improved its systems.

As we noted in our discussion of outsourcing, one way to absorb excess capacity is to sell the use of that capacity to an external organization. Some insurers with excess capacity in a particular functional area are also serving as outsource providers to other companies. Such arrangements help both the outsourcing company and the company taking on the outsourced work. A company with excess capacity is able to lower its unit costs by more fully utilizing its operational capabilities.

Another way insurers put excess capacity to work is by assuming reinsurance. The assumption of reinsurance as a means of profiting from excess capacity is discussed in Chapter 14.

Combating Fraud

One approach insurers are taking to reduce expenses is to vigorously combat fraud. Health care fraud alone is estimated to cost $100 billion a year in the United States, or 10 percent of the nation's total health care expenditure.[5] Fraud is also common with life insurance and annuities. By successfully combating fraud, insurers can decrease unnecessary expenses.

Fraud can be perpetrated by parties both internal and external to the insurance company. The sources of internal fraud include the insurer's employees and agents. Common types of agent and employee fraud include the following:

- Submission or approval of fictitious policies, or policies that have not been authorized by the supposed customer
- Approval of fictitious claims
- Theft of payments that the customer intends to pay to the insurer
- Theft of policy values the insurer intends to pay to the customer

External perpetrators of life and health insurance fraud include insureds, health care providers, and third party administrators (TPAs).

Fraud by insureds usually takes the form of claims submitted for feigned or non-existent injuries or illnesses, and in some extreme cases, can take the form of claims submitted for deaths that did not occur. Fraud by health care providers generally involves providers seeking reimbursement for unnecessary services or services that were never provided, overcharging for services provided, or charging higher rates for insured patients than for uninsured patients. TPA fraud occurs when a third party administrator provides false information and/or incorrect reimbursement to an insurer or customer.

In January 1994, the Coalition Against Insurance Fraud recommended that the U.S. government combat insurance fraud by tightening statutes and regulations, stiffening penalties, and establishing state offices to combat insurance fraud. In the meantime, many insurers are taking their own measures to detect and combat fraud. Figure 20-3, taken from a 1994 LOMA survey, lists 27 anti-fraud controls used by 78 insurers.

In addition, some insurers are implementing extensive and innovative programs designed to identify instances of fraud, particularly provider fraud. Many of these programs make use of sophisticated forms of expert systems and artificial intelligence software. Provider fraud is most commonly associated with health insurance claims; insurance companies and government programs, such as Medicare, have been faced with damaging amounts of fraudulent claims submitted by dishonest practitioners. Insight 20-5 tells of one program to identify and halt such abuses.

Achieving Revenue Growth by Focusing on Core Competencies

Management theorists Gary Hamel and C.K. Prahalad recently published a book—*Competing for the Future*—that presents a revenue-based approach to improving profitability. Hamel and Prahalad have been joined by a host of other theorists who suggest that businesses can best achieve revenue growth by identifying and leveraging their core competencies in pursuit of their strategic intent. In discussing these ideas, we first address the subject of strategic intent and then that of core competencies. Finally, we discuss some of the management implications for insurance companies of organizing strategy around their core competencies.

Strategic Intent

A company's ***strategic intent*** is a brief, precise, ambitious, and motivational expression of the company's long-term corporate goal or reason

Figure 20-3. Controls insurers use to combat fraud.*

1. Agents not allowed to use company name on personal or business checking account (55 installed).
2. Permanent audit trail record for each critical policy transaction—including identification of individual who entered the transaction into the system (54 installed, 7 plan).
3. Confirmations to all clients of agent(s) suspected of wrong-doing or fraud (50 installed, 1 plan).
4. Background checks on prospective agents (49 installed, 4 plan).
5. Formal written policy on fraud that identifies when and to whom to report questionable activities (45 installed, 14 plan).
6. Prohibition of agent's check as payment for client's policies (42 installed, 4 plan).
7. Wording on application in bold letters instructing applicant to make checks payable to the company only (39 installed).
8. Confirmation to policyholder whenever payout checks are sent to someone other than the policyholder (39 installed, 1 plan).
9. Random confirmation for established policies (35 installed, 1 plan).
10. Program to monitor premium payments from agents for client's policies (32 installed, 1 plan).
11. Investigate undeliverable mail sent to new policyholders to identify possible fictitious policies (29 installed, 1 plan).
12. Review endorsement on disbursement checks (28 installed, 1 plan).
13. Background check on prospective home office employees (27 installed, 1 plan).
14. Fraud awareness presentations for employees (27 installed, 12 plan).
15. Random confirmations for newly issued policies (25 installed, 6 plan).
16. Fraud awareness presentations for field management (25 installed, 11 plan).
17. Review for and follow-up of agent dishonored payment checks (21 installed, 1 plan).
18. Confirmation to old address when address change is followed by withdrawal of policy values (i.e., loans or surrenders) within *x* days after address change (19 installed, 9 plan).
19. Confirmation if policy values are used to pay premium for new policy (18 installed, 4 plan).
20. Computer program to identify when cash values from existing policies are used to pay premiums for new policies (16 installed, 3 plan).
21. Confidential method of reporting possible fraud, such as 800 number (16 installed, 8 plan).
22. Confirmation to old address for every address change (15 installed, 11 plan).
23. Confirmation to previous owner when ownership changes (14 installed, 3 plan).
24. Regular review of sample of agent's client files (13 installed, 5 plan).
25. Phone call to policyowner to confirm large policy loans/surrenders (11 installed, 1 plan).
26. Computer report of address changes or new policy addresses that are the same as the agent's addresses—for follow-up with the agent (8 installed, 6 plan).
27. Use of secret PIN code for phone withdrawals (loans and surrenders) (3 installed, 3 plan).

The survey also asked respondents to document any additional controls installed. The most significant include

- Drug testing of all new employees
- Monitoring ratio of total policy loans to total cash value for each agent's clients
- Monitoring number of complaints per agent

The number of controls installed at each company depends to a great extent on each company's experience and control environment.

* *The parentheses following each fraud control measure indicate the number of insurers who used each control and the number who planned to implement each control.*

for being. Although similar to a mission statement, a strategic intent is generally more hard-hitting and to the point, more difficult for the organization to achieve and more motivational; a strategic intent should make the company's employees excited to come to work each day. One example that has been used to illustrate strategic intent is President Kennedy's bold proclamation during his presidency that within eight years the United States would put an astronaut on the moon and bring the astronaut safely back.

Insight 20-5 Cigna, IBM Tech Tool Targets Health Care Fraud

Stepping up its battle against health care fraud and abuse, Cigna HealthCare has joined with IBM to develop and implement a technological tool that analyzes providers' behavior patterns to identify potential abusers.

The Fraud and Abuse Management System (FAMS) uses claim data to examine the billing and medical practices of health care providers to help determine the most likely abusers.

High-risk providers are identified through the use of a behavior "profiler" based on fuzzy logic technology.

This relatively new technology enables FAMS to detect and measure subtle variations in behavior and to construct a hierarchy of scores that reflect a provider's composite abnormality relative to others in the same peer group, said Tom Schamber, manager of IBM's Technology Services Group.

"We may have a provider who orders three or four lab tests for every office visit or who shows many services rendered on weekends or holidays," said Susan Mitchell, director of claim review services for Bloomfield, Connecticut-based Cigna HealthCare.

"These are providers we want to look at more closely," she added.

FAMS can find such patterns as well as provide sophisticated analyses, said Mr. Schamber.

"A typical artificial intelligence system might red-flag all office visits for which the patient was charged more than $100," he said.

But that may not be outrageous in some (medical) specialties and in some geographic locations, he added.

FAMS' analyses, he said, are based on specialty, geographic region and claims data over a given period.

The system uses multiple behavior within each specialty to come up with ranking, said Mr. Schamber.

For example, he said the system might look at the practice patterns of chiropractors in a certain region.

Using comparative data, FAMS would highlight those with higher-than-average charges or those treating many patients under age six, said the IBM official.

FAMS, he said, would also spotlight a provider who was regularly treating every member of one family.

The system can also produce management reports to build a case on a suspect provider, or generate a letter to a provider pointing out specific problem areas.

IBM's role in the joint venture has been to provide the technological expertise, while Cigna has contributed claim data for analysis as well as its experience in provider fraud and abuse detection and investigation.

Cigna said that FAMS will improve the capabilities of its health care fraud investigations unit.

Ms. Mitchell noted that while the original goal of Cigna's relationship with IBM was to create a system to detect highly suspect providers, it became clear during the development process that the fuzzy logic-based FAMS could also provide significant support for the investigation of cases brought to the insurer's attention through other internal and external referrals, including those from the FBI and regulatory agencies.

"From what we've seen so far," she said, "we're enthusiastic about the potential of this system in enhancing our fraud detection and investigative efforts."

With FAMS, said Ms. Mitchell, "We're increasing the odds that we're focusing our time on what we call the biggest and the baddest."

Source: *"Cigna, IBM Tech Tool Targets Health Care Fraud." Reprinted with permission from* National Underwriter, *copyright © 1996, The National Underwriter Company* Life & Health/Financial Services Edition, *September 19, 1994, p. 30.*

Core Competencies

According to Hamel and Prahalad, an organization's strategic intent should be derived from, and the organization's activities should be focused on, the organization's core competencies.* A ***core competency*** is a set of skills that provides an organization with a competitive advantage in several products or markets. Let's examine each of the elements of this definition separately.

1. "A core competency is a set of skills." A core competency is something an organization *does*, and, therefore, the description of a core competency should refer to an action. For example, one of an insurer's core competencies might be "distributing products"; another might be "pricing risks" or "managing investments."

2. "A core competency is a source of competitive advantage." The organization does this activity better, faster, or at a lower cost than the majority of its competitors. Therefore, the activity adds considerable value to end products from the customer's point of view. For example, an insurer's rapid response time to customer requests might be a source of competitive advantage.

3. "A core competency is transferable to several products or markets." For example, an insurer's investment expertise is a valuable asset to many products and important to many consumers.

FAST FACT

"McKinsey & Co. did a study in 1994 that identified over a 5-, 10-, and 15-year period the most successful insurance companies and found that the one thing they had in common (there were only about a dozen companies) was that they had a strong underwriting culture and they were not driven by market share or budgetary goals or other factors that were extraneous. They viewed themselves as being in the business of putting a price on risk, and they were willing to take risk—in some cases, large amounts of risk—because of their skills in doing that. Over time, it led them to higher returns."[6]

Figure 20-4 lists some areas that could potentially be the core competencies of an insurance company. Note that Figure 20-4 is not a complete list. There is no fixed group of potential core competencies.

Core Competencies as a Key to Growing New Revenues

According to proponents of the core competency perspective, organizations should seek long-term revenue growth by focusing their efforts on their core competencies. By concentrating on core competencies, organizations can further improve their expertise in those areas, and thus increase their ability to provide value to the customer. By providing more value to the customer, organizations can improve their revenues. Additionally, because core competencies are transferable to new products and markets, organizations can improve their revenues by using their core competencies to create new products and to serve new markets.

The decision to focus on core competencies has a number of implications for an organization's structure and way of doing business.

* For more information about their observations, refer to the article by Gary Hamel and C.K. Prahalad "Competing for the Future," as appeared in *Harvard Business Review*, July–August, 1994.

Figure 20-4. Potential core competencies for an insurer.

- Pricing for mortality risk
- Managing morbidity risk
- Managing investments
- Distributing products
- Responding to customers
- Providing financial advice
- Meeting financial needs
- Providing tax-sheltering opportunities
- Administering employee benefits

In general, a focus on core competencies can be supported by an increased use of outsourcing and a new approach to resource allocation within an organization.

Core Competencies and Outsourcing

Outsourcing can help an organization focus on its core competencies. If a function is not central to an organization's competitive advantage, then the organization may benefit from outsourcing that function.

However, a company should not outsource functions that are part of its core competencies. Companies must retain control over those factors that create competitive advantage.

Core Competencies and Resource Allocation

Many companies are organized into departments or strategic business units (SBUs) that perform different functions, produce different products, or serve different markets. One of the primary responsibilities of corporate management is to allocate resources—human, material, and financial—among the company's operating units. Focusing on core competencies may require an organization to make changes to both its resource allocation system and its incentive system. Pay incentives must be structured to reward staff for their contributions to the organization's overall success in exploiting its core competencies and making progress toward its strategic intent.

Improving Profitability by Focusing on Loyalty

The relationship between loyalty and profitability is becoming easier to quantify and, consequently, efforts to promote and enhance loyalty are becoming more widespread. Insurers can profit from the loyalty of customers, distributors, employees, vendors, or any other groups with which insurers do business. Companies are finding that the economic benefits of loyalty are well worth the added expenses that companies may incur to earn that loyalty.*

Building Customer Loyalty

In the insurance industry, customer loyalty translates into improved profitability through both revenue increases and cost reductions. Loyal customers are persistent, repeat customers—they are less likely to allow coverages to lapse and are more likely to purchase additional products from the company. Repeat customers cost the company less in acquisition costs and remain customers long enough to generate a profitable revenue stream. Statistics show that in the life insurance business, even a small increase in customer retention can result in a significant reduction in policy costs.

A loyalty-based management approach requires some preliminary research in order for this approach to result in improved profitability. First, they need to discover which customers are the primary sources of their profitability. For example, customers who are primarily price driven may not be a company's best source of profits. Such customers may switch insurers whenever they can obtain a slightly better price elsewhere. In such situations, efforts to retain such customers may not be worth the costs.

The next step in building customer loyalty is determining what targeted customers value. To find out what customers value, insurers can survey current customers and departing customers. Companies can also monitor customer behavior, gaining insights into customer values and motivations by studying customer actions. Finding out why customers stay with a company and continue to purchase its products and why customers quit buying a company's products gives the company the information needed to design administrative systems that fulfill customer needs and to develop the product, pricing, promotion, and distribution strategies necessary to reach those customers.

Next, companies need to compute the costs of losing targeted customers and the benefits of retaining those customers. This difficult step is essential, because without a true "bottom-line" analysis of such costs and benefits, companies are reluctant to commit the resources needed to build loyalty. Building loyalty may initially increase the company's expenses, a difficult "sell" to company owners and management. However, if the link is made between such an

* For more complete information about the role of loyalty and company management, refer to Frederick F. Reichheld, with Thomas Teal, *The Loyalty Effect: The Hidden Force Behind Growth, Profits, and Lasting Value* (Boston, MA: Bain & Company, Inc., 1996).

increase and a larger increase in profits, the case becomes easier. For example, if the development of a new customer service system results in a higher level of customer satisfaction, and the higher level of customer satisfaction leads to higher customer retention, and the higher customer retention results in higher long-term profits, then the company's investment in the customer service system can be shown to have a specific, measurable return. Without such quantifiable measures, building customer loyalty is a good idea, but one that will not receive financial backing.

Building Loyalty in Other Business Relationships

Loyalty in an insurance company's other business relationships can be just as important as customer loyalty. For example, distributor loyalty results in both lower costs and increased revenues. The costs of hiring and training agents are very high, and companies that wish to cut such costs often find they need to spend more money initially on selecting and training agents in order to spend less money later on finding and training replacements. State Farm, for example, has a four-year agent retention rate of 80 percent, compared to industry averages of from 20 percent to 40 percent. One reason cited for this retention rate is that State Farm spends as much as a year selecting and recruiting an agent. The payoff of this effort is the high agent retention rate and an agent productivity rate that is nearly 50 percent above industry averages.[7]

Similarly, the costs of hiring new employees and of seeking reliable vendors and suppliers can be high, so it is to the insurer's advantage to develop loyalty in all types of relationships. Also, loyal, long-term employees acquire valuable knowledge that can in fact be one of a company's core competencies. When employees leave a company, they take with them knowledge that can be difficult, costly, or impossible to replace.

The Value Exchange

To quantify the relationship between loyalty and profitability, companies need to focus on what some theorists call the "value exchange." Essentially, the value exchange is the association between the company's financial investment in a business relationship and the return that the business relationship generates. By carefully studying this association, companies can determine which customer segments, types of employees, and vendors add the most value and, correspondingly, warrant the greatest attention. Additionally, companies can determine whether increasing their investment in a business relationship will result in greater profitability. For example, companies may estimate that a 5 percent price reduction will result in a 20 percent increase in a customer group's retention and a 25 percent increase in profitability from that customer group. To determine the exact profitability effect derived from increasing the investment in a relationship, companies need to look at long-term measures of profitability such as those obtained using an economic value added approach. Particularly for insurance companies, the relationships that are the most profitable are those that extend well beyond the current accounting period.

Adopting an International Perspective

Because of recent growth in international trade, the world has, to some extent, become a single marketplace where money, goods, and services freely cross borders. The free flow of international trade presents new challenges and new opportunities. In this environment, taking an international perspective in their operations can be profitable for insurance companies.

In a single global market, insurers can potentially sell their products around the world, purchase supplies and equipment from any country, invest in the financial markets on any continent, relocate business units, and outsource non-core functions overseas. Insurers can shop the global market for the best deals and the most reliable customers, and they can spread risk among a world-wide pool of insureds.

Revenue Growth through International Expansion

For U.S. and Canadian insurers, one approach to increasing revenues is through expansion into markets outside of North America. After Japan, the United States is the second largest insurance market in the world in terms of total premiums, but the U.S. market is growing more slowly than almost every other insurance market in the world. The Canadian insurance market is growing faster than the U.S. market, but its current and potential size are no match for those of many other countries. Many markets outside of North America, though presently small in terms of premium volume, are growing extremely quickly and have enormous potential for further growth. By expanding operations into one of these small, growing markets, an insurer opens up the possibility of a new, highly profitable source of revenue.

Several factors combine to determine how viable and how attractive expansion into a given market is for an insurer. These factors include

- *Low insurance penetration.* Current insurance holdings in a market determine whether the market is saturated, mature, or growing. The lower a market's current penetration, the greater the potential that market is considered to have.

- *Economic stability.* Insurance operations depend on a stable currency and stable financial markets. In the absence of economic stability, it is difficult for insurers to operate.
- *Political stability.* Insurance operations are difficult and risky in an environment of political instability. Owing to political change, an insurer may cease to be welcome in a given country. In such situations, some of the insurer's assets may even be confiscated by the government.
- *Market access.* Some governments limit the ability of foreign companies to operate in their countries.
- *Economic prosperity.* In order for an insurer's venture in a given market to be successful, the customers in that market must have money to purchase the insurer's products.
- *Consumer demand for insurance and financial products.* Consumers must have a need for insurance and financial products. If a government provides elaborate social security programs, then its citizens will have little need for many types of financial and insurance products.

Several recent economic and political developments are combining to increase the attractiveness to insurers of expanding into a number of countries and regions of the world. The primary economic factor is the recent increase in the number of manufacturing jobs in developing countries. The increase in manufacturing jobs is creating economic booms in many countries and increasing the wealth of much of the population. Many developing countries are seeing the creation of a substantial middle class, which is considered essential to a successful insurance industry.

On the political front, many formerly closed economies are becoming more open. Eastern Europe and the former Soviet Union have recently opened up to trade with the rest of the world. In addition, many other closed or restricted economies, particularly in Asia, are gradually becoming more open. Many Asian economies are also benefiting from economic development. At the same time, many governments are reducing the social security protections they provide to their citizens. As a consequence, many of the citizens of these countries must look for private sources of insurance and retirement protection.

Different countries and regions exhibit different advantages and disadvantages as potential targets for international expansion by insurers. Here, we discuss the pros and cons of expansion into Latin America, Western Europe, Eastern Europe, and Asia.

Latin America

The major advantages of Latin America as a market are its increasing prosperity, its increasing political and economic stability, the privatization of government social security systems in several countries, and the lack of insurance coverage of most of the population. Although many Latin American countries have had life insurance companies since around 1900, rampant inflation and government instability severely impaired the industry's ability to function. However, the move toward market economies in leading Latin American countries such as Mexico, Chile, and Argentina has brought economic growth and at least some measure of relative financial stability. Since the liberalization of Chile's insurance market in 1980 and the privatization of its pension programs, insurance markets have also opened up in the other more developed Latin American countries. International insurers are attracted to expansion into these markets because of the growth rate achievable in an underinsured region.

The main drawback of Latin America as a potential market is the risk of a return to economic and political instability. Most of the Latin American countries that are moving toward market economies are still very early in that process, and many have political opposition to market reforms. Major changes in the governing party could wreak economic havoc. In Mexico, for example, a combination of political scandals and economic setbacks in late 1994 and early 1995 forced a devaluation of the peso that threatened to cause an economic collapse.

Western Europe

The main advantages of Western Europe as a potential market are the prosperity of its population, its political and economic stability, and the fact that the populations of several Western European nations are distinctly underinsured. In addition, the disparate nations of Western Europe are forming an economic union that could create a single huge market from a number of smaller markets. Economic union should bring harmonization of insurance regulation and should mean that an insurer need only set up operations in one nation in order to be able to operate in all the member nations of the union.

The drawbacks of Western Europe as a market include the fact that a number of European countries are decidedly not underinsured, and have a well-developed insurance industry. In addition, economic union has been delayed by disagreements among the countries involved. In the meantime, major differences concern such matters as capital requirements for insurers, the types of financial products that may be sold, life insurance taxation, and social security systems.

Eastern Europe

Since the fall of the Iron Curtain, the economies of Eastern Europe have been increasingly privatized and opened up to foreign investment. As the economies have been privatized, the social security systems have been reduced, creating a market for private security products, such as insurance and retirement products.

Economic prosperity and economic and political stability vary from country to country in Eastern Europe. Some countries, like Poland, Hungary, and the Czech Republic are considered to be promising markets. Unfortunately, Russia, the largest potential market in the region, is generally considered to be politically or economically unstable, and its progress toward economic prosperity has been limited.

Asia

With the notable exception of Japan, Asian countries tend to be underinsured. Most of Asia holds a vast, underinsured population whose economic fortunes are continually improving. A number of Asian countries have been the principal beneficiaries of the increase in manufacturing jobs and the accompanying increase in economic prosperity we discussed earlier in this section. Over the long term, Asia is almost certainly the region offering the greatest growth potential for insurers.

Asia contains many countries with various political and cultural characteristics and in various stages of economic development. Most of these countries present some level of political risk. In some countries, such as China, the risk exists that the winds of political change could close down foreign investment altogether. In other countries, the political risk is present, but probably less extreme. For example, in some countries, insurance regulations may change dramatically from one administration to the next.

In some Asian countries, foreign company access to the insurance market is restricted. Such is the case in three of the largest potential markets in the world: Japan, India, and China. Japan already has developed its own insurance industry, and the access of foreign insurers to the Japanese market is restricted. Only a few non-Japanese insurers are permitted to operate in Japan, although preliminary agreements have been made to open up the Japanese market. In India and China, state-owned monopolies have dominated their respective insurance industries. Both countries have been considering opening their insurance markets to foreign companies only since the beginning of the 1990s. In India, market reform has been proposed by a special commission, but is yet to be implemented. In order even to be considered for a license to operate in China, a foreign insurer must have been in business at least 50 years, have $5 billion in assets under management, and have maintained a representative office in China for three years. Only a few non-Chinese insurers have so far met these criteria and have obtained licenses to operate in China.

Ethics

The concept of ethics can be quite subjective. Ethics often means different things to different people. The concept has a long history and has often been pondered by philosophers. For the purpose of this discussion, we define ***ethics*** as standards of moral conduct. Applying this definition, ***ethical behavior*** is behavior that meets accepted standards of moral conduct.

Insurance companies can encourage ethical behavior by requiring training in ethics for their employees, by establishing an ethics office or ethics hotline, and by incorporating ethical guidelines into the company's mission statement. For an ethics program to truly succeed, top management must be involved, and the principles of ethics must be incorporated into everyday business decisions. A management team that preaches ethics without practicing or rewarding it may leave the company in more of an ethical dilemma than before.[8]

The middle 1990s have seen an erosion in public confidence in the insurance industry. A 1994 Monitoring Attitudes of the Public (MAP) survey revealed that one quarter of the population of the United States does not believe that the life insurance industry is fair, trustworthy, or caring. A few big stories of insurance industry scandals have contributed to this shrinking confidence. Yet the life insurance industry continues to pride itself as the protector of the world's financial security.[9] In order to better maintain high standards of fairness and responsibility and to combat the public perception that insurers are not trustworthy, insurers are focusing more on *ethics.*

The Profitability of Ethics

Many people believe that the only responsibility of a corporation is to produce profits for its owners or shareholders. Many experts believe that maintaining a high standard of ethics can actually be a valuable asset in a company's efforts to earn a profit. The positive effect of ethics on profitability holds especially true among insurance companies because the business of insurance involves a significant financial trust between insurers and their customers. A focus on ethics can increase profitability in the following ways:

- As a rule, customers are more likely to want to do business with a company or industry that they perceive as ethical.

- Strong ethical business practices help engender the loyalty of customers, employees, shareholders, and distributors.
- An effective ethics program can improve employee morale in an insurance company. Focusing on the insurance industry's responsibility to its customers can energize a workforce and bring it together.[10]
- Every year the insurance industry loses millions of dollars because of employee fraud. A company can reduce the chance that it will be defrauded by employees by offering ethics training and emphasizing ethics in all of its business practices.
- By maintaining a high standard of ethics, insurers can avoid costly lawsuits, antitrust actions, and even criminal prosecution.
- If the industry adheres to ethical behavior, there will be fewer calls for costly government regulations.

The Ethics of Solvency

Throughout this book we have discussed the ways that insurance companies balance the pursuit of profitability with the need to protect solvency. In the final analysis, protecting solvency means protecting customers—the insurance industry's highest ethical responsibility. The reason it is so important for insurance companies to protect solvency is that the money insurance companies manage actually belongs to their customers. The money has been entrusted with the insurance industry because of the insurance industry's promise to provide financial security. Because of this trust, no other industry is held to a higher moral and ethical standard than is the insurance industry.[11]

In Conclusion

As the insurance industry evolves, new approaches to improving profitability continue to emerge. In this chapter we have covered only some of the recent approaches insurers have developed to reduce costs and increase revenues. First, we focused on controlling administrative expenses through downsizing, reengineering, and the outsourcing of non-core functions. Then we examined some new methods of insurance product distribution. Next we discussed mergers, the importance of combating fraud, and uses for excess technology capacity. Then we explained how understanding its core competencies can help an insurer achieve greater profitability. Finally, we explored loyalty in business relationships, the possibilities of the global marketplace, and the importance of ethics.

Key Terms and Concepts

downsizing
attrition
early retirement program
layoff
reengineering
continuous process improvement
outsourcing
core competencies
levelized commission schedule
direct response marketing
worksite marketing
low-load products
cost efficiencies
unit cost
fixed costs
total variable costs
excess capacity
strategic intent
ethics
ethical behavior

References

1. *Information Technology . . . Its Impact on the Insurance Industry* (Atlanta, GA: LOMA, 1986), p. 3.

2. ACLI *1995 Life Insurance Fact Book,* p. 37.

3. *Reengineering the Life Insurance Company: Integrating Technology, People, and Work* (Atlanta, GA: LOMA, 1994), pp. 81–91.

4. *The Internet and Online Services: Opportunities for Insurance and Financial Services Companies* (Atlanta, GA: LOMA, 1995), pp. 1–3.

5. Rick Pullen, "Group Offers Blueprint for Making Insurers a Smaller Target for Fraud," *BestWeek,* Life/Health Edition (January 17, 1994), p. 15.

6. From a speech by Alice D. Schroeder, quoted in "Why Invest in Insurance Stocks When Other Industries Offer Better Returns?" *BestWeek,* Life/Health Edition (November 27, 1995), pp. 5–16.

7. Frederick F. Reichheld, "Loyalty-Based Management," *Harvard Business Review* (March–April 1993), p. 72.

8. Lawrence A. Berger, "Train All Employees to Solve Ethical Dilemmas," *Best's Review,* Life/Health Edition (March 1995), p. 72.

9. Therese Mruk Garrett, "An Ethical Dilemma," *Resource* (October 1995), p. 44.

10. Berger, *op. cit.,* p. 70.

11. Garrett, *op. cit.,* p. 44.

Appendix

Figure A-1. Future Value Interest Factor Table, FVIF (*n*, *i*).

# of periods	Interest rate (*i*)									
(*n*)	1%	2%	3%	4%	5%	6%	7%	8%	9%	10%
½	1.005	1.010	1.015	1.020	1.025	1.030	1.034	1.039	1.044	1.049
1	1.010	1.020	1.030	1.040	1.050	1.060	1.070	1.080	1.090	1.100
1½	1.015	1.030	1.045	1.061	1.076	1.091	1.107	1.122	1.138	1.154
2	1.020	1.040	1.061	1.082	1.103	1.124	1.145	1.166	1.188	1.210
2½	1.025	1.051	1.077	1.103	1.130	1.157	1.184	1.212	1.240	1.269
3	1.030	1.061	1.093	1.125	1.158	1.191	1.225	1.260	1.295	1.331
3½	1.035	1.072	1.109	1.147	1.186	1.226	1.267	1.309	1.352	1.396
4	1.041	1.082	1.126	1.170	1.216	1.262	1.311	1.360	1.412	1.464
4½	1.046	1.093	1.142	1.193	1.246	1.300	1.356	1.414	1.474	1.536
5	1.051	1.104	1.159	1.217	1.276	1.338	1.403	1.469	1.539	1.611
5½	1.056	1.115	1.177	1.241	1.308	1.378	1.451	1.527	1.606	1.689
6	1.062	1.126	1.194	1.265	1.340	1.419	1.501	1.587	1.677	1.772
6½	1.067	1.137	1.212	1.290	1.373	1.460	1.552	1.649	1.751	1.858
7	1.072	1.149	1.230	1.316	1.407	1.504	1.606	1.714	1.828	1.949
7½	1.077	1.160	1.248	1.342	1.442	1.548	1.661	1.781	1.909	2.044
8	1.083	1.172	1.267	1.369	1.477	1.594	1.718	1.851	1.993	2.144
8½	1.088	1.183	1.286	1.396	1.514	1.641	1.777	1.924	2.080	2.248
9	1.094	1.195	1.305	1.423	1.551	1.689	1.838	1.999	2.172	2.358
9½	1.099	1.207	1.324	1.451	1.590	1.739	1.902	2.077	2.268	2.473
10	1.105	1.219	1.344	1.480	1.629	1.791	1.967	2.159	2.367	2.594
10½	1.110	1.231	1.364	1.510	1.669	1.844	2.035	2.244	2.472	2.720
11	1.116	1.243	1.384	1.539	1.710	1.898	2.105	2.332	2.580	2.853
11½	1.121	1.256	1.405	1.570	1.753	1.954	2.177	2.423	2.694	2.992
12	1.127	1.268	1.426	1.601	1.796	2.012	2.252	2.518	2.813	3.138
12½	1.132	1.281	1.447	1.633	1.840	2.072	2.330	2.617	2.937	3.292
13	1.138	1.294	1.469	1.665	1.886	2.133	2.410	2.720	3.066	3.452
13½	1.144	1.306	1.490	1.698	1.932	2.196	2.493	2.826	3.201	3.621
14	1.149	1.319	1.513	1.732	1.980	2.261	2.579	2.937	3.342	3.797
14½	1.155	1.333	1.535	1.766	2.029	2.328	2.667	3.052	3.489	3.983
15	1.161	1.346	1.558	1.801	2.079	2.397	2.759	3.172	3.642	4.177

Figure A-2. Future Value Interest Factor of an Annuity Table, FVIFA (*n*, *i*).

# of periods	Interest rate (*i*)									
(*n*)	1%	2%	3%	4%	5%	6%	7%	8%	9%	10%
½	0.499	0.498	0.496	0.495	0.494	0.493	0.492	0.490	0.489	0.488
1	1.000	1.000	1.000	1.000	1.000	1.000	1.000	1.000	1.000	1.000
1½	1.504	1.507	1.511	1.515	1.519	1.522	1.526	1.530	1.533	1.537
2	2.010	2.020	2.030	2.040	2.050	2.060	2.070	2.080	2.090	2.100
2½	2.519	2.538	2.557	2.575	2.595	2.614	2.633	2.652	2.671	2.691
3	3.030	3.060	3.091	3.122	3.152	3.184	3.215	3.246	3.278	3.310
3½	3.544	3.588	3.633	3.679	3.724	3.770	3.817	3.864	3.912	3.960
4	4.060	4.122	4.184	4.246	4.310	4.375	4.440	4.506	4.573	4.641
4½	4.579	4.660	4.742	4.826	4.910	4.997	5.084	5.173	5.264	5.356
5	5.101	5.204	5.309	5.416	5.526	5.637	5.751	5.867	5.985	6.105
5½	5.625	5.753	5.884	6.019	6.156	6.296	6.440	6.587	6.737	6.891
6	6.152	6.308	6.468	6.633	6.802	6.975	7.153	7.336	7.523	7.716
6½	6.681	6.868	7.061	7.259	7.464	7.674	7.891	8.114	8.344	8.580
7	7.214	7.434	7.662	7.898	8.142	8.394	8.654	8.923	9.200	9.487
7½	7.748	8.006	8.273	8.550	8.837	9.135	9.443	9.763	10.095	10.438
8	8.286	8.583	8.892	9.214	9.549	9.897	10.260	10.637	11.028	11.436
8½	8.826	9.166	9.521	9.892	10.279	10.683	11.104	11.544	12.003	12.482
9	9.369	9.755	10.159	10.583	11.027	11.491	11.978	12.488	13.021	13.579
9½	9.914	10.349	10.807	11.287	11.793	12.324	12.882	13.468	14.084	14.730
10	10.462	10.950	11.464	12.006	12.578	13.181	13.816	14.487	15.193	15.937
10½	11.013	11.556	12.131	12.739	13.382	14.063	14.783	15.545	16.351	17.203
11	11.567	12.169	12.808	13.486	14.207	14.972	15.784	16.645	17.560	18.531
11½	12.123	12.787	13.495	14.249	15.052	15.907	16.818	17.789	18.823	19.924
12	12.683	13.412	14.192	15.026	15.917	16.870	17.888	18.977	20.141	21.384
12½	13.245	14.043	14.900	15.818	16.804	17.861	18.996	20.212	21.517	22.916
13	13.809	14.680	15.618	16.627	17.713	18.882	20.141	21.495	22.953	24.523
13½	14.377	15.324	16.347	17.451	18.644	19.933	21.325	22.829	24.453	26.208
14	14.947	15.974	17.086	18.292	19.599	21.015	22.550	24.215	26.019	27.975
14½	15.521	16.630	18.837	19.149	20.577	22.129	23.818	25.655	27.654	29.828
15	16.097	17.293	18.599	20.024	21.579	23.276	25.129	27.152	29.361	31.772

Figure A-3. Present Value Interest Factor Table, PVIF (*n*, *i*).

# of periods	Interest rate (*i*)									
(*n*)	1%	2%	3%	4%	5%	6%	7%	8%	9%	10%
½	0.995	0.990	0.985	0.981	0.976	0.971	0.967	0.962	0.958	0.953
1	0.990	0.980	0.971	0.962	0.952	0.943	0.935	0.926	0.917	0.909
1½	0.985	0.971	0.957	0.943	0.929	0.916	0.903	0.891	0.879	0.867
2	0.980	0.961	0.943	0.925	0.907	0.890	0.873	0.857	0.842	0.826
2½	0.975	0.952	0.929	0.907	0.885	0.864	0.844	0.825	0.806	0.788
3	0.971	0.942	0.915	0.889	0.864	0.840	0.816	0.794	0.772	0.751
3½	0.966	0.933	0.902	0.872	0.843	0.816	0.789	0.764	0.740	0.716
4	0.961	0.924	0.888	0.855	0.823	0.792	0.763	0.735	0.708	0.683
4½	0.956	0.915	0.875	0.838	0.803	0.769	0.738	0.707	0.679	0.651
5	0.951	0.906	0.863	0.822	0.784	0.747	0.713	0.681	0.650	0.621
5½	0.947	0.897	0.850	0.806	0.765	0.726	0.689	0.655	0.623	0.592
6	0.942	0.888	0.837	0.790	0.746	0.705	0.666	0.630	0.596	0.564
6½	0.937	0.879	0.825	0.775	0.728	0.685	0.644	0.606	0.571	0.538
7	0.933	0.871	0.813	0.760	0.711	0.665	0.623	0.583	0.547	0.513
7½	0.928	0.862	0.801	0.745	0.694	0.646	0.602	0.561	0.524	0.489
8	0.923	0.853	0.789	0.731	0.677	0.627	0.582	0.540	0.502	0.467
8½	0.919	0.845	0.778	0.717	0.661	0.609	0.563	0.520	0.481	0.445
9	0.914	0.837	0.766	0.703	0.645	0.592	0.544	0.500	0.460	0.424
9½	0.910	0.829	0.755	0.689	0.629	0.575	0.526	0.481	0.441	0.404
10	0.905	0.820	0.744	0.676	0.614	0.558	0.508	0.463	0.422	0.386
10½	0.901	0.812	0.733	0.662	0.599	0.542	0.491	0.446	0.405	0.368
11	0.896	0.804	0.722	0.650	0.585	0.527	0.475	0.429	0.388	0.350
11½	0.892	0.796	0.712	0.637	0.571	0.512	0.459	0.413	0.371	0.334
12	0.887	0.788	0.701	0.625	0.557	0.497	0.444	0.397	0.356	0.319
12½	0.883	0.781	0.691	0.612	0.543	0.483	0.429	0.382	0.341	0.304
13	0.879	0.773	0.681	0.601	0.530	0.469	0.415	0.368	0.326	0.290
13½	0.874	0.765	0.671	0.589	0.518	0.455	0.401	0.354	0.312	0.276
14	0.870	0.758	0.661	0.577	0.505	0.442	0.388	0.340	0.299	0.263
14½	0.866	0.750	0.651	0.566	0.493	0.430	0.375	0.328	0.287	0.251
15	0.861	0.743	0.642	0.555	0.481	0.417	0.362	0.315	0.275	0.239

Figure A-4. Present Value Interest Factor of an Annuity Table, PVIFA (*n*, *i*).

# of periods	Interest rate (*i*)									
(*n*)	1%	2%	3%	4%	5%	6%	7%	8%	9%	10%
½	0.496	0.493	0.489	0.485	0.482	0.479	0.475	0.472	0.469	0.465
1	0.990	0.980	0.971	0.962	0.952	0.943	0.935	0.926	0.917	0.909
1½	1.481	1.463	1.446	1.428	1.411	1.395	1.379	1.363	1.347	1.332
2	1.970	1.942	1.913	1.886	1.859	1.833	1.808	1.783	1.759	1.736
2½	2.457	2.415	2.374	2.335	2.297	2.259	2.223	2.188	2.154	2.120
3	2.941	2.884	2.829	2.775	2.723	2.673	2.624	2.577	2.531	2.487
3½	3.423	3.348	3.276	3.207	3.140	3.075	3.012	2.952	2.893	2.836
4	3.902	3.808	3.717	3.630	3.546	3.465	3.387	3.312	3.240	3.170
4½	4.379	4.263	4.152	4.045	3.942	3.844	3.750	3.659	3.572	3.488
5	4.853	4.713	4.580	4.452	4.329	4.212	4.100	3.993	3.890	3.791
5½	5.326	5.160	5.002	4.851	4.707	4.570	4.439	4.314	4.194	4.080
6	5.795	5.601	5.417	5.242	5.076	4.917	4.767	4.623	4.486	4.355
6½	6.263	6.039	5.827	5.626	5.435	5.255	5.083	4.920	4.765	4.618
7	6.728	6.472	6.230	6.002	5.786	5.582	5.389	5.206	5.033	4.868
7½	7.197	6.901	6.628	6.371	6.129	5.901	5.685	5.482	5.289	5.107
8	7.652	7.325	7.020	6.733	6.463	6.210	5.971	5.747	5.535	5.335
8½	8.110	7.746	7.406	7.087	6.789	6.510	6.248	6.002	5.770	5.552
9	8.566	8.162	7.786	7.435	7.108	6.802	6.515	6.247	5.995	5.759
9½	9.020	8.574	8.161	7.776	7.419	7.085	6.774	6.483	6.211	5.956
10	9.471	8.983	8.530	8.111	7.722	7.360	7.024	6.710	6.418	6.145
10½	9.921	9.387	8.894	8.439	8.018	7.627	7.265	6.929	6.616	6.324
11	10.368	9.787	9.253	8.760	8.306	7.887	7.499	7.139	6.805	6.495
11½	10.812	10.183	9.606	9.076	9.588	8.139	7.724	7.341	6.987	6.658
12	11.255	10.575	9.954	9.385	8.863	8.384	7.943	7.536	7.167	6.814
12½	11.696	10.964	10.297	9.688	9.132	8.622	8.154	7.723	7.327	6.962
13	12.134	11.348	10.635	9.986	9.394	8.853	8.358	7.904	7.487	7.103
13½	12.570	11.729	10.968	10.277	9.649	9.077	8.555	8.077	7.640	7.238
14	13.004	12.106	11.296	10.563	9.899	9.295	8.745	8.244	7.786	7.367
14½	13.435	12.480	11.619	10.843	10.142	9.507	8.930	8.405	7.926	7.489
15	13.865	12.849	11.938	11.118	10.380	9.712	9.108	8.559	8.061	7.606

Glossary

absorption costing. See *full costing.* (7)*

accounting policies note. A note in a company's annual report that describes the accounting conventions used during the past year. (15)

accumulated cost of insurance. At any time during the life of a block of policies, the amount the insurer has paid in benefits since the beginning of the contract, accumulated at interest. (9)

acquisition. A transaction wherein one corporation purchases a controlling interest in another corporation. (19)

acquisition expenses. Expenses related to procuring, underwriting, and issuing new insurance business. (7)

actual margin. The margin that emerges after a financial product has been in force; the difference between the assumed values for benefit costs, expenses, or investment income, and the actual values realized for these factors. (7)

actual solvency. The condition of having positive net worth; a condition that exists when a company's total assets exceed or equal its total liabilities. (16)

actual values. In reference to product profitability calculations, the values that materialize after a financial product is sold to the public. Contrast with *assumed values* or *expected values.* (7)

actuarial assumptions. In reference to product design calculations, the values set by actuaries—for such elements of product design as interest rates, mortality or morbidity rates, withdrawal rates, and reserve valuation method—and on which an insurer bases its policy reserve or product pricing calculations. Compare with *assumed values.* Contrast with *actual values* or *expected values.* (9)

actuarial opinion and memorandum (AOM). A formal declaration and filing attesting that a valuation actuary has tested the insurer's cash flows under the required scenarios and that the insurer's reserves make adequate provision for the insurer to meet future obligations to customers, considering the assets that are backing the reserves. (3) The actuarial *opinion* may further be distinguished from the actuarial *memorandum.* (17).

Actuarial Opinion and Memorandum (AOM) model law. A 1991 model law promulgated by the NAIC and adopted in many states, requiring many insurers to appoint a valuation actuary and to perform cash-flow testing. The law mandates actuarial modeling of risks connected with issuing interest-sensitive products. (16)

actuary. An expert in the mathematics of insurance, annuities, and financial instruments. (4)

adequate capitalization. The condition wherein an insurer has enough financial resources to conduct its business over the long run. (2)

adequate liquidity. The condition wherein an insurer has enough cash—or assets that can easily be converted into cash—available as needed to pay bills and meet other obligations as they come due. (2)

adequate rates. Premium rates that are high enough to provide an insurer with enough money on hand to pay both an insurance policy's operating expenses and policy benefits when they come due. (7)

adjusted capital and surplus. The amount of capital and surplus that results after a series of adjustments to the reported value of capital and surplus. These adjustments are often related to the asset valuation reserve and optional reserves. (15)

adjusted liabilities. The amount of liabilities that results after a series of adjustments to reported liabilities. These adjustments often involve subtracting from a company's statutory reserves the asset valuation reserve, possibly the interest maintenance reserve, and certain optional reserves. (15)

adjusted premium. A premium amount used in the calculation of cash values; the adjusted premium for a policy is equal to the policy's valuation net annual premium plus an amount added to account for the insurer's expenses. (9)

administrative supervision. A legal status, usually associated with financial impairment, in which an insurer can be required to obtain permission from the insurance commissioner in order to take any of a variety of specified actions. (18)

* The number(s) in parentheses after glossary entries indicate the chapter(s) in which the term is discussed.

adverse deviation. Any one of the actual policy values that differ from actuarial assumptions, thus reducing a company's revenues, increasing its expenses or increasing its benefit payments. (3)

affiliation. Between corporations, a relationship involving common elements of ownership. (19)

agents' debit balances. Amounts that sales agents have collected from customers and now owe to the company. (12)

aggregate mortality table. A mortality table combining select mortality data and ultimate mortality data to arrive at a single mortality rate for each age. (8)

aggressive financial strategy. A financial management approach that places unusually strong emphasis on profitability and de-emphasizes solvency. (2)

ALM. See *asset/liability management.* (16)

ALM steering committee. In an insurance company, the standing committee that oversees the company's asset/liability management program. (16)

ALM team. Any asset/liability management technical working group. A task team of experts in finance, actuarial mathematics, and other functions, providing technical support to a company's asset/liability management analysis and reporting. (16)

Amendments to the Standard Valuation Law. The NAIC's official 1980 revisions to the older Standard Valuation Law. The original Standard Valuation Law and the amendments set forth criteria for setting nonforfeiture values and policy reserves. (16)

analytical phase of IRIS. In a situation in which an insurer does not pass the statistical phase of IRIS, the process of applying qualitative and quantitative standards to analyze the insurer's Annual Statement data. (18)

annuity. In actuarial terminology, any series of equal payments made over equally spaced time periods. (5)

annuity certain. A type of annuity in which the insurer pays benefits for a specified number of years, whether the annuitant lives or dies during that period, known as a *period certain.* (8)

annuity due. A type of annuity for which a periodic payment is made at the beginning of each payment period. (5)

annuity immediate. See *ordinary annuity.* (5)

annuity in advance. See *annuity due.* (5)

annuity in arrears. See *ordinary annuity.* (5)

annuity unit. A unit of ownership in a variable annuity contract; the unit value increases and decreases reflecting the investment performance of a designated portfolio. (8)

antitrust laws. Laws designed to prevent monopolies, restraint of trade, and any ownership changes that could materially diminish competition in the marketplace. (19)

appropriated surplus. See *contingency reserves.* (9)

assessment. A charge imposed by a public authority for the public good. (18)

asset. An item of value. (1)

asset-backed securities. New securities that are secured by the values of other assets. (12)

asset-driven ALM. An approach to asset/liability management guided by the belief that product design should take into account the nature of the financial assets available in financial markets. (16)

asset/liability management (ALM). A management program for coordinating the financial effects from the insurer's portfolio of products on the one hand and its investment portfolio on the other hand. (16)

asset purchase acquisition. A type of corporate acquisition transaction in which one company purchases another company's assets. Contrast with *stock purchase.* (19)

asset share. The net amount of cash per unit of coverage—often per $1,000 of face value in force—that an insurance or annuity product has accumulated at a given time. (6)

asset-share model. A mathematical simulation model used by insurance companies to indicate how a product's assets can be expected to grow and when the product can be expected to become profitable. (6)

asset valuation reserve (AVR). In U.S. statutory accounting, an Annual Statement account that absorbs both realized and unrealized credit-related capital gains and losses. (9)

assigned surplus. See *contingency reserves.* (9)

association examination. An on-site regulatory examination that conforms to the procedures outlined in the NAIC's ***Examiners Handbook.*** (18)

assumed rate. *a.* In product pricing or profitability, the value attached to any actuarial assumption. *b.* For bundled products, the interest rate that the insurance company assumes when pricing the product. See also *actuarial assumption* and *assumed value.* (7)

assumed margin. In product pricing, before actual product results are known, the assumed value of a product's margin. Contrast with *actual margin* and *expected margin.* (7)

assumed values. Values that actuaries use in establishing a product's price. (7)

assuming company. In a reinsurance transaction, the insurance company that reinsures the risk on a contract issued by another insurance company. (14)

assumption. From an assuming company's standpoint, the acceptance of risk in an insurance or a reinsurance transaction. (14)

assumption certificate. A new insurance certificate issued on an existing insurance contract in order to indicate that a reinsurer has assumed from the ceding company all of the risk under the contract. (14)

assumption reinsurance. A broad type of reinsurance that effects a complete, permanent, and total transfer of in-force (not newly written) business. (14)

attrition. A naturally occurring and gradual reduction in membership. (20)

automatic binding limit. In a reinsurance transaction, a maximum limit on the amount of coverage that can be ceded automatically. (14)

automatic reinsurance. A type of reinsurance agreement providing for the assuming company to automatically accept, within limits, the amount of risk presented by the ceding company. (14)

back-end load. An amount charged to an insurance company customer when the customer withdraws money from some types of products. (7)

balance sheet. A type of financial statement—showing assets, liabilities, and owners' equity—that provides a snapshot of a company's financial position as of a given date. (1)

banding. A pricing system for bundled products under which an insurer establishes several premium rate ranges (bands) according to the face amount of a policy. The premium rate decreases as the face amount increases. (7)

basic mortality table. A type of mortality table with no safety margin built into the mortality rates. (8)

basic statutory merger. The merger of one corporate entity into another and, in the United States, conforming to state legal requirements for a merger between two corporations. See also *statutory merger.* (19)

basis point. One one-hundredth of a percent (0.01 percent). A unit often used in measuring interest rates. (6)

blended rating. In the pricing of group business, a combination of manual and experience ratings. (8)

block of business. A distinctive group of contracts issued on the same basis, but issued on a variety of insureds. (8) See also *block of policies.*

block of insureds. A group of insureds or annuitants of the same age, sex, and risk classification. (8)

block of policies. A group of policies issued on insureds or annuitants of the same age, sex, and risk classification. A large number of similar policies. (8)

board of representatives. The ultimate governing body of a state guaranty association. (18)

book of business. A distinctive group of contracts issued on the same basis, but issued on a variety of insureds. (8)

break-even point. The point where a product's earnings equal the initial investment in the product. A point where there is no profit and no loss. (6)

bundled products. A broad classification of insurance products for which the insurer expresses the product's pricing elements as a single gross premium amount, which it charges to the customer. (7)

business volume. The amount of an insurer's new sales. (14)

C-1 risk. Asset risk. Risk that the insurer will lose money because of defaults or losses in market value on the company's investments in stocks, bonds, mortgages, and real estate. (2)

C-2 risk. Pricing risk. Risk that the insurer's mortality or morbidity experience will differ significantly from the insurer's assumptions, causing the insurer to lose money on its products. (2)

C-3 risk. Interest-rate risk. Risk that interest rates will shift, causing the insurer to lose money. (2)

C-4 risk. General management risk. The risk of losses resulting from ineffective general business practices, including losses resulting from fraud and litigation. (2)

Canadian Life and Health Insurance Compensation Corporation. See *CompCorp.* (18)

cap. A type of interest-rate swap contract, sometimes used for fine-tuning a portfolio's duration and convexity. (17)

capital. *a.* Investments by owners in a company. Owners' equity. (1) *b.* Long-term funds. (1)

capital and surplus. See *owners' equity* and *capital.* (1)

capital budgeting. The analysis of decisions about investing in long-term projects. (3)

capital charge. In economic value added analysis, a dollar cost of capital employed in a given investment project; equal to the monetary investment multiplied by the percentage cost of capital. (15)

capital impairment restriction. A prohibition whereby a stock company cannot pay out as stockholder dividends any portion of its legal capital. (13)

capital investment projects. Long-term investment projects. (1)

capital management. An administrative system used to plan for, obtain, and control a company's long-term funds. (10)

cash flows. Any movement of cash into or out of a company. (1)

cash-flow based surplus (CFS). A technical measure of net worth, equal to the present value of expected cash flows for existing assets minus the present value of expected cash flows for existing liabilities, all discounted at a specific interest rate. (11)

cash-flow matching. An ideal and theoretical condition wherein the insurer's cash inflows exactly match in timing and amount the insurer's needs for meeting its cash obligations. (16)

cash-flow testing (CFT). A type of interest-sensitive cash-flow analysis that involves projecting and comparing, as of a given valuation date, the timing and amount of cash flows after the valuation date. (3) (16)

cash management. The management of short-term funds. (10)

cash surrender value. See *cash value.* (9)

cash value. For some types of insurance products, the amount of a cash payment made available to a policyowner whose policy lapses or is surrendered. (9)

causal model. A quantitative model that expresses the value of one variable, the *dependent* variable, as a function of the value of one or more *independent* variables. (3)

CBO. See *collateralized bond obligation.* (12)

ceding commission. See *reinsurance commission.* (14)

ceding company. In a reinsurance transaction, the company that transfers risk to another company. Also called the *primary insurer* or the *direct writing company.* (14)

cession. From a ceding company's viewpoint, the transfer of risk in a reinsurance transaction. Also, the paperwork documenting such a transaction. (14)

CFT. See *cash-flow testing.* (2) (16)

CFS. See *cash-flow based surplus.* (11)

claim reserve. A type of liability account reflecting amounts that an insurer will pay in the future on claims that have been incurred but which the insurer has not yet paid in full. (9)

Clayton Anti-Trust Act. Landmark 1914 U.S. federal legislation that regulates local price discrimination, interlocking directorates, holding company structures, and other issues directed toward maintaining competitive forces. (19)

closing. The event in which legal documents are executed and financial values are exchanged during an asset purchase or a corporate merger transaction. (19)

CMO. See *collateralized mortgage obligation.* (12)

collateralized bond obligation (CBO). A type of bond that is secured by a pool of bonds. (12)

collateralized mortgage obligation (CMO). A type of bond that is secured by a pool of mortgages. (12)

Commissioners' Reserve Valuation Method (CRVM). A part of the Model Standard Valuation Law that outlines methods insurers must use to calculate minimum statutory reserves for life insurance. (9)

common costs. See *indirect expenses.* (7)

CompCorp. The Canadian Life and Health Insurance Compensation Corporation, the guaranty association of the Canadian life and health insurance industry. (18)

Competition Act. 1986 Canadian federal legislation designed to prevent undesirable monopolies, price-fixing, and various other anticompetitive or deceptive trade practices. (19)

compliance. All activities undertaken to fulfill regulatory requirements. (19)

compound interest. The amount of interest payable on a principal amount and also on all accumulated interest. (5)

confidence level. A point estimate expressing the probability of achieving a predicted outcome. (17)

confidence limit. A range estimate expressing the range of probabilities that a predicted outcome will fall within a certain range. (3) (17)

conglomerate. A group of corporations in unrelated businesses, all under the control of one holding company. (19)

conservative financial strategy. A management approach that de-emphasizes profitability and places unusually strong emphasis on solvency. (2)

conservator. See *receiver.* (18)

conservatorship. See *receivership.* (18)

consideration. *a.* The price an insurer charges for a particular annuity product. (7) *b.* The values exchanged in settlement of a contract for purchase/sale. (19)

consolidation. *a.* A transaction wherein two corporations combine to form a distinct new corporation. See also *merger.* (19) *b.* Also, a trend toward fewer separate businesses within a given industry. (19)

consortium. A shared business venture involving three or more businesses. (14)

contingencies. Unexpected events that cause actual expenses, investment earnings, mortality rates, morbidity rates, or persistency rates to depart significantly from company forecasts or assumptions. (3)

contingency reserve. In statutory accounting, a reserve created by insurers as a cushion against various special risks. (9)

contingency risks. See *C risks.* (2)

continuance table. A type of morbidity table showing the proportion of disabilities that are expected to last various lengths of time; used by insurers to help forecast the length of a disability. (8)

continuous process improvement. The ongoing, repeated analysis and redesign of some of a company's work processes. (20) Contrast with *reengineering.*

contribution to surplus. A term insurance companies use to refer to the excess of revenue over expenditures. Equivalent to the term *profit.* (1)

convexity statistic. A measure of the stability of the duration statistic. (17)

core competency. A set of skills that provides an organization with a competitive advantage in several products or markets. (20)

corporate plan. See *corporate strategic plan.* (11)

cost efficiencies. Cost savings. (20)

costing. The process used to estimate a product's costs for pricing purposes. (7)

cost of benefits. The total amount of contractually required benefits a product is expected to pay. (4)

cost of capital. The overall rate of interest or dollar amount that a company pays for the long-term funds it employs. (2) (10) See also *weighted average cost of capital.*

credibility. In pricing group business, a measure of how relevant an insurer believes the group's past experience to be. (8)

crediting rate. The interest rate that an insurer awards (pays) its customers on interest-sensitive products. (6) (17)

crediting-rate resolution. A formal declaration by a company's board of directors of the rate of interest that an insurer will credit on customers' money held in interest-sensitive products. Also known as a *crediting resolution,* an *interest resolution,* or an *interest-rate resolution.* (17)

crediting resolution. See *crediting-rate resolution.* (17)

C risks. Crucial areas of risk that actuaries have identified as being vital to insurance company cash flows. Also known as *contingency risks.* (2)

critical mass. The theoretical minimum size that an insurance company must achieve in order to survive, prosper, and benefit from economies of scale. (2)

cross-sectional analysis. A type of financial analysis designed for comparing one company's financial performance to the performance of one or more similar firms or else to industry-wide norms. (15)

cumulative dividends. Dividends that amass on preferred stock and must be paid before any dividends can be paid on the company's common stock. (13)

current liquidity. The ratio of all of an insurer's assets not invested in affiliates to all of the insurer's liabilities. (15)

customer-driven management. An approach to management guided by the belief that management processes should focus foremost on meeting customers' needs. (16)

debt financing. Corporate funds raised by issuing debt instruments that represent funds owed to bondholders. (13)

debt instruments. Financial securities that represent debts that the issuing corporation owes to the bondholders. (13)

debt service. The repaying of principal and interest on debt obligations. (1)

decision criterion. For making a selection between alternatives, a rule that helps determine which decision alternative to select. (6)

default risk. The risk of incurring capital losses or defaults on investments; a component of C-1 risk. (17)

deferred acquisition costs (DAC). Under GAAP accounting for insurers, an asset account used in order to counterbalance the accounting entries for the amortization of first-year acquisition expenses. (9)

Delphi method. A type of expert opinion poll in which a questionnaire is sent to a number of experts who are knowledgeable about a specified activity. (3)

demutualization. The process by which a mutual insurer changes its corporate form to that of a stock insurer. (19)

denominator. The number or expression in the bottom part of a fraction. (15)

dependent variable. A variable whose value is predicted by a forecasting model. Contrast with *independent variable.* (3)

derivatives. Financial assets based on other securities. (17)

dilution of earnings. A situation in which an increased number of shares of a company's stock has an ownership claim on the company's earnings. (13)

direct costing. See *marginal costing.* (7)

direct expenses. Expenses that can be directly attributed to a specific product. (7)

direct response marketing. The sale of a product through direct contact between the customer and the company selling the product. (20)

direct writing company. See *ceding company.* (14)

discontinuities. One-time changes that cannot be predicted with any degree of accuracy and which are so influential that the past is no longer a reliable predictor of the future. (3)

discounting. In finance, a process for converting a future value to its present value. (5)

disintermediation. A phenomenon in which customers remove money from a financial intermediary. (3)

disintermediation risk. The risk of unexpectedly high levels of customer withdrawals from a financial institution; includes lapse risk, withdrawal risk, and the risk of a run on assets. (17)

disposition committee. A committee of NOLHGA that works with guaranty associations in cases of multi-state insolvencies to arrange equitable settlements for the customers of a failed insurance company. (18)

distribution expense. Money spent in relation to sales distribution of a company's products. (4)

diversification. In finance, the use of a variety of asset types in an effort to limit exposure to risk. (16)

divestiture. A corporation's disposition of an asset, investment, or operation by any means, including outright sale, sale to employees, or liquidation. (19)

dividend. *a.* On common stock or preferred stock, a payment of a share of the company's profits to corporate shareholders. (13) *b.* For participating insurance policies, see *policy dividend.* (4) *c.* For group insurance, see *experience rating refund.* (8)

dividend liability. A liability account to back policy dividends and experience rating refunds that have been declared but that have not yet been paid. (9)

divisible surplus. A portion of an insurer's capital and surplus, set aside annually from current earnings, and earmarked for distribution to owners of participating policies. (4)

downsizing. A reduction in the size of a company's workforce. (20)

downstream holding company. A company owned or controlled by the corporation that formed it and operating in order to control subsidiary corporations. (19)

DST. See *dynamic solvency testing.* (3)

due diligence. A legal duty of care required of any party in a fiduciary position. Upholding such a duty of care generally requires performing a thorough investigation on behalf of those whose interests a fiduciary must protect. (13)

due diligence investigation. In a merger or reinsurance transaction, a thorough analysis by one party of the other party's assets, liabilities, and future prospects. (14) (19)

duration and convexity matching. The effort to construct asset portfolios that match specified blocks of liabilities in terms of duration and convexity. (17)

duration creep. A phenomenon whereby, as a result of slight changes in interest rates, duration statistics become obsolete and must be recalculated. (17)

duration gap. In paired asset and liability portfolio segments, the difference between the weighted-average duration of the assets and that of the liabilities. (17)

duration gap report. A report that describes the results of duration analysis of an insurer's investment portfolios. (17)

duration mismatch. See *duration gap.* (17)

duration statistic. A measure of the responsiveness of asset market values or liability values to changes in market interest rates. (16) (17)

dynamic forecasting models. Mathematical simulation models based upon projections of a number of future scenarios. (17)

dynamic solvency testing (DST). The use of simulation modeling to project into a future period an insurance company's existing and future business in terms of assets, liabilities, and owners' equity. (3)

early retirement program. An employer's systematic effort to force or encourage the immediate retirement of employees who have not yet reached the company's normal retirement age. (20)

earmarked surplus. See *contingency reserves.* (9)

earnings. For an insurance product, the amount that the product adds to a company's capital and surplus in a given period. (6)

earnings before interest and taxes (EBIT). See *net gain (loss) from operations.* (1)

econometric forecast. A type of forecast that provides information about the expected general level of activity for the economy as a whole. (3)

economic value added (EVA). A measure of profitability of a company, business unit, line of business, or block of business which takes into consideration both return and overall cost of capital. Also known as *embedded value, residual income,* and *value added.* (15)

economies of scale. The savings achievable from increased size of operations. (2) (19)

equitable rates. Product prices that vary based only on factors affecting the product's costs. (7)

equity financing. A process by which a corporation raises funds by issuing financial instruments that represent an ownership (equity) interest in the issuing corporation. (13)

equity instruments. Financial instruments such as common and preferred stock that represent an ownership (equity) interest in the issuing corporation. (13)

ethical behavior. Behavior that meets accepted standards of moral conduct. (20)

ethics. Standards of moral conduct. (20)

EVA. See *economic value added.* (15)

examination report. The document submitted to state regulators and insurance company officers which communicates the results of any NAIC examination. (18)

examiners. State insurance department representatives who perform on-site regulatory examinations of insurance companies. (18)

Examiners Handbook. An NAIC guide that outlines standard procedures for performing either a financial condition examination or a market conduct examination. (18)

excess capacity. The situation wherein an insurer has the technological capacity to produce or process more units than it is currently producing or processing. (20)

exclusion provisions. Policy provisions that limit an insurer's liability if an insured loss results from specified causes. (4)

expected interest margin. The profit or margin from investment (or interest) an insurer forecasts before a product is in force. (7)

expected margin. Before a product is in force, an insurer's forecast values for the product's profits. (7)

expected values. In product design and pricing, the values that the insurer's actuaries believe are most likely to occur. (7)

expense charge. Portion of a product's price designed to reimburse an insurer for its operating expenses—specifically, commissions, premium taxes, and general operating expenses. (7)

expense margin. For an insurance product, the difference between actual expenses and the expense level the insurer assumed in pricing the product. (7)

experience rating. For group insurance, a method of calculating premium rates by using morbidity or mortality rates based on the group's actual claims experience. (8)

experience rating refund. In group insurance, an insurer's refund to a customer in connection with a retrospective experience rating of a group. (8)

external forecast. A forecast that concerns factors beyond an insurer's control. (3) Also, a forecast developed by sources outside of the company.

facultative reinsurance. A type of reinsurance treaty giving the reinsurer the option of accepting or declining a risk based on its own underwriting evaluation. (14)

favorable deviation. For an insurance product, any variation of actual values from assumed values which results in better-than-expected revenues or costs for the insurer. (7)

Federal Trade Commission Act. Landmark 1914 U.S. federal legislation that created the Federal Trade Commission to oversee interstate commerce. (19)

Financial Analysis and Solvency Tracking (FAST) system. A formal system of financial analysis that the NAIC applies to the financial statements of insurers that write business in at least 17 states and have gross premiums greater than $50 million. (18)

financial condition. An insurer's prospects for surviving and prospering long into the future, taking into account current financial position and future business. (17) Contrast with *financial position.*

financial condition examination. The type of on-site regulatory examination that is intended to identify and monitor any threats to the insurer's solvency. (18)

financial engineering. In a context of insurance company capital management, tactics for uncovering hidden capital. (12)

financial leverage. The effect whereby incurring fixed financing costs—usually borrowing funds—automatically magnifies a company's risks and potential returns. (15)

financial management. The process of managing a company's financial resources. (1)

financial position. An insurer's current financial status, ignoring any future business the insurer is likely to issue. (17) Contrast with *financial condition.*

financial ratio analysis. Calculation of the relationships between various financial statement values for the purpose of assessing a company's financial performance and financial condition. (15)

financial reengineering. See *financial engineering.* (12)

financial restructuring. See *financial engineering.* (12)

financial statement analysis. The process of evaluating the information presented in financial statements. (15)

fixed assumptions. With regard to asset-share models, the assumptions built into the design of an asset-share model. (6)

fixed costs. Costs incurred regardless of the number of units produced or processed. (20)

fixed dividends. On preferred stock, dividends that are fixed in both schedule and amount. (13)

flight to quality. The tendency of consumers and sales agents to do business only with insurers having high quality ratings. (15)

floor. A type of interest-rate swap used for fine-tuning a portfolio's duration and convexity. (17)

flotation costs. Expenses associated with issuing securities. (13)

forecast. A prediction of future conditions or events. (3)

formal forecasting method. A standardized procedure for making predictions based on objective data or the opinions of more than one expert. (3)

forward contract. A negotiable instrument representing a limited-time agreement to buy or sell an asset for a stated price at a future date. (17)

forward triangular merger. A type of merger in which a target company merges into a subsidiary of the purchaser, rather than directly into the purchaser itself. (19)

front-end load. In unbundled products, an amount deducted from the amount of the customer's premium or investment. It is intended to pay for the product's loading. (7)

fronting arrangement. An arrangement in which one company acts as a primary insurer and issues policies that another company, a reinsurer, has underwritten; then the primary insurer cedes most of the risk to the same reinsurer. (14)

fronting company. The primary insurer in a fronting arrangement. (14)

full costing. A method of costing in which both direct and indirect expenses are treated as product expenses. (7)

full preliminary term method. A modified reserving method according to which the first-year policy reserve is equal to the end-of-year reserve of a one-year term policy, which is $0. (9)

functional-area plan. A type of long-term plan created for the various functional areas of an organization. (11)

futures contract. A negotiable financial instrument representing a limited-time agreement to buy or sell an asset in the future for a stated price. (17)

future value (FV). In finance, the value of a sum after a given number of compounding periods (n) at a given interest rate (i). (5)

future value interest factor (FVIF). In finance, a factor equal to the future value of a $1 sum after a given number of compounding periods (n) at a given interest rate (i). An amount can be multiplied by the FVIF to calculate the future value of that amount. (5)

future value interest factor of an annuity (FVIFA). In finance, a factor equal to the future value of a $1 annuity for a given number of payments (n), earning a given interest rate (i). An amount can be multiplied by the FVIFA to calculate the future value of an annuity at that amount. (5)

future value of an annuity (FVA). In finance, the amount that a series of annuity payments plus the interest earned on these payments will accumulate after a given number of compounding periods (n) at a given interest rate (i). (5)

gap. In asset/liability management, a mismatch in the cash flows of paired asset and liability portfolio segments. (17)

gap analysis. The asset/liability management technique for evaluating paired asset and liability segments in an effort to predict and understand gaps. (17)

goals. In the context of corporate planning, the results that a business activity is designed to achieve. (11)

goodwill. The value of a company's name, its relations with its customers, the knowledge, skills, and morale of its workforce, and all of the other intangible assets a company possesses. (2)

gross leverage ratio. See *insurance leverage ratio.* (15)

gross premium. The amount charged to a consumer for an insurance company product. (4)

gross profit ratio. The ratio of an insurer's contributions to capital and surplus for one period to the insurer's beginning capital and surplus for the period; measures the growth in an insurer's capital and surplus. (15)

guaranty association. In the United States, a type of state agency responsible for ensuring that customers of an insolvent insurer are treated equitably when the insurer is closed down and its assets are distributed. (18)

guaranty-fund assessment. A charge levied upon sound insurers by a guaranty association as a contribution toward the unsupported customer obligations of a failed insurer that operated in a jurisdiction where the surviving insurer does business. (18)

hedging. A strategy of investing in a given asset in order to limit the overall riskiness of a given portfolio's asset mix. (17)

holding company. A company that owns another corporation or other corporations. (19)

horizontal analysis. A type of financial analysis designed for identifying changes in one company's financial statement values over the course of several financial reporting periods. (15)

horizontal communication. Communication across departmental lines. (16)

hurdle rate. In capital budgeting, the minimum percentage rate of return on capital—or other profitability measure—that a company must earn in order to recoup its cost of capital. (10)

implementation. See *product implementation.* (4)

income risk. The risk associated with the level and timing of income. (17)

income statement. A type of financial statement used to show the increase or decrease in capital and surplus—that is, the profit or loss—resulting from a company's operations. (1)

indemnity reinsurance. A broad type of reinsurance that effects a usually partial transfer of business and forms the basis for sharing the insurance or financial risks of the insurance business. (14)

independent variable. In quantitative modeling, a variable whose value is used as input to a forecasting model. (3) Contrast with *dependent variable.*

indirect expenses. Expenses that are not directly attributable to any specific product. An insurer incurs the same level of indirect expenses whether or not it offers a specific product. (7)

industry outlook report. A report that discusses the likely impact of external factors on firms operating in a given industry. (3)

initial investment. *a.* In product planning, the amount of capital that an insurer must invest to establish a new product. (6) *b.* In capital budgeting in general, the relevant cash outflow at the outset of a long-term investment project.

initial public offering (IPO). An offering of a new company's stock for sale. (12)

insolvency. The inability of a company to meet its financial obligations on time. In the United States and Canada, an insurer can be declared insolvent only by the judgment of a court. (1)

Insurance Holding Company Acts. U.S. state laws that require any company proposing to acquire control of a domestic insurer to file a comprehensive application for approval with the target company's home state. (19)

insurance leverage ratio. The ratio of contractual reserves to capital and surplus. (15)

insurance liquidity ratio. The ratio of an insurer's liquid assets at market value to the insurer's total reserves. (15)

Insurance Regulatory Information System (IRIS). A system established by the NAIC to monitor the financial condition of insurers with a view toward preventing insolvencies. (15)

interest. In business and finance, compensation paid for the use of money. (5)

interest crediting strategies. The formulas and criteria a company uses to set the interest rates it will credit to interest-sensitive products. (17)

interest maintenance reserve (IMR). In U.S. statutory accounting, an account that absorbs the investment portfolio's realized capital gains and losses caused by changes in interest rates. (9)

interest margin. *a.* The actual value of an interest margin is the difference between the interest rate an insurer earns and the rate the insurer credits to its customers. (6) *b.* Under MCCSR, the difference between the amount of investment income an insurer earns and the investment income the insurer either credits to the product or else assumed when pricing the product. (18) See also *investment margin.*

interest margin pricing risk. In MCCSR, the risk that, in the aftermath of changes in market interest rates, an insurer's realized interest margins could be smaller than expected, and the insurer's product-related cash flows would then exceed its product reserves. (18)

interest rate. The percentage factor that is applied to a sum of money to derive the amount of compensation paid for the use of that money. (5)

interest-rate sensitivity match. For paired asset and liability portfolio segments, a condition in which the interest-rate sensitivity of the assets equals that of the liabilities. (17)

interest-rate sensitivity matching. An asset/liability management technique that pairs an asset portfolio segment with a liability portfolio segment. (17)

interest-rate swap. A negotiable instrument consisting of a contractual agreement between two parties to exchange a pair of cash flow streams, typically with one based on a fixed interest rate and the other based on a variable interest rate. (17)

interest-sensitive cash-flow analysis. An approach for analyzing the sensitivity of cash flows to the changed assumptions of various interest-rate scenarios. (3)

interest spread. See *interest margin* or *investment margin.* (6)

internal forecast. A forecast concerning factors that are at least partially within an insurer's control. (3) Also, a forecast prepared by a company's own staff.

internal rate of return (IRR). The percentage rate at which the earnings from an insurance product or other investment must be discounted in order to exactly repay the initial investment. (6)

investment. Any expenditure of money or assets in an attempt to earn a return. An asset. (2)

investment activity report. A type of asset/liability management report that presents the specifics about all investment transactions, including all asset purchases and all dispositions of assets through sales, prepayments, or repayment at maturity. (17)

investment banking company. A type of financial intermediary whose business is to take new issues of securities to market. (13)

Investment Limitation Model Law. A 1989 NAIC model law adopted in many states, this law sets maximum percentages on insurers' holding of specified classes of assets and on their holding of the securities of any one issuer. The purpose of these limitations was to mandate investment diversification. (16)

investment margin. The difference between the amount of investment income an insurer earns and the investment income the insurer credits to a product or assumes when pricing the product. (7) See also *interest margin.*

investment portfolio performance review. A report communicating the results of a comprehensive formal review of the company's investment performance, submitted by the asset/liability management team to the company's board of directors. (17)

investment yield ratio. The ratio of an insurer's investment income to the insurer's average invested assets; indicates the effectiveness of the insurer's investment managers in earning returns on the investment portfolio. (15)

IPO. See *initial public offering.* (12)

IRIS. See *Insurance Regulatory Information System.* (15)

IRIS ratios. A series of twelve financial ratio tests applied by the NAIC to an insurer's statutory Annual Statement in the United States. (18)

IRR. See *internal rate of return.* (6)

joint venture. A type of partnership arrangement between two otherwise independent businesses, providing for the two businesses to undertake a specific project for a specified time period. (14)

judgment forecasting. Also known as *judgmental forecasting.* See *qualitative forecasting methods.* (3)

lapse rate. The percentage share of an insurer's business that customers voluntarily terminate over a specified period. (4)

lateral communication. See *horizontal communication.* (16)

layoff. A permanent dismissal or temporary suspension of employees. (20)

legal capital. The total par value of a company's outstanding stock. (13)

letter of intent. A usually nonbinding letter from a prospective purchaser to a target company outlining the understanding of both parties prior to the beginning of contractual negotiations in a merger or an acquisition transaction. (14)

levelized commission schedule. In contrast to traditional agents' commission schedules, an approach to agent compensation that pays a smaller-than-traditional first-year commission and larger-than-traditional renewal commissions. (20)

leverage. A financial effect in which fixed costs—either operating costs or financing costs—are incurred, usually in order to gain access to greater resources. (15)

liabilities. A company's financial obligations. (1)

liability-driven ALM. An approach to asset/liability management guided by the belief that the asset management process should be driven by the nature of liability portfolios. (16)

Life and Health Insurance Guaranty Association Model Act. An NAIC model act that recommends the standards for states to use when establishing guaranty associations. (18)

life annuity. A type of annuity in which the annuity benefit is payable only for so long as the annuitant lives. (8)

life annuity with period certain. An annuity in which, whether the annuitant lives or dies, the insurer guarantees to pay the annuity benefit for a stated number of years, known as a *period certain.* After the period certain, the insurer pays the annuity benefit only for so long as the annuitant lives. (8)

life income with refund annuity. An annuity in which the insurer pays benefits so long as the annuitant remains alive, with the added condition that, if the annuitant dies before the insurer has made annuity payments at least equal to the amount of premiums paid for the annuity, the insurer will refund an amount based on the difference between the premiums paid for the contract and the benefits the annuitant received. (8)

life insurance company tax status. For the purposes of U.S. federal income taxation, the classification of a company as a "life insurance company." (14)

limited-scope regulatory examination. An NAIC examination that focuses on one or more areas requiring immediate attention rather than covering the full extent of the insurer's operations and financial situation. (18)

line diagram. A visual device that illustrates the timing of essential elements of a particular financial transaction. (5)

line of business. From an accounting viewpoint, a segment of products that has a cost pattern distinctively different from that of other segments. (1)

liquid assets. Cash and other readily marketable assets. (15)

liquidation. A condition under which a receiver either transfers all of the insurer's business and assets to other insurers, or sells the insurer's assets and terminates its business. (18)

liquidity. The ease with which an asset can be converted into cash for an approximation of its true value. (2) (15)

loading. In traditional individual insurance products, an amount added to the net premium which covers the insurer's expenses of doing business. (4) (7)

low-load products. Insurance products whose front-end loads or other expense charges are relatively small. (20)

Macauley duration. See *weighted-average maturity.* Contrast with *option-adjusted durations.* (17)

macroeconomic forecasts. See *econometric forecasts.* (3)

maintenance expenses. In product design, product expenses that arise once a product is in force. (7)

manual. An insurer's book of rates for use in setting premium charges. (8)

manual rates. Premium rates derived using the manual rating method. (8)

manual rating. A method of calculating premium rates whereby the insurer calculates a group's expected cost of benefits based on the claims experience of an "average" group. (8)

margin. The amount by which a product's price exceeds its costs. (7)

marginal costing. A method of costing in which only direct expenses are treated as product expenses. (7)

market analysis. A study of all factors that might affect sales. (4)

market conduct examination. The type of routine NAIC examination intended to verify that an insurer is complying with all applicable statutes and regulations regarding sales, advertising, underwriting, and claims. (18)

market-driven management. An approach to management guided by the belief that management processes should focus foremost on market imperatives such as competitive forces, the economic environments, and meeting customers' needs. (16)

marketing plan. A tactical plan that deals primarily with the product, price, distribution, and promotion strategies that a company will follow in order to reach potential customers and meet their needs. (4)

market signaling. Any action on the part of company insiders that informs participants in public financial markets about the level of management's overall confidence in the company. (13)

market survey methods. Research activities—such as telephone surveys, mail questionnaires, and interviews with consumer panels—that are used to gain information about businesses' and consumers' future purchase and other plans. (3)

matrix organization. A form of organization in which *ad hoc* committees or teams of experts from various disciplines work to support a single project or program. (16)

maturity gap. The dollar-value difference between the weighted-average maturity of an asset portfolio and that of the associated portfolio of liabilities. (17)

maturity gap formula. A formula that helps determine the difference between the weighted-average maturities of a paired asset and liability portfolio segment. (17)

maturity mismatch. See *maturity gap.* (17)

MCCSR. See *Minimum Continuing Capital and Surplus Requirements.* (2) (18)

merger. A transaction joining two business corporations to form a distinct new corporation. (12) (19)

minimum capital and surplus requirements. Requirements setting a minimum dollar amount of capital and surplus that a company must maintain. (2)

Minimum Continuing Capital and Surplus Requirements (MCCSR). Risk-Based Capital requirements established by the Canadian Life and Health Association for federally licensed companies in Canada. A series of calculations weights each insurer's assets and liabilities to reflect their inherent riskiness. The company must meet a specified ratio value to be considered solvent. (2) (18)

minimum reserve requirements. Guidelines required under the Standard Valuation Law for insurers to apply in calculating U.S. statutory policy reserves. (9)

mismatch formula. See *maturity gap formula.* (17)

mismatch risk. The risk of not achieving expected patterns of cash flows for a pairing of asset and liability portfolios. (17)

model Hazardous Condition Regulation. An NAIC model act that prescribes the actions regulators can take for companies deemed to be in hazardous financial condition. (18)

model Rehabilitation Act. An NAIC model act that prescribes the actions regulators can take for companies deemed to be in need of rehabilitation and possible liquidation. (18) See also *rehabilitation.*

model Supervision Act. An NAIC model act that prescribes the actions regulators can take for companies deemed to be in need of administrative supervision. (18) See also *supervision.*

modified reserve method. A method for calculating U.S. statutory policy reserves which creates smaller first-year statutory reserves than those calculated using the net level premium reserve valuation method. (9) Contrast with *net level premium reserve valuation method.*

moral suasion. Regulators' application of informal pressure in an effort to encourage voluntary actions by financial institutions. (18)

morbidity. Injury, sickness, or failure of health. (8)

morbidity rate. The rate at which injury, sickness, or failure of health occur among a defined group of people. (8)

mortality rate. The rate at which death occurs among a defined group of people. (8)

mortality table. A type of actuarial table showing the mortality rates by age of a given group of people. (8)

NAIC. See *National Association of Insurance Commissioners.* (2)

NAIC's RBC ratio calculation. A measure of insurance company solvency that is calculated by dividing an insurer's reported capital by the risk-weighted minimum (required) capital that regulators regard as being sufficient. (18)

National Association of Insurance Commissioners (NAIC). In the United States, an association of state insurance commissioners designed to promote consistent insurance regulation from state to state. (2)

National Exchange Market System Act. Landmark 1975 U.S. federal legislation that established a nationwide system for clearance and settlement of securities transactions and prohibited the fixing of commission rates for selling securities. (19)

National Organization of Life and Health Guaranty Associations (NOLHGA). An organization created by state guaranty associations to coordinate multi-state insolvencies. (18)

negative leverage effect. The diminished return that can result from the presence of leverage. (15)

negative net cash flow. A condition that exists when cash outflows exceed or equal cash inflows. (16)

net amount at risk. For life insurance policies, the difference between the amount of coverage promised by the policy and the policy reserve. (4)

net annual premium. An annual premium established to cover precisely the costs of a product's benefit payments. (7)

net cash flows. For an insurance product, the cash inflows (from premiums, investments, and other sources) generated by that product minus the cash outflows (benefit payments, commissions, expenses, etc.) generated by the product. (Cash flows can be measured with respect to any investment.) (6)

net cash inflow. See *positive net cash flow.* (16)

net earnings. See *net income.* (1)

net GAAP reserves. GAAP policy reserves minus deferred acquisition costs. (9)

net gain. See *net income* and *net gain from operations.* (1)

net gain (loss) from operations. On an insurer's income statement, revenue minus expenses. (1)

net gain to total income. The ratio of an insurer's net gain from operations to its total income plus its realized capital gains and losses. This profitability measure highlights the share of an insurer's operating income that represents a profit. (15)

net income. On an insurer's income statement, net gain from operations minus amounts paid out in dividends to policyowners and the amount of income taxes paid by the insurer. (1)

net level premium. A type of periodic net premium representing an amount expected to precisely cover a product's benefit cost at the moment the product is issued. Compare to *net annual premium.* Contrast with *net single premium.*

net level premium reserve valuation method. An approach to calculating policy reserves which assumes that a policy's net premiums are level. (9) Contrast with *modified reserve method.*

net premium. The amount calculated to precisely convey a product's cost of benefits. (4)

net premiums written (NPW). Premiums written, adjusted to exclude the effects of reinsurance. (15)

net present value. For an investment project, the present value of earnings minus the initial investment. An approach to capital budgeting. (6)

net profit. See *net income.* (1)

net single premium. A type of net premium amount expected to precisely cover a product's benefit cost, calculated by finding the present value of a product's benefit payments at the moment the product is issued. (7) Contrast with *net level premium.*

net worth. See *owners' equity.* (1)

new business strain. See *surplus strain.* (9)

new money. Initial deposits into interest-sensitive products. (17)

NOLHGA. See *National Organization of Life and Health Guaranty Associations.* (18)

nonadmitted assets. Assets that a U.S. insurer may not apply to back its statutory reserves and which do not appear as asset values on the insurer's statutory balance sheet. (10)

non-life insurance company tax status. For the purposes of U.S. federal income taxation, the classification of a company as *not* being a "life insurance company," according to amount of insurance business written or other standards. (14)

nonresident corporation. Under Canadian law, a company incorporated outside of Canada. Contrast with *resident corporation.* (19)

NPV. See *net present value.* (6)

numerator. The number or expression in the top part of a fraction. (15)

objective. In the context of corporate planning, the result that a business activity is designed to achieve. (11)

Office of the Superintendent of Financial Institutions (OSFI). The office of the Canadian federal government responsible for monitoring federally licensed insurers. (18)

old money. Money already on deposit in an interest-sensitive product. (17)

operating income (loss). See *net gain (loss) from operations.* (1)

operating leverage. The effect whereby incurring fixed operating costs automatically magnifies a company's risks and potential returns. (15)

operational plan. See *tactical plan.* (11)

optimization modeling. A form of mathematical modeling that involves finding an optimum simultaneous solution to several equations. (17)

optimum price. The price level at which a seller maximizes revenue from selling a specified product. (4)

optimum results. The maximum or minimum results that can be achieved for a chosen objective. (17)

option. In finance and investments, a limited-time negotiable contract giving a contract owner the right to buy or sell a specified asset for a stated price. (17)

option-adjusted duration statistic. A measure insurance companies use for expressing the relationship between interest-rate changes and changes in the market valuation of an asset or a portfolio. See *duration statistic.* Contrast with *maturity-weighted duration statistic.* (17)

ordinary annuity. A type of annuity for which payment occurs at the end of each payment period. (5)

OSFI. See *Office of the Superintendent of Financial Institutions.* (18)

outsourcing. The practice of hiring an outside vendor to perform a business function. (20)

owners' equity. The excess of assets over liabilities; for an insurer, consists of two components: capital and surplus. Also know as *net worth.* (1)

panel consensus method. A format for expert opinion polls in which a group of experts meets face-to-face to discuss a question. (3)

parent corporation. A corporation that creates another corporation. The parent corporation may either own subsidiaries itself or it may create a holding company that owns the subsidiaries. (19)

participating (par) policies. Policies on which policy dividends are payable. (4)

payback period. The length of time that elapses before the cumulative earnings that an insurance product or other investment produces equal the initial investment in the product. The time required for an investment to break even. (6)

performance profile. In asset/liability management, the specified set of desired outcomes for a portfolio segment. (17)

period certain. In reference to annuity contracts, a minimum period during which the insurer guarantees to continue paying annuity benefits, even if the annuitant does not survive to the end of the period.

periodic fee. With reference to unbundled products, an amount that must be paid at predetermined intervals—for example, every six months—to compensate the insurer for its investment management expenses, or its administrative expenses, or both. (7)

persistency bonus. In insurance, a bonus paid to a customer upon completion of a specified number of contract years. (4) Also, a bonus paid to sales agents based on the persistency of the business they sell. (20)

persistency rate. In insurance, the share of business that remains in force for a specified period. (4)

planning. The process of establishing objectives and then formulating the strategies, tactics, and other supporting activities needed to achieve those objectives. (11)

planning hierarchy. Together, the different levels of formal corporate plans—including corporate strategic plans, functional-area plans, and tactical plans—that make up a company's overall planning process. (11)

point estimate. A single forecasted value assigned to a variable. Contrast with *range estimate.* (3)

policy dividend. The amount an insurer credits to the owners of participating policies at the end of a policy year and which represents a return of premiums. (4)

policy fee system. A pricing system for unbundled products whereby the customer pays a flat amount—called the *policy fee*—plus a specific rate per $1,000 face amount. (7)

policy filing. The process of obtaining legal approval for a product from all appropriate jurisdictions. (4)

Policy Loan Interest Rate Model Law. A 1980 NAIC model law adopted in many states, this law permitted insurers to adjust policy-loan interest rates after policy issue and thus to reflect changing market interest rates. (16)

policy premium method (PPM). A version of the prospective method of calculating policy reserves that uses gross premiums instead of net premiums. Insurers in Canada are required to use the PPM to calculate policy reserves. (9)

policy reserve. A liability account that identifies the amount that, together with the future premiums to be received from an insurer's in-force products and interest earned, is expected to be sufficient to pay future benefits on those in-force policies. (4) (9)

policy rider. An amendment to an insurance policy that either expands or limits the benefits payable under the policy. (4)

portfolio. A collection of financial assets. (16)

portfolio insurance. Asset portfolio management activities that set absolute limits upon potential investment losses. (17)

portfolio performance specifications. See *performance profile.* (17)

portfolio segment. A portion of an insurer's portfolio set aside into a separate unit for convenience of management. (17)

portfolio segmentation. The process of classifying assets into distinct groupings having similar characteristics. (17)

positive leverage effect. The effect of earning an enhanced return because of the presence of leverage. (15)

positive net cash flow. A condition when cash inflows exceed cash outflows. (16)

preferred stock. A type of equity instrument having some features of both bonds and common stock. Fixed dividends on preferred stock are paid on a regular schedule, and at a stated rate. These dividends must be paid before the issuer can pay any dividends on common stock. (13)

premature withdrawals. A withdrawal of account values prior to the occurrence of an insured event or a scheduled payout date. (4)

premium. The price charged for an insurance-company product. (4)

premium deficiency reserve. A reserve required in the United States when a policy's gross premium is less than the net premium used to calculate the statutory policy reserve. (9)

premium offset policy. A policy with a rapid build-up of cash values, structured with the expectation that, after the policy has remained in force for a specified period, no further premiums are expected to be necessary. (4)

premiums paid in advance. A premium paid in one accounting period for insurance coverage that does not begin until the next period. (9)

prepayment. Early repayment of a loan. (3)

present value (PV). In finance, the amount of money that, if invested now at a specified interest rate, would grow to equal a specified future sum. (5)

present value interest factor (PVIF). A factor equal to the present value of $1 for a given number of discounting periods (n) at a given interest rate (i). The PVIF can be multiplied by an amount to calculate the present value of that amount. (5)

present value interest factor of an annuity (PVIFA). A factor equal to the present value of a $1 annuity of a given number of periods (n) and earning a given interest rate (i). The PVIFA can be multiplied by an amount to calculate the present value of an annuity of that amount. (5)

present value of an annuity (PVA). The amount that must be invested now in order to provide for a specified series of equal future payments, given a specified interest rate and a specified number of periods. (5)

price-elastic. The condition wherein the percentage change in quantity demanded of a product is greater than the percentage change in price. (4)

price elasticity. A quality that represents the relationship between the quantity demanded of a product and the price of that product. Price elasticity can be calculated as the percentage change in quantity demanded resulting from a change in price, divided by the percentage change in price. (4)

price-inelastic. The condition when the percentage change in quantity demanded of a product is less than the percentage change in price. (4)

primary insurer. See *ceding company.* (14)

principal. The amount an investor pays for an asset. (5)

product design objectives. For a proposed insurance product, the basic characteristics, features, benefits, issue limits, age limits, underwriting classes, and the manner in which benefits will be provided. (4)

product development. The process of taking an idea for a new product from the initial phase of idea generation to the final phase of its introduction to the marketplace. (4)

product development expense. The expense related to taking a new product idea from the initial phase of idea generation to the final phase of its introduction to the marketplace. (4)

product implementation. Relative to developing an insurance-company product, establishment of all the administrative structures and processes necessary to take a new product to market. (4)

professional reinsurers. Insurance companies that specialize in the reinsurance market. (14)

profit. The excess of revenue over expenditures. (1)

profitability. A business operation's degree of success in generating returns to its owners. (1)

profit margin. *a.* In general business, the ratio of profit to sales revenue. (6) *b.* For insurance products, the ratio of present value of profits to present value of premiums. (6) *c.* For an entire insurance company, the difference between the company's return on capital and its cost of capital. (10)

projection method. Relative to financial calculations, a method of modifying tabular rates in which the insurer multiplies the mortality rate found in a mortality table by a certain fraction or percentage. (8)

proprietary mortality table. A type of mortality table that an insurer develops for itself, based largely on its own experience with insureds. (8)

prospective experience rating. A system of experience rating in which the insurer uses a group's own previous experience to set that group's premium rates for the coming year (or other future rating period). Contrast with *retrospective experience rating.* (8)

prospective method. A method of calculating policy reserves by looking ahead at a policy's future benefits and premiums so that the policy reserve is equal to the difference between the present value of future benefits and the present value of future premiums. Contrast with *retrospective method.* (9)

provision for adverse deviation. A safety margin in GAAP policy reserves that allows for unfavorable variations from actuarial assumptions. (9)

published mortality table. Mortality tables available to the general public that are based on the experience of the public at large or the general insured population. (8)

qualitative forecasting methods. Forecasting methods that rely primarily on expert opinion and other subjective factors as a basis for predicting future events. (3)

quality rating. A rating or grade assigned to an insurance company by an independent rating agency to reflect the insurer's claims-paying ability, credit worthiness, or financial strength. (10)

quantitative forecasting methods. A forecasting method that uses mathematical data and models to predict future events. (3)

quantity demanded. The volume of a product or service that consumers will buy at different price levels. (7)

quick liquidity. The ratio of an insurer's liquid assets at statutory value to the insurer's contractual reserves. (15)

range estimate. The predicted extent of variation in possible values for a predicted outcome. Contrast with *point estimate.* (3)

rating agencies. Organizations—owned independently of any insurer or government body—that evaluate the financial condition of insurers and provide information to potential customers of and investors in insurance companies. (15)

rating downgrade. A reduction in an insurer's quality rating. (15)

ratio. A comparison of two values that results in a measurement expressed as a percentage or a fraction. (15)

realized capital gain or loss. The monetary result of the actual sale of an asset. (9)

reasonable rates. In reference to insurance premiums, rates that do not exceed the level needed to cover an insurer's expenses and provide the insurer with a fair profit. (7)

recapture provision. A contractual clause specifying a procedure that would allow the ceding company to end the reinsurance arrangement on a given block of business. (14)

receivable. A type of asset based upon an outside party's promise to pay cash to the holder of the receivable. Also known as an *account receivable.* (12)

receivable for agents' debit balances. An asset based on agents' obligations to pay cash owed to an insurance company. (12)

receivables purchase agreement. A contract through which receivables are sold for cash. (12)

receiver. The person—usually the state insurance commissioner or someone acting on the commissioner's behalf—responsible for formulating a plan to distribute a troubled insurer's assets and for making sure that the insurer's obligations to customers are met to the extent possible. (18)

receivership. A condition wherein a state insurance commissioner, acting for the state court, takes control of and administers an insurer's assets and liabilities because of the insurer's serious financial difficulties. (18)

reengineering. The comprehensive and systematic analysis and redesign of an organization's work processes with a goal of dramatically improving efficiency and increasing customer satisfaction. (20)

refinance. To repay a debt and make new borrowing arrangements. (16)

regulatory capital. The amount of capital that an insurer holds in order to comply with regulatory standards for minimum capital. (10)

rehabilitation. In an insurance receivership, a condition wherein an insurer regains financial stability and thus continues to exist after the receivership. (18)

reinsurance. Insurance taken out by an insurance company to cover insurance policies that the company has issued. (14)

reinsurance commission. An allowance that a reinsurer grants to the ceding company and which is intended to cover part or all of the ceding company's acquisition costs and other costs related to reinsured business. (14)

reinsurance premium. In reinsurance, the consideration paid by a ceding company to an assuming company. (14)

reinsurance recoverable. A balance that a reinsurer owes to an insurer. (12)

reinsurance treaty. A contract for reinsurance. (14)

reinsurer. See *assuming company.* (14)

reinvestment risk. The risk that funds generated from an asset portfolio will be reinvested at market interest rates lower than the rates they had been earning. (17)

relevant cash flows. Cash flows that are attributable to a particular investment project. (3)

required capital. For insurance companies, the minimum capital requirements set by regulatory authorities, independent rating agencies, and a company's internal management. (10)

reserve credit. In a reinsurance transaction, the accounting treatment for recording a transfer of reserves on the books of the ceding company. (14)

reserve destrengthening. The process of reducing an insurer's reserve liability amount. (9) (12)

reserves. Accounts that an insurer maintains to set aside funds for meeting future business obligations. Compare to *policy reserves.* (9)

reserve strengthening. The process of increasing an insurer's reserve amount. (9) (12)

reserve valuation. *a.* The process of establishing a value for an insurer's reserves. (12) *b.* The value that is established by actuarial methods for an insurer's reserves. (12)

resident corporation. Under Canadian law, a company incorporated in Canada. Contrast with *nonresident corporation.* (19)

retention charge. For calculating a group product's gross premium, an amount added to the net premium to account for the insurer's expenses, contingencies, and an expense margin. (8)

retention limit. A stated maximum amount of insurance that a reinsurer will assume on any one risk. (14)

retroceded. See *retrocession.* (14)

retrocession. A reinsurer's obtaining reinsurance on some of the risk that it has assumed on a policy. (14)

retrocessionaire. An insurance company's role in providing reinsurance to a reinsurer. (14)

retrospective experience rating. In group insurance, a type of experience rating in which the insurer refunds part of a group's premium after the rating period is over if the group's experience during the period has been better than expected. Contrast with *prospective experience rating.* (7) (8)

retrospective method. A method of calculating policy reserves by looking back at a policy's past premiums and benefits, so that the policy reserve is equal to the difference between the accumulated value of net premiums and the accumulated cost of insurance. Contrast with *prospective method.* (9)

return. The reward, profit, or compensation an investor hopes to earn for taking a risk. (2)

return on capital. A measure of profitability; the ratio of the insurer's earnings to its capital and surplus at the beginning of an accounting period. (1)

return on invested assets ratio. The ratio of an insurer's net gain from operations to the insurer's average amount of invested assets for the same period; measures the efficiency with which a company used its investment portfolio to earn a return. (15)

reverse merger. A merger procedure for spinning off a business operation and then reabsorbing the same operation. (12)

reverse triangular merger. A reverse merger transaction in which a subsidiary company of the acquiring company is merged into the target company so that the target company then becomes a subsidiary of the acquiring company. (19)

risk. For an investor, the possibility of experiencing a loss or failing to earn a return. (2)

risk-adjustment factor. A percentage factor used in capital planning for the purpose of reflecting exposure to risk. (10)

risk augmentation. Regarding capital planning, in the presence of an interaction between corporate line-of-business risk exposures, the effect wherein such an interaction produces a corporate risk exposure greater than the sum of the line-of-business risk exposures. Contrast with *risk offset.* (11)

Risk-Based Capital (RBC) Ratio Requirements. A requirement devised by the NAIC for U.S. companies prescribing a ratio formula and a minimum ratio value that each insurer must meet in order to be considered solvent. (2) (18)

risk-based capital ratios. Ratios that compare a dollar amount of capital to a measure of risk. (10)

risk charge. In group insurance, an amount added to a product's loading to protect the insurer and its customers from the potentially damaging financial results of adverse deviations. (7) (8)

risk offset. In capital planning, in the presence of an interaction between corporate line-of-business risk exposures, the effect wherein such an interaction produces a corporate risk exposure lesser than the sum of the line-of-business risk exposures. Contrast with *risk augmentation.* (11)

risk-return tradeoff. The interplay between risk and return in finance. The higher the risk associated with an investment, the greater the potential return must be in order to offset the risk the investor is taking. The lower a risk on an investment, the lower the potential return can be and still attract investors. (2)

ROIA ratio. See *return on invested assets ratio.* (15)

run on assets. A sustained outflow of funds when many customers withdraw their funds from a financial institution within a short period of time. (15)

run on the bank. See *run on assets.* (15)

sale-leaseback transaction. A lease arrangement wherein the original owner of an asset sells the asset to another party in exchange for cash and then leases the asset back from the new owner. (12)

scenario analysis. In quantitative modeling, a process that involves altering assumptions in a model to determine how assumption changes will affect results. (3)

scheduled retention limit. In a reinsurance transaction, a maximum limit on the amount of risk that a ceding company will assume. (14)

SEC. See *Securities and Exchange Commission.* (4)

Securities Act. Landmark 1933 U.S. federal legislation that regulated disclosure concerning sales of securities and required registration of securities, public disclosure, and publication of a prospectus. (19)

Securities and Exchange Commission (SEC). The U.S. federal authority charged with regulating transactions in financial securities. (4)

Securities Exchange Act. Landmark 1934 U.S. federal legislation that created the Securities and Exchange Commission to enforce compliance with securities laws. (19)

securities laws. Laws designed to ensure full disclosure of companies' financial information to interested investors. (19)

securitization. The creation of new securities based on assets in a pool or portfolio of securities dedicated to that purpose. (12)

select and ultimate mortality table. A type of mortality table containing both select mortality rates and ultimate mortality rates. (8)

select mortality table. A type of mortality table showing the expected mortality rates of people who have recently been underwritten for insurance policies. (8)

select period. On a select mortality table, the length of time during which the effects of selection (underwriting) are assumed to be observable and significant. (8)

sensitivity analysis. With respect to quantitative modeling, measuring the impact that changing any one independent variable has on the results of a model. (3)

setback method. A method of modifying tabular rates in which the insurer forecasts the mortality rate for insureds or annuitants of a certain age by using the mortality rate shown in the table for people of a younger age. (8)

sex-distinct mortality table. A mortality table that shows different mortality rates for males and females, reflecting the fact that women, as a group, experience lower mortality at all ages than men. (8)

Sherman Anti-Trust Act. Landmark 1890 U.S. federal legislation that prohibits business dealings that tend to create monopolies. (19)

simple interest. Interest payable only on the original principal. Contrast with *compound interest.* (5)

simulation. In quantitative modeling, the use of models to represent a complex system in order to study how the system behaves under various circumstances. (3)

small insurance company tax status. For purposes related to federal tax filings, a U.S. life insurance company with less than $15 million in taxable income and less than $500 million in assets. (14)

solvency. Generally defined as a business organization's ability to meet its financial obligations on time; for insurers, solvency refers to the legal minimum standard of capital and surplus that every insurance company must maintain. (1)

special surplus. See *contingency reserves.* (9)

spin-off. A transaction wherein a company reorganizes a discrete internal operating unit into an independently operating subsidiary company. (12) (19)

spread. See *profit margin.* (7) (10)

spread compression. The narrowing of an insurer's interest-rate spread that occurs when market interest rates rise, and insurers are forced to take a smaller spread because customers demand to get the higher market rate credited immediately, even though the average yield or the insurer's investment portfolio rises only very slowly. Contrast with *spread expansion.* (16)

spread expansion. The widening of an insurer's interest-rate spread that occurs when market interest rates fall, and insurers are able to reduce crediting rates while they continue to earn an average portfolio rate of return that is higher than the current market rates. Contrast with *spread compression.* (16)

standard costs. Estimates of the average expenses an insurer incurs in the course of specified activities or functions. (7)

Standard Nonforfeiture Law for Individual Deferred Annuities. A model law established by the NAIC which specifies methods of calculating cash surrender values for individual deferred annuities. (9)

Standard Nonforfeiture Law for Life Insurance. A model law established by the NAIC which specifies methods of calculating cash surrender values for life insurance products. (9)

standing committee. A work group formed on a permanent basis to meet a more or less permanent organizational need and often having the authority to make decisions for the organization within a limited area of responsibility. (16)

statistical phase of IRIS. The process of applying the 12 financial ratios that make up IRIS. (18)

statutory merger. In the United States, a merger that meets state legal requirements for a merger between two corporations. See also *basic statutory merger.* (19)

statutory policy reserves. Policy reserves established to satisfy the requirements of state insurance regulators. (8)

stock purchase acquisition. An acquisition transaction in which one company acquires another company by purchasing that company's stock. Contrast with *asset purchase acquisition.* (19)

stock repurchase. A transaction in which a company buys back its own outstanding stock. (13)

stock swap. A transaction wherein two companies exchange shares of stock in their companies. (12)

straight life annuity. An annuity that pays a benefit so long as the annuitant is alive. (8)

strategic intent. A brief, precise, ambitious, and motivational expression of a company's long-term corporate goals or reason for being. (20)

strategies. Broad plans or methods for achieving objectives. (11)

subordinated. In reference to financial instruments, a condition in which payment of one set of obligations is assigned a lower priority than payment of another set of obligations. (13)

subsidiary. A corporation that is owned by another corporation. (19)

surplus. The total net profits that have been earned from a company's operations and left to accumulate since the company's inception. (1)

surplus debenture. See *surplus note.* (13)

surplus note. A type of unsecured debt instrument that is issued only by insurance companies and that has characteristics of both traditional equity instruments and traditional debt instruments. (13)

surplus relief. Any action that an insurer takes to relieve the effects of surplus strain. (14)

surplus relief ratio. A comparison of an insurer's net cost for—or net earnings from—ceding reinsurance relative to the insurer's capital and surplus. (15)

surplus strain. The decrease in an insurer's capital and surplus caused by high first-year costs and the reserving requirements associated with new products. (9)

surrender charge. Amount that a customer must pay upon terminating a financial product within a given period after the purchase. (4) See also *back-end load.* (7)

surrender value. See *cash value.* (9)

swap contract. A negotiable financial instrument conveying a limited-time agreement to exchange the cash flow from one asset for the cash flow of another asset. See also *interest-rate swap.* (17)

tabular rates. The rates shown in mortality or morbidity tables, or in other types of actuarial tables. (8)

tactical plan. A type of corporate plan for the day-to-day implementation of the corporation's strategic plan. (11)

tactics. Specific action plans for accomplishing strategies. (11)

takeover. A transaction wherein one corporation purchases a controlling interest in another corporation. (19)

target capital. In capital planning, the amount of capital—equal to the sum of an insurer's required and uncommitted capital—that the insurer chooses to hold in support of both existing and future business obligations. (10)

target corporation. A corporation that is the focus of another corporation's efforts to purchase it. (19)

target quality rating. An insurance company's ideal level of quality rating that supports the insurance company's goals for making new sales and raising new capital. (10)

task team. A work group assigned with fulfilling a long-term or permanent mission, and having membership chosen on the basis of individual expertise and ability to carry out the team's mission. (16)

technical product design. The phase of the product development process during which the product language, product provisions, pricing and dividend structures, and underwriting and issue specifications are created. (4)

technical solvency. The condition of being able to pay obligations as they come due. (16)

temporary life annuity. An annuity that pays a benefit throughout a specified period, so long as the annuitant is still alive. If the annuitant dies before the end of that period, the annuity ceases paying benefits. (8)

thin margin. A small profit margin. (7)

timeline. See *line diagram.* (5)

time-series analysis. See *horizontal analysis.* (15)

time-series model. A quantitative model that forecasts the future value of a variable by performing a mathematical operation on the value of the same variable in one or more past periods. (3)

time value of money. The concept that the value of a sum of money at one point in time will be different from its value at another point in time as a result of the effect of interest. (5)

top-down, bottom-up approach. In reference to strategic planning, an approach that involves sending for revision a proposed strategic plan down through the levels of the organizational hierarchy—from the corporate level to the lowest operating levels of management—and then back up again to the corporate level. (11)

total leverage. The combined effect of operating leverage and financial leverage. (15)

total variable costs. Variable costs per unit times the number of units produced. (20)

traditional indemnity reinsurance. A broad type of reinsurance that effects a partial and permanent, but recapturable, transfer of newly written business. (14)

transaction costs. Legal and administrative costs associated with planning and executing a financial exchange. (12)

transfer fee. A fee charged when a customer transfers money from one fund to another. (7)

treasury management. See *cash management.* (10)

trend analysis. See *horizontal analysis.* (15)

triangular merger. A type of corporate merger involving three corporate entities: (1) the purchaser, (2) a subsidiary of the purchaser, and (3) the target company. (19)

ultimate mortality table. A mortality table showing mortality rates for people who have not recently been underwritten. (8)

unauthorized reinsurer. A reinsurer that is not authorized by the regulatory authorities in the direct writing insurer's state of domicile. (14)

unbundled products. A broad classification of insurance products for which the insurer specifies to the customer which portions of the product's total price reflect the insurer's expenses, the cost of benefits, and the interest being credited to the customer. (7)

uncommitted capital. In capital planning, capital an insurer elects to hold to support financial obligations related to issuing and maintaining future business commitments. (10)

uncovering hidden capital. Making capital appear on a balance sheet as a result of cosmetic accounting or financial changes. (12)

undervalued. A condition in which an asset's statutory book value is lower than its hypothetical market value. (12)

underwriting depth and experience. The adequacy of an insurer's underwriting staff and other resources to evaluate and process applications. (14)

underwriting guidelines. General rules that an underwriting staff uses in assigning applicants to an insurance company's different premium classifications. (4)

underwriting margin. The difference between a product's actual benefit costs and the benefit costs the insurer assumes in its pricing; applies only to products with an insurance component. (7)

underwriting philosophy. For an insurance company, a body of standards and goals for guiding the risk assessment process. (4)

unearned premium reserve. A liability account that includes premiums paid for coverage occurring in a future accounting period. (9)

Uniform Insurers Liquidation Act. In some states, a law—older than the NAIC's model Rehabilitation Act—that governs rehabilitations and liquidations. (18)

unisex mortality table. A type of mortality table that shows a single set of mortality rates to be used for both males and females. (8)

unit cost. The incurred expense that can be attributed to a single measured unit of work. (20)

unit of coverage. A basic amount of insurance coverage that insurers use when calculating premiums for their products. For life insurance, a common unit of coverage is $1,000 of face value. (4)

Universal Life Model Regulation. Model regulation created by the NAIC to establish reserve requirements for flexible-premium and interest-sensitive life insurance products. (9)

unrealized capital gain or loss. The monetary result that would occur if the insurer were to sell an asset at its market price at a given moment. A capital gain or loss remains unrealized as long as the insurer holds the asset. (9)

upstream holding company. A company that owns the company that created it, and may also own other corporate subsidiaries. (19)

user-defined assumptions. The assumptions under the control of the end-user of an asset-share model. (6)

validation point. The point at which a product in an asset-share model breaks even. Calculated as the first year that a product's asset share is greater than its reserve. (6)

valuation actuary. An actuary who specializes in setting the proper values for an insurance company's assets, reserves, and capital and surplus. (3)

valuation date. The date as of which the value of a financial transaction is determined. (5)

valuation mortality table. A mortality table intended for use in calculating statutory policy reserves. (8)

value added. See *economic value added.* (20)

vanishing premium policy. See *premium offset policy.* (4)

variable. An item of data that is incorporated in a model or an equation and that is subject to change. (3)

variable costing. See *marginal costing.* (7)

variable policy-loan interest rate. An insurance product feature in which the interest rate that a policyowner must pay on policy loans fluctuates according to prevailing interest rates in the economy. (4)

vertical analysis. A type of ratio analysis designed for examining the financial structure of one company at one point in time. (15)

vertical communication. Communication up and down the lines of an organizational hierarchy. (16)

wealth. The combination of goodwill and the monetary value that a company has built up over the years from successive periods of profits. (2)

wealth maximization. Maximizing of a company's stock price, which in turn maximizes the return that the organization's owners receive for their investment in the company. (2)

weighted average cost of capital (WACC). A weighted value or percentage, reflecting the overall cost that a company pays to obtain new funds from all sources. (15)

weighted-average maturity. The dollar-weighted average time period remaining until the instruments held in a portfolio expire or reach full value. (17)

weighted value. An amount that has been multiplied by a percentage. (15)

wide margin. A relatively large profit margin. (7)

withdrawal charge. See *back-end load.* (7)

withdrawal fees. An amount that a customer must pay if the customer withdraws part of the account value from a financial product within a given period after purchasing the product. (4)

withdrawal rate. See *lapse rate.* (4)

working capital management. See *cash management.* (10)

worksite marketing. The marketing of insurance products to people at their place of work. (20)

yearly renewable term reinsurance method. A reinsurance premium method under which, on the anniversary date of each policy reinsured, the ceding company is required to pay a one-year term premium to the assuming company. (14)

Index

A

B

D

J–K

L

M

N

S

T

To Install *ExecuView* to Your Computer's Hard Drive . . .

1. Insert the *ExecuView* Setup disk into drive A or drive B.
2. In Windows 3.1 or 3.11, select File menu and choose Run. In Windows 95, select Start button and choose Run.
3. Type "a:\setup" (or "b:\setup") and press ENTER.
4. Follow the onscreen instructions.

For instructions on the operation of *ExecuView,* please refer to the *ExecuView* User's Guide section of this textbook.

IMPORTANT—READ CAREFULLY BEFORE REMOVING THE *EXECUVIEW* DISK FROM ITS JACKET. *By installing this LOMA-provided software, you indicate your agreement to be bound by the following provisions governing any use of said software. If you have any questions about any of these provisions, please contact LOMA's Information Services Help Desk at (770) 984-3782.*

LOMA LICENSE AGREEMENT
This is a legal agreement between you (individual or company) and LOMA. By removing the disk from its jacket you are agreeing to be bound by the terms of this agreement.

Grant of License. LOMA grants you the right to use one copy of *ExecuView* (hereinafter referred to as "the software") on a single computer. The software is in "use" on a computer when it is loaded into temporary memory (RAM) or installed into permanent memory (hard disk, CD-ROM, or other storage device) of that computer.

Copyright. The software is owned by LOMA and is protected by U.S. copyright laws and international treaty provisions. Therefore, you must treat the software like any other copyrighted material (e.g., a book or musical recording) EXCEPT that you may either make one copy of the software solely for back-up or archival purposes or transfer the software to a single hard disk provided you keep the original solely for backup or archival purposes.

Other restrictions. You may not rent or lease the software. You may not reverse engineer, decompile, or disassemble the software or in any way duplicate the contents of the code and other elements therein.

Warranty. LOMA warrants that all software provided by LOMA has been treated with a virus detection, removal, and prevention system before the LOMA software is shipped to the User. Before installing the software, it is the User's responsibility to re-check the software and verify that it is free from any virus, bug, or any other problem whatsoever that may affect User's hardware, software, network, data, database, or any other equipment, material, or operations whatsoever.

Disclaimer of Warranty. LOMA MAKES NO OTHER WARRANTY EXPRESSED OR IMPLIED INCLUDING, WITHOUT LIMITATION, NO WARRANTY OF MERCHANTABILITY OR FITNESS OR SUITABILITY FOR A PARTICULAR PURPOSE. In the event of LOMA's breach of its warranty above, User's sole remedy shall be replacement of the defective LOMA software or refund of the purchase price thereof, as determined at LOMA's sole option. UNDER NO CIRCUMSTANCES SHALL LOMA BE LIABLE TO USER OR ANY THIRD PARTY FOR ANY INCIDENTAL OR CONSEQUENTIAL DAMAGES WHATSOEVER.

Limitation of Liability. User agrees to indemnify and hold harmless LOMA, its employees, its agents, and their successors and assigns against any loss, liability, cost or expense (including reasonable attorneys' fees) asserted against or suffered or incurred by LOMA as a consequence of, or in the defense of, any claim arising from or based upon any alleged negligence, act or failure to act, whatsoever of LOMA, its employees, their successors, agents, heirs, and/or assigns with respect to the aforementioned software.

DISCLAIMER
The *ExecuView* program in designed solely to provide information for educational purposes. The models therein are not designed for use in corporate decision making. *ExecuView* is sold and distributed with the understanding that the publisher is not engaged in rendering legal, accounting, financial, or other professional service. If such advice or other expert assistance is required, the services of a competent professional person should be sought.